The Adams Papers

L. H. BUTTERFIELD, EDITOR IN CHIEF

SERIES I

DIARIES

Diary and Autobiography of John Adams

Diary and Autobiography of John Adams

L. H. BUTTERFIELD, *EDITOR*

LEONARD C. FABER AND WENDELL D. GARRETT

ASSISTANT EDITORS

———————— ☆ ————————

Volume 1 · *Diary* 1755–1770

THE BELKNAP PRESS

OF HARVARD UNIVERSITY PRESS

CAMBRIDGE, MASSACHUSETTS

1961

Distributed in Great Britain by Oxford University Press · London

Funds for editing *The Adams Papers* have been provided by Time, Inc.,
on behalf of *Life*, to the Massachusetts Historical Society, under whose
supervision the editorial work is being done.

Library of Congress Catalog Card Number 60–5387 · Printed in the United States of America

This edition of *The Adams Papers*
is sponsored by the MASSACHUSETTS HISTORICAL SOCIETY
to which the ADAMS MANUSCRIPT TRUST
by a deed of gift dated 4 April 1956
gave ultimate custody of the personal and public papers
written, accumulated, and preserved over a span of three centuries
by the Adams family of Massachusetts

The Adams Papers

The acorn and oakleaf device on the preceding page is redrawn from a seal cut for John Quincy Adams after 1830. The motto is from Statius as quoted by Cicero in the First Tusculan Disputation: *Serit arbores quæ alteri seculo prosint* ("He plants trees for the benefit of later generations").

Contents

Contents

Illustrations

house on the far left was that occupied by John Adams after his marriage in 1764 and was the birthplace of John Quincy Adams. The house next to it was the home of Deacon John Adams and the birthplace of John Adams. The house on the far right was that of the schoolmaster Joseph Marsh where John Adams was prepared for college. The abrupt hills rising on the opposite side of the valley were the site of the later famous Quincy granite quarries; Dorchester Heights and the city of Boston may be seen in the distance. This view was taken from Penn's Hill. See a note under Adams' Diary entry of 17 March 1756 at p. 15. (Courtesy of the Massachusetts Historical Society.)

6. MOUNT WOLLASTON, THE FORMER SEAT OF COLONEL JOHN QUINCY, 1822, BY ELIZA SUSAN QUINCY   256

Water color in the first volume of Eliza Susan Quincy's manuscript "Memoir." Mount Wollaston Farm, which included the site of Thomas Morton's "Merrymount," was the estate of Abigail Adams' maternal grandfather, Colonel John Quincy. In 1767 it passed into the hands of his son Norton Quincy, and it was from here that John and John Quincy Adams took ship for France in February 1778. After Norton Quincy's death in 1801 the property passed into the hands of the Adamses. In 1875 Eliza Susan Quincy noted on the back of the drawing: "The Lime tree in the foreground of this sketch stood behind the house formerly the residence of Rev. Mr. Hancock, the birthplace of his distinguished son — John Hancock. . . . The splendid limetrees in front of the house of John Quincy, seen in the distance, in this sketch, are yet standing, although the house is gone." See the Diary entries of [25 June] 1760, 13 August 1769, and 13 February 1778 and notes in the present volume p. 141, 340–341, and vol. 2:269–270. (Courtesy of the Massachusetts Historical Society.)

7. QUINCY FROM PRESIDENTS HILL, 1822, BY ELIZA SUSAN QUINCY   257

Water color in the second volume of Eliza Susan Quincy's manuscript "Memoir." The First or North Parish Church, built in 1732 and enlarged in 1805, dominates the scene. John Adams was baptized in this church by the Reverend John Hancock in 1735. On the right, Eliza Susan Quincy's number 1, is the house of the Reverend Peter Whitney, minister of the First Church, 1800–1843. On the left, number 2, is the "former residence of Gov. Shirley." Far in the distance, number 3, is the Germantown estate of Joseph Palmer, the glass manufacturer, where John Adams was frequently a visitor. Number 4 is the former residence of the Reverend Anthony Wibird, minister of the First Church, 1775–1800. It was here that John Adams spent a night in January 1759 "reading the Reflections on Courtship and Marriage"; see p. 72. (Courtesy of the Massachusetts Historical Society.)

A 19th-century engraving from William S. Bartlet's *Frontier Missionary: A Memoir of the Life of the Rev. Jacob Bailey* . . . , Boston, 1853, p. 79. The three-story wooden courthouse was built in 1761, as the seat of government for Lincoln County. Gershom Flagg, a Boston housewright, was the builder. The courtroom was on the second floor; the lower floor was occupied as a dwelling by Major Samuel Goodwin. After 1794 the court functions were transferred to Wiscasset, but the old courthouse still stands. See the note on John Adams' Accounts, 7–12 June 1765, at p. 259. For his description of a trip to Pownalborough in 1765, see his Autobiography, vol. 3:281–282.

A 1769 impression, with revisions and additions, of Captain John Bonner's map of Boston originally engraved in 1722. The changes in the new edition consisted primarily in the addition of new streets on and around Beacon Hill. John Adams' residences in Boston from 1768 to 1774 were in Brattle Square, Cole Lane, again in Brattle Square, and finally in Queen Street. See Diary entries and notes in the present volume, p. 339; vol. 2:63–64, 68; also vol. 3:286–287, 291, 296–297. (Courtesy of the New York Public Library.)

Rex *v.* Preston, the first of the trials growing out of the "Boston Massacre," was tried in the Suffolk Superior Court, 24–30 October 1770, John Adams serving as co-counsel for Preston in one of the most famous cases in his career as a lawyer. See the note on Diary entry of 10 January 1771, vol. 2:1–2, and Autobiography, vol. 3:292–294. (Courtesy of the Massachusetts Historical Society.)

Introduction

1. AN ARTICULATE FAMILY

The earliest document in the manuscript records of the Adams family, upon which the present edition is mainly based, is an agreement by which William Tyng of Boston mortgaged to William Coddington of Aquedneck certain lands at Mount Wollaston, now a part of Quincy, Massachusetts. This large and handsome indenture is dated 10 April 1639, and the lands were probably among those which the Adamses eventually acquired through Abigail Adams' descent from the Quincys, long the chief landowners at "The Mount." But for more than a century after 1639 there remain only a few wills, deeds, receipts, printed fast-day proclamations, and scraps of correspondence to document the history of a family of farmers, maltsters, and holders of town offices who lived their lives below the level of historical scrutiny.

Then, in 1755, John Adams (1735–1826), second of his name and great-great-grandson of the first Adams to settle in Massachusetts Bay, was jolted by an earthquake into starting a diary. With this record of a young schoolmaster's daily thoughts and experiences, the family records may be said truly to begin. Once begun, they were continued with a diligence that is almost staggering to contemplate, and preserved with exemplary care by one generation after another, each of which in turn of course added to the bulk. The habit of making and keeping written records became as persistent a trait among the Adamses as the distinctive conformation of their skulls.

"Copied into my Letter-Book the Letter written last Evening to my wife," John Quincy Adams (1767–1848) recorded in the thirty-ninth volume of his manuscript journal while supposedly vacationing at Quincy between terms of Congress.

This is noisome, and to me useless labour [he went on], consuming time which might be fruitfully employed. But in my father's first Letter-Book, I find him saying on the 2d. of June 1776 that in all the correspondences he had maintained, during a course of twenty years at least that he had been a writer of Letters, he never kept a single copy. And he adds, This negligence and inaccuracy has been a great misfortune to him on many occasions. A Letter Book, a Diary, a Book of receipts and expenses—these three Books, kept without intermission, should be the rule of duty of every man who can read and write. But to keep them perseveringly requires a character given to very few of the Sons of men. Above all it requires a character to which toil is a pleasure, and of which untiring Patience is an essential Element.[1]

Patience was not a conspicuous trait in any Adams statesman before Charles Francis Adams (1807–1886). But toil at their writing desks was as natural to them as eating or walking, and those who lacked patience made up for it by self-discipline. The combined product of their labors was briefly and admirably described by Edward Everett Hale about 1888, soon after C. F. Adams had laid down his pen for good. Of a visit to the Stone Library on the grounds of the Adams homestead in Quincy, Hale wrote:

You enter by the lordly fireplace, you turn to the right, and there is the diary of the first Adams when he left college in 1755. You walk on and you walk on, turning the corners as they come, and at the fireplace end, after your walk, a hundred paces more or less, you have seen the manuscript history of America in the diaries and correspondence of two Presidents and of that Minister to England who spoke the decisive word which saved England and America from a third war.[2]

Hale's "hundred paces more or less" is perhaps as good a measure for the physical bulk of the family archives as one needs. The microfilm edition of the Adams Papers, 1639–1889, runs to 27,464 feet of 35-mm. film. No one has attempted to count the pages or is likely to. If to the records created and accumulated by the three generations of statesmen were added those of Charles Francis Adams' sons, three of whom were extremely articulate and lived well into the present century, the total would certainly run to 400,000 pages and perhaps substantially more.

The story told by these massed documents begins in a farmer's cottage in Braintree during the year of Braddock's defeat near Fort Duquesne, moves through the excitements of Massachusetts' quarrel with the British ministry and crown as recorded by a young and highly observant lawyer, and then enlarges, first, to the Continental Congress in Philadelphia, Baltimore, and York, and, before long, to the

[1] 20 July 1834. Unless otherwise indicated, all manuscripts cited in the Introduction are in the Adams Papers.

[2] Edward Everett Hale, *Memories of a Hundred Years*, New York and London, 1902, 2:138–139.

theater of world politics and diplomacy as viewed from Paris, Amsterdam, The Hague, London, and occasionally St. Petersburg. "I have written more to Congress, since my Arrival in Paris," John Adams told a friend in the spring of 1780, "than they ever received from Europe put it all together since the Revolution [began]."[3] This boast may not have been far from the literal truth, and Adams maintained a comparable output for eight years longer.

Then, after a decade of contending with wily foreign secretaries and rubbing elbows with generals, dukes, mistresses of salons, Dutch bankers and burgomasters, and the most eminent philosophers of the day, Deacon John Adams' son, a former village schoolmaster, returned home and was elected in turn the first Vice President and the second President of the United States. His administration was torn by strife not only between parties but within his own party. But being convinced that war would be disastrous, he kept the peace and found himself repudiated by both parties, thereby setting an example of independence and isolation followed more than once by his descendants. John Adams retired to the house in Quincy he name "Peacefield," where he chewed the cud of frustration and relived his public life in long self-justifying letters and memoirs.

Gradually his love of farming, of books, of his country, of life itself, aided by the tireless support and care of a matchless partner, Abigail Adams, restored him. He resumed his correspondence with friends like Benjamin Rush and Thomas Jefferson who had differed with him during the heat of the day, by turns entertaining them with his jocularity and astounding them with his learning. His greatest satisfaction lay in watching the progress of his son in public life, and his greatest excitement in joining that son in new political battles that presented remarkable parallels with those which he himself had fought long ago.

John Quincy Adams' records begin at a relatively earlier stage of his life than do those of his father—a tribute no doubt to parental training. He was not quite eleven when he wrote John Adams, then in the Continental Congress, that he loved "to recieve Letters very well much better than I love to write them," and that he made "but a poor figure at Composition" because his thoughts were always "running after birds eggs, play and trifles, till I get vexd with my Self, Mamma has a troublesome task to keep me Steady." Hoping to do better, he requested his father's advice "how to proportion my Studies and my Play," and in a postscript promised that if he were sent "a Blank book

---

[3] To Elbridge Gerry, 23 May 1780 (Yale University Library).

I will transcribe the most remarkable occurances I mett with in my reading which will Serve to fix them upon my mind."[4] During the next eight years this boy visited most of the capitals of Europe, served as his father's amanuensis and as French interpreter to the first United States diplomatic mission to Russia, and instructed French diplomats in the mysteries of the English language. Franklin, Lafayette, and Jay became familiar figures to him, and many years later his father reminded Thomas Jefferson that "when you was at Cul de sac at Paris, he appeared to me to be almost as much your boy as mine."[5]

After taking his degree at Harvard and spending a few years in unprofitable law practice and much more successful political journalism, John Quincy Adams, then twenty-six, was appointed by President Washington American minister to the Netherlands—familiar ground to him because he had attended schools in Amsterdam and Leyden and had lived with his father in the first of all American legation buildings in Europe, at The Hague. Here began the remarkable series of dispatches that was to stretch (with an interval while he served in the United States Senate and as Boylston professor of rhetoric and oratory at Harvard) from 1794 to 1817, first from The Hague, then from Berlin, St. Petersburg, Ghent, Paris, and London, the originals filling volume after volume among the records of the State Department in the National Archives and the drafts and bound letterbook copies filling other shelves in the Adams Papers. The panorama they unfold of Napoleonic and post-Napoleonic Europe is probably unsurpassed, especially when supported by his incredibly detailed diary entries, even in that age studded with brilliant and articulate diplomatists.

Called home to serve as secretary of state in Monroe's cabinet, Adams spent eight laborious and highly effective years in that office. They were followed by a single term as a minority President, equally laborious but devoid of accomplishment because, like his father before him, Adams found himself a leader without a party. Looking back after his defeat by Jackson in 1828, he reflected that he would have to content himself "with the slender portion of [posterity's] regard which may be yielded to barren good Intentions, and Aspirations beyond the temper of the Age."[6] But even as he wrote, the way was being opened to his "second career," as a member of Congress from Massachusetts, the founder of the Smithsonian Institution, and the indomitable champion of the right of popular petition. There were many who thought it a mistake, because beneath him, for the ex-President to

[4] 2 June 1777.
[5] 22 January 1825 (Library of Congress).
[6] To Charles Miner, 11 October 1830.

return to Congress. But Adams himself esteemed the suffrage of his neighbors the highest tribute ever paid him. The nation looked on with growing wonder as the bald little old man with his high-pitched voice fought the Southern phalanx in the House to a standstill. Emerson described the spectacle and summed up Adams' character better than anyone else when he wrote:

> Mr. Adams chose wisely and according to his constitution, when, on leaving the Presidency, he went into Congress. He is no literary old gentleman, but a bruiser, and loves the *mêlée*. When they talk about his age and venerableness and nearness to the grave, he knows better, he is like one of those old cardinals, who, as quick as he is chosen Pope, throws away his crutches and his crookedness, and is as straight as a boy. He is an old *roué* who cannot live on slops, but must have sulphuric acid in his tea.[7]

Among those who thought John Quincy Adams lost dignity by reentering political life was his son Charles Francis. Considering his upbringing, this is not surprising. The only young man who has ever been both a son and grandson of Presidents, taught by his father in Russia and enrolled in British schools while his father served as American minister in London, Charles Francis was inclined both by temperament and training to take the proprieties of life with great seriousness. His mother pampered him, and his father by turns forgot him for long intervals and then lectured him sternly and at length on what his family and his country expected of him. His closest companion during his young manhood, as one of his own sons noted with exasperation, was a diary. "He took to diary writing early, and he took to it bad," the younger Charles Francis observed while preparing a biography of his father. Worse than that, his diary displayed no humor, no picturesqueness, no imagination, no love of nature or of sports or even of gossip, "no eye to the dramatic, ... no touches of sympathy or fun. ... He studied the classics and read Clarissa Harlowe to his young wife—who evidently was bored to extinction." He went to church because it was the right thing to do, but even though he was bored by the sermons he conscientiously epitomized them in his journal.[8]

To this private indictment, much softened in the son's published biography, another son made a public reply. In Henry's opinion

Charles Francis Adams possessed the only perfectly balanced mind that ever existed in the name. For a hundred years, every newspaper scribbler

[7] Ralph Waldo Emerson, *Journals*, ed. Edward W. Emerson and Waldo E. Forbes, Boston and New York, 1909–1914, 6:349–350.

[8] Charles Francis Adams 2d to Henry Adams, 15 April 1895 (Adams Papers, Fourth Generation).

had, with more or less obvious excuse, derided or abused the older Adamses for want of judgment. They abused Charles Francis for his judgment. . . . Charles Francis Adams was singular for mental poise—absence of self-assertion or self-consciousness—the faculty of standing apart without seeming aware that he was alone—a balance of mind and temper that neither challenged nor avoided notice, nor admitted question of superiority or inferiority, of jealousy, of personal motives, from any source, even under great pressure. . . . [His] memory was hardly above the average; his mind was not bold like his grandfather's or restless like his father's, or imaginative or oratorical—still less mathematical; but it worked with singular perfection, admirable self-restraint, and instinctive mastery of form. Within its range it was a model.[9]

None of the qualities singled out for praise or blame by either son was of the kind likely to create a popular following. Charles Francis Adams therefore enjoyed limited success as a politician. He served reputably in the Massachusetts House and Senate in the 1840's. In 1848, at the birth of the Free Soil Party in Buffalo, he was nominated as a running-mate for, of all people, Martin Van Buren. But this seems to have been largely a gesture of homage to the memory of John Quincy Adams, who had died earlier that year. After the poor showing of the Free Soilers in the national election, Adams returned contentedly to his labors on the family papers and specifically to the editing of John Adams' *Works*. A whole decade passed before he was lured back into politics. In 1858 he took his father's seat in Congress and filled it with distinction during one term and the beginning of a second. This was the last elective office he was to hold. His name and his extraordinary resemblance to the Adams Presidents caused him to be put forward with more or less enthusiasm for high national office in almost every election year until 1876. But as often as this happened he doused his supporters' hopes with the cold water of a self-restraint that could as well be called inverted pride. As early as 1852 a former political associate described him as "the greatest Iceberg in the Northern hemisphere,"[1] and in the popular mind a chill always clung to his name.

But if Charles Francis' prudence, self-restraint, and coolness handicapped him as a political leader, they served him well in his two diplomatic missions—in London from 1861 to 1868 and in Geneva as United States arbitrator of the *Alabama* claims in 1871–1872. Both his historian sons have treated the London years well—Henry with the dramatic flourishes characteristic of his style, Charles more soberly.

[9] *The Education of Henry Adams: An Autobiography*, Boston, 1918, p. 26–27.
[1] Marcus Morton to John Van Buren, 4 October 1852, quoted in Arthur B. Darling, *Political Changes in Massachusetts, 1824–1848*, New Haven, 1925, p. 352.

Neither of them provided a better key to his conduct and to his success in coping with the denizens of Downing Street and Mayfair during critical periods in Anglo-American relations than a sentence or two the Minister himself wrote in a letter to his eldest son in 1863. "My practice," he said, "has been never to manifest feeling of any kind, either of elation or of depression. In this, some Englishmen have taken occasion to intimate that I have been thought quite successful." [2]

So it was to be again during the delicate and protracted arbitration proceedings at Geneva, the outcome of which was another tribute to Adams' patience and firmness. Thereafter he could retire with genuine relief to his beloved books and his editorial work on his father's diary, alternating with the seasons between the Stone Library he had built at the homestead in Quincy and the well-stocked shelves of the Boston Athenæum.

This bare summary of the story the family papers tell has so far dealt only with the Adams statesmen, with emphasis on their preparation for and their accomplishments in public life. But the papers are quite as remarkable when considered in a wholly different light, not as documentation for momentous events but as sources for the history of a uniquely gifted family. The diaries, correspondence, and other writings of John, John Quincy, and Charles Francis Adams are embedded in a much larger body of manuscript records to which many other members of the family have contributed. For a period of more than a century the husbands and wives, the sisters and brothers, the parents and children, the grandparents and grandchildren in the Adams family found themselves dispersed in vantage points for observation on both sides of the Atlantic and maintained a highly effective communication system by correspondence. Abigail Adams (born Abigail Smith, 1744–1818) set the pattern, first as a young mother left in charge of a farm and a house full of children, servants, and refugees from British-occupied Boston; later at her husband's side in Paris and London, but never unmindful for a day of her boys at home or of her sisters and their families; ultimately as a matriarch, the balance wheel of her roving family, reporting charmingly on her garden, tirelessly on news of the family and neighbors, tartly on public affairs, and chiding young and old alike when they did not write regularly to her. "It is a habit the pleasure of which increases with the practise," she pointed out as one who knew, "but becomes urksome by neglect." [3] "To know that you are well that you have Bread to Eat, and Raiment

[2] To John Quincy Adams 2d, 21 August 1863.
[3] To her daughter, Abigail Adams Smith, 8 May 1808 (Massachusetts Historical Society).

to cloath you, are subjects of no trivial import, and communicate pleasure to me, as the reverse would be most painfull."[4] To the end she kept up the flow of news from Quincy to New York, Philadelphia, and Washington, to St. Petersburg, Ghent, and London. Writing a young relative who lived no farther away than Boston but whom she was very fond of, Mrs. Adams said that her epistolary activity had provoked local comment but this would by no means deter her from going on. "I beleive the post man thinkes us very important correspondents, as one observed that it was well the P[resident] had the priviledge of Franking. I have no scruples upon that head. As it is the only gratuity his country ever bestowed upon him, I mean to place a high value upon it, by as frequent a use of it as I have occasion for."[5]

Mrs. John Quincy Adams (born Louisa Catherine Johnson, 1775–1852) was cast in a less heroic mold than her mother-in-law. One of the most dramatic moments in the entire history of the family occurred when Louisa Catherine confronted Abigail Adams for the first time, at the Old House in Quincy during the Thanksgiving season of 1801. The daughter-in-law's antecedents were Southern and English; she had grown up in London and France and had passed her first four years of married life at the Court of Berlin. Her sudden translation to the village of Quincy in a wintry season was more than her delicate temperament and breeding could stand. "Had I steped into Noah's Ark," she recalled later, "I do not think I could have been more utterly astonished." The rustic relatives and neighbors, the queer hours, dress, food, and manners, "Even the Church, its forms, the snuffling through the nose," dismayed and depressed her. And in the presence of the all-competent Abigail she knew she was conspicuously ill-qualified to conduct a household according to Quincy standards. "I was literally and without knowing it a *fine* Lady," which was to say contemptible in the eyes of Quincy folk. Her one comfort was that "the old Gentleman took a fancy to me."[6]

John Adams' affection was rewarded by his daughter-in-law's unswerving devotion. Louisa Catherine accompanied her husband on his further diplomatic travels, which were extensive, and she contributed splendidly to the surviving annals of the family by writing long journal-letters home. These grew even longer after Abigail died and "the old Gentleman" lived on until he was nearly ninety-one.

[4] To the same, 3 October 1808 (Massachusetts Historical Society).
[5] To Harriet Welsh, 3 March 1815.
[6] Louisa Catherine Adams, "The Adventures of a Nobody" (an autobiographical narrative written July 1840 and later).

After her first traumatic experience Louisa Catherine never adapted herself to the Quincy climate. Her visits there were few and usually short, though her memory haunts the chamber at the Old House where her grandson Henry described her unforgettably—"a fragile creature, ... an exotic, like her Sèvres china"—seated at her writing desk with sets of *Peregrine Pickle* and *Tom Jones* in 18th-century bindings behind its little glass doors.[7] Her desk and books are still to be seen there.

Louisa Catherine's fragility was perhaps more apparent than real. She not only survived more than fifty years of married life with John Quincy Adams but outlived him by four years. To those who have studied the mountainous masses of records he created and left behind him, John Quincy Adams sometimes appears to have had more of the attributes of a natural force than of a human being. Certainly we must grant his lifetime partner endurance. But if this, together with wifely loyalty and submission, is her most visible trait, her main contribution to the family was a love of letters. The Adamses had not lacked for books before her time, but their taste ran to folios of law, history, diplomacy, and philosophy. Louisa Catherine loved literature as an elegant art. Volume upon volume of her poetical compositions, both originals and translations from the French, remain among the family archives. In a prose sketch dated from the White House and entitled "The Metropolitan Kaleidoscope or Varieties of Winter" there are echoes of Goldsmith and Irving; and several short dramatic pieces (for example, "Juvenile Indiscretions or Grand Papa a Farce in one Act" and "The Captives of Scio or The Liberal American. A Melo-Drame") suggest that she tried lightening the atmosphere of a grimly earnest household with amateur theatricals. How well she succeeded is an open question, but along with the "quarter taint of Maryland blood" her grandson Henry acknowledged from her there obviously came much that was new and leavening in the Adams strain.

Mrs. Charles Francis Adams (1808–1889) was much less articulate than the other Adams statesmen's wives. The daughter of a Medford capitalist, Abigail Brooks was, or became, as prosy as her innumerable relatives who were always on hand and had made Charles Francis' courtship of her (very fully recorded in his diary) almost unendurable. But if she was as Victorian as Victoria, whom she came to resemble remarkably in later years, her fortune, handled with acumen by her husband, guaranteed family solvency for several generations. And she more than compensated for her own want of brilliance by rearing

[7] *The Education of Henry Adams*, p. 16–19.

four extraordinarily gifted sons. The eldest, named John Quincy (1833–1894) after his grandfather, was a lawyer, moderator of town meetings, member of the General Court, gentleman farmer, and Fellow of Harvard College, but deliberately broke with family tradition not only by becoming a Democrat but by abandoning what he called "the vile family habit of preserving letters." [8] Yet such of his own letters as survive, mainly addressed to his father and brothers during the Civil War and Reconstruction, are among the liveliest that any Adams ever wrote. The next brother, Charles Francis 2d (1835–1915), Union Army officer, railroad commissioner and executive, capitalist, historian and biographer, and president of the Massachusetts Historical Society, became the most prolific publicist in the whole history of the family. His diaries and correspondence remain in large part intact among the family papers and constitute a mass almost as formidable as the manuscript records of any of his statesmen-forebears. The two younger brothers, Henry (1838–1918) and Brooks (1848–1927), while still boys helped their father in his editorial work on the family papers and thus began adult life with a thirst for printer's ink. Henry's taste for it ran its course and declined as he grew old and world-weary; Brooks' never diminished. A niece of theirs, Mrs. Robert Homans of Boston, has told the editor in chief of *The Adams Papers* that when as a girl she visited the Adams homestead she would find her Uncle Brooks in the house itself at work on a philosophical treatise, perhaps *The Law of Civilization and Decay*, her Uncle Henry in the Stone Library writing the *History of the United States*, and her Uncle Charles in his house on Presidents Hill across the way narrating the settlement of Boston Bay for his *Three Episodes of Massachusetts History*. She once asked her father, John Quincy Adams 2d, why her uncles were always writing and he very seldom did. "My dear," he answered without much hesitation, "it amuses them."

Students of the past, and students of human nature too, may be glad that the Adamses were amused or otherwise satisfied by writing. The assembled results of their activity with their pens embody a long, dense, and rich record of experience on two continents, by turns entertaining and moving and always informative. Those of us who have lived and worked with the Adams Papers have properly sensed, we hope, both the unique privilege and the high responsibility conferred on us as the agents through whom the family's written records are being presented to the public.

[8] John Quincy Adams 2d to his father, Charles Francis Adams, 5 February 1867.

2. HISTORY AND PLAN OF *THE ADAMS PAPERS*

Family Custody and Use of the Papers

Each generation of the Adams family displayed its concern to get itself on record, and to preserve the records thus created, in its own characteristic way.[9] John Adams wrote up his diary (though with lapses for which he reproached himself) as a matter of course, and he evidently preserved every scrap of writing, no matter how cryptic, relative to his law practice because it was good business to do so. At an inn in Danvers, upon hearing the news that he had been elected to what became the First Continental Congress, Adams wrote that although he felt "unequal" to the "grand Scene" now opening before him, he could at least "keep an exact Diary, of my Journey, as well as a Journal of the Proceedings of the Congress."[1] He discharged this pledge with less than perfect fidelity; nevertheless, he told more about the birth of the United States in the years 1774–1776 than any of his colleagues did. On the eve of the Declaration of Independence he discovered the virtues of letterbooks, purchased some, and from then until his death a half-century later pretty regularly continued the practice of making copies of all the letters he sent out. On his arrival in Paris in 1778 he was shocked by the casual record-keeping practices of the American mission in Europe, and hastened "to procure some blank books, and to apply myself with Diligence to Business."[2] The result is a matchless body of records documenting many of the crucial transactions concerning American finances and treaty-making in Europe throughout the decade that followed.

Their survival is owing to a combination of solicitude and good luck. Conveying them safely from one European capital to another required endless arrangements and correspondence. In 1784 Adams sent the accumulation in a trunk to his bankers in Amsterdam and asked that they be treated "as a Sacred Deposit."[3] A year later they were brought to London with the Minister's household goods from the Legation at The Hague in order to avoid growing dangers from

[9] This section of the Introduction is mainly a condensation of an article by L. H. Butterfield, "The Papers of the Adams Family: Some Account of Their History," Massachusetts Historical Society, *Proceedings*, 71 (1953–1957): 328–356.

[1] Diary, 20 June 1774 (vol. 2:96).

References to the present edition are in the form given here.

[2] Autobiography under date of 21 April 1778 (vol. 4:77).

[3] To the Willinks, Van Staphorsts, and De la Lande & Fynje, 3 August 1784.

Dutch political disturbances. In 1787 Adams found a trusty hand to send them home by and seized the opportunity. Writing his friend and agent Cotton Tufts back home in Weymouth, he explained:

There is so much Appearance of War, that I thought it a Precaution of Prudence to send my Manuscript Letter Books, and Collections of Papers, relative to all my Transactions in France and Holland, home by Mr. Jenks. They are contained in a large Trunk, and are so numerous as to fill it, so that there is no room for any Thing else in it. I suppose the Custom house officers will let it pass: but they may open it if they please. Yet I hope they will not disturb the order of the Papers. These I suppose are neither prohibited Goods, nor liable to Duties. Let my pray you Sir, to send them to Braintree, to the Care of Mr. Cranch till my Return.[4]

These, in the main, were the papers from which Adams prepared the sprawling autobiographical writings of his old age, important segments of which are presented in the third and fourth volumes of the current publication. Immediately after his wife's death, late in 1818, he made an effort to put his accumulations in order. "Tell Mr. A.," he wrote Mrs. John Quincy Adams in Washington, "that I am assiduously and sedulously employed in Exertions to save him trouble, by collecting all my Papers. What a Mass!"[5] And two days later he informed his son directly that he was

deeply immersed in researches, not astro[no]mical or mineralogical or metaphisical; but after old Papers. Trunks, Boxes, Desks, Drawers locked up for thirty Years have been broken open because the Keys are lost. Nothing stands in my Way. Every Scrap shall be found and preserved for your Affliction [or] for your good.... I shall leave you an inheritance sufficiently tormenting, for example, The huge Pile of family Letters, will make you Alternatly laugh and cry, fret and fume, stamp and scold as they do me.[6]

As good as his word, the old gentleman on the day he signed his will, 27 September 1819, signed a separate deed of gift by which he conveyed to John Quincy Adams "all my Manuscript Letter Books, and Account Books, Letters, Journals, and Manuscript papers," contained in several trunks, a bureau, and an escritoire, each carefully identified.

The son's own accumulations were by this time at least as formidable; they continued to increase until his death, and he was never to find (or for that matter to seek) the leisure to put them in order. Like his father before him he had usually if not invariably acted as the penman for the committees and the commissions on which he served.

[4] 16 October 1787 (Princeton University Library).

[5] 22 December 1818.

[6] 24 December 1818.

Introduction

In the long negotiation at Ghent the younger Adams' relations with
Henry Clay, who liked cards and cigars better than drafting treaty
articles, paralleled those of John Adams with Benjamin Franklin three
or four decades earlier. And in order to complete his own files J. Q.
Adams stayed in Ghent, laboriously copying documents and correspondence, while his wife and little son Charles made their way from
St. Petersburg across Europe, alone, in the dead of winter, and with
Napoleon's veterans gathering for what was to be known to history
as the Hundred Days.[7]

A letter of Abigail Adams' shows how her son entered on his duties
as secretary of state two years and a half later. The new secretary and
his family had been in Quincy about a week after their arrival from
London when Abigail wrote that she had finally been able to persuade
Louisa Catherine to take a short holiday in Boston,

and leave me to see the House put in a little order, which is covered with
trunks, Books and papers, not confined to my sleeping room and the
parlour, but every chamber in the House. For instance, in your uncles
room, ranged in two rows, lie—I will get up and count them—no less than
Eighteen large packages, addrest to all the Govenours in the United States,
with Eighteen Circular Letters of half a page each, all Copied by your
Aunt and Charles Foster, for she has become his private Secretary. Copies
all his private letters into his Letter Books to save his hand and Eyes, his
Eyes being very weak, and his right hand of which he complaind to me
you remember, much upon the tremble like his Fathers. Heaven preserve
both his Eyes and hands, for I am sure he is like to have labour enough
for them; if he fulfills half the additional dutys which Congress by their
direction to the office of States have laid upon him.[8]

This was the way it was always to be with Abigail's son during his
eight-year secretaryship, his four years as President, and his seventeen
years in Congress. He took it upon himself to do the research and to
write a report during hot Washington summers "relative to the regulations and standards for weights and measures in the several states, and
relative to proceedings in foreign countries, for establishing uniformity

[7] Characteristically, Louisa Catherine Adams later wrote an account of this harrowing journey, of which the original, dated at the end 27 June 1836, and a copy are both in the Adams Papers. Her grandson Brooks prepared a rather heavily edited version of her "Narrative of a Journey from St. Petersburg to Paris in February, 1815," and published it in *Scribner's Magazine*, 34:449–463 (October 1903). Her travel costs, in-cluding the purchase of a carriage, were neatly itemized and converted into dollars from rubles, thalers, florins, and francs by her husband in one of his account books surviving in the Adams Papers. The total came to $1606.38.

[8] To Susan Boylston Adams Clark, 26 August 1817 (original owned by Robert Treat Crane Sr., Stonington, Connecticut, 1957; photostat in New York Public Library).

in weights and measures," with accompanying recommendations, which had been called for by Congress before he took office as secretary.[9] Later, in Congress, he laboriously calendared every one of the thousands of anti-slavery petitions that poured in on him during his eight-year fight against successive "gag rules" imposed on the House by Southern congressmen and their allies from the North. In the midst of this fight, when Adams was nearly seventy-three, he tripped on some matting newly laid on the House floor, fell heavily, and dislocated his right shoulder. The first attempt to reset it failed. He was carried out of the chamber and physicians reset the bone. Next day he reported in his diary that he had had "rather an uneasy night" and that his arm was in a sling. "I write against the kindest remonstrances of my family, and attended the morning sitting of the House against those of both my doctors." But in his view such "occasional disabilities" were "admonitions and chastisements of Providence" for his own good, certainly not excuses for leaving the field of action or giving up his record of it.[1]

During the brief interval between his Presidency and his election to Congress, Adams sorted and examined his father's papers and undertook a memoir of him, to contain or be amplified by diary extracts and selected correspondence. The son's diary reveals the slow progress of the work and how little taste he had for it. And it may be added that the two chapters he produced show how little aptitude he had for such a task. They bring John Adams to his thirty-fifth year, breaking off with the Boston Massacre in 1770, and are exceedingly discursive and heavy-handed.[2] Clearly he was only too happy in 1831 to dismiss the "stale excitements" of a former age and buckle on his armor for new political battles that were to continue through the rest of his life. Despairing of ever putting his own papers in order, he left both them and his father's papers to his son Charles, enjoining him, "as soon as he shall find it suit his own convenience," to build a fireproof building in which to keep them.[3]

Charles had already taken up with energy the task his father had dropped with relief. Sorting and reading family papers suited his lonely

[9] *Report upon Weights and Measures, by John Quincy Adams, Secretary of State of the United States. Prepared in Obedience to a Resolution of the Senate of the Third March, 1817*, Washington, 1821. Voluminous notes, drafts, and correspondence pertaining to this *Report* remain in the Adams Papers.

[1] Diary, 18–20 May 1840.

[2] John Adams, *Works ... with a Life of the Author*, ed. Charles Francis Adams, Boston, 1850–1856, 1:3–89. J. Q. Adams' manuscript draft bears evidence that he was struggling as late as 1839 to get on with this filial duty.

[3] Signed copy of J. Q. Adams' will, dated 18 January 1847.

temperament; he loved history; and he developed a talent for historical analysis and editing. His first publication from the family archives was a collection of his grandmother's letters.[4] He offered them to the public with some trepidation because of their intimate character, but to his surprise the book met with immediate and enthusiastic acceptance for that very reason.[5] His next venture was a matching collection of *Letters of John Adams, Addressed to His Wife*.[6] For it he wrote a preface that is a landmark of good sense in an age of irresponsible editing. On the subject of textual fidelity he said:

> If there is one recommendation to a literary work more than any other to be prized, it is that it should present the mind of the writer in as distinct a shape and as free from all extrinsic modeling as possible.... At no time in his life was John Adams a man of many concealments.... There was no hypocrisy in him whilst alive and it would scarcely be doing him justice to invest him with a share of it after his death.... We are beginning to forget that the patriots of former days were men like ourselves, acting and acted upon like the present race, and we are almost irresistibly led to ascribe to them in our imaginations certain gigantic proportions and superhuman qualities, without reflecting that this at once robs their characters of consistency and their virtues of all merit. It is imitating the conduct of those poets and romancers who laud their heroes for courage after having made them invulnerable. Fancy may do as it pleases as its purpose is only to amuse, but history has a nobler object.[7]

In the great task to which he addressed himself after his father's death and the Free Soil campaign of 1848, Charles Francis Adams adhered to these principles as no other historical editor of that period did or even tried to do. In view of the difficulties he faced and the lack of good precedents for the editing of statesmen's papers, his edition of the *Works of John Adams*, published between 1850 and 1856, was a remarkable accomplishment. As a single example, his presentation of the Massachusetts Constitution of 1780, in which he attempted to indicate in his editorial apparatus all the changes that instrument "underwent after it left [John Adams'] hands," from

[4] *Letters of Mrs. Adams, the Wife of John Adams. With an Introductory Memoir*, ed. Charles Francis Adams, Boston, 1840.
[5] A second edition appeared within a few months of first publication, a third in 1841, and a fourth in 1848. The contents vary to some extent in all the editions, the most complete being the last. More easily obtainable than any of

these is the now classic *Familiar Letters of John Adams and His Wife Abigail Adams, during the Revolution*, New York, 1876, a selection, with additions, from both the earlier collections, and a splendid contribution to the literature of the centennial year of the United States.
[6] Boston, 1841; 2 vols.
[7] 1:x–xiv.

1779 to 1840, shows a grasp of scholarly standards and methods not equaled until the work of Paul and Worthington Ford almost half a century later.[8] Generally speaking, C. F. Adams' annotation throughout the volumes is also excellent. In other respects, however, the family edition has not stood up well. The format itself is repellent— "funereal," as Mr. Zoltán Haraszti has said—and the publishers having used inferior materials, the volumes themselves fall apart when used with any frequency. These are faults not attributable to the editor, but both his selection and arrangement of material are decidedly open to question. Happily he printed large portions of both the Diary and Autobiography in the second and third volumes, but thereafter he concentrated, unhappily for John Adams' subsequent reputation, on public writings and official correspondence until the middle of the ninth volume. At this point he announced that room was left for only "a rigid selection" of his grandfather's private letters, although

Probably not a single leading actor of the revolutionary period has left nearly so many as Mr. Adams.... Especially is it matter of regret that room could not be found for the familiar letters as well of Mr. Adams as of his wife, a small portion of which were collected and published by the Editor in another shape some years ago. A number of letters addressed to Mr. Adams by distinguished men, which had been prepared, are likewise excluded, for the same reason. These materials, however, are not lost. They await a later period, when they may be presented in a shape not less durable than the present, to illustrate the heroic age of the United American States.[9]

The effect of these decisions, though of course unintended, was to exaggerate the formal and pompous traits of John Adams' character and literary style, and to minimize the warmth, pungency, humor, and incurable playfulness that are seldom absent from his personal writings. Almost equally unfortunate was C. F. Adams' complicated classification by subject or type of the materials he selected for editing, an arrangement that results in half a dozen or more overlapping chronological sequences, deprives the record of the writer's career of all continuity, and almost guarantees that one will not find a given letter or document where one expects to. Many, many times students must have consulted the volumes, searched for an item that ought to be there, and put them aside without finding what they wanted— even though it was there, perhaps tucked away in an appendix, a footnote, or an introductory commentary on some other document.

The prospectus for "The Life and Works of John Adams," issued

[8] John Adams, *Works*, 4:213–267.   [9] Same, 9:331.

by Little & Brown of Boston in February 1849, stated that if this publication were well received, the editor and publishers would "be encouraged to go on and perfect the other and later part of it, the Life and Works of the no less distinguished son, JOHN QUINCY ADAMS." At that time the family editor obviously viewed his double task as a unified enterprise. But with the approach of the Civil War he was drawn back into politics, and from politics into diplomacy, so that it was to be many years before he could undertake the work of memorializing his father's career. In preparation for it and in fulfillment of his father's injunction, he built a fireproof library adjacent to the Old House in Quincy.[1] After returning from the arbitration tribunal at Geneva he settled down in 1873 to edit John Quincy Adams' diary, for he had now decided that this one monumental document, extending (with a few early gaps) over seventy years, would serve his father's memory better than a biography and a selection of his papers after the pattern of the *Works of John Adams*. Or perhaps, understandably, he quailed in the face of "the super-abundance of the materials."[2] The preface to the *Memoirs of John Quincy Adams* set forth clearly and tersely the editor's principles of selection. To be omitted were "details of common life and events of no interest to the public." To be reduced were "the moral and religious speculations, in which the work abounds." Nothing was to be excluded merely because it might be or seem unfavorable to either the diarist or any of his contemporaries. And there was to be no "modification of the sentiments or the very words, and substitution of what might seem better ones."[3] So far as the present editors' knowledge now extends, these principles were faithfully applied. The chief deficiencies of the *Memoirs* are, first, that such a very great deal had to be left out, especially relative to the writer's personal as distinct from his public life, in order to compress the text into twelve large octavo volumes—twice as many as the editor and publisher had planned on; and, second, the almost total absence of editorial notes and commentary. A lesser fault, but a serious one in so large a work, is the woefully inadequate index.

Whatever faults may be found with C. F. Adams' editing, he accomplished an astonishing amount of work as family archivist and editor, and performed that work with great skill and intelligence. He was beyond question the ablest historical editor of his time in the

[1] The Stone Library was designed by Edward Clark Cabot and constructed in 1869–1870.

[2] John Quincy Adams, *Memoirs ...,*

Comprising Portions of His Diary from 1795 to 1848, ed. Charles Francis Adams, Philadelphia, 1874–1877, 1:vi.

[3] Same, p. viii.

United States. In 1886 he died, leaving his "papers, manuscripts and printed books ... to such of my four sons as may survive me, and the survivors and survivor of them, in trust," to be kept together in the Stone Library at Quincy as long as "any of my male descendants bearing the family name shall continue to reside upon the said mansion house estate." [4] All four of his sons survived him. Three of them had literary and historical tastes and made use of the family papers for one scholarly purpose or another. Henry used them surprisingly little and before long grew inexpressibly bored with anything that concerned family history.[5] Brooks made dashes at them from time to time over a long period. To the second Charles Francis fell the task of preparing a suitable literary memorial to his father. But his plans for a massive documentary biography, which was to embrace the whole of American foreign relations during the Civil War, grew so ambitious that they were left unfinished at his death.[6] All that he completed was a succinct, undocumented, but admirable memoir of his father for the American Statesmen series, published in 1900.

As for the disposition of the family papers, which by now embraced the personal and official records of three major American statesmen, the brothers who jointly owned them had difficulty in determining their best course of action. It was the younger Charles Francis who hit upon the Bostonian expedient of placing the papers beyond the dangers of plundering, sale, or dispersal by creating the Adams Manuscript Trust in 1905. By consent of all the heirs of full age to the still undivided estate of the first Charles Francis Adams, the declaration of trust vested in four trustees (the three surviving brothers and their nephew, a third Charles Francis, 1866–1954) the absolute ownership and the care and supervision of the entire family archives. The Trust was to run for fifty years, and the trustees were to appoint their own successors during that period from among other lineal descendants of the first Charles Francis. They were also empowered during the term of the Trust to convey its property, by gift or otherwise, to the United States, the State of Massachusetts, or a chartered institution, and in any case within a year of its expiration they were to transfer ownership of the Trust's property as they saw fit, "with

[4] Will, signed 12 September 1871 (Norfolk County Probate Registry, No. 25,276).

[5] He had printed one major unpublished paper by J. Q. Adams in *Documents Relating to New-England Federalism, 1800–1815*, Boston, 1877, but one may look almost in vain for citations of the Adams Papers in his nine-volume *History of the United States of America* [1801–1817], New York, 1889–1891.

[6] His extensive transcripts from British, French, and United States archives, together with segments of the biography itself, remain in the Adams Papers.

full power first to destroy the whole or such part" of it as they thought best.[7] While the expressed intent of the agreement was to preserve the family papers intact, the trustees' unexpressed purpose was simply to gain time. Not knowing what some of the papers might contain, they were uncertain what would be their best ultimate disposition, and they meant to keep them under close family control until they or their successors could make up their minds.

For their better physical protection the papers themselves had been moved in 1902 from the Stone Library in Quincy to the new building of the Massachusetts Historical Society on the Fenway in Boston. Six years later C. F. Adams 2d, president of the Historical Society, persuaded Worthington C. Ford to become editor of the Society's publications. A scholar of international standing and endowed with incredible energy, Ford had known the Adams brothers well, and he enjoyed enough of their confidence to be given more or less unrestricted access to the Adams family manuscripts. With the brothers' approval—after all, it was a burden lifted from their shoulders—Ford soon projected an edition of John Quincy Adams' letters and other writings. He made rapid progress with it until war shortages caused the publisher, Macmillan, to break off publication with the seventh of an intended twelve-volume set.[8] As late as 1925 Ford hoped to resume and complete the edition, but his hopes proved vain. Probably Brooks Adams, the sole surviving son of Charles Francis the diplomat, opposed the continuation, as he seems in his later years to have opposed any and all use of the family papers. Ford turned to other projects,[9] and after Brooks' death in 1927 the trustees in effect sealed the collection in the double-locked Adams Room on the first floor of the Historical Society building. Exceptions were sometimes made when scholars applied for copies of letters written to Adamses rather than letters and other papers written by them. The late Henry Adams 2d (1875–1951), a trustee from 1927 until his death, was fond of antiquarian pursuits and laboriously typed by the hunt-and-peck system a great many copies of such letters and sent them to inquirers. But in general the policy that he and his cousin Charles Francis 3d agreed on and applied was

[7] The instrument is in the Norfolk County Registry of Deeds, vol. 1016, p. 443; it was signed 14 December and entered 29 December 1905. The Trust included the John and John Quincy Adams birthplaces, which were given to the City of Quincy in 1940, and the Adams mansion (or Old House), which was given to the United States in 1946.

[8] John Quincy Adams, *Writings*, ed. Worthington C. Ford, New York, 1913–1917. The seventh volume ends in the year 1823, short of Adams' Presidency.

[9] On Ford's other editorial ventures involving writings of the Adamses, see L. H. Butterfield's article, cited above, in Massachusetts Historical Society, *Proceedings*, 71:350, note.

that what had been published of the Adamses' writings was all that should be published. As to the ultimate fate of the family archives they preferred to await the expiration of the Trust and the voice of a new generation.

The Present Enterprise

The history of the present editorial enterprise begins with the appointment, following the death of Henry Adams 2d, of two trustees bearing the historic names of Thomas Boylston Adams and John Quincy Adams, great-grandsons of Charles Francis Adams the Civil War diplomat. After preliminary discussions with several historians in Boston, the trustees invited a group of scholars who represented, though unofficially, the Massachusetts Historical Society, the Boston Athenæum, the American Antiquarian Society, the American Council of Learned Societies, the National Park Service, the Institute of Early American History and Culture, and several universities, to meet with them at the Adams National Historic Site in August 1952. To this group gathered in the Stone Library where the first Charles Francis Adams had edited his father's *Memoirs* and where Henry Adams had finished his *History of the United States,* Mr. Thomas B. Adams announced the decision of the trustees to put the Adams Papers freely in the service of history. He then asked how this might best be done. Once the significance of the question and of the moment was grasped, the answer was readily forthcoming: the papers should be published on microfilm as a nonprofit venture in the public interest, the cost to be met by subscriptions from the libraries purchasing sets of the films. An advisory committee of scholars was appointed to plan the edition. Grants for photographic equipment were obtained from the American Philosophical Society and the American Academy of Arts and Sciences, with both of which the Adams family had been associated since the 18th century. Preparation of the papers for filming began at the Historical Society, the sponsoring institution, in the following fall, under the oversight of Dr. Stephen T. Riley, then librarian (now director) of the Society; and technical supervision of the microfilming operation was undertaken by Dr. Vernon D. Tate, then librarian of the Massachusetts Institute of Technology.[1] The microfilm edition of *The Adams Papers,* 1639–1889, was published in four major installments (Part I, Diaries; Part II, Letterbooks; Part III, Miscellany; Part IV, Letters Received and Other Loose Papers) in 608 reels between 1954 and 1959. The

[1] From 1956 Mr. Peter R. Scott, head of the Microreproduction Laboratory, Massachusetts Institute of Technology, served as technical supervisor.

materials filmed have been made freely available for research, but in the interest of the printed edition, hoped for from the outset and later realized, they are protected by copyright.[2]

With the Adams family archives as a whole under scholarly examination for the first time, the possibility of a letterpress edition commensurate with the quantity and importance of the materials could be discussed in realistic terms. Early in 1954 Mr. Thomas J. Wilson, director of Harvard University Press, informed the trustees of the Adams Manuscript Trust that the Press was willing and eager to publish such an edition and was authorized by representatives of the Harvard Corporation to assume all the publishing expenses incident thereto. Mr. Wilson's proposal was made possible by a recent and generous bequest to the Press by the late Waldron P. Belknap Jr. for the publication of important sources and studies in American history, and it was promptly accepted by the Adams trustees. In respect to finances this left only the question of funds to support editorial work. This question too was soon settled. Mr. Roy E. Larsen, chairman of the Visiting Committee of Harvard University Press and president of Time, Inc., shortly proposed that his company purchase first serial publication rights to the Adams Papers on behalf of *Life*. By an agreement signed in August 1954 Time, Inc., pledged itself to pay to the Massachusetts Historical Society the sum of $250,000 over a period of ten years in return for the right to publish serially in *Life*, in advance of book publication, materials prepared for the Belknap Press edition of *The Adams Papers*; and the Society agreed (on behalf of the Adams Manuscript Trust) to be responsible for the editing of the family papers in an acceptable scholarly form. The Society appointed an Administrative Board representing itself, the Press, and the Trust. The Administrative Board appointed an editor in chief and an Editorial Advisory Committee. In the last week of November 1954 the editor took possession of an office adjacent to the Adams manuscripts, by then transferred to the Society's manuscript stack, and editorial work began.

The ultimate event in the physical and legal history of the family archives occurred a year and a half later. By a deed of gift dated 4 April 1956 Thomas Boylston Adams and John Quincy Adams, trustees, transferred and conveyed to the Massachusetts Historical Society

all right, title and interest of the said Trust (including all literary rights, copyrights and rights to future income and proceeds) in, to and from all

[2] Quotation from the filmed documents is permitted on as liberal a scale as possible, but only upon written application to the Massachusetts Historical Society. While editing of the letterpress edition is in progress, the manuscripts themselves (through the year 1889) are not available for consultation.

manuscripts, letters, letter-books, documents, public and private, diaries and other material belonging to the said Trust and now located on the premises of the said Society . . . , being all of the trust property remaining in the hands of the Trustees.

The document is signed by the two trustees, who thereby dissolved the Trust, and by Mr. John Adams, then president of the Society, signifying acceptance of the gift.

After the manner of Adamses, the family had discharged its trust well. The integrity of the records they created, accumulated, and preserved is in marked contrast with the fate of most other bodies of papers comparable in extent and importance—if any have been—in the United States and particularly during the early period of its history. The principal family archivist and editor pointed out more than once, in varying language, that "America is not the place for preservation of papers in the hands of families. The modes of life are too migratory, and the means of subsistence too precarious to be favorable to this object"[3]—which is another way of saying that the shirtsleeves-to-shirtsleeves pattern of American life has usually meant, at least until the present century, the sale and dispersal of accumulations of historical manuscripts. The history of the Adams Papers has been singularly free of such misfortunes. Weeding to be sure did from time to time take place. For example, there must once have existed many more letters written to John Adams before the Revolution than can now be found, and we know from numerous references in the first Charles Francis Adams' diary and correspondence that he destroyed, as inconsequential, the bulk of the letters received by both his grandmother and his mother except those written by members of the family. Among the sons of the first Charles Francis the destruction of their own papers was much heavier: the second John Quincy kept few papers; the second Charles Francis destroyed some of his early diaries (though nothing like what his *Autobiography* appears to imply);[4] Henry burned up virtually all his diaries in 1888, along with a great many of the letters he had received, and such of his own letters as he could recover (though fortunately he did not succeed too well in this last endeavor); and of Brooks Adams' correspondence very little survives except the letters he exchanged with his brother Henry, now in the Houghton Library at Harvard. During the early stages of the autograph-collecting fad in the 19th century both John Quincy Adams

[3] Preface to *Letters of John Adams, Addressed to His Wife,* 1:xiii.
[4] *Charles Francis Adams, 1835–1915: An Autobiography. Prepared for the Massachusetts Historical Society,* Boston and New York, 1916, p. 27–28, 110–111.

and his son Charles Francis occasionally pilfered from the manuscripts to gratify requests from institutions, charity fairs, and even individuals.[5] But no evidence is known to the present editors of the sale of a single scrap of manuscript from the family archives in their entire history.

Whatever losses of these kinds may have been sustained, the assemblage was still so enormous in 1954 that it required extended exploration. The first task of the editor and the small staff he gathered in the following months was to prepare an item-by-item inventory of the papers as the family custodians had left them. The purpose of the inventory was not merely to extend a preliminary control over the mass but also to make it possible to determine at a later stage (if it proved desirable for editorial purposes—and it often has) the location and context of any given item according to the family's arrangement of the manuscripts. About 650 entries appear in the inventory, most of them representing bound volumes and containers of loose manuscripts with some identity of their own, but ranging in size from the four-page sheet on which John Adams made his copy of Jefferson's draft of the Declaration of Independence while it was still in committee, to a gigantic folio containing the Geneva Arbitration documents, some 800 pages in all, assembled by the first C. F. Adams and bound up by his son Henry.

As the volumes, boxes, portfolios, and bundles were inventoried, all the unbound materials were placed in a single chronological sequence, and to these were added, after decasing and repairing, letters and other papers that had originally been separate pieces but had been arranged and bound by various family custodians according to their notions of convenience—by correspondent, by office, by subject, by period, and the like. Decasing of groups of manuscripts sewed into heavy leather bindings was essential in order both to photograph them and to establish a control over individual pieces (that is, to be able to find them when wanted). For the latter purpose it was also necessary to number serially every letter and other document copied into the three statesmen's letterbooks, totaling about 21,000 items. The method of control—a simplified catalogue or finding list on slips in duplicate arranged both by date and alphabetically by the names of writers and recipients of letters and other papers—was borrowed from Mr. Julian P. Boyd's system in the editorial office of *The Papers of Thomas*

---

[5] Among the beneficiaries were such well-known autograph collectors as Lewis J. Cist, Lyman C. Draper, Frank M. Etting, and Israel K. Tefft. Eventually C. F. Adams grew more chary in gratifying such requests.

Jefferson at Princeton, but with modifications and elaborations because in the Adams Papers there is no single focal figure but many.

These operations required two full years, to the end of 1956. But they were not the only ones performed by the Adams Papers staff during that time and that have continued into the period of transcription and editing. There was, first of all, the problem of locating and adding to the editorial files photocopies of pertinent Adams materials outside the family's own archives. Several hundred inquiries were sent to likely repositories in this country and abroad requesting lists of Adams materials held by them; the lists returned were studied for essential and nonessential items; orders for photoduplicates were placed for those considered essential, and the others were recorded in the control file for their possible relevance later on. Filmed materials were printed up on paper and processed as if originals (though stored in a file of "accessions" separate from the Adams Papers proper). The chief concentrations of material, as anticipated, have been found in the Boston area, where we have been able to do our own searching, and in the great Federal repositories in Washington, where we have had the invaluable help of the staff of the National Historical Publications Commission. Among the manuscript collections of the Massachusetts Historical Society alone over 2,600 supplementary items have been located, and the search is still incomplete. Harvard, the Boston Public Library, the Massachusetts Archives, and the American Antiquarian Society have all contributed heavily. A rich mine of material has also been found in the Clerk's Office of the Supreme Judicial Court, County of Suffolk. Some hundreds of papers documenting John Adams' legal career before the Revolution have been earmarked among the early court files there but have not yet been photocopied for this enterprise. From Washington the Library of Congress had at the end of 1960 furnished the Adams Papers with more than 1,250 supplementary letters and other writings in photofacsimile, chiefly dating before 1800 because searches had so far been concentrated in this early period. From the National Archives the Adams Papers staff had accessioned by the same date more than 1,050 pieces, but literally thousands more had been received in the form of microfilm publications of United States diplomatic correspondence during John Quincy Adams' long public career and were awaiting processing while John Adams' Diary and Autobiography were being edited. The total number of supplementary items processed at the end of 1960 was something over 11,000, drawn from 204 different institutional and private sources.

Searches of printed sources, of dealers' catalogues, and of auction records have been carried on in the Adams editorial office as time and hands permitted, and the findings recorded in the control file. Such searches, though tedious, yield quantities of pertinent material, some of it of first importance, that would otherwise be overlooked. They can never, of course, be considered complete.

Other editorial aids have been developed as circumstances allowed. Of prime importance is an Adams Bibliography, based on Library of Congress author and subject cards but so vastly amplified that no guess beyond "thousands" can be made as to the number of entries by and about members of the Adams family this file contains. The editors hope that sooner or later the bibliography can be edited and published as a reference tool of independent value. The Adamses collected as well as published books on a heroic scale, and what is more they read their books and put them to use in performing their public duties. The editorial staff has therefore made a start on a union catalogue of all books known to have been owned by the Adamses, wherever they are now located, incorporating information on place and date of purchase, marginalia, and the like.[6] A third working aid that has been carefully nurtured is a documented and indexed genealogy of the Presidential line of the Adamses and their close connections by blood and marriage. The editors plan to present this in print in conjunction with the Adams Family Correspondence (Series II of the present edition). And a fourth editorial aid, to mention no more, is a compilation of data and photographs concerning Adams iconography: portraits, views of residences and other sites associated with the family, and physical survivals of all sorts. This file serves not only as a stockpile of material for illustrations for the volumes being published but frequently, like the others that have already been mentioned, as a ready means of interpreting and annotating allusions in the Adams diaries and correspondence.

Plan of the Edition as a Whole

This summary of work done and in progress has run ahead of the main story of editorial planning for the letterpress edition of *The Adams Papers*. Planning began as soon as the work of inventorying

[6] John Adams' library, given to the town of Quincy in 1822, has come to rest, more or less intact, in the Boston Public Library. Though John Quincy Adams' books remain for the most part in the Stone Library at the former family homestead in Quincy, his pamphlet collection, numbering thousands of titles, was given to the Boston Athenæum by his son in 1848, and others of his books have been placed on deposit there in more recent times. The main collection of Henry Adams' books was given to the Massachusetts Historical Society in 1919, though a portion had been given by the owner during his lifetime to Western Reserve University. Many of the second Charles Francis' books are at the Old House in Quincy; his extensive collection of bound pamphlets is in the Massachusetts Historical Society.

and arranging the papers was completed. Two major decisions were made at an early stage by the editor in chief with the concurrence of the Editorial Advisory Committee and the Syndics of the Harvard University Press. The first decision established the year 1889 as the cut-off date for materials to be included in the edition. Some terminus had to be fixed in a body of papers that extended well into the 20th century, and the year chosen was that in which Abigail Brooks Adams, wife of the first Charles Francis, died. Since she was the last of the "third generation," there was logic in the choice, but there was also common sense, because the three highly articulate members of the fourth generation—Charles Francis 2d, Henry, and Brooks—have either been receiving or can be counted on to receive adequate scholarly attention outside the present editorial undertaking. Content with documents spanning exactly two and a half centuries, the editors have turned over to the Massachusetts Historical Society, to be served to readers like its other manuscript collections, all Adams papers dated from 1890 onward.

The other major decision was that the letterpress edition, with the exception of the diaries of the statesmen, is to be selective rather than all-inclusive in the pattern of the Jefferson, Franklin, and a number of other documentary publications now in progress. Confronting a mass of papers running to several hundred thousand pages emanating from famous and obscure Adamses and their correspondents, the editor and his advisers were never in doubt on this score. Not all the writings and all the "recorded actions"[7] of all the Adamses, it was agreed, deserve perpetuation in type; it will be proper, and sufficient, to make available the entire corpus of the family archives on microfilm, but to publish in volumes only those portions which have substantial human or historical interest. Under this arrangement readers will be disburdened of much they do not want, and scholars will not be deprived of anything they do.

These decisions having been made, the character of the papers themselves has shaped the edition in its main outlines. It will consist of three principal series of volumes, numbered I, II, and III merely for convenience and not as an indication of the order in which they will appear.

Series I will embrace the Adams Diaries and will be divided into at least three parts of disparate length: one for each of the Adams statesmen and possibly a fourth for the diary fragments and autobio-

[7] Julian P. Boyd's phrase in his introduction to *The Papers of Thomas Jefferson*, Princeton, 1950– , 1:vii.

graphical writings of Louisa Catherine Adams. The texts of the diaries of the statesmen will be published complete, without regard to previous publication of parts of some of them. To publish still another selection would simply leave the job to be done over again later, as has so often happened before with important diaries. The first part of Series I, the Diary of John Adams from 1755 to 1804, amplified by the three large fragments of his Autobiography, by three brief journals kept by Abigail Adams, and by certain other diary-like material from his papers, is presented in the four volumes now published. The second part, John Quincy Adams' Diary from 1779 to 1848, of which perhaps half has never been published before, will run to an estimated twenty to twenty-four volumes. The third part, Charles Francis Adams' Diary, 1820–1880, of which only a few snippets have ever appeared in print, may run to sixteen or eighteen volumes. Mrs. J. Q. Adams' journals and recollections, if published by themselves, will fill a volume.

Series II will be devoted to the Adams Family Correspondence. It will extend in a single chronological sequence from the courtship letters exchanged by John and Abigail Adams beginning in 1762, through three generations and part of a fourth, to the death of Abigail Brooks Adams in 1889. The second Abigail in the family (later Mrs. William Stephens Smith) remarked in one of her long journal-letters from London to her brother John Quincy in 1785 that the members of their family were brought up "Strangers to each other" because of their continuous foreign travels.[8] This habit increased among the Adamses of the next century, but so did their habit of letter-writing to compensate for it, and the network of family communication grew ever wider and at the same time more closely meshed. Distinctive portions of it have been put into print, for example in the early collections of John Adams' and Abigail Adams' *Letters* mentioned above in this Introduction; in Stewart Mitchell's *New Letters of Abigail Adams, 1788–1801* (1947), based on a collection of Mrs. Adams' letters to her sister Mary Cranch in the American Antiquarian Society; and in Worthington C. Ford's edition of the three-way correspondence of the first Charles Francis and his sons Charles and Henry during the Civil War, entitled *A Cycle of Adams Letters* (1920; 2 vols.). It may seem hardly credible, but these are only samplings from the mine. The greatest merit of the Adams family correspondence is its continuity. It is an unbroken record of changing modes of domestic life, religious views and habits, travel, servants, dress, food, schooling,

[8] Letter of 4 July–11 August 1785.

reading, health and medical care, diversions, and every other conceivable aspect of manners and taste among the members of a substantial New England family who lived on both sides of the Atlantic and wrote industriously to each other over a period of more than a century. The editors recognize that separating family from general correspondence and thus creating an additional chronological sequence has disadvantages. But the advantages of presenting the story of the family, as told by the family, appear to them to be greater. Among other things it enables the women of the family (whether they were born into it or married into it) to be heard fully, and they are worth hearing.

Series II will be selective, but the term "family" will be broadly interpreted in choosing letters for inclusion. The criteria governing selection have not been precisely formulated and perhaps neither can nor should be. Those letters between members of the family, together with other letters written and received by the Adams ladies, will be included which reveal something of consequence about one or more members of the family. Previous publication will be disregarded in selecting letters. Since this is a very elastic formula, only a wild guess can be made concerning the length of Series II. It may possibly extend to twenty volumes.

Series III will have the over-all title General Correspondence and Other Papers and, like Series I, will be divided into three parts: The Papers of John Adams, The Papers of John Quincy Adams, and The Papers of Charles Francis Adams. Each part will contain a comprehensive selection from the letters written by and to the statesman concerned (excluding letters exchanged between him and members of his family) and from his other writings, such as committee reports, diplomatic dispatches, newspaper communications, speeches and messages, literary productions, and the like. The scale of inclusiveness remains to be determined. Presumably the statesmen's correspondence, without regard to previous publication, together with unpublished, inadequately edited, and inaccessible political writings and diplomatic dispatches, will have the highest priority. Certain bulky works pose special problems. John Adams' *Defence of the Constitutions of Government of the United States of America* (1787–1788), for example, appears to be more in need of a bibliographical monograph than of a new edition. The same is true of John Quincy Adams' two-volume *Lectures on Rhetoric and Oratory ...* (1810), the product of his Boylston professorship at Harvard. Probably few of either J. Q. Adams' or C. F. Adams' occasional speeches deserve republication, though their speeches in the Massachusetts legislature and in Congress must certainly be represented. From the immense number of J. Q. Adams' poetical effusions, ranging from sonnets for young ladies' autograph albums to a mock-epic on a theme in Irish medieval history, and filling over twenty volumes in the Adams Papers Miscellany, a light sampling will suffice. On the other hand, his great *Report on Weights and Measures* does deserve a modern scholarly edition; and John Adams' legal records, fragmentary and cryptic as many of them are, would, if adequately edited, contribute significantly to our knowledge of the judicial system and modes of legal practice in Massachusetts prior to the Revolution, as well as to the social history of that period.

Too many questions of this kind remain unanswered to permit sensible guesses about the length of Series III or any of its parts. The number of volumes in *The Adams Papers*, if completed on a scale commensurate with the bulk, variety, and importance of the materials available, will run at least to eighty and possibly to a hundred. Not even so rough an estimate could have been made before prolonged study was given to the Adams Papers at large, an undertaking not feasible until the present editorial enterprise was agreed to and its funds allotted. No one, in other words, had thoroughly explored this ocean until the present principal editor launched his open boat upon it. In view of his findings he labors under no illusion that he will live to see the publication completed. But he has felt he has had no choice but to plan it in as nearly ideal terms as possible, and to execute that part of it he is privileged to execute without regard to immediate limitations of time and funds. To have done less would have been to add another to the long series of editions of statesmen's papers that are monuments to inadequate planning, duplicative effort, and little faith.

3. JOHN ADAMS' DIARY AND AUTOBIOGRAPHY: THE MANUSCRIPTS AND EARLIER PUBLICATION

The Diary Manuscript

John Adams' Diary consists physically of fifty-one manuscript pieces, though to be perfectly accurate some of these are themselves multiple pieces or scraps. Of the fifty-one pieces the greater part (including the first twenty-four, which extend from 1755 to 1775) are stitched or unstitched gatherings of leaves of pocket size (6″ x 4″, more or less), sometimes protected by wrappers of marbled paper or a piece of contemporary newsprint and sometimes altogether unprotected. Some notion of their appearance can be obtained from the reproductions in the present volume of the first two pages of the earliest Diary booklet. John Quincy Adams referred to the early booklets as his father's "Journal Fragments"; Charles Francis Adams called them "Paper Books" (sometimes shortened to "P.B."). Later units of the Diary as arranged and left by the family custodians are assemblages of folded sheets of various sizes, small memorandum books bound in soft or hard covers, and larger, bound journal books.

C. F. Adams numbered the pieces of this heterogeneous collection serially through No. 31. The Adams Papers staff has preserved and extended this numbering in order to facilitate references to particular parts of the manuscript. The present numbering is as follows: D/JA/1–22, 22A, 22B, 23–49. It has not seemed necessary to furnish here a tabulation of all the booklets, loose sheets, and bound journals, with the respective dates they cover, but in the present edition the first entry drawn from a new unit of the manuscript is signaled in a footnote, and the complex dovetailing of entries from overlapping parts of the manuscript is also indicated, because it sometimes explains passages that would otherwise be meaningless.

J. Q. Adams' term "Journal Fragments" is a little ambiguous. It should not be taken to mean that there was once more of John Adams' Diary than now exists, but rather that what does exist is full of gaps, the Diary seldom having been kept regularly and whole years sometimes passing without any entries whatever. One cannot pronounce on the matter beyond all possibility of doubt, but probably no manuscripts existed that have not survived. In a very few instances leaves may possibly have been removed from the fragile early booklets, or much more likely simply lost in handling.[9] For only two entries in the entire Diary have the present editors had to rely on C. F. Adams' printed text rather than on a manuscript source.[1]

Both the nature of the entries and the physical condition of the manuscripts show that John Adams carried the paper booklets of his Diary in his pocket as he rode the court circuits from county to county before the Revolution and as he traveled to and from the Continental Congress. Until he began his record of debates in Congress in Septem-

[9] See notes at vol. 1:71, 102, 216.

[1] 10 August and first entry of 15 August 1774 (vol. 2:97–98). C. F. Adams' source was probably a separate page of Diary entries later accidentally lost. Concerning an important segment of the Diary (D/JA/8) which strayed at an unknown time from the family archives and was returned to them in 1913, see vol. 1:226, note 1.

ber 1775, which was the third session he attended, he evidently did not indulge himself in a durable, store-bought notebook for diary purposes. The home-made booklets he used until then (D/JA/1–22B) were usually ill-protected against wear and, before he put them aside, often became so badly worn that their front and back pages are now scarcely legible and their fore-edges are ragged and chipped away. Since in early life he wrote in a fine hand and economized on paper by leaving no margins whatever, transcription of the early Diary has been tedious and difficult work. Nor has it been facilitated by Adams' careless habits in writing up his journal. He often kept several booklets going at once, sometimes proceeded simultaneously from the front and back of the same booklet, used old partially filled booklets for much later entries, and occasionally went long periods without dating his entries at all. There are also cases where the threads holding the sheets together have parted and the booklets are now mere assemblages of loose leaves without determinable order.

John Quincy Adams was the first person to read the Diary as his father had left it. In the summer of 1829 he set himself the task of examining John Adams' papers and preparing an extended memoir interspersed with excerpts from his father's Diary and letters.[2] Finding the early parts of the manuscript fragile, "scarcely legible," and in confused order, he set two young men to work copying them: his nephew Thomas Boylston Adams Jr. ("the Lieutenant") and a neighbor who was also a relative, William Cranch Greenleaf. This work went on into November and probably from time to time in later years. While we must be grateful for it, because the early transcripts preserve some passages of the Diary texts now utterly lost through the physical deterioration of the originals, the transcription could hardly have been done worse. J. Q. Adams thriftily chose to have the copies written into two of his father's larger, bound journal books;[3] the boys (for they were hardly more than that) could neither read nor understand much of what they were copying; and they were given little or no guidance concerning the order in which the material should be copied. The results were a fearful hodgepodge. They remained such until C. F. Adams went to work on his edition of John Adams' Diary and, by his careful correction of the texts, filling in of gaps, and indi-

[2] See John Quincy Adams' Diary, July–November 1829; also p. xxvi, above.

[3] D/JA/47 and 48. A third, new bound volume (D/JA/49) was later obtained in which to continue the transcripts. The first forty-four pages of D/JA/49 are in Louisa Catherine Adams' hand, and sundry other hands appear in this volume. The transcripts of the Diary booklets end with the entry of 18 December 1773, in D/JA/19.

cating correspondences between the originals and the copies, rendered the copies of some use to himself and his successors.

The Autobiography Manuscript

The manuscript of John Adams' Autobiography consists of three large fragments, none of them bearing that title. All three parts were written on folio sheets folded once to make four quarto pages that are mostly of precisely the same size (8⅞″ x 7″), but with a few larger sheets that have plagued his editors because the three outer edges of these long ago grew brittle from exposure to the air, have partly cracked off, and have carried away some words and passages beyond recovery.

The manuscript as a whole runs to about 450 pages. Disregarding one or two false starts, the three main segments may be described as follows:

Part One, entitled "John Adams," in 53 numbered sheets (plus a few insertions), is dated at the head of the text 5 October 1802; a few pages farther on it is said to have been resumed on 30 November 1804; and it contains later references in the text to 21 February, 8 March, and 7 June 1805 as contemporary with the composition of the manuscript—the last of these dates appearing near the end. Part One begins with what the writer knew about the coming of the Adamses to Massachusetts Bay in the 1630's and ends with John Adams' departure from the Continental Congress for Braintree in mid-October 1776.

Part Two, entitled "Travels, and Negotiations," in 37 numbered sheets (plus a number of insertions), is dated at the head of the text 1 December 1806; about a third of the way through the writer refers to the current year as still 1806. Part Two begins chronologically in November 1777 with the writer's return to Braintree from Congress and his appointment immediately thereafter as joint American commissioner to France; it breaks off with a copy of a letter dated at Passy, 25 July 1778.

Part Three, entitled "Peace," in 18 numbered sheets (plus one insertion), bears no date of composition, but an entry in it dated 14 December 1779 refers to 1807 as the current year, and the entire fragment was doubtless written during that year. It begins with a copy of a letter from the Chevalier de La Luzerne, Philadelphia, 29 September 1779, congratulating Adams on his appointment to negotiate a peace with Great Britain, and it ends after the first few lines of a copy of Adams' letter to Vergennes written at Paris, 21 March 1780.[4]

[4] On the composition of the Autobiography and its sudden termination, see further p. lxx–lxxi, below.

This summary gives no notion of the complex—a better word might be chaotic—structure of John Adams' Autobiography. A glance through the last portion of Part One ("John Adams") will, however, do so. Adams wrote most of this first large fragment from an unaided memory, never stopping to consult his own Diary or files of correspondence or the contemporaneously published *Journals* of the Continental Congress which he had in multiple copies on his bookshelves. In this manner he carried the narrative rapidly through the sessions of Congress in 1774, 1775, and 1776 up to the drafting of the Declaration of Independence and the appointment of a committee "for preparing the Model of a Treaty to be proposed to France" in June 1776.[5] But in his account of this last measure he left a blank for the names of the members of the committee, for here it evidently occurred to him that he could look these names up in the printed *Journals*. Although he never did supply the missing names, his very next paragraph begins with the remark: "I have omitted some things in 1775 which must be inserted."[6] His glance at the first volume of the *Journals* reminded him of all sorts of things he had not dealt with sufficiently or at all up to the point he had reached in his narrative. He at once reverted to affairs in Congress in September 1775 and, browsing at large, began to copy freely from the volume in hand, with remarks, through the point when he left Congress in December of that year.[7] Having launched upon this method of combining excerpts and commentary— no new method of composition, to be sure, for him—he found it so suited to his taste that he now went back still farther. Observing that he "should be a little more particular, in relating the Rise and Progress of the new Governments of the States," he reviewed the first volume of the *Journals* for material pertinent to that subject from 2 June 1775, touching as well on some matters that were *not* pertinent to it, until he had again brought the story up to mid-1776 with the voting of independence and the adoption of the Declaration of Independence.[8] He now simply continued his review, from early July through his journey with Benjamin Franklin and Edward Rutledge to confer with Lord Howe at Staten Island in September and the report of that mission.[9] At this point, for no discernible reason, it occurred to him for the first time in composing his Autobiography to look at his old letterbooks. "To a few of my most confidential friends," he remarked by way of transition, "I expressed my feelings, in a very few Words,

[5] See vol. 3:337.
[6] Vol. 3:338.
[7] Vol. 3:338–351, including one wholly unexpected leap forward to his

appointment on 12 June 1776 as president of the Board of War (p. 342).
[8] Vol. 3:351–398.
[9] Vol. 3:398–423.

which I found time to write: and all the Letters, of which I find Copies, in my Letter Book, are here subjoined, relative to this Transaction [Gen. John Sullivan's invitation from Howe and the conference which followed] from its Beginning to its End."[1] The rest of Part One is largely a collection of letter copies from August through early October. At length Adams noted that "Some time in the month of October ... I asked Leave of Congress to be absent, which they readily granted." But "before I proceed to relate the Occurrences of this Journey, I will copy some other Letters which ought to be inserted in this place, or perhaps they would be better thrown into an Appendix all together."[2] Then, after copying in a single letter of the preceding August, he stopped flat. He never related "the Occurrences of this Journey" home, and he never filled in the gap between October 1776 and November 1777, where Part Two of the Autobiography begins.

These details are tedious, but they show the disorderly and fitful way in which Adams worked. This was to be his way again when he composed the other two parts of his Autobiography, with this principal difference, that in the meantime he had rediscovered his old diaries and drew so heavily upon them, as well as upon his letterbooks, throughout "Travels and Negotiations" and "Peace" that these two parts of the Autobiography have more of the character of compilations than of original compositions.

After John Quincy Adams was launched on his memoir of his father, he discovered "two collections of loose sheets of autobiography," but he made very little use of them in his chapters on John Adams' early life.[3] With his usual excellent editorial judgment, Charles Francis Adams recognized both the value and the limitations of his grandfather's autobiographical fragments and included large portions of them in his edition of John Adams' *Works*. What Charles Francis with his tidy habits and orderly cast of mind must have thought of his grandfather's method of composition, or want thereof, he kept to himself. There were other things too that he could not approve in the Autobiography. On the brown paper wrapper in which he tied up and put away the original manuscript he wrote: "J.A. Autobiography. [Cop]ied, perused, extracts taken and printed—to remain for the future among the secret papers. C.F.A. 16. September. 1854."

---

[1] Vol. 3:423–424.
[2] Vol. 3:447.
[3] J. Q. Adams, Diary, 22 September 1829. One extract from the Autobiography, on the choice of a profession, will be found in J. Q. Adams' chapters (John Adams, *Works*, 1:41–44).

Introduction

Charles Francis Adams' Edition of the Diary and Autobiography

John Adams' Diary and Autobiography as edited by his grandson fill the whole of the second and most of the third volume of *The Works of John Adams*, these being the first volumes published in that edition, in the years 1850 and 1851 respectively. The editor decided to combine the texts of the documents, preferring the contemporary Diary entries when available and using the retrospective narrative both to fill in gaps in the Diary and to amplify the contemporary record when the Autobiography provided what seemed to him significant additions by way of new information or comment. The additions were introduced in several ways—by subjoining them in footnotes, by inserting them within or tacking them on to Diary entries *in the text* but distinguishing them by enclosing them in square brackets, and by giving two long passages, the last section of Part One and the first section of Part Two, the independent heading "Autobiography."[4]

The general principle of placing material in the form of recollections and commentary *with* the record made some decades earlier has the advantage of enabling the reader to see precisely what the writer later added and modified. But its disadvantages, at least as applied by the editor of John Adams' *Works*, are much greater. It led him to omit a very great deal of matter from the Autobiography that, while partly repetitious, was also partly "new," or at least different because it contained both significant shadings of language and occasional interpretive comments, brief or extended. Moreover, despite the use of brackets around material interpolated in the Diary text, the blending of the two documents does lead to confusion, especially when the interpolations are so long that the reader forgets he is reading later rather than contemporary testimony. And finally, in working in some of the amplifications, the family editor sometimes altered the language and even dates of passages drawn from the Autobiography for the sake of mere editorial convenience. The total effect is an overintricate and somewhat sophisticated text.

At the same time it can hardly be overemphasized that Charles Francis Adams was honest and conscientious beyond the scholarly standards of his day. These were, to be sure, low. The most productive historical editor of the period was Jared Sparks, who was also the most notorious exemplar of the school of editing that placed its heroes on

---

[4] *Works*, 2:503–517; 3:3–93, covering, in irregular order, Congress' proceedings from September 1775 to October 1776, and the appointment of John Adams to his first European mission, November 1777–February 1778.

stilts by suppressing or "improving" any passages in their writings that were indecorous or, in the eyes of their filiopietistic editors, otherwise possibly discreditable. Sparks' methods characterized "family editing" of diaries and letters throughout the 19th and is by no means unknown in the 20th century.[5] C. F. Adams repudiated them from the outset. Sparks, he said in a disdainful note in his Diary while editing John Adams' *Works*, "is a general whitewasher who regards differences of shading in human character as in the highest degree disfiguring to the beauty of human action."[6] He had stated his own very different rationale of editing in philosophical terms in the preface to the *Letters of John Adams* (1841), which is a critique of Sparks without mentioning Sparks' name.[7] In presenting John Adams' Diary to the public, he said—so admirably as to have said it for all time:

It is proper, in cases of publication like this, to define the extent to which it has been carried. The editor has suppressed or altered nothing in the Diary, which might be considered as bearing either against the author himself, or against any other person, for that reason alone. Wherever any omission has been made, it has been from other motives than those of fear or favor. The main purpose has been to present to the public a fair and unbiased picture of the mind and heart of an individual, so far as this may be supposed to command any interest. To do this, it is as necessary to retain the favorable or unfavorable opinions expressed of men, including himself, as those of things or of events. No true, honestly written Diary can be regarded as in itself a correct general history. It is good always as biography, often as furnishing materials for history, and that just in proportion as it appears on its face never to have been written or prepared for publication. But if this be true, it is obviously perverting its character to attempt to make patchwork of it, by selecting to be seen only such passages as show a single side. Rather than this, it were wise not to publish at all. The effect is to make an opinion for the reader instead of allowing him to form one for himself, to control rather than to develop

[5] Mrs. Hawthorne's editing of Nathaniel Hawthorne's journals is a famous (or notorious) example; see Randall Stewart's introduction to his edition of Hawthorne's *American Notebooks*, New Haven, 1932, p. xiii–xxi. The editors of the new edition of Emerson's *Journals and Miscellaneous Notebooks*, Cambridge, 1960– , have recently shown that Emerson's son and nephew, the editors of the *Journals* as published in 1909–1914, had the same compulsion to keep the public image of a great man elevated, which is to say genteel, by never letting him indulge, in print, in earthy language or grotesque thoughts. In a brilliant essay on "Manasseh Cutler's Writings: A Note on Editorial Practice" (*Mississippi Valley Historical Review*, 37:88–101 [June 1960]), Lee N. Newcomer has shown how, by slight but persistent editorial manipulation, editors who were striving to glorify a forebear actually succeeded in accomplishing the opposite, robbing their subject of his human attributes.

[6] 22 January 1852.

[7] Quoted above in this Introduction, p. xxvii.

his judgment. In the present instance at least, the fact may be relied on, that no experiment of the kind has been tried. The reader is more likely to feel disposed to find fault with being supplied beyond his wants than with having less than he might get.[8]

The text of John Adams' Diary and Autobiography as edited by C. F. Adams upholds his principle of representativeness in selection very well, and that of fidelity to the manuscript originals fairly well. Much that seemed to the editor dull and inconsequential, such as jottings about legal cases and indications where the diarist supped and what the weather was like, he stripped away without compunction. Some other suppressions, scarcely of this harmless kind, will be spoken of a little farther on. His principle of textual fidelity did not of course extend to matters of mere form. He standardized spelling, punctuation, and capitalization, corrected crudities of grammar according to the somewhat overelegant standards of the 1850's, and usually if not invariably formalized dialect and colloquial phrasing, so that John Adams and his friends were never permitted to say "Canady" (for Canada), "arning" (for "awning"), "he don't," "you wasn't," "we sat off for Philadelphia," "he eat strawberries," "she aint obliged," and the like. His editorial improvements extended also to John Adams' exceedingly careless French and Latin. But since the family editor was an extremely accurate copy reader, seldom failing to understand and convey what the diarist meant, little distortion of substance results from all these practices, though the informality and intimacy of the original record have been largely drained off.[9]

In order "to present to the public a fair and unbiased picture of the mind and heart" of John Adams, C. F. Adams was courageous enough to breach, upon occasion, the canons of Victorian taste. An early entry in the Diary relates an anecdote of a rustic seduction. Its purpose is didactic of course, but it is told in racy language, and the family editor did not flinch from preserving the unhappy girl's "three-farth-

[8] John Adams, *Works*, 2:viii.
[9] After the most exhaustive scrutiny of C. F. Adams' printed texts (always *after* collating typed copy with the manuscripts), the present editors remain deeply impressed with his extraordinary skill in reading the manuscripts and his accuracy as a copy and proof reader. Curiously enough, in the first entry of the Diary he left out a figure at the beginning of a sentence (omitting "7" before "Chimnies"), but for scores of pages on end he is not to be caught out, and time and again his editorial resourcefulness has furnished us with undoubtedly the right reading of a tricky word or passage. On the other hand, he sometimes resorted to the practice, doubtless justified in his own mind by his selective policy, of skipping over serious difficulties; and he was addicted to the inexcusable and (to his successors) exasperating practice of silently altering and supplying dates for misdated and undated entries.

ing bastard" in the text.[1] It it doubtful whether any other historical editor of his time would have done so. But he did flinch sometimes. His avowedly selective policy enabled him to suppress material of several kinds when the language in which it was couched seemed too strong. He omitted all sheer indecencies, such as a bawdy story told at Richard Cranch's wedding party.[2] He omitted passages containing suggestive words or actions, and thus wholly cut out a wonderfully colorful account of a ship-launching frolic, with Negroes fiddling and "Young fellows and Girls dancing in the Chamber as if they would kick the floor thro."[3] Later on, John Adams was himself shocked by things he heard and saw in French society, but he put them down. His grandson either suppressed them or modified the diarist's language. Thus an amusing conversation at a Bordeaux dinner table, in which John Adams demonstrated great presence of mind when a French lady asked him if he could explain how Adam and Eve had learned "the Art of lying together," was omitted altogether.[4] And the diarist's reports of a prostitute's appearance at a Longchamps fête and of Louis XV's relations with Madame de Pompadour were bowdlerized by the family editor.[5]

Gentility also prompted C. F. Adams to suppress a good many, though not all, of his grandfather's frequent references to the coarser side of farm and barnyard life. Whether at home or abroad, John Adams had an irrepressible habit of comparing his own manure piles with others' and boasting of the superiority of his own. But C. F. Adams, who had been brought up in foreign courts, had no enthusiasm for farming, to say nothing of the composition of manure heaps, and he therefore omitted or docked much of the material in the Diary relative to farm life and operations. Perhaps little was lost thereby, because most of these entries are routine enough, but the losses in the farm journal kept by John Adams during the summer of 1796, on the eve of his election to the Presidency, are more serious. For example, along with other things jettisoned went an account of Dr. Tufts' dinner of "salted Beef and shell beans with a Whortleberry Pudden and his Cyder," which John Adams said with some gusto made "a Luxurious Treat" for an August day.[6]

Here, of course, the criterion for rejection was something else again.

[1] 15 March 1756 (vol. 1:14). Compare John Adams, *Works*, 2:10.

[2] 30 November 1762 (vol. 1:231–232). Many other examples could be cited.

[3] 25 November 1760 (vol. 1:172–173).

[4] Autobiography under date of 2 April 1778 (vol. 4:36–37).

[5] Autobiography under dates of 17 April and 2 June 1778 (vol. 4:62–63, 121–122). Compare John Adams, *Works*, 3:133, 170.

[6] 4 August 1796 (vol. 3:238).

This rustic feast was evidently thought not quite suited to the dignity
of a Vice-President about to become President of the United States.
Earlier in the Diary the editor had been more tolerant of matter illus-
trative of his forebears' country ways. But even there he balked at too
revealing glimpses of the diarist and his family. Thus, while he left
in several incidents showing John Adams' long and rather tortured
interest in Hannah Quincy, who seems to have been an outrageous
flirt, he excised much more and thus gave the impression that his
grandfather, after a single narrow escape from her allurements, sensibly and without regret resigned Hannah to another young man, though
this was far from the truth of the matter.[7] The family editor in fact
laid a very heavy hand on John Adams' moonings and mopings, his
"gallanting" and "hustling" with the girls of the neighborhood, throughout the years in which he was endeavoring to establish himself as a
lawyer in Braintree. The diarist's first impressions of Abigail Smith
(whom he later married), though on record in the manuscript, were
not allowed to appear in print. She had wit, John Adams decided, but
not Hannah Quincy's "Tenderness."[8] This was months after he had
supposedly given up all interest in Hannah. Another example of C. F.
Adams' excisions in the interest of respectability is the vivid account of
"a conjugal Spat" in the Adams cottage in the winter of 1758. Deacon
John Adams had brought home a destitute girl to work as a servant,
and Mrs. Adams, who had a temper to which her son certainly owed
something, thought her husband had made a doubtful bargain with
the town authorities. Mrs. Adams raged, Mr. Adams stayed cool and
firm, the servant girls blubbered, John scolded his younger brother
Peter for listening on the backstairs—and then put it all down in detail,
with reflections, in his Diary.[9]

Expurgations of this kind extended to unsavory descriptions of, and
harsh observations on, the diarist's acquaintances. Repellent sketches
of Parson Wibird of Braintree and Parson Smith of Weymouth (later
John Adams' father-in-law) were entirely suppressed.[1] A good many
examples of Colonel Quincy's egotism and boastfulness were elimi-
nated, probably in deference to his numerous descendants who were
friends of the Adams family. It is a little hard, however, to understand why the whole delightful episode of John Adams' "fishing frolick"
with the Colonel also disappeared, unless the editor thought so eminent a citizen of Braintree should not be shown suffering the effects of

[7] See vol. 1:87–88, 104, 113–114. [1] Spring 1759 (vol. 1:92–93); Sum-
[8] Summer 1759 (vol. 1:108–109). mer 1759 (vol. 1:108).
[9] 30 December 1758 (vol. 1:65–66).

seasickness.[2] Sometimes the editor dealt with passages unflattering to the diarist's contemporaries by reducing their names to initials or blanks.

In editing the Autobiography, which contains so much matter duplicating the Diary entries, C. F. Adams' selective policy and his natural caution were reinforced by a desire to avoid retrospective judgments—especially when unfriendly—on the diarist's political associates. Such judgments when introduced into the Diary text, even if bracketed, would appear anachronistic, as indeed they were. It seemed best, therefore, to leave them out. Examples of what may be called political expurgation in the Autobiography are the omission of John Adams' comments on Hancock's and Samuel Adams' jealousy of him after his appointment to France in 1777; of Jefferson's alleged "gross insult on Religion" in the Continental Congress and his threat to the Federal judiciary; and a captious but scintillating description of Franklin's frivolous life in Paris in 1778.[3] The Autobiography was written while John Adams was smarting from Hamilton's *Letter ... concerning the Public Conduct and Character of John Adams, Esq.* (1800), and contains a number of passages explicitly answering Hamilton's charges in that pamphlet. C. F. Adams either suppressed these passages, one of which is perhaps the bitterest personal attack John Adams ever directed against anyone, or silently emended them to avoid the mention of Hamilton's name.[4] The reader is thus robbed of the means to measure the strength of the feelings that divided the leaders of the Federalist Party in 1800.

4. THE EDITORIAL METHOD

Materials Included and Their Arrangement

The present edition of the Diary and Autobiography of John Adams contains the following materials:

(1) The entire text of the manuscript (or manuscripts) of Adams' Diary, 1755–1804, as identified, selectively edited, and put away by Charles Francis Adams in the 1850's.[5] So far as possible every entry

---

[2] 25 June 1760 (vol. 1:140–141).
[3] See vol. 3:324, 335, 298; vol. 4:118–119.
[4] See vol. 3:386–388, and compare John Adams, *Works*, 3:47–49. See also vol. 3:434–435 for a paragraph on Hamilton totally suppressed in Adams' *Works*.
[5] See the description of the manuscripts, p. xli–xliv, above.

has been printed in its precise chronological position in a single over-all sequence.

(2) A few supplementary materials of a diary-like character, drawn alike from John Adams' papers in the family archives and from other sources. Examples are: dated or datable marginalia in Adams' copy of John Winthrop's *Lecture on Earthquakes* (1755), now in the Boston Public Library; scattered accounts and itineraries recorded while Adams was riding the court circuit as a lawyer and serving in Congress and in Europe, found among his letterbooks and other papers; a few receipted bills for traveling and living expenses as a dele-gate to the Continental Congress, preserved in the Massachusetts Archives; memoranda on visits paid and received, persons to consult, and the like, written while he was in diplomatic service and scattered here and there among his papers. Though all these materials together do not bulk large, they piece out the Diary where it is meager or quite lacking; and they are precisely of the kind that Adams often entered in his Diary.

(3) Three fragmentary journals kept by Abigail Adams and in-serted here (from originals in the Adams Papers) under their respec-tive beginning dates. They cover her voyage from Boston to Deal to join John Adams in London, June–July 1784; part of the Adams family's tour to the west of England, July 1787; and the beginning of her and her husband's return trip to America, March–May 1788. These are the only diaries known to survive from Mrs. Adams' hand, and, as far as they go, they helpfully fill in gaps in her husband's Diary.

The material listed above comprises the text of the first two volumes of the present edition and approximately the first half of the third volume. It is followed by

(4) The entire text of the three fragmentary parts of John Adams' Autobiography. Part One, "John Adams," completes the third volume. Part Two, "Travels and Negotiations," and Part Three, "Peace," to-gether constitute the entire text of the fourth and final volume.[6] The editors' decision to print all three parts *in toto*, including their inserted letter copies, transcripts of entries from the original edition of the *Journals* of the Continental Congress, and copies and paraphrases of Adams' Diary entries, was not made without difficulty. Up to the point where Adams began consulting the *Journals*, Part One is entirely new matter, having been written wholly from recollection. Part Two, com-piled to a large extent from his letterbooks and Diary, contains less fresh matter, and Part Three still less. Where, then, is one to draw the line?

[6] The manuscripts are described at p. xliv–xlvi, above.

It has seemed on the whole best to draw no line, since all three parts of the Autobiography contain some important new information, numerous altered judgments on men and events, and countless subtle shadings of language that one would not willingly lose and that to select from would merely distort. If we are so fortunate as to have from a man of John Adams' stature and gifts of style both a contemporaneous and a retrospective record of his career, it would seem desirable to preserve both, in full, for purposes of comparison.

We have stopped short, however, of including the text of a second autobiography that Adams wrote a few years after breaking off his first one. This is his tremendous series of letters of reminiscence communicated to the *Boston Patriot* from 1809 to 1812, a fraction of which were reprinted in serial parts, running to 572 pages, and still smaller portions of which were in turn included by C. F. Adams in his edition of his grandfather's *Works*.[7] This distended and chaotic work contains so much documentation and so relatively little comment, and it deals so largely with Adams' Presidency, which is not covered by either his Diary or his Autobiography, that it has been omitted from the present edition except for occasional passages of highly pertinent narrative and comment that are introduced into the editorial notes.[8] The circumstances that led to and accompanied the composition of what we have called Adams' second autobiography, together with the public and private comment it evoked, form an important chapter in his later life that has not hitherto been told. The present editors plan to tell it soon but not in these volumes.

All materials introduced from sources other than the Diary and Autobiography manuscripts, whether in the text or in the footnotes, have of course been identified and credited to their respective sources at the points where they occur. Materials printed here but not printed in C. F. Adams' edition of 1850–1851 have not been systematically indicated, though occasionally an interesting or significant omission has been pointed out. What proportion of the present text is now printed for the first time would be impossible to say accurately without word counts of both the old edition and the new—a chore the editors have not thought worth the time it would take. An informed guess is that not less than a quarter of the combined text of the Diary

[7] *Correspondence of the Late President Adams. Originally Published in the Boston Patriot* ..., 10 parts, Boston, 1809[-1810]. C. F. Adams' selections are in John Adams, *Works*, 9:239–330.

[8] For example on Adams' stay at Auteuil during his illness in the fall of 1783 (vol. 3:143–144), and on his first visit to England and winter crossing of the North Sea to save the credit of the United States in Amsterdam, 1783–1784 (vol. 3:149–154).

and Autobiography as now printed, and quite possibly as much as a third, has never been published before.

Textual Policy

The general principles and specific rules for rendering the text that are stated here are intended to apply to both this first published unit of *The Adams Papers* and to the edition as a whole. But it would be futile to assume that we could anticipate at the outset every textual problem that may be encountered in so large and complex a publication program. As the edition moves from one generation of the family to another, and from diaries to letters and other types of material, the rules now stated will be enlarged according to need, and exceptions for particular cases will doubtless have to be made, but always with due notice and, it is expected, without modification of the general textual policy here laid down.

That policy has been admirably stated and is being followed by the editors of two forerunners of the present work, namely *The Papers of Thomas Jefferson* and *The Papers of Benjamin Franklin.* Both endeavor to follow "a middle course" between "exact reproduction," that is to say a printed text as near a facsimile of the handwritten original as possible, and "complete modernization" of the text. "The purpose," as the *Franklin* editors say, "is to preserve as faithfully as possible the form and spirit in which the authors composed their documents, and at the same time to reproduce their words in a manner intelligible to the present-day reader and within the normal range of modern typographical equipment and techniques."[9]

In the opinion of the editors of *The Adams Papers* it is a happy omen for historical scholarship that this common-sense policy appears to be prevailing more and more widely. For on the one hand type simply cannot reproduce the idiosyncrasies of old handwriting—the blots and flourishes, the scribal signs and contractions, the interlineations and cancelations—with perfect fidelity. Attempts to make it do so are usually unsatisfactory or worse; it is far better to go directly to facsimile reproduction, and some documents can be presented adequately only by such a method.[1] On the other hand, if it is recognized that a limited

[9] *The Papers of Benjamin Franklin,* ed. Leonard W. Labaree and Whitfield J. Bell Jr., New Haven, 1959– , 1:xl. See also Mr. Boyd's statement in *The Papers of Thomas Jefferson,* 1:xxix.

[1] For admirable examples of this method see *Thomas Jefferson's Farm Book . . . ,* ed. Edwin M. Betts, Princeton, 1953; and the pages from Lincoln's early "Sum Book" reproduced in the first volume of *The Collected Writings of Abraham Lincoln,* ed. Roy P. Basler and others, New Brunswick, 1953–1955.

degree of conventionalization is unavoidable and if due care is taken in converting manuscript originals into readable print, the *essential* "form and spirit" of the hastily jotted diary entry or the letter written in a mood of agitation or serenity, frustration or triumph, need not be sacrificed to type and type-composing machinery.

The principal rules for rendering the text that are being followed in *The Adams Papers* and specifically the text of John Adams' Diary and Autobiography may be summarized as follows. They may be regarded as devices for maintaining the desired middle ground between pedantic fidelity and readability. The scholar concerned with the ultimate niceties of a critical passage in the text may always resort to the photographic facsimiles of the manuscripts available in the microfilm edition of the Adams Papers.

Spelling is preserved as found in the manuscripts. But mere slips of the pen are silently corrected: *Gentlement* is corrected to *Gentlemen*, and *punisment* to *punishment*. If, however, such a slip appears to have psychological or other significance, it is retained, as in *travailing* (for *traveling*), or *faignt* and *feignt* (for *faint*). Proper names are given as the writers spelled them, no matter how erratically, though if a misspelling is seriously misleading it is corrected at its first appearance either by a bracketed insertion which follows it in the text, or by a footnote. A great many misspelled or inconsistently spelled names are corrected only in the index, with cross-references from the variant and erroneous forms.

Grammar and syntax are preserved as found in the manuscripts. Errors and oddities in grammatical forms and sentence structure are not given emphasis by *sic*-marks, but essential corrections may be furnished by bracketed insertions, and if the writer's error creates a serious ambiguity a clarifying editorial note is subjoined. Inadvertent repetitions of words are corrected, usually without notice.

Capitalization is preserved as found in the manuscripts, with these exceptions: (1) All sentences begin with capital letters. (2) All personal and geographical names and honorifics attached to the former are capitalized; for example *major leonard* is rendered as *Major Leonard*, and *cape ann* as *Cape Ann*. (3) In indeterminate cases, where one cannot be sure whether the writer meant a capital or lower-case letter, modern usage is followed.

Punctuation is normally preserved as found in the manuscripts, but a few rules of conventionalization have been systematically applied in preparing John Adams' Diary and Autobiography for publication. Most of these have been forced upon us by peculiarities in the manuscripts themselves. For one thing, Adams commonly wrote all the way to the margins of the "paper books" of his Diary, leaving no room for punctuation at the ends of lines. He seems in fact to have regarded a line end itself as sufficient for medial punctuation (commas) and often for terminal punctuation (periods) as well.[2] One may run through scores if not hundreds of lines of the Diary in succession and find no punctuation marks at the ends of lines. To add to the problem, Adams long persisted in "pointing" by making marks that may be interpreted as either commas or periods. And finally, he seems to have had a visual difficulty in placing his commas, since they are very frequently one or two words before or after the place where they belong according to punctuation usage either then or now.

Accordingly we have established the following rules, and they will be applied throughout *The Adams Papers* unless special circumstances call for a departure from them:

(1) Every sentence ends with a period.

(2) Dashes obviously intended to be terminal marks are converted to periods, and superfluous dashes are removed. Dashes evidently intended to indicate breaks or shifts in thought or used as semi-paragraphing devices are of course retained.

(3) Intrusive commas are omitted. For example, the sentence *I, muse, I, mope, I, ruminate* is rendered *I muse, I mope, I ruminate.*

(4) Minimum punctuation for intelligibility is supplied between members of a series, particularly in lists of names of persons whose forenames and family names John Adams tended to run together chaotically.

(5) Minimum punctuation for intelligibility is supplied in dialogue and quoted matter. John Adams was fortunately fond of recording conversations in his Diary and elsewhere, but he was also exceedingly casual in punctuating such passages. When, as often, the speakers' names are given as in the script of a play, the names are arbitrarily italicized in our printed text, and each speaker's remarks are set off in a paragraph of their own. If quotation marks appear only at one end or the other of a passage of direct discourse, the matching pair is silently supplied *when its location is clearly determinable*, but quotation marks are not systematically inserted according to modern usage. Quotations within quotations, when they demand editorial attention, are treated according to modern rules.

Aware of the possibility of distorting a writer's meaning by altering,

---

[2] Miss J. E. Norton has pointed out that this was also the historian Gibbon's practice; see her edition of *The Letters of Edward Gibbon,* New York, 1956, 1:xvi.

suppressing, or supplying punctuation, the editors have refrained from applying any of the rules of conventionalization stated above when it has seemed risky to do so. Passages that are truly ambiguous because of faulty pointing have been allowed to stand, and the editors have suggested possible clarifications in footnotes.

Abbreviations and contractions are preserved as found in names of persons and places; in the datelines, salutations, and leavetakings of letters; in endorsements and docketings; in units of money and measurement; and in accounts and other tabular documents. They are also retained elsewhere if they are still in use or are readily recognizable by a modern reader. For example, such forms as *Coll.* and *Colo.* (for *Colonel*), *N. Yk.* (for *New York*), and *Septr.* (for *September*) are allowed to stand. But in all cases where they are retained, the superscript letters once so commonly used to indicate contractions are brought down to the line. With the exceptions mentioned above, unfamiliar contractions are silently expanded in our text; for example, *abt.* to *about*, *cd.* to *could*, *Commee.* to *Committee*, *dft.* to *defendant*, *Dn.* to *Deacon, Mes.* to *Messrs.*, and the like. Scribal devices in such forms as *Comĩsion, petñ, yt*, and *yrfr* are disregarded and these words rendered as *Commission, petition, that*, and *therefore*. The ampersand (&) is retained in the form *&c.* (for *etc.*) and in the names of firms, but elsewhere it is rendered as *and*.

Missing and illegible matter is indicated by square brackets ([ ]) enclosing the editors' conjectural readings (with a question mark appended if the reading is doubtful), or by suspension points (...) if no reading can be given. If only a portion of a word is missing, it may be silently supplied when there is no doubt about the reading. When the missing or illegible matter amounts to more than one or two words, a footnote estimating its amount is subjoined. See the Guide to Editorial Apparatus, p. lxxx, below.

Canceled matter in the manuscripts (scored-out or erased passages) is disregarded unless it is of real stylistic, psychological, or historical interest. When included in our text, such passages are italicized and enclosed in angle brackets (< >). If a revised equivalent of a canceled passage remains in the text, the canceled matter always precedes it. For a document that consists largely of canceled matter and in which the cancelations are of extreme importance and have therefore been restored, see Adams' draft letter to Vergennes of 10–11 February 1779 (vol. 2:347–350).

Variant readings (variations in text between two or more versions of the same letter or document) are ordinarily indicated only when they are significant enough to warrant recording, and then always in footnotes keyed to the basic text that is printed in full. In John Adams' Diary the texts of the inserted letters are sometimes drafts, but in the Autobiography they are always copies from his letterbooks. Whatever version is found *in the manuscripts being edited* has perforce been considered the "basic" text in the present volume. Other available texts have, however, been collated with the texts of the same letters in the Diary and Autobiography, and significant differences noted.

Editorial insertions are italicized and enclosed in square brackets, for example [*Enclosure*], [*In the margin*], [*sentence unfinished*]. When, however, the editors have expanded initials or have inserted clarifying equivalents for names and the like, the insertions are not italicized. Thus "Coll. Q[uincy]," "P[arson] Wib[ird]," "at Slewmans [Slumans]," "sent of [off]."

Problems of Dating

One arbitrary change of form has been imposed by the editors upon the text of John Adams' Diary. The dates of the entries in the manuscript are normally part of the entries themselves, being the first word or several words therein. Because the eye has extreme difficulty in picking up short dates (for example, "3d.") and changes of date in sequences of entries that are of irregular length (very short entries often being intermingled with very long ones), the editors have decided to print the diarist's dates as centered captions above the entries. We believe that students who have tried to find their way around C. F. Adams' edition of his grandfather's Diary, where, as in the manuscript, the dates are often effectually buried in blocks of text, will be grateful.

Many entries and even whole sequences of entries in the early booklets of the Diary are vaguely dated or wholly undated, and cannot be given specific dates. These have been assigned by the editors to a month, season, or year according to the best evidence available, and the assigned dates have been bracketed.

Semidetached or "floating" entries, separated in a Diary booklet by small or large intervals of space, or by lines across the page, from dated entries preceding them, have been printed after the dated entries they follow in the manuscript, without captions but set off by an arbitrary measure of blank space. In some cases they probably belong to the same day as the entry preceding; in others to dates either soon or considerably afterward.

Examples of all these problems and of the editors' methods of handling them by furnishing readers with the best guidance possible, will be found in the Diary entries for the early months of 1759 and the editorial notes that are appended to many of those undated and often cryptic entries (vol. 1:66 ff.).

Annotation

Both the magnitude and the complex publication plan of *The Adams Papers* have made the formulation of a satisfactory policy for editorial annotation difficult. In presenting so densely packed a mass of documents extending over so long a period, one can of course count on the documents' annotating each other to a considerable degree. The diaries and letters of members of the family living at the same time repeatedly cover the same events—births, marriages, deaths, appointments and elections to office, departures and returns—from different points of view; and in this family, besides, there were always some members of later generations who were studying and commenting upon the lives and writings of their forebears. The result is a grand though uncontrived fugal pattern which ideally should be allowed to unfold itself with the least possible interference or manipulation.

On the other hand it can scarcely be assumed that everyone interested in a particular member of the family or his times will also be interested in other Adamses and *their* times, and so each major segment (series or part of a series as the case may be) of *The Adams Papers* has been designed to stand as self-sustainingly as possible. Where, in such a scheme involving several overlapping chronological sequences, is the "first reference" to a person or an event requiring annotation? And should an equivalent note be furnished in each later segment of the edition, or will a cross-reference be sufficient? For that matter, how much cross-referring between parallel materials is necessary or desirable—for example between John Quincy Adams' Diary in St. Petersburg (in Series I, Part 2) and his diplomatic dispatches written from there (in Series III, Part 2)?

In the face of problems like these, the editors have adopted a few general principles of annotation policy applicable to the entire edition rather than a body of specific rules. The principles can be stated briefly and will be amplified as necessary in later parts of the edition.

(1) *Persons, personal names.* It is impracticable in so large a work to try to furnish identifying notes on the thousands of persons who will be mentioned in the documents. Members of the immediate family and other relatives who played a significant part in the family's history

are to be identified. In the volumes now published they are ordinarily noted upon first appearance, but in Series II a systematic effort will be made to place and identify all members of the "Presidential line" by means of an Adams Genealogy based on the family papers, to be issued first in a trial form and then printed for permanent reference in the final volume of the Family Correspondence. Notes on persons who are not well known to history but who were closely associated with one or more of the Adamses are to be furnished at what seem to the editors the most strategic points. Thus while generals in the Continental Army and delegates to the Continental Congress are not identified in the present work (because they may be looked up in common works of reference), such elusive figures as C. W. F. Dumas and Edmund Jenings are sketched, especially with respect to their relations with John Adams, whose close friends and correspondents they were. Such sketches as these will simply be referred to when their subjects reappear in John Adams' general correspondence in Series III of *The Adams Papers.* In the early years of John Adams' Diary the editors have been rather more liberal with such identifying notes on the diarist's contemporaries, especially his associates at the bar, because of the comparative meagerness of parallel documentation in the family archives during the pre-Revolutionary period.

Names seriously misspelled or represented in the manuscript by initials are clarified either by a corrected or full version inserted in the text within brackets or by a footnote. Names of persons likely to be confused with others bearing the same or similar names are given clarifying notes; for example, in the present volumes, the various Colonel Chandlers of Worcester and the two Jonathan Williamses. An attempt has been made and will be continued by the editors to verify and fill out partially recorded names of all but inconsequential persons, *but their findings will appear far more often in the indexes to the various series than in footnotes.*

(2) *Place names* are to be corrected by bracketed insertions in the text or by footnotes when they are seriously misspelled or otherwise confusing; but as with personal names most of the results of the editors' verification of geographical names will appear in the indexes. Special attention has been and will continue to be given in the notes to purely local (and now often lost) names in the Braintree-Quincy area.

(3) *Books and other publications.* References in the documents to writings by the Adamses and to books they purchased or were reading

are given particular attention in the annotation, and even when no notes appear the authors' names and the titles of books mentioned have been or will be, if possible, verified for listing in the indexes. In the present volumes the bibliographical annotation and verification fall well short of the ideal, because, for one thing, some of John Adams' publications present bibliographical problems demanding further study, and for another thing, books once owned and read by him keep turning up unexpectedly—an indication that we have much less than the complete control we would like over the Adamses' libraries.

(4) *Other subjects* are to be annotated on an *ad hoc* basis, primarily in order to clarify the text. Examples of our *ad hoc* method will be found in the notes in the present volumes relative to John Adams' law practice. Adams often alluded in his Diary to cases in which he was active, and he occasionally entered memoranda for his use in court; but his references, of whatever kind, are frequently obscure. Much closer study of both his own legal papers and the voluminous pre-Revolutionary records preserved in the Suffolk County Court House must precede full annotation of his allusions of this kind. With the aid of several consultants on colonial law, the editors have done something but not enough. A select edition of Adams' legal papers, perhaps accompanied by a monograph on his legal studies and practice, remains a desideratum.

(5) *Textual problems.* The method of annotating the text and dealing with special problems therein has been explained above under Textual Policy. See also the Guide to Editorial Apparatus, below.

(6) *Gaps in the Diary record.* This is a special and continuous problem in John Adams' Diary, which, unlike his son's and grandson's, was kept only fitfully from first to last. Gaps of months and even years appear frequently. The editors have attempted to fill in these gaps, in a fashion, by summarizing, chiefly from Adams' correspondence, the principal events that occurred during the intervals. If John Adams' Diary were the only diary being published in *The Adams Papers*, a different method from the one they have chosen would have been preferable. But in the interest of uniformity of design among all the Adams statesmen's diaries, the editors have not placed their summaries as connecting tissue between portions of the text; they have instead presented them as footnotes. Notes of this kind are usually attached to the first entry following a long break in the Diary; in a few special cases they are attached to the last entry preceding the break. Some of the summaries have an unavoidably awkward appearance because they are very long notes on very short entries.

5. JOHN ADAMS AS DIARIST AND AUTOBIOGRAPHER

As a Diarist

In introducing John Adams' Diary to the public for the first time, now more than a century ago, Charles Francis Adams stressed its representativeness of the writer's time and place. During the years covered by the first part of the Diary, the family editor observed in neatly balanced sentences,

Puritan Massachusetts, whilst dropping much of her early religious bigotry, was yet nursing in the French wars the stern qualities that carried her successfully through the fiery trial of the Revolution. She contained one, whilst Virginia furnished the other, of the two germs of public sentiment which have since spread extensively over this continent, and which bid fair yet to develop themselves indefinitely. To these two types of mind all classes of American opinion may be ultimately reduced. The state of society through which the first of these was evolved, until from a religious it took a political direction, and the influences through which the change was shaped, gain much illustration from the following pages.[3]

This is plausible and in some degree true, reinforcing the point of someone's epigram that the American Revolution was the product of a temporary alliance between the Adamses and the Lees. But C. F. Adams' theorem obscures another truth and the most conspicuous and valuable quality of his grandfather's Diary. John Adams was no "type" at all, but a unique human being, individualistic to the point of eccentricity. "Passion, Accident, Freak, Humour, govern in this House," he wrote a little ruefully at his parents' home in Braintree in 1758.[4] They were to govern much of Adams' life, because—there is no other word for it—he was a "character." And though he of course possessed Yankee traits, to call him a Yankee character is inadequate if not misleading. What traits of mind and personality did he share, for example, with Samuel Adams, with James Otis, or with John Hancock, his temporary colleagues in Massachusetts' struggles against the British government? John Adams would have been a character at any time and in any part of the world. Some men who knew him well thought his touchiness and tantrums went beyond eccentricity. "I am persuaded," said Franklin, who had endured much from Adams' jealousy and suspicion, "that he means well for his Country, is always an honest Man, often a wise one, but sometimes, and in some things, absolutely out of his

[3] John Adams, *Works*, 2:v–vi.
[4] Diary, 30 December 1758 (vol. 1:66).

senses."[5] During Adams' Presidency, Hamilton, Pickering, and Mc-Henry, among others, would have concurred in only the last part of this judgment.

The primary value of Adams' Diary lies in its faithful, because almost wholly unselfconscious, revelation of a complex human being who was endlessly curious about himself and all that went on around him, and who was at the same time endowed with an unsurpassed gift for idiomatic and robust language—for what Mr. Bernard Bailyn has called "fist-like phrases."[6] If we learn much from the Diary—as we do—about village life in New England during the 1750's and 1760's, about the origins of resistance in Massachusetts, and about the ordeals and triumphs of the Revolution itself in Congress and in European courts, these are dividends not to be undervalued. But the information in the Diary is secondary to its picture of a remarkable human being—self-important, impetuous, pugnacious, tormented by self-doubts and yet stubborn to the point of mulishness, vain, jealous, and suspicious almost to the point of paranoia; and yet at the same time deeply affectionate and warm-hearted, "as sociable as any Marblehead man,"[7] irrepressibly humorous, passionately devoted all his life to the welfare of his country, and as courageous a statesman and diplomat as his country has ever had.

Both the physical nature of the manuscripts and the text itself provide abundant proof that the Diary was intended as a wholly private record. John Quincy Adams accurately described the early booklets as "effusions of mind; committed from time to time to paper, probably without the design of preserving them."[8] The booklets are too fragile ever to have been supposed a permanent record, and only by continuous good luck have they survived at all, worn and tattered as they are. Like most of his kind, the writer began with the notion that a diary is an aid to memory and self-cultivation: "A Journal, scrawled with Algebraical signs, and interspersed with Questions of Law, Husbandry, natural History &c., will be a useful Thing."[9] "A Pen," he added a little later, " is certainly an excellent Instrument, to fix a Mans Attention and to inflame his Ambition."[1] These entries he

[5] To Robert R. Livingston, 22 July 1783 (Benjamin Franklin, *Writings*, ed. Albert Henry Smyth, New York and London, 1905–1907, 9:62).

[6] "Boyd's Jefferson: Notes for a Sketch," *New England Quarterly*, 33: 393 (September 1960).

[7] The opinion of Captain Samuel Tucker of the Continental Navy, quoted in Adams' Diary, 11 May 1779 (vol. 2:368).

[8] Memorandum dated November 1829, in "Rubbish 1," a volume of draft entries for his Diary and other miscellaneous material (Adams Papers, Microfilms, Reel No. 49).

[9] 29 May 1760 (vol. 1:127).

[1] 14 November 1760 (vol. 1:168).

"scrawled" while trying to gain a footing as a lawyer in the village of Braintree, when he felt sorry for himself because he had so little to do, and the road to eminence seemed long and hard. ("It is my Destiny to dig Treasures with my own fingers."[2]) A decade later, having been drawn into Boston's struggle with royal authority backed by military force, he felt sorry for himself because he had so much to do. But his Diary was still helpful: "The only Way to compose myself and collect my Thoughts is to set down at my Table, place my Diary before me, and take my Pen into my Hand. This Apparatus takes off my Attention from other Objects."[3]

But his success in this form of self-discipline was limited. There is no discernible relationship between the regularity and length of his journal entries on the one hand and the amount of his legal, political, and other business on the other hand. He did better while he was in Congress from 1774 to 1776 than he had done a decade earlier when he was only occasionally occupied with public affairs, or than he was to do a decade later in France and England when his diplomatic tasks were light. During his Presidency he kept no journal at all, though in preparation for it he had taken up his Diary, after long neglect, in the summer of 1796.[4] And for the quarter-century of his retirement only a handful of farming memoranda exist.[5]

The text of the Diary is almost wholly free of indications that the writer supposed anyone, including himself, would read it later. While on circuit in Maine in 1770, Adams recorded how his horse leaped out of her "bare Pasture into a neighbouring Lott of mowing Ground," and then added: "These are important Materials for History no doubt. My Biographer will scarcely introduce my little Mare, and her Adventures in quest of Feed and Water."[6] But such remarks, and others like them to the effect that his Diary might amuse him in old age, or entertain his children after his death, are merely conventional and signify little.[7] By the time he came to write his Autobiography he had himself so nearly forgotten his Diary, or rated it so poorly, that he did not consult it at all until he had reached the year 1778 in his narrative. Having discovered it, he drew heavily on it from that point on.[8] But fortunately in the course of his reading, copying, and paraphrasing his old journals he seems to have felt no temptation at all to tamper with what he found there. After the most intensive study of the Diary

[2] 18 December 1758 (vol. 1:63).
[3] 27 June 1770 (vol. 1:352).
[4] See entry of 12 July 1796 (vol. 3:226).
[5] Vol. 3:249–250.

[6] 1 July 1770 (vol. 1:355).
[7] See entries of 13 June 1771, 21 November (2d entry) 1772 (vol. 2:34, 67).
[8] See vol. 4:6.

manuscripts the editors are convinced that Adams let everything stand in them as first hastily written and never revised—faults in grammar, unfinished sentences, mistakes of fact and opinion that he could not have helped recognizing, indiscretions, improprieties, and self-betrayals of every sort.[9] The strongest possible assurances may therefore be given that the contemporaneous record has suffered nothing from suppressions, additions, or corrections. The integrity of the text reflects the integrity of a man who would have scorned sophisticating a record, and endows the Diary with an immediacy and authenticity rare in historical literature.

For none of the other founders of the republic do we have anything remotely comparable. Franklin wrote enchantingly of his early life in Boston and Philadelphia, but many years afterward and with a detachment as suitable for a character he could have invented as for himself when young. Jefferson's autobiographical recollections were composed when he was seventy-seven and condense his entire career before he entered the Continental Congress in 1775 into fifteen printed pages. George Washington as a young man fortunately kept diaries, but being the least introspective of men he recorded only what he thought might prove to be useful information—the weather, state of the crops, distances, prices, "Where, how, or with whom my time is Spent." One will look in vain for opinions on issues or persons. Washington was present as a member of the Virginia Convention of March 1775 on the day Patrick Henry made his speech ending "Give me liberty or give me death," but his diary entry for that day reads: "Dined at Mr. Patrick Coote's and lodgd where I had done the Night before." [1]

Precisely the opposite qualities distinguish the present Diary. It

[9] A single possible exception is the crossed-out expression of hurt pride in the entry of 26 May 1766 (vol. 1:312–313). The editors believe this obliteration was made soon after the passage was written, certainly not when Adams wrote his Autobiography, for he did not even consult these earlier Diary booklets at that time. It may be added that Adams was equally scrupulous in copying letters and other documents from his old letterbooks into his Autobiography. He repunctuated freely, sometimes (but rarely) made slight improvements in grammar and supplied missing words, and translated French passages into English; but all other changes in the copies he then made seem to have been merely inadvertent. The point is emphasized because then and long afterward it was a common and acceptable practice to correct one's own records before giving them to the public or leaving them to posterity. Washington made improvements in style in his Revolutionary correspondence when he caused it to be copied at the close of the war. Madison had an incurable habit of doctoring his papers in the light of later knowledge and opinion. Gideon Welles, Lincoln's secretary of the navy, rewrote his famous *Diary* in his retirement, and it was subsequently published as if it were a wholly contemporaneous record.

[1] George Washington, *Diaries, 1748–1799*, ed. John C. Fitzpatrick, Boston and New York, 1925, 2:189.

is both intimate and copious. The entries of the first dozen years—in many ways the most fascinating and also the most heavily cut in the only previous edition—chronicle the inner life of a young man who deeply yearned for recognition and fame and who recorded and pondered every step forward and backward in his quest. "Shall I look out for a Cause to Speak to," he asks himself soon after setting up his office in Braintree, "and exert all the Soul and all the Body I own, to cut a flash, strike amazement, to catch the Vulgar," and thus "take one bold determined Leap into the Midst of some Cash and Business?" Or "shall I walk a lingering, heavy Pace [?] ... Shall I creep or fly [?]"[2] He is almost an 18th-century Dale Carnegie in his painstaking efforts to learn the "Arts ... of Living in the World" and of "Popularity." He studies Lawyer Putnam's well-timed "Sneer" and Parson Wibird's habit of playing "with Babes and young Children that begin to prattle" and of talking with their mothers.[3] Immediately after his narrow escape from Hannah Quincy's wiles he adjures himself: "Now let me collect my Thoughts, which have been long scattered, among Girls, father, Mother, Grandmother, Brothers, Matrimony, Husling, Chatt, Provisions, Cloathing, fewel, servants for a family, and apply them, with steady Resolution and an aspiring Spirit, to the Prosecution of my studies."[4] But his resolutions of this kind always prove infirm, and his repeated backslidings are set down as fully as his successes in obtaining new clients and his progress in reading legal treatises.

With a footing gained in the law, as shown by the increasing number of memoranda for pleadings, Adams soon sought another—and, for the time, the most natural—path to recognition, namely writing for the press. Beginning in 1760 the booklets of his Diary are strewn with notes and drafts for essays on all manner of subjects: on the evils of taverns, on demagogic orators, on feasting at church ordinations, on political issues and personalities of the day, on the cultivation of hemp, and even one, addressed to "Dear Nieces," on the conduct of young ladies, a wonderfully gay and frank little essay that the family editor omitted, possibly because it recommended bundling.[5] None of Adams' earliest literary efforts seem to have been accepted by the printers, if he ever actually submitted them, but from 1763 onward he was a more or less steady contributor to the Boston papers, and the Diary is a repository of both hitherto unidentified published writings by him and of materials, sometimes of considerable interest, that he pruned away before publishing his newspaper pieces.

By 1770 his substantial success at the bar and his repute as a writer

[2] 14 March 1759 (vol. 1:78). [4] Spring 1759 (vol. 1:87).
[3] Spring 1759 (vol. 1:96, 84, 97). [5] January 1761 (vol. 1:193–196).

brought him the recognition he had so long and earnestly craved. How he fulfilled his own and others' expectations on the successive stages of provincial, continental, and international politics is recorded in the pages that follow, at times with the same detail (though with sad lacunae) and always with the same vividness and candor. John Adams never learned to govern his tongue or his pen. "Mr. Adams is a decided Character," Admiral Howe remarked during his conference with three delegates from Congress at Staten Island.[6] Most of Adams' difficulties in public life sprang from his decidedness, which he was perfectly incapable of concealing even if he had wanted to. But so did most of his triumphs—in his campaigns for new state governments and for American independence, in obtaining Dutch recognition and financial aid for the United States, and in keeping the country out of war in 1799–1800. When his thoughts were once formed, they exploded. Reading his Diary is something like watching a display of fireworks. It is also the best of all antidotes for the false idea that the nation was founded by a set of lawgivers dignified in mien and inspired by heaven. The scuffles and turmoil, the mingled pettiness and courage, the frequent foolishness and the flashes of wisdom are all here, recorded by a witness and participant who was also a master of words.

As an Autobiographer

The germ of John Adams' Autobiography will be found in a Diary entry he wrote at Paris in 1782 a few days after he had placed his signature on the Preliminary Treaty between the United States and Great Britain. He hoped, he said, that it would be permitted to himself "or to some other who can do it better, some Ten or fifteen Years hence, to collect together in one View [his] little Negotiations in Europe. Fifty Years hence it may be published, perhaps 20." Whatever his accomplishments and mistakes as a diplomat may have been, "the Situations I have been in between angry Nations and more angry Factions" had surely been among "the most singular and interesting that ever happened to any Man. The Fury of Ennemies as well as of Elements, the Subtilty and Arrogance of Allies, and what has been worse than all, the Jealousy, Envy, and little Pranks of Friends and CoPatriots, would form one of the most instructive Lessons in Morals and Politicks, that ever was committed to Paper."[7]

In this spirit he began in the fall of 1802 the narrative of his life. So far as we know, he did not tell even the members of his own family

[6] Autobiography under date of 17 September 1776 (vol. 3:423).
[7] 4 December 1782 (vol. 3:89).

about the venture, though his first paragraph states that he has undertaken it for his own children and "not for the Public." He proceeded only as far as to get himself into Harvard College in 1751 before he tired of his task and broke off. Two years passed and then his son John Quincy, now in the United States Senate, wrote to renew a request he had apparently made verbally earlier, that his father "commit to writing, an account of the principal incidents" of his life. This would prove "a lasting and cordial gratification to your children" and ultimately, no doubt, "a benefit to your Country." Its composition would "also amuse many hours which otherwise may pass heavily."[8] J. Q. Adams had another reason for wishing his father would occupy himself with his reminiscences. To his brother Thomas Boylston Adams, who had recently returned from Philadelphia to live in Quincy, he wrote soon afterward that since his "most ardent wish" was that their father "may in future enjoy *tranquility of mind*, I wish it were possible he could see the course of things with more indifference. Try to engage his mind in something other than public affairs. For these will henceforth never affect him but unpleasantly, and the less he feels on this subject, the more he will enjoy."[9]

John Adams promptly told his son that the suggestion was a poor one. He could remember no part of his public life, he said, "without pain," and the persecutions he had suffered had been so great and constant that he could not look back on his career "without a kind of Scepticism in my own memory and a doubt whether I should be believed even by my own Children," say nothing of other readers, who would certainly consider such a narrative a mere "Hymn to Vanity." A week later he added: "You have recommended to me, a Work, which instead of increasing my indifference to public affairs, would engage my feelings and enflame my Passions. In many Passages it would set me on fire and I should have Occasion for a Bucket of Water constantly by my side to put it out." And further, as if putting the idea quite out of his mind: "I wish not to be reminded of my Mortifications, Disappointments or Resentments. As to my good deeds if I have ever done any they will be recorded in Heaven: but I shall never be rewarded, nor will they ever be acknowledged upon Earth."[1] Yet on the very day that he had written the first of these letters John Adams went to work again and during the next seven months or so completed what is now designated Part One of his Autobiography, to October 1776. He evidently did not intimate to his son that he had done so.

[8] 19 November 1804.
[9] 26 November 1804.

[1] 30 November, 6, 22 December 1804.

Before long, similar appeals came to the ex-President from old friends around the country. Writing from Oldenbarneveld, New York, F. A. Van der Kemp, a friend and admirer from the time of Adams' Dutch missions, said that by failing to furnish his memoirs Adams "would wrong your Self—you would wrong us—you would wrong our children." [2] And from Philadelphia Dr. Benjamin Rush, who had strong feelings about the way in which the history of the Revolution was being written, or miswritten, wrote to say that only actual participants would be able to counteract the errors and myths fast gaining currency as truth. [3] To both friends Adams returned evasive answers. He told Van der Kemp that "The twelve Books of the Æneid, the twenty four of the Iliad, and all the Odissy, the forty Volumes of Thuanus would not be enough" for such a purpose; and besides, "My Life is already written in my Letter books.... There I shall appear as I wish with all my imperfections on my head." [4] To Rush he said that rummaging through "Trunks, Letter books, bits of Journals and great heaps and bundles of papers, is a dreadful bondage to old Age, and an extinguisher of old eyes.... The few traces that remain of me, must I believe go down to posterity in much confusion and distraction, as my life has been passed." [5]

Yet once again, at the beginning of December 1806, he resumed his chore and apparently did not halt for any length of time until he had written Parts Two and Three of his Autobiography as we now have them, carrying the story to an abrupt ending in March 1780. Of this he gave a hint to John Quincy Adams, but to no one else unless to his wife. [6] From innumerable indications in the text of the three fragments it is clear that the author expected to continue his narrative through the peace negotiations of 1782–1783, his other diplomatic missions, his Vice-Presidency, and his term as President. [7] But for a reason not too hard to discern, he did not.

Having taken care, in various parts of the narrative he had so far written, of a number of those who had publicly criticized him, Adams was at length diverted by another assailant from going on with it at all. In 1805 Mercy Otis Warren published her three-volume *History of the Rise, Progress and Termination of the American Revolution. Interspersed with Biographical, Political and Moral Observations.* James and Mercy Warren had been friends of John and Abigail Adams

[2] 18 February 1806.
[3] 11 July 1806.
[4] 9 March, 30 April 1806.
[5] 23 July 1806 (Historical Society of Pennsylvania).

[6] John Adams to John Quincy Adams, 7 January 1807.
[7] See, for example, vol. 3:383, 447; 4:147, 187.

since before the Revolution, but during the 1790's the winds of party strife had blown them apart, and in the election of 1800 the Warrens had supported Jefferson against Adams. With some of the facts Mrs. Warren furnished and with a great many of her "Observations" of all sorts, John Adams was therefore bound to disagree. He began to read her book when it came out, but in a random way, and satisfied himself temporarily with a sarcastic reference in his "Travels and Negotiations" to "My quondam Friend Mrs. Warren."[8] As he read more, or perhaps as he reflected further on what he had already read, his resentment grew and the inevitable explosion took place. In July 1807 he sat down and began a letter to her in which he proposed "in the Spirit of Friendship" to point out "some" of her errors "in those Passages which relate personally to me," so that they could be corrected "for any future Edition of the Work."[9] He began by attempting to refute a passage in which she asserted that although he possessed "penetration and ability ... his prejudices and his passions were sometimes too strong for his sagacity and judgment."[1] As he warmed to his work he demonstrated the truth of her assertion overwhelmingly. Abandoning anything like "the Spirit of Friendship," he rained down hammer blows on the lady's head in a series of ten tremendous letters, some of them running to twenty or more pages of quarto letter paper. Mrs. Warren quite properly resented his "angry and indigested" tirades, and answered with skill and spirit, though less often and less lengthily. Refusing to be interrupted, Adams continued his serial self-vindication over a period of six weeks without regard to anything his correspondent said, reviewing much of his life since 1761, inserting copies of documents which she said she had no use for, and in short writing another version of his autobiographical memoirs addressed solely to a person who did not want to read them.[2]

This feverish effort put an end to the Autobiography John Adams had begun in 1802. He apparently never looked back at the abandoned manuscript, though much if not most of what he was to write in his remaining years was autobiographical. Early in 1809 critical questions relating to American foreign policy, in which his son John Quincy had been deeply involved as a senator, lured John Adams back into political journalism and led directly to his long series of letters of reminiscence that he stuffed with documents from his old files and

---

[8] See the Autobiography under date of 27 May 1778 (vol. 4:118).
[9] 11 July 1807 (Massachusetts Historical Society).

[1] Mercy Warren, *History*, 3:392.
[2] Their exchanges are printed in Massachusetts Historical Society, *Collections*, 5th series, 4(1878):321–491.

contributed to a Jeffersonian newspaper, the *Boston Patriot*.[3] Such
as they were, in all their disorder, written at white heat, fired off to
the printer without copies being retained or opportunity for revision,
and printed with incredible carelessness, they constituted John Adams'
public testament.[4]

As for the Autobiography proper, written as a private record only,
something has already been said of its chaotic structure, the windings
and turnings of the narrative in Part One, the indiscriminate copying
in all its parts, and its deplorable gaps. As the writer himself was more
or less aware, those sections written from memory contained a great
many minor and some serious inaccuracies. The present editors have
checked Adams' statements, dates, and names whenever they could
be checked, but readers must be warned that some innocent-looking
mistakes may have eluded editorial attention. Yet with all its faults John
Adams' Autobiography is a valuable and generally a highly readable document. It contains much that is "new" (in the sense of not being available elsewhere) on Adams' early life, notably on his education, his choice
of a profession, his beginnings in the law, and his involvement in provincial politics. Whereas, for example, the Diary has only the barest hint of
Adams' part in the trials growing out of the "Boston Massacre," the Autobiography devotes several pages to what happened in King Street on
that momentous evening and to the trials that followed. Adams'
retrospective account of the First Continental Congress is of course
less reliable than his contemporaneous notes in his Diary, but if he
had not written an autobiography we would not have had his record
of the dramatic conference in Carpenters Hall between the Massachusetts delegates and the Baptists from New England supported by
Philadelphia Quakers "with their broad brimmed Beavers on their
Heads"[5]—an incident important in the history of religious liberty.
Even the tedious extracts from the printed *Journals* of Congress in
1775–1776 tell us much about the crushing burden of routine business
and the often insoluble problems that were laid on the shoulders of

[3] Adams' four letters on "The Inad-
missible Principles of the King of England's Proclamation of October 16, 1807,
Considered," dated 9 January–25 April
1809, were published in the *Boston
Patriot*, 19 April–3 May 1809, and then
reprinted in pamphlet form. The first of
his series of 130 autobiographical and
self-justifying letters to the *Patriot* was
dated 10 April and was published on
15 April 1809.

[4] "They are not generally read by any

Party and cannot be expected to be so.—
I am not anxious to have them read by
the present Age. I wish them to be preserved to Posterity, that the Truth may
be known, without Panegyrics on one
hand or Reproaches on the other, which
I have not deserved" (Adams to Joseph
Ward, 31 August 1809, Chicago Historical Society). See C. F. Adams' dry
comments on this expectation, in John
Adams' *Works*, 1:614–615.

[5] Vol. 3:311.

a little group of fallible men. Amplified as the extracts are by frequent and sometimes detailed commentaries, and embellished by glimpses and sketches, affectionate or acidulous, of leaders like Dickinson, Stephen Hopkins, Hancock, Jefferson, Harrison, and Charles Thomson, they are full of nuggets for the casual reader and the scholar alike.

But it is when he reaches Europe that Adams' method of combining extracts with clarifying comments provides the richest fare. For though his Diary supplied him with notes of travel and his files of correspondence with a record of business transacted, he had experienced twenty further years of bruising diplomatic and political life before he sat down to recount his memories and ultimate views on the origins of American foreign policy. As he knew well enough at the time, he had been but a "raw American" when in 1778 he was unexpectedly thrust into "this great Theatre of Arts, Sciences, Commerce and War." [6] He had braced himself for contrasts between New England and French ways of life, so that he contrived to maintain outward composure when asked questions that shocked his moral sense at his first dinner party in France that included ladies, and a little later when he was introduced to *"amies"* of dukes and other grandees at their family dinner tables. He could even tolerate the extravagance of aristocratic life in and around Paris, though he hoped nothing like it would be introduced into America. Sometimes, to be sure, he blurted out his feelings, as he did once to a gentleman who showed him around his ornamental gardens and boasted that the collection of a thousand curious rocks he had assembled had cost several thousand guineas. Adams, who knew something about rocks because he had lived most of his life on a farm in the neighborhood of granite quarries, told his host that he "would sell him a thousand times as many for half a Guinea." [7] What he was totally unprepared for, however, was the bitter conflict between factions of Americans in France, a conflict in which the French government more or less directly participated and which, Adams despairingly thought, paralyzed American diplomacy. In reviewing his first European mission in his Autobiography he furnished a brilliant behind-the-scenes narrative and analysis which cannot, of course, be taken at face value but which, like his review of his years in the Continental Congress, adds a whole new dimension to the official records. To mention only a single example, his series of pen portraits of his co-commissioners and of the American and French satellites who gyrated around them is unparalleled in the literature of the time. And it is a sharp reminder of what we have

[6] Vol. 4:132, 33.　　　　　　　　　[7] 26 May 1778 (vol. 4:117).

lost by Adams' failure to continue his narrative through the later years of his public service, both abroad and at home.

"If my business had been travel," Adams remarked at the end of the last letter he contributed to the *Boston Patriot*, "I might write a book."[8] He never wrote such a book, but it would have been a superb contribution if to his other intellectual and literary gifts had been added some sense of form and structure. In spite of the numerous entries that appear under his name in library catalogues and bibliographies, Adams never really wrote a book. He was too much at the mercy of both his moods and his materials to do so. His best writing is always in short forms—in diary entries, in letters and dispatches (some of which, however, are brief treatises in themselves), and in comments that sizzle and sparkle in the margins of the books he read or between passages from other writers (or even himself) that stirred him, as in his Autobiography now first printed entire. Of the architecture of writing he knew nothing. But of unforgettable phrases and sentences, portraits of great and little men, homely and momentous scenes, insights into the nature of man in all conditions and of society on two sides of the Atlantic, he has left us at least as many as any of his great contemporaries whose writings have hitherto been better known. Best of all, he has left us a living likeness of a subject he never gave up studying—himself.

On board the *Alliance* in the Loire in 1779, impatient to sail home to America, John Adams examined himself and concluded: "There is a Feebleness and a Languor in my Nature. My Mind and Body both partake of this Weakness. By my Physical Constitution, I am but an ordinary Man. The Times alone have destined me to Fame—and even these have not been able to give me, much." Then he added: "Yet some great Events, some cutting Expressions, some mean Hypocrisies, have at Times, thrown this Assemblage of Sloth, Sleep, and littleness into Rage a little like a Lion."[9]

Here in these pages is John Adams the "ordinary Man," and here also is John Adams the "Lion."

[8] Letter dated 17 February 1812, concluded in the *Boston Patriot*, 16 May 1812.
[9] Diary, 26 April 1779 (vol. 2:362–363).

Acknowledgments

If, as John Donne said, "no man is an island, entire of itself," but "a piece of the continent, a part of the main," so also, in not too different a sense, is every undertaking in documentary publication. The editors set up their apparatus in one place—a library or other institution of learning—but they cannot work effectively without drawing on the resources of scores of other institutions and upon the generous services and specialized knowledge of uncounted and uncountable co-workers. No kind of scholarship is more truly and completely collaborative and interinstitutional than large-scale historical editing. No kind more naturally and necessarily incurs scholarly debts that cannot even be enumerated, say nothing of being repaid.

The editors of *The Adams Papers* are keenly aware of these considerations as they go to press. Any listing they might make of help they have so far received would run to many pages and still be far from complete. What follows is a mere token, in which a few names must stand for many, like a stage army.

The editors wish to express thanks to the following individuals, groups, and institutions for help specifically in the course of setting up the Adams enterprise and the editing and production of John Adams' *Diary and Autobiography*:

To the members of the Administrative Board, three gentlemen representing the Adams family, Harvard University Press, and the Massachusetts Historical Society. Their names appear at the head of this volume, but such a listing cannot remotely suggest the vision and effort they have contributed to this enterprise.

To the members of the Editorial Advisory Committee, listed in the same place, who have strengthened the editors' hands whenever help has been asked for, and have left the editors' hands free at other times.

To the living members of the Adams family, whose interest in a publication containing their family history has naturally been strong but has been expressed exclusively by confidence in the editors, patient answers to their questions, and generous actions forwarding their labors.

To Time, Inc., which on behalf of *Life* provided the funds to edit these papers. There is something highly fitting and gratifying in the realization that large portions of the writings of a family that for three generations devoted itself to national service should be presented to the American public in the numbers of a magazine that reaches millions of readers. "Mausauleums, Statues, Monuments will never be erected to me," John Adams told a friend in 1809. "Panegyrical Romances will never be written, nor flattering Orations spoken, to transmit me to Posterity in brilliant Colours." He was right in only the most limited sense. If few monuments have been erected to John Adams, he has, at length, something better. Thanks to a great publishing corporation, his life and the lives of his descendants, who never courted popularity either, are to be spread amply before their countrymen in their own words.

To the John Simon Guggenheim Memorial Foundation for a generous fellowship enabling the editor in chief to follow the footsteps of the Adamses through Europe and to document their travels and residences abroad with pictorial as well as printed and manuscript materials that have greatly enriched the present volumes and will continue to enrich those that follow.

To Harvard University Press and its staff in all its departments for their extraordinary professional competence, constructive interest at every stage of the work, and understanding and forbearance during times of editorial stress.

To the Harvard University Printing Office for high standards of craftsmanship maintained in tandem with efficiency and dispatch in performance.

To the Massachusetts Historical Society for the inspiration of its long record of distinguished documentary publications, for hospitable space, for unrivaled facilities for the study of New England history, for the daily and almost hourly help of its director and staff, and for the kindness of members of its Publications Committee in reading the galley proofs of these volumes.

To a number of neighboring libraries and their officials, especially the Boston Athenæum, the Boston Public Library, the Harvard College Library, and the American Antiquarian Society in Worcester, for the liberality with which they have placed their rich resources at the disposal of the Adams editorial enterprise.

To the librarians, archivists, and curators of scores of other institutions in this country and abroad who have furnished lists and photoduplicates of Adams documents, have patiently and efficiently answered our inquiries on all kinds of topics, and who continue to volunteer information they know will be pertinent to our work.

Acknowledgments

To the National Historical Publications Commission and its staff in Washington. For the Adams Papers, as for other large-scale editorial enterprises, the staff of the Commission has carried on searches for documents in the Library of Congress and the National Archives with a comprehensiveness that none of the enterprises individually could have equaled, and it has made available microfilm publications of the National Archives that augment our files and support our research at many points.

To those collectors, dealers, and other private owners of Adams letters and manuscripts who have graciously permitted them to be photocopied for our editorial files.

To our fellow editors engaged in similar undertakings, some of whom have shown and lighted the way for us and all of whom have shared with us their discoveries and their specialized knowledge of the Adamses' contemporaries and their writings.

To the present and former members of *The Adams Papers* staff. Here we must break through the anonymity so far maintained in this listing and name names. It is revealing no secret to point out that the names of the titlepage of a publication like the present one are only the exposed part of an iceberg. A whole band of co-workers, some for long periods, some for short, have contributed their skills, intelligence, and devotion to the work so far done. Miss Eleanor Bates must lead the list and be placed in a class by herself. She served as assistant editor during the period when the papers were being inventoried and brought under control and the edition was being planned. Though she left for other fruitful work before any edited copy was handed to the press for production, her successors, Leonard C. Faber and Wendell D. Garrett (whose terms as assistant editors have only briefly overlapped each other) and the editor in chief have had daily proofs that if she took much away with her she also left much behind on which we continue to build with confidence. Other former and current members of the staff have been Mrs. Harriet R. Cabot, Mrs. Paul W. Cherington, Miss Nancy Hugo, Mrs. R. Tenney Johnson, Mrs. Nadia M. Kun, Mrs. John A. Malcolm, Miss Anna K. Moses, Mr. W. Lyon Phelps, Miss Veronica Ruzicka, and Miss Jean Willcutt. The editors tender their warmest thanks to each one of them.

When confronting special problems the editors have drawn on an ever-widening circle of friends and of consultants to the enterprise. The present volumes have particularly benefited from the specialized knowledge of the following persons:

On matters relative to British manuscripts, archives, topography, and the like: Mr. Francis L. Berkeley Jr., University of Virginia Library; Miss W. D. Coates, National Registry of Archives, Historical Manuscripts Commission, London; Sir David Evans, Public Record Office, London; Sir Frank C. Francis, The British Museum; Mr. A. Taylor Milne, Institute of Historical Research, University of London; Mr. J. R. Pole, University of London; Mr. R. A. Skelton, The British Museum.

On Dutch archives, history, language, and topography: Mr. Meyer Elte, The Hague; Professor Pieter Geyl, University of Utrecht; Dr. Simon Hart, Gemeentlijke Archiefdienst, Amsterdam; Dr. H. M. Mensonides, Gemeente-Archief, The Hague; Mrs. Francis O'Loughlin, Cambridge, Mass.; Dr. A. van der Poest Clement, Algemeen Rijksarchief, The Hague; Professor P. J. van Winter, University of Groningen; Mrs. van Winter.

On French archives, language, and topography: M. Jean Baillou, Ministère des Affaires Etrangères, Paris; Dr. Howard C. Rice Jr., Princeton University Library; Mrs. W. Kenneth Thompson, Boston; Mr. William R. Tyler, Bonn, Germany; M. Pierre Verlet, Musée du Louvre, Paris.

On classical languages: Mr. and Mrs. Van Courtlandt Elliott, Cambridge; Professor Sterling Dow, Harvard University; Dr. Richard M. Gummere, Cambridge; Professor Johannes E. Gaertner, Lafayette College; Professor Mason Hammond, Harvard University; Sir Ronald Syme, Oxford University; Mr. Herbert H. Yeames, Boston.

On cartography: Mr. Ernest S. Dodge, Peabody Museum of Salem; Dr. Lawrence C. Wroth, John Carter Brown Library.

On legal history and the interpretation of 18th-century legal manuscripts: Professor Mark DeWolfe Howe, Harvard University; and a succession of students and graduates of the Harvard Law School—Messrs. R. Tenney Johnson, L. Kinvin Wroth, and Hiller Zobel—who, with the active encouragement of Professor Howe and Dean Erwin N. Griswold, have annotated John Adams' legal papers and identified and listed related materials in the early files of Massachusetts courts in the Suffolk County Court House.

On military history in the 18th century: Colonel Edward P. Hamilton of Milton, Mass., and Fort Ticonderoga, N.Y.

On American naval history: Mr. Marion V. Brewington, Peabody Museum of Salem; Mr. William Bell Clark, Brevard, N.C.; Rear Admiral E. M. Eller, Bureau of Naval History, U.S. Navy.

On Philadelphia local history: Miss Lois V. Given and Nicholas B. Wainwright, both of the Historical Society of Pennsylvania.

Acknowledgments

On printing, illustrations, and related matters: Mr. P. J. Conkwright, Princeton University Press; Mr. Harold Hugo, Meriden Gravure Company, Meriden, Conn.; Mr. Rudolph Ruzicka, Boston.

On Quincy local history: Mr. John Adams, Lincoln, Mass.; Mr. William C. Edwards, Quincy, Mass.; Mr. H. Hobart Holly, Braintree, Mass.

Mr. Charles F. Adams of Dover, Mass., very generously provided funds for a checklist of the books in the Old House and the Stone Library at Quincy. The work was carried out by Mr. Lloyd A. Brown and has proved constantly useful.

Mr. Roger Butterfield and Miss Alison Kallman have in the preparation of the text and illustrations for the articles on *The Adams Papers* appearing or to appear in *Life* added a new dimension to the editors' labors.

Mr. George M. Cushing Jr. of Boston has been our constant resource in everything relating to photography, as our lists of illustrations in these volumes show.

Mr. Zoltán Haraszti of the Boston Public Library graciously turned over to the editors for their unrestricted use his transcripts and notes, compiled over many years, relating to the marginalia John Adams wrote in the books he read.

Mrs. Frank E. Harris, superintendent of the Adams National Historic Site ("the Old House") at Quincy, administered by the National Park Service, has proved so warm and resourceful a friend to this enterprise that the editors have again and again sought her aid, and they have never sought in vain.

Jane Coolidge Whitehill of North Andover, Mass., has given voluntary help to the Adams enterprise on all kinds of problems from time to time and over long periods of time. It is not easy to think of terms in which to express our thanks to her.

Jane N. Garrett and Elizabeth E. Butterfield have not only furnished cheer and comfort during the long struggle to launch these volumes, but during its final and most arduous stages have plunged into and shared that struggle fully. John Adams often, and rightly, congratulated himself on the peerless qualities of his partner in marriage. Fortunately wifely virtues did not pass from the world with Abigail Adams.

Guide to Editorial Apparatus

1. TEXTUAL DEVICES

The following devices will be used throughout *The Adams Papers* to clarify the presentation of the text.

[...], [....]	One or two words missing and not conjecturable.
[...]¹, [....]¹	More than two words missing and not conjecturable; subjoined footnote estimates amount of missing matter.
[ ]	Number or part of a number missing or illegible. Amount of blank space inside brackets approximates the number of missing or illegible digits.
[roman]	Conjectural reading for missing or illegible matter. A question mark is inserted before the closing bracket if the conjectural reading is seriously doubtful.
⟨*italic*⟩	Matter canceled in the manuscript but restored in our text.
[*italic*]	Editorial insertion in the text.

2. ADAMS FAMILY CODE NAMES

In dealing with an assemblage of papers extending over several generations and written by so many members of a family who often bore the same or similar names, the editors have been obliged to devise short but unmistakable forms for the names of the persons principally concerned. They could not be forever adding dates and epithets to distinguish between the two or more Abigails, Charles Francises, Johns, John Quincys, and Louisa Catherines in the family. The following table lists the short forms that will be used in the annotation throughout *The Adams Papers*, together with their full equivalents and identifying dates. It includes the principal writing members of the "Presidential line" of the Adamses and certain others in that line (and their husbands and wives) who either appear frequently in the family story or have been important in the history of the family papers. Users should bear in mind that this table is *highly selective*, being a mere epitome of the Adams Genealogy that is being prepared to accompany the Family Correspondence in Series II of the present edition.

First Generation

JA	John Adams (1735–1826)
AA	Abigail Smith (1744–1818), *m.* JA 1764

Second Generation

JQA	John Quincy Adams (1767–1848), son of JA and AA
LCA	Louisa Catherine Johnson (1775–1852), *m.* JQA 1797
CA	Charles Adams (1770–1800), son of JA and AA
Mrs. CA	Sarah Smith (1769–1828), sister of WSS, *m.* CA 1795
TBA	Thomas Boylston Adams (1772–1832), son of JA and AA
Mrs. TBA	Ann Harrod (1774–1846), *m.* TBA 1805
AA2	Abigail Adams (1765–1813), daughter of JA and AA, *m.* WSS 1786
WSS	William Stephens Smith (1755–1816), brother of Mrs. CA

Third Generation

GWA	George Washington Adams (1801–1829), son of JQA and LCA
JA2	John Adams (1803–1834), son of JQA and LCA
Mrs. JA2	Mary Catherine Hellen (1807–1870), *m.* JA2 1828
CFA	Charles Francis Adams (1807–1886), son of JQA and LCA
ABA	Abigail Brown Brooks (1808–1889), *m.* CFA 1829
ECA	Elizabeth Coombs Adams (1808–1903), daughter of TBA and Mrs. TBA

Fourth Generation

JQA2	John Quincy Adams (1833–1894), son of CFA and ABA
CFA2	Charles Francis Adams (1835–1915), son of CFA and ABA
HA	Henry Adams (1838–1918), son of CFA and ABA
MHA	Marian Hooper (1842–1885), *m.* HA 1872
BA	Brooks Adams (1848–1927), son of CFA and ABA
LCA2	Louisa Catherine Adams (1831–1870), daughter of CFA and ABA, *m.* Charles Kuhn 1854
MA	Mary Adams (1845–1928), daughter of CFA and ABA, *m.* Henry Parker Quincy 1877

Fifth Generation

CFA3   Charles Francis Adams (1866–1954), son of JQA2
HA2   Henry Adams (1875–1951), son of CFA2

3. DESCRIPTIVE SYMBOLS

The following symbols will be employed throughout *The Adams Papers* to describe or identify in brief form the various kinds of manuscript originals.

D
: Diary (Used only to designate a diary written by a member of the Adams family and always in combination with the short form of the writer's name and a serial number, as follows: D/JA/23, i.e. the twenty-third fascicle or volume of John Adams' manuscript Diary.)

Dft
: draft

Dupl
: duplicate

FC
: file copy (Ordinarily a copy of a letter retained by a correspondent *other than an Adams,* for example Jefferson's press copies and polygraph copies, since all three of the Adams statesmen systematically entered copies of their outgoing letters in letterbooks.)

Lb
: Letterbook (Used only to designate Adams letterbooks and always in combination with the short form of the writer's name and a serial number, as follows: Lb/JQA/29, i.e. the twenty-ninth volume of John Quincy Adams' Letterbooks.)

LbC
: letterbook copy

M
: Miscellany (Used only to designate materials in the section of the Adams Papers known as the "Miscellany" and always in combination with the short form of the writer's name and a serial number, as follows: M/CFA/32, i.e. the thirty-second volume of the Charles Francis Adams Miscellany—a ledger volume mainly containing transcripts made by CFA in 1833 of selections from the family papers.)

MS, MSS
: manuscript, manuscripts

RC
: recipient's copy

Tr
: transcript (A copy, handwritten or typewritten, made substantially later than the original or than other copies—

such as duplicates, file copies, letterbook copies—that were made contemporaneously.)

Tripl   triplicate

4. LOCATION SYMBOLS

The originals of most of the manuscript documents to be printed, quoted, and cited in this edition are in the Adams Papers in the Massachusetts Historical Society. But the originals of the Adamses' outgoing letters and dispatches and of many other papers by them, not to mention papers pertaining to them, are preserved in numerous public and private archives and collections in this country and elsewhere. Locations of documents privately owned and of documents in public institutions outside the United States are to be given in expanded form. Locations of documents held by public institutions in the United States are to be indicated by the short, logical, and unmistakable institutional symbols used in the National Union Catalog in the Library of Congress, of which a published listing is available and which do not vary significantly from the library location symbols in the familiar *Union List of Serials.* (For a brief explanation of how these symbols are formed, see the headnote to the list of Location Symbols in *The Papers of Thomas Jefferson,* 1:xl.)

The following list gives the symbols and their expanded equivalents for institutions owning originals drawn upon in the four volumes of John Adams' *Diary and Autobiography.* The listing will be appropriately revised in each series, or part of a series, of *The Adams Papers* as the several series and parts are published.

CSmH	Henry E. Huntington Library and Art Gallery
CtHi	Connecticut Historical Society
CtY	Yale University Library
DLC	Library of Congress
DNA	The National Archives
DSI	Smithsonian Institution
DeHi	Historical Society of Delaware
M-Ar	Massachusetts Archives
MB	Boston Public Library
MBM	Boston Medical Library
MH	Harvard College Library
MHi	Massachusetts Historical Society
MQA	Adams National Historic Site, Quincy, Massachusetts

MWA   American Antiquarian Society
MiU-C   William L. Clements Library, University of Michigan
NHi   New-York Historical Society
NHpR   Franklin D. Roosevelt Library, Hyde Park, New York
NN   New York Public Library
NNMC   Museum of the City of New York
NNP   Pierpont Morgan Library
NhD   Dartmouth College Library
NhHi   New Hampshire Historical Society
NjP   Princeton University Library
PHi   Historical Society of Pennsylvania
PPAmP American Philosophical Society
ViHi   Virginia Historical Society
ViU   University of Virginia Library

5. OTHER ABBREVIATIONS AND CONVENTIONAL TERMS

Adams Papers

> Manuscripts and other materials, 1639–1889, in the Adams Manuscript Trust collection given to the Massachusetts Historical Society in 1956 and enlarged by a few additions of family papers since then. Citations in the present edition are simply by date of the original document if the original is in the main chronological series of the Papers and therefore readily found in the microfilm edition of the Adams Papers (see below). The location of materials in the Letterbooks and the Miscellany is given more fully, and often, if the original would be hard to locate, by the microfilm reel number.

Adams Papers Editorial Files

> Other materials in the Adams Papers editorial office, Massachusetts Historical Society. These include photoduplicated documents (normally cited by the location of the originals), photographs, correspondence, and bibliographical and other aids compiled and accumulated by the editorial staff.

Adams Papers, Fourth Generation

> Adams manuscripts dating 1890 or later, now separated from the Trust collection and administered by the Massachusetts Historical Society on the same footing with its other manuscript collections.

Adams Papers, Microfilms
The corpus of the Adams Papers, 1639–1889, as published on microfilm by the Massachusetts Historical Society, 1954–1959, in 608 reels. Cited in the present work, when necessary, by reel number. Available in research libraries throughout the United States and in a few libraries in Europe.

The Adams Papers
The present edition in letterpress, published by The Belknap Press of Harvard University Press. References between volumes of any given unit will take this form: vol. 3:171. Since there will be no over-all volume numbering for the edition, references from one series, or unit of a series, to another will be by title, volume, and page; for example, JQA, *Papers,* 4:205.

Corr. pol.
Correspondance politique, in the Archives du Ministère des Affaires Etrangères, Paris.

PCC
Papers of the Continental Congress. Originals in the National Archives; microfilm edition, completed in 1961, in 204 reels. Usually cited in the present work from the microfilms, but according to the original series and volume numbering devised in the State Department in the early 19th century; for example, PCC, No. 93, III, i.e. the third volume of series 93.

Quincy, First Church, MS Records
First Church of Quincy, Mass., MS Records, 1639–1854; transcript in possession of William C. Edwards, city historian.

Quincy Town Records, 1791–1891
Quincy, Mass., MS Town Records, 1791–1891, 6 vols., in the archives of the City of Quincy; positive microfilm, 2 reels, in the Massachusetts Historical Society.

RG
Record Group. Used, with appropriate numbers, to designate the location of documents in the National Archives.

Suffolk County Court House, Early Court Files, &c.
Early Court Files and Miscellaneous Papers in the Office of the Clerk of the Massachusetts Supreme Judicial Court, Suffolk County, Suffolk County Court House, Boston.

Superior Court of Judicature, Minute Books, Records
Massachusetts Superior Court of Judicature, Minute Books and Records in the Office of the Clerk of the Supreme Judicial Court, Suffolk County, Suffolk County Court House, Boston.

Thwing Catalogue, MHi
Annie Haven Thwing, comp., Inhabitants and Estates of the Town of Boston, 1630–1800; typed card catalogue, with supplementary bound typescripts, in Massachusetts Historical Society.

6. SHORT TITLES OF WORKS FREQUENTLY CITED

AA, *Letters*, ed. CFA, 1848
Letters of Mrs. Adams, the Wife of John Adams. With an Introductory Memoir by Her Grandson, Charles Francis Adams, 4th edn., Boston, 1848.

AA, *New Letters*
New Letters of Abigail Adams, 1788–1801, ed. Stewart Mitchell, Boston, 1947.

AA2, *Jour. and Corr.*
Journal and Correspondence of Miss Adams, Daughter of John Adams, . . . edited by Her Daughter [Caroline Amelia (Smith) de Windt], New York and London, 1841–1842; 2 vols.

A. N. Adams, *Geneal. Hist. of Henry Adams of Braintree*
Andrew N. Adams, *A Genealogical History of Henry Adams, of Braintree, Mass., and His Descendants*, Rutland, Vt., 1898.

Samuel Adams, *Writings*
The Writings of Samuel Adams, ed. Harry Alonzo Cushing, New York and London, 1904–1908; 4 vols.

AHR
American Historical Review.

Almanach royal, 1778 [and later years]
Almanach royal, année M.DCC.LXXVIII [&c.]. *Présenté à sa majesté pour la première fois en 1699*, Paris, no date.

Annals of Congress
The Debates and Proceedings in the Congress of the United States [1789–1824], Washington, 1834–1856; 42 vols.

Appletons' Cyclo. Amer. Biog.
James Grant Wilson and John Fiske, eds., *Appletons' Cyclopædia of American Biography*, New York, 1887–1889; 6 vols.

Austin, *Gerry*
James T. Austin, *The Life of Elbridge Gerry. With Contemporary Letters,* Boston, 1828–1829; 2 vols. [Vol. 1:] *To the Close of the American Revolution*; [vol. 2:] *From the Close of the American Revolution.*

Bartlett, *Henry Adams of Somersetshire*
J. Gardner Bartlett, *Henry Adams of Somersetshire, England, and Braintree, Mass.: His English Ancestry and Some of His Descendants,* New York, 1927.

Bemis, *Diplomacy of the Amer. Revolution*
Samuel Flagg Bemis, *The Diplomacy of the American Revolution: The Foundations of American Diplomacy,* 1775–1823, New York and London, 1935.

Bemis, *JQA*
Samuel Flagg Bemis, *John Quincy Adams,* New York, 1949–1956; 2 vols. [Vol. 1:] *John Quincy Adams and the Foundations of American Foreign Policy*; [vol. 2:] *John Quincy Adams and the Union.*

Biddle, *Old Family Letters*
Old Family Letters: Copied from the Originals for Alexander Biddle, Series A, Philadelphia, 1892.

Biog. Dir. Cong.
Biographical Directory of the American Congress, 1774–1949, Washington, 1950.

Blanck, *Bibliog. Amer. Lit.*
Jacob Blanck, comp., *Bibliography of American Literature ... Compiled for the Bibliographical Society of America,* New Haven, 1955– .

BM, *Catalogue*
The British Museum Catalogue of Printed Books, 1881–1900, Ann Arbor, 1946; 58 vols. *Supplement,* 1900–1905, Ann Arbor, 1950; 10 vols.

Boston Record Commissioners, *Reports*
City of Boston, Record Commissioners, *Reports,* Boston, 1876–1909; 39 vols.

Boston Streets, &c., 1910
City of Boston, Street Commissioners, *A Record of the Streets, Alleys, Places, Etc., in the City of Boston,* Boston, 1910.

Bouvier, *Law Dictionary*
> John Bouvier, *A Law Dictionary, Adapted to the Constitution and Laws of the United States*, 14th edn., Philadelphia, 1871; 2 vols.

Braintree Town Records
> Samuel A. Bates, ed., *Records of the Town of Braintree, 1640 to 1793*, Randolph, Mass., 1886.

Burnett, *Continental Congress*
> Edmund C. Burnett, *The Continental Congress*, New York, 1941.

Burnett, ed., *Letters of Members*
> Edmund C. Burnett, ed., *Letters of Members of the Continental Congress*, Washington, 1921–1936; 8 vols.

Cal. Franklin Papers, A.P.S.
> I. Minis Hays, comp., *Calendar of the Papers of Benjamin Franklin in the Library of the American Philosophical Society*, Philadelphia, 1908; 5 vols.

Catalogue of JA's Library
> *Catalogue of the John Adams Library in the Public Library of the City of Boston*, Boston, 1917.

Catalogue of JQA's Books
> Worthington C. Ford, ed., *A Catalogue of the Books of John Quincy Adams Deposited in the Boston Athenæum. With Notes on Books, Adams Seals and Book-Plates*, by Henry Adams, Boston, 1938.

CFA2, *Three Episodes*
> Charles Francis Adams, *Three Episodes of Massachusetts History: The Settlement of Boston Bay; The Antinomian Controversy; A Study of Church and Town Government*, Boston and New York, 1892; 2 vols.

Col. Soc. Mass., *Pubns.*
> Colonial Society of Massachusetts, *Publications.*

Commonwealth Hist. of Mass.
> Albert Bushnell Hart, ed., *Commonwealth History of Massachusetts: Colony, Province and State*, New York, 1927–1930; 5 vols.

Currier, *Newburyport*
> John J. Currier, *History of Newburyport, Massachusetts, 1764–1905*, Newburyport, 1906–1909; 2 vols.

Curwen, *Journal and Letters*, 4th edn., 1864
> *The Journal and Letters of Samuel Curwen, ... from 1775 to 1783; with an Appendix of Biographical Sketches*, ed. George Atkinson Ward, 4th edn., Boston, 1864.

DAB
Allen Johnson and Dumas Malone, eds., *Dictionary of American Biography*, New York, 1928–1936; 20 vols. plus index and supplements.

DAH
James Truslow Adams and R. V. Coleman, eds., *Dictionary of American History*, New York, 1940; 5 vols. and index.

Deane Papers
Papers of Silas Deane, 1774–1790, in New-York Historical Society, *Collections, Publication Fund Series*, vols. 19–23, New York, 1887–1891; 5 vols.

Dexter, *Yale Graduates*
Franklin Bowditch Dexter, *Biographical Sketches of the Graduates of Yale College, with Annals of the College History*, New York, 1885–1912; 6 vols.

Dezallier, *Environs de Paris*, 1779
[Antoine Nicolas Dezallier d'Argenville,] *Voyage pittoresque des environs de Paris*, 4e. édn., Paris, 1779.

Dict. de la noblesse
François Alexandre Aubert de La Chesnaye-Desbois and —— Badier, *Dictionnaire de la noblesse*, Paris, 3d edn., 1863–1876; 19 vols.

Dict. of Americanisms
Mitford M. Mathews, ed., *A Dictionary of Americanisms on Historical Principles*, Chicago, 1951.

Dipl. Corr., 1783–1789
[William A. Weaver, ed.,] *The Diplomatic Correspondence of the United States of America, from* ... 1783, *to* ... 1789, Washington, 1837 [actually 1855]; 3 vols.

DNB
Leslie Stephen and Sidney Lee, eds., *The Dictionary of National Biography*, New York and London, 1885–1900; 63 vols. plus supplements.

Doniol, *Histoire*
Henri Doniol, *Histoire de la participation de la France à l'établissement des Etats-Unis d'Amérique: correspondance diplomatique et documents*, Paris, 1886–1892; 5 vols.

Eliot, *Biog. Dict. of N.E.*
John Eliot, *Biographical Dictionary, Containing a Brief Account of the First Settlers, and Other Eminent Characters* ... *in New-England*, Salem and Boston, 1809.

Evans

Charles Evans, and others, comps., *American Bibliography: A Chronological Dictionary of All Books, Pamphlets and Periodical Publications Printed in the United States of America* [1639–1800], Chicago and Worcester, 1903–1959; 14 vols.

Farrand, *Records of the Federal Convention*

Max Farrand, ed., *The Records of the Federal Convention of* 1787, New Haven, 1911–1937; 4 vols.

Forbes, *Paul Revere*

Esther Forbes, *Paul Revere and the World He Lived In*, Boston, 1942.

Force, *Archives*

[Peter Force, ed.,] *American Archives: Consisting of a Collection of Authentick Records, State Papers, Debates, and Letters and Other Notices of Publick Affairs*, Washington, 1837–1853; 9 vols.

Ford, ed., *Statesman and Friend*

Worthington C. Ford, ed., *Statesman and Friend: Correspondence of John Adams with Benjamin Waterhouse,* 1784–1822, Boston, 1927.

Franklin, *Papers,* ed. Labaree and Bell

The Papers of Benjamin Franklin, ed. Leonard W. Labaree and Whitfield J. Bell Jr., New Haven, 1959– .

Franklin, *Writings,* ed. Smyth

The Writings of Benjamin Franklin, ed. Albert Henry Smyth, New York and London, 1905–1907; 10 vols.

Freeman, *Washington*

Douglas Southall Freeman, *George Washington: A Biography*, New York, 1948–1952; 6 vols. Vol. 7, by John Alexander Carroll and Mary Wells Ashworth, New York, 1957.

Gage, *Corr.*

The Correspondence of General Thomas Gage with the Secretaries of State, 1763–1775, ed. Clarence E. Carter, New Haven, 1931–1933; 2 vols.

Gérard, *Despatches and Instructions*

Despatches and Instructions of Conrad Alexandre Gérard, 1778–1780: *Correspondence of the First French Minister to the United States with the Comte de Vergennes,* ed. John J. Meng, Baltimore, 1939.

Gottschalk, *Lafayette*

Louis Gottschalk, *Lafayette,* Chicago, 1935–1950; 4 vols. [Vol. 1:]

Lafayette Comes to America; [vol. 2:] *Lafayette Joins the American Army*; [vol. 3:] *Lafayette and the Close of the American Revolution*; [vol. 4:] *Lafayette between the American and the French Revolution* (1783–1789).

La grande encyclopédie
La grande encyclopédie: inventaire raisonné des sciences, des lettres et des arts, Paris [1886–1902]; 31 vols.

HA, *Gallatin*
Henry Adams, *The Life of Albert Gallatin*, Philadelphia, 1879.

HA2, *Birthplaces*
Henry Adams, *The Birthplaces of Presidents John and John Quincy Adams in Quincy, Massachusetts*, Quincy, 1936.

Hamilton, *Works*, ed. Hamilton
The Works of Alexander Hamilton, ed. John C. Hamilton, New York, 1850–1851; 7 vols.

Haraszti, *JA and the Prophets of Progress*
Zoltán Haraszti, *John Adams and the Prophets of Progress*, Cambridge, 1952.

Harvard Quinquennial Cat.
Harvard University, *Quinquennial Catalogue of the Officers and Graduates, 1636–1930*, Cambridge, 1930.

Heitman, *Register Continental Army*
Francis B. Heitman, comp., *Historical Register of Officers of the Continental Army during the War of the Revolution*, new edn., Washington, 1914.

Hoefer, *Nouv. biog. générale*
J. C. F. Hoefer, ed., *Nouvelle biographie générale depuis les temps les plus reculés jusqu'à nos jours*, Paris, 1852–1866; 46 vols.

Hutchinson, *Diary and Letters*
The Diary and Letters of His Excellency Thomas Hutchinson, ed. Peter Orlando Hutchinson, Boston, 1884–1886; 2 vols.

Hutchinson, *Massachusetts Bay*, ed. Mayo
Thomas Hutchinson, *The History of the Colony and Province of Massachusetts-Bay*, ed. Lawrence Shaw Mayo, Cambridge, 1936; 3 vols.

JA, *Corr. in the Boston Patriot*
Correspondence of the Late President Adams. Originally Published in the Boston Patriot. In a Series of Letters, Boston, 1809[–1810]; 10 pts.

JA, *Defence*
John Adams, *A Defence of the Constitutions of Government of the United States of America*, London, 1787–1788; 3 vols.

JA, *Letters*, ed. CFA
Letters of John Adams, Addressed to His Wife, ed. Charles Francis Adams, Boston, 1841; 2 vols.

JA, *Works*
The Works of John Adams, Second President of the United States: with a Life of the Author, ed. Charles Francis Adams, Boston, 1850–1856; 10 vols.

JA-AA, *Familiar Letters*
Familiar Letters of John Adams and His Wife Abigail Adams, during the Revolution. With a Memoir of Mrs. Adams, ed. Charles Francis Adams, New York, 1876.

Jay, *Correspondence and Public Papers*
The Correspondence and Public Papers of John Jay, ed. Henry P. Johnston, New York and London, 1890–1893; 4 vols.

JCC
Worthington C. Ford and others, eds., *Journals of the Continental Congress, 1774–1789*, Washington, 1904–1937; 34 vols.

Jefferson, *Papers*, ed. Boyd
The Papers of Thomas Jefferson, ed. Julian P. Boyd and others, Princeton, 1950– .

Jefferson, *Writings*, ed. Ford
The Writings of Thomas Jefferson, ed. Paul Leicester Ford, New York and London, 1892–1899; 10 vols.

Jones, *Loyalists of Mass.*
E. Alfred Jones, *The Loyalists of Massachusetts: Their Memorials, Petitions and Claims*, London, 1930.

JQA, *Life in a New England Town*
Life in a New England Town: 1787, 1788. Diary of John Quincy Adams, While a Student in the Office of Theophilus Parsons at Newburyport, Boston, 1903.

JQA, *Memoirs*
Memoirs of John Quincy Adams, Comprising Portions of His Diary from 1795 to 1848, ed. Charles Francis Adams, Philadelphia, 1874–1877; 12 vols.

JQA, *Writings*
> The Writings of John Quincy Adams, ed. Worthington C. Ford, New York, 1913–1917; 7 vols.

Lasseray, *Les français sous les treize étoiles*
> André Lasseray, *Les français sous les treize étoiles* (1775–1783), Macon and Paris, 1935; 2 vols.

LC, *Catalog*
> A Catalog of Books Represented by Library of Congress Printed Cards, Ann Arbor, 1942–1946; 167 vols. *Supplement*, Ann Arbor, 1948; 42 vols.

R. H. Lee, *Arthur Lee*
> Richard Henry Lee, *Life of Arthur Lee*, Boston, 1829; 2 vols.

R. H. Lee, *Letters*, ed. Ballagh
> The Letters of Richard Henry Lee, ed. James C. Ballagh, New York, 1911–1914; 2 vols.

William Lee, *Letters*
> Letters of William Lee, ... 1766–1783, ed. Worthington C. Ford, Brooklyn, 1891; 3 vols.

Lincoln, *Worcester*
> William Lincoln, *History of Worcester, Massachusetts, from Its Earliest Settlement to September, 1836*, Worcester, 1837; 2 vols.

Maclay, *Journal*, 1890
> Journal of William Maclay, United States Senator from Pennsylvania, 1789–1791, ed. Edgar S. Maclay, New York, 1890.

Mass. Constitutional Convention, 1779–1780, *Journal*
> Journal of the Convention for Framing a Constitution of Government for the State of Massachusetts Bay, ... September 1, 1779, ... to June 16, 1780, Boston, 1832.

Mass., *House Jour.*
> Journals of the House of Representatives of Massachusetts [1715–], Boston, reprinted by the Massachusetts Historical Society, 1919– . (For the years for which reprints are not yet available, the original printings are cited, by year and session.)

Mass., *Province Laws*
> The Acts and Resolves, Public and Private, of the Province of the Massachusetts Bay, Boston, 1869–1922; 21 vols.

Mass. Provincial Congress, *Jours.*
> William Lincoln, ed., *The Journals of Each Provincial Congress of*

Massachusetts in 1774 and 1775, and of the Committee of Safety, Boston, 1838.

Mass. Soldiers and Sailors
Massachusetts Soldiers and Sailors of the Revolutionary War, Boston, 1896–1908; 17 vols.

Mass., *Speeches of the Governors, &c.,* 1765–1775
[Alden Bradford, ed.,] *Speeches of the Governors of Massachusetts, from 1765 to 1775 ...,* Boston, 1818.

MHS, *Colls., Procs.*
Massachusetts Historical Society, *Collections* and *Proceedings.*

Michaud, *Biog. universelle*
Biographie universelle, ancienne et moderne, Paris: Michaud Frères, 1811–1862; 85 vols.

Miller, ed., *Treaties*
Hunter Miller, ed., *Treaties and Other International Acts of the United States of America,* Washington, 1931–1948; 8 vols.

MVHR
Mississippi Valley Historical Review.

NEHGR
New England Historical and Genealogical Register.

NEQ
New England Quarterly.

Nieuw Ned. *Biog. Woordenboek*
P. C. Molhuysen and others, eds., *Nieuw Nederlandsche Biografisch Woordenboek,* Leyden, 1911–1937; 10 vols.

OED
The Oxford English Dictionary, Oxford, 1933; 12 vols. and supplement.

Parliamentary Hist.
The Parliamentary History of England, from the Earliest Period to the Year 1803, London: Hansard, 1806–1820; 36 vols.

Pattee, *Old Braintree and Quincy*
William S. Pattee, *A History of Old Braintree and Quincy, with a Sketch of Randolph and Holbrook,* Quincy, 1878.

Paullin, *Atlas*
Charles O. Paullin and John K. Wright, eds., *Atlas of the Historical Geography of the United States,* Washington and New York, 1932.

Pickering and Upham, *Pickering*
Octavius Pickering and Charles W. Upham, *The Life of Timothy Pickering*, Boston, 1867–1873; 4 vols.

PMHB
Pennsylvania Magazine of History and Biography.

Quincy, *History of Harvard Univ.*
Josiah Quincy, *The History of Harvard University*, 2d edn., Boston, 1860; 2 vols.

Quincy, *Reports*
Josiah Quincy Jr., *Reports of Cases Argued and Adjudged in the Superior Court of Judicature of the Province of Massachusetts Bay, between 1761 and 1772*, ed. Samuel M. Quincy, Boston, 1865.

Josiah Quincy, *Josiah Quincy, Jr.*
Josiah Quincy, *Memoir of Josiah Quincy, Junior, of Massachusetts: 1744–1775*, 2d edn., ed. Eliza Susan Quincy, Boston, 1874.

Rowe, *Letters and Diary*
Letters and Diary of John Rowe, Boston Merchant, 1759–1762, 1764–1779, ed. Anne Rowe Cunningham, Boston, 1903.

Benjamin Rush, *Autobiography*
The Autobiography of Benjamin Rush: His "Travels through Life," Together with His Commonplace Book for 1789–1813, ed. George W. Corner, Princeton, 1948.

Benjamin Rush, *Letters*
Letters of Benjamin Rush, ed. L. H. Butterfield, Princeton, 1951; 2 vols.

Sabin
Joseph Sabin and others, comps., *A Dictionary of Books Relating to America, from Its Discovery to the Present Time*, New York, 1868–1936; 29 vols.

Sabine, *Loyalists*
Lorenzo Sabine, *Biographical Sketches of Loyalists of the American Revolution, with an Historical Essay*, Boston, 1864; 2 vols.

Salisbury, *Family-Memorials*
Edward E. Salisbury, *Family-Memorials: A Series of Genealogical and Biographical Monographs*, New Haven, 1885; 2 vols. and 1 portfolio.

Scharf and Westcott, *History of Philadelphia*
J. Thomas Scharf and Thompson Westcott, *History of Philadelphia, 1609–1884*, Philadelphia, 1884; 3 vols.

Sheppard, *Tucker*
John H. Sheppard, *The Life of Samuel Tucker, Commodore in the American Revolution*, Boston, 1868.

Shurtleff, *Description of Boston*
Nathaniel B. Shurtleff, *A Topographical and Historical Description of Boston*, 3d edn., Boston, 1890.

Sibley-Shipton, *Harvard Graduates*
John Langdon Sibley and Clifford K. Shipton, *Biographical Sketches of Graduates of Harvard University, in Cambridge, Massachusetts*, Cambridge and Boston, 1873– .

Sprague, *Annals Amer. Pulpit*
William B. Sprague, *Annals of the American Pulpit; or Commemorative Notices of Distinguished American Clergymen of Various Denominations*, New York, 1857–1869; 9 vols.

Stark, *Loyalists of Mass.*
James H. Stark, *The Loyalists of Massachusetts and the Other Side of the American Revolution*, Boston, 1910.

Stevens, *Facsimiles*
B. F. *Stevens's Facsimiles of Manuscripts in European Archives Relating to America, 1773–1783*, London, 1889–1898; 25 vols.

Stiles, *Literary Diary*
The Literary Diary of Ezra Stiles, D.D., LL.D., President of Yale College, ed. Franklin Bowditch Dexter, New York, 1901; 3 vols.

Stillé, *Dickinson*
Charles J. Stillé, *The Life and Times of John Dickinson, 1732–1808*, Philadelphia, 1891.

Stokes, *Iconography of Manhattan Island*
I. N. Phelps Stokes, *The Iconography of Manhattan Island, 1498–1919*, New York, 1915–1928; 6 vols.

Thacher, *Amer. Medical Biog.*
James Thacher, *American Medical Biography: or Memoirs of Eminent Physicians Who Have Flourished in America*, Boston, 1828; 2 vols.

Thiéry, *Almanach du voyageur à Paris*
Luc Vincent Thiéry, *Almanach du voyageur à Paris . . ., année 1784*, Paris [1784].

Thomas, *Columbia Univ. Officers and Alumni*
Milton Halsey Thomas, comp., *Columbia University Officers and Alumni, 1754–1857*, New York, 1936.

Thorpe, *Federal and State Constitutions*
Francis N. Thorpe, ed., *The Federal and State Constitutions, Colonial Charters, and Other Organic Laws of the States, Territories, and Colonies Now or Heretofore Forming the United States of America,* Washington, 1909; 7 vols.

Tudor, *James Otis*
William Tudor, *The Life of James Otis, of Massachusetts,* Boston, 1823.

VMHB
Virginia Magazine of History and Biography.

Walpole, *Corr.,* ed. W. S. Lewis
The Yale Edition of Horace Walpole's Correspondence, ed. W. S. Lewis and others, New Haven, 1937- .

Walpole, *Letters,* ed. Mrs. Toynbee
The Letters of Horace Walpole, Fourth Earl of Orford, ed. Mrs. Paget Toynbee, Oxford, 1903–1905; 16 vols.

Warren-Adams Letters
Warren-Adams Letters: Being Chiefly a Correspondence among John Adams, Samuel Adams, and James Warren (Massachusetts Historical Society, *Collections,* vols. 72–73), Boston, 1917–1925; 2 vols.

Washington, *Writings,* ed. Fitzpatrick
The Writings of George Washington from the Original Manuscript Sources, 1745–1799, ed. John C. Fitzpatrick, Washington, 1931–1944; 39 vols.

Washington, *Writings,* ed. Sparks
The Writings of George Washington, … with a Life of the Author, ed. Jared Sparks, Boston, 1839–1840; 12 vols.

Weis, *Colonial Clergy of N.E.*
Frederick Lewis Weis, comp., *The Colonial Clergy and the Colonial Churches of New England,* Lancaster, Mass., 1936.

Wells, *Samuel Adams*
William V. Wells, *The Life and Public Services of Samuel Adams,* Boston, 1865; 3 vols.

Wharton, ed., *Dipl. Corr. Amer. Rev.*
Francis Wharton, ed., *The Revolutionary Diplomatic Correspondence of the United States,* Washington, 1889; 6 vols.

Wheatley, *London Past and Present*
    Henry B. Wheatley, *London Past and Present: Its History, Associations, and Traditions,* London, 1891; 3 vols.

Whitmore, *Mass. Civil List*
    William H. Whitmore, comp., *The Massachusetts Civil List for the Colonial and Provincial Periods,* 1630–1774, Albany, 1870.

Wilson, *Where Amer. Independence Began*
    Daniel Munro Wilson, *Where American Independence Began: Quincy, Its Famous Group of Patriots; Their Deeds, Homes, and Descendants,* 2d edn., Boston and New York, 1904.

Winsor, *Memorial History of Boston*
    Justin Winsor, ed., *The Memorial History of Boston, Including Suffolk County,* 1630–1880, Boston, 1880–1881; 4 vols.

WMQ
    William and Mary Quarterly.

VOLUME I

Diary 1755–1770

Diary of John Adams

NOVEMBER 18TH. 1755.[1]

We had a severe Shock of an Earthquake. It continued near four minutes. I was then at my Fathers in Braintree,[2] and awoke out of my sleep in the midst of it. The house seemed to rock and reel and crack as if it would fall in ruins about us. 7 Chimnies were shatter'd by it within one mile of my Fathers house.[3]

[1] First entry in "Paper book No. 1" (D/JA/1), which is the first in the series of stitched booklets that make up the greater part of JA's MS Diary. MS notations by JQA on the front cover of the booklet indicate that its contents were copied into the "Small Quarto" series of early transcripts of the Diary and that JQA compared the transcripts with the original entries, 22 Sept. 1832.

[2] John Adams (1691–1761), father of JA, is usually called Deacon John Adams in order to distinguish him from his son, and he will be so designated in this edition. Farmer, cordwainer (shoemaker), tithingman, constable (tax collector), militia officer, nine times selectman, and for fourteen years a deacon of the North Precinct church, he was "a typical New England yeoman" (CFA2, Three Episodes, 2:715). JA, who paid repeated and very high tributes to his father's character, said that "almost all the Business of the Town [was] managed by him for 20 Years together" (Memoranda on a copy of Deacon John Adams' Will, 10 July 1761, Adams Papers, Wills and Deeds).
There is a note on the Deacon's two houses in Braintree, the birthplaces of the two Adams Presidents, under 17 March 1756, below.

[3] This earthquake, a fairly severe one in New England, occurred a little after 4 A.M., Tuesday, 18 Nov., and was one of an intermittent series of seismic shocks on both sides of the Atlantic, the most memorable of which had virtually destroyed the city of Lisbon on the morning of 1 Nov. Besides jolting JA into beginning a diary, the earthquake of the 18th produced a public controversy between Rev. Thomas Prince of Boston and Professor John Winthrop of Harvard that has been engagingly recounted by Eleanor M. Tilton in "Lightning-Rods and the Earthquake of 1755," NEQ, 13:85–97 (March 1940). JA sided with the scientist rather than with the divine, though he appears to have kept his thoughts on the subject to himself; see his marginalia in Winthrop's Lecture on Earthquakes under Dec. 1758, below. A very full description of the physical effects of the earthquake on the town of Boston was printed in the Boston Gazette, 24 Nov. 1755.

JANUARY THE 14TH. 1756.

At Worcester. A very rainy Day. Kept school in the forenoon; but not in the afternoon, because of the weather and my own indisposition.[1]

[1] JA had come to Worcester "about three weeks after [his] commencement" at Harvard to keep a school. (Commencement in 1755 fell on 16 July.) The circumstances of his appointment are related in his Autobiography. The

I

school he kept was the "Center School," built in 1738 close to the site of the present Worcester County Court House in Lincoln Square, where a plaque now memorializes his brief career as a pedagogue (Daughters of the Amer. Rev., *Report of the Committee on Historical Research and Marking Local Sites of the Colonel Timothy Bigelow Chapter,* Worcester, 1903, *passim*). The town appropriated £75 for the support of its center and several outlying schools in 1755, but part of JA's compensation was his keep ("Worcester Town Records," Worcester Soc. of Antiquity, *Colls.,* 4 [1882]:20).

During a later visit to Worcester JA recorded the names of some of the pupils he had taught at the Center School (entry of 2 June 1771, below).

15.

A fair morning and pretty warm. Kept school. Drank Tea at Mr. Swan's, with Mr. Thayer.

16 FRYDAY.

A fine morning. A large white frost upon the ground. Reading Hutcheson's Introduction to moral Phylosophy.[1] A beautiful Day and Evening. Din'd with Major Chandler.[2]

[1] Francis Hutcheson, *A Short Introduction to Moral Philosophy, in Three Books; Containing the Elements of Ethicks and the Law of Nature,* Glasgow, 1747, and later edns., was long a popular textbook in Scotland and America. A number of works by Hutcheson survive among JA's books in the Boston Public Library; see *Catalogue of JA's Library.*

[2] Gardiner Chandler (1723–1782), son of the third John Chandler (1693?–1762) and brother of the fourth John Chandler (1721–1800), with all of whom JA was on friendly terms during his years in Worcester. The leading family in pre-Revolutionary Worcester, the Chandlers tended to multiply and succeed each other in civil and military offices in a manner that often makes it difficult to tell which of them JA refers to in his jottings. "Major Chandler," "the Major," and "Gardiner" clearly signify Gardiner Chandler; "Judge Chandler" and "the Judge" always mean the third John Chandler; and "Colonel Chandler Jur." the Judge's son John. References to "Colonel Chandler" or "the Colonel" are, however, often ambiguous, especially after 1757, when all three Chandlers held the rank of colonel.

17 SATURDAY.

A clowdy, dull, Day. Some snow about noon, and rain towards night. σπίζημαι, τα καθαρματα Ψυχησ.[1] Plato.

[1] This passage remains a puzzle after examination by several authorities on Greek. It is not an accurate quotation from Plato, and nothing in the context gives a clue to what JA intended by the first word, which makes neither sense nor grammar as it stands. If we may read the first word as the noun ἐπιστῆμαι, then the passage may be translated: "Sciences (or studies), the things that cleanse the soul."

18 SUNDAY.

A fair morning. Heard Mr. Maccarty.[1]

[1] Rev. Thaddeus Maccarty (1721–1784), who at the preceding Harvard commencement had singled out JA to serve as schoolmaster in Worcester.

19 MONDAY.

A rainy Day.

20 TUESDAY.

A fair, warm spring like Day. Drank Tea and supped at Mr. Greenes.[1]

[1] For the first few months after he came to Worcester JA had "boarded with one Green at the Expence of the Town" (JA, Autobiography), but since there were numerous Greens in Worcester at this period and since JA writes this name as "Green" and "Greene" interchangeably, none of those mentioned in the early Diary can be certainly identified.

21 WEDNESDAY.

A very rainy day. Dined with Coll. Chandlers Jur. Spent the Eve at Mr. Maccarty's. Kept school. Nothing more.

22 THURDSDAY.

A fair morning. Fresh and lively Air. Drank Tea and supped at Mrs. Paine's.[1]

[1] Presumably Sarah (Chandler) Paine, daughter of Colonel or Judge John Chandler and wife of Timothy Paine (1730–1793), currently a member of the General Court (Stark, *Loyalists of Mass.*, p. 382–385).

23 FRYDAY.

A fair and agreable Day. Kept School. Drank Tea, at Coll. Chandler's Jur., and spent the Evening at Major Gardiners.

24 SATURDAY.

A very high west Wind. Warm and cloudy. P.M. warm and fair.

25 SUNDAY.

A cold Weather. Heard friend Thayer preach two ingenious discourses, from Jeremy 10th. 6. and 7. Supped att Coll. Chandlers.

26 MONDAY.

A sharp piercing Air. Sat out for Uxbridge, arrived 2'O clock.

27 TUESDAY.

Att my Uncles.[1]

[1] Rev. Nathan Webb (1705–1772), who in 1731 had married Ruth, a younger sister of Deacon John Adams of Braintree. Webb, who graduated at Harvard in 1725, was settled as the first minister at Uxbridge, Mass., in the year of his marriage and enjoyed a pastorate there of over forty years (Sibley-Shipton, *Harvard Graduates*, 7:617–619).

28 WEDNESDAY.

Ditto. Thick weather, and some rain.

29 THURSDAY.

Still, cloudy Weather. Set out for Worcester, Drank Tea in Sutton, with my class mate, Wheeler and arrived at Worcester about 7 o clock. Supped with Major Chandler. Very miry Roads.

30 FRIDAY.

Still, foggy, damp Weather. Kept School and dined at Mr. Greenes.

31 SATURDAY.

A warm, spring-like Day. Kept School. Lodged at Mr. Maccartys, at night.

FEBRUARY. 1756. 1 SUNDAY.

Pretty cold. Staid at Home, A.M.   P.M. heard Mr. Maccarty. Lodg'd with him at night.

2 MONDAY.

Wrote to John Wentworth[1] by Coll. Josiah Willard. Spent the Eve, sup'd and lodg'd at Major Chandler's, with that universal Scholar, gay Companion, and accomplish'd Gentleman Mr. Robert Treat Pain.[2] Misty, thick Weather.

[1] This letter to a classmate, who was to become the last royal governor of New Hampshire and subsequently lieutenant governor of Nova Scotia (see *DAB*), has not been found.

[2] Robert Treat Paine (1731–1814) preceded JA into the law by a few years, and the two became keen professional rivals. The eulogistic phrases in this first mention of Paine in the Diary are not untouched by sarcasm; many of JA's later references are in the same tone. Paine became a member of the first and later Continental Congresses and a judge of the Massachusetts Supreme Court. His papers (in MHi) are being edited for publication by the Society.

3 TUESDAY.

Breakfasted at Gardiners. This morn the Weather clear'd away. As warm and brilliant as May. Kept School all Day.

4 WEDNESDAY.

A charming warm Day. Dined at Coll. Chandler's with Mr. Pain, Abel Willard and Ebenr. Thayer. Drank Tea at Mr. [Timothy?] Paines and supp'd and spent the Eve at Major Chandlers with the same Company, very gaily.

5 THURDSDAY.

A fair morning but some symptoms of a Change of Weather. Kept School. Spent the evening with Messrs. Paine, Putnam,[1] Willard, Thayer, partly at home and partly at Mr. Putnams.

[1] James Putnam (1726–1789), who was to teach JA law.

6 FRYDAY.

A cloudy morning. About 10 [the sun][1] brake out. A warm Day. Dined at Mr. Paines. Kept school. Spent the Evening at home. A windy Evening.

[1] Here and occasionally elsewhere in his early Diary JA used a symbolic sketch of the sun.

7 SATURDAY.

A Fair warm, day. Dined at the Judges. Drank Tea at Major Gardiners.

8 SUNDAY.

Heard Mr. Maccarty. Fine Weather.

9 MONDAY.

Fine Weather. Settled roads. Drank Tea and spent the Evening at Coll. Chandlers, very gaily, with much Company.

10 TUESDAY.

Fair Weather. Spent the Evening at Major Chandlers, with Major Greene and Mr. Maccarty. Charming Weather. Roads Setled.

5

11 WEDNESDAY.

Serene Weather, but somewhat cool. I am constantly forming, but never executing good resolutions. I take great Pleasure, in viewing and examining the magnificent Prospects of Nature, that lie before us in this Town. If I cast my Eyes one Way, I am entertained with the Savage and unsightly appearance of naked woods and leafless Forests. In another place a chain of broken and irregular mountains, throws my mind into a pleasing kind of astonishment. But if I turn my self round, I perceive a wide extensive Tract before me, made up of Woods, and meadows, wandring streams, and barren Planes, covered in various places by herds of grazing Cattle, and terminated by the distant View of the Town.

12 THURSDAY.

A cool, but pleasant morning. Heard Mr. Welman [Wellman] preach the Lecture, and drank Tea, with him, at home where he made this observation, (viz.) That Dr. Mayhew was a smart man, but he embraced some doctrines, not generally approved.[1]

[1] Jonathan Mayhew (1720–1766), Harvard 1744; D.D., Aberdeen 1749; minister of the West Church, Boston; early famous for his radical theological and political views. JA admired him as "a transcendent genius" whose character would require "a dozen volumes" to delineate; and there can be no question that Mayhew's numerous published discourses profoundly influenced young JA. (*DAB*; Clinton Rossiter, "The Life and Mind of Jonathan Mayhew," *WMQ*, 3d ser., 7:531–558 [Oct. 1950]; JA, *Works*, 10:288.) See also 17 March, below.

13 FRYDAY.

A pleasant morning. Saw my classmates Gardner, and Wheeler. Wheeler dined, spent the afternoon, and drank Tea with me. Supped at Major Gardiners, and ingag'd to keep School at Bristol, provided Worcester People, at their insuing March meeting, should change this into a moving School, not otherwise.[1] Major Greene this Evening fell into some conversation with me about the Divinity and Satisfaction of Jesus Christ.[2] All the Argument he advanced was, "that a mere creature, or finite Being, could not make Satisfaction to infinite Justice, for any Crimes," and that "these things are very misterious."

[*In the margin:*] Thus mystery is made a convenient Cover for absurdity.

[1] Prior to the formation of school districts, schoolmasters were obliged to keep school for stated periods in different parts of a town (township), so that the children of all those who supported schools by taxes would have equal access to them; this arrangement was called a "moving school" (*DAH*, under School,

6

District). Extract from the Worcester Town Records, 1 March 1756: "Voted that the School[s] be Kept in the same way and manner as they were the Last year and that John Chandler Junr. and Timo. Paine Esq. and Mr. Asa Moore be a Comitte for provid[ing] a master for the Center School" (Worcester Soc. of Antiquity, *Colls.*, 4 [1882]:23).

[2] See *OED* under Satisfaction, 3: "*Theol.* The atonement made by Christ for sin, according to the view that His sufferings and merits are accepted by the Divine justice as an equivalent for the penalty due for the sins of the world." In recent published sermons Jonathan Mayhew had called in question the divinity of Christ; see 17 March, below.

14 SATURDAY.

Good Weather. This afternoon took a Vomit of Tartar Emet. and Turbith mineral,[1] that worked 7 Times, and wrecked me much.

[1] Turpeth, turbith: "A cathartic drug prepared from the root of East Indian jalap, *Ipomœa Turpethum*" (*OED*).

15 SUNDAY.

Charming Weather. A.M. staid at home reading the Independent Whig.[1] Very often Shepherds that are hired, to take care of their Masters sheep, go about their own Concern's and leave the flock to the Care of their Dog. So Byshops, who are appointed to oversee the flock of Christ, take the Fees themslves, but leave the Drudgery to their Dogs, alias i.e. curates and understrappers.

[1] [Thomas Gordon and John Trenchard,] *The Independent Whig*, originally a periodical publication but issued as a volume, London, 1721. There were numerous later enlarged editions, some bearing the subtitle "A Defence of Primitive Christianity." Gordon and Trenchard attacked the high-church party in England and became still more influential as anticlerical and whig propagandists through their *Cato's Letters* (London, 1724; 4 vols.), which was a popular book in America. JA owned several of their works. (Article on Gordon in *DNB*; BM, *Catalogue*; Josiah Quincy, *Josiah Quincy, Jr.*, p. 289; *Catalogue of JA's Library*, p. 106, 247.)

16 MONDAY.

A most beautiful morning. We have the most moderate Winter that ever was known in this country. For a long time together we have had serene and temperate Weather and all the Roads perfectly settled and smooth like Summer.—The Church of Rome has made it an Article of Faith that no man can be saved out of their Church, and all other religious Sects approach to this dreadfull opinion in proportion to their Ignorance, and the Influence of ignorant or wicked Priests. Still reading the Independent Whigg. Oh! that I could wear out of my mind every mean and base affectation, conquer my natural Pride and Self Conceit, expect no more defference from my fellows than I deserve, acquire that meekness, and humility, which are the sure marks and Characters of a great and generous Soul, and subdue every unworthy Passion and treat all men as I wish to be treated by all. How happy should I then be, in the favour and good will of all honest men, and the sure prospect of a happy immortality!

17 TUESDAY.

A clowdy Day. Dined at Mr. Greenes.

18 WEDNESDAY.

A charming morning. My Classmate Gardner drank Tea with me. Spent an Hour in the beginning of the evening at Major Gardiners, where it was thought that the design of Christianity was not to make men good Riddle Solvers or good mystery mongers, but good men, good majestrates and good Subjects, good Husbands and good Wives, good Parents and good Children, good masters and good servants. The following Question may be answered some time or other—viz. Where do we find a præcept in the Gospell, requiring Ecclesiastical Synods, Convocations, Councils, Decrees, Creeds, Confessions, Oaths, Subscriptions and whole Cartloads of other trumpery, that we find Religion incumbered with in these Days?

19 THURDSDAY.

No man is intirely free from weakness and imperfection in this life. Men of the most exalted Genius and active minds, are generally perfect slaves to the Love of Fame. They sometimes descend to as mean tricks and artifices, in pursuit of Honour or Reputation, as the Miser descends to, in pursuit of Gold. The greatest men have been the most envious, malicious, and revengeful. The miser toils by night and Day, fasts and watches, till he emaciates his Body, to fatten his purse and increase his coffers. The ambitious man rolls and tumbles in his bed, a stranger to refreshing sleep and repose thro anxiety about a preferment he has in view. The Phylosopher sweats and labours at his Book, and ruminates in his closet, till his bearded and grim Countenance exhibit the effigies of pale Want and Care, and Death, in quest [of] hard Words, solemn nonsense, and ridiculous grimace. The gay Gentleman rambles over half the Globe, Buys one Thing and Steals another, murders one man, and disables another, and gets his own limbs and head broke, for a few transitory flashes of happiness. Is this perfection, or downright madness and distraction?—A cold day.

20 FRYDAY.

A dull Day. Symptoms of Snow. Writing Tillotson.[1]

[1] That is, copying out extracts from the published sermons of John Tillotson (1630–1694), sometime Archbishop of Canterbury and a celebrated preacher (*DNB*). There survives among JA's papers a literary commonplace book (Adams Papers, Microfilms, Reel No. 187) containing a good many exercises of this kind during his years in Worcester.

21 SATURDAY.

A Snowy day. Snow about ancle deep. I find by repeated experiment and observation, in my School, that human nature is more easily wrought upon and governed, by promises and incouragement and praise than by punishment, and threatning and Blame. But we must be cautious and sparing of our praise, lest it become too familiar, and cheap and so contemptible. Corporal as well as disgraceful punishments, depress the spirits, but commendation enlivens and stimulates them to a noble ardor and emulation.

22 SUNDAY.

Suppos a nation in some distant Region, should take the Bible for their only law Book, and every member should regulate his conduct by the precepts there exhibited. Every member would be obliged in Concience to temperance and frugality and industry, to justice and kindness and Charity towards his fellow men, and to Piety and Love, and reverence towards almighty God. In this Commonwealth, no man would impair his health by Gluttony, drunkenness, or Lust—no man would sacrifice his most precious time to cards, or any other trifling and mean amusement—no man would steal or lie or any way defraud his neighbour, but would live in peace and good will with all men—no man would blaspheme his maker or prophane his Worship, but a rational and manly, a sincere and unaffected Piety and devotion, would reign in all hearts. What a Eutopa, what a Paradise would this region be. Heard Thayer all Day. He preach'd well.

Spent the Evening at Coll. Chandlers, with Putnam, Gardiner, Thayer, the Dr. and his Lady,[1] in Conversation, upon the present scituation of publick affairs, with a few observations concerning Heroes and great Commanders. Alexander, Charles 12th., Cromwel.

[1] Probably Dr. and Mrs. Nahum Willard, who came to Worcester about the same time JA did and with whom JA was now boarding at the cost of the town (JA, Autobiography; Lincoln, *Worcester*, p. 254).

23 MONDAY.

Fair weather. Crawford spent the Evening here.

24 TUESDAY.

A fine morning. We are told that Demosthenes transcribed the history of Thucidides 8 times, in order to imbibe and familiarize the elegance and strength of his stile. Will it not then be worth while for a candidate for the ministry to transcribe Dr. Tillotson's Works.

25 WEDNESDAY.

Fair and cold Weather. An extream cold night.

26 THURSDAY.

Fair cold morning. An extream cold Day.

27 FRYDAY.

A fair, cold day. Drank Tea at Mrs. Paines. All day, in high health, and spirits. Writing Tillotson. That Comet which appeared in 1682, is expected again this year, and we have intelligence, that it has been seen, about 10 days since, near midnight, in the East.[1]—I find my self very much inclin'd to an unreasonable absence of mind, and to a morose, unsociable disposition. Let it therefore be my constant endeavour to reform these great faults.

[1] The reference is to Halley's comet, named for the British astronomer who had worked out the periodicity of its appearance, approximately every three-quarters of a century. Its next return after 1682 was in April-May 1759, so that the reports JA had heard were mistaken. Professor John Winthrop provided an account of Halley's comet in an appendix to his *Two Lectures on Comets, Read in the Chapel of Harvard-College . . . in April, 1759*, Boston, 1759.

28 SATURDAY.

A raw cold day. Attended Mrs. Brown's funeral. Let this, and every other Instance of human frailty and mortality, prompt me to endeavour after a temper of mind, fit to undergo this great Change.

29 SUNDAY.

Went to Leicester with Thayer. Heard him preach all Day. Dined at Mr. Whitneys. Returned home and drank Tea, and spent the Evening at Mr. Paines.

MARCH. 1756. I MONDAY.

Wrote out Bolingbrokes reflections on Exile.[1]

[1] For JA's lifelong study of, and his extensive commentaries on, the writings of Henry St. John, first Viscount Boling-broke, see Haraszti, *JA and the Prophets* *of Progress*, ch. 4. JA's own copies of Bolingbroke's writings are now divided between the Boston Athenæum and the Boston Public Library.

2 TUESDAY.

A snow fall last night, half leg deep. Began this afternoon, my 3rd. quarter. The great and almighty Author of nature, who at first established those rules which regulate the World, can as easily Suspend those Laws whenever his providence sees sufficient reason for such suspension. This can be no objection, then, to the miracles of J[esus] C[hrist]. Altho' some very thoughtfull, and contemplative men among the heathen, attained a strong persuasion of the great Principles of Religion, yet the far greater number having little time for speculation, gradually sunk in to the grossest Opinions and the grossest Practices. These therefore could not be made to embrace the true religion, till their attention was roused by some astonishing and miraculous appearances. The reasonings of Phylosophers having nothing surprizing in them, could not overcome the force of Prejudice, Custom, Passion, and Bigotry. But when wise and virtuous men, commisioned from heaven, by miracles awakened mens attention to their Reasonings the force of Truth made its way, with ease to their minds.

3 WEDNESDAY.

Fair Weather. Natural Phylosophy is the Art of deducing the generall laws and properties of material substances, from a series of analogous observations. The manner of reasoning in this art is not strictly demonstrative, and by Consequence the knowledge hence acquired, not absolutely Scientifical, because the facts that we reason upon, are perceived by Sence and not by the internal Action of the mind Contemplating its Ideas. But these Facts being presumed true in the form of Axioms, subsequent reasonings about them may be in the strictest sence, scientifical. This Art informs us, in what manner bodies will influence us and each other in given Circumstances, and so teaches us, to avoid the noxious and imbrace the beneficial qualities of matter. By this Art too, many curious Engines have been constructed to facilitate Business, to avert impending Calamities, and to procure desired advantages.

4 THURSDAY.

A fine morn.

5 FRYDAY.

Dined at home, Mr. Barnes dined here, drank Tea, and spent the evening at Coll. Chandlers.[1]

[1] The ambiguous punctuation of the MS has been retained. JA probably intended a full stop after "dined here."

6 SATURDAY.

Rose 1/2 after 4. A clowdy morn. Wrote Bolinbrokes letter on retirement and study.

7 SUNDAY.

Heard Mr. Maccarty all day. Spent the Evening and supped at Mr. Greenes, with Thayer. Honesty, Sincerity and openness, I esteem essential marks of a good mind. I am therefore of opinion, that men ought, (after they have examined with unbiassed Judgments, every System of Religion, and chosen one System on their own Authority, for themselves) to avow their Opinions and defend them with boldness.

8 MONDAY.

Spent the Evening at Major Chandlers. Fair Weather.

9 TUESDAY.

A charming Day. Spent the evening up Chamber.

10 WEDNESDAY.

A misty morning. [Sun] brake out about noon. Spent Evening at Gardiners.

11 THURSDAY.

Dined at the Colonels. Drank Tea at Mr. Paines with a number of Ladies, and spent the Evening at Major Chandlers, with Thayer.

12 FRYDAY.

Clowdy. Laid a pair of Gloves with Mrs. Willard that she would not see me chew tobacco this month.[1]

[1] We do not know who won this wager. We do know something about JA's use of tobacco. In 1805 his friend Dr. Benjamin Waterhouse of the Harvard Medical School published a tract entitled *Cautions to Young Persons concerning*

Health in a Public Lecture . . . ; containing the General Doctrine of Chronic Diseases; Shewing the Evil Tendency of the Use of Tobacco upon Young Persons; More Especially the Pernicious Effects of Smoking Cigarrs. The lecture had been delivered to Harvard undergraduates, and in it Waterhouse declared that in his twenty-three years at Harvard he had never observed "so many palid faces, and so many marks of declining health; nor ever knew so many hectical habits and consumptive affections" among the students as now (p. 27). These he attributed in large measure to the increasing use of tobacco. A copy sent by the author to JA evoked several letters of reminiscence, in which among other things JA said he had "learned the Use of [tobacco] upon Ponds of Ice, when Skaiting with Boys at Eight Years of Age," and though he had given it up at certain periods, including his sojourns abroad, he had, to his regret, been a frequent user of tobacco in one form or another for sixty years (JA to Waterhouse, 19 and 13 Feb. 1805, MHi:Adams-Waterhouse Coll.).

13 SATURDAY.

Some Snow last night, a clowdy, raw morning.

14 SUNDAY.

Heard Mr. Maccarty all Day upon Abrahams Faith, in offering up Isaac. Spent the Evening, very Sociably at Mr. Putnams. Several observations concerning Mr. Franklin of Phyladelphia, a prodigious Genius cultivated with prodigious industry.

15 MONDAY.

I sometimes, in my sprightly moments, consider my self, in my great Chair at School, as some Dictator at the head of a commonwealth. In this little State I can discover all the great Genius's, all the surprizing actions and revolutions of the great World in miniature. I have severall renowned Generalls but 3 feet high, and several deep-projecting Politicians in peticoats. I have others catching and dissecting Flies, accumulating remarkable pebbles, cockle shells &c., with as ardent Curiosity as any Virtuoso in the royal society. Some rattle and Thunder out A, B, C, with as much Fire and impetuosity, as Alexander fought, and very often sit down and cry as heartily, upon being out spelt, as Cesar did, when at Alexanders sepulchre he recollected that the Macedonian Hero had conquered the World before his Age. At one Table sits Mr. Insipid foppling and fluttering, spinning his whirligig, or playing with his fingers as gaily and wittily as any frenchified coxcomb brandishes his Cane or rattles his snuff box. At another sitts the polemical Divine, plodding and wrangling in his mind about Adam's fall in which we sinned all as his primmer has it. In short my little school like the great World, is made up of Kings, Politicians, Divines, L.D. [LL.D.'s?], Fops, Buffoons, Fidlers, Sychophants, Fools, Coxcombs, chimney sweepers, and every other Character drawn in History or seen in the World. Is it not then the highest Pleasure my Friend to preside in this little World, to bestow the proper applause upon virtuous and generous Actions, to blame and punish every vicious and contracted Trick, to wear out of the tender mind every thing that is mean and little, and fire the new born soul with a noble ardor and Emulation. The World affords no greater Pleasure. Let others waste the bloom of Life, at the Card or biliard Table, among rakes and fools, and when their minds are sufficiently fretted with losses, and inflamed by Wine, ramble through the Streets, assaulting innocent People, breaking Windows or debauching young Girls. I envy not their exalted happiness. I had rather sit in school and consider which of my pupils will turn out in his future Life, a Hero, and which a rake, which a phylosopher, and which a parasite, than change breasts with them, tho possest of 20 lac'd wast coats and £1000 a year. Methinks I hear you say, this is odd talk for J. Adams. I'll tell you, then the Ocasion of it. About 4 months since a poor Girl in this neighbourhood walking by the meeting H[ouse] upon some Ocasion, in the evening, met a fine Gentleman with laced hat and wast coat, and a sword who sollicited her to turn aside with him into the horse Stable. The Girl relucted a little, upon which he gave her 3 Guineas, and wished he might be damned if he did not have her in 3 months. Into the horse Stable they went. The 3 Guineas proved 3 farthings—and the Girl proves with Child, without a Friend upon Earth that will own her, or knowing the father of her 3 farthing Bastard.

16 TUESDAY.

Sat out for Uxbridge, arrived about 12, dined. Rode to Aldridges after Mr. Webb, and brought him with me to my Uncles. Spent the Evening there. Lodged with Webb.[1]

[1] Presumably Nathan Webb (1734–1760), Harvard 1754, nephew and namesake of JA's "Uncle Webb"; he is said to have practiced medicine, and it was to him that JA addressed his first letter that survives, 1 Sept. 1755 (Adams Papers; JA, MS note appended to a copy of his letter to Webb, 12 Oct. 1755, same).

17 WEDNESDAY.

A fine morning. Proceeded on my Journey towards Braintree. Stop'ed at Josiah Adams's.[1] Baited at Clarks of Medway. Dined at Clarks of Medfield. Stopd to see Mr. Haven of Dedham, who told me very civilly that he supposed I took my faith on Trust from Dr. Mayhew, and added that he believed the doctrine of the satisfaction of J[esus]

C[hrist] to be essential to Cristianity, and that he would not believe this satisfaction, unless he believed the Divinity of C[hrist]. Mr. Balch was there too, and observed that he would not be a Christian if he did not believe the Mysterys of the Gospel. That he could bear with an Arminian, but when, with Dr. Mayhew, they denied the Divinity and Satisfaction of J[esus] C[hrist] he had no more to do with them. That he knew not what to make of Dr. Mayhews two discourses upon the Expected Dissolution of all Things.[2] They gave him an Idea of a Cart whose wheels want'd greazing. It rumbled on in a hoarse rough manner. There was a good deal of ingenious Talk in them, but it was thrown together in a jumbled confused order. He believed the Dr. wrote it in a great Pannick. He added farther that Arminians, however stiffly they maintain their opinions in health, always, he takes notice, retract when they come to Die, and chose to die Calvinists.—Sat out for Braintree and arrived about sun set. Spent the Evening partly at home and partly at the Drs.[3]

[1] Josiah Adams (1696–1802) was a younger brother of Deacon John Adams; he moved from Braintree to Mendon in 1735 (A. N. Adams, *Geneal. Hist. of Henry Adams of Braintree*, p. 395; Quincy, First Church, MS Records).

[2] *The Expected Dissolution of All Things, a Motive to Universal Holiness*, Boston, 1755, comprises two sermons preached by Mayhew on the Sunday following the earthquake of 18 Nov. 1755. They were intended as "a religious improvement of these visitations of divine providence" (p. 58), and to a modern eye seem sufficiently orthodox.

[3] Dr. Elisha Savil (this name is variously spelled in contemporary records) and his wife, the former Ann Adams, a niece by blood of both of JA's parents. At this time the Savils rented the more southerly of the two cottages on Deacon John Adams' farm at the foot of Penn's Hill in the North Precinct of Braintree. The cottages were separated by only a cartway; on the northern side was the home of JA's parents, now known as the John Adams Birthplace; and on the southern, the home of JA and AA after their marriage in 1764, now known as the John Quincy Adams Birthplace. Owned by descendants of the two Presidents until 1940, when they were presented to the City of Quincy, the Birthplaces (at 129 and 131 Franklin Street) are open to the public under the care of the Quincy Historical Society. See HA2, *The Birthplaces of Presidents John and John Quincy Adams*, Quincy, 1936 (repr. from *Old-Time New England*, 26:79–99 [Jan. 1936]); and Quincy Historical Society, *A Brief Story of the Birthplaces of the Presidents John and John Quincy Adams*, Quincy, Mass., Quincy, 1954. While the present volume was in press the Quincy Historical Society published *The President John Adams and the President John Quincy Adams Birthplaces*, by Waldo C. Sprague, Quincy, 1959, much the fullest historical and descriptive account of these houses yet written.

18 THURSDAY.

A cloudy morning. Spent the afternoon at my Uncles,[1] and part of the Evening at the Doctor's.

[1] Ebenezer Adams (1704–1769?), youngest brother of Deacon John Adams; his

wife was Ann, sister of Susanna Boylston, JA's mother; their daughter Ann was Mrs. Elisha Savil, mentioned in the preceding note (*Braintree Town Records*, p. 685, 766, 815).

19 FRYDAY.

A rainy morning. Went down in the afternoon, to the Point. Spent the afternoon and Evening and lodged with my dear Friend Cranch, in the usuall social friendly Strain.[1]

[1] Richard Cranch (1726–1811), who in 1762 became AA's brother-in-law before her marriage to JA. Cranch conducted a glass manufactory at a settlement called Germantown (from the German artisans who worked there), on a point of land forming Town River Bay in Braintree, now Quincy (Pattee, *Old Braintree and Quincy*, p. 490).

20 SATURDAY.

After breakfast, rode to my Uncle Hunts, dined there, came Home, went to see my Aunt Owen,[1] drank Tea at Deacon Webbs with Mrs. Nabby [Webb?]. Came home. Spent the evening at the Drs.

[1] JA's aunt Hannah Adams had married Benjamin Owen of Braintree, 1725; his aunt Bethiah Adams had married Ebenezer Hunt of Weymouth, 1737 (A. N. Adams, *Geneal. Hist. of Henry Adams of Braintree*, p. 395).

21 SUNDAY.

Vernal Equinox. Heard Mr. Wibird preach two excellent Discourses from Eccles. 9.12.[1] Spent the Evening at Mr. Wibirds with Messrs. Quincy,[2] Cranch, Savel, in Conversation upon the present Scituation of publick affairs. Mr. Quincy exerted his Talents in the most Eloquent Harrangue. Mr. Cranch quoted the bishop of Quebecks Letter concerning the french Missionaries among the Indians.[3] Some, he says, are very good men.

[1] Rev. Anthony Wibird (1729–1800), minister in the North Precinct of Braintree (afterward Quincy) from 1754 until his death.

[2] Presumably the elder Josiah Quincy (1710–1784), more often referred to in this Diary as Colonel Quincy.

[3] A confusing and perhaps confused reference. CFA's explanation (JA, *Works*, 2:11, note) is not satisfactory, since "A Letter from Canada," which he cites and which was printed in the *Boston Evening Post*, 8 Sept. 1755, was not written by the Bishop of Quebec and did not purport to be from his hand. (It is a transparent fabrication, designed to stir up anti-French and anti-Catholic feeling in New England.) But the discussion at Parson Wibird's house no doubt related to the activities of such men as Le Loutre, the Bishop of Quebec's vicar-general in maritime Canada. Le Loutre's work among the French Neutrals, or Acadians, had led directly to their enforced exile from Nova Scotia in 1755. Shiploads of these unfortunate people were arriving at intervals in Boston Harbor during 1755–1756, and they were naturally the subject of frequent conversation. See Hutchinson, *Massachusetts Bay*, ed. Mayo, 3:28–31; Francis Parkman, *Montcalm and Wolfe*, Boston, 1907, vol. 1:

chs. 4, 8; Lawrence H. Gipson, *The British Empire before the American Revo-* *lution*, Caldwell, Idaho, and N.Y., 1936– , vol. 6: chs. 8–10.

22 MONDAY.

A fair but cool morn. Mounted for Boston, arrived about 11 o'clock, went to friend Wm. Belchers, drank a bowl of punch, dined at my Uncle Sympsons,[1] rode to Cambridge, drank Tea with Tom Wentworth. Spent the Evening partly at Hills Chamber, partly at Slewmans [Sluman's], and partly at Trumbles [Trumbull's] and partly at Harry Hills. Lodged with John Hill.

[1] Nathan Simpson, a blacksmith of Boston, who in 1740 had married Mary, sister of Susanna (Boylston) Adams, JA's mother (*NEHGR*, 7 [1853]:146, 150).

23 TUESDAY.

A fine morn. Breakfasted with Slewman at Prentices, mounted for Braintree, arrived about 1, dined, went to Dr. Millers, to see friend Sam.[1] Drank Tea there with Mrs. Veasey[2] and Mrs. Mary Miller, stopped in my return at Dr. Marshes, smoked a pipe there, came home, went to my Uncles and spent the Evening. Returned home and went to bed.

[1] Samuel Miller, Harvard 1756, was a son of Ebenezer Miller, D.D., Oxford 1747, for many years minister of Christ Church, the first Episcopal church in Braintree (Sibley-Shipton, *Harvard Graduates*, 7:93–100).

[2] The Veaseys (also spelled Veazie, Vesey, &c.) were a numerous family in Braintree, some of whom were prominent in the affairs of Christ Church (Pattee, *Old Braintree and Quincy*, p. 248–249).

24 WEDNESDAY.

Sat out for Worcester. Dined at Dedham and rode from thence in the rain to Mendon, supped and lodged at Josiah Adamses.

25 THURDSDAY.

Rode to Uxbridge. Tarried at my Uncle Webbs and lodged with Mr. Nathan [Webb].

26 FRYDAY.

A delightful morning. Rode to Grafton, dined at Josiah Rawsons. He exerted his rawsonian Talents concerning the felicity of Heaven. I sat and heard for it is vain to resist so impetuous a Torrent. Proceeded to Worcester, drank Tea at Mr. Maccarty's and spent the evening at Major Gardiner's.

27 SATURDAY.

The Stream of Life sometimes glides smoothly on, through flowry meadows and enamell'd planes. At other times it draggs a winding reluctant Course through offensive Boggs and dismal gloomy Swamps. The same road now leads us thro' a spacious Country fraught with evry delightful object, Then plunges us at once, into miry Sloughs, or stops our passage with craggy and inaccessible mountains. The free roving Songster of the forest, now rambles unconfin'd, and hopps from Spray to Spray but the next hour perhaps he alights to pick the scattered Grain and is entangled in the Snare. The Ship, which, wafted by a favourable gale, sails prosperously upon the peaceful Surface, by a sudden Change of weather may be tossed by the Tempest, and driven by furious, opposite winds, upon rocks or quicksands. In short nothing in this world enjoys a constant Series of Joy and prosperity.

28 SUNDAY.

Heard Mr. Maccarty, spent the Evening at Coll. Chandlers, in Conversation concerning Lands and Farms &c.

29 MONDAY.

A little hail and rain fell to Day. We find our Selves capable of comprehending many Things, of acquiring considerable Degrees of Knowledge by our slender and contracted Faculties. Now may we not suppose our minds strengthened, and Capacities dilated, so as fully to comprehend this Globe of Earth, with its numerous appendages? May we not suppose them further enlarged to take in the Solar System, in all its relations? Nay why may we not go further and suppose them increased to comprehend the Whole created Universe, with all its inhabitants, their various Relations, Dependencies, Duties and necessities. If this is supposeable, then a Being of such great Capacity, indowed with sufficient Power, would be an accomplished Judge of all rational Beings ...[1] would be fit to dispense rewards to Virtue and Punishments to Vice.

[1] Suspension points in MS.

30 TUESDAY.

A fair day. Drank Tea and spent the Evening at Mr. Putnams, with Mr. Maccarty, very Sociably.

31 WEDNESDAY.

A cool morning. Drank Tea with the Ladies at the Judges. Spent the Evening at Gardiners with the Coll., Mr. Putnam and Thayer.

APRIL 1756. 1 THURSDAY.

A very rainy Day. A little Snow.[1]

[1] On this day JA wrote a remarkable letter to his classmate Charles Cushing, who was then keeping a school in Newbury, on the choice of a profession. Extracts are printed in JA, *Works*, 1:29–30, 32; a complete text is in MHS, *Procs.*, 46 (1912–1913):410–412.

2. FRYDAY.

Cool and very windy. Drank Tea, and Spent the Evening at Coll. Chandlers.

3 SATURDAY.

Dined, Spent the afternoon and drank Tea at Coll. Chandlers.

4 SUNDAY.

Heard Mr. Davis of Holden all Day. Spent the Evening at Mr. Putnams.

5 MONDAY.

A warm pleasant Day. Drank Tea at Mrs. Paines, came home, lodged with Dr. Upham.

6 TUESDAY.

A fair Day. Drank Tea at Coll. Chandlers, and fixt[1] a Letter for Cushing, Wentworth, Dalton, Lock [Locke], my Father, and Dr. Savel.

[1] Fix: to set down in writing (*OED*, fix, vb., 5b). None of the six letters enumerated here, the first four of which were addressed to Harvard classmates, has been found.

7 WEDNESDAY.

A fair Morning. Mr. Thayer set out for Coll. [Harvard College?].

8 THURSDAY.

Heard Mr. Maccarty preach the Lecture, drank Tea with him, and spent the Evening at Mr. Putnams.

9 FRYDAY.

Drank Tea at Coll. Chandlers, spent the Evening at home with My Friend Eliot, lodged with him.

10 SATURDAY.

A raw cold day. The man to whom Nature has given a great and Surprizing Genius, will perform Great and Surprizing Atchievments, but a Soul originally narrow and confined, will never be enlarged to a distinguishing Capacity. Such a one must be content to grovel amidst pebles, and Butterflies thro the whole of his Life. By dilligence and Attention, indeed, he may possibly get the Character of a Man of Sence, but never that of a great Man.

11 SUNDAY.

Heard Mr. Maccarty preach all Day. Spent the Evening at Mr. Paines, and supped upon fresh Fish with the Coll., Mr. Putnam, Major Gardiner and his Lady. Talking about Law and Pollitics.

12 MONDAY.

Signs of Rain. Cleard off about 10. A most beautiful Day. Drank Tea with Coll. Chandler, and spent the Evening, at Major Gardiners, with the Coll., Messrs. Maccarty, Paine, Putnam, Green.

12 [*i.e.* 13] TUESDAY.

A fine morning. A Charming warm Day. Every thing looks gay and lively. The Grass begins to spring, and the sprightly sunbeams gleam upon the houses. The windows are opened, the insects begin to buz, and every thing wellcomes the Joyful Spring.—Went to the Drs. Farm.

13 [*i.e.* 14] WEDNESDAY.

A pleasant morning. Wheeler drank Tea here. I went with him in the Evening, to Capt. Stearns.

14 [*i.e.* 15] THURDSDAY.

Wheeler and I breakfasted at Mr. Maccarty's. Went to Mr. Dyers.[1] Very warm. Drank Tea and spent the Evening at Mr. Putnams, in conversation concerning Christianity. He is of Opinion that the Apostles were a Company of Enthusiasts. He says we have only their word, to prove that they spoke with different Tongues, raised the Dead, and healed the Sick &c.[2]

[1] Joseph Dyer, "an excentric Charac- ter ... who had removed from Boston and lived on a Farm of Mr. Thomas Handcock, Uncle of the late Governor,

and kept a Shop" (JA, Autobiography). [2] Putnam's religious opinions are de- scribed more fully in JA's Autobiography.

15 [*i.e.* 16] FRYDAY.

A Stormy Day.

16 [*i.e.* 17] SATURDAY.

A Stormy Day.

17 [*i.e.* 18] SUNDAY.

A Stormy Day. For these 3 days past there has been a severe N.E. Storm. Heard Mr. Maccarty. Spent the Evening at Major Gardiners.

18 [*i.e.* 19] MONDAY.

The Storm continues.

19 [*i.e.* 20] TUESDAY.

A lovely Day after the Storm. Drank Tea at Major Chandlers. Walked with the Coll. to his Saw-mill Farm.

20 [*i.e.* 21] WEDNESDAY.

Charming Weather. The Fields begin to look verdant. The leaves begin to shew themselves on the apple Trees, and Blossoms on the peach Trees. Drank Tea at Mr. Putnams. Spent the Evening at the Majors.

21 [*i.e.* 22] THURDSDAY.

Cloudy, black morning. Cleared away very pleasant about 9. Dined at Capt. Stearns's, with the Officers of the Militia in this Place. Spent the Evening at Mr. Greenes.

22 [*i.e.* 23] FRYDAY.

A pleasant Day. I can as easily still the fierce Tempests or Stop the rapid Thunderbolt, as command the motions and operations of my own mind. I am dull, and inactive, and all my Resolution, all the Spirits I can muster, are insufficient to rouse me from this senseless Torpitude. My Brains seem constantly in as great Confusion, and wild disorder, as Miltons Chaos. They are numb, dead. I have never any bright, refulgent Ideas. Every Thing appears in my mind, dim and obscure like objects seen thro' a dirty glass or roiled water. Drank Tea at the Colonels. Spent the Evening at Mr. Putnams.

23 [*i.e.* 24] SATURDAY.

A cloudy morn. All my Time seems to roll away unnoticed. I long to study sometimes, but have no opportunity. I long to be a master of Greek and Latin. I long to prosecute the mathematical and philosophical Sciences. I long to know a little of Ethicks and moral Philosophy. But I have no Books, no Time, no Friends. I must therefore be contented to live and die an ignorant, obscure fellow. A showery Day.

24 [*i.e.* 25] SUNDAY.

Astronomers tell us, with good Reason, that not only all the Planets and Satellites in our Solar System, but all the unnumbered Worlds that revolve round the fixt Starrs are inhabited, as well as this Globe of Earth. If this is the Case all Mankind are no more in comparison of the whole rational Creation of God, than a point to the Orbit of Saturn. Perhaps all these different Ranks of Rational Beings have in a greater or less Degree, committed moral Wickedness. If so, I ask a Calvinist, whether he will subscribe to this Alternitive, "either God almighty must assume the respective shapes of all these different Species, and suffer the Penalties of their Crimes, in their Stead, or else all these Being[s] must be consigned to everlasting Perdition? " Heard Mr. Maccarty. Spent the Evening at the Colonels.

25 [*i.e.* 26] MONDAY.

The Reflection that I penned Yesterday, appears upon the review to be weak enough. For 1st. we know not that the Inhabitants of other Globes have sinned. Nothing can be argued in this manner, till it is proved at least probable that all those Species of rational Beings have revolted from their rightful Sovereign.—When I examine the little Prospect that lies before me, and find an infinite variety of Bodies in one Horizon of perhaps two miles diameter, how many Millions of such Prospects there are upon the Surface of this Earth, how many millions of Globes there are within our View, each of which has as many of these prospects upon its own surface as our Planet—great! and marvellous are thy works! &c.

26 [*i.e.* 27] TUESDAY.

We had a few soft, vernal Showers to Day.

27 [*i.e.* 28] WEDNESDAY.

A cool but pleasant morning. Dined at Mr. Paines. Drank Tea at Mr. Putnams. Walked with him to his Farm. Talked about all Nature.

28 [*i.e.* 29] THURDSDAY.

Fast day. Heard Mr. Maccarty. Spent the Evening at Mr. Putnams. Our proper Business in this Life is, not to accumulate large Fortunes, not to gain high Honours and important offices in the State, not to waste our Health and Spirits in Pursuit of the Sciences, but constantly to improve our selves in Habits of Piety and Virtue. Consequently, the meanest Mechanick, who endeavours in proportion to his Ability, to promote the happiness of his fellow men, deserves better of Society, and should be held in higher Esteem than the Greatest Magistrate, who uses his power for his own Pleasures or Avarice or Ambition.

29 [*i.e.* 30] FRYDAY.

A hazy, dull Day. Reading Milton. That mans Soul, it seems to me, was distended as wide as Creation. His Powr over the human mind was absolute and unlimited. His Genius was great beyond Conception, and his Learning without Bounds. I can only gaze at him with astonishment, without comprehending the vast Compass of his Capacity.

30 [APRIL, *i.e.* 1 MAY] SATURDAY.

A rainy Day. If we consider a little of this our Globe we find an endless Variety of Substances, mutually connected with and dependent on Each other. In the Wilderness we see an amazing profusion of vegetables, which afford Sustenance and covering to the wild Beasts. The cultivated Planes and Meadows produce grass for Cattle, and Herbs for the service of man. The milk and the Flesh of other Animals, afford a delicious provision for mankind. A great Part of the human Species are obliged to provide food and nourishment for other helpless and improvident Animals. Vegetables sustain some Animals. These animals are devoured by others, and these others are continually cultivating and improving the vegetable Species. Thus nature, upon our Earth, is in a continual Rotation. If we rise higher, we find the sun and moon to a very great degree influencing us. Tides are produced in the ocean, Clouds in the Atmosphere, all nature is made to flourish and look gay by these enlivening and invigorating Luminaries. Yea Life and Chearfulness is diffused to all the other Planets, as well as ours, upon the sprightly Sunbeams. No doubt There is as great a multitude and variety of Bodies upon each Planet in proportion to its magnitude, as there is upon ours. These Bodies are connected with and influenced by each other. Thus we see the amazing harmony of our Solar System. The minutest Particle in one of Saturns Sattelites, may have some influence upon the most distant Regions of the System. The Stupendous Plan of operation was projected by him who rules the universe, and a part assigned to every particle of matter to act, in this great and complicated Drama. The Creator looked into the remotest Futurity, and saw his great Designs accomplished by this inextricable, this mysterious Complication of Causes. But to rise still higher this Solar System is but one, very small wheel in the great the astonishing Machine of the World. Those Starrs that twinkle in the Heavens have each of them a Choir of Planets, Comets, and Satellites dancing round them, playing mutually on each other, and all together playing on the other Systems that lie around them. Our System, considered as [one] body[1] hanging on its Center of Gravity, may affect and be affected by all the other Systems, within the Compass of Creation. Thus it is highly probable every Particle of matter, influences, and is influenced by every other Particle in the whole collective Universe. A stormy Day.

[1] This phrase is only partly legible. JA may perhaps have written "only a body."

MAY. 1756. 1 [*i.e.* 2] SUNDAY.

Last night we had rain all night accompanied with a very high Wind, and the storm continues. Heard Mr. Camel [Campbell] of Oxford. About noon cleard away. I think it necessary to call my self to a strict account, how I spend my Time, once a week at least. Since the 14th of April I have been studying the 1st Part of Butlers Analogy.[1] Spent the Evening at home with Mes[srs]. Camel, Green.

[1] Copious extracts from Joseph Butler's celebrated *Analogy of Religion, Natural and Revealed, to the Constitution and Course of Nature*, first published in London, 1736, will be found in JA's early commonplace book (Adams Papers, Microfilms, Reel No. 187).

3 MONDAY.

I was mistaken one Day in my reckoning.[1] A pleasant Day. Spent the Evening and supped at Mr. Maccartys. The Love of Fame naturally betrays a man into several weaknesses and Fopperies that tend very much to diminish his Reputation, and so defeats itself. Vanity I am sensible, is my cardinal Vice and cardinal Folly, and I am in continual Danger, when in Company, of being led an ignis fatuus Chase by it, without the strictest Caution and watchfulness over my self.

[1] That is, in the preceding entries from 13 April through 2 May.

4 TUESDAY.

Let any man, suppose of the most improved understanding, look upon a watch, when the Parts of it are separated. Let him examine every Wheel and spring seperately by itself. Yet if the Use and Application of these springs and Wheels is not explained to him, he will not be able to judge of the Use and Advantage of particular Parts, much less will he be able, if he sees only one wheel. In like manner We who see but a few coggs in one Wheel of the great Machine of the Universe, can make no right Judgment of particular Phœnomena in Nature.— Spent the Evening at Mr. Swans.

5 WEDNESDAY.

A very cold Day. Drank Tea at the Colonels. Spent the Evening at the Majors.

6 THURDSDAY.

A cold day. Spent the Evening and supped at Mr. Putnams.

7 FRYDAY.

Spent the Evening and supped at Mr. Maccartys. A mans observing the Flux of the Tide to Day, renders it credible that the same Phenomenon may be observed tomorrow. In the same manner, our Experience that the Author of Nature has annexed Pain to Vice, and Pleasure to Virtue, in general I mean, renders it credible that the same or a like Disposition of Things may take place hereafter. Our observing that the State of minority was designed to be an Education for mature Life, and that our good or ill Success in a mature Life, depends upon our good or ill improvement of our Advantages in Minority, renders it credible that this Life was designed to be an Education, for a future one, and that our Happiness or Misery in a future life will be alloted us, according as our Characters shall be virtuous or vicious. For G[od] governs his great Kingdom the World by very general Laws. We cannot indeed observe many Instances of these Laws. But wherever we see any particular Disposition of Things, we may strongly presume that there are other dispositions of Things in other Systems of Nature, analogous and of a Piece with them.

8 SATURDAY.

Went a Shooting with Mr. Putnam. Drank Tea with him and his Lady.

9 SUNDAY.

Since last Sunday I have wrote a few Papers of the Spectators, read the last Part of Butlers Analogy, wrote out the Tract upon personal Identity, and that upon the nature of Virtue.[1] A poor Weeks Work! Spent the Evening at Mr. Greenes.

[1] These tracts were appended to Butler's *Analogy of Religion.*

10 MONDAY.

A pleasant Day.

11 TUESDAY.

A pleasant [day]. The first Day of Court. Nature and Truth or rather Truth and right are invariably the same in all Times and in all Places. And Reason, pure unbiassed Reason perceives them alike in all Times and in all Places. But Passion, Prejudice, Interest, Custom and Fancy are infinitely precarious. If therefore we suffer our Understandings to be blinded or perverted by any of these, the Chance is that of millions to one, that we shall embrace error. And hence arises that endless Variety of Opinions entertained by Mankind.—The Weather and the Season are beyond expression delightful. The Fields are coverd with a bright and lively Verdure. The Trees are all in bloom, and the atmosphere is filled with a ravishing Fragrance. The Air is soft and yielding and the Setting sun Sprinkled his departing Rays over the Face of Nature, and enlivened all the Land skips around me. The Trees put forth their Leaves and the Birds fill the Spray. Supd at Gardiners.

12 WEDNESDAY.

Rambled about all Day, gaping and gazing.

12 [*i.e.* 13] THURSDAY.

Spent the Evening with Mr. Swan at home.

13 [*i.e.* 14]. FRIDAY.

Drank Tea at the Colonels.—Not one new Idea this Week.

14 [*i.e.* 15]. SATURDAY.

A lovely Day. Soft vernal Showers. Exercise invigorates, and enlivens all the Faculties of Body and of mind. It arouses our Animal Spirits, it disperses Melancholy. It spreads a gladness and Satisfaction over our minds and qualifies us for every Sort of Buisiness, and every Sort of Pleasure.

15 [*i.e.* 16]. SUNDAY.

A pleasant morning. The Week past was Court week. I was interrupted by Company, and the noisy Bustle of the publick Occasion, so that I have neither read or wrote any Thing worth mentioning.—Heard Mr. Thayer, and spent the Evening at Mr. Putnams, very sociably.

16 [*i.e.* 17] MONDAY.

The Elephant and the Lion, when their Strength is directed and applyd by Man, can exert a prodigious Force. But their Strength, great and surprizing as it is, can produce no great Effects, when applyed by no higher Ingenuity than their own. But Man, allthough the Powers of his Body are but small and contemptible, by the Exercise of his Reason can invent Engines and Instruments, to take advantage of the Powers in Nature, and accomplish the most astonishing Designs. He can rear the Valley into a lofty mountain, and reduce the mountain to a humble Vale. He can rend the Rocks and level the proudest Trees. At his Pleasure the Forest is cleard and Palaces rise. When He pleases, the soaring Eagle is precipitated to Earth, and the light footed Roe is stop'd in his Career. He can cultivate and assist Nature in her own Productions. By pruning the Tree, and manuring the Land, he makes the former produce larger and fairer Fruit, and the latter bring forth better and greater Plenty of Grain. He can form a Communication between remotest Regions, for the benefit of Trade and Commerce, over the yielding and fluctuating Element of water. The Telescope has settled the Regions of Heaven, and the Microscope has brought up to View innumerable millions of Animals that Escape the observation of our naked sight.

17 [*i.e.* 18] TUESDAY.

27

18 [*i.e.* 19] WEDNESDAY.

19 [*i.e.* 20] THURSDAY.

Spent the Evening at Gardiners.

20 [*i.e.* 21] FRYDAY.

After School, rode to Shrewsbury, went to Capt. Hows, to see Dr. Flynt, spent an Hour, and then rode to Mr. Howards, talked a little with him, and returned home.

21 [*i.e.* 22] SATURDAY.

Dined at Judge Chandlers.

22 [*i.e.* 23] SUNDAY.

Heard Mr. Maccarty. He is particularly fond of the following Expressions. Carnal, ungodly Persons. Sensuality and voluptuousness. Walking with God. Unregeneracy. Rebellion against God. Believers. All Things come alike to all. There is one Event to the Righteous and to the Wicked. Shut out of the Presence of God. Solid, substantial and permanent Joys. Joys springing up in the Soul. The Shines of G[od]s Countenance.

When we consider the vast and incomprehensible extent of the material Universe, those myriads of fixed Stars that emerge out of the remote Regions of Space to our View by Glasses, and the finer our Glasses the more of these Systems we discover. When we consider that Space is absolutely infinite and boundless, that the Power of the Deity is strictly omnipotent, and his Goodness without Limitation, who can come to a Stop in his Thoughts, and say hither does the Universe extend and no farther?

"Nothing can proceed from Nothing." But Something can proceed from Something, and Thus the Deity produced this vast and beautiful Frame of the Universe out of Nothing, i.e. He had no preexistent matter to work upon or to change from a Chaos into a World. But He produced a World into Being by his almighty Fiat, perhaps in a manner analogous to the Production of Resolutions in our minds.

This week I have read one Volume of Duncan Forbes Works[1] and 1/2 Bentleys Sermons at the Boilean Lectures. Spent the Evening at the Collonels.

[1] JA's own copy of the *Whole Works* of Duncan Forbes of Culloden (2 vols., Edinburgh [1755?]) survives among his books in the Boston Public Library. In

28

his early commonplace book JA copied long extracts from Forbes' "Letter to a Bishop concerning Some Important Discoveries in Philosophy and Theology," first published in 1732 (Adams Papers, Microfilms, Reel No. 187).

23 [*i.e.* 24] MONDAY.

A pleasant morning. Drank Tea at the Colonells.—Had the projectile Force in the Planets been greater than it is, they would not describe Circles but very excentrical Elipses round the Sun. And then the Inhabitants would be tormented yea destroyed and the Planets left barren and uninhabitable Wastes by Extreme Vicissitudes of Heat and cold. It was many million Times as likely that some other degree of Velocity would have been lighted on, as that the present would, if Chance had the Disposal of it, and any other Degree would have absolutely destroyed all animal and sensitive if not vegetable Inhabitants. Ergo an intelligent and benevolent mind had the Disposal and determination of these Things.

24 [*i.e.* 25] TUESDAY.

A cool, but pleasant Day.

25 [*i.e.* 26] WEDNESDAY.

Election Day. I have spent all this Day at Home reading a little and eating a little Election Cake.

26 [*i.e.* 27] THURSDAY.

Drank Tea at the Colonels with a Number of Ladies. Spent the Evening partly at Putnams and partly at Gardiners.

27 [*i.e.* 28] FRYDAY.

Dined at the Majors. A pleasant Day.—If we examine critically the little Prospect that lies around us at one view we behold an almost infinite Variety of substances. Over our heads the sun blazes in divine Effulgence, the Clouds tinged with various Colors by the refracted Sunbeams exhibit most beautiful appearances in the Atmosphere, the cultivated Planes and meadows are attired in a delightful Verdure and variegated with the gay enamell of Flowers and Roses. On one hand we see an extensive Forest, a whole Kingdom of Vegetables of the noblest Kind. Upon the Hills we discern Flocks of Grazing Cattle, and on the other hand a City rises up to View, with its Spires among the Clouds. All these and many more objects encounter our Eyes in the

Prospect of one Horizon, perhaps 2, or 3 miles [in] diameter. Now every Animal that we see in this Prospect, Men and Beasts, are endued with most curiously organized Bodies. They consist of Bones, and Blood, and muscles, and nerves, and ligaments and Tendons, and Chile [Chyle] and a million other things, all exactly fitted for the purposes of Life and motion, and Action. Every Plant has almost as complex and curious a structure, as animals, and the minutest Twigg is supported, and supplied with Juices and Life, by organs and Filaments proper to draw this Nutrition of the Earth. It would be endless to consider minutely every Substance or Species of Substances that falls under our Eyes in this one Prospect. Now let us for a minute Consider how many million such Prospects there are upon this single Planet, all of which contain as great and some a much Greater Variety of animals and Vegetables. When we have been sufficiently astonished at this incomprehensible multitude of substances, let us rise in our Thoughts and consider, how many Planets and Sattellites and Comets there are in this one solar system, each of which has as many such Prospects upon its surface as our Earth. Such a View as this may suffice to show us our Ignorance. But if [we] rise still higher in our Thoughts, and consider that stupendous Army of fixt Starrs that is hung up in the immense Space, as so many Suns, each placed in Center of his respective system and diffusing his inlivening and invigorating Influences to his whole Choir of Planets, Comets and sattellites, and that each of this unnumbered multitude has as much superficies, and as many Prospects as our Earth, we find our selves lost and swallowed up in this incomprehensible I had almost said infinite Magnificence of Nature. Our Imaginations after a few feignt Efforts, sink down into a profound Admiration of what they cannot comprehend. God whose almighty Fiat first produced this amazing Universe, had the whole Plan in View from all Eternity, intimately and perfectly knew the Nature and all the Properties of all these his Creatures. He looked forward through all Duration and perfectly knew all the Effects, all the events and Revolutions, that could possibly, and would actually take place, Throughout Eternity.[1]

[1] A detached, undated fragment among JA's literary notes appears to belong to the series of reflections entered in his Diary at this time. It reads:

"There seems by the late discoveries to be as great a Variety of Genera and Species of Globes and Spheres in the Heavens as there are of animals and Vegetables upon Earth.—Clusters of Worlds, Groups of Systems, and Clumps of combinations of Systems, as thick as of Groves and forests of Trees and shrubbs here below.—Variegated too in Colour as much as in magnitude, in decoration as much as in Use" (Adams Papers, Microfilms, Reel No. 188).

28 [*i.e.* 29] SATURDAY.

Drank Tea at Mr. Putnams.—What is the proper Business of Mankind in this Life? We come into the World naked and destitute of all the Conveniences and necessaries of Life. And if we were not provided for, and nourished by our Parents or others should inevitably perish as soon as born. We increase in strength of Body and mind by slow and insensible Degrees. 1/3 of our Time is consumed in sleep, and 3/4 of the remainder, is spent in procuring a mere animal sustenance. And if we live to the Age of three score and Ten and then set down to make an estimate in our minds of the Happiness we have enjoyed and the Misery we have suffered, We shall find I am apt to think, that the overballance of Happiness is quite inconsiderable. We shall find that we have been through the greatest Part of our Lives pursuing Shadows, and empty but glittering Phantoms rather than substances. We shall find that we have applied our whole Vigour, all our Faculties, in the Pursuit of Honour, or Wealth, or Learning or some other such delusive Trifle, instead of the real and everlasting Excellences of Piety and Virtue. Habits of Contemplating the Deity and his transcendent Excellences, and correspondent Habits of complacency in and Dependence upon him, Habits of Reverence and Gratitude, to God, and Habits of Love and Compassion to our fellow men and Habits of Temperance, Recollection and self Government will afford us a real and substantial Pleasure. We may then exult in a Conciousness of the Favour of God, and the Prospect of everlasting Felicity.

29 [*i.e.* 30] SUNDAY.

Heard Mr. Maccarty. "You who are sinners, are in continual Danger of being swallowed up quick and born away by the mighty Torrent of Gods wrath and Justice. It is now as it were restrained and banked up by his Goodness. But he will by and by, unless Repentance prevent, let it out in full Fury upon you." This week I have wrote the [8th?] Sermon of Bentleys Boilean Lectures. Read part of the 1st Volume of Voltairs Age of Lewis 14th.[1]—I make poor Weeks Works.

[1] Lengthy extracts from Voltaire's *Age of Louis XIV*, first published in 1751, appear in JA's commonplace book kept in Worcester (Adams Papers, Microfilms, Reel No. 187).

30 [*i.e.* 31] MONDAY.

When we see or feel any Body, we discern nothing but Bulk and Extention. We can change this Extention into a great Variety of Shapes and Figures, and by applying our senses to it can get Ideas of those different Figures, But can do nothing more than change the Figure. If we pulverize Glass or Salt, the original constituent matter remains the same, only we have altered the Contexture of its Parts. Large loads and heaps of matter as mountains and Rocks lie obstinate, inactive and motionless, and eternally will remain so unless moved by some Force extrinsick to themselves. Dissolve the Cohesion, and reduce these Mountains to their primogeneal Atoms, these Atoms are as dull and senseless as they were when combined into the Shape of a mountain. In short matter has no Consciousness of its own Existence, has no power of its own, no active Power I mean, but is wholly passive. Nor can Thought be ever produced by any modification of it. To say that God can superadd to matter a Capacity of Thought is palpable nonsense and Contradiction. Such a Capacity is inconsistent with the most essential Properties of matter.

JUNE 1756. 1 TUESDAY.

Drank Tea at the Majors. The Reasoning of Mathematicians is founded on certain and infallible Principles. Every Word they Use, conveys a determinate Idea, and by accurate Definitions they excite the same Ideas in the mind of the Reader that were in the mind of the Writer. When they have defined the Terms they intend to make use of, they premise a few Axioms, or Self evident Principles, that every man must assent to as soon as proposed. They then take for granted certain Postulates, that no one can deny them, such as, that a right Line may be drawn from one given Point to another, and from these plain simple Principles, they have raised most astonishing Speculations, and proved the Extent of the human mind to be more spacious and capable than any other Science.

2 WEDNESDAY.

Went to Spencer in the afternoon.—When we come into the World, our minds are destitute of all Sorts of Ideas. Our senses inform us of various Qualities in the substances around us. As we grow up our Acquaintance with Things enlarges and spreads. Colours are painted in our minds through our Eyes. All the various Modulations of Sounds, enter by our Ears. Fragrance and Fœtor, are perceived by the Smell, Extention and Bulk by the Touch. These Ideas that enter simple and uncompounded thro our Senses are called simple Ideas, because they are absolutely one and indivisible. Thus the Whiteness of Snow can not be divided or seperated into 2 or more Whitenesses. The same may

1. JOHN ADAMS IN 1766, BY BENJAMIN BLYTH

2. ABIGAIL ADAMS IN 1766, BY BENJAMIN BLYTH

be said of all other Colours. It is indeed in our Power to mix and compound Colours into new and more beautiful Appearances, than any that are to be found in Nature. So We can combine various Sounds into one melodious Tune. In Short we can modify and dispose the Simple Ideas of Sensation, into whatever shape we please. But these Ideas can enter our minds no other Way but thro the senses. A man born blind will never gain one Idea of Light or Colour. One born deaf will never get an Idea of sound.

3 THURSDAY.

Heard Mr. Maccarty preach the Lecture, drank Tea with him, and spent the Evening at the Majors.

4 FRIDAY.

5 SATURDAY.

Dreamed away the afternoon.

6 SUNDAY.

Heard Mr. Maccarty all Day. Drank Tea at home with Crawford. Spent the Evening at home with Mr. Maccarty and Capt. Doolittle.[1] A great deal of Thunder and Lightning.

[1] Ephraim Doolittle, on whom JA has much more to say in his Autobiography.

7 [–13] MONDAY, TUESDAY, WEDNESDAY, THURSDAY, FRYDAY, SATURDAY, SUNDAY.

14 MONDAY.

Drank Tea at Mr. Putnams. Spent the Evening at the Majors, with Esqrs. Chandler of Woodstock and Brewer of Worcester.—He is not a wise man and is unfit to fill any important Station in Society, that has left one Passion in his Soul unsubdued. The Love of Glory will make a General sacrifice the Interest of his Nation, to his own Fame. Avarice exposes some to Corruption and all to a Thousand meannesses and villanies destructive to Society. Love has deposed lawful Kings, and aggrandiz'd unlawful, ill deserving Courtiers. Envy is more Studious of eclipsing the Lustre of other men by indirect Strategems, than of brightening its own Lustre by great and meritorious Actions. These Passions should be bound fast and brought under the Yoke. Untamed they are lawless Bulls, they roar and bluster, defy all Controul, and some times murder their proper owner. But properly inured to Obedience, they take their Places under the Yoke without Noise and labour vigorously in their masters Service. From a sense of the Government of God, and a Regard to the Laws established by his Providence, should all our Actions for ourselves or for other men, primarily originate. And This master Passion in a good mans soul, like the larger Fishes of Prey will swallow up and destroy all the rest.

15 TUESDAY.

Consider, for one minute, the Changes produced in this Country, within the Space of 200 years. Then, the whole Continent was one continued dismall Wilderness, the haunt of Wolves and Bears and more savage men. Now, the Forests are removed, the Land coverd with fields of Corn, orchards bending with fruit, and the magnificent Habitations of rational and civilized People. Then our Rivers flowed through gloomy deserts and offensive Swamps. Now the same Rivers glide smoothly on through rich Countries fraught with every delightful Object, and through Meadows painted with the most beautyful scenery of Nature, and of Art. The narrow Hutts of the Indians have been removed and in their room have arisen fair and lofty Edifices, large and well compacted Cities.

20 SUNDAY.

Supped and spent the Evening at the Majors.

21 MONDAY.

A cool Day.

22 TUESDAY.

A rainy Day. Drank Tea and spent Evening at Put[nam's].

23 WEDNESDAY.

Went with Mr. Thayer and Mrs. Willard, to Mr. Richardsons of Sutton.

24 [–27] THURSDAY. FRYDAY. SATURDAY. SUNDAY.

Spent the Evening at the Colonels.[1]

[1] Presumably the text of this entry pertains to the last day in the heading (Sunday, 27 June).

28 MONDAY.

JULY. 1756. 19. MONDAY.

Sat out for Boston. Borrowed the Idea of a Patriot King of Ned. Quincy.[1] Rode to Cambridge. Lodgd. Rode the next morning to Worcester.

[1] Edmund Quincy (1733–1768), son of the first Josiah Quincy; Harvard 1752. Bolingbroke's *Idea of a Patriot King* was first published in 1749.

20 TUESDAY.

Eliot and Trumble lodged here with me.

21 WEDNESDAY.

Kept School.—I am now entering on another Year,[1] and I am resolved not to neglect my Time as I did last Year. I am resolved to rise with the Sun and to study the Scriptures, on Thursday, Fryday, Saturday, and Sunday mornings, and to study some Latin author the other 3 mornings. Noons and Nights I intend to read English Authors. This is my fixt Determination, and I will set down every neglect and every compliance with this Resolution. May I blush whenever I suffer one hour to pass unimproved. I will rouse up my mind, and fix my Attention. I will stand collected within my self and think upon what I read and what I see. I will strive with all my soul to be something more than Persons who have had less Advantages than myself.

[1] Since his graduation from Harvard, or since his arrival in Worcester? It was not exactly a year since either of these events; see note on entry of 14 Jan. 1756, above.

22 THURSDAY.

Fast day. Rose not till 7 o clock. This is the usual Fate of my Resolutions! Wrote the 3 first Chapters of St. James. Wrote in Bolinbroke pretty industriously. Spent the Evening at Mr. Paines.—The Years of my Youth are marked by divine Providence with various and with great Events. The last Year is rendered conspicuous in the memorials of past Ages, by a Series of very remarkable Events, of various Kinds. The Year opened with the Projection of 3 Expeditions, to prevent the further, and remove the present Depredations, and Encroachments of our turbulent french Neighbours. I shall not minute the graduall Steps, advanced by each Army, but only the Issue of each. Braddock the Commander of the Forces, destind against Duquesne, and 6 or 700 of his men, were butchered in a manner unexampled in History. All, routed and destroyed without doing the least Injury that we know of, to the Enemy. Johnson, with his Army, was attacked by the Baron

Dieskeau, but happily maintaind his Ground and routed the Enemy, taking Dieskeau prisoner. Moncton and Winslow at Nova Scotia, gaind their Point, took the Fortresses and sent of [off] the Inhabitants into these Provinces. Boskawen bravely defended our Coast with his Fleet, and made great Havock among the french merchant Ships. All these Actions were performed in a Time of Peace. Sed paulo majora canamus. God almighty has exerted the Strength of his tremendous Arm and shook one of the finest, richest, and most populous Cities in Europe, into Ruin and Desolation, by an Earthquake. The greatest Part of Europe and the greatest Part of America, has been in violent Convulsions, and admonished the Inhabitants of both, that neither Riches nor Honours, nor the solid Globe itself is a proper Basis, on which to build our hopes of Security. The british Nation has been making very expensive and very formidable Preparations, to Secure its Territories against an Invasion by the French, and to humble the insolent Tempers, and aspiring Prospects of that ambitious and faithless Nation. The gathering of the Clouds, seems to forebode very tempestuous Weather, and none can tell but the Storm will break heavy upon himself in particular. Is it not then the highest Frensy and Distraction to neglect these Expostulations of Providence and continue a Rebellion against that Potentate who alone has Wisdom enough to perceive and Power enough to procure for us the only certain means of Happiness and goodness enough to prompt him to both.

23 FRIDAY.

Rose at 7. Wrote the 2 last Chapters of St. James. Spent the Evening at the Majors and drank Tea at Putnams.

24 SATURDAY.

Rose at 7. Wrote a little in Greek. Afternoon wrote Bolinbroke.

25 SUNDAY.

Rose 1/2 after 6.—Good Sense, some say, is enough to regulate our Conduct, to dictate Thoughts and Actions which are proper upon certain Occasions. This they say will soften and refine the Motions of our Limbs into an easy and agreable Air altho the Dancing Master never was applied to, and this will suggest good Answers, good Observations and good Expressions to us better than refined Breeding. Good sense will make us remember that others have as good a right to think for themselves and to speak their own Opinions as I have, that another mans making a silly Speech, does not warrant my ill nature and Pride in grasping the Opportunity to ridicule him, and show my Witt. A puffy, vain, conceited Conversation, never fails to bring a Man into Contempt, altho his natural Endowments be ever so great, and his Application and Industry ever so intense. No Accomplishments, no Virtues are a sufficient Attonement for Vanity, and a haughty over-bearing Temper in Conversation. And such is [the] Humour of the World the greater a mans Parts and the nobler his Virtues in other Respects, the more Derision and Ridicule does this one Vice and Folly throw him into. Good sense is generally attended with a very lively sense and delight in Applause. The Love of Fame in such men is generally much stronger than in other People, and this Passion it must be confessed is apt to betray men into impertinent Exertions of their Talents, sometimes into censorious Remarks upon others, often into little meannesses to sound the opinions of others and oftenest of all into a childish Affectation of Wit and Gaiety. I must own my self to have been, to a very heinous Degree, guilty in this Respect. When in Company with Persons much superior to my self in Years and Place, I have talked to shew my Learning. I have been too bold with great men, which Boldness will no doubt be called Self Conceit. I have made ill natured Remarks upon the Intellectuals, manners, Practice &c. of other People. I have foolishly aimed at Wit and Spirit, at making a shining Figure in gay Company, but instead of shining briter I only clouded the few Rays that before rendered me visible. Such has been my unhappy Fate.—I now resolve for the future, never to say an ill naturd Thing, concerning Ministers or the ministerial Profession, never to say an envious Thing concerning Governors, Judges, Ministers, Clerks, Sheriffs, Lawyers, or any other honorable or Lucrative offices or officers, never to affect Wit upon laced Wastecoats or large Estates or their Professors [Possessors?], never to shew my own Importance or Superiority, by remarking the Foibles, Vices, or Inferiority of others. But I now resolve as far as lies in me, to take Notice chiefly of the amiable Qualities of other People, to put the most favourable Construction upon the Weaknesses, Bigotry, and Errors of others, &c. and to labour more for an inoffensive and amiable than for a shining and invidious Character.—Heard Crawford in the morning, and Harding in the afternoon.

26 MONDAY.

Rose at 7. Read carefully 30 lines in Virgil.

Rose at 7. Read carefully 30 lines, in Virgil. Wrote a little in Bolingbroke at noon and a little at night. Spent the Evening at Mr. Putnams.

Read about 40 lines in Virgil, and wrote a little at noon. Nothing more.

Rose half after 6. Read a little Greek.

A very rainy Day. Dreamed away the Time.

A rainy forenoon. Dined at Mr. Paines. A fair after[noon]. The Nature and Essence of the material World is not less conceal'd from our knowledge than the Nature and Essence of God. We see our selves surrounded on all sides with a vast expanse of Heavens, and we feel our selves astonished at the Grandeur, the blazing Pomp of those Starrs with which it is adorned. The Birds fly over our Heads and our fellow animals Labour and sport around us, the Trees wave and murmur in the Winds, the Clouds float and shine on high, the surging billows rise in the Sea, and Ships break through the Tempest. Here rises a spacious City, and yonder is spread out an extensive Plain. These Objects are so common and familiar, that we think our selves fully Acquainted with them; but these are only Effects and Properties, the substance from whence they flow is hid from us in impenetrable Obscurity.

God is said to be self existent, and that therefore he may have existed from Eternity, and throughout Immensity. God exists by an absolute Necessity in his own Nature. That is, it implies a Contradiction to suppose him not to exist. To ask what this Necessity is, is as if you should ask what the Necessity of the Equality between twice 2 and 4, is. Twice 2 are necessarily in their own nature equal to 4, not only here but in every Point of Space, not only now, but in every Point of Duration. In the same manner God necessarily exists not only here but throughout unlimited Space, not only now but throughout all Duration, past, and future.

We observe, in the animate and in the inanimate Creation, a surprizing Diversity, and a surprizing Uniformity. Of inanimate Substances, there is a great variety, from the Pebble in the Streets, quite up to the Vegetables in the Forrest. Of animals there is no less a Variety of Species from the Animalculs that escape our naked sight, quite through the intermediate Kinds up to Elephants, Horses, men. Yet notwithstanding this Variety, there is, from the highest Species of animals upon this Globe which is generally thought to be Man, a regular and uniform Subordination of one Tribe to another down to the apparently insignificant animalcules in pepper Water, and the same Subordination continues quite through the Vegetable Kingdom. And it is worth observing that each Species regularly and uniformly preserve all their essential and peculiar properties, without partaking of the peculiar Properties of others. We dont see Chickens hatched with fins to swim, nor Fishes spawned with wings to fly. We dont see a Colt folded [foaled] with Claws like a Bird, nor men with the Cloathing or Armour which his Reason renders him capable of procuring for himself. Every Species has its distinguishing Properties, and every Individual that is born has all those Properties without any of the distinguishing Properties of another Species. What now can preserve this prodigious Variety of Species's and this inflexible Uniformity among the Individuals, but the continual and vigilant Providence of God.

AUGUST. 1756. 1 SUNDAY.

Heard Mr. Maccarty all Day. Spent the Evening at the Collonels.— The Event Shews that my Resolutions are of a very thin and vapory Consistence. Almost a fortnight has passed since I came to Worcester the last Time. Some part of the Time, I have spent as frugally and industriously as I possibly could. But the greatest Part I have dreamed away as Usual. I am now entering upon a new month, and a new Week, and I should think that one month would carry me forward considerably, If I could keep up a continual Presence of mind, and a close Application, at all proper Times. This I will Labour after.

2 MONDAY.

Agreably to the Design laid last night, I arose this Morning before the sun. Dined at Pains. Lodgd at Putnams.

3 TUESDAY.

Dind at the Colonels. Lodged at Put[nam's].

Breakfasted at Put[nam']s.

All this past Week my designs have been interrupted, by the Troubles and Confusion of the House. I shall be able to resume the Thread of my Studies I hope now. Wrote pretty industriously in Bolinbroke.— I have never looked attentively into my own Breast. I have never considered, (as I ought) the surprizing Faculties and Opperations of the Mind. Our minds are capable of receiving an infinite Variety of Ideas, from those numerous material objects with which we are surrounded. And the vigourous Impressions which we receive from these, our minds are capable of retaining, compounding and arranging into all the Varieties of Picture and of Figure. Our minds are able to retain distinct Comprehensions of an infinite multitude of Things without the least Labour or fatigue, by curiously enquiring into the Scituation, Fruits, Produce, Manufactures, &c. of our own, and by travailing into or reading about other Countries, we can gain distinct Ideas of almost every Thing upon this Earth, at present, and by looking into Hystory we can settle in our minds a clear and a comprehensive View of This Earth at its Creation, of its various changes and Revolutions, of its various Catastrophes, of its progressive Cultivation, sudden depopulation, and graduall repeopling, of the growth of several Kingdoms and Empires, of their Wealth and Commerce, Warrs and Politicks, of the Characters of their principal Leading Men, of their Grandeur and Power, of their Virtues and Vices, and of their insensible Decays at first, and of their swift Destruction at last. In fine we can attend the Earth from its Nativity thro all the various turns of Fortune, through all its successive Changes, through all the events that happen on its surface, and thro all the successive Generations of Mankind, to the final Conflagration when the whole Earth with its Appendages shall be consumed and dissolved by the furious Element of Fire. And after our minds are furnished with this ample Store of Ideas, far from feeling burdened or overloaded, our thoughts are more free and active and clear than before, and we are capable of diffusing our Acquaintance with things, much further. We are not satiated with Knowledge, our Curiosity is only improved, and increased, Our Thoughts rove beyond the visible diurnal sphere, they range thro the Heavens and loose themselves amidst a Labyrinth of Worlds, and not contented with what is, they run forward into futurity and search for new Employment there. Here they can never stop. The wide, the boundless Prospect lies before them. Here alone they find Objects adequate to their desires.

I know not by what Fatality it happens, but I seem to have a Necessity upon me of trifling away my Time. Have not read 50 lines in Virgil this Week. Have wrote very little.

12[-13] THURSDSAY. FRYDAY.

I know not what became of these days.

14 SATURDAY.

I seem to have lost sight of the Object that I resolved to pursue. Dreams and slumbers, sloth and negligence, will be the ruin of my schemes. However I seem to be awake now. Why cant I keep awake? I have wrote Scripture pretty industriously this morning.—Why am I so unreasonable, as to expect Happiness, and a solid undisturbed Contentment amidst all the Disorders, and the continual Rotations of worldly Affairs? Stability is no where to be found in that Part of the Universe that lies within our observation. The natural and the moral World, are continually changing. The Planets, with all their Appendages, strike out their amazing Circles round the Sun. Upon the Earth, one Day is serene, and clear, no cloud intercepts the kind influence of the Sun, and all Nature seems to flourish and look gay. But these delightfull scenes soon vanish, and are succeeded by the gloom and Darkness of the Night. And before the morning Appears, the Clouds gather, the Winds rise, Lightnings glare, and Thunders bellow through the vast of Heaven. Man is sometimes flushed with Joy and transported with the full Fury of sensual Pleasure, and the next Hour, lies groaning under the bitter Pangs of Disappointments and adverse Fortune. Thus God has told us, by the general Constitution of the World, by the Nature of all terrestrial Enjoyments, and by the Constitution of our own Bodies, that This World was not designed for a lasting and a happy State, but rather for a State of moral Discipline, that we might have a fair Opportunity and continual Excitements to labour after a cheerful Resignation to all the Events of Providence, after Habits of Virtue, Self Government, and Piety. And this Temper of mind is in our Power to acquire, and this alone can secure us against all the Adversities of Fortune, against all the Malice of men, against all the Opperations of Nature. A World in Flames, and a whole System tumbling in Ruins to the Center, has nothing terrifying in it to a man whose Security is builded on the adamantine Basis of good

Conscience and confirmed Piety. If I could but conform my Life and Conversation to my Speculations, I should be happy.—Have I hardiness enough to contend with omnipotence? Or have I cunning enough to elude infinite Wisdom, or Ingratitude enough to Spurn at infinite Goodness? The Scituation that I am in, and the Advantages that I enjoy, are thought to be the best for me by him who alone is a competent Judge of Fitness and Propriety. Shall I then complain? Oh Madness, Pride, Impiety.

15 SUNDAY.

If one Man or Being, out of pure Generosity, and without any Expectation of Returns, is about to confer any Favour or Emolument upon Another, he has a right and is at Liberty to choose in what manner, and by what means, to confer it. He may convey the Favour by his own Hand or by the Hand of his Servant, and the Obligation to Gratitude is equally strong upon the benefited Being. The mode of bestowing does not diminish the kindness, provided the Commodity or good is brought to us equally perfect and without our Expence. But on the other Hand, If our Being is the original Cause of Pain, Sorrow or Suffering to another, voluntarily and without provocation, it is injurious to that other, whatever means he might employ and whatever Circumstances the Conveyance of the Injury might be attended with. Thus we are equally obliged to the Supream Being for the Information he has given us of our Duty, whether by the Constitution of our Minds and Bodies or by a supernatural Revelation. For an instance of the latter let us take original sin. Some say that Adams sin was enough to damn the whole human Race, without any actual Crimes committed by any of them. Now this Guilt is brought upon them not by their own rashness and Indiscretion, not by their own Wickedness and Vice, but by the Supream Being. This Guilt brought upon us is a real Injury and Misfortune because it renders us worse than not to be, and therefore making us guilty upon account of Adams Delegation, or Representing all of us, is not in the least diminishing the Injury and Injustice but only changing the mode of conveyance.

22 SUNDAY.

Yesterday I compleated a Contract with Mr. Putnam, to study Law under his Inspection for two years.[1] I ought to begin with a Resolution to oblige and please him and his Lady in a particular Manner. I ought to endeavour to oblige and please every Body, but them in particular.

Necessity drove me to this Determination, but my Inclination I think was to preach. However that would not do. But I set out with firm Resolutions I think never to commit any meanness or injustice in the Practice of Law. The Study and Practice of Law, I am sure does not dissolve the obligations of morality or of Religion. And altho the Reason of my quitting Divinity was my Opinion concerning some disputed Points, I hope I shall not give Reason of offence to any in that Profession by imprudent Warmth.

Heard Crawford upon the Love of God. The Obligation that is upon us to love God, he says, arises from the Instances of his Love and Goodness to us. He has given us an Existence and a Nature which renders us capable of enjoying Happiness and of suffering Misery. He has given us several senses and has furnished the World around us with a Variety of Objects proper to delight and entertain them. He has hung up in the Heavens over our Heads, and has spread in the Fields of Nature around about us, those glorious Shows and Appearances, by which our Eyes and our Imaginations are so extremely delighted. We are pleased with the Beautyful Appearance of the Flower, we are agreably entertaind with the Prospect of Forrests and Meadows, of verdant Field and mountains coverd with Flocks, we are thrown into a kind of transport and amazement when we behold the amazing concave of Heaven sprinkled and glittering with Starrs. He has also bestowed upon the Vegetable Species a fragrance, that can almost as [agreeably?] entertain our sense of smell. He has so wonderfully constituted the Air that by giving it a particular Kind of Vibration, it produces in us as intense sensation of Pleasure as the organs of our Bodies can bear, in all the Varieties of Harmony and Concord. But all the Provision[s] that he has [made?] for the Gratification of our senses, tho very engaging and unmerited Instances of goodness, are much inferior to the Provision, the wonderful Provision that he has made for the gratification of our nobler Powers of Intelligence and Reason. He has given us Reason, to find out the Truth, and the real Design and true End of our Existence, and has made all Endeavours to promote them agreable to our minds, and attended with a conscious pleasure and Complacency. On the Contrary he has made a different Course of Life, a Course of Impiety and Injustice, of Malevolence and Intemperance, appear Shocking and deformed to our first Reflections. And since it was necessary to make us liable to some Infirmities and Distempers of Body, he has plentifully stored the Bowells and the surface of the Earth with Minerals and Vegetables that are proper to defend us from some Deseases and to restore us to health from others.

Besides the Powers of our Reason and Invention have enabled us to devize Engines and Instruments to take advantage of the Powers that we find in Nature to avert many Calamities that would other wise befall us, and to procure many Enjoyments and Pleasures that we could not other wise attain. He has connected the greatest Pleasure with the Discovery of Truth and made it our Interest to pursue with Eagerness these intense Pleasures. Have we not the greatest Reason then, yea is it not our indispensible Duty to return our sincere Love and Gratitude to this greatest, kindest and most profuse Benefactor. Would it not shew the deepest Baseness and most infamous Ingratitude to despize or to disregard a Being to whose inexhausted Beneficence we are so deeply indebted.

¹ The terms were that JA would continue to keep the Worcester school, the town paying Mrs. Putnam for his board, and that JA would pay Putnam "an hundred dollars, when I should find it convenient" (JA, Autobiography).

23 MONDAY.

Came to Mr. Putnams and began Law. And studied not very closely this Week.

29 SUNDAY.

BRAINTREE OCTR. 5TH. 1758.¹

Yesterday arrived here from Worcester.² I am this Day about beginning Justinians Institutions with Arnold Vinnius's Notes. I took it out of the Library at Colledge.³ It is intituled, D. Justiniani Sacratissimi Principis Institutionum sive Elementorum Libri quatuor, Notis perpetuis multo, quam hucusque, dilligentius illustrati, Cura & Studio, Arnoldi Vinnii J.C. Editio novissima priori Progressu Juris civilis Romani, Fragmentis XII. Tabularum & Rerum Nominumque Indice Auctior, ut ex Præfatione nostra patet.—Now I shall have an opportunity of judging of a dutch Commentator whom the Dedicat[ion] calls celeberrimus suâ Etate in hac Academiâ Doctor.—Let me read with Attention, Deliberation, Distinction. Let me admire with Knowledge. It is low to admire a Dutch Commentator m[erely] because he uses latin, and greek Phraseology. Let me be able to draw the True Character both of the Text of Justinian, and of the Notes of his Commentator, when I have finished the Book. Few of my Contemporary Beginners, in the Study of the Law, have the Resolution, to aim at much Knowledge in the Civil Law. Let me therefore distinguish my self from them, by the Study of the Civil Law, in its native languages, those of Greece and Rome. I shall gain the Consideration and perhaps favour of Mr. Gridley and Mr. Pratt by this means.[4]—As a stimulus let me insert in this Place Justinians Adhortationem ad Studium Juris. "Summa itaque ope et alacri Studio has Leges nostras accipite: et vosmet ipsos sic eruditos ostendite, ut Spes vos pulcherrima foveat, toto legitimo Opere perfecto, posse etiam nostram Rem publicam in Partibus ejus vobis credendis gubernari." Data Constantinopoli XI. Kalendas Decembris, Domino Justiniano, perpetuo Augusto tertium Consule.—Cic. 1. de Orat.—Pergite, ut facitis, Adolescentes, atque in id Studium in quo estis incumbite ut et vobis honori, et Amicis Utilitati, et Reipublicæ emolumento esse possitis.—Arnoldus Vinnius in Academia Leidensi Juris Professor fuit celeberrimus.

I have read about 10 Pages in Justinian and Translated about 4 Pages into English. This is the whole of my Days Work. I have smoaked, chatted, trifled, loitered away this whole day almost. By much the greatest Part of this day has been spent, in unloading a Cart, in cutting oven Wood, in making and recruiting my own fire, in eating nuts and apples, in drinking Tea, cutting and smoaking Tobacco and in chatting with the Doctor's Wife[5] at their House and at this.[6] Chores, Chatt, Tobacco, Tea, Steal away Time. But I am resolved to translate Justinian and his Commentators Notes by day light and read Gilberts Tenures by Night till I am master of both, and I will meddle with no other Book in this Chamber on a Week day. On a Sunday I will read the Inquiry into the Nature of the human Soul, and for Amusement I will sometimes read Ovids Art of Love to Mrs. Savel.—This shall be my Method.—I have read Gilberts 1st Section, of feuds, this evening but am not a Master of it.

[1] First entry in JA's booklet "No. 2," as numbered by CFA (our D/JA/2). Actually this is a collection of loose leaves, not a stitched gathering, and many of the leaves are badly chipped and worn at the edges. Where illegible or partly missing words or phrases can be reconstructed from the early transcripts prepared for JQA and carefully corrected by CFA, the editors have not ordinarily used square brackets, reserving them for very doubtful readings.

[2] JA had recently finished his two-year period of legal studies under the "Inspection" of James Putnam. He kept no diary during that period and wrote almost no letters that have been preserved. A few incidents of his life in Worcester, 1756–1758, are recorded in his Autobiography, q.v. On 19 July 1758 he had attended commencement in Cambridge and argued, for his master of arts degree, the affirmative side of the *quæstio, An Imperium civile, Hominibus prorsus necessarium, sit* (Harvard *Quæstiones,* 1758, broadside).

[3] This copy of Vinnius' Justinian, which was probably of the edition published at Leyden, 1730, is no longer in the Harvard College Library.

[4] Jeremiah (or Jeremy) Gridley (1702–1767), Harvard 1725, and Benjamin Prat (1711–1763), Harvard 1737 and later chief justice of New York Province, were at this time the two leading lawyers of Boston.

[5] Mrs. Elisha Savil; see entry of 17 March 1756 above, and note 3 there.

⁶ This sentence, falling at the foot of one page of the MS and the top of the next, is partly worn away. The present text follows the early transcript as corrected by CFA.

FRYDAY. OCT. 6.

Rose about sun rise. Unpitched a Load of Hay. Translated 2 Leaves more of Justinian, and in the afternoon walked to Deacon Webbs, then round by the Mill Pond home. Smoaked a Pipe with Webb at the Drs. and am now about reading over again Gilberts section of feudal Tenures.

SATURDAY [7 OCTOBER].

Read in Gilbert. Rode with Webb to Mr. Cranche's. Dined and drank Tea with him, and then home. Saturday night.

SUNDAY [8 OCTOBER].

Read a few Leaves in Baxters Enquiry into the Nature of the human Soul. He has explaind with great Exactness, the Resistance, which Matter makes to any Change of its State or Condition, whether of motion or of Rest. The Vis Inertiæ, the positive Inactivity of matter not barely its Inactivity, but its AntiActivity. For it not only is destitute of a Power of changing its state from Rest to motion or from motion to Rest, but it has the possitive Power, each single Particle has a Possitive Power of Resisting any force that attempts to change its state. But a leaden Ball, held between my fingers, as soon as I withdraw my fingers, will of itself for ought I see change its State from rest to motion and fall suddenly to the floor. This Phenomenon is not Vis Inertiæ, 'tis by no Reluctance or Aversion to motion that it moves, but it seems to be a Tendency to motion, an Active Principle. If it is passive the Agent that presses it downwards is invisible. But because matter in all the Experiments I have tried, resists a Change from rest to motion upwards, will it follow, that all matter essentially resists a Change from rest to motion, downwards. Is it a Posteriori from Experiments, that he deduces this Proposition, that all matter essentially resists any Change of State, or is it a Priori from some Property that is essentially included in our Idea of Matter that he demonstratively [argues?] this Vis Inertiæ. Is Inactivity, and AntiActivity, included in our Idea of Matter? Are Activity, Perceptivity &c. Properties that we by only comparing Ideas can see to be incompatible to any Properties of matter.

If nothing is Matter which has not this antiactive Principle, then human Minds are not matter for they have no such Principle. We are

46

conscious, that we can begin and end motion of ourselves. If he argues a Posteriori from Experiments, he can pretend only to Probability. For Unless he was certain that he had made the Experiment and found the Property in every Particle of Matter that ever was created, he could not be certain, that there was no Particle in the World, without this Property, tho he had tried all but one and found that they had it. We have tried but a few Parcells of Matter. The Utmost we can say is, that all we have tried are inactive. But for Argument sake I will deny, that all the Parcels that we have tried, have this Property. On the Contrary I will say that all have a motive Power downwards. Powder has an Active Power springing every Way &c. Thus Experiment is turned against the Doctrine. I cant yet see how he will prove all matter Anti inactive a Priori from Properties of matter before known essential, with which he must shew this to be necessarily connected.

MONDAY OCTR. 9.

Read in Gilberts Tenures. I must and will make that Book familiar to me.

TUESDAY [10 OCTOBER].

Read in Gilbert. I read him slowly, but I gain Ideas and Knowledge as I go along, which I dont always, when I read.

WEDNESDAY [11 OCTOBER].

Rode to Boston. Conversed with Ned Quincy and Saml.,[1] Peter Chardon &c. By the Way Peter Chardon is a promising Youth. He aspires, and will reach to a considerable Height. He has a sense of the Dignity and Importance of his Profession, that of the Law. He has a just Contempt of the idle, incurious, Pleasure hunting young fellows of the Town, who pretend to study Law. He scorns the Character, and he aims at a nobler. He talks of exulting in an unlimited field of natural, civil and common Law, talks of nerving, sharpening the mind by the Study of Law and Mathematicks, quotes Locks Conduct of the Understanding and transcribes Points of Law into a Common-Place Book on Locks Modell.[2] This fellows Thoughts are not employed on Songs and Girls, nor his Time, on flutes, fiddles, Concerts and Card Tables. He will make something.[3]

[1] Samuel Quincy (1735–1789), son of Col. Josiah Quincy; Harvard 1754; lawyer; loyalist.

[2] A self-indexing commonplace book or collection of quotations arranged under topical headings. Locke's explanation of his plan is in a letter to M. Toignard (*The Works of John Locke.*

A *New Edition, Corrected*, London, 1823, 3:331–349). Among CFA's papers is such a book, partly filled up by him, with a printed titlepage and the imprint of Cummings and Hilliard, Boston, 1821 (Adams Papers, Microfilms, Reel No. 312).

[3] This prophecy was not borne out, as CFA points out in a note on this passage; Chardon, Harvard 1757, admitted barrister in the Superior Court, March term, 1763, died in Barbadoes in 1766 (JA, *Works*, 2:39, note; Superior Court of Judicature, Minute Book 79).

THURSDAY [12 OCTOBER].

Examined the Laws of this Province concerning Pads,[1] Cattle, fences &c. and read in Gilbert. This small volume will take me a fortnight, but I will be master of it.

[1] Pad: "A path, track; the road, the way. Orig. *slang*, now also *dial.*" (*OED*).

FRYDAY [13 OCTOBER].

Read Gilbert. Went in the Evening to Coll. Quincys. Heard a Tryal before him, as a Justice between Jos. Field and Luke Lambert.[1] The Case was this. Lamberts Horse broke into Fields Inclosure, and lay there some time, damage feasant. When Lambert found that his Horse was there he enters the Inclosure and altho Feild called to him and forbid it, waved his Hat, and Screamed at the Horse, and drove him away, with[out] tendering Feild his Damages. This was a Rescous of the Horse, out of Feilds Hands, for altho Lambert had a Right to enter and take out his [Horse] tendering the Damages, yet, as [the] Words [of] the Law are "that whoever shall rescous any Creature out of the Hands of any Person about to drive them to pound, whereby the Party injured shall be liable to lose his Damages, and the Law be eluded, shall forfeit &c.," and as Feild was actually about to drive them to Pound, and Lambert offered him no Damages, this was compleatly a Rescous. Feild, after the Rescous, went to Coll. Quincy, made Complaint against Lambert and requested and obtained a Warrant. The Warrant was directed to the Constable, who brought the Offender before the Justice, attended with the Complainant, and the Witnesses ordered to be summoned. Quincy, for Defendant, took Exception on the Warrant, to the Jurisdiction of the Justice, because the sum originally sued for, consisting of the forfeiture of 40s. to the Poor, and the Parties Damages estimated at 9d. which was 40s. 9d., was a greater sum than the Justice can take Cognisance of, and because the Words of this Act of the Province are, that this 40s. to the Poor, and these Damages to the Party injured shall be recovered, by Action &c., in any of his Majesties Courts of Record. Now as the Court of a single Justice is not one of his Majesties Courts of record the forfeiture and Damages prayed for in this Complaint, cannot be recovered in this Court. The Justice adjourned his Court till 8 o'clock monday morning, in order to inform himself, 1st. Whether the Court of a single Justice of the Peace was one of his Majesties Courts of Record? 2. Whether a single Justice can take Cognisance of any Matter, in which the sum originally prosecuted for is more than 40s.? If upon Examination the Coll. shall find, that, a single Justice has no Authority to hear and determine such a Rescous, at the Adjournment the Proceedings will be quashed, and the Complainant must begin de Novo, but if he finds, that a single Justice has Authority, to determine the matter, he will proceed to Judgment.—The Questions that arise, in my mind, on this Case are these.

1. What is the true Idea, and Definition of a Court of Record? What Courts in England and what in this Province are Courts of Record and what are not? Wood, Jacobs, &c.

2. Whether a Justice has Authority, by Warrant, to hear and determine of any offence the Penalty of which, or the forfeiture to the K[ing], the Poor, the Informer &c. is more than 40s.?

[3.] Whether a Court is denominated a Court of Record from its keeping Records of its Proceedings? Whether every Court is a Court of Record, whose President is a Judge of Record? For it seems plain in Dalton that a Justice of the Peace is a Judge of Record?

4. On supposition the Warrant should be quashed, who should pay the Cost of the original Warrant, of the Defendants attendance, and of Witness[es'] Oaths and attendance? The Complainant, who was mistaken thro Ignorance in going to the Justice for a Remedy, or the Justice who was mistaken, in the same manner, in Acting upon the Complaint beyond his Authority?

5. What are the Steps of prosecuting by Information? Is not a motion made in Court, that the Information may be amended or filed? Are Informations ever filed, but by Attorney General? When the Penalty sued for by the Information is half to the King or half to the Poor and the other half to the Informer, is the Defendant committed till he discharges the Penalty? Or is an Execution ever issued?

[6.] Tis said Courts of Record alone have Power to impose a fine, or Imprison. Q[uery] which?

7. A Rescous is a Breach of Law and a Breach of the Peace, and Remedy for it may be by Action of Trespass, which is always contra Pacem.

8. Are not Justices Warrants confined to criminal matters? May a Warrant be issued for a Trespass Quare Clausum fregit?[2] It may

for a Trespass of assault and Battery. Justices may punish by fine, Imprisonment, Stripes &c.

The Coll. inquired, what Punishment he could inflict on a Constable for Disobedience to his Warrant, for not making Return of his Doings? And he found a Case ruled in K[ing]'s Bench that a Constable is a subordinate officer to a Justice of the Peace and is indictable at common Law for neglect of Duty. The Malefeasance or Nonfeasance of officers are Crimes and offences that may be inquired of, indicted or presented by the grand Jury at Common Law.

Feild took Lamberts Horses Damage feasant in his Close once before and impounded them, and gave him verbal Notice, that his Horses were in Pound, but neglected to give either Lambert or the Pound keeper an account of the Damages the Horses had done him. Lambert went to the Pound keeper and demanded his Horses, tendering the Poundkeepers fees, and the Pound keeper delivered them up.

Now Q. Whether Feild is injoined by any Law of the Province, to get his Damages appraised and to lodge an account of them with the Pound keeper?

2. Whether as he neglected this, the Pound keeper cant justify his resigning of them to the owner?

3. If Feild had lodged an Estimation of his Damages with the Pound keeper, and the Pound keeper had nevertheless resigned the Creatures up, without taking the Damages, would not an Action lay against him as an Action lies against a Prison keeper for a voluntary Escape? And Quere what Action would be proper. I want a form of an Action of Escape, now.

4. It cant be called an indirect Way of delivering his Creatures out of Pound, to pay or tender the Poundkeeper his fees and demand and receive his Cattle of him, when he has unlocked and opened the Pound Gate and turned the Creatures out? So that it will not admit a Quere whether Lambert is liable to an Action for receiving his Horses of the Pound keeper. Tis plain I think he is not.

[1] Field *v.* Lambert (or Lambard), in which JA served as counsel for the plaintiff, was evidently JA's first case as a practicing lawyer. As later entries show, it caused him great concern and vexation because his writ proved defective. The cause was heard by Justice Josiah Quincy, whose son Samuel was the defendant's counsel.

[2] "because he has broken the close" (Bouvier, *Law Dictionary*, 2:610).

MONDAY [16 OCTOBER].

Read a few Pages in Gilbert. I proceed very slowly.

TUESDAY [17 OCTOBER].

Read in Gilbert. Went to Monatiquot to see the Raising of the new Meeting House.[1] No Observations worth noting.

I have not Spirits, and Presence of mind, to seek out scenes of Observation, and to watch critically the Air, Countenances, Actions and Speeches of old men, and young men, of old Women and young Girls, of Physicians and Priests, of old Maids and Batchelors. I should chatter with a Girl, and watch her Behaviour, her answers to Questions, the workings of Vanity and other Passions in her Breast. But objects before me dont suggest proper Questions to ask, and proper Observations to make, so dull and confused at present is my mind.—Betsy Niles affects to trip lightly across the floor, to act with a Sprightly Air, and to be polite. But she is under Restraint, and awe, from her Unacquaintance with Company. Saw Lawyer Thachers Father,[2] at Mr. Niles's. He said old Coll. Thatcher of Barnstable was an excellent man. "He was a very holy man. I used to love to hear him pray. He was a Counsellor, and a Deacon. I have heard him say, that of all his Titles, that of a Deacon, he tho't the most honourable."[3]—Q[uery] is he a new Light? Old Age has commonly a sense of the Importance and Dignity of Religion. I dare say, he is not well pleased with his son's professing the Law. He had rather have him a Deacon.

[1] Monatiquot (variously spelled) was an ancient name frequently used by JA and others for the settlement on the Monatiquot River in present Braintree—at that time the Middle Precinct of Braintree. The "new Meeting House" was that of the Second Parish, to which Rev. Samuel Niles, Harvard 1699, had long ministered. See Pattee, *Old Braintree and Quincy*, p. 7, 56, 285-286; also map in CFA2, *Three Episodes*, vol. 2: following p. 578.

[2] Oxenbridge Thacher the elder (1681-1772), Harvard 1698, father of the eminent Boston lawyer of the same name who will be frequently mentioned in these pages.

[3] Quotation marks supplied, here and above, around what is certainly a direct quotation from old Mr. Thacher.

WEDNESDAY [18 OCTOBER].

Went to Boston.

Bob Paine. I have ruined myself, by a too eager Pursuit of Wisdom. I have now neither Health enough for an active Life, nor Knowledge enough for a sedentary one.

Quincy. We shall never make your great fellows.

Thus Paine and Quincy both are verging to Despair.

Paine. If I attempt a Composition, my Thoughts are slow and dull.

Paine is discouraged, and Quincy has not Courage enough to harbour a Thought of acquiring a great Character. In short, none of them have a foundation that will support them. P. Chardon seemed to me in the directest Road to Superiority. Pains Face has lost its Bloom, and his Eye its Vivacity and fire. His Eye is weak, his Countenance pale and his Attention unsteady. And what is worse, he suffers this decline of Health to retard, almost to Stop his studies. And Q's dastard soul is afraid to aim at great Acquisition.

Paine (to me). You dont intend to be a Sage, I suppose.

Oh! P. has not Penetration to reach the Bottom of my mind. He dont know me. Next time I will answer him, A Sage, no. Knowledge eno' to keep out of fire and Water, is all that I aim at.

THURSDAY [19 OCTOBER].

I borrowed yesterday of Quincy, the 1st Volume of Batista Angeloni's Letters,[1] and a general Treatise of naval Trade and Commerce as founded on the Laws and Statutes of this Realm in which those (Laws and Statutes I suppose) relating to his Majesties Customs, Merchants, Masters of Ships, Mariners, Letters of Marque, Privateers, Prizes, Convoys, Cruizers &c. are particularly considered and treated with due Care under all the necessary Heads from the earliest time down to the present, 2d Edition in 2. Volumes.[2] Read Angeloni thro I believe, and studied, carefully, about a dozen Pages in mercantile Law. Angelonis Letters are all of a Piece. He has an odd System of Faith, viz. that Utility is Truth and therefore that Transubstantiation is true, and Auricular Confession is true because they are useful, they promote the Happiness of mankind. Therefore Rain is true because it is useful in promoting the Growth of Herbs, and fruits and flowers, and consequently of Animals for mans Use. This is very different from Mathematical Truth, and this Explanation of his meaning gives Room to suspect that he disbelieves a Revelation, himself, tho he thinks it useful for the World to believe it.

He reasons, who can conceive that a Being of infinite Wisdom, Justice and Goodness, would suffer the World to be governed 2000 [years] by a Religion that was false. But may not this Question be asked of the Mahometan, the Chinese, in short of every Religion under the sun, and will not the Argument equally prove them all to be true?

What Passion is most active and prevalent in Dr. Savel's mind?[3] The Desire of Money. He retails Sugar by the Pound, [...] by the bunch, Pins, Pen knifes, to save these Articles in his family, and neat[4] a few Shillings Profit. He makes poor People who are in his Debt pay him in Labour. He bargains with his Debtors in the 2 other Parishes for Wood, which he sends to the Landing Place, and to Dr. Marshes. Thus by practice of Physick, by trading and bargaining and scheming he picks up a Subsistance for his family and gathers very gradually, Additions to his Stock. But this is low. The same Application, and scheming in his Profession, would raise and spread him a Character, procure him profitable Business and make his fortune. But by this contemptible Dissipation of mind, among Pins, Needles, Tea, Snuff Boxes, Vendues, Loads of Wood, day labour &c. he is negligent of the Theory of his Profession, and will live and die unknown.—These driveling souls, oh! He aims not at fame, only at a Living and a fortune!

[1] *Letters on the English Nation*, London, 1755, 2 vols., purporting to be "by Batista Angeloni, a Jesuit," were actually the work of John Shebbeare (see *DNB*), a British political writer whose identity JA had discovered by the time of his next reference to this book; see 19 March 1759, below. JA's own copy of the *Letters*, now in the Boston Public Library, contains a few marginal notes in his hand and some underscoring, though none in Letter IX, on religion, from which the paraphrase below is largely derived.

[2] The first volume of JA's own copy of this edition survives, as does the first volume of his copy of the first edition, London, 1740 (*Catalogue of JA's Library*, p. 101).

[3] The present paragraph is separated from the preceding ones by a line across the page in the MS; it may therefore have been written on either 19 or 20 Oct.

[4] Neat, vb.: to clear or net (a sum of money) (*OED*).

SATURDAY [21 OCTOBER].

Rose with the sun. Brot up the Horse and took a Ride over Penns Hill, as far as John Haywards in a cold, keen, blustering N. Wester. Returned and breakfasted. I feel brac'd, as if the cold clear Air had given a Spring to the System.—I am now sett down to the Laws relating to naval Trade and Commerce. Let me inquire of the next Master of a Ship that I see, what is a Bill of Lading, what the Pursers Book. What Invoices they keep. What Account they keep of Goods received on Board, and of Goods delivered out, at another Port, &c.

SUNDAY [22 OCTOBER].

Conversed with Capt. Thatcher about commercial affairs.—When he receives a freight of Goods on board his Vessell, he signs 3 Bills of Lading (a Bill of Lading, by the Way, is a List of the several Articles, and the Receipt of them signed by the Master) two of which the Merchant keeps, and the other he incloses in a Letter to his Correspondent to whom he sends the Goods and sends it by the Vessell. When the Master arrives at the Port he is destined to, he delivers the Letter, and then the Goods to his Employers Correspondent, who upon Receipt indorses the Bill of Lading, and delivers it up to the Master, and this

Bill thus endorsed, will [...] the other two in the Merchants Hands. The Receiver of Goods pays the freight.

Some Voyages, We have nothing to do, but receive Goods on board, keep them safely on the Voyage and deliver them safely to the Merchant to whom they are directed. But sometimes we make Trading Voyages. We carry a Cargo of Goods, to sell for money or exchange for other Goods, in the most profitable manner we can. Here we keep a regular Account, make the owners Debtors for Goods that we buy or receive, and give them Credit for Goods that we deliver out.

MONDAY [23 OCTOBER].

TUESDAY [24 OCTOBER].

Rode to Boston. Arrived about 1/2 after 10. Went into the Court House, and sett down by Mr. Paine att the Lawyers Table. I felt Shy, under Awe and concern, for Mr. Gridley, Mr. Prat, Mr. Otis,[1] Mr. Kent,[2] and Mr. Thatcher were all present and looked sour. I had no Acquaintance with any Body but Paine and Quincy and they took but little Notice. However I attended Court Steadily all Day, and at night, went to Consort with Samll. Quincy and Dr. Gardiner.[3] There I saw the most Spacious and elegant Room, the gayest Company of Gentlemen and the finest Row of Ladies, that ever I saw. But the weather was so dull and I so disordered that I could not make one half the observations that I wanted to make.

[1] James Otis Jr. (1725–1783), Harvard 1743, the celebrated lawyer and pamphleteer.
[2] Benjamin Kent (1708–1788), Harvard 1727, another leading lawyer and later attorney general of the Province.
[3] Silvester Gardiner (1707–1786), Boston physician and druggist; founder of Gardiner, Maine; one of JA's early law clients.

WEDNESDAY [25 OCTOBER].

Went in the morning to Mr. Gridleys, and asked the favour of his Advice what Steps to take for an Introduction to the Practice of Law in this County.[1] He answered "get sworn."

Ego. But in order to that, sir, as I have no Patron, in this County.

G. I will recommend you to the Court. Mark the Day the Court adjourns to in order to make up Judgments. Come to Town that Day, and in the mean Time I will speak to the Bar for the Bar must be consulted, because the Court always inquires, if it be with Consent of the Bar.

Then Mr. Gridley inquired what Method of Study I had pursued, what Latin Books I read, what Greek, what French. What I had read upon Rhetorick. Then he took his Common Place Book and gave me Ld. Hales Advice to a Student of the Common Law, and when I had read that, he gave me Ld. C[hief] J[ustice] Reeves Advice [to] his Nephew, in the Study of the common Law. Then He gave me a Letter from Dr. Dickins, Regius Professor of Law at the University of Cambridge, to him, pointing out a Method of Studying the civil Law. Then he turned to a Letter He wrote himself to Judge Lightfoot, Judge of the Admiralty in Rhode Island, directing to a Method of Studying the Admiralty Law. Then Mr. Gridley run a Comparison between the Business and studies of a Lawyer or Gentleman of the Bar, in England, and that of one here. A Lawyer in this Country must study common Law and civil Law, and natural Law, and Admiralty Law, and must do the duty of a Counsellor, a Lawyer, an Attorney, a sollicitor, and even of a scrivener, so that the Difficulties of the Profession are much greater here than in England.

The Difficulties that attend the study may discourage some, but they never discouraged me. [Here is conscious superiority.] [2]

I have a few Pieces of Advice to give you Mr. Adams. One is to pursue the Study of the Law rather than the Gain of it. Pursue the Gain of it enough to keep out of the Briars, but give your main Attention to the study of it.

The next is, not to marry early. For an early Marriage will obstruct your Improvement, and in the next Place, twill involve you in Expence.

Another Thing is not to keep much Company. For the application of a Man who aims to be a lawyer must be incessant. His Attention to his Books must be constant, which is inconsistent with keeping much Company.

In the study of Law the common Law be sure deserves your first and last Attention, and He has conquered all the Difficulties of this Law, who is Master of the Institutes. You must conquer the Institutes. The Road of Science is much easier, now, than it was when I sett out. I began with Co. Litt.[3] and broke thro.

I asked his Advice about studying Greek. He answered it is a matter of meer Curiosity.—After this long and familiar Conversation we went to Court. Attended all Day and in the Evening I went to ask Mr. Thatchers Concurrence with the Bar. Drank Tea and spent the whole Evening, upon original sin, Origin of Evil, the Plan of the Universe, and at last, upon Law. He says He is sorry that he neglected to keep a common Place Book when he began to study Law, and he is half a mind to begin now. Thatcher thinks, this County is full.[4]

[1] The account of this momentous interview in JA's Autobiography differs so widely in details from this contemporary record of it as to suggest that JA did not consult his Diary in composing the later account.

[2] Brackets in MS.

[3] Coke upon Littleton, the famous *Institutes of the Laws of England*, London, 1628–1644, in four parts, which consisted of Sir Thomas Littleton's treatise on tenures with an elaborate commentary by Sir Edward Coke, long the standard authority on real property in England and America.

[4] Of lawyers.

THURSDAY [26 OCTOBER].

Went in the morning to wait on Mr. Prat. He inquired if I had been sworn at Worcester? No. Have you a Letter from Mr. Putnam to the Court? No. It would have been most proper to have done one of them things first. When a young Gentleman goes from me into another County, I always write in his favour to the Court in that County, or if you had been sworn, there, you would have been intitled to be sworn here. But now, no Body in this County knows any Thing about you. So no Body can say any Thing in your favour, but by hearsay. I believe you have made a proper Proficiency in science, and that you will do very well from what I have heard, but that is only hearsay. [How different is this from Gridleys Treatment? Besides it is weak, for neither the Court nor the Bar will question the Veracity of Mr. Gridly and Mr. Prat, so that the only Uncertainty that can remain is whether Mr. Putnam was in Earnest, in the Account he gave of my Morals and Studies to them Gentleman, which cannot be removed by a Line from him, or by my being sworn at Worcester, or any other Way than by getting Mr. Putnam sworn.][1] After this, he asked me a few, short Questions about the Course of my studies which I answered, and then came off as full of Wrath as [I] was full of Gratitude when I left Gridley the morning before. Prat is infinitely harder of Access than Gridley. He is ill natured, and Gridley is good natured. —Attended Court all Day, and at night waited on Otis at his office where I conversed with him and he, with great Ease and familiarity, promised me to join the Bar in recommending me to the Court. Mr. Gridley lent me Van Muydens Compendiosa Institutionum Justiniani Tractatio in usum Collegiorum. Editio tertia prioribus Auctior et emendatior. Pax Artium Altrix.[2]—After I have mastered this, I must read Hoppius's Commentary on Justinian. The Design of this Book is [to] explain the technical Terms of the civil Law, and to settle the Divisions and Distributions of the civil Law. By the Way this is the first Thing a student ought to aim at, viz. distinct Ideas under the terms and a clear apprehension of the Divisions and Distributions of the science. This is one of the principal Excellences of Hawkins's

Pleas of the Crown,[3] and it is the very End of this Book of Van Muyden's.

Let me remarke here one important neglect of the last Week. I omitted minuting the Names of the Cases at Trial in my Ivory Book, and I omitted to keep Pen, Ink and Paper at my Lodgings, in order to comitt to Writing, at Night, the Cases and Points of Law that were argued and adjudged in the Day.

Let me remember to mark in my Memorandum Book, the Names of the Cases, and the Terms and Points of Law that occur in each Case, to look these Terms and Points in the Books at Otis's, Prats or any other office, and to digest and write down the whole in the Evening at my Lodgings. This will be reaping some real Advantage, by my Attendance on the Courts, and, without this, the Observations that I may make will lie in total Confusion in my mind.

[1] Brackets in MS.
[2] JA later acquired this book (as he did others) from Gridley's library, and it survives among JA's books in the Boston Public Library.

[3] JA's copy of William Hawkins, *A Treatise of the Pleas of the Crown*, 4th edn., London, 1762, 2 vols. in 1, is in the Boston Public Library. It bears his autograph and that of his son Charles.

FRIDAY, SATURDAY, SUNDAY, MONDAY [27–30 OCTOBER].

All Spent in absolute Idleness, or what is worse, gallanting the Girls.

TUESDAY [31 OCTOBER].

Set down, and recollected my self, and read a little in Van Muyden, a little in naval Trade and Commerce.

WEDNESDAY [1 NOVEMBER].

Read a little in Van Muyden, and a little in naval Trade and Commerce.

THURSDAY [2 NOVEMBER].

Rode as far as Smelt Brook. Breakfasted, made my fire and am now set down to Van Muyden in Earnest. His latin is easy, his deffinitions are pretty clear, and his Divisions of the subject, are judicious.

SUNDAY [5? NOVEMBER].

Drank Tea at Coll. Quincy's. He read to me a Letter Coll. Gouch [1] wrote him in answer to his Questions, whether a Justices Court was a Court of Record? and then concluded, "So that Sammy was right, for he was all along of that Opinion. I have forgot what your Opinion was?" [This must be a Lye, or else Partiality and parental affection have blotted out the Remembrance that I first started to his son Sam and him too, the Doubt whether he had Jurisdiction as a Justice—and made him really imagine, what he wished had been true viz. that Samll. had started it. If he did remember he knew it was insult to me. But I bore it. Was forgetfulness, was Partiality, or was a cunning Design to try if I was not vain of being the Starter of the Doubt, the true Cause of his saying, He forgot what my Opinion was.] [2]

Sam has the utmost Reason to be grateful to Mr. Pratt. He will have an opportunity 100 times better than Mr. Prat had of rising into the Practice and Reputation of the Law. I want to see and hear Sam at the Bar. I want to know how he will succeed. I am concerned for him. The Govr.[3] likes Sam much better than Ned. He has seen or heard some of Neds freaks. This is a Partiality in favor of one Child and against another quite indecent in a father. Tis great Weakness to expose himself so before Strangers.

[1] Joseph Gooch, on whom see further the entry of 9 Aug. 1760, below.
[2] Initial bracket in MS; closing bracket supplied.
[3] Evidently a sobriquet for Col. Josiah Quincy; possibly an inadvertence for "the Colonel."

MONDAY [6? NOVEMBER].[1]

Went to Town. Went to Mr. Gridleys office, but he had not returned to Town from Brookline. Went again. Not returned. Attended Court till after 12 and began to grow uneasy expecting that Quincy would be sworn and I have no Patron, when Mr. Gridly made his Appearance, and on sight of me, whispered to Mr. Prat, Dana,[2] Kent, Thatcher &c. about me. Mr. Prat said no Body knew me. Yes, says Gridley, I have tried him, he is a very sensible Fellow.—At last He rose up and bowed to his right Hand and said "Mr. Quincy," when Quincy rose up, then bowed to me, "Mr. Adams," when I walked out. "May it please your Honours, I have 2 young Gentlemen Mr. Q. and Mr. Adams to present for the Oath of an Attorney. Of Mr. Q. it is sufficient for me to say he has lived 3 Years with Mr. Prat. Of Mr. Adams, as he is unknown to your Honours, It is necessary to say that he has lived between 2 and 3 Years with Mr. Put[nam] of Worcester, has a good Character from him, and all others who know him, and that he was with me the other day several Hours, and I take it he is qualified to study the Law by his scholarship and that he has made a very considerable, a very great Proficiency in the Principles of the Law, and therefore that the Clients Interest may be safely intrusted in his Hands. I therefore recommend him with the Consent of the Bar to your

Honors for the Oath." Then Mr. Prat said 2 or 3 Words and the Clerk was ordered to swear us. After the Oath Mr. Gridley took me by the Hand, wished me much Joy and recommended me to the Bar. I shook Hands with the Bar, and received their Congratulations, and invited them over to Stones to drink some Punch. Where the most of us resorted, and had a very chearful [Chat?].

[1] In his Autobiography JA twice says, in varying language, that his admission as attorney to the Suffolk bar (which is to say his swearing-in before the Inferior Court of Common Pleas for Suffolk County) occurred on the last Friday (i.e. the 27th) of October 1758. Since the records of the Suffolk Inferior Court for this period have been lost, the date cannot be finally established, but there can be little doubt that the present Diary entry has been correctly dated as 6 Nov.

even though this date has had to be assigned, and, accordingly, that the swearing-in occurred on that day. Note again how widely the account in the Autobiography varies from that written at the time.

[2] Richard Dana (1700–1772), Harvard 1718, often called "Father Dana" by JA to distinguish him from his son Francis, who also became a lawyer and, later, JA's secretary in Europe, a diplomat, and a judge.

TUESDAY. DECEMBER 3 OR 4 [*i.e.* 5?].[1]

Bob Paine is conceited and pretends to more Knowledge and Genius than he has. I have heard him say that he took more Pleasure in solving a Problem in Algebra than in a frolick. He told me the other day, that he was as curious after a minute and particular Knowledge of Mathematicks and Phylosophy, as I could be about the Laws of Antiquity. By his Boldness in Company, he makes himself a great many Enemies. His Aim in Company is to be admired, not to be beloved. He asked me what Duch Commentator I meant? I said Vinnius.—Vinnius, says he, (with a flash of real Envy, but pretended Contempt,) you cant understand one Page of Vinnius.—He must know that human Nature is disgusted with such incomplaisant Behaviour. Besides he has no Right to say that I dont understand every Word in Vinnius, or even in [...] for he knows nothing of me. For the future let me act the Part of a critical spy upon him, not that of an open unsuspicious friend.—Last Superiour Court at Worcester he dined in Company with Mr. Gridly, Mr. Trowbridge,[2] and several others, at Mr. Putnams, and altho a modest attentive Behaviour would have best become him in such a Company, yet he tried to ingross the whole Conversation to himself. He did the same, in the Evening, when all the Judges of the Superiour Court with Mr. Winthrop, Sewall, &c. were present, and he did the same last Thanksgiving day, at Coll. Quincies, when Mr. Wibirt, Mr. Cranch &c. were present. This Impudence may sett the Million a Gape at him but will make all Persons of Sense despize him, or hate him.

That evening at Put[nam]s, he called me, a Numbskull and a Blunder Buss before all the Superiour Judges. I was not present indeed, but such expressions were indecent and tended to give the Judges a low Opinion of me, as if I was despized by my Acquaintance. He is an impudent, ill-bred, conceited fellow. Yet he has Witt, sense, and Learning, and a great deal of Humour, and has Virtue and Piety except his fretful, peevish, Childish Complaints against the Disposition of Things. This Character is drawn with Resentment of his ungenerous Treatment of me, and Allowances must therefore be made, but these are unexaggerated facts.

Lambert setts up for a Witt and a Humourist. He is like a little nurley[3] ill natured Horse that kicks at every Horse of his own size, but lears and shears off from every one that is larger. I should mind what I say before him for he [is] always watching for wry Words to make into a droll story to laugh at. He laughs at John Thayer, for saying, "Lambert, I am sorry [I] am your good Friend I am sorry. This will cost you between 2 and 3 hundred Pounds."[4] And it was a silly, [... impertinent?], ignorant Speech. He laughs at Field for being nettled at his laughter. Field complained that he laughed at him. Lambert said, I will laugh when I please. If you carry me to the Rat hole I will laugh all the Way, and after I get there.—Such fellows are hated by all mankind, yet they rise and make a figure, and People dred them.

Altho men of bitter witt, are hated and feared, yet they are respected, by the World.

Quære, was there ever a Witt, who had much Humanity and Compassion, much Tenderness of Nature? Mr. Congreve was tender, extreamly tender of giving offence to any man. Dr. Arbuthnot was a[s] great a Wit and Humourist, yet he was tender, and prudent. Mr. Cranch has Witt, and is tender and [gentle?].[5]

The other Night I happened to be at the Drs., with Ben. Veasey. He began to prate upon the Presumption of Philosophers in erecting Iron Rods to draw the Lightning from the Clouds. His Brains were in a ferment with strong Liquor and he railed, and foamed against those Points and the Presumption that erected them, in Language taken partly from Scripture and partly from the drunken Disputes of Tavern Philosophy, in as wild mad a manner as King Lear raves, against his Daughters Disobedience and Ingratitude, and against the meaness of the Storm in joining with his Daughter against him in Shakespears Lear. He talked of presuming upon God as Peter attempted to walk upon the Water, attempting to controul the Artilry of Heaven, an Execution that Mortal man cant Stay—the Elements of Heaven, fire, Heat, Rain, Wind, &c.

Let me search for the Clue, which Led great Shakespeare into the Labyrinth of mental Nature! Let me examine how men think. Shakespeare had never seen in real Life Persons under the Influence of all those Scenes of Pleasure and distress, which he has described in his Works, but he imagined how a Person of such a Character would behave in such Circumstances, by analogy from the Behaviour of others that were most like that Character in nearly similar Circumstances, which he had seen.

[1] If JA was correct in giving the day of the week as Tuesday, this entry should be dated 5 Dec.

[2] Edmund Trowbridge (1709–1793), of Cambridge; Harvard 1728; attorney general and later a justice of the Superior Court. JA sometimes calls him Goffe, a name Trowbridge used in college and for a time thereafter because his guardian was a great-uncle named Edmund Goffe.

[3] Dwarfish, gnarled (*OED*, under "knurly").

[4] The point of this anecdote is now lost, perhaps owing to JA's punctuation, which stands here as in the MS except for moving back the closing quotation mark to this point from its original position after the first use of the word "sorry" in the preceding sentence.

[5] The following two paragraphs are separated from the present entry and from each other by lines drawn across the page in the MS; they may have been written at any time between 5 and 18 Dec.

[MARGINALIA IN WINTHROP'S *Lecture on Earthquakes*, DECEMBER 1758?] [1]

"O! there is no getting out of the mighty hand of GOD!" [2]

This Exclamation was very popular, for the Audience in general like the rest of the Province, consider Thunder, and Lightning as well as Earthquakes, only as Judgments, Punishments, Warnings &c. and have no Conception of any Uses they can serve in Nature. I have heard some Persons of the highest Rank among us, say, that they really thought the Erection of Iron Points, was an impious attempt to robb the almighty of his Thunder, to wrest the Bolt of Vengeance out of his Hand. And others, that Thunder was designed, as an Execution upon Criminals, that no Mortal can stay. That the attempt was foolish as well as impious. And no Instances, even those of Steeples struck, where Iron Bars have by Accident conveyed the Electricity as far as they reached without damage, which one would think would force Conviction, have no weight at all. [3]

This Invention of Iron Points, to prevent the Danger of Thunder, has met with all that opposition from the superstition, affectation of Piety, and Jealousy of new Inventions, that Inoculation to prevent the Danger of the Small Pox, and all other usefull Discoveries, have met with in all ages of the World.

I am not able to satisfy myself, whether the very general if not universal apprehension that Thunder, Earthquakes, Pestilence, Famine &c. are designed merely as Punishments of sins and Warnings to forsake, is natural to Mankind, or whether it was artfully propagated, or whether it was derived from Revelation.

An Imagination that those Things are of no Use in Nature but to punish and alarm and arouse sinners, could not be derived from real Revelation, because it is far from being true, tho few Persons can be persuaded to think so.

[1] The two following paragraphs were written, without indication of date, in JA's copy of John Winthrop, *A Lecture on Earthquakes; Read in the Chapel of Harvard-College in Cambridge*, N.E. November 26th 1755, Boston, 1755, the first at p. 37 and the second on a blank final leaf. This copy is in the Boston Public Library, and Mr. Zoltán Haraszti has published the marginalia, with a helpful commentary, in "Young John Adams on Franklin's Iron Points," *Isis*, 41:11–14 (March 1950). See also entries of 18 Nov. 1755, above, and 12 March 1761, below.

[2] This sentence is quoted in Winthrop's text from Rev. Thomas Prince's *Earthquakes the Works of God*, Boston, 1755, a sermon first published in 1727 and reissued with a new appendix after the earthquake of 18 Nov. 1755. In the appendix Prince took a very dim view of the recent invention by "the sagacious Mr. Franklin." "The more *Points of Iron* are erected round the *Earth* to draw the *Electrical Substance* out of the *Air*; the more the *Earth* must needs be charged with it," and consequently the more earthquakes. "In *Boston* are more erected than any where else in *New England*; and *Boston* seems to be more dreadfully shaken. Oh! there is no getting out of the mighty Hand of God! If we think to avoid it in the *Air*, we cannot in the *Earth*: Yea it may grow more fatal." To this Winthrop replied in an appendix of his own: "I should think, though with the utmost deference to superior judgements, that the pathetic exclamation, which comes next, might well enough have been spared. 'O! there is no getting out of the mighty hand of GOD!' For I cannot believe, that in the whole town of *Boston*, where so many iron points are erected, there is so much as one person, who is so weak, so ignorant, so foolish, or, to say all in one word, so atheistical, as ever to have entertained a single thought, that it is possible, by the help of a few yards of wire, to 'get out of the mighty hand of GOD.' " JA's comments are attached to this paragraph of Winthrop's.

[3] JA's faulty grammar is retained as in MS.

MONDAY. DECEMBER 18TH. 1758

I this Evening delivered to Mr. Field, a Declaration in Trespass for a Rescue.[1] I was obliged to finish it, without sufficient examination. If it should escape an Abatement, it is quite indigested, and unclerk-like. I am ashamed of it, and concerned for it. If my first Writt should be abated, if I should throw a large Bill of Costs on my first Client, my

Character and Business will suffer greatly. It will be said, I dont understand my Business. No one will trust his Interest in my hands. I never Saw a Writt, on that Law of the Province. I was perplexed, and am very anxious about it. Now I feel the Dissadvantages of Putnams Insociability, and neglect of me. Had he given me now and then a few Hints concerning Practice, I should be able to judge better at this Hour than I can now. I have Reason to complain of him. But, it is my Destiny to dig Treasures with my own fingers. No Body will lend me or sell me a Pick axe. How this first Undertaking will terminate, I know not. I hope the Dispute will be settled between them, or submitted, and so my Writt never come to an Examination. But if it should I must take the Consequences. I must assume a Resolution, to bear without freting.

Heard Parson Wibirt exert his Casuistry to J. Spear.[2] Warned him against selling his [drowned?] Sheep for merchantable Mutton. It was not so nutritive nor palatable as Mutton butchered and dressed, and therefore, was not worth the same Price, and it would be an Imposition and a Cheat that his Conscience must disapprove to describe it and sell it as good Mutton. He could not [*sentence unfinished*]

[1] In the case of Field *v.* Lambert.
[2] This detached paragraph may have been written on 19 December.

WEDNESDAY [20 DECEMBER].

I am this forenoon, resuming the Study of Van Muyden. I begin at the 99th Page.

THURDSDAY [21 DECEMBER].

Yesterday and to day I have read loud, Tullius 4 Orations against Cataline. The Sweetness and Grandeur of his sounds, and the Harmony of his Numbers give Pleasure enough to reward the Reading if one understood none of his meaning. Besides I find it, a noble Exercise. It exercises my Lungs, raises my Spirits, opens my Porr[s], quickens the Circulations, and so contributes much to Health.

TUESDAY, 26 OF DECEMBER.

Being the Evening after Christmas, the Dr. and I spent the Evening with Mr. Cleverly[1] and Major Miller.[2] Mr. Cleverly was chearful, alert, sociable and complaisant. So much good sense, and knowledge, so much good Humour and Contentment, and so much Poverty, are not to be found, in any other House I believe in this Province. I am amazed that a man of his Inginuity, and sprightliness, can be so shiftless. But what avails a noisy fame, a plentiful fortune, and great figure and Consideration in the World? Neither Prat nor Gridley, Mayhew nor Eliot, Stockbridge nor Hersey appear more easy and happy with all their wealth and Reputation, than he with neither. Major Miller was sedate, but the Conversation was not to his Taste. He began to tell what this and that fellow said, what Coll. Oliver[3] did at Dorchester and what he did at Deadham, but he said very little on the whole. Both of them took unused freedoms with Coll. Quincy and his Brother.[4] They are determined to esteem them both Knaves and fools.

[1] Probably Joseph Cleverly (1713–1802), Harvard 1733, JA's first schoolmaster.

[2] Ebenezer Miller (1730–1811), of Braintree; militia officer, selectman, Episcopalian, and loyalist.

[3] Andrew Oliver (1706–1774), Harvard 1724; secretary of the Province and later lieutenant governor.

[4] Edmund Quincy (1703–1788), fourth of his name and brother of "Colonel" Josiah. His Boston mercantile firm having gone into bankruptcy, Edmund was currently a farmer in Braintree, living in what is now known as the "Dorothy Q." house, still standing on Hancock Street in Quincy.

FRIDAY [29 DECEMBER].

Let me see, if Bob P[aine] dont pick up this Story to laugh at. Lambert will laugh no doubt, and will tell the story to every man he sees, and will squib me about it, whenever he sees me. He is impudent and unfair enough, to turn this on every Occasion to my Disadvantage. Impudence, Drollery, Villany, in Lambert, Indiscretion, Inconsideration, Irresolution, and ill Luck in me, and Stinginess as well as ill Luck on the Side of Field, all unnite in this Case to injure me.

Fields Wrath waxed hot this morning. When he found himself defeated a second time.[1] He wished the affair in Hell, called Lambert a Devil and said, "That's always the Way in this Town, when any strange Devil comes into Town, he has all the Priviledges of the Town."

Let me Note the fatal Consequences of Precipitation. My first Determination, what to do in this affair was right. I determined not to meddle. But By the cruel Reproaches of my Mother, by the Importunity of Field, and by the fear of having it thought I was incapable of drawing the Writt, I was seduced from that determination, and what is the Consequence? The Writt is defective. It will be said, I undertook the Case but was unable to manage it. This Nonsuit will be in the mouth of every Body. Lambert will proclaim it.

November 18th 1755 We had a severe
Shock of an Earthquake. It continued near
four Minutes. I was then at my father's
in Braintree, and awoke out of my Sleep
in the midst of it. the house seemed to roak
and reel and crack as if it would fall in
ruins about us. 7 Chimnies were shook
by it within one mile of my father's house.

January the 14th. 1756

14   At Worcester, a very rainy Day, kept School
      in the forenoon, but after it the afternoon
      because of the weather & my own indisposition.
      A fair morning & pretty warm. Kept School.

15   Drank Tea at Mr Swan's, with mr Thayer.

16   Fryday. a fine morning. a large white
      Frost upon the ground. Reading Hutcheson's
      Introduction to moral Phylosophy. a cloudy
      Day, an Evening. Mr Charles Mayor Chandler...

17   Saturday. a cloudy, dull Day. Some frost
      about noon. N rain. towards night
      Μισήμαι, τα καθαρμιατα [τ]ο ν η ς. Plato.

18   Sunday. a fair morning. Heard mr Maccarty
      Monday. a rainy Day.

19
20   Tuesday. a fair, warm, Spring like Day.
      Drank Tea & Supped at mr Greene's.

21   Wednesday. a very rainy day. dined
      with Coll Chandler. Spent the Eve...
      at mr maccartys. kept School, returning...

      Thursday. a rainy morning, froze & pretty
23   air, drank Tea & Supped at mr Barns.
      Fryday. a fair & agreable Day. kept School.
      Drank Tea at Coll Chandler's, and spent
      the Evening at major Gardiners.

24   Saturday. a very high, cold wind. warm...
      & cloudy. P.M. warm & fair.
25   Sunday. a cold Weather. heard mr Thayer
      preach. very ingenious discourses...
      From 10 to 6 & Supped att Coll Chandlers

26   Monday. a sharp [thickening] fire. got out for
      weather. arrived 20 cloc[k]

27   Tuesday. att my uncles.
28   Wednesday. Letto which weather. Very raw...
29   Thursday. Still cloudy weather. Set out for

3. JOHN ADAMS BEGINS HIS DIARY

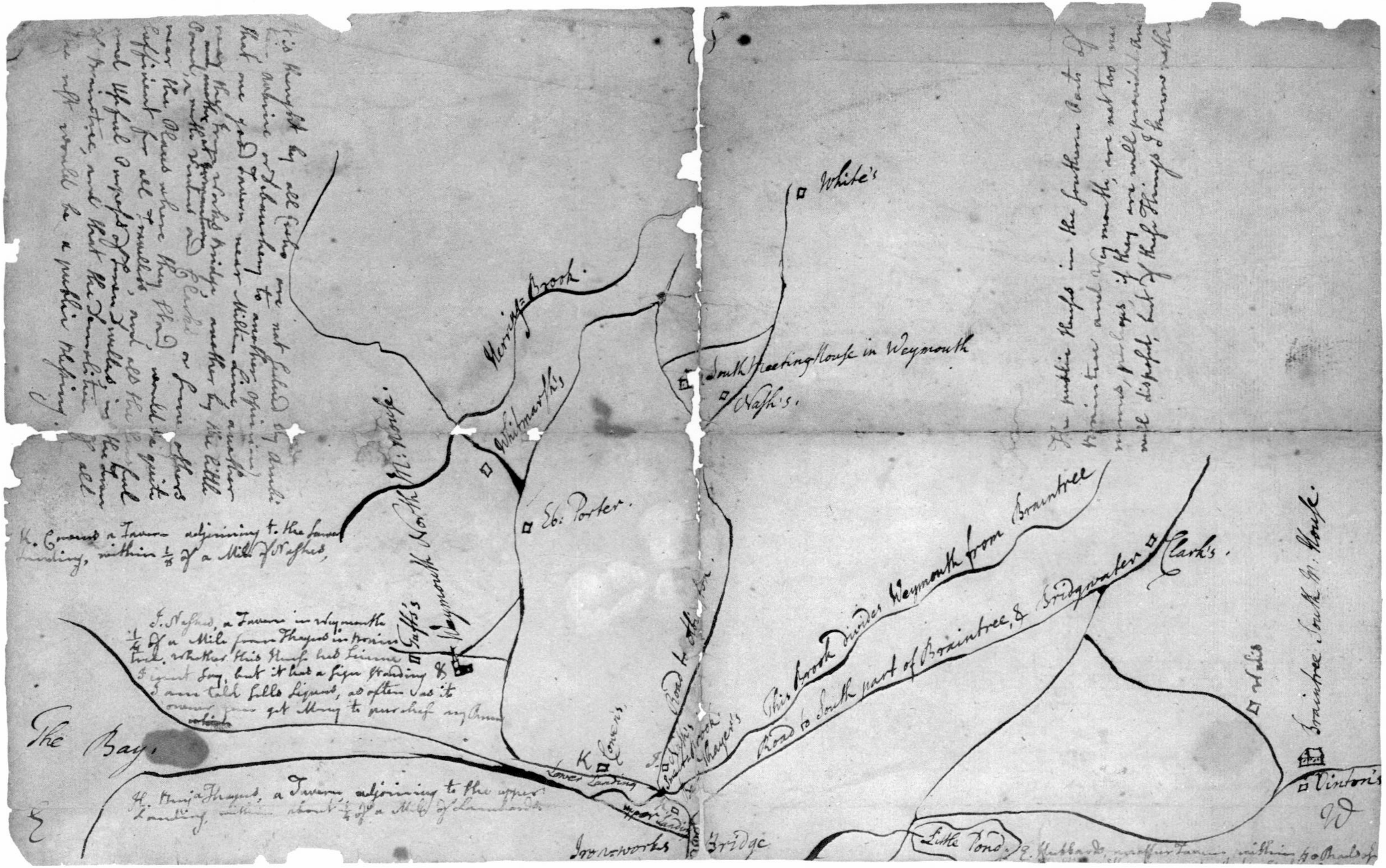

4. JOHN ADAMS' SKETCH MAP OF TAVERNS IN BRAINTREE AND WEYMOUTH, ABOUT 1761

Let me never undertake to draw a Writt, without sufficient Time to examine, and digest in my mind all the Doubts, Queries, Objections that may arise.—But no Body will know of any Abatement except this omission of the County.

An opinion will spread among the People, that I have not Cunning enough to cope with Lambert. I should endeavour at my first setting out to possess the People with an Opinion of my subtilty[2] and Cunning. But this affair certainly looks like a strong Proof of the Contrary.

[1] Sentences punctuated as in MS.
[2] MS: "sublilty."

SATURDAY [30 DECEMBER].

How a whole Family is put into a Broil sometimes by a Trifle.[1] My P. and M.[2] disagreed in Opinion about boarding Judah, that Difference occasioned passionate Expressions, those Expressions made Dolly and Judah snivell, Peter[3] observed and mentioned it, I faulted him for it, which made him mad and all was breaking into a flame, when I quitted the Room, and took up Tully to compose myself. My P. continued cool and pleasant a good while, but had his Temper roused at last, tho he uttered not a rash Word, but resolutely asserted his Right to govern. My Mamma was determined to know what my P. charged a Week for the Girls Board. P. said he had not determined what to charge but would have her say what it was worth. She absolutely refused to say. But "I will know if I live and breath. I can read yet. Why dont you tell me, what you charge? You do it on purpose to teaze me. You are mighty arch this morning. I wont have all the Towns Poor brought here, stark naked, for me to clothe for nothing. I wont be a slave to other folks folk for nothing."—And after the 2 Girls cryed.—"I must not speak a Word [to][4] your Girls, Wenches, Drabbs. I'le kick both their fathers, presently. [You][5] want to put your Girls over me, to make me a slave to your Wenches." Thus when the Passions of Anger and Resentment are roused one Word will inflame them into Rage.

This was properly a conjugal Spat. A Spat between Husband and Wife. I might have made more critical observations on the Course and Progress of human Passions if I had steadily observed the faces, Eyes, Actions and Expressions of both Husband and Wife this morning.

M. seems to have no Scheme and Design in her Mind to persuade P. to resign his Trust of Selectman. But when she feels the Trouble and Difficulties that attend it she fretts, squibs, scolds, rages, raves.

None of her Speeches seem the Effect of any Design to get rid of the Trouble, but only natural Expressions of the Pain and Uneasiness, which that Trouble occasions. Cool Reasoning upon the Point with my Father, would soon bring her to his mind or him to hers.

Let me from this remark distinctly the Different Effects of Reason and Rage. Reason, Design, Scheme, governs pretty constantly in Put[nam]s House, but, Passion, Accident, Freak, Humour, govern in this House. Put knows what he wants, and knows the Proper means to procure it, and how to employ them. He employs, Reason, Ridicule, Contempt, to work upon his Wife.

I feel a fluttering concern upon my mind.[6]

Andrew Oliver is a very sagacious Trifler.[7] He can decypher, with surprizing Penetration and Patience, any Thing wrote in signs, whether English, Latin, or French. But to what Purpose? Tis like great skill and Dexterity in Gaming, used only for Amuzement. With all his Expertness he never wins any Thing. But this is his Way to fame. One man would be a famous Orator, another a famous Physician, another a famous Phylosopher, or a 4th a famous Dancer, and he would be a famous Decypherer. But I am quite content with the 24 Letters without inventing all the possible Marks that might signify the same Things. Ned Q[uincy] is learning to be such another Nugator Sagax, an ar[t]ificial arrangement of Dots and Squares.

[1] The whole of the entry recounting this domestic incident was omitted by CFA in editing JA's Diary.

[2] Papa and Mama, or Pater and Mater. Susanna (1709-1797), daughter of Peter and Ann (White) Boylston of Muddy River, or Brookline, married Deacon John Adams on 31 Oct. 1734; she married, 2d, John Hall, 3 Dec. 1766.

[3] JA's younger brother, Peter Boylston Adams (1738-1823); later a captain in the militia and holder of numerous local offices.

[4] MS reads "for"—clearly an inadvertence by the diarist.

[5] MS: "I"—another inadvertence.

[6] This and the following paragraph, each separated in the MS by lines across the page from what precedes, may have been written on either 30 or 31 Dec. 1758 or even in Jan. 1759 preceding the several undated entries that apparently belong to that month.

[7] Andrew Oliver Jr. (1731-1799), Harvard 1749, who published an *Essay on Comets*, Salem, 1772 (Eliot, *Biog. Dict. of N.E.*).

WEDNESDAY [JANUARY 1759].[1]

Drank Tea at Coll. Quincies. Spent the Evening there, and the next morning. In the afternoon, rode out to German Town. H[annah] Q[uincy] or O.[2] Suppose you was in your Study, engaged in the Investigation of some Point of Law, or Philosophy, and your Wife should interrupt you accidentally and break the Thread of your Thoughts, so that you never could recover it?

Ego. No man, but a crooked Richard, would blame his Wife, for such an accidental Interruption. And No Woman, but a Xantippe, would insist upon her Husbands Company, after he had given her his Reasons for desiring to be alone.

O. Should you like to spend your Evenings, at Home in reading and conversing with your Wife, rather than to spend them abroad in Taverns or with other Company?

Ego. Should prefer the Company of an agreable Wife, to any other Company for the most Part, not always. I should not like to be imprisoned at home.

O. Suppose you had been abroad, and came home fatigued and perplexed, with Business, or came out of your Study, wearied and perplexed with Study, and your Wife should meet you with an unpleasant, or an inattentive face, how should you feel?

I would flee my Country, or she should.

O. How shall a Pair avoid falling into Passion or out of humour, upon some Occasions, and treating each other unkindly.

Ego. By resolving against it. Forbid angry words &c.? [3] Every Person knows that all are liable to mistakes, and Errors, and if the Husband finds his Wife in one he should [...] reasonably [4] and convince her of it, instead of being angry, and so on the Contrary. But if it happens, that both get out of humour and an angry dispute ensues, yet both will be sorry when their anger subsides, and mutually forgive and ask forgiveness, and love each other the better for it, for the future.

O. thinks more than most of her Sex. She is always thinking or Reading. She sitts and looks steadily, one way, very often, several minutes together in thought. E. [5] looks pert, sprightly, gay, but thinks and reads much less than O.

[...] [6] expos'd himself to Ridicule, by affectation, by Pretensions to Strength of mind and Resolution, to depth and Penetration. Pretensions to Wisdom and Virtue, superiour to all the World, will not be supported by Words only. If I tell a man I am wiser and better than he or any other man, he will either despize, or hate, or pity me, or perhaps all 3.—I have not conversed enough with the World, to behave rightly. I talk to Paine about Greek, that makes him laugh. I talk to Sam Quincy about Resolution, and being a great Man, and study and improving Time, which makes him laugh. I talk to Ned, about the

Folly of affecting to be a Heretick, which makes him mad. I talk to Hannah and Easther about the folly of Love, about despizing it, about being above it, pretend to be insensible of tender Passions, which makes them laugh. I talk to Mr. Wibirt about the Decline of Learning, tell him, I know no young fellow who promises to make a figure, cast Sneers on Dr. Marsh for not knowing the Value of old Greek and Roman Authors, ask "when will a Genius rise, that will shave his Beard, or let it grow rather and sink himself in a Cell, in order to make a figure." I talk to Parson Smith [7] about despizing gay Dress, grand Buildings, great Estates, fame, &c. and being contented with what will satisfy the real Wants of Nature.

All This is Affectation and Ostentation. 'Tis Affectation of Learning, and Virtue and Wisdom, which I have not, and it is a weak fondness to shew all that I have, and to be thot to have more than I have.

Besides this I have insensibly fallen into a Habit of affecting Wit and Humour, of Shrugging my Shoulders, and moving [and] distorting the Muscles of my face. My Motions are stiff and uneasy, ungraceful, and my attention is unsteady and irregular.

These are Reflections on myself that I make. They are faults, Defects, Fopperies and follies, and Disadvantages. Can I mend these faults and supply these Defects?

O. makes Observations on Actions, Characters, Events, in Popes Homer, Milton, Popes Poems, any Plays, Romances &c. that she reads and asks Questions about them in Company. What do you think of Helen? What do you think of Hector &c. What Character do you like best? Did you wish the Plot had not been discovered in Venice preserved? [8] These are Questions that prove a thinking Mind. E. asks none such.

Thus in a Wild Campaign, a dissipating Party of Pleasure, observations and Improvement may be made. Some Foppery, and folly and Vice, may be discerned in ones self, and Motives, and Methods may be collected to subdue it. Some Virtue, or agreable Quality may be observed in ones self and improved and cherished, or in another and transplanted into ones self.

O. Tho O. knows and can practice the Art of pleasing, yet she fails, sometimes. She lets us see a face of Ridicule, and Spying, sometimes, inadvertently, tho she looks familiarly, and pleasantly for the most part. She is apparently frank, but really reserved, seemingly pleased, and almost charmed, when she is really laughing with Contempt. Her face and Hart have no Correspondence.

Hannah checks Parson Wibirt with Irony.—It was very sawcy to disturb you, very sawcy Im sure &c.

I am very thankful for these Checks. Good Treatment makes me think I am admired, beloved, and [my] own Vanity will be indulged in me. So I dismiss my Gard and grow weak, silly, vain, conceited, ostentatious. But a Check, a frown, a sneer, a Sarcasm rouses my Spirits, makes me more careful and considerate. It may in short be made a Question, whether good Treatment or bad is the best for me, i.e. wether Smiles, kind Words, respectful Actions, dont betray me into Weaknesses and Littlenesses, that frowns, Satirical Speeches and contemptuous Behaviour, make me avoid.

Mr. Wibirt has not an unsuspicious openness of face. You may see in his face, a silly Pain when he hears the Girls, a whispering, and snickering.

Is Mrs. Palmer[9] so infinitely sensible of such soft, tender scenes and actions, or, does she affect to appear so? Or is it partly affected and partly real?

Popularity, next to Virtue and Wisdom, ought to be aimed at. For it is the Dictate of Wisdom, and is necessary to the practice of Virtue in most.

Yesterday, went down to defend an Action for an old Horse vs. Samll. Spear. This was undertaking the relief of distressed Poverty, the Defence of Innocence and Justice, vs. Oppression, and Injustice. Capt. Thayer[10] and Major Crosby too had told the Plaintiff that he could not maintain his Action, and advised him to drop it or agree it. And Thayer spoke out, "I would have these Parties agree." I did not clearly understand the Case, had no Time to prepare to fix in my mind beforehand the Steps that I should take. And Capt. Hollis, Major Miller, and Captn. Thayer, were all 3 very active, and busy and interested themselves in the suit. It was a scene of absolute Confusion. Major Crosby persuading an Agreement, the Parties raging and scolding, I arguing and the 3 Voluntiers proposing each one his Project. And all the Spectators smiling, whispering &c. My Attention was dissipated. I committed oversights, omissions, inexpert Management. I should have adhered to the Relation my Client gave me, and believed nothing that came from the other side, without Proof. I should have insisted upon the Entry, and opposed any Motion for an Adjournment till next Week or Continuance till next Hour, to send for Witnesses. For Madam Q. could not swear any Thing, that can support this Action. Should have offered to admit all she could say. If I had strictly pursued the story, that my Client told me, I should have demanded an Entry of the Action, or else a Dismission of the Defendant with Costs. It was equally idle and tame [lame?] to continue the Action, to send for a Witness, and to submit it to referees. For the Witness if sent for could not support the Action, and to submit the original Debt to Referees, was to submit nothing. For by the original Agreement, nothing was due. Agreement was to take the Horse and keep him, and if he lived till April, to pay 2 dollars for him, but if he died before, to pay nothing. Now he actually died in February, and therefore nothing by Contract was to be paid. The Keeping of so old an Horse was more than the service he could do, was worth. The Hay he eat would have hired more riding and drawing than that Horse did thro that Winter.

If Spear had applied to such as know, he would not have brot that Writ. But Deputy Sheriffs, petit Justices, and pettifogging Meddlers, like Faxon, Niles, Hollis, attempt to draw Writts, and draw them wrong oftener than they do right.

The Declaration was an Indeb[itatus] Ass[umpsit] with an Account annexed, for a Horse, sold and delivered. He could have proved, by Spears Confession, that he had the Horse, but could not prove the Sale or Delivery of the Horse, nor could he prove any Price agreed on by the Parties. Far from producing Proof of any express Price agreed on by the Parties at the sale and Delivery, he cant prove the Sale and delivery itself. Now to maintain an Action on an Indeb. Ass. the Plaintiff must aver in his Declaration, and prove at the Trial, a certain, express Price, agreed on by the Parties, or else a customary Price. Tis true there is this Exception to the general Rule, that Merchants and Tradesmen, who keep running Accounts open with their Customers, and deal out their Commodities and Manufactures in small Parcells, shall be allowed to produce their Account Books in Evidence, and if they will swear that they made the Entries of the several Articles att the times they were delivered, and that they charged the Price for them, that was at that time customary, they shall be allowed to recover. But is this Case like that. Will Mr. Spear swear that he entered this Article at the time of the Sale and delivery, and will he swear that he charged the customary Price? Pray what is the Customary Price of a

Horse. Are not some customar[il]y bot for £100 and some for less than £100.

I must study how to manage Eb. and Atherton Thayer and Hollis, and Eb. Miller and Faxon. They are meddlers, hinters, and Projectors. I should have made a Motion to the Justice, that either the Defendant or I might be consulted in the settlement of this Affair, and that Miller, Hollis and Thayer who had no concern with it, might not determine it, as they please.—I pray your Honour to silence the Clamour of those who have no Concern with the Matter, that those who have may be heard.

Capt. Thayer pretends to great Knowledge in the Law. He could not bear to lose the Honor of knowing and telling Mr. Spear, that an Indeb. Ass. could not lie, but that Quant[um] Mer[uit] could [in] this Case. He was proud, bragged of it before all the Company, bragged, boast[ed], was ostentatious of his Knowledge in Law. So many hinting advice, making Proposals, &c., make Confusion.

O. Pain aims at so many Things, but especially at getting Cash, that he will be distracted. He pursues Cash with all his Hart and soul. He writes well and tells a very droll story, but he is very peevish, fretful, odd tempered. He thinks himself in high favour with the Ladies, but he little thinks how he is blasted sometimes.

[1] This is one of only two entries in Jan. 1759 that bear even an indication of the day of the week on which they were written, the next fully dated entry being that of 1 Feb. 1759. The January entries have therefore been placed in two groups but with intervals of space between what may be entries written on different days. A word of caution: since the pages of the MS are loose, *it is not always possible to tell with certainty what the original order of the entries was.* Their order as printed by CFA is highly arbitrary.

[2] In the MS the words "H.Q. or" have been crossed out but in so halfhearted a way that they provide a key to the name of a girl who courted JA rather more energetically than he courted her. This was Hannah (1736–1826), daughter of Col. Josiah Quincy, who was in 1760 to marry Dr. Bela Lincoln. The initial "O." stands for a fanciful name that may have been Olinda or Orlinda (Salisbury, *Family-Memorials*, 1:359; JA to Richard Cranch [1759?], in Adams Papers).

[3] In the MS this sentence is badly rubbed, and some words have been scored out; the present reading is highly conjectural.

[4] The illegible verb may be "use," in which case JA meant to write "use reason," as CFA rendered this passage.

[5] Esther (1738–1810), daughter of Edmund Quincy and Hannah's first cousin; she married JA's friend Jonathan Sewall in 1764.

[6] Apparently two initials, now illegible.

[7] Rev. William Smith (1707–1783), Harvard 1725, of Weymouth, who was in 1764 to become JA's father-in-law.

[8] *Venice Preserv'd*, a play by Thomas Otway produced and published in London in 1682.

[9] Mary (Cranch) Palmer (d. 1790), wife of Deacon Joseph Palmer of Germantown and sister of JA's friend Richard Cranch.

[10] Capt. Ebenezer Thayer (1721–1794), son and father of other Ebenezer Thayers, was for many years a Braintree

selectman and representative to the General Court. JA disliked him on two counts: he kept a tavern in the Middle Precinct and dabbled in legal practice.

TUESDAY [JANUARY 1759].

Took a ride after Dinner to Gullivers Brook in Milton, returned home. Went over to Deacon Belchers and drank Tea, and in the Evening walked home with O. Strolled by the House down to Mr. Borlands, then back down the farm Lane as far as the Gate, then back, up the Hill, and home.[1] Met Mr. Wibirt at the Coll's door, went with him to his Lodgings, slept with him and spent all the next day with him, reading the Reflections on Courtship and Marriage, and afternoon the 4 Satires of John Oldham on the Jesuits, and his Satyr on a Woman who by breaking her Engagement had killed his friend, and his Bion, or Lamentation on the Death of the Earl of Rochester, a Pastoral in Imitation of the Greek of Moschus, a Piece as soft, and tender, as his Satyrs are nervous and malignant, or perhaps more properly indignant.

The other night, the Choice of Hercules came into my mind, and left Impressions there which I hope will never be effaced nor long unheeded. I thought of writing a Fable, on the same Plan, but accommodated, by omitting some Circumstances and inserting others, to my own Case.

Let Virtue address me—"Which, dear Youth, will you prefer? a Life of Effeminacy, Indolence and obscurity, or a Life of Industry, Temperance, and Honour? Take my Advice, rise and mount your Horse, by the Mornings dawn, and shake away amidst the great and beautiful scenes of Nature, that appear at that Time of the day, all the Crudities that are left in your stomach, and all the obstructions that are left in your Brains. Then return to your Study, and bend your whole soul to the Institutes of the Law, and the Reports of Cases, that have been adjudged by the Rules, in the Institutes. Let no trifling Diversion or amuzement or Company decoy you from your Books, i.e. let no Girl, no Gun, no Cards, no flutes, no Violins, no Dress, no Tobacco, no Laziness, decoy you from your Books. (By the Way, Laziness, Languor, Inattention, are my Bane, am too lazy to rise early and make a fire, and when my fire is made, at 10 o'clock my Passion for knowledge, fame, fortune or any good, is too languid, to make me apply with Spirit to my Books. And by Reason of my Inattention my mind is liable to be[2] called off from Law, by a Girl, a Pipe, a Poem, a Love Letter, a Spectator, a Play, &c.) But, keep your Law Book or some Point of Law in your mind at least 6 Hours in a day. (I grow too minute and lengthy.)

Labour to get distinct Ideas of Law, Right, Wrong, Justice, Equity. Search for them in your own mind, in Roman, grecian, french, English Treatises of natural, civil, common, Statute Law. Aim at an exact Knowledge of the Nature, End, and Means of Government. Compare the different forms of it with each other and each of them with their Effects on public and private Happiness. Study Seneca, Cicero, and all other good moral Writers. Study Montesque, Bolinbroke, [Vinnius?], &c. and all other good, civil Writers, &c."

Prat. There is not a Page in Flavels Works without several sentences of Latin. Yet the common People admire him. They admire his Latin as much as his English, and understand it as well. [...][3] preached the best sermon that ever I heard. It was plain common sense. But other sermons have no sense at all. They take the Parts of them out of their Concordances and connect them together Hed and Tail.

How greatly elevated, above common People, and above Divines is this Lawyer. Is not this Vanity, littleness of mind?

What am I doing? Shall I sleep away my whole 70 Years. No by every Thing I swear I will renounce the Contemplative, and betake myself to an active roving Life by Sea or Land, or else I will attempt some uncommon unexpected Enterprize in Law. Let me lay the Plan and arouse Spirit enough to push boldly. I swear I will push myself into Business. I will watch my Opportunity, to speak in Court, and will strike with surprize—surprize Bench, Bar, Jury, Auditors and all. Activity, Boldness, Forwardness, will draw attention. Ile not lean, with my Elbows on the Table, forever like Read, Swift, Fitch,[4] Skinner, Story, &c. But I'le not forego the Pleasure of ranging the Woods, Climbing Cliffs, walking in fields, Meadows, by Rivers, Lakes, &c., and confine my self to a Chamber for nothing. Ile have some Boon, in Return, Exchange, fame, fortune, or something.

Here are 2 nights, and one day and an half, spent in a softening, enervating, dissipating, series of hustling, pratling, Poetry, Love, Courtship, Marriage. During all this Time, I was seduced into the Course of unmanly Pleasures, that Vice describes to Hercules, forgetful of the glorious Promises of Fame, Immortality, and a good Conscience, which Virtue, makes to the same Hero, as Rewards of a hardy, toilsome, watchful Life, in the service of Man kind. I could reflect with more satisfaction on an equal space of Time spent in a painful Research of the Principles of Law, or a resolute attempt of the Powers of Eloquence.

But where is my Attention? Is it fixed from sunrise to midnight, on grecian, roman, gallic, british Law, History, Virtue, Eloquence? I dont see clearly The objects, that I am after. They are often out of Sight. Moats, Attoms, feathers, are blown into my Eyes, and blind me. Who can see distinctly the Course he is to take, and the objects that he pursues, when in the midst of a whirl Wind of dust, straws, attoms and feathers.

Let me make this Remark. In P[arson] Wib[ird]s Company, Something is to be learned, of human Nature, human Life, Love, Court Ship, Marriage. He has spent much of his Life, from his Youth, in Conversation with young and old Persons of both sexes, maried and unmaried, and therefore has his Mind stuffed with Remarks and stories of human Virtues, and Vices, Wisdom and folly, &c. But his Opinion, out of Poetry, Love, Court ship, Mariage, Politicks, War, Beauty, Grace, Decency &c. is not very valuable. His Soul is lost, in a dronish effeminacy. Ide rather be lost in a Whirlwind of Activity, Study, Business, great and good Designs of promoting the Honour, Grandeur, Wealth, Happiness of Mankind.

He says he has not Resolution enough to court a Woman. He wants to find one that will charm, conquer him and rouse his spirit. He is like a Turkey, retiring to Roost. She is difficult, looks a[t] several Places, to roost on, before she fixes on any, and when she has fixed on one she stretches her Neck, squats, and changes her Posture several Times before she flies up. This Simile is pretty and humorous enough. He is benevolent, sociable, friendly, and has a pretty Imagination, Wit, some Humour but little grandeur, Strength, Penetration of m[ind.] In short, he has an amiable and elegant, not a great mind. Paine has neither an amiable nor a great Mind. There is too much Malignance, Envy, Conceit and ostentation, in it, to be amiable, and too much Unsteadiness to be great.

Wib[ir]t exposes very freely to me his Disposition, the past and present state of his mind, his susceptibility of Impressions from Beauty &c., his Being amourous, and inclined to love, his Want of Resolution to Court, his Regard, fondness, for O.,[5] his Intimacy and dalliance with her &c. He has if I mistake not a good many half born Thoughts, of courting O.

[1] On this sentimental stroll JA and Hannah Quincy walked past her father's house (on the site of the old Adams Academy building in present Quincy Square) and then down past the house and into the farm that were later to become JA's own homestead upon his return from Europe twenty-nine years later.

"Mr. Borland" was John Borland (1728–1775), who in 1750 had married Anna, daughter of the late Leonard Vassall, a wealthy sugar-planter from the West Indies. Vassall had settled in Boston and built, probably in 1731, a summer home in the northern part of Braintree on the "old coast road" that ran from Boston to Plymouth. His daughter inherited the property, but the Borlands lived here only occasionally, their principal residence being in Cambridge. At the very beginning of the siege of Boston John Borland died. "He lost his life by a fall in attempting to get upon the top of his house [in Boston] to see an expedition to Hog Island" (Jonathan Sewall to Thomas Robie, 7 June 1775, MHS, *Procs.*, 2d ser., 10 [1895–1896]:412). This circumstance aided his widow, who in 1776 fled with other loyalists to England, to recover her Braintree property at the close of the Revolution; she promptly sold it to her son Leonard Vassall Borland; and in 1787, while still in England, JA bought it through agents in Boston. Thereafter Adamses were to occupy it, expanding the house and dependencies and improving the grounds in each generation, until 1927, when BA, its last occupant, died. In 1946 the family, which had formed the Adams Memorial Association to care for it, presented the homestead, long simply known as "the Old House," to the United States, and it is now the Adams National His-

toric Site, 135 Adams Street, Quincy.

On the Vassalls and Borlands see *NEHGR*, 17 (1863):56–61, 113–128; Lucius R. Paige, *History of Cambridge*, Boston, 1877, p. 493, 674–675; Jones, *Loyalists of Mass.*, p. 41–42. A profusely illustrated historical and descriptive sketch of the Old House was published by HA2, "The Adams Mansion," *Old-Time New England*, 19:3–17 (July 1928); an enlarged reprint was issued by the Adams Memorial Association, Quincy, 1935. Also available is an eight-page leaflet, *Adams National Historic Site*, issued by the National Park Service. There is no substitute, however, for a visit to homestead itself. No other house in the United States has been the home of so many successive generations of political and intellectual leaders, and no restored structures and sites can quite compare with originals that have been altered only by time and are still furnished with the possessions of those who lived there.

[2] MS: "me."

[3] Possibly "Friend Park [Parke, Parkes?]."

[4] Samuel Fitch (1724–1799), Yale 1742; Boston lawyer and member of JA's legal "sodality"; loyalist.

[5] The initials "H.Q." have been deleted in the MS before "O."

FEB. 1.

I intend a Journey to Worcester to morrow. How many observations shall I make on the People at West Town, and Worcester, and how many new Ideas, Hints, Rules of Law, and Eloquence, shall I acquire before I return? Let my Journal answer this Question, after my Return.

FEB. 2. 1759.

At Westtown, in Dr. Webbs Chamber at Hammonds. His landlady is an odd Woman. She seems good Natured, and obliging to[o], but she has so many shruggs, grimaces, affectations of Witt, Cunning, and Humour, as make her ridiculous. She is awkward, shamefaced, bashful, yet would fain seem sprightly, witty, &c. She is a Squaddy,[1] masculine, Creature, with a swarthy pale face, a great staring, rolling Eye, a rare Collection of disagreable Qualities.

I have read several Letters, this afternoon and Evening, in the Turkish Spy.[2]

[1] Squaddy: "Short and thick-set; squat, squab" (*OED*).

[2] *Letters Writ by a Turkish Spy* ... *at Paris*, prototype of numerous "secret histories," was first published in Paris, 1684, was later greatly amplified, and became a popular work in both French and English. On its multiple and probably international authorship see Joseph E. Tucker, "On the Authorship of *The Turkish Spy* ...," Bibliog. Soc. of Amer., *Papers*, 52 (1958):34–47, and references there.

WORCESTER FEB. 11. 1759.

I have been in this Town a Week this night. How much have I improved my Health by Exercise, or my mind by Study or Conversation, in this Space? I have exercised little, eat and drank and slept intemperately. Have inquired a little, of Mr. Putnam and of Abel Willard, concerning some Points of Practice in Law. But dining once at Coll. Chandlers, once at Mr. Pains, once at the Doctors, drinking Tea once at Mr. Paines, once at the Drs. and spending one Evening at the Drs., one at Gardi[ner]s and several at Putnams in Company has wasted insensibly the greatest and best Part of my time since I have been in Town. Oh how I have fulfilled the vain Boast I made to Dr. Webb, of reading 12 Hours a day! What a fine scene of study is this office! a fine Collection of Law, oratory, History, and Phylosophy. But I must not stay. I must return to Braintree. I must attend a long Superiour Court at Boston. How shall I pursue my Plan of Study?

Bo[b] Paine acted a scene that happened on the Com[mon] when the Troops were reviewed by the Governor.[1] People crouded very near to the Troops, till a highland serjeant of a gigantic size, and accoutred with a Variety of Instruments of Cruelty and Death, stalked out with his vast Halbert to drive them back. He brandished his Halbert and smote it on the Ground and cryed with a broad, Roaring Voice, Sta ban, i.e. Stand back. Sta ba. His size, armour, Phyz and Voice, frighted People so that they presd backwards and almost trampled on one another. But in the highest of his fury, he sprung onward, and shri[ek]ed out Sta, but then saw some Ladies before him, which softened him. At once, he drops his Halbert, takes off his Bonnet, and makes a very complaisant Bow, pray Ladies, please to stand a little back, you will see a great deal better.

Pain lifts up his Eyes and Hands to Heaven and cryes, of all Instruments of Defence, good Heavens, give me Beauty. It could soften the ferocity of your highland serjeant.

76

Paine and Dr. Wendel took Katy Quincy and Polly Jackson, and led them into a retired Room and there laughed, and screamed, and kissed and hussled. They came out glowing like furnaces.

Mr. Marsh.[2] Father Flynt has been very gay and sprightly, this sickness.[3] Coll. Quincy was to see him, a fast day, and was or appeared to be, as he was about taking leave of the old Gentleman, very much affected. The Tears flowed very fast.—I hope Sir says he in [a] Voice of Grief, you will excuse my Passions.—Ay, prithy, says the old Man, I dont care much for you, nor your Passions neither.

F. Morris said to him, "you are going Sir to Abrahams Bosom, but I dont know but I shall reach there first."—"Ay if you are a going there, I dont want to go."

I spent one Evening this Week at Billy Belchers. I sat, book in Hand, on one side of the fire, while Dr. Wendell, Billy Belcher and Stephen Cleverly and another young Gentleman sat, in silence, round the Card Table, all the Evening. Two Evenings I spent att Samll. Quincys, in the same manner, Dr. Gardiner, Henry Q., Ned Q., and S.Q. all playing Cards the whole Evening. This is the wise and salutary amuzement, that young Gentlemen take every Evening in this Town, playing Cards, drinking Punch and Wine, Smoaking Tobacco, swearing &c. while 100 of the best Books lie on the shelves, Desks, and Chairs, in the same room. This is not Misspence of Time. This is a wise, a profitable, Improvement of Time. Cards, and Back Gammon, are fashionable Diversions. I'le be curst if any young fellow can study, in this town. What Pleasure can a young Gentleman, who is capable of thinking, take, in playing Cards? It gratifies none of the Senses, nor Sight, Hearing, taste, smell, feeling. It can entertain the Mind only by hushing its Clamours. Cards, Back Gammon are the great antidotes to Reflection, to thinking, that cruel Tyrant within Us. What Learning, or Sense, are we to expect from young Gentlemen, in whom a fondness for Cards, &c. outgrows and choaks the Desire of Knowledge?

[1] This detached entry and the following ones, all recording incidents at Braintree, must have been written at least several days after the preceding entry dated at Worcester, 11 February. The leaves of the MS being loose at this point, one cannot be sure of the original order of entries, but very likely these revealing fragments belong to late February or early March.

[2] Joseph Marsh (1710–1761?), Har-vard 1728, who had prepared JA for Harvard.

[3] Henry Flynt (1675–1760), Harvard 1693, usually known as "Tutor" Flynt from his long service as a Harvard tutor. His sister Dorothy married Judge Edmund Quincy (1681–1738), and he was thus an uncle of Col. Josiah Quincy and of Edmund Quincy (1703–1788), in whose house he frequently stayed. (Sibley-Shipton, *Harvard Graduates,*

4:162–167.) In the Adams Papers there is a paper endorsed "Of Father Flynt's Journey to Portsmouth and back to Cambridge Æ. 80," i.e. in 1754, written by David Sewall and probably sent by Sewall to his Harvard classmate JA in 1821. This entertaining account of a famous Harvard character was communicated by CFA to the Massachusetts Historical Society and was printed in its *Proceedings*, 1st ser., 16 (1878):5–11.

MARCH 14. 1759.

Reputation ought to be the perpetual subject of my Thoughts, and Aim of my Behaviour. How shall I gain a Reputation! How shall I Spread an Opinion of myself as a Lawyer of distinguished Genius, Learning, and Virtue. Shall I make frequent Visits in the Neighbourhood and converse familiarly with Men, Women and Children in their own Style, on the common Tittletattle of the Town, and the ordinary Concerns of a family, and so take every fair opportunity of shewing my Knowledge in the Law? But this will require much Thought, and Time, and a very particular Knowledge of the Province Law, and common Matters, of which I know much less than I do of the Roman Law. This would take up too much Thought and Time and Province Law.

Shall I endeavour to renew my Acquaintance with those young Gentlemen in Boston who were at Colledge with me and to extend my Acquaintance among Merchants, Shop keepers, Tradesmen, &c. and mingle with the Crowd upon Change, and trapes the Town house floor, with one and another, in order to get a Character in Town. But this too will be a lingering method and will require more Art and Address, and Patience too than I am Master of.

Shall I, by making Remarks, and proposing Questions [to] the Lawyers att the Bar, endeavour to get a great Character for Understanding and Learning with them. But this is slow and tedious, and will be ineffectual, for Envy, Jealousy, and self Intrest, will not suffer them to give a young fellow a free generous Character, especially me. Neither of these Projects will bear Examination, will avail.

Shall I look out for a Cause to Speak to, and exert all the Soul and all the Body I own, to cut a flash, strike amazement, to catch the Vulgar? In short shall I walk a lingering, heavy Pace or shall I take one bold determined Leap into the Midst of some Cash and Business? That is the Question. A bold Push, a resolute attempt, a determined Enterprize, or a slow, silent, imperceptible creeping. Shall I creep or fly.

Walked, this afternoon, along the side of the [Bushy?] Pond.[1] The Blackbirds were perched on the Trees round the Borders of the Pond, and singing. I saw a large flock of Crow Blackbirds alight on the Ground, in search of Grain or Worms, I suppose. The Birds that were behind were perpetually flying over the Heads of all the rest, and alighting in the front of the flock, so that each Bird was in the front and Rear by turns, and all were chattering. It looked like a hovering, half walking, half flying flock of Blackbirds. Soon after, they rose, and alighted on the neighbouring Apple Trees, chattering, and singing all the Time. At the same time, a Number of Crows were croaking, at a little distance on one side, and a wood Pecker and a blue bird were whistling, and cackling, at a little Distance on the other.—This is the first vernal scene I have observed this season. So many Birds of several different species, all singing, chattering, whistling, fluttering, flying, hopping, leaping, on the ground, in the Air, and on the Trees, was a very pleasant Amuzement to me. It is very pleasant to see and hear the flocks of Birds, at their first Appearance in the Spring. The Ground looks naked, and lifeless yet. The Colour of the Ground, before the green [rises?] upp, is pale, lifeless, dead. There is very little beauty [in] the face of the Earth now, but the Vegetables will soon spring fresh and green, and young and sprightly Grass, and flowers, and Roses, will appear on the Ground, buds, blossoms, leaves on the Trees, and 100 species of Birds, flying in Air, alighting on the Ground and on Trees, herds of Cattle, Sheep, horses, grazing and lowing in the Pastures. Oh Nature! how [bright?] and beautiful thou art.

Means not but blunders round about a meaning.[2]

M.[3] has a very confused, blundering Way of asking Questions. She never knows distinctly what she is [after?], but asks at Random, any Thing, and has a difficulty in recollecting the Names of Things. The Names of Things dont flow naturally into My Mind, when I have occasion to use them. I had the Idea of the General Court in my Mind when I said to Otis, the Judges had [some?] important Business to do in &c., but the Words General Court did not arise with the Idea and therefore Otis thought I made [a] silly Speech. My Aunt Cunningham[4] has the same difficulty, recollecting Words and Ideas too, especially, of Things that are sometime past. A slothful Memory, a slow, heavy Memory, in oposition to a quick prompt Memory.

[I?] read a letter from one in St.K. to one in P. concerning M. Chateleu going to this Coast.[5] M. asks what is that. How confused is this Question? It wants much explanation and restriction, before an Answer can be given, for [. . .] she ask,[6] who is that letter from or who to, or what Place from or to, or what about, and what Place was

Chateleu going to. She knows not what she asks. Tis [owing?] to the Hurry and Impatience of Thought—which is the fault of us all.

Common People are not incapable of discerning the Motives and Springs of Words and Actions.

[1] This and the following detached entry may have been written any day between 14 and 17 or 18 March.

[2] Doubtless a quotation.

[3] Presumably JA's mother.

[4] Elizabeth Boylston, sister of JA's mother, married James Cunningham in 1742 (Boston Record Commissioners, 28*th Report*, p. 240).

[5] An extract of the letter in question, dated 9 Jan., was printed in the *Boston Post Boy*, 12 March 1759. It was from Jamaica, not St. K[itts], was addressed to a gentleman in Philadelphia, and reported the arrival in the West Indies of the French naval commander Chateleau and his intention to raid Delaware Bay.

[6] This passage is obscure. Perhaps JA meant to write: "for should she not ask ...?"

MARCH 18 [*i.e.* 19?]. MONDAY.[1]

This whole Day is dedicated to walking, riding, talk, &c. No Reading to day.

Twas Avarice, not Compassion that induced [...] [2] to pass the last Court. He was afraid that Pen [3] would be provoked to appeal both to the Superior Court if he put both in suit, and so keep him out of his Money for 6 or 8 months. 6 months without Interest. Tis fear of loosing the Interest upon Interest that induces him to pass this Court.—Oh Love of Money!—oh, Avarice, disguised under the shew of Compassion!

I feel vexed, fretted, chafed, the Thought of no Business mortifies, stings me. I feel angry, vexed with my Uncle Field,[4] &c. But Let me banish these Fears. Let me assume a Fortitude, a Greatness of Mind.

In such a gradual ascent to fame and fortune, and Business, the Pleasure that they give will be imperceptible, but by a bold, sudden rise, I shall feel all the Joys of each at once. Have I Genius and Resolution and Health enough for such an attchievement?

> Oh but a Wit can study in the Streets
> and raise his mind above the Mob he meets.

Who can study in Boston Streets. I am unable to observe the various Objects, that I meet, with sufficient Precision. My Eyes are so diverted with Chimney Sweeps, Carriers of Wood, Merchants, Ladies, Priests, Carts, Horses, Oxen, Coaches, Market men and Women, Soldiers, Sailors, and my Ears with the Rattle Gabble of them all that I cant think long enough in the Street upon any one Thing to start and pursue a Thought. I cant raise my mind above this mob Croud[5] of Men, Women, Beasts and Carriages, to think steadily. My Attention is sollicited every moment by some new object of sight, or some new sound. A Coach, Cart, a Lady or a Priest, may at any Time, by breaking a Couplet, disconcert a whole Page of excellent Thoughts.

What is meant by a nodding Beam, and pig of Lead.[6] He means that his Attention is necessary to preserve his Life and Limbs, as he walks the streets, for Sheets of Lead may fall from the Roofs of Houses. I know of no nodding Beam, except at the Hay Market.

Shybeares Dedication is in a strain of ironical, Humorous Satyr.[7] He reasons as warmly and positively as if in earnest in his favour, but his Reasoning is so manifestly weak and in some places ambiguous that every Reader knows his true Intention. This System of Religion is indeed new. Religious Institutions are mere means of increasing and preserving Piety and Virtue in the World, and any Thing, that will produce public and private advantages on the Happiness and Morals of a Nation, however repugnant to common sense, as Transubstantiation e.g. is true.

[1] Monday fell on 19, not 18, March 1759. Some of the detached entries that follow may extend into April, since the next entry dated by JA is that of 8 April.

[2] Name (probably an initial) either omitted by JA or lost in the frayed margin.

[3] This name is more or less conjectural.

[4] The Fields were neighbors but not close relatives of the Adamses, and JA evidently uses the term "Uncle" in a loose sense.

[5] This word, written between the lines, was probably intended to replace the preceding word, not crossed out.

[6] From Pope, *The Second Epistle of the Second Book of Horace*, from which the couplet at the head of this paragraph is also taken: "And then a nodding beam, or pig of lead, / God knows, may hurt the very ablest head."

[7] The reference is to John Shebbeare's *Letters on the English Nation*, which satirizes the first Duke of Newcastle; see 19 Oct. 1758, above.

SUNDAY. APRIL 8TH. 1759.

Spent the Evening at Captain Bracketts. A Case was proposed and my Opinion asked, which gave me Opportunity to display some Knowledge of Law but betrayed me into mistaken Dogmatism. I frequently expose my Ignorance of the Province Law, but [things?] are started that put me upon Exn. [Examination?].

Coll. Q.[1] I value not the Governor's favours, more than this Pinch of Snuff, in Comparison of my Honour and my Duty to my Town.

B. Fessenden: The Coll. said to Field, when he was building his pen, "I had rather have it said on my Tomb Stone, here lies the good Mr. Quincy, than here lies the rich Mr. Apthorp." [2] He told me that People were angry with him, because he was so fond of Honesty.

These reiterated Protestations in favour of Honesty, Goodness, Patriotism, or rather these verbal Pretensions to these Qualities raise Suspicions and Jealousies. Too much talk, Prate. Praise him self. He praises himself as much as other People censure him. Populus me sibilat sed plaudo meipsum. The People hiss him, and curse him, and reproach him, but he applauds, praises, admires himself. Does he believe what he says?

Fessenden, Nash, Field, Marsh, &c. &c. sneer, hiss, curse him. Most secretly despise, hate him, but they fear him too.

Tis in vain to expect felicity, without an habitual Contempt of Fortune, Fame, Beauty, Praise, and all such Things. Unaffected Benevolence to Men and conscious Integrity are sufficient supports. I have no Money. But I have an easy Heart, a quiet Mind. G[od] made us to be happy. I distress my self. This Animi Magnitudo and Rerum humanarum Contemptio, are alone secure of Happiness.

Oh Stoicks you are wise.[3]

What Passions or affections in human Nature are affected by Satyr, by Humour, and Drollery?

There is some Affection in human Nature that is delighted with Humour and Satyr, for a good deal of it is to be seen and heard in all Nations, and among all Ranks of People. It prevails in every Country Parish, may be found in every Tavern, at every Town meeting thro the Province.

F.[4] Oh blessed Storm. The Storm blowed me away. Oh blessed storm.

This was spoke in Person of one of the new Select Men, as Bracket, Thayer &c. and upon this secret Principle, that an Advantage had been meanly taken of the thinness of the Meeting to get a Change of Town officers. So that it hinted at the meanness, and want of Influence in Town. Their Influence was not sufficient, to have carried a Vote, had the Town been together. But they were mean enough to seize that Opportunity when 3/4 of the Town were detained at Home by the storm, to assemble their Crew of Debtors and Labourers, and accomplish their Projects as they pleased. Thus, the Wit of this lay in hinting at their Meanness of Soul, and Insignificancy in the Town. It hinted that the Point was carried, not by Merit, nor by real Popularity, but by mean and clandestine Artifice, and Plotting.

How great is the Dread of Satyr and Ridicule in human Nature. Mrs. S. is afraid C[olonel] Q. and his [...] H.[5] will laugh at her shape, dress, Behavior. Afraid of Laughter. I used to dread J[ames] O[tis] and B[enjamin] K[ent] because I suspected they laughed at me. I used to dread Put[nam], because of his satirical and contemptuous smiles.

Another reason. We were pleased to see the old Gent diverting himself and laughing at the success of their Artifices to depose him, instead of being angry and scolding.

What Passions are pleased in the Reader or Hear[er], and what are vexed in the Person ridiculed.

Dr.[6] S. after L.R. had turned him off, went into Church one day, and into the same Pew where L. was. She smiled, and almost giggled at him. That stung him. He cryed a nasty, stinking Jade, he did not think she was such a nasty yellow Jade, before. Thus the Dr. diverted him self with her Colour. He laughed at her yellow Colour, in Revenge of her Ridicule on him.

Thus human Nature, when despized and laughed at, is vexed, naturally vexed, and looks about for some Imperfection, Deformity, folly or Vice to laugh at in turn. And when a Man is deposed in T[own] meeting, he naturally imputes it to some mean Contrivance &c.

Ruggles's Grandeur consists in the quickness of his apprehension, Steadiness of his attention, the boldness and Strength of his Thoughts and Expressions, his strict Honour, conscious Superiority, Contempt of Meanness &c. People approach him with Dread and Terror.[7]

Gridleys Grandeur consists in his great Learning, his great Parts and his majestic Manner. But is diminished by stiffness and affectation.

Ruggles is as proud, as lordly as Gridley. But he is more popular. He conceals it more. He times it better. And it is easy and natural in him, but is stiff and affected in Gridley.

Tis an Advantage to Ruggles's Character, but a Disadvantage to Gridley's.

Gridley has a bold, spirited Manner of Speaking, but is too stiff, has too little Command of the Muscles of his face. His Words seem to pierce and search, have something quick and animating. He is a great Reasoner, and has a very vivid Imagination.

Prat has a strong, elastic Spring, or what we call Smartness, and Strength in his Mind. His Ideas seem to lie deep and to be brot up with a strong Effort of the Mind. His Ideas are vivid, and he sees their

Differences. Otis is extreamly quick and elastic. His Apprehension is as quick as his Temper. He springs, and twitches his Muscles about in thinking.

Thatcher has not this same Strength and Elasticity. He is sensible, but slow of Conception and Communication. He is queer, and affected. He is not easy.

Coll. Q. I learn'd to write Letters of Pope and Swift &c. I should not have wrote a Letter with so much Correctness as I can, if I had not read and imitated them. The Faculty has come to me, strangely, without any formed Design of acquiring it.

There is a concealed Encomium on himself, his own Letters, in this Remark, but there is an Observation too, which is worth considering. Men [wear?] themselves, by slow and imperceptible Degrees, into confirmed Habits of thinking, Speaking, and Acting. He began early in Life, I suppose perhaps at Colledge, to read these smooth, soft, Writers, and altho he never formed any Design of imitating their Ease and Politeness, yet he gradually wore it into his Mind. He learned to write as Children learn to Speak, without thinking what they do. Perhaps had he formed a Design in his Youth of acquiring that Faculty and read Authors with that Design, he would have acquired it much sooner and more perfectly.

The Principle in Nature is Imitation, Association of Ideas, and contrasting Habits. How naturally we imitate, without Design or with, Modes of thinking, Speaking, Acting, that please us! Thus we conform gradually to the Manners and Customs of our own family, Neighbourhood, Town, Province, Nation &c. A[t] Worcester, I learned several Turns of Mind of Putnam, and at Boston I find my self imitating Otis, &c.—But Q[uery], Who will learn the Art soonest, and most perfectly, he who reads without a Design of extracting Beauties or he who reads with? The last undoubtedly. Design attends, and observes nicely, and critically. I learned with Design to imitate Put's Sneer, his sly look, and his look of Contempt. This look may serve good Ends in Life, may procure Respect.

To form a style, therefore, read constantly the best Authors. Get a Habit of clear Thinking and strength and Propriety and Harmony of Expression. This one Principle of Imitation would lead me thro the whole human System. A Faculty acquired accidentally, without any Endeavours or forsight of the Effect. He read for Amuzement, not to learn to write.

Let me recollect, and con over, all the Phenomena of Imitation that

I may take advantage of this Principle in my own make, that I may learn easier and sooner.

Mem. To look in the Clerk's office, for the Files of the Dispute concerning the Registry of Vessells belonging to Newbury, viz. Mr. Prats state or Questions, and Mr. Gridleys Answers.

[1] This and the following more or less detached entries were probably written soon after 8 April but cannot be dated with any certainty.

[2] Closing quotation mark supplied. It is likely, but not certain, that the following sentence is a part of Fessenden's statement rather than a statement by JA. Charles Apthorp (1698–1758) was a wealthy Boston merchant and prominent Anglican (Winsor, *Memorial History of Boston*, 2:545–546).

[3] CFA's reading. The two or three last words are now scarcely legible.

[4] JA's father. At a town meeting on 3 March 1759 three of the five Braintree selectmen were replaced. Among them was Deacon John Adams, and among those newly elected were Capt. Richard Brackett and Capt. Ebenezer Thayer (*Braintree Town Records*, p. 360, 365.

[5] His daughter Hannah?

[6] Perhaps "Dn." (for Deacon), as also a few lines below in the same paragraph. The subjects of this anecdote cannot now be identified.

[7] Timothy Ruggles (1711–1795), Harvard 1732, of Hardwick; lawyer, legislator, chief justice of the Worcester Court of Common Pleas, and ardent loyalist. Mr. Shipton's sketch of Ruggles (Sibley-Shipton, *Harvard Graduates*, 9:199–223) is a brilliantly lifelike portrait, painted *con amore*.

[SPRING 1759.] [1]

The Road is walled on each side with a Grove of Trees. The stillness, silence, and the uniformity of the Prospect puts the Mind into a stirring, thoughtful Mood.

But the Reflections that are made in a Grove, are forgotten in the Town, and the Man who resembles a saint in his Thoughts in the first, shall resemble [a] Devil in his Actions in the last.

In such silent scenes, as riding or walking thro the Woods or sitting alone in my Chamber, or lying awake in my Bed, my Thoughts commonly run upon Knowledge, Virtue, Books, &c. tho I am apt to forget these, in the distracting Bustle of the Town, and ceremonious Converse with Mankind.

This morning rode to Moses Frenchs to get him to serve a Writ for me. He told me he was not yet sworn, but was obliged to me for coming to him, and would be glad to serve me at any Time, and would now rather than It should be any Damage to me. Thus he was pleased, I hope secured. Men are only secured by falling in with their Inclination, by favouring their Hopes, clearing their Prospects.

Then I went to Wales'. He was not at home. I followed him to Germantown. He served the Writt. We returned together. He seemed quite pleasant. Told me the Practice of the two Thayers, of Hollis, Niles, &c. They drive a great stroke. There is two Thayers, 2 Niles's, Faxon, Hollis, Wales, Moses French, W. Penniman, are all pettifogging Dabblers in Iniquity and Law. I might except 2 Niles's, Wales and French, and perhaps Faxon from the Iniquitous part. I hope that Wales and French are secured to me. How they love Thayer I cant say. I hope they will recommend me to Persons that they hear Speaking of Business, as Wm. Veasey did. Veasey knew me, and mentioned me, to Shaw.

The Difference between a whole Day and a divided scattered Day.
Q[uery]. Can any Man take a Book in his hand, in the Morning, and confine his Thoughts to that till Night. Is not such a Uniformity tiresome? Is not Variety more agreable, and profitable too? Read one Book one Hour, then think an Hour, then Exercise an Hour, then read another Book an Hour, then dine, smoke, walk, cutt Wood, read another Hour loud, then think, &c. and thus spend the whole day in perpetual Variations, from Reading to thinking, Exercise, Company, &c. But what is to be acquired by this Wavering Life, but a Habit of Levity, and Impatience of Thought?
I never spent a whole Day upon one Book in my Life.
What is the Reason that I cant remove all Papers and Books from my Table, take one Volume into my Hands, and read it, and then reflect upon it, till night, without wishing for my Pen and Ink to write a Letter, or taking down any other Book, or thinking of the Girls? Because I cant command my attention. My Thoughts are roving from Girls to friends, from friends to Court, to Worcester, to Piscataquay,[2] Newbury, and then to Greece and Rome, then to France, from Poetry to oratory, and Law, and Oh, a rambling, Imagination. Could I fix my attention, and keep off every fluttering Thought that attempts to intrude upon the present subject, I could read a Book all Day. Wisdom, curse on it, will come soon or late.
I have to smooth and harmonise my Mind, teach every Thought within its Bounds, to roll, and keep the equal Measure of the Soul.

H. went up to the Negroes Chamber over this little Room and awakened Jack and Ruby. Ruby was frightened and screamed till H. pacified her at last. Jack got up to alight a Candle and see if his Master was abed and if he found him up was to say he got up to get some thing for his Child. Thus a Girls Invention is alone sufficient for every Intrigue of this sort.

Accidents, as we call them, govern a great Part of the World, especially Marriages. Sewal [3] and Esther broke in upon H. and me and interrupted a Conversation that would have terminated in a Courtship, which would in spight of the Dr.[4] have terminated in a Marriage, which Marriage might have depressed me to absolute Poverty and obscurity, to the End of my Life. But the Accident seperated us, and gave room for Lincolns addresses, which have delivered me from very dangerous shackles, and left me at Liberty, if I will but mind my studies, of making a Character and a fortune.[5]

I never began an Explanation of my Designs and Thoughts so that she was obliged to act without certain Knowledge. She had peculiar Reasons to desire an immediate Marriage, viz. a young and a very fruitful Mother in Law,[6] on whom her father fondly doats, &c. and she had peculiar Reasons to receive the Drs. Addresses viz. The fondness of her father and his father, for the Match. The Drs. family, Business, and Character. And, in oposition to these Inducements, she had no Certainty of my Passions or Reason or Designs in her favour, but a strong suspicion that I was apprised of the Drs. Designs, and determined to see her no more.—But the Thing is ended. A tender scene! a great sacrifice to Reason!

Now let me collect my Thoughts, which have been long scattered, among Girls, father, Mother, Grandmother, Brothers, Matrimony, Husling, Chatt, Provisions, Cloathing, fewel, servants for a family, and apply them, with steady Resolution and an aspiring Spirit, to the Prosecution of my studies. Now Let me form the great Habits of Thinking, Writing, Speaking. Let my whole Courtship be applyed to win the Applause and Admiration of Gridley, Prat, Otis, Thatcher &c. Let Love and Vanity be extinguished and the great Passions of Ambition, Patriotism, break out and burn. Let little objects be neglected and forgot, and great ones engross, arouse and exalt my soul.

The Mind must be aroused, or it will slumber. To make and [confirm?] in his Mind a Contempt of Cowardice, and an Admiration of Bravery.

I found a Passion growing in my heart and a consequent Habit of thinking, forming and strengthening in my Mind, that would have eat out every seed of ambition, in the first, and every wise Design or Plan in the last.

A Young fellow of fond amorous Passions, may appear quite cold and insensible. The Love of Knowledge may prevail over the Love of

Girls. Old Men may be mistaken in their opinion of young ones. Mr. Goffe[7] and Mr. Putnam, especially Goffe, thought me incapable of Gallantry and Intrigue.

Should have drawn a Confession from her (by shewing the Imprudence, Danger, Cruelty, and Wickedness of her Conduct without that supposition) that she loved me, and was determined to run all Hazards with me, to run the chance of Business, and success. Should have tryed, what the Imputation of Jilting, and Wheedling, and hinting, for a Courtship, in order to Torment, or at least to secure one for fear another should fail, would have produced. Should have said, H. you was dissatisfied with your situation and desirous of a Husband. In order to get one, you Wheedled Wibirt; you wheedled Lincoln. You gave each of them hints and Encouragement to Court you. But especially you wheedled me. For 6 months past you and I have never been alone together but you have given me broad Hints, that you desired I should court you, &c. &c.

Used to say how moderate her Desires were. She cared not for Riches or Dress, nor Gentility. She could live upon common Necessaries. Such Speeches used to be frequently dropped to me, and before me. She used before their House was burned[8] to say frequently before me in Company, and to me alone, she should admire to be Courted a great while. She should admire a long Courtship. She would not be married by any means, these 4 or 5 years; but since she lost that House and her Agreable Retirement, solitude, and especially since her mother has been with Child again, she has said to me, that nothing should persuade her to be married these seven Years if it were not for her fathers young Wife, that [nothing?][9]

Deed from Stephen Dudley, of Exeter, in N. Hampshire, Cordwainer, to Wm. Cunningham of Boston Glaiser, of 150 Acres of Land, to be taken out of the Tract of Land that Capt. Peter Renewitt and Abigail his Squaw gave to said Stephen by deed of Gift 7 of Jan. 1718, which Tract begins on the River 3 miles above Petuckaway mill in Exeter and running 3 miles in breadth on Each side of said River and Ten miles in Length up said River.

I will get an Husbandmans Common Place Book.[10]

I will make me a Common Place Book of Agriculture—and Place Wheat, Rye, Corn, and Pease, Beans, [*sentence unfinished*]

A Common Place Book of Husbandry and Gardening—and Place in the Index Wheat, Rye, Corn, Pease, Beans, Turnips, Potatoes. Apples, Cyder, Trees, Elms, Butten Woods, Locusts, Cherry Trees, Plumb Trees, Quince Trees, &c. Nurseries. Lands, Grounds, Plough land, Pasture, mowing Land. Meadow, Upland, fields, Groves, forests. Hills, Valleys, Ditches. Fresh Meadows, gravelly Land, clay Land. Loomy Land. Springy Land, &c. Horses, oxen, Cows, Calves, sheep, Hogs. Scrub Oak Plains, pitch Pine Plains. Rocks. Wall. Posts, Rails, fence. Red Ceder, Juniper, Savine, Oaks, Pine, Hemlock, Holly. Apple Trees, Pear Trees. Orchard. Salt Meadow. Manure. Rock Wick [Weed?], sea Weed. Dung, Ashes, Marl, Chips, sticks, straw, &c. Weeds, Nature of Weeds, methods of destroying, and extirpating them. Barbery Bushes, Cadlock, White Weed, yellow Weeds. Grasses, Clover, while [white?] honey suckle, fowl medow Grass, fox Tail or Herds Grass. St. foin, Tree foin, &c. Roots, fibres, saps, Juices, Vessells, Circulation, Inoculation, Engraftments, scients [scions], &c.

Currants. Goose Berries. Currants, white and red, Goose Berries, strawberries.

Husbandry may be studied by me either as a Phylsopher inquisitive into the secrets of Nature in Vegetation, Generation, and of Art in Manufacture or as a Politician and Patriot, desirous of promoting the Improvement of Laws &c. for the Interest of the Public, or as a Private Man, selfishly [thirsting?] after Profit, in order to make money.

I would fill my Yard with Geese, Turkies, Ducks, Guinea Hens, Peacocks, fowls. Bees, &c.

Labour, Howing, Ploughing. Ploughs, mathematical Principles on which Ploughs are constructed. Raking, Mowing, scythes, &c. Carts, Waggons, Wheelbarrows. Harrow. Utensils of Husbandry. Sleds. Methods of subduing Land, cutting Wood and Bushes, burning wood and Bushes, eradicating Stumps, Plowing new Ground, &c.

Potatoes, different sorts. Cabbages, different sorts. Colly flower, sellery, &c. Peas, different sorts. Beans, English and others, different sorts, white black, red, large, small, &c. Turnips. Bates for rats. Parsnips, Parsley, Pepper Grass, Horse radish, Mustard, Onions, shyves [chives], Herbs. Hog Weed, red rood [root?]. Pursley, Dandelyons, &c. Balm, Sage, Penny Royal, Hyssop, &c. Pinks, Tulips.

Roses, white and Red Peonies, &c.

Yesterday afternoon, a Plea, Puis darrien Continuance,[11] was argued by Mr. Prat for the Plea, and G[ridley] and O[tis] against it. The Plea was, that after the last Continuance and before the 1st day of the sitting of this Court this Term, viz. on such a day, one Allin one of the Plaintiffs died. Mr. Prat argued that the Writ must abate, for it was clear Law, that the Writt in this Case was ipso facto abated and might be dismissed at the Motion of any Person as amicus Curiæ. And of this opinion was the whole Court. G. took an Exception to the Plea as imperfect in not giving the Plaintiff a better Writ. The whole Afternoon was Spent in arguing this Point, and 20 Volumes of Institutes and Reporters, I suppose were produced as authorities.[12]

(*Otis aside.* It makes me laugh to see Pratt lugg a Cart load of Books into Court to prove a Point as clear as the Sun. The Action is as dead as a Hubb.)

Otis. I will grant, Mr. Prat, very readily, that there has been a time since Wm. the Conqueror when this Plea would have abated this Writ in England. But I take it that Abatements at this day are rather odious than favored and I dont believe that this Plea would abate this Writ at any time within this Century in Westminster Hall.

This morning, the Action Patten vs. Basen was argued.[13] It was [a] Case for not returning an Ex[ecutio]n. Prat and the Court, an Action will not lie against the officer for not returning without averring and proving Special Damages, as that the Party was broke, run away, or dead, leaving nothing. Then the special Damage may be laid equal to the whole Debt. Gruchy v. Hews [Hughes] comes on this afternoon.[14]

Of Abatement by the Death of Parties.

The Rule is "That wherever the Death of any Party happens pending the Writt and yet the Plea is in the same Condition, as if such Party were living, there such death makes no Alteration; for where the death of the Parties makes no Change of Proceeding, it would be unreasonable that the surviving Parties should make any Alteration in their Writt; for if such Writ and Proscess were changed, twould let [...] but in the same Condition they were at the Death of the Parties; and 'twould be absurd that what made no alteration should change the Writ and the Proscess;"[15] and on this Rule all the Diversities turn.

1. Inst. 139. The first Difference is in Real Actions; where there are several Pleadings, there is summons and severance, as there is in the most real Actions, there the death of one of the Parties abates the suit; but in Personal and mixed Actions, where one entire Thing is to be recovered, there the Death of the Parties does not abate the Writt; and the Reason of the Difference is, where there are two Jointenants

and the one goes on to recover his Moiety, and the other will not proceed, there is no Reason that he that is willing to proceed should not recover his Ritt, since such tenant has a distinct Moiety, and therefore should have an Action to recover it. But no Summons and severance lies in Personal Actions; as if Trespass be committed in such Jointenants, they must both join in the Action, for as one may release the whole, so the other may refuse to go on, and the other cant recover his Part of the Damage without him; and so in Debt by an obligation to two, there can be no summons and severance, because one of the joint obligees may release the Bond, and therefore may not go in the Action; but if a Man appoint two men Executors, there shall be summons and severance, because tho one of the Executors may release, the such a Release is a Devastavit in him; but if he will not proceed at Law, tis no Devastavit; and therefore both Executors being only Trustees for the Person deceased, they shall not both be compelled to go on together; but if one refuses, the other may bring his Action in the name of both, and have summons and severance; for otherwise each Coexecutor might by Collusion with the Debtor and not proceeding, keep the other from recovering the assitts, and not create a Devastavit in himself.

Coll. Hunt.

A single Adventure, Expedition, Undertaking or Incident in a Mans Life often renders him forever afterwards attentive to Matters of that sort.

Coll. Hunt was highly entertained and gratified with my Relation of the Gallant bloody Action between an English Privateer and two frenchmen in the West Indies. It Engaged his Attention, and gave him a high Pleasure, which Mr. Olivers Project of improving Husbandry, and making Profits, was not able to do.

He hearkened to the story of the fight, but was cold to the Project of inriching his Country. He acquired at Louisbourg this Admiration of Bravery, which all the Perplexity, Disgrace, and Indigence, which he has been brought to endure, since his Return from that Expedition, has never been able to extinguish.

There he saw frequent Instances of daring Actions, and he heard such Actions applauded. There he saw frequent Instances of Cowardice; and he heard such Persons despized, which hightened the Distinction, which it is natural to Mankind to [16]

Justice with a Band, a Veil before her Eyes, sitting on the Globle, with a Pair of scales and a sword in her right Hand, the scales hang below her hand, the sword points to the Zenith with a Crown upon it, and with four pieces of something in her left Hand. With her left foot she treads upon a Lion, the Emblem of strength, i.e. Violence, and with her right upon a serpent, the Emblem of subtlety, i.e. fraud. The Roman Eagle, with her Wings hovering, half spread, stands on her right Claw foot, upon the Globle, by the left side of Justice, and extending her left Claw, in which she grasps some Arrows, perhaps, towards the East.

Behind the Globle on the right hand of Justice, you see some stately Buildings, with a fine Row of Roman statues, round the Roofs, and with the statue of an Horse and Man on the Top of a Chimney almost behind Justice.

On the left Hand of Justice, you see the Roman Army, entrenched, and picketted in, with a large Castle, and flag flying at a Distance.

At the Foot of Justice, on the left Hand, stands truth arrayed in a roman Habit with her curled Hair, decently yet negligently tyed, pointing with her left Hand to Justice, and with her Right, extending her Torch, over to an old Gentleman, who stands, at the feet of Justice on the Right, with a large Book in his left Hand, a Pen in his Right, and seems in a listening attentive Posture, taking down the Dictates of Justice by the light of Truth. Q[uery], is this old Gentleman Justinian? There are four figures, or there is a Groupe of figures, at the feet of this old Gentleman, which I am unable to decypher. They are habited differently. One is black like a Negro, with a Chain of Beeds about his Neck and a Crown of Feathers on his Head. Is this an African? The next is black too, but without any Beeds or Crown, but he seems to wear the Proboscis of an Elephant, upon his C[ap?]. The other two are clothed in Roman Habits, one in Armour. The three last are on their Knees, and seem to shrink from the sight of Justice and Truth. Q.—was not the Architecture and statuary, behind the Globle and Justice, designed to represent the roman skill in those Arts. They must have had Master Architects to build those grand and beautiful Piles, and Master Statuaries, to make those statues, round the Roofs, and on the Chimney Tops.

And is not the entrenched Army on the left Hand designed to represent the Glory and Terror of their Arms.

I cannot decypher half these figures.

P[arson] W[ibird] is crooked, his Head bends forwards, his shoulders are round and his Body is writhed, and bended, his head and half his Body, have a list one Way, the other half declines the other Way, and his lower Parts from his Middle, incline another Way. His features are as coarse and crooked as his Limbs. His Nose is a large roman Nose with a prodigious Bunch Protuberance, upon the Upper Part of it. His Mouth is large, and irregular, his Teeth black and foul, and craggy. His Lips [...] to command, when he speakes, they dont move easily and limberly pliant. His lips are stiff, rigid, not pliant and supple. His Eyes are a little squinted, his Visage is long, and lank, his Complexion wan, his Cheeks are fallen, his Chin is long, large, and lean. These are the Features, these the Limbs, and this the Figure of the worthy Mr. Wibirt.

But his Air, and Gesture, is still more extraordinary. When he stands, He stands, bended, in and out before and behind and to both Right and left; he tosses his Head on one side. When he prays at home, he raises one Knee upon the Chair, and throws one Hand over the back of it. With the other he scratches his Neck, pulls the Hair of his Wigg, strokes his Beard, rubbs his Eyes, and Lips.

When he Walks, he heaves away, and swaggs on one side, and steps almost twice as far with one foot, as with the other.

When he sitts, he sometimes lolls on the arms of his Chair, sometimes on the Table. He entwines his leggs round the Leggs of his Chair, lays hold of the Iron Rod of the stand with one Hand. Sometimes throws him self, over the back of his Chair, and scratches his Hed, Vibrates the foretop of his Wigg, thrusts his Hand up under his Wigg, &c.

When he speakes, he cocks and rolls his Eyes, shakes his Head, and jerks his Body about.

Thus clumsy, careless, slovenly, and lazy is this sensible Man.

It is surprizing to me that the Delicacy of his Mind has not corrected these Indecent, as well as ungraceful Instances of Behaviour. He has Wit, and he has Fancy, and he has Judgment. He is a Genius. But he has no Industry, no Delicacy, no Politeness. Tho' he seems to have a sort of Civility, and Cleverness in his Manners. A civil, clever Man. He observes that in Dana which I have observed—a cleverness, a good Humored look.

What is it, that Settles Men's opinions of others? It is Avidity, Envy, Revenge, Interest.

C[olonel] Q[uincy] will represent Eb. Thayer as one of the worst of Men, as a Conspirator against his Country, as a Cataline.

C[olonel's] Friendship is not worth a wise Mans seeking, nor his

Enmity worth fearing. As long as you flatter his Vanity, gratify his avarice, or favour his Ambition, you will be a great Genius, an honest Man, a good man, in short you will be every thing, but as soon as you obstruct any of his Views you will be a silly man, a Knave, in short every thing that is bad.

While the Governor as he thought, had a great Opinion of him, the Governor was wise, learned, industrious &c., but when he found the Governor despized him, the Governor had no Principles, was guided by self Interest &c.[17]

Coll. Q. I have discovered the Phylosophers stone in military Matters.

[...] this is the darling, favorite Theme still. Tho every Man who hears this scheme conceives at once the most contemptible Opinion of it, yet no one chuses to shew his Disapprobation of it. A few Queries, and distant Proposals, are the Utmost that has been said against it, to him.—Thus he is flattered to his face by Nods, and Winks, of seeming Assent and compliance, and cursed behind his back as a Villain and a fool. Oh, envied State of Greatness.

He calls it a scheme to do men good in spight of their Teeth—forcing food down a hungry Mans Throat. The Philosophers Stone &c. Others say he is a cursed Rogue, a dutiful son of his father the Devil, he wants to get Money into his Pocket. Thus the Coll. and some of his Company differ in Opinion, of his Contrivance. He thinks, tis fatherly, patriotical, sagacious. They think it inimical, diabolical and silly!

You may hint to him particular Defects of his Plan, and he will contrive Amendments, but the general Plan would never be [exploded?] by his Consent. I will not attempt to undeceive him any more. This scheme is Mentis gratissimus Error. demptus, Error, gratissimus Error the most agreable Error mentis of the Mind, demptus taken away, per Vim, by violence. Pol. by Pollux, amici my friends, occidistis you have killed me, non servastis [you] have not preserved me, [saved?] me alive, cui, sic extorta Voluptas—Pleasure extorted, torn away, cui from which thus.[18]

This political scheme is mentis gratissimus Error Mentis [...] Error. It will be told to the Disadvantage of [his] Character, for sense and Honesty. Twill furnish his Enemies with a topick of scandal and will introduce Jealosy's and suspicions into the Minds of his friends. He will suffer the most by it.

The Notes will give offence. A rich Man will be allowed to give a Note, but a poor Man must pay the Money. This will be a Distinction between poor and rich, a Partiality to the rich and Oppression of the poor. It will occasion such Ravings, and swearing and Impudence and Insolence as was never seen by a military officer in this Company. Bass and my Uncle told him, how it would be received. He is wrongheadedly Headstrong, headstrongly Wrongheaded.

Ned tells a story tolerably well. He told of [*illegible name*]. He was a better Prophet than Elijah for he stretched himself on her but once to bring her to Life whereas Elijah did 3 times.[19] He breathed into her the Breath of Life. Ned told the Duke of Whartons Character and Life, &c. Ned was sociable, told the stories he had read pretty well, &c. Billy was sociable too, but awed, afraid.

They told of the wickedest jokes that had been put upon Nat Hurd, by some fellows in Boston, who found out that he had such a Girl at his shop, at such a time. One went to him and pretended to make a confidant of him. Oh god, what shall I do? That Girl, [...] her, has given me the Clap. That scared him and made him cry, Oh damn her, what shall I do? I saw her such a Night. I am [peppered?]. He went to the Dr. [...] and was salivated for the Clap. Then they sent him before Justice Phillips, then before Justice Tyler, in short they played upon him till they provoked him so that he swore, he would beat the Brains out of the first man that came into his shop, to plague him with his [...].

I think it is an equal Proof of Piety, Wit, and sensuality.—This was affected. I thought it witty, wise, smart. It could not but disgust.

Why have I not Genius to start some new Thought. Some thing that will surprize the World. New, grand, wild, yet regular Thought that may raise me at once to fame.

Where is my Soul? where are my Thoughts.

When shall I start some new Thought, make some new Discovery, that shall surprize the World with its Novelty and Grandeur?

Coll. Q['s] End is Popularity. He intends to procure Votes by his schemes for raising Men, but if he had used all his Ingenuity to contrive a scheme to disgust People, to raise scruples, Jealousies, and Contempt, he could not have found a better. He will loose more Votes than he will get by this Project.

Would it not save trouble to give the Men that he shall impress after 4 o'clock, leave to inlist and date their Inlistment a few days sooner?

Is it not absurd to study all Arts but that of Living in the World, and all sciences but that of Mankind? Popularity is the Way to gain and figure.

The Arts of Gain are necessary. You may get more by studying Town meeting, and Training Days, than you can by reading Justinian and all his voluminous and heavy Commentators.

Mix with the Croud in a Tavern, in the Meeting House or the Training Field, and grow popular by your agreable assistance in the Tittle tattle of the Hour, never think of the deep hidden Principles of natural, civil, or common Law, for thoughts like these will give you a gloomy Countenance and a stiff Behaviour.

I should talk with Tirrells, Lamberts, Clarks, Thayers, Faxons, Beal, Wales, French &c. about changing Horses. Offer to change or sell, trade in any Thing.

It is certain that Retirement will loose its Charms if it is not interrupted, by Business, and Activity. I must converse and deal with Mankind, and move and stir from one scene of Action and Debate and Business, and Pleasure, and Conversation, to another and grow weary of all before I shall feel the strong Desire of retiring to contemplation on Men and Business and Pleasure and Books.

After hard Labour at Husbandry, Reading and Reflection in Retirement will be a Relief and a high refined Pleasure. After attending a Town Meeting, watching the Intrigues, Acts, Passions, Speeches, that pass there, a Retreat to reflect, compare, distinguish will be highly delightful. So after a Training Day, after noting the Murmurs, Complaints, Jealousies, Impudence, Envy that pass in the field, I shall be pleased with my solitude.

Transitions from study to Business, from Business to Conversation and Pleasure, will make the Revolution of study still more agreable and perhaps not less profitable, for we are very apt, in total Retirement, to forget the sciences, and to smoak, and trifle and drone it too much.

I have been very negligent and faulty, in not treating Deacon Savil,

Nat. Belcher, Deacon Belcher &c. with more Attention, and sprightliness. I should bow and look pleasant to Deacon Savil, and talk with him about News, War, Ministers, Sermons &c. Should watch critically every Word that Nat Belcher says, and let him see by the Motions of the Muscles of my face, that I have discernment between wise and foolish, witty and silly, candid and ill natured, grave and humourous speeches and let him know on proper occasions I can vent a Smart Repartee. Should always speak and shake Hands with the Deacon, inquire after his Wife, Sons, S[amuel], W[illiam], E[lijah], and humour his talkative Disposition.—It is of no small Importance to sett the Tongues of old and young Men and Women a prating in ones favour.

As to Dr. Savil and his Wife, I have dismissed all my Guards before Them, and acted and spoke at Random. But I might easily gain their warmest Words and assiduous Assistance, by visiting seldomer, by using tender and soothing, instead of rough and reproachful Language, and by complying with their Requests of riding out with her, and reading Plays, once in a while, to them in the Evening.

But I have been rash, boastful, prophane, uncivil, Blustering, threatning, before them.

Let me remark P[arson] Wibirts Popularity. He plays with Babes and young Children that begin to prattle, and talks with their Mothers, asks them familiar, pleasant Questions, about their affection to their Children. His familiar careless way of conversing with People, Men and Women. He has Wit, and Humour.

Ripping, i.e., using the Words faith, Devil, I swear, damnable, [cursed?], &c., displease the Dr. but especially his Wife.

Threatning to Quarrell with Thayer, Penniman, Hollis &c., disgust[s] them, especially her.

Asserting dogmatically on Points of Province Law which he knows more of than I, by several Years experience, and Conversation with People concerning their Estates, Law suits, &c., and being fretted, disgusts them very much.—I have more faults, Mistakes, Imprudences, follies, rashness to answer for in the Drs. House than in all the Town besides.

I am to attend a Vendue this afternoon at Lamberts. My F[ather], C[aptain] Bracket and Thayer are a Committee to lease out the Town Lands to the highest Bidder. Let me remark the Management of the

97

sale, and the Behaviour of Persons especially of Thayer and Bracket, watch his Treatment of People, and their Treatment of him.

Let me ask myself this Question when I return. What have I seen, heard, learned? What hint observed to lift myself into Business, what Reputation or Disgrace have I got, by attending this Vendue. My Character will be Spread, and mended or injured by it.

I was consulted by 2 Men this afternoon, who would not have applied to me if I had not been at Vendue, E. Niles and Elijah Belcher. And the Questions they asked, have led me into Useful Thoughts and Inquiries. I find hints, and Inquiries, arise sooner in the World than in my Study.

It would be an agreable and useful speculation to inquire into that Faculty which we call Imagination. Define it, enquire the Good Ends it answers in the human system, and the Evils it sometimes produces.

What is the Use of Imagination? It is the Repository of Knowledge. By this faculty, are retained all the Ideas of visible objects, all the observations we have made in the Course of Life on Men and Things, our selves &c.

I am conscious that I have the faculty of Imagination, that I can at Pleasure review in my Thoughts, the Ideas and Assemblages of Ideas that have been before in my Mind. Can revive the scenes, Diversions, sports of Childhood, Youth. Can recall my youthful Rambles, to the farms,[20] frolicks, Dalliances, my lonely Walks thro the Groves, and swamps, and fields, and Meadows at Worcester. Can imagine my self with the wildest Tribe of Indians in America in their Hunting, their Warrs, their tedious Marches, thro wild swamps and Mountains. Can fly by this faculty to the Moon, Planets, fixed Starrs, unnumbered Worlds. Can cross the Atlantic and fancy my self in Westminster Hall, hearing Causes in the Courts of Justice, or the Debates in the Houses of Commons or Lords.—As all our knowledge is acquired by Experience, i.e. by sensation or Reflection, this faculty is necessary to retain the Ideas we receive and the observations we make, and to recall them, for our Use, as Occasion requires.

I am conscious too, that this faculty is very active and stirring. It is constantly in Action unless interrupted by the Presence of external Objects, by Reading, or restrained by Attention. It hates Restrain[t], it runs backward to past scenes &c. or forward to the future. It flyes into the Air, dives in the sea, rambles to foreign Countries, or makes excursions [to] foreign planetary starry Worlds. These are but Hints, irregular observations, not digested into order.

But [what] are the Defects of this faculty? What are the Errors, Vices, Habits, it may betray us into, if not curbed? What is the Danger.

I must know all the Ends of this faculty, and all its Phenomena, before I can know all its Defects. Its Phenomena are infinitely various, in different Men, and its Ends are different. Therefore its Defects must be almost infinitely various. But all its Defects may be reduced to general Laws.

The Sphere of Imagination includes both Actuality and Possibility, not only what is but what may be.

One Use of Imagination, is to facilitate the Acquisition and Communication of Knowledge. How does it facilitate the Acquisition. It lays up, It retains, the Ideas of Things and the Observations we make upon them. By reviving past scenes, or creating new, it suggests Thoughts and inquiries. Starts Hints and doubts, and furnishes Reason with Materials in our retired Hours. In the Hours of solitude, Imagination recalls the Ideas of Things, Men, Actions, Characters, and Reason reduces them to order, and forms Inferences and Deductions from them.

How does it help to communicate? Why by recalling our Knowledge, and by comparing abstract Notions with sensible Images—by Metaphor, allusion &c.

Another End of Imagination, may be personal Pleasure and Entertainment. We take Pleasure in viewing the Works of Nature, and the Productions of Art, as Painting, Statuary, Poetry, oratory &c., but are not these rather objects and Pleasures of sense than of Imagination?

We take Pleasure in recollecting the Sports, Diversions, Business, scenes of Nature &c. that we have seen in our past Lives. We take Pleasure in fancying our selves in Places, among Objects, Persons, Pleasures, when we are not; and a still greater Pleasure in the Prospect which Imagination constantly gives us of future Pleasure, Business, Wealth, fame &c.

This Prospect of futurity, which Imagination gilds and brightens, is the greatest Spur to Industry and Application. The scholars spur to study. The Commanders spur [to] Activity and Courage. The Statesmans Spur to the Invention and Execution of Plans of Politicks. The Lovers Spur to assiduity, and &c.

Coll. [Quincy] told the Compliment the Governor passed on him in calling him one of the most active Members, before 20 Persons [in a Tavern?], and one was lolling out his Tongue, another shrugging his shoulders and another sneering all the Time.

Men are aspiring and ambitious in their souls [and hearts?] as their Imaginations are vivid.

I had an acking Void within my Breast, this night. I feel anxious, eager, after something. What is it? I feel my own Ignorance. I feel concern for Knowledge, and fame. I have a dread of Contempt, a quick sense of Neglect, a strong Desire of Distinction.

Went this morning to D.B. [Deacon Belcher?] and L.B. to see the Leases under which they held the Town Lands. I learned enough to reward me for the Trouble, tho I could not see the Leases. I find that as much knowledge in my Profession is to be acquired by Conversing with common People about the Division of Estates, Proceedings of Judge of Probate, Cases that they have heard as Jurors, Witnesses, Parties, as is to be acquired by Books. Talked familiarly with Deacon B. and his Wife. Talked to N.B. [Nathaniel Belcher?] about The Ile of Orleans, and the Contrast between the present and the last administration, to J. Curtis, of Husbandry, and the Tittletattle of the Town. Thus I believe I have lost no Credit yet, but have gained Credit as a knowing as well as a familiar young fellow. I must sett the Town to talking about me.

What shall I say to Majr. Crosby to procure his Love and Admiration too? Ask him for Executions, Writs, News Papers, what days he usually attends at Home to try Causes. What say to Deacon Webb, to procure his Love and Ad[miration?]. Papers.

As I rode under the Rocks and savines in the common the Project darted into my Head of writing a Poem under the Title of the matrimonial Ballance, or the Ballance of Celibacy. A Ballance for weighing the Pleasures of Matrimony against the Pains, the Inconveniences vs. the Conveniences. Let me invent the Fable. Wisdom appears to a young fellow, as he sits meditating on Celibacy and Matrimony, and presents him with these scales. How shall I describe Wisdom? the Scales? that every Air, Shape, Colour, may convey some moral Instruction.

B[illy] B[elcher] has a very mean Opinion of all the Quincies, all 3 Neds, and Jos[iah] and Samll. and Henry.

Cranch has been mean since, if Q[uincy] was before the first difference between them.

Billy B. He says he will charge you with 1/2 the Rent of the Warehouse in B[oston]. If he does, I can swear that he declared to me in a very solemn manner that he kept the Warehouse open only to oblige me.[21]

This might be new. The Coll. and all his sons are insincere. They make a greater shew, more Expressions of Kindness and Friendship, than they really have for any Man. He wanted to convince B. that he was a great Benefactor to him. Perhaps he wanted his good Words at home at Braintree, to his father and Brother.

M[aster?] Cleverly. I have no Opinion of our Courts. They act as the spirit moves them. There is no Dependance upon Judge Sewall,[22] nor Judge Hutchinson,[23] the Governor &c.

He is as hungry after Vices and Follies in the Characters of the Quincies, and of our Courts, as a Wolf ever was for Prey. An Instance of Weakness or Wickedness practiced by any Quincy gratifies him to the quick. He has no Candour, no Charity. He is censorious. He is spightful.

Dr. Savil. Ephraim Thayer told a Story the other day that he saw a small ground Squirrell run away with 2 large Ears. He introduced it with a solemn Train of Circumstances. He raised a great deal of Corn, and could not imagine how it went. He could not suspect any of his Neighbours, and he thought no Creature but Man could take it of[f] so fast. At last he lay and watched it and soon found that the squirrells were the Thieves for he saw one single ground squirrell run out of his fold with 2 Ears.—This Pun.

Another time he was a gunning and he saw at a little distance a Partridge at the foot of a Tree and a grey Squirell, at the Top of it. He wanted to get both, but he knew if he shot at the squirrel the Partridge would fly, and if he shot at the Partridge the squirrel would run away before he could charge his Gun a second time. He tho't he would contrive to kill both at once, and he crept round in fair Sight of both, and shot and killed both at once. Now one must be very quick and [very expert?] to hold the Gun just at the Root long eno' to kill the Partridge and then raise it to the Top in order to kill with the other half of the Charge the squirrel at the Top. But the Riddle was, The Tree was blown down, and he got the Partridge and Squirrel in a very fair Range.

An Advocate. The Patron of the Cause, assisting the Litigant with his Advice, the Person who pleads or represents the Cause of his Client. They should not be interrupted in their studies by [...]. De quota litis.[24] Tis a public off[ence?].

[1] This approximate and indefinite date is the best that can be assigned to the long series of wholly undated entries that begin JA's Diary booklet "No. 3." This "paper book" (our D/JA/3) is made up of loose leaves and small gatherings, some originally stitched together with thread and some apparently not. Since such stitching as there once was has now largely worn away, and since in composing his Diary JA sometimes left blank pages, or portions of pages, that he filled in later, it is now impossible to determine the original order of some of the entries. It may only be said that the earliest ones in this booklet were legal notes, set down before JA had filled up the preceding "paper book" (D/JA/2) early in April 1759; these are now embedded among diary entries that extend into the summer of 1759 and possibly later. The MS contains entries in small blank spaces in the margins, others written upside down on pages bearing other matter, some entries begun but never finished by the diarist, and still others that he may have completed on pages now lost from the MS. Only one entry was fully dated by JA, that of 29 June 1759, about halfway through D/JA/3.

Most of the entries were written in a hasty, slipshod way, and some whole pages are badly worn and faded, necessitating at times a reconstruction of the text that is not wholly satisfactory to the editors. It is perhaps for these reasons that large portions of D/JA/3 were omitted in the early transcripts made for JQA and corrected by CFA. Moreover, in his edition of JA's Diary CFA omitted all but a few selections from this booklet. These selections give only a hint or two of JA's protracted affair with Hannah Quincy and no hint at all of JA's first impressions of Miss Abigail Smith of Weymouth, who five years later became his wife.

After careful study the editors have decided that they have no good choice but to print all the entries in their present physical order in the MS,

scrambled though they may be, simply grouping them under the assigned dates of Spring 1759 and Summer 1759 according to whether they precede or follow the single dated entry of 29 June.

[2] Spelling very doubtful. The Piscataqua River empties into the Atlantic at Portsmouth, N.H.

[3] Jonathan Sewall (1728–1796), Harvard 1748; lawyer, loyalist, and, until their separation by the events leading up to the Revolution, JA's intimate friend. He married Esther Quincy in 1764.

[4] Bela Lincoln (1734–1773), Harvard 1754; a physician of Hingham; married Hannah Quincy, 1 May 1760 (*History of Hingham*, Hingham, 1893, vol. 1: pt. ii, p. 317–318; JQA's extracts from Braintree Church Records, Adams Papers).

[5] The following paragraph and a number of later entries in D/JA/3 touching on JA's romantic interest in Hannah Quincy were omitted by CFA in editing the Diary. Evidently that interest was by no means ended by the incident recorded in the present entry, though, as explained above, the chronological sequence of numerous undated entries in this part of the MS is very uncertain.

[6] Elizabeth (Waldron) Quincy, 2d wife of Col. Josiah Quincy. She had married Quincy in 1756 and is said to have died later in the present year (Salisbury, *Family-Memorials*, 1:356); but see the entry of 2 Dec. 1760 and note 3 there.

[7] That is, Edmund Trowbridge, the Cambridge lawyer and judge, who as a young man had used the name Goffe.

[8] Col. Josiah Quincy's house was burned on 17 May 1759 (*Boston Evening Post*, 21 May 1759). Though the allusion to this event very strongly suggests that the present entry is out of chronological order and belongs later in the Diary, there is nothing in the MS itself to support this conjecture. See also p. 111–113, below.

[9] The entry breaks off thus at the end

of a left-hand page in MS. A leaf or leaves may therefore be missing from the MS, but there are instances in this booklet of JA's deliberately leaving sentences unfinished.

[10] This and the following detached paragraphs on husbandry were omitted by CFA in editing the Diary.

[11] Puis darrein continuance: "A plea which is put in after issue joined, for the purpose of introducing new matter" (Bouvier, *Law Dictionary*, 2:394).

[12] The case was that of William Thompson, appellant, *v.* John Allen et al., appellees, in the Superior Court, Suffolk, Feb. term, 1759. The argument JA records took place on 1 March (Superior Court of Judicature, Minute Book 71; Records, 1757–1759, fol. 522–523). These notes by JA must therefore have been taken down on 2 March, well before the regular Diary entries in D/JA/3 begin (see note 1, above).

[13] Probably in the Suffolk Inferior Court, whose records for this period are missing.

[14] In the Superior Court (Minute Book 71; Records, 1757–1759, fol. 534–535).

[15] Closing quotation mark conjecturally supplied.

[16] Text breaks off thus at the end of a

left-hand page in MS. A leaf or leaves may therefore be missing.

[17] Thomas Pownall was governor of Massachusetts Bay, 1757–1760.

[18] This passage is only semilegible. JA is quoting Horace, Epistle II, Book II, lines 138–140:

"Pol me occidistis, amici,
Non servastis," ait; "cui sic extorta voluptas
Et demptus per vim mentis gratissimus error."

[19] See 1 Kings, 17:21.

[20] The Farms was long the local name for an area later known as North Quincy (Pattee, *Old Braintree and Quincy*, p. 56; *Braintree Town Records*, p. 430).

[21] This is in all probability the end of Billy Belcher's remarks, and what follows is doubtless JA's comment thereon. In the MS, however, there is no indication of such a shift.

[22] Chief Justice Stephen Sewall (1702–1760); Harvard 1721 (Sibley-Shipton, *Harvard Graduates*, 6:561–567).

[23] Doubtless Eliakim Hutchinson (1711–1775), chief justice of the Suffolk Inferior Court of Common Pleas; Harvard 1730 (Sibley-Shipton, *Harvard Graduates*, 8:726–729).

[24] See Bouvier, *Law Dictionary*, 1:430.

JUNE 29. 1759.

Have this moment finished Woods new Institute of the Imperial or civil Law.[1] It is a great Help in the study of Van Muyden and Justinian. I understand Wood much better for having read Van Muyden, and shall now understand Van Muyden much better for having read Wood.

[1] Thomas Wood, *A New Institute of the Imperial or Civil Law*, London, 1704, went through several editions.

[SUMMER 1759.][1]

Mr. Wibirt. Ld. Chancellor Hardwick used at night to take off the Robes of his office and lay them aside. "There Ld. Chancellor lie there till morning." This Story means that he assumed the state and Dignity of his office, when he was in the Exercise of it, but threw off all state with his Robes and shewed the sociable Friend and Companion.

P[arson] W[ibird]. Out of H[annah] and E[sther] might be made a very personable Woman but not a great soul.

She is pleased. I find that the Chat I had with H. is uppermost in my mind. While my Eyes are on my Book, my Attention, my Imagination is playing and prating with her. These scenes of Pleasure make too deep Impressions on my Imagination.

K.[2] I see H. have such an one, and asked her who it was for?

Again I find my Thoughts ruminating the idle Chat, and Banter, I had with K. and Easther. A Contest, a Combat between Reason and Passion is unequal. A struggle between Reflections upon Law and Reflections upon Love, between an Inclination to study and an Inclination to ruminate on the Prate, Banter, laughter, looks, airs of the Girls, is likely to be followed by Victory on the side of Trifles.

I asked Mr. Wibirt if he made the fowl eat his Comb and Gills to make him couragious?—and Nan.[3] broke out into a triumphant, awkward, silly, shamefaced, malignant Laugh, and cryed, why some has been cutt off of your Head, lately, did you eat it to make you couragious? You eat it I believe and that made you so couragious.— This is ill breeding.

I find, that by walking, riding, and talking so much, I have got a restless Habit. As I set, writing or reading a Thought, a Desire of running over to the Drs. will dart into my Head, and I feel a [damp?] in suppressing of it. Next minute a Thought and desire of running down to Dr. Webbs, John Mills's &c. Thus Reflections upon past and Projects for future Pleasures, interrupt my studies.

Enim for omnis Res, every Thing. Virtus, Virtue. Fame, Decorum, both divine and human Things, obey, bow with Reverence to fair Riches: which, whoever has accumulated, heaped up, he will be handsome, valiant, just [...] wise, and a King, and what ever he will.

Novation.[4] An obligation is abolished, by Novation. A Transfer of the 1st Obligation into another. Transfer the obligation by Changing the Person, shift the Debtor. I take A.B. for my Debtor, for that Debt which was owed me by B.C. Dr. Savel owes me 10 Dollars, I discharge him and take J. Field for Paymaster. Tis only a Transfer, a shifting the obligation from the Dr. to Field. That obligation which lay on Sempronius to pay me 10 Dolls. is now on Titius. Or Novation may be by transferring one obligation into another while the same Persons continue.

Sempronious owes me £10 on Account. This £10 by mutual Consent is acknowledged to be due to [me?] as [money?] lent him, cui Bono.

May I call them 2 sorts of Novation. Quibus Modis, by what Ways—by what Means, by what Ways, an obligation is taken away or abolished. Concerning Novation or Renewal. This Conversion is made by Words or Stipulation. Besides an obligation is taken away by Renewal, as, if that which Sejus owed you, if that which Savil owed you, you should stipulate to be [given?] by Titius. If you should stipulate that that should be given paid by Titius which Sejus owed you. For by the Intervention of a new Person, a new obligation is born, springs, grows, and the 1st is abolished, translata in Posteriorum, is transferred on the latter, so that some times, altho the latter stipulation is useless, yet the first by the Law of Renewal is taken away. As if that which you owe to Titius, and he stipulated by the Pupil without the Authority of a Tutor. There are many ways, in which by the Law itself an Obligation is abolished. In this Title only 4 are related. Novation is a transfusion and Translation of a former Debt, into another obligation, civil or natural, and is either voluntary, which is made by the Agreement of Parties, or necessary, which is made [...]5 by a Joining of Issues and the sentence of the Judge. This does not diminish the Right of the Plaintiff.

Novation moreover is made either the Persons of the Creditor and Debtor remaining: or these Persons changed. Continuing which either the Cause of [...] is changed or a new quality is added, or an old one substituted, so that it be acted among the Contracting Parties. A Mutation Change of Persons happens [three] Ways, either the Person of the Creditor being changed, or of the Debtor, which in specie [*i.e. in this form*] is called Delegation, or by changing the Person of both. In Delegation a twofold Act ought to be considered, the first between the delegating and the delegated in which naked Consent is sufficient, declared by Writing or a Nod or by any other manner, in which Consent it may be [defined?].

Delegation is a Command, by which a Debtor substitutes his Debtor in his own Place to his own Creditor. Another Act is committed between a Delegate and him to whom the Delegation is made in which a stipulation is required. A stipulation, by which a Debtor delegate to a stipulating Creditor to [whom?] delegated, promises that [he] is about to pay the Debt, in whose Name the Delegation is made.

Acceptilation is an imaginary Payment, an Acknowledgment of the Creditor, that he has been paid when in truth he has not, with Design to discharge the Debtor. Acceptilation is a stipulation by which a

Creditor, with a design of dissolving the obligation answers the Debtor interrogating, that he has received his Debt when [indeed?] he has not. Simple Acceptilation is that by which is abolished only an Obligation contracted by Words. An Exception is an Exclusion, barring of an Action [...] by law.

Consider what figure is fittest for you to make. Consider what Profession you have chosen? The Law. What Rule and Method must I observe to make a figure to be useful, and respectable in that Station. Ask this Question upon every Occasion, of what Use to the Lawyer? of what use at the Bar—[to have?] perfection of Knowledge in Theory or Expertness in Practice, or Eloquence at Bar? Let my Views concenter, and terminate in one focus, in one Point, a great, useful, virtuous Lawyer. With this View I might plan a system of study for seven Years to come, that should take in most Parts of Science and Literature. I might study Mathematics, and Poetry and Rhetorick and Logick, as auxiliary Sciences and Arts, but my principal Attention should be directed at british Law, and roman and Grecian Antiquities.

Gad. Chd.[6] I set out once for a merry, jovial fellow. Merriment and Jollity, a thoughtless, careless Air, humming a Tune, &c. are esteemed the Supream Excellence of human Nature by some Men.

I have slid insensibly of late into a Channell of Prattle with Dr. Savel that will carry me into folly if I dont get out of it. I talk ⟨dogmatically⟩ big, impudent, bully like, and think it wit, sense and Eloquence.
Let me avoid such silly and indecent freedoms with the Dr. and such silly, affected drollery with his Wife and Niese.
I shall loose the natural Course of my Thoughts.

Trumbull has nothing new upon the Subject. His Principles are all taken from ancient Moralists, and from Dr. Clark, Mr. Hutchinson, Bp. Butler, Ld. Shaftesbury and Mr. Pope.

Nat. Gard[ner].[7] I can never recollect Mens Names. I remembered your Face, and Person, but I could not recollect your Name.
This is a Habit of Inattention, a Habit of ruminating on Poetry, &c., on what he has read as he walks the Streets. This slowness of Memory, is consistent with ready Wit.
His Memory is very quick and prompt sometimes, tho it is very slow

at others.—Ruggles now is a contrast. Ruggles has the most constant Presence of Mind. He never makes Blunders thro Inattention. He received Money from 1/2 a dozen Gentlemen, and then rummaged his Pocketts, and dropd [8] with John Chandler with as much Composure as if he had been a week in studying how to behave. And, upon that sudden Occasion, at Worcester, he planned his scheme in a moment, and he managed every Part of it with as much Readiness and Propriety as he could have done, if he had prepared himself for it, a week before hand.

N. Gard[ner] is heedless, and inattentive, has no Presence of Mind. Ruggles is the Man for Attention.

Dan. [Treadwell].[9] There is a linear, a superficial and a solid Amplification. Thus if a Globe of one Inch in Diameter, appears thro a Microscope, 10 Inches in Diameter, This Microscope magnifies lineally 10 times, superficially 100 times and in solidity 1000 times, because the solidity is amplified in a cubical and the superficies in a quadratical Proportion to the Amplification of the Diameter. So that a Glass which magnifies in Diameter only 10 times, magnifies in solidity 1000 times.

Any Attraction or Repulsion that should accelerate or retard the Motion of the Comet would alter the Excentricity of its Elipsis and its Inclination too, if the attracting or repelling Body was without the Plane of the Comets Orbit.

Treadwell and I were four Hours on the Road to Boston. Our Horses never went out of a Walk and I believe, sometimes almost stood still, while we were engaged in Conversation upon Mathematicks, Physicks, Astronomy, optics &c. I am ashamed of my self. Treadwell [h]as had great Advantages, and has greatly improved them. He bears a great share in all Conversation, upon Politicks, War, Geography, Physicks &c.

Treadwell. The Rule for determining the Specific Gravity of a Body is to multiply not its Superficies, but its Capacity, its solid Contents into its Weight. For two Bodies of the same Metal of the same specific Gravity but of different Figures as a Sphere and a Cube e.g. may have equal surfaces but unequal solid Contents, and on the other Hand equall solid Contents or Capacity and unequal surfaces. Suppose a Sphere and Cube of Gold, of equal superficies, the Sphere will have the greatest Capacity.

The solid Content, the real Magnitude multiplied into the absolute

Gravity or absolute Weight determines its Specific Gravity or relative Weight.

Treadwell. Sewall and Mr. Langdon together made a very great Blunder.[10] They made just observations of the Comet, but they drew several false Consiquences from those observations. I was sorry for Sewall is a very ingenious, young fellow. I blamed him for printing so hastily.

Quere, does the Capacity, the Solid Content, bear the same Proportion to the Weight, when the Matter is in one Sphere, as it does when divided into 20 Spheres.

Take a Sphere of gold one foot in Diameter, and divide it into 12 Globes, Quere, will the solid Content, the Capacity be increased?

Parson Smith has no small share of Priest Craft.[11]—He conceals his own Wealth, from his Parish, that they may not be hindered by knowing it from sending him Presents.—He talks very familiarly with the People, Men and Women of his Parish, to gain their affection.— He is [a] crafty designing Man.—He watches Peoples Looks and Behaviour.—He laughs at Parson Wibirts careless Air and Behaviour—his Walk across the Room, his long step and his Clapping his naked sides and Breasts with his Hands before the Girls.—He made just Remarks on the Character of Mr. Maccarty.—his Conceit, his orthodoxy, his Ignorance &c. and I caught him, several times, looking earnestly at my face.—He is not one of the heedless, inattentive Crew, that take no Notice of Mens Behaviour and Conversation and form no Judgment of their Characters.

Polly and Nabby are Wits.[12] Ned will not take Account of all of every Colour that spring from the Quincys. Easthers Simile.

A Man of fond Passions. Cranch was fond of his Friend, fond of his Girl, and would have been fond of his Wife and Children. Tender and fond. Loving and compassionate. H.Q. is of the same Character, fond of her Brother, fond of herself and tender[ly] pitiful. Q[uery], are fondness and Wit compatible? P[arson] S[mith]s Girls have not this fondness, nor this Tenderness.

Fondling and Indulgence. They are the faulty Effects of good Nature. Good nature is H's universal Character. She will be a fond, tender Wife, and a fond indulgent Mother. Cranch is endeavoring to amend this Defect, to correct this fault in his Character, he affects an Asperity, to the Children, to his old Friends. His former Complaisance is vanished.—Do real Fondness, and Frankness, always go together. They met in C. and they met in H.—Fondness and Candour, and Frankness. Frankness, and Simplicity. Fondness is doting Love. Candor is a Disposition to palliate faults and Mistakes, to put the best Construction upon Words and Actions, and to forgive Injuries. Simplicity is a direct, open, artless, undisguised, Behaviour.

Are S Gils [the Smith Girls] either Frank or fond, or even candid.— Not fond, not frank, not candid.

[Draft of a Letter to Samuel Quincy.] [13]

Dear Sam

I am seated, to write you a most humble Petition for, what you have already repeatedly promised to grant, the favour of a Letter. I have, in this Place, none to converse with but the dead, and altho their Conversation is generally very entertaining and instructive yet I find in my Heart, sometimes an Inclination to speak to the Living, but as that Priviledge is denied me, I would be satisfied with Writing to them, if that could interceed for an Answer. For my own Part, I flatter my self sometimes, that I have an uncommon share of Benevolence, sociability and friendship in my Composition, since I feel the strongest Desire of talking and writing, to you and many others, but upon a closer Reflection I find it is self at Bottom that hungers for the Instruction that others can give. Your situation, in the most busy office, in the Center of one of the best Libraries, and under the Instructions and Advice of one of the ablest Masters in America, not to mention (least you should suspect me of Compliment) the early youthful friendship between us, nor your happy Talents for such a Correspondence, have made me wish most heartily for a constant Correspondence with you.

Cards, Fiddles, and Girls, are the objects of Sam. Cards, Fiddles and Girls. Kissing, fidling and gaming. A flute, a Girl, and a Pack of Cards.

Note. I am liable [to] absence and Inattention, stupidity. I called at [Baldwins?] with J. Crosby and Mr. W[...] and left W. to pay for my Oats. [T. Lyde?] asked me for an Account. I took 3 or 4 [wrong?] Papers before I could find the [...]. [L.?] bid me open the [Door?], and I shut it.

Thatcher. Pownalls style is better than Shirleys. Shirley never promoted any Man for Merit alone. If Satan himself were incarnate and in Competition with Parson Wells for the Election, I would vote for old Harry. I cant think that any Man of true good sense can be so vain, and fond of talking of himself as Parson Wells. Tully was not a vain Man. The vainest Thing that ever he said was, in his oration for Murena, that if they provoked him, he would profess himself a Lawyer in 3 days. I wish my self a soldier. I look upon these private soldiers with their Guns upon their shoulders, as superiour to me.

These are all wild, extravagant, loose Opinions and Expressions. He expresses himself as madly as Coll. Chandler. Wild flights. He has not considered that these crude Thoughts and wild Expressions are catched and treasured, as Proofs of his Character. He is extreamly tender, and sensible of Pleasure and of Paine.

Kent is for fun, Drollery, Humour, flouts, Jeers, Contempt. He has an irregular immethodical Head, but his Thoughts are often good and his Expressions happy.

Thatchers Passions are easily touched, his shame, his Compassions, his fear, his Anger, &c.

Worthington.[14] A Man may be in Duress as well by an Injury to his Estate as by a Restraint of his Liberty, or by Menaces to his Person. I remember a Case in Sir John Stayer [Sir James Stair?] to this Purpose. A Man borrowed of his Neighbour £100 for 6 months, and gave him a Pawn of twice that Value, for security. When the 6 months were expired, he offered to pay the Money and the lawful Interest for it, and redeem his Pawn, but the Pawnee refused to resign it, without £10 for the Interest of his £100 for the 6 months. The Owner of the Pawn accordingly paid the £10, and redeemed his Pawn and afterwards brought his Action against Pawnee, for the £10 he had paid him as Interest, and it was pleaded, that he paid it voluntarily, and Volenti non fit Injuria, i.e. as he had paid it voluntarily, he was not injured. But it was adjudged that he should recover, for he was under a Constraint, a Necessity, in Point of Interest, i.e. in order to regain his Pawn, to pay the ten Pounds, and therefore, it should be considered as extorted from him by Duress.

Thatcher. The Speaker of the House of Commons in some former age, was impeached before the House, of Bribery. And was obliged to sett in the Chair, and hear the whole Examination of his own Conduct, and all the Debates of the Members upon it, till the House was ready for a Vote, and then was obliged to put the Vote himself whether he should be expelled the House? The poor Man earnestly prayed to be excused, but could not, for while he was Speaker he alone could demand the Vote, which he did at last, and it passed in the Affirmative.

Divorce. Is it for the Benefit of Society, for the Convenience and Happiness of human Life, to allow of Divorces, in any Cases. I think it is. I think that either Adultery or Impotence are sufficient Reasons of Divorce. But Quere, if Dissonance of Dispositions is a sufficient Reason. This may be known, if sufficient Caution is taken beforehand. But the others cannot. By Conversation with a Lady, and Tryals of her Temper, and by Inquiry of her Acquaintance, a Man may know, whether her Temper will suit him or not. But he can never know whether she will be fruitful or barren, continent or incontinent.

But would an unlimited Toleration of Divorces promote the multiplication of Mankind or the happiness of Life.

Suppose every Man had a Power by Law, to repudiate his Wife and marry another at his Pleasure. Would not such a Power produce confusion, and Misery? After a Man and Woman had cohabited 7 years and had as many Children a seperation would be very inconvenient and unhappy. If either retained all the Children the other would be deprived of the Pleasure of educating, and seeing [them]. But if the Children were divided, each would want to see and provide for the others half.

Fortune has burned Coll. Quincys House, and some of his Furniture.[15] Fortune is a capricious Goddess. She diverts herself with Men. She bestows her favours sometimes with very great Profusion on a Man, and within a few Years she strips him even of Necessaries. Tis a fluctuating state. We are tossed on the Waves sometimes to Heaven, and then sunk down to the Bottom. That House and Furniture clung and twined round his Heart, and could not be torn away without tearing to the quick.

Is it possible to preserve a serene undisturbed Mind, thro such a fire, and the Consequences of it.

There is in human Nature an attainable Magnanimity, which can see a valuable House, full of furniture, consuming in flames, a Friend, a Child, a Wife, struggling in the Agonies of Death, without a sigh, a Tear, or a painful sensation or Reflection. The Felicis Animi immota Tranquilitas, the immovable Tranquility of a happy Mind, unmoved by Perils of Water or of fire, unmoved by any Losses, Accidents, by Loss of Wealth, of fame, of friends, &c. Happy Mind indeed. Cant a

Mind be called happy, unless its Tranquility, its Ease, its Rest, is immovable, invincible.

It is not at all surprizing, that the Coll. is more dejected than his Brother was, for tho his Brothers Reduction was more compleat, yet the Coll's was less expected.[16] Ned was reduced to be worse than nothing. Josa.[Josiah] has a Competency left. But Josa.['s] loss was entirely unforeseen, unexpected, and unprepared for. But Neds was, I presume, familiarly known and considered, by him at least beforehand.

Edmund lost a son as suddenly as the Coll. lost his House. And he shew[ed] as much Anxiety too. He could not sleep, all night, after he heard of it. The Colls Grief is more eloquent than Neds.

Dissappointments are Misery. If a Man takes Pride and Pleasure in a House, or in rich furniture, or Cloathing, or in any Thing, how is it possible for him to be satisfied when they are lost, destroyed, consumed.

Not to admire is all the Art I know, to make men happy and to keep them so. Coll. admired his House, tis burned, he is unhappy, &c. They are burned. He is unhappy.

It is a natural, immutable Law that the Buyer ought not to take Advantage of the sellers Necessity, to purchase at too low a Price. Suppose Money was very scarce, and a Man was under a Necessity of procuring a £100 within 2 Hours to satisfy an Execution, or else go to Goal. He has a Quantity of Goods worth £500 that he would sell. He finds a Buyer who would give him £100 for them all, and no more. The poor Man is constrained to sell £500s worth for £100. Here the seller is wronged, tho he sell [them?] voluntarily in one sense. Yet, the Injustice, that may be done by some Mens availing them selves of their Neighbours Necessities, is not so Great as the Inconvenience to Trade would be if all Contracts were to be void which were made upon insufficient Considerations. But Q. What Damage to Trade, what Inconvenience, if all Contracts made upon insufficient Considerations were void.

I made some observation[s] on Barbery Bushes, Shoe make [Sumach], Cater Pillars, &c.

Inquire the Properties of Isinglass, and of Carpenters Glew. How the 1st attracts all the Pumice and Sediment in Cyder to the Bottom and the latter to the Top?

Inquire how the Juice lies in the Apple. What is the Cause of its natural Fermentation and inquire the operation of artificial fermentation.

[*Draft of a Letter to Colonel Josiah Quincy.*] [17]
You regret your Loss. But why? Was you fond of seeing, or of thinking that others saw and admired, so stately a Pile? Or was you pleased with viewing the convenient and elegant Contrivance of the inside, and with shewing to others how neatly it was finished. Is it the Pleasure of seeing, with your own Eyes, the Elegance, and Grandeur of your House, or is it the Pleasure of imagining that others admired it and admired or envyed you for it that you regrett the Loss of? Did you suppose that you was esteemed and regarded for the Beauty and Conveniency of your House? Or are you mortified to think that your Enemies will be gratified, at your Misfortune. If these are the sources of your Grief, it is irrational, unmanly. For the Friendship, that is founded on your figure and Estate, is not worth preserving, and the Man who can rejoice, at your Loss, is not worth attention. But if you consider it as a punishment of your Vices and follies, as a frown that is designed to arrouse your attention, to Things of a more permanent Nature, you should not grieve, but rejoice, that the great Parent of the World has thus corrected you for your good.

Figure, and shew, may indeed attract the Eyes, and Admiration of the Vulgar, but are little very little regarded by wise Men. Is it not rational, noble, to dote of the Pleasure of viewing a fine Horse, and being seen by others to ride such a one. A fine Horse, a fine House, Riches, Learning, make People stare at me and talk about me, and a mighty Boon this to be stared at, and talked of by People that I despize, and all that I regard will love and Honor me for Acquisitions that I have Power to [make?] and which cant be torn from me. Wisdom and Virtue are not dependent on the Elements of fire or Water, Air or Earth.

How should I bear Bob Pains Detraction? Should I be angry, and take Vengeance by scandalizing him? or should I be easy, undisturbed, and praise him, as far as he is Praise worthy. Return good for Evil. I should have been as well pleased if he had said I was a very ingenious, promising young fellow, but as it is I am pretty easy.—I should not have been sorry if you had called at our House.

Try her [Hannah Quincy's] Prudence. See if you cant draw from

her saucy disrespectfull Expressions concerning her Mother in Law.—
Was not you very intimate with your Mother, when she was Bty.
Waldron?—as intimate as you are with N. Marsh. She assumes the
Authority of the Step mother.—She wears more Airs of Reserve, and
Distance, and Superiority than your father.—She[18] is elated with her
Match.—She is not the most discreet Woman. She told the Behaviour
of the People, at the Tavern they were at in the Country about the
Tea, before all the Monatiquot officers, shoe string fellows that never
use Tea and would use it as [awkwardly?] as the Landlady did. That
was quite imprudent [and] impopular. It was designed to divert
and please, but it had a contrary Effect. It made them all jealous and
suspicious that they were remarked and laughed at as much to the
next Company. And her unguarded Expressions about Peoples being
afraid, backward to go near the fire, and about their Eating her Sweet
meats, drinking their Brandy, and stealing their [. . .] and Cloathing
have given offence to many People.

These are Indiscretions, that some Women would have avoided.

H. was very imprudent, to endeavour to exasperate Mr. Cranch, for
she is sensible, that he knows a story to her Disadvantage, and she
should remember that Love turned to Hatred, is like the best Wine
turned to Vinegar, the most acrid in the World. He will seek Revenge.
Arise black Vengeance from the hollow Hell is the language of Othello.
I expect to hear very soon that he has divulged that story.

By saying you have corresponded with Dr. Lincoln so long and by
saying I can tell you how J. Brackett carries your Letters to Captn.
Hews's, and leaves them there, and takes Lincolns Letters to you, she
judged, that J. Brackett had told me she held a correspondence with
Lincoln, and went to clearing herself. She declared and protested, she
never wrote a Line to him in her Life, excepting one Billet, relating to
those Reflections on Courtship and Marriage which she sent with that
Book. So I got satisfied.

H. I dont know who has been plagued most, Mr. Cranch or I. I
think I have as much Reason to complain of being plagued as he.

Parson Wiberts Hints. I am not obliged to answer his Hints. I could
see a good deal of Passion mixed with his Raillery. This is bragging.
She will drop such Hints, by and by, that I am in Love with her, and
will tell others, that she aint obliged to take my meaning by my saying,

but let me explain my self, and then I shall receive a [...] Repulse. My Father gave me my Choice, left me at Liberty. I am not controuled nor constrained. My own Pleasure and Inclinations are to be my Guide.

Suppose I should hear that J. Went[worth], [Dan.?] Lock, B. Crawford, Mr. Cranch was dead, what Sentiment would rise? A tender Grief, sorrow, mourning. But should Hannah die, what sentiment? Should not I be more affected with her Death than with Cranch's? I cant say. But should my father or Mother die or my Brothers, how should I feel? But the Deaths of Acquaintances, Relations, Friends, are but one sort of sorrowful Events. Losses by Shipwreck, Bankruptcy, or fire, are another sort. How should I bear a sudden Consumption [of] a fine Estate, by any such Accident? How should [I] bear acute Pain, or frequent sickness, or a lingering chronical Disorder? The latter I have born, the former never tryed. Scorn Grief, and create Joy. Create, and maintain out of your own Thoughts a constant Satisfaction of Mind, by considering the Littleness of Grief, and the Magnanimity of Resignation.
Littleness of Mind alone can be grieved, and grumble at what it cannot help, and what it would be foolish to help if it could.

An habit of Indolence, and Listlessness is growing very fast upon me.

I am unable to think patiently, for any Length of Time.

Secondat says, that a Man, in the State of Nature i.e. unimproved by Education or Experience, would feel Nothing but his own Impotence and would tremble at the motion of a Leaf, and fly from every Shadow.[19]
But Q.—What proof can be given of this Assertion? What Reason is there to think that Timidity, rather than Confidence or Presumption, would hold the Ascendancy in him? Is it not as reasonable to think he would be too bold, as too timorous, and engage oak Trees, unwieldy Rocks, or wild Beasts, [&c.?] as that he would fly from every Shadow? The scarcity of Phenomena, make it impossible to decide. There never was more than one or two Men found, at full Age, who had grown up with the Beasts in the Woods and never seen a human Creature, and they were not very critically observed. What does he mean by a Man in a State of Nature? Suppose a Child, confined in a Room, and supplied with Necessaries, by some secret invisible avenue, till 20

115

year[s] old, without ever seeing a human Creature. That Man would be in a State of Nature, i.e. unimproved by Experience and human Conversation. ⟨*Suppose, this Man at 20, brought from his Cell.*⟩ Suppose a Man of the same Age and size let into this poor fellows Cell. What would be the Effect of the Meeting. Would the savage be frightened, or pleased. Surprized he would be, but agreably, or disagreably. Would his fears make him fly, or his Curiosity examine, or his Presumption assault the new object?

In a total Inexperience and Ignorance, how would human Passions operate? I cant say. A Child, at its first Entrance upon the World, discovers no signs of Terror or Surprize at the new scenes and objects, that lie around it, and if the Child is not terrified, why should the Man be. The Child is pleased as soon as its Eyes are first opened with bright and luminous objects, not frightened. It will smile not cry. Suppose then a whole Army of Persons, trained up in this manner in single seperate Cells, brought together, would they mutually dred and fly each other, or be pleased with the sight of each other, and by consequence allured gradually to a more intimate Acquaintance or would they fall together by the Ears for the Mastery as two Herds of strange Cattle do? Would the State of Nature be a State of War or Peace? Two might meet, and be pleased with each others looks, and fall to play, like two Lambs. Two others might meet, and one might apply his Hands to the others Body and hurt him, and then both fall afighting like 2 Dogs. So that both Friendship and Squabbles might be the Consequences of the first Congress. But Passions work so differently in different men especially when several of them are complicated together, and several, as Surprize, Joy, fear, Curiosity would in this Case be combined, that we cant judge what the Consequences would be in such an imaginary Congress.

Hobbes thinks, that Men like Cattle, if in a state of Nature, would mutually desire and strive for the Mastery, and I think Secondat's Argument from the Complexity of the Idea of Dominion, is not a Refutation of Hobbes's Hypothesis, for Cattle fight for Dominion, and Men in the State of Nature may be supposed to have as clear an Idea of Dominion as the Cattle have. The Laws received in a State of Nature i.e. before the Establishment of society, are the Laws of Nature. How can man be considered out of Society, before the Establishment of Society. We put possible imaginable Cases, and then ask what would be the Effect. The Species cant subsist, without Society, but an Individual may, as the wild Man found in a forrest, or a Child bred alone in a Cell out of all Human sight. Now suppose 1000 such Individuals should exist at once and all be collected and turned loose together in the same forrest. What would succeed. Some squabbles, wild [staring?], and some plays, [sports?], Copulation would soon succeed.

[...] Lust of Dominion could not at first produce a War of all against all. They would not feel any such Desire of ruling and subduing. They would soon feel hunger and thirst, and desire of Copulation and Calf, and would endeavour to supply these Wants and gratify these Desires, but would not yet conceive the Thought and Wish of governing all the Rest. Peace, Nourishment, Copulation, and Society. Recur [to] this by all means, when I get into a thotless dissipated [Mood?], set down and write my self into [steady?] thinking.

Law is human Reason. It governs all the Inhabitants of the Earth; the political and civil Laws of each Nation should be only the particular Cases, in which human Reason is applied.

Let me attend to the Principle of Government. The Laws of Britain, should be adapted to the Principle of the british Government, to the Climate of Britain, to the Soil, to its situation, as an Island, and its Extent, to the manner of living of the Natives as Merchants, Manufacturers and Husbandmen, to the Religion of the Inhabitants.

This is a succession in Capita. Suppose my father should die, and leave me and my 3 Brothers. In that Case The Inheritance, all my fathers Estate must be divided into 3 Parts. And if he had left 4 or 5 or 6 Children, his Estate must have been divided into 4 or 5 or 6 Parts or shares. The Inheritance is to be divided according to the Number of Heads, that are to succeed.

This is a succession in stirpes. Suppose I had a family and should die leaving 3 Children and afterwards my father should die, leaving my two Brothers alive, in this Case my 3 Children must succeed to my fathers Estate in my stead and my fathers Inheritance must be divided into 3 parts, one of which should be inherited by my three Children. Here it is divided not according to the No. of Heads but according to the Number of stocks, that spring from the common Root which is my father.

An alliance between the Emperor and the States to which England acceded. England and Holland obliged themselves to assist the House of Austria, in taking and keeping Possession of the Spanish Monarchy, when ever Charles 2d should die without lawful Heirs. France had designs and Pretensions on the Spanish Monarchy. The 1st object of the grand alliance was the Reduction of the Power of France; the 2d to secure the succession of Spain to the H[ouse] of Austria. Charles 2d of Spain whose good Queen could not with all her [...].[20] Right of succeeding would have been in the [Children?] of Maria Theresa, in [whom this?] Right was [...] by [...] 1657–1688.

Have been out of Humour, this Evening, more than I have been for some Weeks if not Months. Reflection, thinking on a Girl, ill Health, Want of Business, &c., wrought me by insensible degrees into a peevish Mood. I felt reduced to Necessities, needy, poor, pennyless, empty Pockets. I have given away at least 10s. this day. Thus decayed Merchants must preserve the Appearances of Affluence. But Poverty is infinitely less deplorable to me than a nervous Languor of the Body. If I have good Digestion and Spirits, I can bear with an easy Mind an empty Purse.

But I have been stupid, to the last Degree, in neglecting to spred my Acquaintance. I have neglected Parson Robbins, Parson Tafte, and Parson Smith too. I have neglected Dr. Tufts[21] and Esqr. Niles, Eben Miller, Dr. Miller, and Edmund Quincy. Dr. Millers &c., Mr. Allins, Mr. Borlands, Mrs. Apthorps, Edd. Quincies. I should aim at an Acquaintance. Not to spend much Time at their Houses but to get their good Word. And behave with Spirit too. I have hitherto behaved with too much Reserve to some and with too stiff a face and air, and with a face and Air and Tone of Voice of pale Timidity. I should look bold, speak with more Spirit. Should talk Divinity with P[arson] Tafte, and gain his Love or else extort his Admiration, or both. Make him love and admire. I ought to hire, or wheedle or allure two or 3 in every Town, to trumpet my Character abroad. But I have no Trumpets in Weighmouth, none in Skadin,[22] none in Milton. Oh! what have I been about? I lay no schemes to raise my Character. I lay no schemes to draw Business. I lay [no?] Schemes to extend my Acquaintance, with young fellows nor young Girls, with Men of figure, Character nor fortune.[23] Am content to live unknown, poor, with the lowest of all our species for Company. This is the Tenor of my Conduct.

Lincoln. My father gave me a serious Lecture last Saturday night. He says I have waited on H.Q. two Journeys, and have called and made Visits there so often, that her Relations among others have said I am courting of her. And the Story has spread so wide now, that, if I dont marry her, she will be said to have Jockied me, or I to have Jockied her, and he says the Girl shall not suffer. A story shall be spread, that she repelled me.

These are the Inconveniences of such Reports. When it has been generally talked and believed that a young fellow is Courting a Girl, if they seperate, if they slacken their Intimacy, the fault will be laid to one or the other—either he would not have her or she would not have him. Oh Tittle Tattle!—subject of Tittle Tattle!

Lincoln. Dependance is, if Inequality is not, inconsistent with a lasting Friendship.

I.[24] A Man cannot maintain, for any Length of Time, a Friendship with another on whom he is dependant, for the Benefactor will expect Condescentions and verbal or other Expressions of Gratitude, that the Receiver will not be always careful to pay.

The Benefactor may, through accident or Passion, or inadvertency, show that he is conscious of the favours he confers, that he expects Submissions and Expressions of Gratitude that the Receiver thro the same Imperfections may not be always careful to perform, and hence Disgusts will arise on both sides. That a Friendship may subsist between two Persons very unequal in Rank and fortune, may be true. Or between two very unequal in Age or Character—as between Gridley and me. But a Friendship between two of equal rank and fortune, of equal Age and Character, has the fairest Probability to continue. But there will be one Tye, that of Gratitude, which ought to have great Strength.

Put this Case. A Gentleman of great Experience and Character in the Profession of the Law as Mr. Gridley, or in that of Physick as Dr. Hersey, may receive a young fellow, just admitted to the Bar as me or just beginning the Practice of Physick as you, to his Friendship. Their Age and Character demand from you and me Deference and Respect, and Gratitude as well as Interest will prompt us to pay it. Yet why may not such a Friendship subsist? Now why should a Dependance for Advice and Assistance in Practice and in the Conduct of Life or for a good Character and Recommendation to the World, be less destructive to friendship than a Dependance for the Necessities of Life, food and Cloathing. There is however a Distinction between Patronage and Friendship. A Patron may advise and assist his Pupil in Practice and may spred his Character with great Advantage to the World, without receiving him to that Intimacy, Confidence, Affection which I distinguish by the Word friendship. It is not natural for old Men to contract intimate, familiar friendships with young ones. For, Experience shows that human Nature is scarcely capable at any Age of Constancy, sincerity, and Virtue enough for a very unreserved friendship, but specially in youth, and young ones are not allured by freedoms and friendly familiarities, to engage with old Men. Yet I cant see why a Man of sense and sentiment too, as well as fortune, might not maintain the strictest friendship, with another of the same Character, tho in very needy Circumstances and tho supported and supplied by him, even with Necessaries. Genius and Virtue might be gratified and improved on both sides. And Generosity, the satisfaction of making the Life of such a friend easy, might be gratified on the Part of the Benefactor, and Gratitude, and Interest on the Part of the Receiver would be ties enough to hold.

P[arson] Gay. Two Countrymen were disputing which did the most good, the Sun or the Moon. One of them asserted that the Moon did the most because that shines in the Night, when without that, we should be in absolute Darkness, but the Sun never shone till it was broad day light, as light as Day. But the Sun never shone but in the day, when there was no need of it.—Oh the stupidity, not to see that the sun was the Cause of the day light without which those Hours that we now call the day would be as dark as the Night without a moon.

Another—at some ordination, a certain Indian, who had never seen a public assembly before, seated himself, in the Alley, very near the Deacon's seat. He sat in Silence with the rest, while the Priests were at Prayer, but when the Psalm was named, and the Deacon rose up [to] set the Tune, he began to stare and grew angry at the Deacon, but when the Deacon had read a Line and the whole Congregation broke out with him, the Indian grew quite mad and rushing up to the Deacon, layed on upon him most unmercifully. 'Tis you says he are the Cause of all this plaguey Rout.

Eunice Paine.[25] Thunder and Lightning have a physical Effect upon me. I am always sick when it thunders. My Mother had a Child that was born in the latter Part of the fall, it lived thro the Winter and Spring, and when warm Weather came there was a violent storm of Thunder and Lightning one afternoon. As soon as the Storm began the Child was thrown into Convulsions. It twitched and trembled from Head to foot, its Nails and its face turned black, and it continued so till the Storm was over, and then it recovered. Sometime afterwards another Thunder Gust happened and the Child was taken exactly in the same manner. We sent for the Dr. but before he got there, the Thunder Cloud was blown over, and the Child as well as ever.

What effluvia, what Physical Virtue, can a Cloud or Thunder or Lightning, diffuse to the Earth that should convulse that Child, (or make Mrs. Eunice Vomit). An Imagination prompted by Hystericks and by fear, might possibly occasion Mrs. Eunices sickness, but not the Childs. No Habit of fear, no association of Terror, Horror with the Idea of Lightning, had yet been formed in the Childs Mind. So that Either the sight of the flashes of Lightning, which it is unlikely the Child saw, or the sound of the Thunder, which the Child no Doubt heard, or else some unknown Effluvia emitted by the Clouds, meeting with some peculiar Property in that Childs Constitution, was the Occasion of its Convulsions.

E.P. My Brother says there is no such Thing as fancy distinct from Judgment. A Man may prefer a Woman, or a Woman a Man, for some Property or Qualification, that he or she may be unable to name. They may be unable to give a reason for their Choice. But [*sentence unfinished*]

Deacon Belcher. I have buried father and Mother, but I never felt, before, as I feel now. I am almost overwhelmed.—The Deacon and his Wife too, were in [Trouble?]. The Pangs of her Grief were violent.— What a pleasant Child have I lost? What a pleasant sister has Billy lost? The Loss of Moses was nothing to this. Oh how deceitful is my Heart? I thought, If Moses had died at home and I could have followed him decently to his Grave, it would have been an alleviation. But I find I was mistaken.

She was so full at the first sight of me, that she could not speak plainly. She sighs and groans and weeps, most bitterly. The father and the mother with throbbing Hearts bewail the Death of their only Daughter. These are Sensations that I never felt. I can reflect on these sorrowful Events with great Serenity. I feel none of that Anguish, which the Parent feels. But cant I fortify my Mind with Patience, with an entire Resignation to the Dispensations of Heaven?

Make Preparation to bear Misfortunes. Prepare your Mind, furnish your Mind with Reflections, Considerations, that will support you and mitigate your Grief.

[1] This arbitrary date has been assigned to all of the entries that follow the sole dated entry in D/JA/3, that of 29 June 1759, preceding.

[2] Probably Hannah's cousin Katharine (b. 1733), daugher of Edmund Quincy (1703–1788) (Salisbury, *Family-Memorials*, 1:324).

[3] Perhaps Ann Marsh, who in 1762 became Col. Josiah Quincy's third wife (*Braintree Town Records*, p. 872).

[4] The notes that follow are in part quotations or translations and in part paraphrases of two works on civil law JA was studying, namely Wood's *New Institute of the Imperial or Civil Law* (see bk. 3, ch. 9) and Johannes van Muyden's *Compendiosa institutionum Justiniana tractatio* (see Titulus XXX, "Quibus Modis Tollitur Obligatio"). It has been necessary to resort to the passages JA was abstracting in order to construct an even passably readable text of these notes, because they were written in a highly abbreviated form and with little regard for punctuation. Gaps in language and sense remain, and even those passages directly translated from Latin are faulty. It is clear that the diarist's mind was not on his books when he made these memoranda, but was "roving from Girls to friends" and other matters not closely related to law.

[5] Three or four words missing.

[6] Probably Gardiner Chandler. From several entries below it appears that JA was in Worcester about this time.

[7] Nathaniel Gardner (1719–1760) kept the South Grammar School in Boston and had some reputation as a poet (Sibley-Shipton, *Harvard Graduates*, 10:366–368).

[8] Thus in MS. Some words have evidently been omitted.

[9] Daniel Treadwell (d. 1760), Harvard 1754, had been since 1757 a fellow and professor at King's College (Thomas, *Columbia Univ. Officers and Alumni*).

[10] Sewall is doubtless David Sewall, a Harvard classmate of JA's; he was at this time studying law in Portsmouth, N.H., and compiling a series of almanacs published there; he later settled at York, Maine, and held important judicial offices. Samuel Langdon (1723–1797), minister of the First Church in Portsmouth, became in 1774 the thirteenth president of Harvard (Sibley-Shipton, *Harvard Graduates*, 10:508–528).

[11] This entry may signalize JA's first visit to the Smith household in Weymouth, where, before long, his initially unfavorable impressions were reversed and his visits became frequent. In printing this entry, which is nothing if not candid, the editors have tried to follow with special care the diarist's ambiguous punctuation and capitalization, leaving it to readers to decide whether certain disapproving comments therein were intended for Parson Smith or for others mentioned incidentally.

[12] Mary Smith (1740–1811), who in 1762 married Richard Cranch; and her sister Abigail (1744–1818), who on 25 Oct. 1764 married JA. The allusions that follow are obscure. The Smith girls' mother was a Quincy (Elizabeth, daughter of Col. John Quincy).

[13] No other version of this letter has been found. Quincy was presumably still in the Boston office of Benjamin Prat, where he had studied for the bar.

[14] John Worthington (1719–1800), Yale 1740, was a prominent lawyer in Springfield, Mass., prior to the Revolution; a loyalist, he did not resume practice after the war (Dexter, *Yale Graduates*, 1:658–660).

[15] This entry, together with the partial draft of a letter to Col. Josiah Quincy on the same subject, below, was in all likelihood written earlier than the entries that immediately precede them. Quincy's house burned on 17 May 1759, and it is natural to suppose that these reflections and the letter were written very soon thereafter.

[16] Edmund Quincy's Boston mercantile firm went into bankruptcy in 1757; the year before, Quincy's son Abraham had been drowned in Boston Harbor (Sibley-Shipton, *Harvard Graduates*, 7:109–110).

[17] No other version of this remarkable letter has been found. It is apparently incomplete and was quite possibly never sent.

[18] The antecedent may be either Betsy (Waldron) Quincy or her stepdaughter Hannah Quincy (whose "Match" could be her engagement to Bela Lincoln), but it is more likely the former than the latter. The allusions that follow are too private to interpret, and the passage was written so rapidly and carelessly that both words and meaning are sometimes doubtful.

[19] JA was reading Montesquieu's *Spirit of Laws*. (Secondat was the family name of the Baron de la Brède et de Montesquieu.) His own copy of this work was Nugent's translation, "Second Edition corrected and considerably improved," London, 1752; 2 vols. This copy is now in the possession of Mrs. Arthur Adams, Charles River Village, Mass., and has in its margins what JA (in his Diary entry for 26 June 1760) calls "a sort of Index to every Paragraph" in JA's hand, though it has no additional remarks or commentary. The passage on which JA is commenting is in bk. 1, ch. 2, "Of the Laws of Nature": "Man in a state of nature ... would feel nothing in himself at first but impotency and weakness; his fears and apprehensions would be excessive; as appears from instances ... of savages found in forests, trembling at the motion of a leaf, and flying from every shadow" (1:5).

Since in the entry for 26 June 1760 JA says that he has "begun to read the Spirit of Laws," one might conjecture that the present entry is badly out of place; but it is more likely that he sampled the book in 1759 and began a year or so later to read it "in order and with Attention," compiling a marginal digest as he did so.

[20] Three or four words illegible. The rest of the entry is only semilegible.

[21] Cotton Tufts, a Weymouth physician. He had married Lucy, daughter of Col. John Quincy, and was thus an uncle by marriage of AA.

[22] A local and now forgotten name, often spelled Scadding, for the South Precinct of Braintree, later incorporated as the town of Randolph (Pattee, *Old Braintree and Quincy*, p. 56). Moses Taft's meetinghouse was in the South Precinct.

[23] This sentence contains words rubbed out and is obviously faulty as JA left it.

[24] This reading is somewhat conjectural, since the initial "I" was inserted between the lines and is not clear beyond question. There is no paragraph break in the MS, but there is a heavy dash preceding this initial. Thus Lincoln *may* have spoken the next several sentences, but if that is so, JA failed to indicate in the next paragraph just where he himself began elaborating the same theme in rejoinder to Lincoln.

[25] Eunice Paine, sister of Robert Treat Paine; a frequent visitor in the Cranch-Palmer circle at Germantown. Richard Cranch had courted her in 1753, but her father opposed the match and she never married. See Ralph Davol, *Two Men of Taunton*, Taunton, 1912, ch. 10, where some of her correspondence is published; also entry of 1 Feb. 1763, below.

EXTRACT OF A LETTER TO JONA. SEWALL, OCTR. 1759.[1]

The true End, which we ought to have in View, is that præclarum ac Singulare quiddam, which follows here.

Tis impossible to employ with full Advantage the Forces of our own minds, in study, in Council or in Argument, without examining with great Attention and Exactness, all our mental Faculties, in all their Operations, as explained by Writers on the human Understanding, and as exerted by Geometricians.

Tis impossible to judge with much Præcision of the true Motives and Qualities of human Actions, or of the Propriety of Rules contrived to govern them, without considering with like Attention, all the Passions, Appetites, Affections in Nature from which they flow. An intimate Knowledge therefore of the intellectual and moral World is the sole foundation on which a stable structure of Knowledge can be erected.

And the structure of british Laws, is composed of such a vast and various Collection of materials, taken partly from Saxony, Normandy and Denmark, partly from Greece and Rome, and partly from the cannon and feudal Law, that, 'tis impossible for any Builder to comprehend the whole vast Design, and see what is well and what [ill] contrived or jointed, without Acquainting himself with Saxon, Danish, Norman [as] well as Greek and Roman History, with civil, [feu]dal and Cannon Law.

[Be]sides all this, tis impossible to avail our selves of the genuine Powers of Eloquence, without examining in their Elements and first Principles, the Force and Harmony of Numbers, as employed by the Poets and orators of ancient and modern times, and without considering the natural Powers of Imagination, and the Disposition of Mankind to Metaphor and figure, which will require the Knowledge of the true Principles of Grammar, and Rhetoric, and of the best classical Authors.

Now to what higher object, to what greater Character, can any Mortal aspire, than to be possessed of all this Knowledge, well digested, and ready at Command, to assist the feeble and Friendless, to discountenance the haughty and lawless, to procure Redress of Wrongs, the Advancement of Right, to assert and maintain Liberty and Virtue, to discourage and abolish Tyranny and Vice.

[1] First entry in booklet "No. 4" as numbered by CFA (our D/JA/4); CFA noted on the paper cover that the contents had been "copied" and "compared" (collated). D/JA/4 contains only a handful of scattered entries, nearly all relative to JA's studies and reading, from 12 Oct. 1759 to 21 Nov. 1772; all but the first two and the last were written in 1760–1761.

No other version of the present letter to Sewall, the draft of which is obviously incomplete, has been found. The earliest letter known to survive in the correspondence between the two young lawyers is that of Sewall to JA, 29 Sept. 1759 (Adams Papers; partly printed in JA, *Works*, 2:80, note), but from internal evidence it is clear that the correspondence began earlier.

1759.

Began Octr. 12th, in Pursuance of the foregoing Plan to transcribe from Brightlands english Grammar, Answer's to Mr. Gridleys Questions for that Grammar.

I have begun too, to compare Dr. Cowells Institutes of the Laws of England, with Justinians Institutes of the Laws of Rome, Title by Title, that each may reflect Light upon the other, and that I may advance my Knowledge of civil and common Law at the same Time.[1]

[1] There are no more entries in D/JA/4 until 14 Nov. 1760, and very little in the form of correspondence or other papers survives to fill the gap between the

present entry and that of 26 May 1760, from a different MS booklet, which follows.

MONDAY MAY 26TH 1760.[1]

Spent the Evening at Mr. Edd. Quincy's, with Mr. Wibird, and my Cozen Zab. Mr. Quincy told a remarkable Instance of Mr. Ben. Franklin's Activity, and Resolution, to improve the Productions of his own Country, for from that source it must have sprang, or else from an unheard of Stretch of Benevolence to a stranger. Mr. Franklin, happening upon a Visit to his Germantown Friends, to be at Mr. Wibirts Meeting, was asked, after Meeting in the afternoon, to drink Tea, at Mr. Quincys. The Conversation turned upon the Qualities of American soils, and the Different Commodities raised in these Provinces. Among the rest, Mr. Franklin mentioned, that the Rhenish Grape Vines had been introduced, into Pensylvania, and that some had been lately planted in Phyladelphia, and succeeded very well. Mr. Quincy said, upon it, I wish I could get some into my Garden. I doubt not they would do very well in this Province. Mr. Franklin replied, Sir if I can supply you with some of the Cuttings, I shall be glad to. Quincy thanked him and said, I dont know but some time or other I shall presume to trouble you. And so the Conversation passed off. Within a few Weeks Mr. Quincy was surprised with a Letter from some of Franklins friends in Boston, that a Bundle of these Rhenish slips were ready for him. These came by Water. Well, soon afterwards he had another Message that another Parcell of slips were left for him by the Post. The next Time Mr. Franklin was in Boston Mr. Quincy waited on him to thank him for his slips, but I am sorry Sir to give you so much Trouble. Oh Sir, says Franklin the Trouble is nothing Sir, to me, if the Vines do but succeed in your Province. However I was obliged to take more Pains than I expected when I saw you. I had been told, that the Vines were in the City but I found none and was obliged to send up to a Village 70 miles from the City for them. Thus he took the Trouble to hunt over the City, and not finding Vines there, he sends 70 miles into the Country, and then sends one Bundle by Water, and least they should miscarry another by Land, to a Gentleman whom he owed nothing, and was but little acquainted with, purely for the sake of Doing Good in the World by Propagating the Rhenish Wines thro these Provinces. And Mr. Quincy has some of them now growing in his Garden. This is an Instance too of his amazing Capacity for Business. His Memory and Resolution. Amidst so much Business as Counsellor, Post Master, Printer, so many private studies, and so many

Publick Avocations too, to remember such a transient Hint and exert himself, so in answer to it, is surprising.[2]

This Rhenish Wine is made of a Grape that grows in Germany upon the River Rhine and from which it receives its Name, and is very famous, all over Europe. Let me remember to look in Chambers, under Rhenish and in Salmons Geography, under the Produce of the Countries upon the Rhine, for more Particulars of this Vine and Grape, and Wine. The soil it delights in, the Method of Cultivation, what digging, what Manure, what Pruning &c. Let me ask Mr. Quincy, whether the soil of his Garden suits them? and what sorts and how many [sorts?][3] of Grapes he has? Dont they require more Heat than we have for them? Where he got his other slips. Where he got his Lime Trees? &c.

[1] First entry in "Paper book No. 5" (D/JA/5). This booklet, an assemblage of stitched gatherings from which the threads have now largely worn away, contains somewhat irregular entries from 26 May to 25 Nov. 1760.

[2] In an interesting letter to Edmund Quincy from London, 10 Dec. 1761, Franklin touched on the subject of American viniculture. This letter, lacking part of its text, was found among the Adams Papers and was printed by CFA in a footnote to the present Diary entry (JA, *Works*, 2:82). It is now in MHi: Misc. Bound MSS.

[3] Possibly "scients" (i.e. scions).

TUESDAY [27 MAY].

At home. Read, in Naval Trade and Commerce.

WEDNESDAY [28 MAY].

Loitered the forenoon away upon this Question in Arithmetic. 3 men give 20 shillings for a Bushell of Corn. A pays in the Proportion of one half, B in the Proportion of $\frac{1}{3}$ and C in the Proportion of $\frac{1}{4}$. Now how many shillings and Pence does each one pay? I put x, an Algebraicall Expression, for that unknown Quantity, whose $\frac{1}{2}$ $\frac{1}{3}$ and $\frac{1}{4}$ added together would make 20 shillings.

And then formed this Equation. $\dfrac{x}{2} + \dfrac{x}{3} + \dfrac{x}{4} = 20.$

Then to free the Equation of fractions. $x + \dfrac{2x}{3} + \dfrac{2x}{4} = 40.$

Then $3x + 2x + \dfrac{6x}{4} = 120.$

Then $12x + 8x + 6x = 480$

$$26x = 480 \quad 26\overline{)480} \,(18\frac{12}{26}\,\mathrm{s} = 18\mathrm{s}. \quad 5\frac{14}{26}\,\mathrm{d}.$$

$$
\begin{array}{r}
\underline{26} \\
220 \\
\underline{208} \\
12
\end{array}
\qquad
\begin{array}{r}
12 \\
\underline{12} \\
26\overline{)144}\,(5 \\
\underline{130} \\
14 \\
\underline{4} \\
56
\end{array}
$$

In the afternoon, Zab and I wandered down to Germantown on foot—running a Parrallell between the Pleasures, Profits, freedoms, Ease and Uses of the several Professions, especially Physick and Divinity.

1760. MAY 29. THURSDAY.

Rose and breakfasted. Have done nothing yet to day, and God only knows what I shall do. The Question of the Pipe. A Pipe of Wine has 3 Cocks, one of which would discharge it in $\frac{1}{4}$ of an hour, another in $\frac{1}{2}$ an hour and the 3rd in $\frac{3}{4}$ of an hour all open and running at once. Quere in what Time, all three together will empty the Cask? Let me Note these Proportions for the Present.

	Cock	m	Cock	m		C	m	C	m
as	1	15	3	5	as	1	30	3	10

as	1	45	3	15.

Now 5, 10 and 15 added make 30.

	C	m	C	m
Now as	3	30	1	10

Perhaps this may turn out right.

I must run over Fractions again, vulgar and Decimal, as well as algebraical, and now and then, a few Questions in Fenning and Hammond, and Ward, or else I shall totally forget my Numbers. I find that the Art of numbering depends upon Practice, and in a short disuse, they will slip from the Memory. A Journal, scrawled with Algebraical signs, and interspersed with Questions of Law, Husbandry, natural History &c., will be a useful Thing. The Principal Uses however will be to correct my style, and assist my Memory, give me a true Compunction for the Waste of Time, and urge me of Course to a better Improvement of it. Besides Writing is one of the greatest Pleasures, and it sooner rouses my ambition, warms my Imagination, and fixes me in a train of thinking, than any other Thing that I can do—than sitting still with my Eyes shut, or than holding a Book to read.

Mem. Last Sunday after Meeting Mr. Cranch explained to us at Dr. Tufts's, the Machines that are used in the Mines of Coal in New Castle, and of Tin, in Cornwal, to convey up Water from the Bottom of the Mine. They go upon the Principles of elastic Air and rarefyed Vapour. They have hollow Globes of plated Iron, or of Copper, which will hold some Barrells, which they heat with great fires and have Tubes, and Cocks, and can cast up great Quantities of Water, many H[ogshea]ds in a minute. But I have forgot the Construction of the Machines, as well as the Method of Working them. Here is my failing or one of my failings. My Attention has not been keen enough, to understand and fix in my Memory the Explications of many of these Machines. Etter explained to me, his stocking Looms, but I could not when I left him, have run from the first Motion to the compleat formation of a stocking. I did not see thro it. Cranch once explained to me, the Machine that draws Water from the Thames, into the Canals under the City of London, and that sends Water up into their Garretts, Chambers, Rooms and Cellars, so that by Opening a Cock you may draw a Pail of Water from the Thames, in any House in the City almost, but I do not remember the Construction of it. Let me remember to enquire of him about the Construction of these 2, that for Water from the Thames, and that for Water from the Thames [*thus in MS*], and that for Water from the Mines, and to go once more to see the stocking Loom.

Few things I believe have deviated so far from the first Design of their Institution, are so fruitful of destructive Evils or so needful of a speedy Regulation, as Licensed Houses. The Accomodation of Strangers, and perhaps of Town Inhabitants on public occasions, are the only warrantable Intentions of a Tavern and the supply of the Neighbourhood with necessary Liquors, in small Quantities ⟨to be consumed at home⟩ and at the cheapest Rates, are the only excusable Designs of a Retailer; and that these Purposes may be effected, it is necessary, that both should be selected from the most virtuous, and wealthy People who will accept the Trust, and so few of each should be erected, that the Profits may enable them to make the best Provision, at a moderate Price. But at the present Day, such Houses are become the eternal Haunt, of loose disorderly People of the same Town, which renders them offensive and unfit for the Entertainment of a Traveller of the least delicacy; and, it seems that Poverty, and distressed Circumstances are become the strongest Argument, to procure an Approbation, and for this [these?] assigned Reasons, such Multitudes have been lately licensed, that none can afford to make Provision, for any but the trifling, nasty vicious Crew, that most frequent them. The Consequences of these Abuses are obvious. Young People are tempted to waste their Time and Money, and to acquire habits of Intemperance and Idleness that we often see reduce many of them to Beggary, and Vice, and lead some of them at last to Prisons and the Gallows. The Reputation of our County is ruined among Strangers who are apt to infer the Character of a Place from that of the Taverns and the People they see there. But the worst Effect of all, and which ought to make every Man who has the least sense of his Priviledges tremble, these Houses are become in many Places the Nurseries of our Legislators;— An Artful Man, who has neither sense nor sentiment may by gaining a little sway among the Rabble of a Town, multiply Taverns and Dram Shops and thereby secure the Votes of Taverner and Retailer and of all, and the Multiplication of Taverns will make many who may be induced by Phlip and Rum to Vote for any Man whatever.

I dare not presume to point out any Method, to suppress or Restrain these increasing Evils; but I think for these Reasons it would be well worth the Attention of our Legislature, to confine the Number of, and retrieve the Character of Licensed Houses; least, that Impiety, and Prophaneness, that abandoned Intemperance, and Prodigality; that Impudence and brawling Temper, which these abominable Nurseries daily propagate, should arise at length to a degree of strength, that even the Legislature will not be able to controul.

[John Adams] [1]

Pownals Remark, every other House a Tavern. Twelve in this Town. Call upon the select men, not to grant Approbation, upon the grand Jurors to present all bad Houses, &c.

[1] The name has been inserted in an early but unidentified hand.

The foregoing draft of an essay on the evils of licensed houses is the first of a series on this topic found in JA's Diary during 1760–1761. They were doubtless intended for publication, but none has been found in the papers of the day. During this same period JA also drew the rough sketch map showing the locations of a dozen or more taverns in Braintree and Weymouth that is reproduced as an illustration in the present volume.

On 18 May 1761, as a direct result of JA's intensive but short-lived temperance campaign, the town of Braintree passed the following votes:

"Voted, That although Licensed Houses so far as they are conveniently scituated well accommodated and under due Regulation for the Releif and Entertainment of Travellers and Strangers may be a usefull Institution, Yet there is Reason to apprehend that the present prevailing Depravity of Manners through the Land in General and in this Town in particular and the shamefull neglect of Religious and Civil Duties, so highly offensive in the sight of God, and injurious to the peace and Welfare of Society are in a great measure owing to the unnecessary increase of Licensed Houses.

"Voted, That for the future there be no Persons in this Town, Licensd for retailing spiritous Liquors and that there be three persons only approbated by the Selectmen as Inn-holders, suitably situated, one in each Precinct.

"Voted, That the Persons that are approbated as Inn-holders for the ensuing year oblidge themselves by written Instruments under their Hands and Seals to retail spiritous Liquors to the Town Inhabitants as they shall have occasion therefor, at the same price by the Gallon or smaller Quantity as the same are usually sold by Retail in the Town of Boston and upon the performance of the above conditions, there be no Person or Persons approbated by the Selectmen as Retailers.

"Voted, That the Town now proceed by written votes to the choice of the Persons and places they think most conveniently scituated and best Qualifyd, for the purposes aforesaid.... Mr. Samll. Bass Junr. was chosen for the North Precinct, Mr. Benjamin Hayden for the Middle and Mr. Jonathan Wales for the South.

"Voted, That there be a Com[mi]ttee appointed to draw up and present a Humble Memo[randum] to the Justices of the Q[uarter] sessions to be holden at Boston on the first Tuesday of July next, praying that the present proceedings of the Town Respecting Licensd. Houses meet with their approbation, and that an authenticated copy of the votes of the Town be annexed thereto and Presented therewith." (Joseph Crosby, Josiah Quincy, and Samuel Niles were named the members of this committee. *Braintree Town Records*, p. 378–379.)

In his old age JA confessed that his youthful crusade had been a complete failure: "I only acquired the Reputation of a Hypocrite and an ambitious Demagogue by it; the Number of licensed Houses was soon reinstated. Drams Grog and Sotting were not diminished, and remain to this day as deplorable as ever. You may as well preach to the Indians Against Rum as to our People" (letter to Benjamin Rush, 28 Aug. 1811, CtY). JA's difficulties in keeping his farm hands sober confirm this gloomy conclusion; see entries of 13, 18, 21 July 1796, below.

On the general subject of intemperance in early New England see CFA2, *Three Episodes*, 2:783 ff., where it is pointed out that JA elsewhere admitted that gatherings and discussions in the rural taverns were important stimuli to the Revolutionary movement.

MAY 30 1760. FRIDAY.

Rose early. Several Country Towns, within my observation, have at least a Dozen Taverns and Retailers. Here The Time, the Money, the Health and the Modesty, of most that are young and of many old, are wasted; here Diseases, vicious Habits, Bastards and Legislators, are frequently begotten.

Nightingale, Hayden, Saunders, J. Spear, N. Spear, Benoni Spear, would vote for any Man for a little Phlip, or a Dram. N. Belcher, John Spear, O. Gay, James Brackett, John Mills, Wm. Veasey &c. voted for T. for other Reasons.[1]

[1] On 19 May 1760 Capt. Ebenezer Thayer Jr. was elected representative to the General Court, replacing Samuel Niles (*Braintree Town Records*, p. 372).

1760 MAY 31TH. SATURDAY.

Read in naval Trade and Commerce, concerning Factors, Consuls,

Embassadors, &c., and the South Sea Company, &c. [Went?] into Water. Talked with Wm. Veasey about Church &c. He will not allow that Dr. Mayhew has any uncommon Parts. He had haughty Spirits, and Vanity &c.—How the Judgment is darkened and perverted by Party Passions!

Drank Tea with Zab. Ran over the past Passages of my Life. Little Boats, water mills, wind mills, whirly Giggs, Birds Eggs, Bows and Arrows, Guns, singing, pricking Tunes, Girls &c. Ignorance of Parents, Masters Cleverly, Marsh, Tutors Mayhew &c. By a constant Dissipation among Amuzements, in my Childhood, and by the Ignorance of my Instructors, in the more advanced years of my Youth, my Mind has laid uncultivated so that at 25, I am obliged to study Horace and Homer.—Proh Dolor!

JUNE 1ST. SUNDAY.

Read 2 Odes in Horace. Spent the Evening at the Coll's. While we were at supper, the Coll. received Letters from Mr. Turner of London, with a Bill of Lading and Invoice of about £150 sterlings worth of Glass and Hinges and Nails, and Locks &c. for a House. These were the Value of a sum of the Coll's. Money, which Mr. Turner had retained, in his own Hands, about seven Years since, to satisfy a Debt from Mr. Branden, whom the Coll. had so strongly recommended, as in Mr. Turners opinion to make himself Brandens sponsor. So that it was as sudden and unexpected at least as [a] Prize in the Lottery would have been, or one taken at sea; and it had such a joyful Effect.

Coll. Grape vines delight in a rockey, and mountainous soil, like our Commons, which would make excellent Vineyards.—I suppose that most of the Wines of the World, are the Growth of Climates at least as northern as ours. Champaign, and Tockay are more southward, but Burgundy &c. &c. &c. are northward of us.

JUNE 2D. MONDAY.

Wasted the Day, with a Magazine in my Hand. As it was Artillery Election, it seemed absurd to study, and I had no Conveniencies, or Companions for Pleasure either in Walking, riding, drinking, husling, or any thing else.

JUNE 3RD. TUESDAY.

This Day has been lost in much the same, Spiritless manner.

JUNE 4TH. WEDNESDAY.

Read nothing but Magazines as indeed an indisposition rendered me unfit for any Application. Discharged my Venom to Billy Veasey, against the Multitude, Poverty, ill Government, and ill Effects of licensed Houses, and the timorous Temper, as well as criminal Designs of the Select Men, who grant them Approbations. Then Spent the Evening, with Zab, at Mr. Wibirts.

JUNE 5TH. THURSDAY.

Arose late. Feel disordered. 8 o'Clock, 3 1/2 Hours after Sun rise, is a sluggard's rising Time. Tis a stupid Waste of so much Time. Tis getting an Habit hard to conquer, and Tis very hurtful to ones Health. 3 1/2, 1/7 of the 24, is thus spiritlessly dozed away. God grant me an Attention to remark, and a Resolution to pursue every Opportunity, for the Improvement of my Mind, and to save, with the Parsimony of a Miser, every moment of my Time.

JUNE 1760. FRIDAY 6TH. JUNE.

Arose very late. A cold, rainy northeasterly storm, of several Days continuance. I have an ugly Cold, a phlegmatic stomach and a Cholicky Pain in my Bowells this morning. Read Timon of Athens, the Man hater, in the Evening at the Drs.

SATURDAY. 7TH.

Arose late, again. When shall I shake off the shackells of morning slumbers, and arise with the sun? Between sun rise, and Breackfast, I might write, or read, or contemplate, a good deal. I might, before Breakfast, entirely shake off the Drowziness of the Morning, and get my Thoughts into a steady Train, my Imagination raised, my Ambition inflamed, in short every Thing within me and without, into a Preparation for Improvement.—I have some Points [of] Law to examine to day.

SUNDAY, 8TH.

Spent the Evening and Night at the Coll's. in ill natured, invidious, Remarks upon Eb. Thayer, and Morals and General Court &c.

MONDAY. 9TH.

Attended Major Crosbeys Court. Where Capts. Thayer and Hollis made their Appearance. Thayer had taken 2 Accounts of Nathan

Spear, in his own Hand Writing, and got the Writts drawn by Niles. But upon my making a Defence for Hunt, Spear was afraid to enter and so agreed to pay Costs and drop. But poor Thayer had to say, several Times I told him so, but he would have his own Way. This little dirty, petty fogging Trade, Thayer carries on yet.

TUESDAY [10 JUNE].

Altho my Spirits were wasted Yesterday, by sitting so late the Night before, (till one o'Clock I believe) and rising so early Yesterday morning, (by sun rise) and walking in the dewy Grass and damp Air, home to my fathers and then down to Major Crosbeys, yet the Thought of being employed, and of opposing Captn. Thayer and punishing Nathan Spear, and Spreading a Reputation, roused my Faculties, and rolled out Thoughts and Expressions, with a strenth and Rapidity, that I never expected. I remember something of the same sort, when I first waited on Mr. Gridley. The Awe of his Presence, a Desire of his Esteem, and of an Introduction to Practice, quickened my Attention and Memory, and sharpened my Penetration. In short, I never shall shine, till some animating Occasion calls forth all my Powers. I find that the Mind must be agitated with some Passion, either Love, fear, Hope, &c. before she will do her best.

I rambled this Afternoon with the Dr. over the Commons, and amused my self by clearing the Spring and climbing the Ledges of Rocks, thro the Apertures of which, large Trees had grown. But I spend too much Time, in these Walks, these amusing Rambles. I should be more confined to my Chamber. Should read and muse more. Running to Dr., to the Barn, down to meals and for Pipes and Coals and Tobacco &c. take up much of my Time. I have grown habitually indolent and thoughtless. I have scarcely felt a glow, a Pang, a Transport of Ambition, since I left Worcester, since I left my school indeed, for there the Mischievous Tricks, the perpetual invincible Prate, and the stupid Dulness of my scholars, roused my Passions, and with them my Views and Impatience of Ambition. Let me Remember to keep my Chamber, not run Abroad. My Books, naval Trade, Coke, Andrews, Locke, Homer, not Fields and Groves and Springs and Rocks should be the Objects of my Attention. Law and not Poetry, is to be the Business of my Life.

SATURDAY [14 JUNE].

This Week has been spent in Business, i.e. filling Writts, and

Journeys to Boston, Scadding, Weighmouth, Abington. The other Night Cranch explained, to Zab and me, the Fire Engine, with which they throw up Water from the Bottoms of their Tin Mines in Cornwall, and Coal Mines in New: Castle. They have a large Cauldron of Plated Iron, filled with Water, and closely covered, and placed over a large Fire. Out of one side of this Cauldron, proceeds a large Tube of Iron horizontally, which Ends in a capacious iron receiver, shaped like an Egg, which will hold a Tun. Half Way between the Cauldron and the Receiver, in the Tube is a Cock. From the Lower Side of the Receiver perpendicularly goes another Tube, down into the Well or Bottom of the Mine, i.e. into the Water. At the mouth of this Tube, where it communicates with the Receiver is a Valve. From the Top of the same Receiver, perpendicularly upwards goes another Tube, which extends quite up above the surface of the Ground, and at the bottom of this Tube i.e. where it communicates with the Receiver, is another Valve. This is the Description of the Machine. Now when the Water in the Cauldron is made to boil, it sends a hot steem along, thro the Cock which is first opened for that Purpose in the Receiver, which proceeds from the Receiver thro one Valve down to the Water and thro another Valve, up into open Air. By this steem the Air, within, is very soon rarified, so as to be no Ballance for the Pressure of the Air, upon the Water in the Mine without the Tube. Of Course the Water rises and fills the Receiver. Then turn the Cock and stop the Passage of the Steem, and the Water beginning to descend will close down the lower Valve. The Vapour thus confined in the Cauldron by the Cock, and the Water confined in the Receiver by the Lower Cock, as soon as you open the Cock, the furious Vapour flies out and drives before it, all the Water in the Receiver, thro the upper Valve, quite up into open Day, where they have channells &c. to convey it away. And when this Proscess is once compleated, they begin anew. This Engine was an Invention of Capt. Savery. They used Copper originally, but lately, they use plated Iron.

They have a different manner now. They use 2 Concentric Tubes, with a Box, like a Pump Box playing in the central one.

In my Journey to Abbington, my Mind seemed to be confused with the Dust and Heat, and fatigue. I had not Spirit and Attention to make any Observations upon the Lands, Corn, Grass, Grain, Fences, orchards, Houses &c. I dined at Nortons where the two military Companies of the Town, were assembled to raise Voluntiers, Recruits, but I had not Spirits to make Observations, on the Landlord, or Lady, or Officers or soldiers or House, or any Thing. I eat Milk for Breakfast.

1760. JUNE 15TH. SUNDAY.

Rose early, 5 o clock. A pleasant Morning. The more I write the better. Writing is a most useful improving Exercise. Yesterday morning before Break fast I wrought my Mind into a Course of Thinking, by my Pen, which I should not have fallen into the whole day without it; and indeed not resuming my Pen after Breakfast, I insensibly lost my attention.

Let me Aim at Perspicuity, and Correctness more than ornament, in these Papers.

MONDAY. JUNE 16TH.

Arose before the sun. Now I am ignorant of my Future Fortune, what Business, what Reputation, I may get, which is now far from my Expectations. How many Actions shall I secure this Day? What new Client shall I have? I found at Evening, I had secured 6 Actions, but not one new Client, that I know of.

TUESDAY. JUNE 17TH.

Arose before the sun again. This is the last day.[1] What, and who to day? Ebenezer Hayden was altogether new and unexpected. Hollis him self was altogether new and unexpected and John Hayward was altogether new and unexpected. 3 entirely new Clients, all from Captn. Thayers own Parish, and one of whom is himself a Pretender to the Practice, are a considerable Acquisition. I believe, by the Writ and Advice I gave Hayden and the Writt and Advice and the Lecture, concerning Idleness and Petty fogging, given Hollis before Hayward will spread me. Hollis is very near to Beggary and Imprisonment. His oxen are attached, and his Cows, and Pew, and a Number of Writts, and Executions are [out] against [him and] not yet extended. He owes more than his Estate can pay I believe. And I told him that by neglecting his own proper Business, and meddling with Law which he did not understand, he had ruined himself. And it is true, for if he had diligently followed his Trade of making shoes and lived prudently he might at this Day have been clear of Debt and worth an handsome Estate. But shomaking I suppose was too mean and dimi[nu]tive an Occupation for Mr. Thomas Hollis, as Wig making was to Mr. Nat Green, or House Building to Mr. Daniel Willard, and he like them in order to rise in the World procured Deputations from the Sheriff, and after serving long enough in that office to gett a few Copies of common

135

Writts and a most litigious Disposition, left the Sheriff and commenced the Writt Drawer. But poor Hollis is like to be stripped of all he has, if he should escape the Goal, which Daniel Willard was obliged to enter, and if he should not be forced to fly like Nat Green. These sudden Transitions from shomaking, Wigg making and House building, to the Deputy Sheriffwick; and from thence to the Practice of Law, commonly hurry Men rapidly to Destruction to Beggary and Goals. Yet Coll. White has rose the same Way, i.e. by a Deputation from the Sheriff. But White had the Advantage of a liberal Education, and had as Rival no Competitor to oppose him, so that he got quickly sworn. E. Taylor too, was naturally smart, and had been long a sheriff, and had the Patronage and Encouragement of Mr. Trowbridge, who was his Brother in Law. Applin and Ruggles are in a higher Class, men of Genius and great Resolution, to combat the World both by Violence and stratagem.

Thayer by his own abject slavery to Coll. Pollard got his Affection and he did every Thing to encourage him. Dana has given him great Numbers of Writts to be served on People in this Town, he takes seven shillings for the Writt, and four shillings always, and some [times] 5 for the service; of this he gives Dana one shilling for his Blank, and reserves 10 or 11 to himself; great Numbers of Writts he has filled himself, and those which he durst not fill he got Niles to fill for 3 shillings so that he takes 3, and four is seven and often times Eight shillings to himself. Thus from Coll. Pollard, from Mr. Dana and Elisha Niles he has got his Estate, as his Legislative Authority, as basely got as Bestia's from the Throne. A little longer Experience will enable me to trace out the whole system of his Policy and iniquity.

The office of a sheriff, has Dangers and Temptations around it. Most of them decline, in Morals or Estate or both. Saml. Penniman is one.

[1] For entering actions for the July sitting of the Suffolk Inferior Court.

1760 JUNE 18TH.

Read but little, thought but little, for the N.E. storm unstrung me.

THURSDAY JUNE 19.

I have been the longer in the Arg[umen]t of this Cause not for the Importance of the Cause itself, for in itself it is infinitely little and contemptible, but for the Importance of its Consequences.[1] These dirty and ridiculous Litigations have been multiplied in this Town, till the very Earth groans and the stones cry out. The Town is become infamous for them throughout the County. I have absolutely heard it used as a Proverb in several Parts of the Province, "as litigious as Braintree." And this Multiplicity is owing to the Multiplicity of Petty foggers among whom Captn. Hollis is one, who has given out that he is a sworn Attorney till 9/10 of this Town really believe it. But I take this Opportunity, publickly to confront him, and undeceive the Town. He knows in his Conscience that he never took the Oath of an Attorney, and that he dare not assume the Impudence to ask to be admitted. He knows that the Notion of his being a sworn Attorney is an Imposture, is an Imposition upon this Town. And I take this opportunity publickly to declare that I will take all legal Advantages, against every Action brought by him or by Captn. Thayer or by any other Petty fogger in this Town. For I am determined if I live in this Town to break up this scene of strife, Vexation and Immorality. (Such suits as this and most others that ever I have seen before a Justice in this Town, have a Tendency to vex and imbitter the Minds of the People, to propagate an idle, brawling, wrangling Temper, in short such suits are an Inlet to all manner of Evils.)

And some [*i.e.* one] of these suit managers, when I first came to this Town, hearing that I had been thro a regular Course of study with a regular Practitioner, and that I was recommended to the Court in Boston, by one of the greatest Lawyers in America, concluded, that I should be enabled by these Advantages, and prompted by my own Interest if by no higher Motive, to put an End to the illegal Course of dirty, quacking Practice in this Town, which he had been in, and thereby enslaved the Minds and Bodyes and Estates of his Neighbours. And to prevent this he set himself to work to destroy my Reputation and prevent my getting Business, by such stratagems as no honest Mind can think of without Horror, such stratagems as I always will resent, and never will forgive till he has made Attonement by his future Repentance and Reformation. I thank God his Malice has been defeated, he has not been able to enslave me, nor to drive me out of Town, but Peoples Eyes begin to open, and I hope they will open wider and wider till they can see like other Towns. Happy shall I be if I can rescue the Souls and Bodies, and Estates of this Town from that Thraldom and slavery, to which these Petty foggers have contributed to depress them; and if I can revive in them a generous Love of Liberty and sense of Honour.—After this long Digression your Honour will let me return to this Cause, and I rely upon it, it is a vexatious one. I rely upon it that many of these Articles were borrowed and not bought, and that therefore this Action cant be maintained for them. I rely upon it, that the Affair of the Hat is a litigious Thing, that it was a mere piece of Tavern Amuzement, and if there was any Thing like Bargain and sale in it, the Bargain was completed, the Hat delivered and the Money paid, and with regard to the other Articles, we have filed an Account that more than ballances them, and therefore I pray your Honours Judgment for Costs.

¹ This entry is obviously a draft of JA's argument, or the closing portion thereof, in the case of Lt. White and the hat. In the very next entry JA redrafted his argument in order to avoid so egotistical a tone.

FRIDAY JUNE 20TH.

I must not say so much about my self, nor so much about Hollis and Thayer by Name. I may declaim against Strife, and a litigious Spirit, and about the dirty Dablers in the Law.

I have a very good Regard for Lt. White, but he must allow me to have a much greater Veneration for the Law. To see the Forms and Processes of Law and Justice thus prostituted, (I must say prostituted) to revenge an imaginary Indignity, offered in a Tavern over a Chereful Bowl or enlivening Mug. To have a mere Piece of Jocular Amuzement, thus hitched into an Action at Law, a mere frolick converted into a Law suit, is a Degree of meanness that deserves no Mercy and shall have none from me. I don't think Lt. White considered the Nature and the Consequences of this Action, before he brought it. If he had he never would have brot it. He has too much Honour to have brot it. But I suppose the Case was this. Lt. White was a little chagrined, that my Client had for once outwitted him, and in a Miff, or a Bravado, I say a Miff or a Bravado, sees Hollis and asks his Opinion. And Hollis glad of an opportunity to draw a Writ, instantly encourages the suit, and the suit was brot. And when once brot, it was too late to repent. But I dare say he has been severely sorry, that he ever brot it, and will have still further Occasion to be sorry before it Ends.

As to the Hat, Either it was a Bargain and Sale or it was not. If it was a Bargain and sale, The Hat is my Clients and the Price agreed upon, which was the Copper, delivered at the very Time, is Lt. Whites. But if it was not a Contract, but only a frolick and no one in Earnest, as I suppose it was, then the Property of the Hat continues in Lt. White, and he is welcome to take it, returning us our Copper.

Rode to Germantown in the morning. Cranch says that the Grind-stone is found in the Coal Mines in Europe. The Coal lies in Apartments, strongly fortified with Partitions of this stone, and this stone forms the Covering over Head, &c. I took Notice of the Rock Weed, they were burning into Kelp and I find there are a great Variety of Species of it. Some of it grows out of the Rock, a small stalk, which soon spreads into several Brainches, and each of those Branches into several others, with those little Bubbles or Bladders, full of Air, scattered along at little Distances, on every Branch and Sprig, but at the End of Each twigg or Sprig, hangs a large Pod, full of seed incased in a spongy substance. We went down to some large stones, which had been thrown over between high Water and low water mark 2 or 3 Years ago. These stones are all grown over with the Rock Weed. The seed, We suppose is deposited by the Water upon the Rock, takes Root and grows. It grows very fast to the Rock and when you pull, you will sometimes break the stalk, sometimes pull off a flake of the Rock with it, and sometimes take the Weed, as it seems to me, fairly up by the roots, and the Roots are little fine Spiculæ, finer than the Point of the finest Needle. These Roots insert themselves into the Pores of the Rock and thence draw Nourishment. And the connoiseurs say, that some Rocks will produce Weeds, large and rank and strong, while others, laid in the same Place at the same time, will produce only a meagre, short, lingering one. They seem to take a deeper and stronger Root, in Timber and Planks, as on the sides of Wharfes, than they do in Rocks. The salt Water seems to be impregnated with the seeds of it, for whenever a Rock is thrown below high Water mark, immediately a Crop of these Weeds Spring up. It is excellent Manure for the Soil. The salts and sulphurs in it are very good. When they thro it into the Kelp Kiln, it is of a dark brown, or a dirty Yellow, but after it has been heated in the Kiln, it turns of a bright clear green. The Fire occasions some Change in the Configuration of the surface, that reflects green Rays most plentifully, where it used to reflect yellow and brown. They burn it into an ashes, which is a fixed salt, which they call Kelp. 20 Tons of the Weeds will produce about one Ton of the ashes. It tastes a little like Gun powder, it smells like marsh Mud, like a muddy Creak, &c. It has a saltish, sulphurous Taste and Smell. —The Deacon shewed us a Sort of Stone, that the old Glass Company brought from Connecticut, to use instead of Grindstone, for the furnace.[1] He called it stone of the asbestus Kind. Dr. Eliot [2] used it in his   and never found the fire made any Impression on it. But the Glass men found it dissolved in about 4 months. They call it a Cotten stone. It seems to have no Gritt at all, it feels as soft as soap. It cost the Company about [...] or £900.—Thus, the first Essays, generally rude, and unsuccessful, prove burdensome instead of profitable.

¹ Deacon Joseph Palmer, later called General Palmer, conducted with his brother-in-law Richard Cranch various business enterprises, including a glass manufactory in the Germantown section of Braintree (*DAB*, under Palmer; Pattee, *Old Braintree and Quincy*, p. 473–

492).
² Doubtless Jared Eliot (1685–1763), Yale 1706, of Killingworth, Conn.; a Congregational minister, physician, and writer on scientific and agricultural subjects (*DAB*).

JUNE 21ST. 1760. SATURDAY.

JUNE 23RD. 1760. MONDAY.

A long obstinate Tryal, before Majr. Crosby, of the most litigious, vexatious suit, I think that ever I heard. Such Disputes begin with ill humour and scurrilous language, and End in a Boxing Bout or a Law suit.

TUESDAY. 24TH. JUNE.

Arose early, a very beautiful Morning. Zab. seems to make insufficient Distinctions between the Vowells. He seems to swallow his own Voice. He neither sounds the Vowells nor Articulates distinctly. The story of Yesterdays Tryal, spreads. Salisbury told my Uncle and my Uncle told Coll. Quincy. They say I was saucy, that I whipped the old Major, &c., that I ripped about the Law suits of this Town And of that House, and that I reminded the Majer of his oath to be of Council to neither Party, and to do Justice equally between the Parties according to Law.

WEDNESDAY [25 JUNE].

Went out with the Coll., in his Canoe, after Tom Codd. Rowed down, in a still calm, and smooth Water, to Rainsford Island, round which we fished in several Places, but had no Bites. Then we went up the Island, and round the Hill. Upon the North Easterly side of the Hill, or Island, is a prodigious Bank or Head, which is perpetually washing away, with Rains and Tides. Heartley says it has been washed away 10 feet since he lived on the Island. The Rocks all round the Island are covered with long, rank, rich Weeds, 3 Years old, which Heartley sells at 5s. a Load.¹

At one of the Clock we took our Mutton and Cyder, under the shade of a fine Tree, and laid our Provisions on a large flat stone which answered for Table, Dish and Plate, and then we dined expecting with much Pleasure an easy sail Home before the Wind, which then bread [2] fresh at East. After Diner we boarded and hoisted sail, and sailed very pleasantly a Mile, when the Wind died away into a Clock Calm and left us to row against the Tide, and presently against the Wind too for that sprung up at south, right a Head of us, and blew afresh. This was hard work. Doubtful what Course to steer, whether to Nut Island, or to Half Moon,[3] or to Hangmans Island or to Sunken Island, Coll. Q. grew sick which determined us to go ashore at Hangmans for that was the nearest. As soon as he set foot on shore he vomited, very heartily, and then weak and faignt, and spiritless, he crawled up to the Gunning House, and wrapping his great Coat round him, lay down on the sea weed and slept, while I rambled round the Island after Weeds and flowers and stones and young Gulls and Gulls Eggs. 500 Gulls I suppose hovered cawing and screaming over the Island, for fear of their Eggs and Young ones, all the time we were there. When the Coll. awoke and found himself strengthened and inspirited, we rowed away, under Half Moon, and then hoisted sail and run home. So much for the Day of Pleasure, The fishing frolick, the Water frolick. We had none of the Pleasure of Angling, very little of the Pleasure of Sailing. We had much of the fatigue of Rowing, and some of the Vexation of Disappointment. However the Exercise and the Air and smell of salt Water is wholesome.

[1] This entire entry was omitted by CFA in editing JA's Diary, perhaps because, though it records a characteristic incident, it shows Col. Josiah Quincy in a momentarily undignified posture. The course of the fishing expedition among the islands of Boston Harbor and Quincy Bay may be traced on the map in Shurtleff, *Description of Boston,* facing p. 518. Hangman or Hangman's Island is about midway between Squantum and Hough's Neck, in shoal water some two miles northeast of the mouth of Black's Creek in present Quincy. Rainsford Island, about two miles farther northeast, had been in use by the town of Boston for quarantine and hospital purposes since 1737 (same, p. 523–525). For present-day details see U.S. Geological Survey map of Hull, Mass.

[2] That is, "bred"? But possibly an end-of-line contraction for "breathed."

[3] Half Moon Island, now submerged except at low tide, formed a half-circle in the flats just off the mouth of Black's Creek. It faced what was called Mount Wollaston Farm, the estate of Col. John Quincy and his son Norton, AA's uncle. After Norton Quincy's death in 1801, Mount Wollaston Farm came into the possession of the Adamses, partly by bequest and partly by purchase. A few years later the title to the island came into dispute because it had long been used by fishing and hunting parties from the neighboring towns. Thereupon JA wrote an historical and legal memorandum that provides an engaging account of Half Moon Island as he had known it since boyhood. This undated memorandum is in the Adams Papers under the assigned date of 1806. On 7 April 1806 a Quincy town meeting voted "To dismiss the article respecting fishing and fowling on half-moon, viz.:—'To know if the town will maintain their right and priviledge, according to old custom, in fishing and fowling on half-moon, and if any inhabitant should be prosecuted on that account, that the town, as a town,

would defend the prosecution'" (Pattee, *Old Braintree and Quincy*, p. 98). Search of the (unpublished) Quincy Town Rec- ords reveals nothing more on this subject.

1760. JUNE 26. THURDSDAY.

Feel indifferently well after my yesterdays walk and sail. I have begun to read the Spirit of Laws, and have resolved to read that Work, thro, in order and with Attention. I have hit upon a Project that will secure my Attention to it, which is to write in the Margin, a sort of Index to every Paragraph.[1]

[1] JA had at least sampled the *Spirit of Laws* earlier; see Summer 1759, above, and note 19 there.

JUNE 27TH. FRIDAY.

Read 100 Pages in the Spirit of Laws. Rambled away to a fine Spring in my Cozen Adam's Land, which gushes thro a Crack in a large flat Rock and gurgles down in a pretty Rill. The Water is clear, sweet, and cool, and is supposed to have a very wholsome Quality, because it issues from a Mountain, and runs towards the North. What Physical Quality its northern Direction may give it, I know not. By its sweetness it flows thro clean Earth, and not minerals. Its Coolness may be owing to its Rise from the Bowells of the Hill.

Zab's Mind is taken up with Arithmetical and Geometrical Problems, Questions, Paradoxes and Riddles. He studies these Things that he may be able to gratify his Vanity by puzzling all the vain Pretenders, to Expertness in Numbers, and that he may be too expert, to be puzzled by any such Questions from others.

There is a set of People, whose Glory, Pride &c. it is to puzzle every Man they meet, with some Question in the Rule of three or fractions, or some other Branch of Arithmetic. Jed. Bass. Moses French. Tom Peniman, &c. &c. Smith, Richard Thayer, &c.

TUESDAY. JULY 1ST. 1760.

Went to Town.

Mr. Thatcher. You have read a great deal, Mr. Adams, in the Roman History, concerning the Modesty of Youth, and their Veneration of the Elders. Now I think these young Gentlemen had very little of that Modesty and Veneration, when they went in the face of Law and against the Remonstrances of all the Elders to act their Plays.

Mr. Otis says there is no Limitation of Attachments. There is no Proportion established between the Demand and the Quantity to be attached, so that a Villain may attach 20,000£ if he pleases as security for £20, and take the whole into the Officers Custody. Tho on second thought, this cant be done without Collusion between the Plaintiff and the officer, for unless the officer is malicious as well as the Plaintiff, he will run the Risque for the Defendant, of making a Common Service, and this is the Reason why there has been no Mischief made of the unlimited Power of Attachment.

THURSDAY JULY 3RD. 1760.

Read pretty diligently in the Spirit of Laws.–Hayden's Consultation suggested the following Questions. Q. Is there any Method of compelling a Grantor to give a new Deed when the Deed he has executed before happens to be burned or lost?–Q. May an Agreement in Writing without seal, or by Parol only be given in Evidence against a Bond sealed and delivered? After Confession of the Forfeiture of the Penalty, any Special Agreement may be given in Evidence.

1760. SATURDAY JULY 5TH.

Last Night Cranch explained to me, the Water Works in the River Thames which convey water, all round the City of London. There is first, a long water Wheel, like the Water Wheel of some saw Mills, which is carried round by the River. On the End of the Axis of this water Wheell are Coggs, which carry round a cogg Wheel. This Cogg wheel has upon the End of its Axis, a Number of Cranks and each of these Cranks lifts up and lets down a Pump Box every Time the Cogg wheel Turns. These Pumps are very large, and prodigious Quantities of Water are pumped away into a general Conveyance and Receiver, from which Pipes are carried to almost every Cellar and to many of the Rooms, and Chambers, and Garrotts, in Gentlemens Houses, thro the City. Cranch says he has seen the Works for Conveying ships up a Cataract, as that between Topsham and Exeter. Vessells are conveyed along, up Hill, so 3 Miles. They rise up hill as far as from the Bottom of the long Wharf to the Top of Bacon [Beacon] Hill. They have Walls of great Thickness and strength built across the River Ex, with Gates, of Timber fortified with Irons, in the Middle. These Gates are opened, and the Vessells float, within the Wall. The gates are then shut, and the fresh running Water of the River let down into that Apartment where the Vessell is which soon raises the Vessell as high as the Top of the lower Walls when the Gates of the second Wall are opened and the Vessell is floated within that. Then the second Gate is shut, and the freshit raises the Vessell up another stair.–

These Gates have several smaller sluice Gates in them that slide up and down. These they slide up, and let out as much Water as they can, before they pretend to open the Great Gates.

This whole Passage and Conveyance is artificial, for the natural Course of the River was at some Distance. This whole Channell was cut by Art. What an Expence! to cutt such a Channell for 3 miles, to erect such and so many Walls across the River, to build such Gates, and such Machines to open them.

Invention has laid under Discouragements in England, for Inventions to facilitate any Manufacture, by which Numbers of People might be thrown out of Business have been prohibited by Act of Parliament. Saw Mills for that Reason were prohibited, That a greater No. of Hands might be employed in sawing, by Hand, Boards and Timber &c. But that Act was of no service. Our Merchants could send to Holland and buy Boards and all sorts of Timber much cheaper, than they could procure them at home. I suppose the Act is expired, and not to be revived, by the Encouragement the society for Encouraging Arts, Manufactures and Commerce, have offered to the Man who shall produce the best Modell of a saw Mill.[1]

The Dutch erected a Dike, some Years since, which shut out the sea for a great Extent of Land, and they erected Wind Mills, at small Distances upon this Dike, which threw all the Water that was left within, over the Dike into the Sea.

Deacon Palmer's Glass Furnace, it seems is a reverberating Furnace. That is, the Heat, which is flashed against the internal surface of the Furnace, when a dry stick of Wood is thrown in, is reverberated, down into the Pots, and melts the Glass, much more than the silent Heat below. So that, rugged Excrescences, prominent Bits of Grindstone, within must be a disadvantage, for if the internal Concave could be polished like a concave Mirror, it would be in its most perfect state. Besides this Furnace is too high. These 2 faults, Hight and internal Ruggedness, the Deacon thinks have wasted him almost a Cord of Wood a Day.

Cowen[2] and Young Thayer the Marketman are full of White and Bowditch. Cowen heard I tore Whites account all to Pieces, and Thayer thought that White had a dirty Case. Few Justices Causes have been more famous, than that. Isaac Tyrrell [Tirrell] had the story too, but he thought Bowditch was to blame, was abusive.

[1] This paragraph, and possibly the next as well, may have been intended as direct discourse by Cranch.

[2] A common name in Weymouth in JA's time; often spelled Cowing in contemporary records.

July 1760

JULY 6TH. SUNDAY.

Heard Mr. Mayhew of Martha's Vineyard.

JULY 9TH. WEDNESDAY.

Gould has got the story of White and Bowditch.

SATURDAY [12 *or* 19 JULY].

I find upon Examination, that a Warrant of Attorney given by an Infant is void; so that, if you intend during your Apprentices Absence, to put the Note you mentioned to me in suit, or to sue for the Detention of the Province Note, or any other wise to prosecute your Right, the only Way I can think of is, for the Lad to elect your father for his Guardian and see to procure the Judge of Probates allowance of it, before he goes off.[1] ⟨*If your father is unwilling to go to Town, you may ride down and wait on this Judge.*⟩ Altho Deacon Bass might have been appointed Guardian to him when a Child, yet you know he has a Right to choose one at fourteen, and he is no doubt willing to choose his Master, but he must give security to the Judge for the faithful Discharge of his Trust.

From the very hasty and imperfect Account of the Case which you gave me, I can think of no other Way at Present, that will have any Safety. So you may Act your own Pleasure.

With Regard to the Notes, as the old Note you mentioned to me, was given to the Lad an Infant, neither He nor his Guardian will be under any Obligation to accept it in Satisfaction for the Province Note, unless they please. So that if that Note is not sufficient to secure the Money, you may bring your Action for the Detention of the Province Note. But in that Case you know you must be able to prove by Witnesses, Confession, or other Circumstances, first that your Apprentice owed the Note, 2dly that French had it in Possession, and 3dly that he converted it to his own Use.

If these Hints are of any service to you, I shall be glad, or if, upon your letting me further into the facts, any Thing further should occur to me, I shall be ready to communicate it.

Yr. svt.,   J. Adams

[1] CFA omitted this draft of a letter to an applicant for legal advice and all of JA's legal notes that follow in July and August.

SUNDAY MORNING [13 *or* 20] JULY 1760.

The week before last Salome Pope appeared before Coll. Quincy, to confess herself with Child, by Jos. Ryford.

Her Intention was to complain against Jos. Ryford and charge him before the Justice with being the father of the Bastard Child with which she is now pregnant. Now what Occasion for taking her Examination upon Oath?—By the Province Law.[1]

[1] Here a line is drawn across the page in the MS and a short entry follows which has been scratched out with two different pens: "Ryford is not only suspected but has been charged to have begotten a Bastard Child; therefore Q. may [now himself perhaps?] bind him to the sessions, But is not [. . .] to do it by the Province Law."

FRYDAY JULY 25TH.

We contend that the Plaintiffs ought to recover nothing on this Bond, because according to the original Agreement it is paid.[1] The Case was this. The Plaintiffs about 15 years ago conveyed to one Tower, a Tract of Land, containing with such and such Boundaries, 30 Acres. And the present Defendants became jointly bound with the Grantee for the Money, which was £750, for which they gave 8 or 10 Bonds, one of which was to be paid off every Year. But at the Time of these Transactions, a suspicion arose, that the Land included within the mentioned Bounds, did not contain so much as 30 Acres, which induced the Defendants to insist upon and the Plaintiffs to enter into an Agreement which they committed to Writing, that the Land should be surveyed, and if it fell short of 30 Acres, the Deficiency should be deducted out of these Bonds. Accordingly an Admeasurement was made, and the Land fell short 7 Acres and 1/2, which in Proportion to the Price of the whole amounted to about the Value of this Bond. With regard to the other Bonds some of them were put in suit, others were paid off and taken up, at length all of them were taken up, but this, and the Reason why this was never taken up was this. The Plaintiff Hollis who had kept all the Bonds in his own Hands never would come to a final settlement with them. The Grantee had made several Payments, and Tower had made several more and Hayden had made several others. Some of these Payments were minuted on the Bonds, but many of them were made abroad upon Hollis Promise to enter them on the Bonds when he went home which was never done, so that these People being Brothers to Hollis and confiding in his Honor have been let [led] on Blindfold, in midnight Darkness, till they have already paid 12 or 1500 Pounds for 750, and when all is done they have no Land. For by some Accident the Deed of this Land is lost, of which Hollis got scent some way or other and has since conveyed away this very Land to another Man. This very land is now mortgaged to Mr. G[oldthwai]t.[2]

The Case of Chambers vs. Bowles was this. Capt. Chambers had sold to one Anthony Lopez a Spaniard of Monto Christo, a Quantity of Merchandizes. Lopez called for the Goods, but when he came to count his Money he found it fell short, 60 Dollars. Chambers, who had no other Dealings with Lopez and was unacquainted with his Circumstances, refused to trust him for the 60 Dollars, and accordingly took back Merchandizes, to that Value. Upon this Captn. Bowles, who was well acquainted with the Spaniard, and knew him to be rich, spoke a few Words to him in Spanish and then turning to Captn. Chambers, said, let Lopez have the goods and I will pay you the Dollars; call upon me tomorrow or any time and Ile pay you the Money.

Mr. Otis said this fell within the Province Law to prevent frauds and Perjuries "that no Action shall be brought whereby to charge the Defendant upon any Special Promise to answer for the Debt, Default or Miscarriages of another Person, unless the Agreement upon which such Action shall be brought, or some Memorandum or Note thereof shall be in Writing, and signed by the Party to be charged therewith," &c. This is, says he, an Agreement to answer for the Debt or Default or Miscarriage of Lopez. The Contract and sale was from Chambers to the Spaniard, not from Chambers to Bowles. No Discrimination was made between the Merchandizes sold to Lopez and these sold to Bowles, but Bowles says let Lopez have the Goods according to your Contract and I will see you paid if he dont.

Thatcher. This is not a conditional Undertaking for Another, but an absolute Undertaking for himself.

I remember a Case in Salkeld precisely parrallel which is this. "A and B go into a Warehouse together and A says to the Merchant, deliver B such and such Merchandizes, and if he dont pay you I will. This Promise is void by the Act of Parliament from which our Province Law was copied. But if A says Let B have such and such Goods and I will be your Pay master, or I will see you paid, or I will be answerable to you, in this Case A's promise is good, is an absolute Undertaking for himself not a conditional Undertaking for Another, and A shall be answerable.—Just so in the Case at Bar. Captn. Bowles says, Let the Spaniard have the Goods and I will pay you, call tomorrow or any time at my Lodgings and I will pay you. Here is an Absolute Undertaking for himself, not a Conditional Undertaking in Case Lopez failed, for We never sold these Goods to Lopez, we have no Demand vs. Lopez for them, we refused to sell them to him: We sold them to Bowles, he sold them to Lopez; He only can demand pay of Lopez and we can demand pay only of him; and we expect your Verdict accordingly.—

This was like Fairbanks v. Brown. There Brown Undertook for the [Govt.?], that the Carter should have such a Price. I will ensure You such a Price. I promise you such a Price, &c.

The Jury gave a Verdict for Chambers in this Case.

[1] This entry is a draft of an argument in which JA was defending Hayden and others against the rapacity of Thomas Hollis, the shoemaker, tavern-keeper, and writ-drawer of Braintree Middle Precinct. The suit was evidently tried in the Suffolk Inferior Court, since Ezekiel Goldthwait, who held the mortgage on the land in question, is mentioned as "Clerk of this Court."

[2] The name is a scrawl in the MS, but is clarified in the entry of next day, which contains another version of JA's argument.

1760. JULY 26.

This Bond has been at [least] once and an half, if not twice, paid. The Case is this. About 15 Years ago, the Plaintiffs sold a tract [of] Land, containing 30 Acres, within such and such Boundaries, to one Tower, for 750£, and He together with the present Defendants became jointly bound to the Plaintiffs, in 10 different Bonds, of which this is one, for the Payment of the Money. But in the Time of it, a suspicion arose that those Bounds did not include 30 Acres; and least they should not an Agreement was made and committed to Writing, that the Land should be surveyed, and if it was found to fall short the Deficiency should be deducted from some of these Bonds. Accordingly the Land was afterwards surveyed, and found to fall short, 7 Acres and an half, which in Proportion to the Price of the whole amounted to about the Value of this Bond. All the other Bonds have been discharged and taken up, and this was set against the Deficiency of Land. But Besides all this, at least one half of it has been paid another Way. For one of these Obligers carried the Money to Hollis and had 1/2 of what was due upon every Bond in his Hands callculated, and paid him down his Money, and Hollis promised to indorse one half, upon every Bond that was left: yet this has never been indorsed; and Hollis has assurance enough to sue for this whole Bond. The Defendants have been extreemely careless, and negligent. Sometimes they paid Money abroad, and took no Receipts, but relied on his Honour to indorse it when he went home. They even left the Agreement that obliged him to make up the wanting Land, in Hollis's own Hands; after the Land was surveyed they left the Plan and survey in his Hands, in short there has been the Utmost Simplicity and Inattention on their Part in every Part of all these Transactions; and there have not been fewer Proofs of Artifice, secresy, and Guile, I must say Guile, on the Part of Hollis, for He always avoided giving Receipts;

he never would suffer any 3d Person to be present, when he did Business. They sometimes would carry with them a Neighbour [who] [1] understood Numbers, better than they, to calculate for them and see that they were not injured, but whenever they did so Hollis would never do any Business with them and at last had the Assurance to tell them that he never would do any Business with them if they brought any Body with them, as long as he lived. So that by one Artifice and another we have been led on to pay, I suppose, £1500 for 750, and what is worse than all the rest, the Deed he gave is accidentally lost. Of this Hollis got a Hint, and has since sold it to another Person. This Hollis has mortgaged this very Land to Mr. Gouldthwat, the Clerk of this Court, since he found We had lost our Deed. Yet he has the assurance to sue this [Bond?]. We have offered him to relinquish his obligation to make good the deficient Land and pay him the 1/2 of this Bond, if he will execute a new Deed of the Land; but he cant do that. He has sold it.

[1] MS: "to"—an obvious slip of the pen.

AUGUST 3D. 1760.

Hollis has appealed. If he prosecutes his Appeal, he shall be paid. I believe there never was an Action in this Court where more Instances of Ignorance, Negligence and Inattention appeared on one side, and of Artifice, Secresy and Guile I must say Guile on the other, since it was erected. Let me draw a Picture of the Defendants stupidity, and of Plaintiffs Knavery. Neglect to acknowledge the Deed, to record it. Then the Loss of it, intrusting the Agreement that obliged him to allow the wanting of Land on these Bonds, in Hollis's own hands; then leaving the survey, in Hollis's Hands. Paying him sums of Money abroad, and confiding in his Honour to indorse them—and consenting to do Business with him alone. On the other side Hollis has been watchful to draw every Tittle of evidence within his own Power. I dare not say he has the Deed of the Land but he has got the Agreement, and he has the survey and he has been careful never to receive money of us before Witness when he could help it, and he never would give any Receipts. He would promise to indorse upon the Bond but he never did it. Nay he had the assurance to tell us at last, that he never would do any Business with us again, if we brought any 3d Person with us. We thought ourselves ill used several Times. We were ignorant of Numbers and Calculations, can but just write our Names, and we had a Desire that somebody better skilled than we should calculate and settle for us. Accordingly we got once or twice some of our Neighbours, to go with us And see that we want [1] defrauded. But he never would do any Business with us, and at last he told them to their Heads, if you ever bring Deacon Penniman, or any other Man with you again when you come to settle with me, I'le go directly off and leave you and will do nothing with you.

I must explain and prove Towers Payment of one half, at large, and then Haydens Payment of £270, and a Book Debt, and the Indorsements which made the 6 Bonds that Hayden took up.

[1] Thus in MS, for "wa'nt" (wasn't or weren't).

1760. AUG. 9TH.

Drank Tea at Coll. Quincys, with Coll. Gooch and Dr. Gardiner. I see Gooch's fiery Spirit, his unguarded Temper. He Swears freely, boldly. He is a Widower, and delights to dwell, in his Conversation, upon Courtship and Marriage. Has a violent aversion to long Courtship. He's a fool, that spends more than a Week, &c. A malignant Witt. A fiery, fierce outragious Enemy. He quarrells with all Men. He quarrelled with Coll. Quincy, and intrigued to dispossess him of his Regiment, by means of Dr. Miller and Mr. Apthorp.[1] He now quarrells with Coll. Miller and Dr. Miller and Eb. Thayer. He curses all Governors. Pownal was a servant, Doorkeeper, Pimp to Ld. Hallifax, and he contracted with Ld. Hallifax to give him 15s. out of every Pound of his salary. So that Pownal had 25 pr. Cent Commissions, for his Agency, under Ld. Hallifax.

Thersites in Homer, was,

> Aw'd by no shame, by no respect controuled
> In scandal busy, in Reproaches bold:
> With witty Malice studious to defame
> Scorn all his Joy and Laughter all his Aim.
> But chief he gloried with licentious style
> To lash the Great and Monarchs to revile.

Thus we see that Gooches lived, as long ago as the siege of Troy.

> Spleen to Mankind his envyous Heart possesst
> And much he hated all, but most the best.
> Long had he liv'd the scorn of every Greek
> Vext when he spoke, yet still they heard him speak.

His daughters have the same fiery Temper; the same witty malice. They have all, to speak decently, very smart Tempers, quick, sharp, and keen.

An Insinuation, of Mr. Pownals giving 3/4 of his salary for his Commission.—This is with licentious style Governors to revile.— Coll. Miller can serve the Devil with as much Cunning, as any Man I know of, but for no other Purpose is he fit.—This is in scandal busy, in Reproaches bold.

Gardiner has a thin Grashopper Voice, and an affected Squeak; a meager Visage, and an awkward, unnatural Complaisance: He is fribble.[2]

Q[uery]. Is this a generous Practice to perpetuate the Shruggs of Witt and the Grimaces of Affectation?

[1] Long afterward JA wrote a detailed account of the method by which Joseph Gooch displaced John Quincy of Mount Wollaston as colonel of the Suffolk militia in 1742; see JA to Jonathan Mason, 3 Oct. 1820, which gives a considerable account of Gooch (Adams Papers; extracts quoted in JA, *Works*, 2:93, note). Since the Quincy and Adams families were united by JA's marriage (his wife being a granddaughter of Col. John Quincy and their eldest son being named for him), any retrospective account by an Adams is likely to be prejudiced. But the reference in JA's Diary, it should be noted, antedates the union of the families.

According to JA, Gooch, who was well-to-do, made a bargain with leading Anglicans, including Rev. Ebenezer Miller, minister of Christ Church in Braintree, offering to build a steeple for Christ Church if his influential friends could persuade Governor Shirley to obtain the colonelcy for Gooch. Shirley did so, but the new colonel proved highly unpopular in Braintree and before long moved to Milton without carrying out his part of the bargain. Deacon John Adams had had a part in this affair, as his son recalled: the elder Adams had been a lieutenant in the militia, but upon being offered a captaincy under Gooch he declined to serve under any other officer than Quincy.

[2] Trifling, frivolous (*OED*). This comment on Dr. Gardiner appears to be JA's own, though by arbitrarily enclosing this paragraph in quotation marks in his text of the Diary CFA attributes it to Gooch and thus makes him the subject of JA's rebuke in the next paragraph; see JA, *Works*, 2:95. It is more likely that JA is rebuking himself.

1760. AUG. 12TH.

Remonstrated at the sessions vers. Licensing Lambard, because the select Men had refused to approbate him, because he never was approbated by the select men, to keep a Tavern in the House he now lives in, because there are already 3 and his would make 4 Taverns besides Retailers, within 3/4 of a Mile, and because he obtained a License from that Court, at April sessions, by artfully concealing his Removal from the Place where he formerly kept, and so by an Imposition on the Court. These Reasons prevailed. Majr. Miller, Coll. Miller and Ruddock, were the only Justices on Lambards side, while I had 8 or 9, Wendells, Coll. Phillips, Mr. Dana, Mr. Storer &c. &c. &c. Mr. Dana enquired, whether those Landing Places at Braintree and Weighmouth or the Road where these 4 Taverns stand was not a great stage for

Travellers. I answered no, and rightly, for the greatest stage that I knew of from Boston to Plymouth, is in the North Precinct of Braintree, where Mr. Bracket, but especially where Mr. Bass now keeps. Where Mr. Bass now keeps, there has been a Tavern, always since my Remembrance, and long before. It is exactly 10 miles from Town, and therefore a very proper stage for Gentlemen who are going from Boston down to Plymouth, and to the Cape, and for People who come from the Cape, towards this Town. And there are very few Travellers either bound to or from Boston, but what stop here, but this stage is 2 or 3 Miles from the Place in Question. These Things I should have said, but they did not then occur.

Dana asked next, what Number of Carters, Boatmen, Shipbuilders &c. were ever employed at a Time, at that Landing Place? I answered half a dozen Carters perhaps. But my Answer should have been this. At some times there are 3 or 4 or half a dozen Ship Carpenters, and it is possible there may have been 2 or 3 Boats at that Wharf at a Time, which will require 1/2 dozen Boatmen, and there has been perhaps 40 Carts in a day with stones, and Wood and Lumber, but these Carts are coming and going all Day long so that it is a rare thing to see half a dozen Carts there at a time. In short there is so much Business done there, as to render one Tavern necessary, but there is not so much Business, there is no such Concourse of Travellers, no such Multitudes of busy People at that Landing as to need all this Cluster of Taverns. One Tavern and one Retailer was tho't by the select Men quite sufficient for that Place. They have Appointed one of each, and pray that your Honors would recognize no more.

1760 AUG. 19TH.

I began Popes Homer, last Saturday Night was a Week, and last Night, which was Monday night I finished it. Thus I found that in seven days I could have easily read the 6 Volumes, Notes, Preface, Essays, that on Homer, and that on Homers Battles and that on the funeral Games of Homer and Virgil &c.[1] Therefore I will be bound that in 6 months I would conquer him in Greek, and make myself able to translate every Line in him elegantly.[2]

Prat. It is a very happy Thing to have People superstitious. They should believe exactly as their Minister believes. They should have no Creeds and Confessions ⟨of Faith⟩. They should not so much as know what they believe. The People ought to be ignorant. And our Free schools are the very bane of society. They make the lowest of the People infinitely conceited. (These Words I heard Prat utter. They would come naturally enough from the mouth of a Tyrant or of a K[ing] or Ministry about introducing an Arbitrary Power; or from the mouth of an ambitious or avaricious Ecclesiastic, but they are base detestable Principles of slavery. He would have 99/100 of the World as ignorant as the wild Beasts of the forest, and as servile as the slaves in a Galley, or as oxen yoked in a Team. He a friend to Liberty? He an Enemy to slavery? He has the very Principles of a Frenchman—worse Principles than a Frenchman, for they know their Belief and can give Reasons for it.)

Prat. It grieves me to see any sect of Religion extinguished. I should be very sorry, to have the Quaker Society dissolved, so I should be sorry to [have] Condy's Anabaptist Society dissolved. I love to see a Variety. A Variety of Religions has the same Beauty in the Moral World, that a Variety of flowers has in a Garden, or a Variety of Trees in a forrest.

This fine speech was Prats. Yet he is sometimes of opinion that all these Sectaries ought to turn Churchmen, and that a Uniform Establishment ought to take place through the whole Nation. I have heard him say, that We had better all of us come into the Church, than pretend to overturn it &c. Thus it is, that fine Speechmakers are sometimes for Uniformity, sometimes for Variety, and Toleration. They dont speak for the Truth or Weight but for the Smartness, and Novelty, singularity of their speech. However I heard him make two Observations, that pleased me much more. One was that People in Years never suppose that young People have any Judgment. Another Was, (when a Deposition was produced taken by Parson Wells, with a very incorrect Caption, a Caption without mention of the Cause in which it was to be used, or certifying that the Adverse Party was present or notifyed) he observed that the Parson could not take a Caption, to save his Life, and that he knew too much to learn any Thing.

[1] For the editions of Pope's translations of the *Iliad* and *Odyssey* owned by JA, see *Catalogue of JA's Library*, p. 122–123.
[2] A line across the page in the MS separates the present paragraph from those reporting Prat's observations that follow; the latter may therefore have been recorded at any time from 19 Aug. to 23 Sept. 1760.

1760. SEPTR. 24TH.[1]

Ephraim Jones, being a Widower and having two Children by a former Wife marries another, and soon after dies, leaving a Widow, and the two Children, mentioned before. The Widow takes one third of the personal Estate, for ever, and is endowed of one third of the real Estate, which she lets out to one Tower, as we say to the Halves. Tower breaks up, and plants 1/2 a dozen Acres of the Land with Corn, which he ploughs and hoes &c. till the 20th of September, when The Widow his Lessor dies, having given by her Will, all her Estate to her Relations, Strangers to her late Husband and his Heirs. Now The Question is whether, the one half of the Produce and profits of this Land which the Widow was by Contract to have had, shall go to the Executor of her Will, and so to her Legatees, or else to the Right Heirs, of the Reversion of the Land, expectant on the Widows Death? And Q. also, whether, the said Right Heirs have the Property of the feed and the Apples, and such other fruits as the Earth produces spontaneously, or at least without any immediate Expence and Industry, of the late Tenant in Dower: and Q. also whether the Possession of the Land vests in the Right [heir] Eo Instante that the Widow dies, so that he has an immediate Right of Entry, or Whether the Lessee has not Possession, so that he must be ejected?

¹ This entry and virtually all of those that follow concerning law cases through 3 Nov. 1760 were omitted by CFA in editing JA's Diary.

SEPTR. 24TH. 1760.¹

If I am the Proprietor of an House, and I lease it to any Man, and bind my self to keep it in Repair, it is reasonable and it is Law, that I should have a Rent. So if I am the owner of a ship, and I let [it] out on a Voyage to the Wist Indies or to Europe it is reasonable, and the maritime Law has made provision that I should have freight. For the sum of Money, that an House or a Ship would Cost, would if placed out, on Interest, bring in Annually 6 pr. Cent for my Use. Now I cant loose the Interest of my money, and besides my House is constantly wearing and decaying and my ship and her Cordage and her Canvas are continually wearing, so that the Rent and the freight ought to be sufficient to enable [me] to make these Repairs: But besides this, all Merchants, all Persons who have Property, in shipping, in Vessells that sail upon the sea, are in a peculiar manner liable to Accidents and Misfortunes. They are in Danger, from storms, from Rocks and sands, and they are in Danger from Pyrates and frenchmen, so that the Law, in establishing the freight of Vessells has made allowance, for these 3 things—for the Interest of Money on the Capital, for the Constant Expences in Repairing the Hull and the Cordage and the sails, and for the peculiar Danger from seas, Winds, Rocks and Enemies, which

154

constantly environ Vessells on the sea. And accordingly the freight or Rent of shipping is very high in all foreign Voyages. Well, now the same Reasons, which have established a freight upon Vessells in foreign Voyages, has by Law established a certain share of the Profits [of] this schooner now in Controversy. But the Case, which is more precisely parrall[el] to this of Mr. Lovell, and which is decisive in this Case, is that of Whaling Voyages. In Whaling Voyages, of[f] the shoals of Nantuckett, and in those to Hudsons Bay, there is frequently, a Master of a Vessell, and a Master of the Voyage i.e. a ship is taken into the service, and Whale Boats put on Board her. The Vessell sails into the Whaling Latitudes, and then puts her Boats to sea after the Whales. The Whales are taken on Board the Vessell, and brought home to Cape Cod we'l say, in a sort of Blubber. Wel there, at Cape Cod they frequently hire other People, People who had no Concern with the Voyage, to boil that Blubber into oil. When that is done the oyl is sent up to Boston and sold by Persons who are allowed Commissions for their Pains and after the Oyl is sold, the Established Rule is, to pay all the Costs of Boiling the Blubber and the Commissions arising on the sales and then the Vessell which went out upon the Voyage draws one Quarter of the whole Profits of the Voyage. But the particular Custom which has prevailed among these small Lighters, and schooners that run out a fishing, where there is not so much Danger of Shipwreck, is that the schooner or Lighter shall draw one fifth Part of the Profits of the Voyage. If a schooner runs out in the Harbour a fishing the schooner draws every fifth fish, and whenever they have taken up any drifted Timber or Shingles or Boards, the same proportion has been observed. I have known several Instances in which our Braintree Boats have taken up valuable things adrift, in Cases where there has been no danger to the Lighter, only her time has been consumed, and the Boat always drew one fifth of such drifted Timber as well as of the fish. The only thing, that I can think of, and which the first [...] [2] to its utmost extent [...] think of, as I believe to distinguish this Case from any of the 3 that I have mentioned, either from that of a ship on a foreign Voyage or of any Vessell on a Whaling Voyage or of common Lighters and schooners on fishing Voyages, is this. That the schooner was not stout enough to weigh the Anchor and they were obliged to hire another Vessell to go down a Weight [*i.e.* and weigh?] it.—I beg your H[onor']s careful Attention to this Point, because I suppose the whole stress of the Cause will be laid upon it, by the other side.—Now this I insist upon it can make no Alteration in the Case at all. For Mr. Lovells Vessell went out, upon the supposition that she should draw 1/5 of the whole Profits of the Voyage, 1/5 of all the fish, that should be caught, and 1/5 of every Thing that he found adrift upon the surface or drawn upon from the Bottom of the Sea. And without this Prospect of 1/5 of the Profits, he would not have let her gone. He could have gone in her himself and made Profits by her or he could have let her out to others who would have minded their fishing, and so have gained Profits for him as well as for themselves. Suppose it had been said to Mr. Lovell, let us have your schooner to go out a fishing, and if we catch any, you shall have a fifth, but if we catch none, you shall have nothing and I believe we shant for we intend to spend most of our time in Poking after an Anchor or a Chest of Gold, that we suppose to be lost out in the Harbour; but if we should find this Anchor or Chest your schooner is not able to weight it, and so you shall have no Part of that.

Would Captn. Lovell have consented to that. No he would have laughed at them for fools to think he would, or have frowned upon them in Resentment of an Affront, for such a Proposal in Earnest would have been an affront. Well now what he could not have been desired reasonably to have consented to before the Voyage Your Honor cant desire him to do, and the Law will not oblige him to do after the Voyage. The Time of [the] Schooner was spent in securing of the anchor, time in which she might have earned him money either in fighting or fishing, his Vessell, his Ropes, and Sails were worn in the service, which will cost him money to repair; and what is worse than both the former, his Property was endangered, his Anchor was in great Risque of being irrecoverably lost in the first Place by its Entanglement with the large Anchor at the Bottom, and afterwards by the Use they made of it in raking at the Bottom to bring up the Cable of the great Anchor. And to say that the great Anchor was not weighed by his schooner is to say nothing. ⟨*It was secured by his schooner, and totally by his schooner.*⟩

I say too that the Whales are not taken, cannot be taken by the ship. They are taken by the Whale Boats: I say too that the ship cant boil the Blubber up into oyl. But what then? The ship's time is spent, she is wearing out, and she is endangered, and therefore she shall draw a Quarter of the Neat Profits of the Voyage after Wages for Boiling and Commissions for selling, are paid. This I rely upon, this schooners being unable to weigh the Anchor, is exactly like the ship in Hudsons bays being unable to chase and take the Whales. And their hiring another Vessell to go down, and weigh it, is like Whale mens hiring other Men to boil their blubber, and to sell their Oyl, and that this schooner has as good a Right to 1/5 of the 2/3 after the one third is taken out, which by Agreement was given to the Vessell that weighed it, as a Whaling Vessell has to one fourth of the whole Profits of the Voyage after enough has been taken out to pay the Boilers and factors.

And nothing can be more reasonable. Suppose I should Agree with a Man, to let him have my Horse to Rhode Island to purchase a Quantity of Goods, and he engages I shall have one fifth or one Qr. of the Profits of his Journey. Well when he gets upon Seachonk Plain, He finds a Number of People there a horse racing. He challenges every Horse upon the Plain to run. At last they run for 100 Guineas which my Horse wins. Would it not be reasonable that I should have a Proportion of that Prize? Shall the Man that I let him to, run the Hazard of breaking the Neck, or Limbs or Wind of my Horse. Shall he strain, and violently drive him so as uterly to mar him very much; and I have no Recompence at all? By no means. Your Honor cant but see, we have a Right, and I dont doubt youl give it us.

Perhaps some Difficulty may arise in your Honours mind about the Propriety of the manner of laying this Action. It is an Ind[ebitatus] Ass[umpsit] for so much Money had and received by the Defendant, to the Use of the Plaintiffs, and it is alledged that the Defendant promised to render a reasonable Account. But this is the constant form of Suing for things of this sort. If I upon a Reckoning and settlement with a man pay him by a Mistake £20 more than is due to him, I may recover it back, by this Action, i.e. he has had and received so much money, which did not belong to him but to me, so if Money is due to me from another man, and some 3d Person goes to him, and under Pretence of Authority from me, receives that Money, I may have this Action against him. And in general if any man has received Money, which did not belong to him, but does belong to me, I may recover it of him by this Action. Now I think it is plain that Mr. Ward has received the sum mentioned in this Writ, that it did not belong to him but it did of right belong to the owners of the schooner the present Plaintiffs, and therefore it follows that he is accountable to us for it, and I dont doubt your honour will think so too.

¹ Second entry so dated. This draft of JA's argument in Lovell *v.* Ward was hastily and carelessly written and a few passages remain obscure.

² Two or three words illegible.

OCTR. 7TH. 1760.

Waited on Mr. Gridley for his Opinion of my Declaration Lambard v. Tirrell, and for his Advice, whether to enter the Action or not.¹ He says the Declaration is bad and the Writ, if Advantage is taken, will abate.

For It is a Declaration on a Parol Lease, not on a Deed, and therefore the Lessee's Occupancy ought to be sett forth very exactly, for it is his Occupancy, not any Contract, that supports the Action.—You have declared, that Defendant by Virtue of the Demise, into the Tenements, entered, and the same Premises had, held and occupied. But you have not declared when he entered, nor how long he occupied. He might enter, and remove again from the Premises in 3 months, for ought appears on this Declaration. You have taken this Declaration from a Precedent of Lillies. But Lilly and Mallorry are not Authorities, Coke and Rastall are, and in them, the Distinction is taken between a Declaration on a Lease Parol, and one on a Deed, an Indenture. In a Declaration on an Indenture, it is not necessary to set forth when the Defendant entered nor how long he held: because by the Indenture he had a Right to enter and occupy, if he would, but whether he occupied, or not, he has indented to pay the Rent, when the time is out: But in a Declaration, on a Parol Lease, it is necessary to set forth, both when he entered and how long he stayed, because the Occupancy is the Cause and foundation of the Action. Besides you have not alledged that the Rent was to be yeilded and payd upon Demand, and this would abate the Writ.—Mr. Gridley sent me to Otis's office to examine in Viners Abrigment, under the Title Rent, and in the Entries, i.e. Lilly, Mallorry, Coke, and Rastal, under the Title Debt, for some Authority to decide the Point whether the Exception was fatal, or not. I could find nothing in Viner, Lilly, or Mallorry, but Mr. Gridley shewed me in Coke and Rastall the Distinction taken between a Declaration on a Parol and on a Written Lease.

G. says, that an Indenture for the Year 1758, att a certain Rent; and the Lessees Continuance in the House, and the Lessors Permission to continue in the House, thro the Year 1759 without any new Indenture, or any Contract or Conversation about any Rent, is presumptive Evidence, that Each Party intended, the Rent should continue the same. The Lessees Continuance, in the House, without taking the Pains of going to the Lessor, to treat about new Terms, is sufficient Evidence of his Satisfaction with the old Terms and of his Consent to pay the old Rent. And the Lessors Permission of his Tenant to continue in the House, without taking the Pains to make a new Contract, is sufficient Evidence of his satisfaction with the old Terms, and of his Consent that they should continue.

[1] JA's client, the plaintiff, recovered £9 6s. 8d. as a result of this action in the Inferior Court; the defendant appealed to the Superior Court at its Feb. 1761 term, but did not prosecute, and judgment was affirmed (Superior Court of Judicature, Records, 1760–1762, fol. 177). The bills of costs in both courts, in JA's hand, are in Suffolk County Court House, Early Court Files, &c., No. 81586. See JA's argument under second entry of 17 Oct., below.

1760. OCT. 9TH.

In Support of Complaint in Case Neal's Action is not entered.[1]

I do not know, nor is it possible for your Honours to determine, what Reason induced the Plantiff to renounce this suit. Whether it was, because the Estate is insolvent, or because he had no Cause of Action, or because his Action was mislayed, or because his Writ was bad, which by the Way is very probable, considering who drew it, that determined the Plantiff, not to enter this Action, I cannot say, and your Honours cannot determine. It appears to your Honours, that the Defendant has been vexed and distressed by this summons, that she has been obliged to take a Journey to this Town, and to attend upon this Court, where it appears there is nothing for her to answer to. All this appears. What Motive induced the Plantiff to drop his Action does not appear, and therefore We have a Right to Costs. As Things are Circumstanced, I will own, that had this Action been commenced by any Gentleman, at this Bar, I would have dispensed [with] this Complaint, but it was drawn by a petty fogging Deputy Sheriff against whom I know it is my Duty, and I think it is my Interest to take all legall Advantages. And he himself cannot think it hard, as he has taken both illegal and iniquitous Advantages against me. Therefore I pray your Honours Judgment for Costs.—Q. If this Action should be entered, what must be done with it? Continued, or dismissed?—A Motion must be made for a Continuance or a Dismission.

[1] Joseph Neal had sued the widow of Capt. Richard Brackett as administratrix of Brackett's estate. JA drafted arguments for this case in several entries below. It is not known how the action, which was entered and continued, presumably in the Inferior Court, came out; but in the case of Joseph Neal v. Nathan Spear, which grew out of it, JA won costs by a plea in abatement of the writ (see an entry under the assigned date of Jan.? 1761, below).

1760. OCT. 11TH.

Neals Action is entered so that I have two Actions to defend by Pleas in Bar and three of the Actions I entered, are to be defended, Clark is to Plead in Abatement and Tirrell and Thayer are, I suppose, to plead to issue. Clark gave a Note of Hand to Captn. Brackett in his Life time, and after his Death, on a Reckoning with the Administratrix, a Ballance was found due to the Estate upon Book, for which he gave a new Note to the Widow as Administratrix. Now I have laid both these Notes in one Declaration in Conformity to the Province Law, which forbids two Bills of Cost, upon Instruments, Bonds, Bills, Notes &c. executed by the same Party, and made payable to one and the same Person, and put in suit at the same Time. Dana pleads in Abatement, that these Notes, tho executed by the same Party, were not made payable to one and the same Person. The first was made payable to Bracket, and the second was made payable to his Wife—and cites 3rd. Salkeld 202. "A. owed to B. £20 as Executor, and £10 more in his own Right. One Action will not lie against him for the whole Money, because there must be several Judgments." And Dana says, that soon after he began Practice, he drew a Writ upon a Note taken by an Executor, as Executor, for a Debt of his Testator, and drew the Writ as if the Note had been taken in the Executors own private Right. Auchmuty[1] for the Defendant, pleaded in Abatement that the Note was given to Plaintiff as Executor, not in his own Right, and the Inferiour Court abated the Writ, but he appealed, and at the Superiour Court, got Mr. Reed to speak for him, who contended that the Words as Executor, were idle, and the Court unanimously set up his Writ.

[1] Robert Auchmuty the elder (d. 1750 or 1751), a Scot trained at the Middle Temple who was prominent in the early Boston bar and other colonial affairs; from 1733 to 1741 he was judge of admiralty for New England. His son Robert was an associate of JA's in the Suffolk bar, notably as co-counsel in the defense of Captain Preston in 1770, but he became a loyalist and left America. A sister of the younger Auchmuty, Isabella, married the lawyer and judge Benjamin Prat. (*DAB*, under both Auchmutys; *NEHGR*, 12 [1858]:69–71.)

1760. OCTR. 13TH. MONDAY.

Attended Mr. Niles's Court this morning for John Holbrook Junior in an Action of his against Benja. Thayer Junior. Holbrook agreed with Thayer, to submit all Demands together with both Actions to 3 men.

Mr. Niles told me, that he consulted Mr. Thatcher about entering his Action against Mrs. Brackett. Thatcher told him, it was as likely that she would recover Costs against him, as that he would recover Judgment against her, And therefore advised him not to enter. Niles's Action is exactly like Neals. How came Thatcher to advise to one Thing and Dana to another? The Answer is Dana dont care, how the Action goes. He is sure of his Fee and attendance, whether he gets or looses his Cause.

Thus I find the Bar is divided. Gridley is at a loss. He told me it was a Point of Law that would require a leisurely Examination. Thatcher is uncertain, but thinks it as likely to go in favour of the Administratrix as against her, and how much more likely he did not say. Kent says, the Administratrix will recover Costs, in Spight of the Devil, and he has recovered many a Time in such a Case.—It is a great object of Ambition to settle this Point of Law, whether a suit brought against an Administrator, who after the Commencement, Entry and several Continuances, represents the Estate Insolvent, shall be barred, and the Administrator allowed Costs?

I cannot be compelled to accept Mr. Dana's agreement not to take Execution. And I insist upon it, if he has Judgment, he may take Execution, and if he takes Execution, what shall hinder the officer, from levying the whole Debt, and then what becomes of the Province Law, relating to insolvent Estates? The Words of the Law are "when the Estate of any Person deceased shall be insolvent, or insufficient to pay all just Debts, which the deceased owed, the same shall be set forth and distributed, among all the Creditors in Proportion to the sums to them owing, so far as the said Estate will extend."

No Debts whatever are excepted from the Average, but Debts due to the Crown and the Charges of the last sickness and of the funeral. The Charges of the funeral, of the last sickness and Crown Debts are to be first paid, and then an Average is to be settled by Commissioners of Insolvency, before the Administrators can pay another Debt. There is no Exception of Debts legally demanded before the Representation of Insolvency. If Debts legally demanded, were to be excepted from the Average, every Debt would be excepted from the average. As soon as the Intestates Breath is gone, every Creditor will bring his Action, will make his legal Demand. If this had been Law and known to be law, 500 suits would have been brought vs. this Administratrix, within a Day after she took Administration. If this Rule of Law should be established, it would prove the Destruction of every Intestate Estate in the Province that is considerably in debt. Every Creditor would bring his suit, immediately, and thus the Costs of Suits would amount to a greater sum, oftentimes than the Debts.

It would indeed, furnish Employment to the Lawyers, and perhaps, a secret Regard to Interest has blinded some to the Inconveniences, that must attend it. I think the Point is clear, that a legal Demand, before the Representation of Insolvency cannot intitle any Creditor to recover his whole Demand.

Now the Q[uestion] is whether, if this Action should be defaulted, and Judgment made up, and Execution should issue, it would not issue for the whole sum; and if it issues for the whole sum, the sheriff must levy the whole sum. So that, if Judgment should be rendered now, the whole Demand would be recovered—for this Court cannot consider an Average, that is not yet settled.

Well, should this Action be continued, along from Court to Court, and Judgment be entered after the.[1]

In answer to Sewals objection, I say, that an Administrator de Bonis non, could not maintain an Action vs. this Defendant, on this Note. But the Administration of this Administratrix must bring the Action, and stand accountable to the Administrator de Bonis non, for the Money, and if this Defendant should break, or die insolvent this would be a good Account.

Her delay to represent this Estate insolvent is of no Consequence at all. She was in Hopes, the Estate would have been sufficient, and she wanted to make a Calculation between the Estate and its Debts, before she made that Representation. She did not want to give the Creditors the Trouble of making out their Claims before Commissioners, if she could pay them without it. She acted in short as every prudent Administrator would do, to save herself and family the Disgrace and Curses of Insolvency, and to save her Creditors, the Trouble of making out their Claims, but People at last grew impatient and some Gentlemen had propagated an Opinion that those who made a legal Demand before the Representation, would recover their whole Debts, and summons's flowed in upon her from all Quarters. Several Actions were brought against her, at Plymouth Court, and several more to this Court, and she saw that Ruin would insue to herself and family if she did not.

Now had this Representation been made when she took Administration, 18 months at least would have been allowed to examine Claims. But 6 months were allowed [over?] so that the Creditors will receive their share quite as soon as they would, if it had been represented sooner.

[1] Thus in MS.

1760. OCTR. 17TH.

What are the Questions, on which Mrs. Bracketts Bars to Danas Actions turn?—The first Question is, whether any Action at all can be maintained vs. the Administrator of an Insolvent Estate excepting for Debt due to the Crown, for sickness and funeral Charges? And the second is, whether an Action brought before the Representation of Insolvency, can be maintained, i.e. Whether an Administrator, by delaying to represent the Insolvency, makes herself liable to any suit, that is brought against her. For I take it to be very clear, that when an Estate is represented insolvent, as soon as an Administrator is appointed no Action can be maintained. All Actions must be barred, bar'd I mean for a Time, till the Commissioners have reported and the Average is settled. So that the only Question is, whether Administrators are liable to suits, till the Representation is made? And with submission I think [it] is certain that they are not. In many Cases it is well known, before a Mans Breath is gone, that he owes more than he is worth, and in such Cases the Administrator would do well to represent the Insolvency, at his first Appointment, but there are many Cases, when it is impossible for the Administrator to know whether his Intestate is solvent or insolvent, the Quantity of his Lands and goods may be unknown, and the Number and Quantity of his Debts is always unknown so that no Computation can possibly be made, and in these Cases, it is certainly reasonable and it is Law, that the Administrator should have some time to examine and calculate before he makes a Representation, for if the Estate is sufficient, it would be folly to draw upon his Intestate and himself and family the Disgrace of Insolvency, and the Curses of the Creditors needlessly, and it would be a Pitty to put the Estate to the Expence of the Commissioners, and the Creditors to the Trouble of making out their Claims before them. In all Cases therefore where it is doubtful whether the Estate is sufficient or insufficient, the Administrator ought to have time to inform himself, and in the mean time, all the Creditors must be debared from suits, or if they will bring them they must do it at their Peril, i.e. if the Estate afterwards proves insolvent, their Actions must be bared and they must pay Costs. Whether some Limitation of the time, is expedient or not, it is not our Business to inquire, if the Laws are imperfect in this respect it is the Business of the Legislature to perfect it, but Mr. Dana cannot avail him self of a Law that has no being.

Now the Case before your Honour, is of the last sort. At the Time of Capt. Bracketts Death, it was very doubtful, with every body, whether he left enough to pay his Debts or not. His Widow, on her appointment, to the Administration, told the Judge, it was uncertain, and asked time to inform herself; and she has been as diligent as she could, considering the distressed situation of her family, in making Enquiry after the Debts. She found Effects enough in her Hands to pay all the Debts that she was apprized of, and so was unwilling to make the Representation, unwilling to put the Estate to needless Charge, and Disgrace, unwilling to put her Creditors to the Trouble of making out their Claims with the Commissioners, till she was satisfyd, there was not enough. But new Creditors are daily making their Appearance, who have large demands, and some who were never so civil as to let her know she owed them, have sent her Writts. She was sued in one Action to this Court for some hundreds, on a Note that she never suspected to be in Being. In short she finds most of the real Estate under Mortgage, so that most, if not all the Personal Estate must go to discharge these Mortgages, and then the real Estate must be sold at Vendue, the Event of which is quite uncertain, and therefore the Estate is not sufficient to pay. And as the Estate is insolvent, these suits must be barred. The Law is express, that No Proscess shall be allowed. And I presume the Reason, why the Law has not confined Administrators to narrow limits, is that People [must?] be restrained from rushing on such Estates, and by stifling all the sentiments of Humanity, bringing Destruction on the fatherless and Widows.

The Time for Enquiry, whether the Estate is insolvent, or not, must be dilated on. It is a momentous Point. Must shew, that the time she has taken, is no more than reasonable.

The Administrator is not liable unless it can be shewn that she has intermeddled with the Goods and made payment of any Debt. She has never paid any Debt.

1760. OCT. 17.[1]

In the Beginning of May 58 Mr. Lambard, the Plantiff, gave a Lease of a House and Barn and Land in Germantown mentioned in the Writ to the Defendant Mr. Tirrell, and this Lease you will have with you. You will find by it, that Tirrill was to give [*illegible initial*] &c. the same Rent, that is sued for, in the present Action. In May 1759, i.e. at the End of the Year, Mr. Lambard went into the service, without making any new Contract, and Mr. Tirrell and his family continued in the House from that time to this. The Plantiff has frequently requested his Rent, but has been always refused, and at last he was obliged to bring his Action. As I said before there was no express Contract between the Parties, for the Year 1759, but as there was an express Contract for 58, and as the Defendant continued with his family, and as the Plantiff permitted him to continue in the House, the natural and legal Presumption is, that each Party was satisfyd with the old Terms, and intended the old Terms should continue. For had the Landlord been dissatisfyd with the Terms, it would have been his Business to have said, you must come upon a new Agreement or else leave the House, and had the Tenant been dissatisfyd he should have said I must have the Place for less Rent or else I must leave. But as each Party was silent, each Party implicitly consented that the old Conditions should remain; especially as the Terms were very reasonable. £70 old Tenor, a Year is a moderate Rent for that Place. There is a very convenient handsome new House, there is a good Barn, and several good Lotts of Land. Besides the House has had Licence for a Tavern for these 7 Years, and Mr. Tirrell has all along kept a Tavern there and does to this day. Now the single Priviledge of keeping a Tavern upon that Place is worth as much annually as this Rent. For Germantown, you all know is a Place of considerable Resort. Hardly any Gentlemen of Curiosity from any of the four Governments come to this Town, without taking a Ride to Germantown to see the Manufactures there, that of Glass and that of Stockings. Great Numbers of People go out from this Town upon Parties of Pleasure to Germantown, and there is a considerable Number of Inhabitants upon the Place and all these must be entertained and supplied, so that considering the House, Barn, Land, and these Priviledges the Rent is quite moderate, and there can be no Reason why each Party should not be confined, to those Terms, which the Defendants silence and Continuance in the House, raise a violent Presumption that he consented to, and I dont doubt, you'l give us the sum sued for accordingly.

¹ Second entry so dated. This is a draft of JA's argument in the case of Lambard (or Lambert) *v.* Tirrell in the Inferior Court; see 7 Oct. and note, above.

[3] NOVR. 1760. MONDAY.

Dana says the Administrator ought not to regard the Disgrace or Trouble or Expence of a Commission of Insolvency, but if it is in the least degree suspicious, that the Estate will not prove sufficient, he must represent it so, at his first Appointment i.e. every Day, that he takes to enquire into the Value of the Estate, and the Number of Debts, is at the Risque of the Creditors, and if any one Creditor brings his Action he must maintain it, at the Expence of the others. For says he, as no Time is limitted an Administrator may wait a whole Year, before he represents the Estate insolvent, and live upon the Estate all that time, to the Injury of the Creditors. Nay he may neglect it two Years, or 10 Years, till he has wasted, spent, or alienated the whole Estate.

I say, it is reasonable that a Time should be allowed the Administrator to enquire, to make a Computation of the Effects, and to enquire into the No. and Quantity of the Debts, that he may be able to judge, whether the Estate is insolvent or not. For a Commission of Insolvency is an Evil, always to be avoided, if Possible. It is always considered as a Disgrace to a family. It is always a great Expence to the Estate. It always provokes the Curses of the Creditors, and puts them to the Trouble in attending the Commissioners to prove their Debts. And it is not only reasonable, that a Time of Enquiry should be allowed, but it is Law. And the Executor or Administrator appointed to any Insolvent Estate, before Payment to any be made, except as aforesaid, shall represent the Condition and Circumstances thereof unto the Judge of Probate. Here is plainly a time allowed him, and there is no Limitation of that time. It is only said the Representation must be made before any Payment is made. And here is an Exception, which clearly gives the Administrator, some time; the Exception is of Debts due to the Crown, of sickness and funeral Charges. These the Administrator, after his Appointment may pay, before he is obliged to represent it insolvent, and he could not pay these any more than any other Debts unless some time was allowed him.

Mr. Danas Objections are in my humble opinion of little Weight. He says, that if the Administrator is not obliged to represent immediately, he may delay it, till she and her family have consumed, or by fraud conveyed away the Estate. But your Honours know that Apprisers are appointed, always directly after the Administrator is appointed, who are to make an Inventory and then the Administrator charges herself with all the Articles in the Inventory, and gives Bonds to be accountable for them at the apprized Value, at the Years End. So that if the Estate is wasted the Administrators Bond may be put in suit. Besides, admitting here is a Defect in the Law, in this Respect, Admitting a new Law is expedient, to limit the Time of [representation], such a Law has no Existence, nor can Mr. Dana avail himself of a Law that has no Being, however expedient it may be, especially when the Representation is made within a reasonable Time, as this was. The Representation was made in 9 months, which was a short space of Time considering the Circumstances of this affair. Brackett was struck out of Life suddenly, left a very distressed family, and a very perplexed and embarrassed Estate, so that it was impossible for the Widow to recover from her surprize, and make any Inquiry so as to satisfy herself whether the Estate was sufficient or not, sooner than she did. And I presume the Reason why the Law has not confined the Administrator to such Estates to narrow limits, is, because Persons, that die so much in Debt, commonly leave Widows and Children behind them, who have been used to decent and reputable living, and will therefore, if some reasonable time is not allowed them to keep together, recover their surprize and look about them, will be driven to absolute Despair. And to this Purpose and that the Estate may not be burdened with Costs, the Law has provided, that no Proscess shall be allowed, while any such Estate is depending as aforesaid, which Words extend as well to the Time, the Estate is depending under the Examination and Enquiry of the Administrator as to that between the Representation of Insolvency and the settling of the Average. And it is quite reasonable that this Action in Particular, should be barred, because it was entered, out of the meer Humour and Obstinacy of the Plantiff. Tho it was commenced before the Representation it was entered afterwards, whereas if he had been a reasonable Man, instead of entering and driving this Action, as he has done, he should have dropd it without Entry.

NOV. 5TH. 1760.

Messrs.[1]

I presume upon the common sense of the World that no offence will be taken at the Freedom of the following Sentiments while the utmost Deference for Authority and Decency of Language is preserved, as Persons of obscure Birth, and Station, and narrow Fortunes have no other Way, but thro the Press to communicate their Tho'ts abroad, either to the high or the low.

The Vacancy, in the highest seat of Justice in the Province occasioned by the Death of J[udge] Sewal, naturally stirrs the Minds of all, who know the Importance of a wise, steady and loyal Administration of Justice, to enquire for a fit Person to fill that Place.[2] Such Persons know, that the Rules of the common Law are extreamly numerous, that Acts of Parliament are numerous, some taken from, or at least in spirit, from the Civil Law, others from the Cannon and feudal Law. Such Persons know that the Histories of Cases and Resolutions of Judges have [been] preserved from a very great Antiquity, and they know also, that every possible Case being thus preserved in Writing, and settled in a Precedent, leaves nothing, or but little to the arbitrary Will or uninformed Reason of Prince or Judge.

And it will be easy, for any Man to conclude what opportunities, Industry, and Genius employd from early Youth, will be necessary to gain a Knowledge, from all these sources, sufficient to decide the Lives, Liberties and fortunes of Mankind, with safety to the Peoples Liberties, as well as the Kings Prerogative, that happy Union, in which the Excellence of british Government consists, and which has often been preserved by the deep Discernment and noble spirit of english Judges.

It will be easy for any Man to conclude that a Man whose Youth and Spirits and Strength, have been spent, in Husbandry Merchandize, Politicks, nay in science or Literature will never master so immense and involved a science: for it may be taken for a never failing Maxim, that Youth is the only Time for lay[ing] the Foundation of a great Improvement in any science or Profession and that an Application in advanced Years, after the Mind is crowded, the Attention divided, or dissipated, and the Memory in part lost will make but a tolerable Artist at best.

[1] This draft of a communication to a newspaper is obviously incomplete and does not appear to have been published.

[2] Chief Justice Stephen Sewall died on 10 Sept. 1760, and a bitter contention ensued over the succession to his post. According to a retrospective account by Edmund Trowbridge, the two candidates who made themselves most conspicuous by their own efforts were William Brattle and the elder James Otis. When, on 13 Nov., Lt. Gov. Thomas Hutchinson was named, the two disappointed candidates were so "very angry with him and every one else they knew or suspected had not favoured their Respective Claims," that much of the subsequent political squabbling in Massachusetts was a result of their irritation (Trowbridge to William Bollan, 15 July 1762, MHS, *Colls.*, 74 [1918]:66). Neither Brattle nor Otis nor Hutchinson had had regular legal training, and so it would appear that JA is arguing against the appointment of any one of the three. If he had completed his article, we would doubtless know whom he was *for*.

NOVR. 14TH. 1760.[1]

Another Year is now gone and upon Recollection, I find I have executed none of my Plans of study. I cannot Satisfy my self that I am much more knowing either from Books, or Men, from this Chamber, or the World, than I was at least a Year ago, when I wrote the foregoing Letter to Sewal.[2] Most of my Time has been spent in Rambling and Dissipation. Riding, and Walking, Smoking Pipes and Spending Evenings, consume a vast Proportion of my Time, and the Cares and Anxieties of Business, damp my Ardor and scatter my attention. But I must stay more at home—and commit more to Writing. A Pen is certainly an excellent Instrument, to fix a Mans Attention and to inflame his Ambition. I am therefore beginning a new literary Year, with the 26th. of my life.[3]

[1] This and the following two entries, all of them bearing the same date, are inserted here from D/JA/4, the journal of studies that JA projected in Oct. 1759 (see entries there) but proceeded to neglect for over a year.

[2] Draft at the beginning of D/JA/4 (p. 123–124, above).

[3] An approximation. JA's 26th birthday fell on 19 Oct. 1760 according to the Old Style calendar; on 30 Oct. according to the New Style.

1760. NOVR. 14TH. FRIDAY.

I am just entered on the 26th Year of my Life, and on the fifth Year of my studies in Law, and I think it is high Time for a Reformation both in the Man, and the Lawyer. 25 Years of the Animal Life is a great Proportion to be spent, to so little Purpose, and four Years, the Space that we spend at Colledge is a great deal of Time to spend for no more Knowledge in the science and no more Employment in the Practice of Law. Let me keep an exact Journal therefore of the Authors I read, in this Paper.[1]

This day I am beginning my Ld. Hales History of the Common Law, a Book borrowed of Mr. Otis, and read once already, Analysis and all, with great Satisfaction. I wish I had Mr. Blackstones Analysis, that I might compare, and see what Improvements he has made upon Hale's.

But what principally pleased me, in the first Reading of Hales History, was his Dissertation upon Descents, and upon Tryals by a Jury.

Hales Analysis, as Mr. Gridley tells me, is an Improvement of one, first planned and sketched by Noy, an Attorney General in the Reign of Charles 1st. And Mr. Blackstone's is an Improvement upon Hales.[2]

[1] That is, this paper booklet or gathering of leaves.

[2] For copies of works by Chief Justice Sir Matthew Hale and Sir William Blackstone still among JA's books at the Boston Public Library, see *Catalogue of JA's Library*, p. 113, 28.

1760. NOVR. 14. FRIDAY.

The Title is "The History of the Common Law of England." The Frontispiece, I cannot comprehend. It is this.

$$\text{'}Ισχυρον \ ὁ \ ΝΟΜΟΣ \ ἐσ[τ]ὶν \ ἄρχοντα \ ^{1}$$

His great Distribution of the Laws of England is into Leges scriptæ and Leges non scriptæ. The first are Acts of Parliament which are originally reduced to writing before they are enacted, or receive any binding Power, every such Law being in the first Instance, formally drawn up in Writing, and made as it were a Tripartite Indenture, between the King, the Lords and Commons.

The Leges non scriptæ, altho there may be some Monument or Memorial of them in Writing (as there is of all of them) yet all of them have not their original in Writing, but have obtained their Force by immemorial Usage or Custom.

[1] Transcribed by JA from the title-page of Sir Matthew Hale's *The History and Analysis of the Common Law of England*, London, 1713. JA could make no sense of it because it is garbled Greek for which the printer may have been re-

sponsible. CFA subjoined the following note on the passage: "Stephanus quotes the following as a proverb,—

Ἰσχυρὸν ὁ νόμος ἐστίν, ἤν ἄρχοντ᾽ ἔχη.

which he translates,—The law is powerful if it have an executor" (JA, *Works*, 2:101). The Stephani, or Estiennes, were 16th-century printers and lexicographers; see *Catalogue of JA's Library*, p. 86. Hale's titlepage motto is evidently a distorted version of this "proverb."

1760. NOVR. 15TH. SAT.

Spent last Evening at Coll. Quincys, with Coll. Lincoln. Several Instances were mentioned, when the Independency and Superiority of the Law in general over particular Departments of officers, civil and military, has been asserted and maintained, by the Judges, at Home. Ld. Cokes Resolution in the Case of —— —— in oposition to the opinion, and even to the orders, and passionate Threatnings of the King. Ld. Holts refusal to give the House of Lords his Reasons, for his Judgment in the Case of —— —— in an extra judicial Manner, i.e. without being legally and constitutionally called before them by a Rit [Writ] of Error, Certiorari, or false Judgment. And C[hief] J[ustice] Wills's resolute spirited assertion of the Rits [Rights] of common Law in opposition to the Court Martial against the Intercession of powerful Friends, and even of the Ministry if not the K[ing] himself.[1]

[1] CFA identifies two of the cases here referred to (JA, *Works*, 2:101).

1760. NOVR. 19TH.

Parson Smith says the Art of Printing like most other Arts, and Instruments, was discovered by Accident. Somebody, at an idle Hour, had whitled his Name, cut his Name out in the Bark of a Tree. And when his Name was fairly cut out, he cut it off [and] put it into his Hankerchief. The Bark was fresh, and full of Sap, and the Sap colored his Hankerchief, i.e. printed his Name upon it. And from observing that he tooke the Hint.

WEDNESDAY [19 NOVEMBER].[1]

Dined at Badcocks, with McKenzie. He pretends to Mechanicks, and Manufactures. He owns the snuff Mill, and he is about setting up some Machine to hull our Barley. One Welsh dined with us, who he said was the best, most ingenious Tradesman, that ever was in this Country. McKenzie and Welsh were very full of the Machinery, in Europe, the Fire Engines, the Water Works, the silk Machines, the Wind Mills, in Holland &c. McKenzie says there are 27,000 Wheels, and 90,000 Movements in the silk Machine. You may see 10,000 Wind Mills going at once in Holland. Thus he tells Wondrous Things, like other Travellers.—I suspect he would be unable to describe the fire Engine or the Water Works. Had I been Master of my self I should have examined him, artfully, but I could not recollect any one Particular of the fire Engine, but the Receiver, and that he says is no Part of the Engine. But he talks about a Center Cylinder.

This conceited Scotchman has been a Rambler I believe. He set up Merchandize in New London. He married a Cunningham, sister to Otis's Wife.—These restless Projectors, in Mechanicks, Husbandry, Merchandize, Manufactures, seldom succeed here. No Manufactury has succeeded here, as yet. And I believe Franklins Reasoning is good, and the Causes he mentions will hinder the growth of Manufactures here in America, for a great While yet to come.[2]

[1] Apparently a second entry for 19 Nov., but the preceding entry should perhaps have been dated a day earlier.
[2] The reference is to Franklin's "Observations concerning the Increase of Mankind, Peopling of Countries, Etc.," written in 1751 and first published four years later in Boston. Franklin reasoned that since land was so plentiful in America, labor would long be costly. "The Danger therefore of these Colonies interfering with their Mother Country in Trades that depend on Labour, Manufactures, &c., is too remote to require the attention of *Great-Britain*" (*Writings*, ed. Smyth, 3:65–66).

1760. NOVR. 21ST. FRIDAY.

This day has been spent to little Purpose. I must confine my Body, or I never shall confine my Tho'ts. Running to Drs., cutting Wood, blowing fires, cutting Tobacco, waste my Time, scatter my Thoughts, and divert my Ambition. A Train of Thought, is hard to procure. Trifles light as Air, break the Chain, interrupt the series.

1760. NOVR. 21ST. FRIDAY.[1]

Finished the History of the Common Law, the second Time. The Dissertation on hereditary Descents, and that on Tryals by Juries, are really, very excellent Performances, and well worth repeated, attentive Reading.

[1] This, the second entry so dated, is from D/JA/4, JA's fragmentary record of studies.

[NOVEMBER] 1760.[1]

Pater was in a very sociable Mood this Evening. He told 3 or 4 merry stories of old Horn. Old Horn, a little crooked old Lawyer in my fathers Youth, who made a Business of Jest and Banter, attacked an old Squaw one Day upon the Neck. The old Squaw made answer,

"You poor smitten Boy, you with your Knife in your Tail and your Loaf on your Back, did your Mother born you so?"

A Man, whom he assaulted at another Time, with his Jests, asked him "Did you come straight from Boston?" And upon being answered yes, replied you have been miserably warped by the Way then.

A Market Girl whom he overtook upon the Neck, and asked to let him jigg her? answered by asking what is that? What good will that do? He replied it will make you fat! Pray be so good then says the Girl as to Gigg my Mare. She's miserably lean.

[1] Presumably written 22, 23, or 24 Nov. 1760.

NOVR. 25TH. 1760.

Rode to the Iron Works Landing to see a Vessell launched. And after Launching went to smoke a Pipe, at Ben. Thayers, where the Rabble filled the House. Every Room, kitchen, Chamber was crowded with People.[1] Negroes with a fiddle. Young fellows and Girls dancing in the Chamber as if they would kick the floor thro. Zab Hayward, not finding admittance to the Chamber, gathered a Circle round him in the lower Room. There He began to shew his Tricks and Postures, and Activity. He has had the Reputation, for at least fifteen Years, of the best Dancer in the World in these Towns. Several attempted, but none could equal him, in nimbleness of heels. But he has no Conception of the Grace, the Air nor the Regularity of dancing. His Air is absurd and wild, desultory, and irregular, as his Countenance is low and ignoble. In short the Air of his Countenance, the Motions of his Body, Hands, and Head, are extreamly silly, and affected and mean.

When he first began, his Behaviour and Speeches were softly silly, but as his Blood grew warm by motion and Liquor, he grew droll. He caught a Girl and danced a Gigg with her, and then led her to one side of the Ring and said, "Stand there, I call for you by and by." This was spoke comically enough, and raised a loud laugh. He caught another Girl, with light Hair, and a Patch on her Chin, and held her by the Hand while he sung a song, describing her as he said. This tickled the Girls Vanity, for the song which he applied to her described a very fine Girl indeed.

One of his witty droll sayings he thought, was this. I am a clever fellow, or else the Devil is in me. That is a Clever Girl or else the Devil is in her. Wm. Swan is such another Funmaking animal of diverting Tricks.

Hayward took one Girl by the Hand, and made a Speech to her.

"I must confess I am an old Man, and as father Smith says hardly capable of doing my Duty." This raised a broad Laugh too.

Thus, in dancing, singing songs, drinking flip, running after one Girl, and married Woman and another, and making these affected, humorous Speeches, he spent the whole Afternoon.—And Zab and I were foolish enough to spend the whole afternoon in gazing and listening.

Gurney danced, but was modest and said nothing. E. Turner danced not, but bawled aloud.—God dam it, and dam it, and the Devil, &c.—And swore he'd go to Captn. Thayers, and be merry and get as drunk as the Devil. He insisted upon it, drunk he would get. And indeed, not 2 pence better than drunk he was.

Fiddling and dancing, in a Chamber full of young fellows and Girls, a wild Rable of both sexes, and all Ages, in the lower Room, singing dancing, fiddling, drinking flip and Toddy, and drams.—This is the Riot and Revelling of Taverns And of Thayers frolicks.

¹ The "Iron Works Landing" and Benjamin Thayer's tavern, on the Monatiquot River where it flows into Fore River Bay, may be seen at the foot of JA's sketch map of taverns in Braintree and Weymouth, reproduced in this volume. This entire entry was omitted by CFA in editing JA's Diary.

1760. NOVR. 26TH. WEDNESDAY.¹

Ten days are now elapsed, since I began Hale the 2d time, and all the Law I have read, for 10 days, is that Book once thro. I read Woods Institute thro the first Time with Mr. Put. in twice that time i.e. in 3 Weeks, and kept a school every day. My present Inattention to Law is intolerable and ruinous.

¹ This entry and those that follow, through 1 Dec. 1760, are again from D/JA/4, JA's record of studies.

1760. NOVR. 26TH WEDNESDAY.

Night before Thanksgiving.—I have read a Multitude of Law Books—mastered but few. Wood. Coke. 2 Vols. Lillies Ab[ridgmen]t. 2 Vols. Salk[eld's] Rep[orts]. Swinburne. Hawkins Pleas of the Crown. Fortescue. Fitzgibbons. Ten Volumes in folio I read, at Worcester, quite thro—besides Octavos and Lesser Volumes, and many others of all sizes that I consulted occasionally, without Reading in Course as Dictionaries, Reporters, Entries, and Abridgments, &c.

I cannot give so good an Account of the Improvement of my two last Years, spent in Braintree. However I have read no small Number of Volumes, upon the Law, the last 2 Years. Justinians Institutes I have read, thro, in Latin with Vinnius's perpetual Notes, Van Muydens Tractatio Institutionum Justiniani, I read thro, and translated, mostly into English, from the same Language. Woods Institute of the Civil Law, I read thro. These on the civil Law; on the Law of England I read Cowells Institute of the Laws of England, in Imitation of Justinian, Dr. and student, Finch's Discourse of Law, Hales History, and some Reporters, Cases in Chancery, Andrews &c. besides occasional searches for Business. Also a general Treatise of naval Trade and Commerce, as founded on the Laws and Statutes. All this series of Reading, has left but faint Impressions, and [a] very Imperfect system of Law in my Head.

I must form a serious Resolution of beginning and pursuing quite thro, the Plans of my Lords Hale, and Reeve. Woods Inst[itutes] of common Law I never read but once, and my Ld. Coke's Com[mentary] on Lit[tleton] I never read but once. These two Authors I must get, and read, over and over again. And I will get em too, and break thro, as Mr. Gridly expressed it, all obstructions.

Besides, I am but a Novice in natural Law and civil Law. There are multitudes of excellent Authors, on natural Law, that I have never read, indeed I never read any Part of the best authors, Puffendorf and Grotius. In the Civil Law, there are Hoppius, and Vinnius, Commentators on Justinian, Domat, &c. besides Institutes of Cannon and feudal Law, that I have to read.

Much may be done in two Years, I have found already. And let it be my Care, that at the End of the next two Years I be better able to shew that no Time has been lost than I ever have been yet.

Let me practice the Rule of Pythagoras.

$$\text{Μηδ' ὕπνον μαλακοῖσίν ἐπ' ὄμμασι προσδέξασθαι}$$
$$\text{πρίν τῶν ἡμερινῶν ἔργων τρὶς ἕκαστον ἐπελθεῖν}$$
$$\text{πῆ παρεβην; τί δ'ερεξα; τι μοι δεον οὐκ ετελεσθη;}^{[1]}$$

Thus let me, every night before I go to bed, write down in this Book, what Book of Law, I have read.

[1] Quoted from the "Golden Verses of Pythagoras," a collection of maxims actually written by disciples of Pythagoras. Professor Johannes A. Gaertner of Lafayette College has kindly furnished the following translation: "Let not sleep be admitted to tiring eyes before going over each of the daily tasks thrice. What have I omitted? What have I achieved? What has not been finished that was my duty?" Years later JA read through the "Golden Verses" in a French translation and wrote a rather bemused marginal commentary on them which has been published by Zoltán Haraszti in *More Books*, 1:106–110 (April 1926). Of the first sentence in the present passage he remarked: "Wise but very difficult." Still later, JQA prefixed a verse translation of this passage to his Diary for 1819; see his *Memoirs*, 4:203.

1760 NOVR. 28TH. FRIDAY.

I have not read one Word of Law, this Day. But several Points, and Queries have been suggested to me, by the Consultors.—In whom is the Fee, and Freehold of our burying Yard? What Right has any Man to erect a Monument, or sink a Tomb there, without the Consent of the Proprietors? In England, the Church Yards are the Places of Burial, and the Parson is seised in fee, of them as of the Ground whereon the Church stands. But our Burying Yards, as well as the Ground, on which our Temples stand, are not vested in our incumbent Ministers, but in the Precinct or Parish, (the Corporation socalled) where they lie, according to the late Resolution in the Dedham Case.

The Property of our Meeting House, is in the Precinct, i.e. the dissenting Part of it,—And I think the Precinct, by its Committee sold the Pews to particular Persons, and perhaps, the Persons who have erected Tombs, might previously ask And obtain the Priviledge of the Precinct.

1760. NOVR. 29TH. SATURDAY.

Read no Law.—An exclusive Property is certainly claimed and enjoyed, by private Persons, in Tombs and Monuments, as well as in Pews. Inhabitants of other Towns, have usually asked Leave of the Select Men, to bury their dead in our burying Place. But I should think the Precinct Assessors, or Parish Committee, had rather the Inspection of our burying Yard. My Father never knew License given nor asked of Town, nor Precinct to sink a Tomb, nor to [raise a] Monument.

Suppose my Father, Wife, Child, friend died, and I order the sexton, or on his Refusal my own servant to open any Tomb in our burying Yard, and without further Ceremony deposit the Corps there, can the pretended Proprietor have any Action, or Remedy against me? The Course of the Descent of these Tombs and Pews, when undisposed by Will, is a matter of uncertainty too. Do they descend to the Heirs, as Inheritances in Houses and Lands, or do they go to the Executor or Administrator, as personal Estate?

There is an Anecdote in the Spectator, of De Wit, the famous dutch Politician. Somebody asked him how he could rid his Hands of that endless Multiplicity and Variety of Business that passed thro them, without Confusion? He answered, "by doing one Thing at once." When he began Any Thing, he applied his whole Attention to it, till he had finished it.—This Rule should be observed in Law. If any Point is to be examined, every Book should be consulted and every Light should be considered, before you proceed to any other Business or study. If any Book is to be read, no other Book should be taken up to divert or interrupt your Attention till that Book is finished.

Order, Method, Regularity in Business or Study have excellent Effects both in saving of Time and in bettering and improving Performance. Business done, in order, is done sooner, and better.

NOVR. 30TH. SUNDAY.

Read no Law. Read Bolinbroke.

1760. DECR. 1ST. MONDAY.

I am beginning a Week and a month, and I arose by the Dawning of the Day. And by sun rise had made my fire and read a number of Pages in Bolinbroke. Tuesday and Wednesday passed, without reading any Law.[1]

[1] There are no further entries in D/JA/4, JA's record of studies, until 27 Jan. 1761.

1760. DECR. 2D. [1]

Spent the Evening at Coll. Q.'s with Captn. Freeman. About the middle of the Evening Dr. Lincoln and his Lady came in. The Dr. gave us an ample Confirmation of our Opinion of his Brutality and Rusticity. He treated his Wife, as no drunken Cobler, or Clothier would have done, before Company. Her father never gave such Looks and Answers to one of his slaves in my Hearing. And he contradicted he Squibd, shrugged, scouled, laughd at the Coll. in such a Manner as the Coll. would have called Boorish, ungentlemanly, unpolite, ridiculous, in any other Man. More of the Clown, is not in the World. A hoggish, ill bred, uncivil, haughty, Coxcomb, as ever I saw. His Wit is forced and affected, his Manners to his father, Wife, and to Company are brutally rustic, he is ostentatious of his Talent at Disputation, forever giving an History, like my Uncle Hottentot,[2] of some Wrangle he has had with this and that Divine. Affects to be thought an Heretic. Disputes against the Eternity of Hell, torments &c. His treatment of his Wife amazed me. Miss Q. asked the Dr. a Question. Miss Lincoln seeing the Dr. engaged with me, gave her Mother an Answer, which however was not satisfactory.[3] Miss Q. repeats it. "Dr. you did not hear my Question."—"Yes I did, replies the Dr., and the Answer to it, my Wife is so pert, she must put in her Oar, or she must blabb, before I could speak." And then shrugged And affected a laugh, to cow her as he used to, the freshmen and sophymores at Colledge.

—She sunk into silence and shame and Grief, as I thought.—After supper, she says "Oh my dear, do let my father see that Letter we read on the road." Bela answers, like the great Mogul, like Nero or Caligula, "he shant."—Why, Dr., do let me have it! do!—He turns his face about as stern as the Devil, sour as Vinegar. "I wont."—Why sir says she, what makes you answer me so sternly, shant and wont?—Because I wont, says he. Then the poor Girl, between shame and Grief and Resentment and Contempt, at last, strives to turn it off with a Laugh.—"I wish I had it. Ide shew it, I know."—Bela really acts the Part of the Tamer of the Shrew in Shakespear. Thus a kind Look, an obliging Air, a civil Answer, is a boon that she cant obtain from her Husband. Farmers, Tradesmen, Soldiers, Sailors, People of no fortune, Figure, Education, are really more civil, obliging, kind, to their Wives than he is.—She always is under Restraint before me. She never dares shew her endearing Airs, nor any fondness for him.

[1] First entry in D/JA/6, an assemblage of loose sheets in which JA made entries at rather irregular intervals until 3 March 1761. About half of these entries, including the present one, were not printed by CFA in his edition of the Diary, and those he did print are frequently incomplete.

[2] This allusion is not now explainable.

[3] The nomenclature in this passage is somewhat puzzling. "Miss Q." can only mean "Mistress Quincy," the wife of Col. Josiah Quincy, since she is immediately identified as the "Mother" (actually stepmother) of "Miss" (i.e. Mistress) Lincoln, that is to say of Hannah (Quincy) Lincoln. From this it is evident that Elizabeth (Waldron) Quincy, the Colonel's 2d wife, was living in Dec. 1760, though the date of her death is usually given as 1759. (Quincy married a third time, but not until 1762.)

DECR. 6TH. 1760.

Talked with Zab about Newton, Bacon, Lock, Martin, Chambers, Rowning, Desaguliers, S'Gravesende &c. I told him I had a low Opinion of the Compilers, Abridgers, and Abstract makers. We had better draw science from its fountain in original Authors. These Writers, the Hirelings of the Booksellers, only vend us the Discoveries of other Philosophers, in another form, and under another Title, in order to get Bread to eat and Raiment to put on.—Zab says, that Martin has made several Discoveries—has invented new Machines, improved and perfected old ones, nay has even detected Errors in Newton. E.g. Newton always thought, the Moon was surrounded by an Atmosphere, but Martin proved it is not; because the Starrs, that appear all round it above, below and on each side of it, are not diminished in their Lustre, as they would appear, if the Rays passed from them thro an Atmosphere.

Then we transited to Dr. Simpson [Simson], Euclid &c. and he asked me to demonstrate, that the 3 Angles of a Triangle are equal to 2 Right. I undertook it. Draw a right Line, A.B. Erect the Perpendicular, C.D. Draw the Hypothenuse D.A. Parallel to A.D. draw the Line C.E.

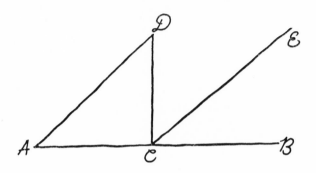

Now I say that the 3 Angles ACD., CDA., and DAC are equal to two right Angles. For it is easy to see that DCA., is a right Angle, and that BCE, which is equal to CAD added to ECD, which is equal to CDA, make another right Angle. But how do I know that BCE is equal to CAD? Let the Triangle ECB, be moved along, to the left hand and by the Hypothesis CE will fall upon AD and CB Upon AC, and of Consequence the 2 Angles are equal. How then do I know that the Angle ECD is equal to ADC? See the Dem[onstration] in Euclid.

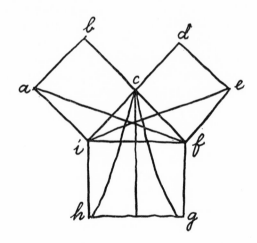

Then we attempted to demonstrate the 47th of the 1st Book. That the Square of the Hypothenuse is equal to the Squares of both the Legs.

I am astonished at my own Ignorance in the french tongue. I find I can neither express my own Thoughts, in it, nor understand others, who express theirs readily in it. I can neither give nor receive Thoughts, by that Instrument.

1760. DECR. 8.

⟨*Began Machiavells* [...] *Machiavell*⟩ [1]

[1] The illegible word begins with "D" but is not "Discourses." JA's lining out is careless; it is possible that he intended to leave "Began Machiavell" as the entry for this day.

DECR. 14TH. 1760.

Hunt v. White. Complaint to Coll. Quincy—of a scandalous Lye, made and published to Hunts Damage.

We appear before your Honour to complain of a very slanderous, and malicious Lye, made and published to our Damage. We complain of a Violation of the Law of this Province against Lying and Libelling. The Law runs thus.—If any Person &c. shall wittingly and willingly make or publish any Lye or Libel tending to the Defamation or Damage &c., make or Spread any false News or Reports &c., and being convicted before one or more Justices, he shall be fined &c. and find sureties.—The Legislature, knowing the quickness and Violence of human Passions saw the Tendency of the Publication of Lyes and false stories, concerning any Person, to raise his Resentment, and provoke him to break the Peace. They knew what a Provocation it was, to recur to Clubbs and fists and swords, the Remedies of Mohocks and Catabaws and to the utter Disturbance of the Peace of society. To prevent therefore the Mischifs and Distraction that might ensue from such Provocations and Resentment they enacted this Law—that Men injured in such a manner might instantly have recourse to a Majestrate and have the Lyar punished for his Malice, and bound to the Behaviour. Now We complain of the Publication of such a Lye— and if we can shew that the Defendant has published such a Lye, i.e. any tending to our Defamation or Damage, that he has spread a false Report, with Intent to abuse us and deceive others, we shall expect your Honours will convict of a breach of this Law, fine him, as this Law directs, and bind him to his good Behaviour. In order to this, I beg leave to lay open as concisely as I can, the previous Facts, which gave Occasion to use the force of the Province Law to this Lye, this false story.

Mr. Hunt, it seems sometime after last Thanksgiving Day, made his application to Mr. Justice Dyer, for a Warrant to search for stolen goods. The Justice administered an oath to him and he swore that on the Night after last Thanksgiving Day, his House was broken and 17£ of Money stolen from his Chest. A Warrant of search was granted and dilligent search was made, but the Money not found. This opportunity it seems, Captn. White took to raise and spread a Lye.—I must be excused, for using these Expressions. The Law has pointed them out to me, and they are the properest that can be found.—A Lye, that has a Tendency, totally and irretrievably to ruin Mr. Hunts Character, to destroy all Confidence in his Probity, to expose him to an infamous Punishment, and to make him avoided as a Pest to Society.

He seems to have made it his Business to ramble about, and publish his Tale to every Man he saw almost both in Weighmouth and Braintree. To one man He says Hunt never lost any Money. To another He stole his Money himself. To a third he enters into a pretended Proof of his story and says—Hunt said in Boston, on Thanksgiving Day Night, which was before his Money was stolen as he swore to Justice Dyer, had told People the story to which he afterwards swore. To another he is more Particular, and says Mr. Ballard of Boston told me, the morning after Thanksgiving, that Hunt told him of the Breach of his House and the Loss of his money the Night before.—Now this we say is the Lye. We never told Mr. Ballard so and Mr. Ballard never told him so. And we say it has a tendency to our Defamation and Damage. If these stories should be believed, every Man will believe us guilty not only of a fraudulent, lying Disposition, but of Perjury. And if the world should believe us guilty of Perjury we are undone, for ever. We shall be dispised. We shall be detested. No man will have the least Confidence in us. We must become Vagabonds upon Earth. I pray the Witnesses may be sworn to prove what we say.

The Crime that is implicitly charged upon the Complainant, is Perjury. What is Perjury? Is it not the worst of Crimes? Is it not, a open deliberate Defyance of Heaven and Earth? Is it not a Challenge of divine Vengence, and a Contemt of all the Infamy and Misery of [three?] of the most severe of civil Punishments? Is it not a Crime that carries with [it] the last Degree of Reproach? It does not indeed strip a Man of the Protection of Society? We cannot, lawfully, hunt down and kill a Perjured Person. But does it not strip us of all the Priviledges of society? Does it not disable us to testify, as Witness on all occasions? Does it not prevent all the World from believing and trusting us?

The Foundation of this Law, is the Tendency of such scandalous stories to the Disturbance of the Peace. The Legislature knew the quickness and Violence of Mens Resentment.

1760. DECR. 16TH. TUESDAY.

Attended the Tryal all day, between Hunt and White before Coll. Quincy, at James Bracketts.

What will be the Consequence of this Tryal? to me, to Hunt, and to White? White has been punished, for his licentious Tittle tatle, but Hunt has gained neither Recompence nor Credit. Benja. Thayer is enraged and Prat and Pitty [Pettee?] were enraged at me for abusing them, by asking them their Thoughts. Ben. Thayer continues so, for aught I know, or care. I fear this unsuccessful Prosecution connected with that of Lovel and Reed, will occasion squibbs, and injure my Reputation in Weighmouth. However in both I am well assured I had good Cause of Action. Lovel and Reed had good Right, tho the Justice was, I dont know what, enough to give his Judgment against them. And stories have been propagated, zealously, industriously propagated by White, with Design I believe to convince Mankind that Hunt had been guilty, or at least from a vain trifling Inclination to shew his Penetration at Hunts Expence; altho the Circumstances of suspicion against Hunt have taken such hold of Mens Minds, that no Conviction of White would have retrieved Hunts Character at all.

It would have been much better, never to have stirred, in this Affair. The more He stirs the worse he stinks.—A Prosecution commenced with so much Temper, pursued with so much Resolution, then supported by so little Evidence and terminated by Agreement, tho in his favour, yet with so small Advantage, will give occasion for Weighmouth Tongues to wanton in obloquy, and to their sides to riot in Laughter.

Virtues, Ambition, Generosity, indulged to excess degenerate in Extravagance which plunges headlong into Villany and folly.

1760 DECR. 18TH. THURDSDAY.

Yesterday spent in Weymouth, in settling the Disputes between old Thos. White and young Isaac French. White has the Remainders of his habitual Trickish lying, cheating Disposition, strongly working to this Day—an infinity of jesuitical Distinctions, and mental Reservations.

He told me he never lost a Cause at Court in his Life—which James White and Mr. Whitmarsh say is a down right Lye.

He owned to me that his Character had been that of a Knave and a Villain: and says every Man of Wit and sense will be called a Villain. —My Principle has been, to deal upon Honour with all men, so long as they deal upon Honour with me, but as soon as they begin to trick me, I think I ought to trick them.

Thus every Knave thinks others, as knavish or more knavish than himself.

What an Intrenchment, is this against the Attacks of his Conscience, is this, "the Knavery of my Neighbours, is superiour to mine." [1]

An old withered, decripit Person, 87 years of Age with a Head full of all the Wiles, and Guile and Artifice of the Infernal serpent, is really a ⟨Phenomenon⟩ mellancholly sight. Ambition of appearing sprightly, cunning, smart, capable of outwitting younger Men. In short I never saw that Guile and subtilty in any Man of that Age. Father Niles has a little of that same serpentine Guile. I never felt the meaning of the Words, Stratagem, Guile, Subtilty, Cunning, Wiles &c. that Milton applies to the Devil [in?] his Plan to effect the Ruin of our first Parents so forcibly, as since I knew that old Man, and his grandson Isaac, who seems to have the same subtilty, and a worse Temper, under a total secresy, and dissembled Intention. He has a smiling face, and a flattering Tongue with a total Concealment of his Designs, tho a devilish malignant, fiery temper appears in his Eyes. He's a Cassius, like Ben. Thayer. Sees thro the Characters of Men, much further, and clearer, than ordinary, never laughs, now and then smiles, or half smiles. Father White, with all his subtilty and Guile, may be easily over reached by Men like him self. He is too open, too ostentatious of his Cunning, and therefore is generally, out witted, and worsted.

Yesterdays Transaction was intended as the final Determination of all Disputes and Concerns between Mr. White and Mr. French—that White should deliver up, or burn all Bonds, Notes, Leases, Indentures, Covenants and Obligations whatever, and that French on his Part should deliver up, or burn, all Indentures, Leases, obligations &c., in his Hands. But as the Indentures and Leases were not destroyed, and some Notes in father Whites Hands not delivered up, I fear, from French's outrageous, and barefaced Declaration, as soon as affairs were over, "that he had got it settled exactly as he would have it," and that "the Receipt did not cut off his Indentures, which would not be in force till his Grandfathers Decease and that he would sue the remaining Notes, out of his Grandfathers Hands" &c., that more Difficulties will yet arise between them. I fear too that my burning of the Arbitration Bonds, and Awards, was a mistaken step, for they might have remained, as Evidence. However, French declared to me, that he would surrender all his Writings, if his Grandfather would surrender his; afterwards in the Evening, at [. . .].[2] But he told me he did not see the Importance of those Indentures.

Five strange Characters I have had Concerns with very lately.—Josiah White, Saml. Hunt, old Thomas White, and Isaac French. Two Fools, and two Knaves—Besides Daniel Nightingale, a Lunatick.

French's Joy, like that of the Devil, when he had compleated the Temptation and fall of Man, was extravagant, but he broke out into too violent a Passion. He broke his own seal of secresy and betrayed his villanous Designs to me. On my Resenting his declared Intention, he grew sensible of his Error, and attempted by soothing to retrieve it. "He was sorry he had broke out so."—"The treatment he had suffered made him in a Passion."—"I raised your Temper too prodigiously."

There is every Year, some new and astonishing scene of Vice, laid open to the Consideration of the Public. Parson Potters Affair, with Mrs. Winchester, and other Women, is hardly forgotten. A Minister, famous for Learning, oratory, orthodoxy, Piety and Gravity, discovered to have the most debauched and polluted of Minds, to have pursued a series of wanton Intrigues, with one Woman and another, to have got his Maid with Child and all that.[3]—Lately Deacon Savils Affair has become public. An old Man 77 Years of Age, a Deacon, whose chief Ambition has always been Prayer, and religious Conversation, and sacerdotal Company, discovered to have been the most salacious, rampant, Stallion, in the Universe—rambling all the Town over, lodging with this and that Boy and Attempting at least the Crime of Buggery. ⟨*Thus Adultery, Buggery, Perjury, are*—⟩

---

[1] Thus in MS (except for closing quotation mark, which has been editorially supplied). Doubtless JA intended to strike out the first "is this."

[2] This name is uncertain. Apparently "Creens," perhaps intended for "Greens."

[3] Nathaniel Potter, College of New Jersey 1753, and honorary A.M., Harvard 1758, was minister at Brookline from 1755 until dismissed in June 1759. Little is said of him in the local histories of Brookline, but the Plymouth church, which seriously considered calling him,

heard in July 1759 "some melancholy things opened with Respect to Mr. Potters moral Charecter." This was just in time to save "this poor Church . . . from Ruine." In 1765 Potter took up with another adventurer, Maj. Robert Rogers, accompanied him to England, and probably had an important hand in Rogers' several literary productions published at that time. With the promise of a good salary as secretary, Potter went with Rogers to Fort Michilimackinac, but quarreled with him in 1767, and died in the English Channel later that year while bringing his charges against Rogers to the British government. (Weis, *Colonial Clergy of N. E.; Plymouth Church Rec-* ords, *1620–1859,* N.Y., 1920–1923, 1:317–318; sources cited in note to entry of 27 Dec. 1765, below, q.v.)

1760. DECR. 18.

Justice Dyer says there is more Occasion for Justices than for Lawyers. Lawyers live upon the sins of the People. If all Men were just, and honest, and pious, and Religious &c. there would be no need of Lawyers. But Justices are necessary to keep men just and honest and pious, and religious.—Oh sagacity!

But, it may be said with equal Truth, that all Magistrates, and all civil officers, and all civil Government, is founded and maintained by the sins of the People. All armies would be needless if Men were universally virtuous. Most manufacturers and Tradesmen would be needless. Nay, some of the natural Passions and sentiments of human Minds, would be needless upon that supposition. Resentment, e.g. which has for its object, Wrong and Injury. No man upon that supposition would ever give another, a just Provocation. And no just Resentment could take Place without a just Provocation. Thus, our natural Resentments are founded on the sins of the People, as much as the Profession of the Law, or that of Arms, or that of Divinity. In short Vice and folly are so interwoven in all human Affairs that they could not possibly be wholly separated from them without tearing and rending the whole system of human Nature, and state. Nothing would remain as it is.

1760. DECR. 18TH [*i.e.* 19TH?] FRYDAY.[1]

Sir

⟨*I am an old Man seventy odd, and as* [I] *had my Education, so I have passed my whole Life in the Country,*⟩ &c.

[1] This is the third entry the diarist dated 18 Dec., but since 19 Dec. 1760 fell on a Friday, an editorial correction seems justified. JA went on with the present canceled draft in an entry conjecturally assigned to Jan. 1761 (p. 190–192, below).

1760. DECR. 22ND. MONDAY.

This day and Tomorrow are the last. I have but one Blank left that I can use.

1760. DECR. 27TH. SATURDAY.

Governor Bernards Speech to the two Houses, at the opening of the present sessions, has several Inaccuracies in it.[1] "The glorious Conclusion of the North American War."—The N. American War is not yet concluded, it continues, obstinate and bloody, with the Cherokees, and will be renewed probably, against the french in Louisiana. However with Regard to this Province, whose Legislature, the Governor was congratulating, it may not very improperly be called a Conclusion.

"The fair Prospect of the security of your Country being settled, upon the most sure and lasting foundations."—Is not this sentence filled with Tautology? The security, being secured upon secure foundations? Emendation—"and the fair Prospect that now Presents itself, of Tranquility, established on lasting foundations."—But it is not Tranquility nor safety, nor Preservation, nor Peace, nor Happiness: but it is security. Then it is not established, fixed, placed: but it is settled: and then it is not stable, permanent: but sure: Here are certainly Words used, mearly for sound.

"This great Contest" &c. Q.—what does he mean, the War, or the Conclusion of the War? If the latter, Conquest should have been his Word: if the former, what follows is not true vizt. we may date the firm Establishment of the british Empire in N. America.—From our late successes and Acquisitions, we may date that Establishment, but not from our Misfortunes and Losses which made no Unmemorable Part of this great **Contest**.

"We form these Pleasing assurances, not only from the more striking Instances of the superiority of its Power, but also from the less obvious observation of the Improvement of its Policy."—Its Power, i.e. the british Empires Power. Instances i.e. Particulars in which it has appeared. Obvious observation, has a good Meaning, but an inelegant, inartificial sound. A Defect of Elegance, Variety, Harmony, at least.

"The improving a Country is a more pleasing Task than the defending it:"—Improving and Defending Participles, used as substantives with the Article the before them, will never be used by a grammarian much less by a Rhetorician. I never could bear such Expressions, in others, and never could use them, myself, unless in Case of absolute Necessity, where there is no substantive to express the same Idea.

"As I have consulted your Convenience in deferring calling you together untill this, the most Leisure time of your whole Year, &c."— "In deferring calling," would never have been used together, by a discerning Ear. He might have said "in deferring this session, untill," &c.—Your whole Year! Why yours, any more than mine or others? Ans[wer]. It is not the most Leisure time of every mans whole Year. It is the most busy time of some Mens year.

Deacon Palmers Observation upon this speech, that "he talks like a weak honest Man," is childish. Tis superficial: Tis Prejudice: Tis a silly thoughtless Repetition of what he has heard others say.

For, tho there are no Marks of Knavery, in it: there are marks of good sense I think. Grammatical and Rhetorical Inaccuracies are by no means Proofs of Weakness, or Ignorance. They may be found in Bacon, Lock, Newton, &c.

¹ This speech by Governor Francis Bernard was delivered to the General Court at the opening of its adjourned session, 17 Dec.; see text in Mass., *House Jour.*, 1760–1761, p. 100–101.

JANY. 2ND. 1760 [*i.e.* 1761]. FRYDAY.

The Representatives in their Address to the Governor, have told him that "Great Britain is the leading and most respectable Power in the whole World." ¹—Let us examine this.—Is she the Leading Power, either in War or Negociation?—In War? She has no Army, not more than 50 or 60 thousand Men, whereas France has a standing Army, of 250,000 men in Camp and in Garrison. And their officers are as gallant and skillful, their Gunners and Engineers, the most accomplished of any in Europe. Their Navy indeed is now inconsiderable, And our Navy alone has given us the Advantage. But our Navy alone will not make us the leading Power. How we can be called the Leading Power I cant see. Holland, Spain, Portugal, Denmark, and all Italy has refused to follow us, and Austria, Russia, Sweeden, and indeed almost all the states of Germany, the Prince of Hesse excepted, have followed France. The only Power, independent Power that has consented to follow us is Prussia, and indeed upon Recollection it seems to me we followed Prussia too, rather than the Contrary.—Thus we are the Leading Power without Followers.

And, if we are not the leading Power, in War, we never have been the Leading Power in Negociation.—It is a common Place observation that the French have regained by Treaty, all the Advantages, which we had gained by Arms. Now whether this arose from the superior Dexterity of the french Plenipotentiaries, or from the universal Complaisance of the other Plenipotentiaries of Europe to France and frenchmen, it equally proves that England is not the leading Power, in Councils.

How are we the most respectable?—The most respected, I am sure, we are not!—else how came all Europe to remain Neuters, or else take Arms against us—how came foreigners, from all Countries, to resort to

France, to learn their Policy, Military Discipline, fortification, Manufactures, Language, Letters, Science, Politeness &c. so much more than to England? How comes the french Language to be studied and spoken as a polite Accomplishment, all over Europe, and how comes all Negociations to be held in french.

And if we consider every Thing, The Religion, Government, Freedom, Navy, Merchandize, Army, Manufactures, Policy, Arts, Sciences, Numbers of Inhabitants and their Virtues, it seems to me, that England falls short in more and more important Particulars, than it exceeds the Kingdom of France.

To determine the Character of "Leading and respectable," as Dr. Savil does, from a few Victories and successes, by which Rules he makes Charles 12th to have been in his day, the leading and most respectable Power, and Oliver Cromwell in his, and the K. of Prussia in this, is most ignorant and silly.

In short, "Leading and Respectable," is not to be determined, either by the Prince, the Policy, the Army, Navy, Arts, Science, Commerce, nor by any other national Advantage, taken singly and abstracted from the rest. But that Power is to be denominated so, whose Aggregate, of component Parts, is most.

[1] This address was read and adopted by the House of Representatives on 23 Dec. 1760; see text in Mass., *House Jour.*, 1760–1761, p. 115–116.

1760 [*i.e.* 1761]. JANY. 2ND. FRIDAY.

Nathl. Bayley Administrator v. Nathll. Niles.—Plea in Abatement. Defendant lives on the Castle,[1] within the Town of Boston but is called of Braintree. It seems he was born in Braintree, owns a House And Land in Braintree, and for about six Weeks past his Wife and family have lived in Braintree. The Question is therefore whether his Non Residence is a good Plea? He has not lived in Town these ten Years, but has been for all that Time, constantly resident, and employed as a serjeant, and a Matross, on Castle William. His Wife and family have lived, in the Town of Dorchester, for some Years past, till about six Weeks ago when they removed to Braintree and at the House where his Wife and family live, the Copy of this Writ was left.—We are not the Man, that is sued in this Writ. We are not the Defendant in this Action. Mr. Nathl. Niles, the young Gentleman now in study with Mr. Marsh, in Preparation for Colledge, is the Man.—And let him Answer.—For

We are called Nathl. Niles of Braintree. Now it has been adjudged, that, when a Man is called of such a Town, the meaning is that he is an Inhabitant of that Town, a legal Inhabitant of that Town, entituled to all the Priviledges, and compellible to bear all the Burdens of that Town. Every Man who is of Braintree i.e. an Inhabitant of Braintree, is to be rated by the assessors of Braintree for his Head. But, my Client never has been rated by our Assessors, for many Years. Suppose my Client was poor, should become a cripple or fall sick, what Town must maintain him? Not Braintree most certainly, but Boston. And why? because he is an Inhabitant of Boston and not of Braintree. There is a Difference between of Braintree and in Braintree, And in Case my Client had come into this Town with his Wife and lived here to this day, tho he could not be called of Braintree because he is no Inhabitant and liable to be warned out every day, yet if he had been styled resident in Braintree that would have done. And this is the style they give the Regular officers, for 3 Winters past several Regular officers have wintered in Boston. Several of these Gentlemen have been sued, but they are never styled of Boston, but only resident in Boston. There's an Instance in this Town. Mr. Gliddens Wife and family, it is well known have lived in this Town chiefly for some Years, tho not constantly, but Mr. Glidden has not. Well now if Mr. Glidden sues any Man must he style himself of Braintree because his Wife and family live here and he comes up, once a fortnight to lodge with her. His Writt would abate, if he should. And I have seen several Writts, wherein he has been concerned as Party, and he has been always styled of Boston. Other Instances innumerable might be quoted. Coll. Brattle is a remarkable one.[2] He did belong to Cambridge. He married a Wife in Boston, and lived with her there in her House, and with her family, so long that People began to take him for a Boston Man and they sued him, several of them sued him by the Name of Wm. Brattle of Boston. He pleaded in Abatement of their Writts, that he was of Cambridge and not of Boston, and he shew'd that [he] had, once or twice a Year, gone up to Cambridge with his family and stayed a month or two. And therefore as an uninterrupted Inhabitancy is necessary to gain a settlement in any Town and he had not Inhabited constantly in Boston, he abated their Writts, a 10 times stronger Case than this.

The Castle Men are all considered as Inhabitants of Boston, so that No Minister will marry a Castle Man, till a Certificate is produced that he has been published in Boston.

[1] That is, on Castle Island, site of Castle William, a fortified post in Boston Harbor.

[2] William Brattle, Harvard 1722, at different times a minister, physician, lawyer, and soldier, with whom JA was to carry on a newspaper dispute in 1773 over the independence of the judiciary (Sibley-Shipton, *Harvard Graduates*, 7:10–23).

JANY. 8TH. 1761.

Last Monday, had a passionate Wrangle, with Eb. Thayer, before Major Crosby. He called me, a petty Lawyer. This I resented.

The Defendant Niles appeared by 10 o'clock, and had his Costs allowed, 1s:6d, for attendance, but nothing for Travel, tho he lived 8 miles off. Upon the first Appearance of the Defendants Daniel White, and Neh. Hayden, the Justice pronounced that they should have no Costs, altho no Plaintiff appeared—because they did not appear by Eleven O Clock. Now in answer to this, I say, that he never made it his Rule to allow no Costs to Defendants, appearing after 11 when no Plaintiff appeared. He has made it his Rule to call out Actions, when the Plaintiffs have appeared, upon the Non Appearance of Defendants after waiting an Hour for them. And he has made it his Rule, to allow Costs to defendants appearing at the time or within the Hour upon the Non Appearance of the Plaintiffs, after waiting an Hour for them. But I believe, he never made it his Rule till that day, to refuse Costs to Defendants appearing soon after the Hour expired when no Plaintiff appeared—so that, had it been certain that these Defendants did not appear within two Hours, he would not have been obliged by any Rule of his own Practice to refuse them Costs. But admitting his Rule had been established and absolute to allow no Costs to any Party not appearing within the Hour—It was not clear in this Case, that the Hour was out. By Captn. Thayers Watch indeed and by mine, it was after 11. But my Watch was set by Guess that morning, and by the Justices own Dial it was not yet Eleven, and by Athertons and several other Persons Judgment of Time, it was not yet Eleven; and some Allowance ought to be made, for the Difficulty of the Weather and the Travelling.

But thirdly, the Justice ought not to establish any such unalterable Rule. The Law has made Provision that the Parties shall be paid for the whole Days Attendance. And these Defendants lived at ⟨seven⟩ 9 or 10 miles distance and could not therefore without great Difficulty, in that severe Weather, and almost impracticable Travelling, have reached the Justices House, by ten O clock:

And to refuse them Costs for Non Compliance with such a rigorous Rule, when those suits had been commenced by Deputy Sheriffs, some of the suits vexatious, and all the Writts abateable; after they had been compelled to ride thro Cold and snow, so many miles, wasting their own and their Witness[es'] Time, and bearing their own Expences,

189

when no Plaintiff appeared and no Body for him dared to enter his Actions; was a Peice of Oppression like that of the Bashaws in Turkey.

[JANUARY? 1761.] [1]

Mess[rs].

I am an old Man, seventy odd, and as I had my Education, so I have spent my whole Life, a few ⟨months⟩ Weeks in a Year excepted, when I commonly took a Journey, in the Country. I was naturally inquisitive, and a little too talkative, in my Youth, which Qualities have perhaps increased with my Age, but as I remember, I used to swear at the vanity and Impertinence of old Nestor whose Speeches I have often read formerly in Popes Homer (a Book of which I was then, and am still very fond) I expect that younger Men will laugh at the like Vanity and Impertinence in me, which it shall be my Care therefore in this Paper, at least to avoid, because I would have the subject of it, candidly weighed.

Indeed, scarcely any Thing that I have observed, in the Course of a long Life, ⟨deserves more Attention⟩ has a greater Influence on the Religion, Moralls, Health, Property, Liberties and Tranquility of the World. I mean public Houses.

The Tempers, and Passions, The Prophaneness and brutal Behaviour inspired by the low sort of Company that frequents such Houses, and by the Liquors they drink there; are not very compatible with the pure and undefiled Religion of Jesus, that Religion whose first Principle is to renounce all filthiness and superfluity of Naughtiness. That Inattention to the public ordinances of Religion as well as to private Devotion which I have Reasons to think is prevalent, in these Times is no unnatural Consequence, of the very generall Resort, to these licentious Houses.

The plentiful Use of spirituous Liquors, begins with producing a strange Confusion of Mind, appetite and Passions, too violent for the Government of Reason; proceeds to involve Men in Debt, and of Consequence, in Lying, cheating, stealing, and sometimes in greater Crimes; and ends in a total, and incurable Dissolution of Manners.

The Effects of such Intemperance upon Health are of two Kinds. It either throws them into some acute and inflammatory fever, which carries them from the Midst of their Vices and their follies, the Mischiefs they do and the ⟨Miseries⟩ Distresses they suffer, at once into their Graves, or else it leads them by insensible Degrees, thro all the Gloom and Languor of a Chronical Distemper, despized by many, hated by more and [pitied?] by a few, to a long expected, and desired death. Thousands, and thousands, are every Year expiring in Europe, and proportionable Numbers in America, the miserable Victims of their own Imprudence, and the ill Policy of Rulers in permitting the Causes of their Ruin to exist. Allured by the smell of these infernal Liquors, like the Ghosts, in Romances, allured by the scent of human Blood, they resort to these Houses, waste their Time, their strength and their Money, which ought to be employed in the Management of their own Affairs and families, till by degrees, much expended, little earned, they contract Habits of Calesness,[2] Idleness, and Intemperance; their Creditors demand, they promise to pay but fail; Writts issue, Charges are multiplied, for the Maintenance of others as idle as themselves, and Executions strip them of all they have, and cast their miserable Bodies into loathsome Prisons.

The Number of these Houses have been lately so much augmented, and the fortunes of their owners so much increased, that an Artful Man has little else to do, but secure the favour of Taverners, in order to secure the suffrages of the Rabbles that attend these Houses, which in many Towns within my observation makes a very large, perhaps the largest Number of Voters. The Consequence is that these offices and Elections, which all the wisest Legislators of the world, in humble Imitation of God and Nature have alloted to Probity and Understanding, may in Time, I dare not say have already become the Gratuity of Tiplers, for Dramms[3] and slops! Good God! where are the Rights of English Men! where is the spirit, that once exalted the souls of Britons and emboldened their [faces?] to look even Princes and Monarchs in the face. But perhaps I am too anxious, and In truth I must own I [so] revere the true Constitution of our Government, founded in those great Principles, that accomplished in a great Antiquity the Destruction of Troy, that extended in a later Period the Bounds of the Roman Empire and that produced in the English History, so many events for the Universe to admire, that I cant think of its evaporating and passing from [the] human Breast with Phlip[4] and Rum, of which Event there is great Danger, without Rage.

Last of all, innumerable Violations of the Peace and order of society, are every Day occurring, that spring originally from the same sources. Quarrells, Boxing, Duels, oaths, Curses, affrays and Riots, are daily hatching from Eggs and Spawns, deposited in the same Nests: in short these Houses, like so many Boxes of Pandora, are sending forth every day innumerable Plagues of every kind, natural, moral and political, that increase and multiply fast enough to lay waste in a little While the whole World.

How different is this, from the state of Things in my Youth. Instead of an unmanly Retreat to the Chimny Corner of a Tavern, the young fellows of my Age were out in the Air, improving their strength and Activity, by Wrestling, running, leaping, lifting, and the like vigorous Diversions, and when satisfyed with these, resorted every one to his Mistress or his Wife. Love, that divine Passion, which Nature has implanted for the Renovation of the species, and the greatest solace of our Lives: virtuous Love, I mean, from whence the greatest Part of human Happiness originates, and which these modern seminaries have almost extinguished or at least changed into filthiness and brutal Debauch, was then considered as God intended it, both a Duty of our Nature and the greatest source of our Bliss. But it is mellancholly to think that the present Prevalent Debauchery, which tends so much to shorten the Lives of the present Generation, tends also, to prevent the Propagation of a succeeding one. I really am afraid that in another Century, unless some wise Precaution should intervene, a Man of my Age will be the rarest Phenomenon.

I should be called talkative indeed if I should attempt to develope the Causes of that strange Multiplication of such Houses, that is lately grown up. But I fear, that some select Men are induced by a foolish Complaisance, and others by Designs of Ambition to give their Approbation to too many Persons who are improper, and perhaps to too many that are proper for that Trust. I am afraid that some Justices may be induced by lucrative Motives, by mercantile Principles to augment the Manufactory or the Importation of Rum or Mollosus, without Attending to the other Consequences, which are plainly pernicious.

But let this Paper be considered as a Warning from one who has seen better days, to Magistrates to suppress, rather than increase within their Department—to select men to discountenance Pretenders rather than encourage [them] in their sphere—to Parents and Masters, to restrain their Children And servants from frequenting. And in short let every Man endeavour to keep one, from suffering any Injury from them, in any Respect.

I was too incautious, and unartful in my Proceeding, but Practice makes perfect. I should have first taken all the summonses, into my own Hand, or Powers of attorney from the Defendants. Then I should have moved that the sheriff should be directed to return his Writts, that against White and that against Hayden. Then I should have drawn a complaint, on each of them, and filed them all. Then I should have desired the Justice to make a Record of his Judgment. This would have been regular, masterly Management, but I had no Time to think and prepare.

This is the third Time I have been before Majr. Crosbey with Thayer. The first time, he was [...] for John Spear. That Action was demolished. The next time he appeared for Nathan Spear against Eph. Hunt and John Vinton. Those Actions were demolished. The last time he appeared for Bayley, against Niles, White, Hayden, &c. These Actions were all demolished. Thus I have come off, pretty triumphantly every time, and he pretty foolishly. Yet I have managed none of these Cases, in the most masterly manner. I see several Inadvertent Mistakes, and omissions. But I grow more expert, less diffident &c. I feel my own strength. I see the complacent Countenances of the Crowd, and I see the respectful face of the Justice, and the fearful faces of Petty foggers, more than I did.

Dear Nieces.[5]

You remember that I wrote you a new Years Address, about two Years since, containing some few Articles of Advice that I then thought would pass with Propriety, considering the Relation between us, from me to you. You are at least two Years older, than you were then, and from a careful observation of your Conduct, I have found few Occasions of Blame, and from your Conversation, and a frequent Inspection of your Compositions, I have reason to think your time has been in general, and in Comparison of the rest of your own sex, not ill improved.

But there are numberless Particulars that I had then no Leisure to discuss, and which some Persons of our sex but more of yours think not worthy to discuss, that will fill the remainder of this Letter and be I hope no unacceptable Present, for the Year 1761.

The first relate to the Delicacy of your own Persons and Houses. It has been the constant observation of foreigners who have lived in England, that the british Ladies are the least careful, to use no harder term, in this Respect than any Ladies, in Christendom. The Brightness of Plate and Dishes, floors, and every other Thing in a House even in a Kitchen, has been always observed by Travellers, even into Holland, where the enormous sizes of the Ladies, and their consequent sloth and Heavyness, one would think would incline them to another extreme. The same Nicety is observed in Italy, France and elsewhere, but the very general Complaint of british Ladies is that their Teeth, Necks, Hair, Perspiration and Respiration, Kichens and even Parlors

193

are no cleaner nor sweeter than they should be. And the same ground of Complaint is in America. For my own Part, tho not very attentive to my own Person, nothing is so disgustful and loathsome to me, and almost all our sex are of my mind, as this Negligence. My own Daughters, whenever they shall grow to Years of Discretion, I am determined to throw into a great Kettle and Boil till they are clean, If I ever find them half so nasty as I have seen some. That you may gain proper sentiments on this Head, and reduce them most religiously to Practice, I recommend to your careful Reading, the Works of Dr. Swift and Dr. Shybear [Shebbeare], especially the former, and let me warn you against any Prejudice to him, or his sentiments on Account of that open Defyance and Contempt in which he held your sex.

2. The next Article is that of Dress. It may be just[ly] considered, as the Principal Design of a young Lady from her Birth to her Marriage, to procure and prepare herself for a worthy Companion in Life. This I believe is modestly enough expressed. Now the finest face, and shape, that ever Nature formed, would be insufficient to attract and fix the Eye of a Gentleman without some Assistance and Decoration of Dress. And I believe an handsome shoe, well judged Variety of Colours, in Linnen, Laces &c., and even the Rustling of silks has determined as many Matches as any natural features, or Proportions or Motions. Hes a fool that is determined wholly by either or by both, but even a wise man will take all these, as well as others less,[6] into Consideration.

I cannot be supposed to be master of the whole Art of Dress, nor to give Rules for your Conduct of it. I only say study it, even of your selves. Study it even as a science, and take in Hogarths mathematicks to your Aid.[7]

3. The 3d is [a] sense of Elegance. This may perhaps include both the former, but I mean in this Place such a Disposition of the Affairs of a family, such a management of an Entertainment, and such a judicious——[*sentence unfinished*]

Neither rich furniture nor dress, nor Provisions, without this, will ever please.

The 4th is Behaviour in mixed Companies. I would not have you Pedants in Greek and Latin nor the Depths of science, nor yet over fond to talk upon any Thing. When your opinion is asked, give it. When you know any Thing, that the Company are at a loss for, disclose it. But what I mean is this. Attend to the Conversation of Gentlemen even when News, Politicks, Morals, Œconomy, nay even when Literature and science but beyond the fathom of your Line make the subject: do not attempt to turn the Conversation to Billy's Prattle—To the

Doggs, or Negroes or Catts, or to any little contemptible tittle tattle of your own.

5thly. Observations of Mankind, or what is called the World. As the House is your Theatre of Action, an Attentive Observation of Domestic Characters should be your Rule. You are in all Probability in some future Part of your Life, to have Husbands. Remark carefully the Behaviour of other Wifes, wherever you go, to their Husbands, but distinguish well between Propriety of Behaviour and the Contrary. You will probably some time or other have Children. Remark then every Mothers Management of her Children, in their Education, Morals, Behaviour, Dress, Diet &c., with the same Distinction.

You may by a Course of Reflection on Instances of this sort among Gentle and simple form to yourselves from reason and Experience, a System of Rules that may one day produce an Hero or a Legislator, a great Statesman or Divine or some other great Character that may do Honour to the World—the Highest Pinacle of Glory to which a Woman can in Modesty aspire.

You will also act hereafter as Mistresses. Let your Attention therefore be fixed on the Behaviour of servants and their Treatment from their Masters and Mistresses.

In short, domestic Morality ought to be your principal study, and you ought not to suffer one Character in the Drama of a family, to be unexamined.

6thly. Under this Head of Conversation with the World falls naturally enough that into which you must if you are not singular, and you will, if you pursue your own Inclinations, sometimes, fall—Conversation with some Person of the other Sex alone: and this before Marriage And even Courtship. Our illustrious young Monarck, indeed, will probably be married by Proxy to some Princess abroad, that he never saw: and this is for Reasons of State, no doubt necessary: Yet it is thought an Hardship, and the prevailing Custom of the World, for this Reason perhaps, allows [a] Prince his Mistress as an alleviation.

And it seems, by what I see and hear, that Persons of Rank and figure even in this Province, are desirous that their Daughters should be married to Men who never saw them, by their prevailing Practice of concealing them from all Males, till a formal Courtship is opened. This Practice must proceed either from deplorable folly, an Awkward Imitation of Majesty, or else from a Consciousness of their Daughters futility and a Dread to expose them.

But be it remembered that no Man that is free and can think, will rush blindfold, into the Arms of any such Ladies, who, tho it is possible they may prove Angells of Light, may yet more probably turn out Haggs of Hell.

You must therefore associate yourselves in some good Degree, and under certain Guards and Restraints, even privately with young fellows. And, tho Discretion must be used, and Caution, yet on [considering] [8] the whole of the Arguments on each side, I cannot wholly disapprove of Bundling.

To Chardon.[9]

Lest a maiden Nicety should prevent the Correspondence, proposed the last Week, I have taken my Pen to open it, upon the lofty subject of Law. We shall be called silly, and tasteless &c. for ought I know, or care. For let the smart sayings of the gay, and the grave Satyrs, even of the wise and learned be what they will, I have for my own Part, and I thank God for it, no bad Opinion of the Law, either as a science, or a Profession.

Why the minute Arteries and Tendons of the human Body, the organization of the human Voice, and mouth, and numberless other subjects of the like sort should be thought worthy of the Attention of a liberal Mind; and the no less Wonderful and much more important combination of Passions, Appetites, Affections, in the human Breast that operate in human society, too futile, or too disagreable, for a wise Mans Examination, I cannot imagine.—Nay if we proceed to the Positive Institutions of the Law, I cannot think them so extreamly dull, uncouth, and unentertaining as you and I have heard them represented, by some whom we love and honour.

Multitudes of needless Matters and some that are nonsensical, it must be confessed have in the Course of Ages, crept into the Law. But I beg to know, what Art or Science can be found in the whole Circle, that has not been taught by silly, senseless, Pedants, and is not stuffed with their Crudities and Jargon.

The Man who intends to become skilful in any science, must be content to study such Authors as have written upon it. No Man will be an adept in Grammar or Rhetoric, or Poetry, or Music or Architecture, without labouring thro a vast deal of Nonsense, and Impertinence—in short, Nonsense seems an unalienable Property of human Affairs. And it is as idle to expect, that any Artist [10] should write well upon any subject, without intermingling some Proportion of it, as it is to expect, that a rapid Torrent should descend from the Mountains without washing some Dirt and Earth along with it.

But if the Grandeur and Importance of a subject, has any share in the Pleasure it communicates, I am sure the Law has by far the Advantage of most other sciences.

Nothing less than the Preservation of the Health and Properties, Lives and Tranquility, Moralls and Liberties of Millions of the human species, is the object and Designs of the Law, and a Comparison of several Constitutions of Government, invented for those Purposes, an Examination of the great Causes of their Danger, as well as those of their safety, must be as Agreable an Employment as can exercise the Mind.

But it is a science that comprises a Multitude. And great Industry, as well as many Helps are needful, to subdue it.

And in truth I do not know a more agreable Help, than the Correspondence of a Friend. Exchange of observations—Proposing Difficulties—stating Cases—repeating Arguments—examining sophisms—will both arouse and support our Ambition, and wear by easy Degrees, a system of Law into the Mind.

The Plan, that I would propose then is this—for you to write me, a Report of any Case you hear argued before the Courts of Admiralty, Court of Probate, Governor and Council, Court of Sessions, Justice of the Peace &c. that you think curious. Propose Questions, for Examination, and write me Answers, to Letters from me on all the foregoing subjects.

And if we will secrete each others Letters, we shall at least avoid the Ridicule of others. But if we should be detected, we can say that Tully and Atticus held some such Correspondence before, that never raised a Laugh in the World. And if we say this we must run off to avoid the Reply, of a Pigs turd to a Pine Apple.

Neal v. Spear. Plea in Abatement. Defendant is a Yeoman, but not a Gentleman, as styled in the Writ.[11]

⟨*This Exception has an Air of Humility, that may be suspected to be feigned.*⟩

This Exception, it must be owned has not a very honourable Air, but if the Circumstances of this Action, are considered, the Defendant will not be blamed.

⟨*My Client is a very Poor Man, but happened to be a Bondsman for Brackett, to the Plaintiff who is rich and in no Want of the Money.*⟩

My Client was bound to this Plaintiff, for Bracket in his Life time, in this Obligation. Bracket died, and this Plaintiff Neal brot his Action last Term against the Administratrix on Bracketts Estate, and that Action is now pending in this Court: But Bracketts Estate proves insolvent: and now Neal has brot this Action against a poor Bondsman. My Client is very poor, and unable to pay this Money, and therefore will be excused for taking all legal Advantages, till he can have some assistance from Bracketts Estate, to pay it.

And, for my own Part I had a further, and a stronger Reason for not discouraging my Client which was this. This Writ was drawn by a Deputy Sheriff, or at least by somebody in the service and Employment of that Deputy Sheriff: and against such Writts your Honours will no doubt commend me for taking all legal Advantages.

And this Exception is, in law fatal. If we are obliged to give any Additions to Parties we should be obliged to give the Right and not call Esquires Labourers, and Labourers Esquires.

If it is of any Consequence to society that Ranks and subordination should be established in it, it is of Consequence that the Titles denoting those Ranks should not be confounded. Now there are no two Titles more distinct from each other than Yeoman and Gentleman. The Yeomanry and Gentry of England is the most ancient and universal of all Divisions of the People.

Now the present Defendant is not a Gentleman in any Respect, neither by Birth, Education, Office, Reputation or Employment: and indeed I have no Reason to think him one in Thought, Word, or Deed. He spring[s] from ordinary Parents, he can scarcely write his Name, his Business is Boating, he never had any Commissions, and therefore to call him Gentlemen is an arrant Prostitution of the Title, and ought to abate the Writ.

[1] Some of the long series of undated and more or less detached entries that follow may extend into February, since the next dated entry in D/JA/6 is that of 9 Feb. 1761. The draft of an essay on the evils of licensed houses, which begins the series, was obviously intended for a newspaper, but no printing has been found. See entry of 29 May 1760, above, and note there.

[2] Thus in MS; seemingly a hybrid of "carelessness" and "callousness."

[3] MS: "Damms."

[4] MS: "Phip."

[5] Draft of another essay intended for a newspaper, probably incomplete. No printing has been found of either the essay or the New Year's "Address" of 1759 mentioned in the first sentence.

[6] Preceding six words added by interlineation in MS and now only partly legible because of fading. The reading given here is that of the early transcript (in D/JA/49), but it may not be correct.

[7] An allusion to William Hogarth's *Analysis of Beauty, Written with a View of Fixing the Fluctuating Ideas of Taste,* London, 1753.

[8] Word omitted in MS and conjecturally supplied by the editors.

[9] Peter Chardon, on whom see the entry of 11 Oct. 1758, above, and note 3 there. Except for the present draft, no letters between JA and Chardon have been found.

[10] CFA reads "Author," which may have been what JA meant, though he did not write it.

[11] For the origin of this case, in which JA served as counsel for the defendant, see entry of 9 Oct. 1760, above, and note. In a fragmentary record of actions,

1761–1763, JA made this notation: "Jo Neal v Nathan Spear. Plea in abatement, which prevailed—recd. Costs of the Con- stable" (MS, Goodspeed's Book Shop, Boston, 1957).

1761. TUESDAY JANY. 27TH.[1]

Last Fryday I borrowed of Mr. Gridley, the second Volume of the Corpus Iuris Canonici Notis illustratum. Gregorii 13 Iussi editum.— complectens Decretum Gratiani. Decretales Gregorii Papæ 9. Sextum Decretalium Bonifacii Papæ 8. Clementinas, Extravagantes Ioannis Papæ 12.[2] Extravagantes communes.—

Accesserunt Constitutiones Novæ summorum Pontificum, nunquam antea editæ, quæ 7. Decretalium Loco esse possint:—Annotationes Ant. Naldi, cum Addit. novis.—Et quæ in Plerisque Editionibus desi- derabantur, Petri Lancelotti, Institutiones Iuris Canonici; Regulæ Cancellariæ Apostolicæ: cum Indicibus &c.[3]

Mr. Gridley about 15 months since, advised me to read an Institute of the Cannon Law—and that Advice lay broiling in my Head, till last Week, when I borrowed the Book.

I am very glad, that he gave, and I took, the Advice, for it will explain many Things in Ecclesiastical History, and open that system of fraud, Bigotry, Nonsense, Impudence, and Superstition, on which the Papal Usurpations are founded, besides increasing my skill in the latin Tongue, and my Acquaintance with civil Law, for in many Respects the Cannon Law is grafted on the civil.

[1] This entry is from D/JA/4, JA's desultory record of studies.

[2] Should be "22" ("XXII" on title- page).

[3] This edition of the *Corpus Juris Canonici* was published at Leon, 1661, and the first volume, bearing the auto- graphs of both Gridley and JA, survives among JA's books in the Boston Public Library (*Catalogue of JA's Library*, p. 64). Except on the titlepage the name of the author of the "Institutiones" ap- pears as Johannes Paulus Lancelottus, a well-known legal scholar of Perugia.

1761. FRIDAY [6] FEBY.[1]

I have now almost finished the first book of Peter Lancelotts In- stitute, which first Book is taken up De Jure Personarum, and is well analized in the 29th Title De Clericis non Residentibus, in these Words vizt. "Personarum quidam Laici sunt, quidam Clerici. Rursus Cleri- corum, quidam sunt in Sacerdotio constituti, quidam in sacris, licet non in sacerdotio, quidam nec in sacris, nec in sacerdotio. Eorum rursus, qui in sacerdotio constituti sunt, quidam sunt in celsiore gradu, ut Episcopi: quidam in inferiore, ut Presbyteri. In sacris vero dicuntur constituti Diaconi et subdiaconi qui vero nec in sacerdotio, nec in sacris reperiuntur, ii sunt, qui sunt in Minoribus ordinibus constituti. Cæterum, quoniam adhuc quidam in Ecclesia sunt, qui non minus in Laicatu, quam in Clericatu constituti Domino Deserviunt, ut sunt Regulares ac Monachi, restat, ut et de his Pauca subjiciamus."

¹ This and the following entry (the first of two dated 9 Feb.) also derive from D/JA/4, JA's journal of studies, which contains no further entries until 20 June, when JA determined to resume reading Lancelotti's work on canon law. Errors in JA's transcription of Lancelotti's Latin have not been corrected.

1761 MONDAY. FEBY. 9TH.

This morning, as I lay abed, I recollected my last Weeks Work. I find I was extreamly diligent, constantly in my Chamber, Spent no Evenings abroad, not more than one at the Drs. Have taken no Walks, never on Horseback the whole Week, excepting once, which was on Tuesday, when I went to Boston. Yet how has this Retirement, and solitude been spent? In too much Rambling and Straggling from one Book to another, from the Corpus Juris Canonici, to Bolingbroke, from him to Pope, from him to Addison, from him to Yoricks sermons, &c. In fine, the whole Week, and all my Diligence has been lost, for want of observing De Wits Maxim, "one Thing at once." This Reflection raised a Determination to re-assume the Corpus Juris, or Rather Lancelots Institutes, read nothing else, and think of nothing else—till sometime.

With the Week then, I begin the second Book Institutionum Juris Canonici.—De Rerum Divisione, atque illorum Administratione. Titulus primus. Res Ecclesiasticæ sunt, aut spirituales, aut temporales.

Res Spirituales sunt aut incorporales, aut corporales: et corporales dividuntur in sacramenta, in res sacras, sanctas et religiosas.

This Institute is a curious Monument of Priestly Ambition, Avarice and subtlety. Tis a system of sacerdotal Guile.

1761. FEB. 9TH.

His Majesty has declared him self, by his Speech to his Parliament to be a Man of Piety, and Candor in Religion, a friend of Liberty, and Property in Government, and a Patron of Merit.¹

"The Blessing of Heaven, I devoutly emplore"—"as the surest Foundation of the whole, (i.e. the Loyalty and affection of his People, his Resolution to strengthen the Constitution, the civil &c. Rights of his subjects and the Prerogatives of his Crown &c.) and the best Means to draw down the divine favour on my Reign, it is my fixed Purpose to countenance and encourage true Religion and Virtue."— These are Proofs of his Piety.

He promises to patronize Religion, Virtue, the british Name and Constitution, in Church and state, the subjects Rights, Liberty, Commerce, military Merit.—These are sentiments worthy of a King—a Patriot King.

[1] George III became king of England 25 Oct. 1760. His first speech to Parliament, 18 Nov., contained the sentence "Born and educated in this country, I glory in the name of Briton," which, together with other sentiments of the same kind quoted (somewhat inaccurately) by JA, for a time endeared him to his subjects both at home and overseas. Text in *Ann. Register* for 1760, p. 248–250.

MARCH 3D. 1761.

Mem. To enquire of Tufts, Gould, Whitmarsh, Hunts, Whites, &c. about their Method of mending High Ways by a Rate.

And to enquire at Worcester, whenever I shall get there of Chanlers, Putnam, Willard, Paine, Swan &c. about their Method. They mended their Ways by a Rate, I am sure.[1]

Saml. Clark, ⟨Jo. Field, Eb. Newcomb⟩ Danl. Nash, the Mirmidons of Thayer.

Luke Lambard, Ben Hayden, Saml. Clark &c. all the Mirmidons of Thayer &c. Mirmidons, Bulldoggs, Hounds, Creatures, Tools.[2]

Weymouth mends her Ways by a Rate. Each Man is rated so much, and a Days Work is estimated at so much, an Horse, a Cart, Yoke of oxen &c. at so much, so each Man has his Choice, to pay his Money or to work it out.—I did not think to ask What sum they expend yearly to mend Ways.

Quære. How they mend their Ways, Streets, Lanes, Alleys &c. in Boston. Whether by a Rate. Is not the Town taxed for Pavement of streets &c. Q. Whether they ever permit those who choose it to work it out themselves.

[1] According to his Autobiography, JA was this month nominated in town meeting, or perhaps only proposed for nomination by his friend and neighbor Elisha Savil, for his first town office, that of surveyor of highways. The usually reliable *Braintree Town Records* do not record his nomination or election at the annual meeting of the town on 3 March 1761 (p. 377). Either this is an error of omission, or else the account in his Autobiography telescopes JA's very early interest in reforming the method of financing highway repairs and his later service (1764–1765) both as a member of a town committee to report a plan for "mending the Ways ... by a Tax" and as an assiduous builder of bridges and highways in the town. See *Braintree Town Records*, p. 395–400; also entry of 21 March, below.

[2] The following two paragraphs are in a different ink and were probably written later than those that precede.

[MARGINAL NOTE IN WINTHROP'S *Lecture on Earthquakes.*][1]

March 12th. 1761. Another Earthquake happened which may perhaps enable us to determine, whereabouts these Earthquakes originate, and what Course they take, for as all Canada is now in English hands, we may have Accounts from Montreal, Quebeck, Oswego, and the several Places upon the River St. Lawrence, at what time this Earthquake happened, its Direction and Degree of Violence.

¹ At foot of p. 16 in JA's copy of John Winthrop's *Lecture* of 1755 (in Boston Public Library; see other marginalia by JA in this copy, following the entry of 5? Dec. 1758, above). At this point in his lecture Winthrop was reporting such scanty data as were available on the direction of movement of earlier earth-quakes in America. On the back of the titlepage of his copy JA recorded, in a separate note, that the earthquake of 12 March 1761 occurred about 2:30 A.M., "resembling 'tho not quite equalling that which gave Occasion to this Discourse, in Violence, or Duration."

[MARCH? 1761.] ¹

Parson Smith's Parsonage.

Vid. 6th. Wm. & M. C. 5. Page 60.—Charter Page 6th &c. from Index to Index. All Lands &c. which any Body politick, or Corporate, Towns, Colledges or Schools, do hold &c. by or under any Grant by any general Court, or by any other lawful Right or Title whatsoever; shall be by such Towns, Colledges or Schools, their respective Heirs, successors and assigns forever [hereafter held and enjoyed],² according to the Purport and Intent of such respective Grant, &c., not withstanding any Want of form.

Now in the Weymouth Case, there is a Deed to a Committee of the Town of Weymouth for the use of the Ministry, &c. and for a convenient settlement of Housing and Lands, for the Ministry, and for no other Use, Intent or Purpose whatsoever. Now I believe it must be agreed that that Committee and their Grant had no Intent or Design, of any thing but that the present Incumbent and his successors should enjoy that House and Land forever. And, it cant be thought that Either Party to that deed entertained a Thought of dividing that House and Land among 50 ministers, that shall happen to settle within the Borders of that Town, tho they may be Churchmen, Anabaptists, Quakers, Separatists, for every one of these sects, have a Minister who may be as well called one of the Ministry of Weymouth as Mr. Bayley can.³

¹ First entry in D/JA/7, a "paper book" without cover, stitching, or docketing.
² The words in brackets, inadvertently omitted in MS, have been supplied from the Massachusetts Charter of 1691 (Thorpe, *Federal and State Constitutions*, 3:1877).
³ James Bayley, Harvard 1719, was minister of the second or south parish of Weymouth from 1723, when Weymouth was divided into North and South Precincts, until his death in 1766. A dispute went on for many years over the interests of the two precincts in the original parsonage property. (Sibley-Shipton, *Harvard Graduates*, 6:293–294; Weymouth Hist. Soc., *History of Weymouth*, 1923, 1:233–236.)

MARCH 21ST. 1761.

Memorandum. To enquire more particularly into the Practice in Weymouth—how they estimate a Days Work for a Man, Horse, Yoke of oxen, Carts, Tools, Pickaxes, Spades, shovells &c.—how much Money or what a sum they assess upon the whole Town, annually, to amend their Ways?—whether the assessment is committed to the surveyor, of all within his District, &c.

Enquire, too, at Boston of Cunningham, how they pave and repair the Pavements of their great Streets, and Lanes and Alleys &c.— whether poor People are left at their Election to work or to pay? and how they apportion their assessment? But I presume it is not according to the Polls Tax but in Proportion to the Province Tax, or Town and County. So that rich Men may contribute in Proportion to their Wealth, to repairing, as they contribute most by their Equipages &c. to the wearing and spoiling the high Ways.

But a Tax upon the Poles, and real and Personal Estates of the Town will not bring the burthen to Equality. We will suppose that John Ruggles and Caleb Hubbard are rated equally for Heads, and real and personal Estates. Caleb Hubbard Carts down £1000 Worth of Wood and Timber to the Landing Places, and so reaps three or £400 a Year Profit by improving the Ways; and by his heavy Loads, and Wheels, he breaks and cutts and crushes the Ways to Pieces. But Mr. Ruggles on the other Hand, confines himself to his farm and [Canoe?] He neither receives Benefit from any High ways, or does any Damage to them, further than riding to Meeting on Sundays, and Town Meetings. Now what Reason, what Propriety can there be in taxing Ruggles and Hubbard equally to the high ways. One gets his living by ruining the Ways, the other neither gets a farthing by them nor does them a farthing Damage.

The Power of a Town. The Proviso in the 11th of George Chaptr. 4th. That this Act shall not extend to the preventing or altering the Practice in any Town of defraying the Charge of repairing or amending the High Ways by a Rate or Tax, or any other Method they have or shall agree upon. The Words "agreed upon," in this Proviso, I presume, signify "determined by the major Part of the Voters," for the same Words "agreed upon" are used, in several other Acts, where their meaning must be so. Thus 6th. W. & M. C. 5, the Act to enable Towns, Villages, Proprietors in common and undivided Lands to sue and be sued.

Messrs.[1]

I am an old Man turned of seventy. When I was young my common amuzement was Reading. I had some Engagements in Business, and was no Enemy to innocent Pleasure. But as my Circumstances were easy, I gave a greater Indulgence to my Curiosity of conversing largely with the World than most Persons of my Age, and Rank. In this Course of Life, I soon found that human Nature, the Dignity of which I heard extolled by some, and debased by others, was far from deserving that Reverence and Admiration, which is due to great Virtue and Intelligence. I found as I thought in that day a Multitude of People, who suffered themselves to be caught by hooks and snares covered over with such Bait, as would not have imposed even on fishes and Birds: and I found as I thought a few others, the Anglers of that Day whose constant Attention and Pursuit was to allure and take that Multitude. The first Instances of this sort that fell under my observation raised my Compassion and Indignation alternately. I pittyd poor deluded simplicity on one hand, and I raged against Cruelty and Wickedness on the other, and could not but think, that to rescue the Lamb from the Jaws of the Wolf would be a noble Adventure. But on further Consideration the Design seemed impracticable. The Attempt was odious. The Knaves would arise in a Combination to ruin the Reformer and the fools would be managed in no other Way than that of their Appetites and Passions. For this Reason and to avoid the pungent Misery of a disappointed, despized Patriot, I determined to make a total alteration in the Course and Nature of my Ideas and sentiments. Whenever I heard or saw an Instance of atrocious Treachery, fraud, Hypocrisy, Injustice, or Cruelty, the common Effects of excessive Ambition, Avarice and Lust, instead of indulging the sentiments of Nature, which I found were a Resentment bordering on Rage, I resolved instantly to set up a Laugh and make my self merry: whenever I saw a simple deluded Creature brot by the Craft of others to brutal Debauchery, sickness, Cold, Hunger, Prison, Whipping Post, Pillory or Gallows, instead of indulging sympathy and feeling, I set my self to laughing. I must own I found a good deal of Difficulty to command my self at first, in this bold Attempt to alter the whole system of Morality: and in spight of my Attention, a flash of Vengeance, or a Thril of Pitty, would sometimes escape me, before I could bring my Muscles into a risible Posture.

But by long Practice I have at last obtained a settled Habit of making my self merry at all the Wickedness and Misery of the World. And the Causes of Ridicule have been every Hour increasing and multiplying from the 25th Year of my Age, when I first attempted the alteration of my Mind, to the present Hour. And now in spight of all the Infirmities of old Age I am the most tittering, giggling Mortal you ever saw.

But the amplest source of my merriment, thru the whole Course of my Life has been the affair of English Priviledges, British Liberty and all that.

I have heard Men every Day for fifty Years boasting, "our Constitution is the finest under heaven. We are governed by our own Laws. No Tyrant can Lord it over us. The King is as accountable for his Conduct as the subject. No Government that ever existed, was so essentially free. Every Man is his own Monarch. His Will, or the Will of his Agent, and no other can bind him." All these gallant, blustering speeches I have heard in Words—and I never failed to raise a Horse laugh. For observe the pleasant course of these Things. The few who have real Honour, Temperance, and Understanding, who are desirous of getting their Bread and Paying their Debts by their own Industry, apply their Attention to their own Business, and leave the Affairs of Towns and Provinces to others. But a young fellow, who happens to be by Nature or by habit indolent, and perhaps profligate, begins by laying schemes by himself or his Friends, to live and get Money without Labour or Care. His first step is to procure a Deputation from some sheriff. By the Help of Writts and Executions, and drawing Writts, or employing some Child to draw them, for a share, 1/3 or 1/4 of the fee, then serving them, and Executions, carrying Tales and Intelligence from one Party to the other, then settling Disputes, vastly compassionating the Party, by taking twice lawful fees, they wheedle themselves into some Connections with the People, and considerable sums of Money into their own Pocketts.

They presently grow capable Men very expert at Calculations, and well acquainted with the real and personal Estates of the Town and so very fit for select Men, and after 2 or 3 Years opposition from the most virtuous and independent Part of a Town they obtain an Election. After this his Reputation increases very fast. He becomes, to those not already grappled to his Interest by fear or affection, very assiduous and obliging. And when the season of the Year approaches, a swarm of Candidates for Approbation to keep Taverns or Dram shops, surround him, for his favour. For one he will use his Utmost Interest. For another, he really thinks there is Occasion for a Public House where he lives. For a Third his Circumstances are so needy he really thinks he ought to be assisted. For a 4th. he is so unable to work, that he must be assisted, and to a fifth, He likes it very well, for he thinks, the more there are the better, the more obliging they will be and the cheaper they will sell.

Taverns and Dram shops are therefore placed in every Corner of the Town, where poor Mankind, allured by the smell of Brandy And Rum, resort, and carouse: waste their Time, spend their Money, run in Debt to Tavern and others, grow attached to the Taverner who is attached to his Patron both by Gratitude and Expectation. The Hero of this Romance, is presently extolled as a public Blessing, as the most useful Man in Town, as a very understanding and [civil?] Man, and is at the next May Meeting set up for a Candidate as Representative. The same Body of wealthy and virtuous Persons, who opposed the first step of his Exaltation, are still resolute to oppose the second, and for the first few Years, he fails. But, by Assiduity and Impudence, by extending and fortifying the Parts of the same system, he increases his Interest, and the virtuous few begin to dread the Consequences, they resolve not to be present and wittnesses of the Disgrace of the Town. They stay at home, and the News is brought them that the Person they despized, and &c. has obtained his Election.

In this manner Men, who are totally ignorant of all Law human and divine, natural, civil, ecclesiastical and common, are employed to make Laws for their Country, while others, who have been led by their Education to search to the Bottom of human Nature, and to examine the Effect of all Laws upon human affairs [*sentence unfinished*]

[1] No contemporary printing of this draft of a newspaper communication has been found.

APRIL 3D. 1761.

Z.[1] tells me, that Jona. Rawson is malicious and cruel as well as conceited. He spights Edd. Quincy and his whole Family. He says that the whole family was prodigal and extravagant, and that he borrowed Money and bought Goods upon Credit, but two days before he housed himself, when he knew that he never should pay, which was no better than Stealing.—Tis fraud. Tis Cheating, Tis Knavery, Tis Villany.— Oh he longs to see Quincys Daughters out at service. It would please him to see them, washing and serving Dishes, Washing Clothes, &c. Why should not they work as well as Mrs. Liddy and I? We are more honourably descended than they!—He longs to hear that Milton select men have warned him out of that Town. He himself was very urgent to have young Edd. warned out of Braintree, when he first came to live with his Father, but never could get a Majority of the select men of his Mind. He hopes that the Church in Milton will refuse him their

Communion. He hears that some Members are uneasy and talk of objecting to his partaking there, and he wishes they would. He was extremely glad to hear, that Mr. Quincy failed of getting Clerk of the General Court. He heard he was a Candidate, and disappointed, and was rejoiced at it. A fine story, that he who wanted discretion to manage his own private Affairs, who rushed headlong to Bankruptcy and Destruction should be intrusted with public affairs. That he who would lye and Cheat, at such a Rate, should stand in public Place.

Thus he seems to wish that poor Mr. Quincy should be excluded from all public Trust, that he should be expelled from any Town that [he] should move into, be excommunicated from the Church, brought to beg his Bread or be maintained by the Town, and his Daughters ⟨*bound out*⟩ sent out to service as Kitchen Maids. This is Malice, Tis Rage, Tis Cruelty, 'Tis Persecution. Tis Hell and the Devil—and by all Probability the Provocation to this Excess of Malevolence, which would strip them of all the means of life temporal and eternal, is a Loss of about forty shillings old Tenor by Mr. Quincy, some way or another. These are dreadful sentiments. This is a woful Temper.

He, and his Brother Josiah, and all the rest of the Family, are very proud of their Descent from Mr. Rawson, an ancient secretary of this Province. Secretary Rawson was his great Grandfather. His father was a tippling, silly old fellow like David Bass, and if his Grandfather was of a like Character, the Dishonour of descending from such a father and Grandfather must have taken away all the Honour of descending from an honorable great Grand father.

Tis vain and mean to esteem oneself for his Ancestors Merit. But he is very avaricious, and very ambitious and excessively vain. Vain of his Descent, his Estate, his Knowledge, his sense, his public Employments, that of Select Man, that of Commissioner of Bankruptcy &c., and of his public Capacity and spirit,—ambitious of public Trust as a select Man, a Representative, a Commissioner &c. And besides all these, he is brutally uncivil and rude in Company. He is an impetuous bauler, a rough, unpolished, ill bred Clown and Coxcomb. These are the Properties of one of the favourites of Braintree.[2]

Is Lawrence to be Styled a Yeoman? or not. For the Negative these Things are to be considered.—1st. Bayley in his Dictionary, defines Yeomen to be the first Degrees of the Commons, Freeholders, who have land of their own, and live on good Husbandry. Sir T. Smith defines a Yeoman to be a free born Englishman, who may lay out of his own free Land in Yearly Revenue, to the sum of 40s.

Now Lawrence is not most certainly one of any of the first degrees of the Commons. He is a poor, low, inferiour sort of Man, to be ranked only among Labourers, and the meanest of the People. He is certainly no freeholder, he has no Land of his own, and he does not live at all upon Husbandry. And if it should be admitted that he was a free born Englishman, according to the first Part of Sir Thos. Smiths Definition, yet he does not answer the last Part of it, for he cannot lay out of his own free Land, in Yearly Revenue to the sum of 40s., for he is not the owner of one foot of Land in the World.

I find in 23: H. 6. 15. Ab[ridgmen]t [of the] Statutes, title Parliament ss. 29. None shall be a Knight of the Shire, which standeth in the Degree of a Yeoman or Under.—By this statute therefore it appears that there are Degrees, or at least a Degree under that of a Yeoman.

In Shep[pard's] Ab[ridgmen]t, Title Name.—So of Commons there be Degrees as Knights, Esquires, Gentlemen, Citizens, Yeomen and Burgesses of several Degrees.—Here Burgesses are a Rank below Yeoman.

Is Lawrence a Yeoman?

For the affirmative these Things are to be considered.—

What was the precise meaning of the Word Yeoman in the ancient Saxon or Teutonic Languages, I cannot say. And whether this Title was or was not in ancient times, most usually given to Land Holders, to Country farmers, is not worth while to inquire, because it is not material to the present Question.—For

It is certain, that in the modern Language both of Courts and History's, all Persons under the Degree of Gentlemen are styled Yeomen. The Gentry and Yeomanry of England comprehend all Degrees of Men from the King to the Beggar, in History, and in the modern Lawbooks a Yeoman is defined to be an ordinary common man.

In Strange's Reports—It is settled over and over again, first that a Trader may be sued by the Addition of his Degree, as that of Yeoman e.g. and the Writ shall not abate unless he pleads another degree. Another Defendant pleaded that he was a Lime merchant, and not a Yeoman. Plaintiff demurred, and the Court held, that every Man be he a trader or not a Trader, has a Degree by which he may be denoted. And that if the Defendant had shewn himself to be a Degree higher than a Yeoman, that would have abated the Writ, but not otherwise.

In modern Cases, Defendant pleaded that he was a Farmer and not a Yeoman. The Plaintiff demurred, and it was held, that if the Defendant is not a Gentleman he must be a Yeoman i.e. an ordinary or common Person.

Besides I find it said in some Dictionaries that the Saxon Word from whence Yeoman is drawn signified a Shepherd. Now a Man may be a shepherd without being a Landholder, and the Word which answers this in the teutonic Language signified a common man. Now every common man is not a Landholder.

But all these Criticisms are Trash and trifling for it is settled Practice in this Court, in Conformity to the late Practice at Home, to call every one of these lower sort of People, who are not Gentlemen and whose Occupation is not known, Yeoman. I have heard common soldiers, styled Yeomen in Indictments, soldiers belonging to the Train who had no Land. I have known a Multitude of Instances where Defendants in civil Actions in this Court, have been called Yeomen, who never owned an Inch of ground in their Lives. But this Man has a better Right to this Addition, for he was born a Yeoman according to this Definition, i.e. a Land holder, and he owned when this Note was given a good farm, a farm worth £3000.

Q[uery]. Is Labourer an Addition of Degree or Mistery? A Labourer is one that has no Trade or Art or Mistery, but it is an Occupation.

It would be worth while to describe all the Transformations of J.Q.'s [3] flatery.—Yet there is always a salvo, which shews his Deceit and Insincerity.

If Mr. Adams should become in 2 or 3 Years, one of the most eminent Lawyers in the County, and remove to Boston, there you would find persons, who have Daughters to dispose of, who have Knowledge of the World, and Prudence enough to look out the ⟨most thriving⟩ best Characters, for Matches to their Daughters. Twenty such Men would have their Eyes upon You; would dress out their Daughters to the best Advantage, contrive Interviews, lay schemes and presently, some one more beautiful, or sensible, or witty or artful, than the rest will take you in. We shall see you, in spight of your Phylosophy, and Contempt for Wife and Mistress and all that, sighing, and dying with Love. [Here, under a specious Pretext of Raillery for my boasted, and affected, Indifference to Ladies, he is insinuating or would make me believe that he designed to insinuate, that I am likely to be the ablest Lawyer on the stage, in 2 or 3 Years, that 20 Gentlemen will Eye me for a Match to their Daughters, and all that. This is the flattery. Yet, in truth he only said, if Mr. Adams should become &c. so that if his Consequences should never take Place, Oh I never expected they would, for I did not expect you would be eminent.—Besides, if he was to speak his real sentiments, I am so illbred, unpolished &c. that I never shall succeed with ladies or the World &c. &c.] [4]

The same Evening, I shew him, my Draught of our Licensed Houses and the Remarks upon it.[5] Oh he was transported! he was ravished! He would introduce that Plan at the sessions, and read the Remarks, and say they were made as well as the Plan by a Gentleman to whom their could be no Exception—&c. He saw an Abstract of the Argument for and against Writts of Assistants—and crys did you take this from those Gentlemen as they delivered it? You can do any Thing! You can do as you please! Gridley did not use that Language. He never was Master of such a style! It is not in him—&c.[6]

I will lay 100 Guineas, that before 20 Years, you will raise the Fees of the Bar 3 fold. If your Eloquence should turn out equal to your Understanding, you will. I know you will!

You have Ld. Bolinbroke by heart! With one cursory Reading you have a deeper Understanding of him and remember more of him, than I do after 3 or 4 Readings, or than I should have after 10 Readings.

With all your Merit, and Learning, and Wit and sense and Spirit, and Vivacity, and all that.—

These are the bold, gross, barefaced Flatteries that I hear every Time I see that Man. Can he think me such a Ninny as to be allured and deceived by such gross Arts? He must think me vastly vain, silly, stupid, if he thinks to impose on me, if he thinks I cant see the Deceit. It must be deceit. It cannot be any Thing else.

Gray v. Paxton. Otis drew a Writ vs. Paxton for Money had and received to the Use of the Province. Prat pleaded in Abatement, That, altho the suit was brot in Greys Name, altho Gray was Plantiff, Yet no Promise was alledged to have been made to Gray. The Defendant is alledged to be indebted to the Province, for Money received to the Provinces Use, and to have promised to pay it to the Province. Yet the Province is not Plantiff. It is Gray vs. Paxton, but it should have been the Province of the Massachusetts Bay v. Paxton.[7]

The Treasurer and Receiver General has not a Right ex Officio, to demand, sue for and recover all Monies that are due to the Province. No more than a Noblemans Steward has to sue for and Recover the Demands of the Nobleman: No more than the Cashier of the Bank of England, has to sue for and Recover all Monies due to the Bank of England. A steward may sue but not in his own Name, he must sue in the Name of his Master. The Cashier may sue, but not in his own Name, he must sue in the Name of the Governor and Company of the

Bank of England. A Corporate Body is one Person in Law and may sue or be sued, and There is an Instance, before the Court, this Term, in your own Dockett, of a suit brot by a Town, the Town of Dorchester vs. A.B. &c. There is a special Law of this Province, which impowers [*sentence unfinished*]

[1] Probably Zabdiel Adams, JA's cousin.

[2] The following semidetached entries may have been written at any time between 3 April and mid-May, though one of them, as indicated below, seems to have been inserted as late as July.

[3] Doubtless Col. Josiah Quincy.

[4] First bracket in MS; closing bracket supplied.

[5] That is, JA's sketch map of tavern locations, which is reproduced in this volume; see entry of 29 May 1760 and note, above. CFA, who mentions the map without reproducing it, prints a passage of JA's accompanying comment which no longer appears on or with the map, as follows:

"N.B. Place one foot of your dividers at Eb. Thayer's house, and extend the other about one mile and a half, and then sweep a circle; you will surround eight public houses, besides one in the centre. There is vastly more travelling and little less business in Milton, Dorchester, and Roxbury, where public houses are thinly scattered, than there is in Braintree; and why poor Braintree men, who have no virtue to boast of, should be solicited with more temptations than others, I can't imagine. This, I will say, that whoever is in fault, or whatever was the design, taverns and dramshops have been systematically and scandalously multiplied in this town; and, like so many boxes of Pandora, they are hourly scattering plagues of every kind, natural, moral, and political, through the whole town" (*Works*, 2:123, note).

[6] This is the only reference in the Diary to the celebrated argument before the Superior Court in Feb. 1761 concerning the legality of writs of assistance. In his Autobiography JA furnished from memory a longer account of what he called the first incident in a "Contest ... to which I could foresee no End." Many of the details in his later account (printed by CFA in JA, *Works*, 2:124, note), repeated with variations and ad-

ditions in his letters to William Tudor, 1817–1818, were questioned and corrected by Horace Gray in a learned appendix on writs of assistance in Quincy's *Reports*, 1865, p. 395–540; see especially p. 408–409; 414, note; 469, note. From some of the language used in the present Diary entry ("an Abstract of the Argument for and against Writts of Assistants"), it would appear that JA showed Col. Quincy his original hasty notes taken during the hearing. These survive as a single large folded sheet with nine pages covered by writing among JA's legal papers (Adams Papers, Microfilms, Reel No. 185; printed in JA, *Works*, 2:521–523, and more literally, with full annotation by Horace Gray, in Quincy, *Reports*, p. 469–482). On the other hand, as Professor Gipson has pointed out, no one could possibly have praised the "style" of these crabbed notes, and it is therefore possible and even probable that JA had already written up his notes of Gridley's argument for the writs and Otis' and Thacher's arguments against them in a discursive form intended to circulate among friends and other interested persons. At any rate, a written-up version *did* circulate some time afterward, if not immediately, for variant texts of such a version appeared in newspapers and in lawyers' commonplace books, and JA acknowledged the authorship of one portion (Otis' speech) that was eventually printed in George Richards Minot's *Continuation of the History of the Province of Massachusetts*, Boston, 1798–1803, 2:91–100. See also JA, *Works*, 2:523–525; Samuel A. Green's remarks on the textual history of Otis' speech in MHS, *Procs.*, 2d ser., 6 (1890–1891):190–196; Lawrence H. Gipson, "Aspects of the Beginning of the American Revolution," Amer. Antiq. Soc., *Procs.*, 67 (1957):23, note; Joseph R. Frese, "James Otis and Writs of Assistance," *NEQ*, 30:496–508 (Dec. 1957). Fortunately it is possible to defer any attempt to reconstruct the text of JA's longer version (of which no MS in his hand has been found) with at least some hope that more evidence may come to light.

⁷ This detached entry appears to be out of place chronologically, since it reports part of Benjamin Prat's plea in abatement of the writ in the case of Gray *v*. Paxton, tried in Suffolk Inferior Court, July 1761. This was a famous case, with marked political overtones. Harrison Gray (1711–1794) was provincial treasurer and receiver-general; Charles Paxton (1707–1788) was a commissioner of customs in Boston (Stark, *Loyalists of Mass.*, p. 334–336, 318–319). The action grew out of Paxton's practice of charging his costs for secret informers entirely against the King's (that is to say, the Province's) one-third share of the value of goods forfeited under admiralty court decisions, while the Governor and the informer each got their full thirds. As a result of a petition from a number of merchants and after much bickering between the House of Representatives and Governor Bernard, the General Court in Jan. 1761 authorized Treasurer Gray to sue Paxton for the alleged deficiencies (more than £357). Much discussed during the spring, the case came on in the Inferior Court in July, and Paxton lost. The Superior Court in its August term supported Prat's plea in abatement and reversed the decision. A new action, Province *v*. Paxton, was thereupon brought in the Inferior Court, Jan. 1762, and judgment was again rendered against Paxton. He again appealed, and, to use Bernard's words, "pursuant to the direction of all the Judges the jury found for the defendant [Paxton]," Feb. 1762. The records of the two cases, with full commentary, are printed by Samuel M. Quincy in Appendix II to Quincy, *Reports*, p. 541–552. It is to Chief Justice Hutchinson's role in the two cases on appeal that JA refers so bitterly in his Diary for 30 Dec. 1765: "Who has made it his constant Endeavor to discountenance the Odium in which Informers are held?" &c.

[DRAFT OF A LETTER TO THE *Boston Gazette,* MAY 1761.] ¹

I am myself an Inhabitant of Boston, and have I think an honest affection for the Town, and a sincere Concern for its Honour: for which Reason I cannot reflect upon the late prevailing Humor of attributing our own follies to the Country without Regret. The late Engagement in your Paper, between two litigating Scribblers, about the Clergy of this Town, and their lawdable Conduct, at the late Installment, forsooth was between two Country laymen: ² and many other Pieces lately published have been in Country Characters; young Gentlemen from the Country, old Batchellers in the Country &c. This is [merely?] fathering our own natural Children on other Men who are more chaste. Such Pieces, every Man who reads them knows, are the Productions of idle fellows in this Town—Persons who have no Business, of more Consequence, to employ their Time and Thoughts, and who happen to grow vain enough in their own Imaginations, to prize highly their own Wit and Talent. Whereas the good People in the Country, whom in Journeys which I often take I have pretty carefully observed, are more dilligent and attentive to their own Business, and much less conceited of their sense and Learning. Besides any Man may observe in these Pieces, a Temper, and Manners quite remote from the honest simplicity and natural, and habitual Benevolence of a Country-man. Tis really doing Injustice to the Country to impute to it such uncandid, illiberal Productions, but no Wonder these Grub-street Garreteers are guilty of this Injustice when, I am sorry to say it, a like Kind is committed by almost all orders of the Town, in many other affairs of much more Consequence.

The affair of Taxes has been a common Place Topic of Complaint against the Country, among all Ranks of Men in this Metropolis for many Years. Our Gentry has given frequent Invitations, to the Country Representatives, and to other Country Gentlemen, who had Acquaint-ance here, to Entertainments. The Productions of every Element and Climate were assembled, and the nicest Art and Cookery employed to regale them. The furniture of our Houses and Tables were proportion-ably rich and gay. Our Persons were cloathed in silks and Laces and Velvet, and our Daughters especially blazed in the rich vestments of Princesses. At the same Time the poor Gentlemen were scarcely able to walk the streets, for the Multitude of Chariots, or to hear themselves speak for the rapid Rattling of Hoofs and Wheels. (Wits and Wags may laugh at my Discription, but Foppery ought to be described in Bombast.) These Appearances at the Churches, assemblies, Concerts, Private Houses and streets, gave the Country an opinion, either that Boston was vastly rich or vastly extravagant, and they dared not, by any public speech or Conduct suppose the latter least they should give offence to us, who had treated them even with assiduous Complaisance and Hospitality.

They endeavoured to Settle the Proportion of public Burdens, (and how should they do otherwise) according to the best Proofs they could procure of Wealth and Ability: And altho People in the Country were obliged to wear Homespun threadbare, eat salt Pork and Beef, drink Cyder and small Beer, and turn every stone, and save every Penny to pay their Taxes, and did it chearfully too: yet we in Boston never would pay ours, without Grumbling, and cursing Country folks, and Country Representatives.

Well, the Country Gentlemen desirous to do Justice, [harkened?] to our Complaints, and set themselves to discover as well as they could, who was and who was not able to support the Pomp they every day saw. They asked our own Representatives and other, the most sensible Inhabitants of the Town, and no better Method was to be found than the Valuation Act.[3] But, this, instead of ⟨quieting⟩ extinguishing only enflamed our Discontent.[4] "What we cry? We obliged to tell upon Oath how much we are worth? must not we drink Madeira, eat in silver and China? Ride in our Chariots? Go to Concerts and assemblies? and let our sons and Daughters spend a few Guineas a Week at Cards without telling the assessors, and having it recorded that we are in Debt for all this, and £10,000 worse than nothing! Oh these vile shoe string Representatives." [5]

We have not in short the Ingenuity of common Debauchees, who will often confess their own folly, in getting Claps and daily Drams, has given them the Hectick: But we are determined to take no shame to ourselves, but charge the natural and unavoidable Consequences of our own Imprudence on the Country. The Country, it is true, is not an unexceptionable Example of Wisdom. Many Things are running Wild. Many simptoms begin to appear, that threaten their Happiness, their Morals, Health, Properties and Liberties, in a very melancholly manner: But even these simptoms are produced, in a great Measure by the inconsiderate Politicks of this Town.—Give me Leave to mention a very flagrant Instance out of a Multitude.

If you ride over this whole Province you will find, that, alltho Taverns are generally too numerous, they are not half so numerous in any one County, in Proportion to the Numbers of People and the Necessity of Business and Travellers, as in this. In most Country Towns, in this County,[6] you will find almost every other House, with a sign of Entertainment before it. If you call, you will find Dirt enough, very miserable Accommodation of Provision and Lodging, for your self and your Horse. Yet if you set the Evening, you will find the House full of People, drinking Drams, Phlip,[7] Toddy, Carrousing, swearing, but especially, plotting, with the Landlord, to get him, at the next Town Meeting an Election, either for select man or Representative. Thus the Multiplicity of these Houses, by dividing the Profits, renders the Landlords careless of Travellers, and allures the poor Country People, who are tired with Labour and hanker after Company, to waste their Time and money, contract Habits of Intemperance and Idleness, and by degrees to loose the natural dignity and freedom of Inglish Minds, and confer those offices, which belong by Nature and the spirit of all Government to Probity and Honesty, on the meanest and weakest and worst of human Characters.

A good deal of this has happened, as I believe, partly from what I have seen and partly from credible Information, in the Country: But who is most to blame! The Court of Sessions has made such Rules for itself, that the Country Justices can seldom attend. The select Men of the several Towns, have been so often disappointed, that they are discouraged. Some Houses to my Knowledge have been licensed which never had any Approbation from any select Man. Other Persons have been licensed whom the select Men have found by Experience, and certified to be, guilty of Misrule, and therefore unfit. Others have been recognized for seven Years together without any Approbation from the select Men, thro that whole Time. Nay a Man has been recognized, tho the select Men certifyed good Reasons for not approbating him—that he was very intemperate, had poor Accommodations, and was subject to fits of Caprice if not Delirium, that made it dangerous to come near him: and altho it was proved, that the same Man, in one of those fits, had but a few days before, Stabbed another, with apparent Design and great Danger of Murder.

Now I agree, that Ambitious Spirits in the Country, who have little Honour, will soon see, that such Houses must be favoured, and multiplied, to promote their own designs, and therefore Retailers and Taverners are generally in the Country Assessors, or select Men, or Representative or Esquires: But are not we more to blame. Are not some of our Justices, Importers of Mollasses? are not others Distillers? and are not all of them fond of a lawful Fee? In short it is owing wholly to Boston Justices, that those Houses have been so shamefully multiplied, in the Country, multiplied so that decent Entertainment for a Traveller is no where to be had.

The Freedom of Censure is a Matter of great Consequence under our Government.[8] There are certain Vices and follies, certain Indecencies of Behaviour, beneath the Inspection and Censure of Law and Magistracy, which must be restrained and corrected by Satyr. And for this Reason, every Piece of just Ridicule in public or private bestowed on any ⟨foppery⟩ wrong or foolish Conduct, gives me great Pleasure, even altho I am myself the Object. From the same Principle I was glad to see some Animadversion on the late inconsistent Conduct of the Ministers of this Town. And nothing but sacerdotal Impudence, and Ecclesiastical Pride, can account for the surly, revengeful Manner in which those Pieces have been received.

[1] This is the last of JA's series of letters on the evils of taverns; see entry of 29 May 1760 and note, above. Though clearly intended for publication in the *Boston Gazette* (see the following note), no printing has been found.

[2] "The late Engagement in your Paper" alludes to a controversy arising from a news item in the *Boston Gazette*, 2 March 1761, describing the installation of Rev. Alexander Cumming as co-pastor with Dr. Joseph Sewall of the Old South Church in Boston a week earlier. The "Entertainment" provided for the "honourable and reverend Guests" was so "very sumptuous and elegant," the notice said, that it had to be held in several houses. "And it is concluded, that many poor People were the better for what remained of so plentiful and splendid a Feast; such as was hardly ever known among us on a similar Occasion." In the

following issue, 9 March, an anonymous writer who described himself as a country layman declared these proceedings "disgusting" to himself and discreditable to the Congregational ministry. He called attention to resolves that a convention of ministers had themselves adopted two years earlier, disapproving "Feasting, Jollity and Revelling" on such occasions, and pointed out that Joseph Sewall had issued the resolves over his own name as moderator of the convention. On 6 April the *Gazette* carried a rejoinder from another "country layman," who ventured the opinion that the guests had enjoyed only the "moderate refreshment" to which any Christian is entitled. The dispute spun itself out until 11 May, when the first writer got the last word by describing the fare in detail, his informant (he said) having been one of the guests:

"There were six tables, that held one with another 18 persons, upon each table a good rich plum pudding, a dish of boil'd pork and fowls, and a corn'd leg of pork, with sauce proper for it, a leg of bacon, a piece of alamode beef, a leg of mutton with caper sauce, a piece of roast beef, a roast line [loin] of veal, a roast turkey, a venison pastee, besides chess cakes and tarts, cheese and butter. Half a dozen cooks were employed upon this occasion, upwards of twenty tenders to wait upon the tables; they had the best of old cyder, one barrel of Lisbon wine, punch in plenty before and after dinner, made of old Barbados spirit. The cost of this moderate dinner was upwards of fifty pounds lawful money."

[3] An Act for Enquiring into the Rateable Estates of this Province, passed 31 Jan. 1761, required all persons to list on oath their real and personal property for the purpose of a new tax assessment (Acts of 1760–1761, ch. 24; Mass., *Province Laws*, 4:422–423).

[4] In an earlier and very fragmentary draft of this essay, just preceding the present draft in the MS, the foregoing sentence reads: "But this threw new fuel into the unquenchable furnace of Boston Passions." There is reason to believe that this alternative draft was once longer but was later removed from the paper booklet; see note 8, below.

[5] Earlier draft reads: "Oh these vile shoe string Country Representatives."

[6] The words "Country" and "County" in this sentence (and frequently elsewhere in JA's early Diary) are indistinguishable as written by JA. In transcribing, one can only go by the sense of the passage.

[7] MS: "Plip."

[8] The present paragraph is separated by an interval of space from the foregoing text. In the margin is written "Beg.," (i.e. "Begin"), which together with the substance indicates that this paragraph was an alternative opening for the essay. It may, however, have been intended as the beginning of the now largely missing draft; see note 4, above.

JUNE 11TH. 1761.

I have been for a Week or fortnight engaged in a Project.[1] Have remarkably succeeded hitherto. Mr. Niles approved in all Things. Major Crosbey approved in all Things. Deacon Palmer approved in all Things. They have given under their Hands a very full and handsome Character and Recommendation of my Brother—much more ample than I expected. They have really Spoken in Hyperbole. They have expressed themselves with Warmth. I expected only a signification of their Consent and Approbation, but they have expressed themselves with Zeal. I ought to consider these Credentials gratefully, as a strong Instance of friendship, and take the first Opportunity of making some Return. Mr. N. has the worst opinion of Thayers Morals. He detests the base Methods of Debauchery, and Lying, and Duplicity, that he has been in. P. despizes him.

But scheming seldom has success. I expect to come off but second best after all. I expect that Thayer will hear of my Design, and in order to defeat it, continue in the office himself. If he should, I shall be pretty [well?]. Intrigue, and making Interest, and Asking favors is a new Employment to me. I'm unpractised in Intrigues for Power.

I begin to feel the Passions of the World. Ambition, Avarice, Intrigue, Party, all must be guarded.[2]

My fears of failing are at last vanished. The scheme succeeded in all Things, and is compleated. B[oylston] is constituted, commissioned, sworn, and this Day, undertaken to officiate. Now a new Train of Anxieties, begins to take Place. Fears of imperfect services, imperfect and false Returns, voluntary and negligent Escapes, miscalculations, Want of strength, Courage, Celerity, Want of Art and Contrivance &c. Rashness, Indolence, Timidity, &c.

The Project was so well planned, that success seemed certain. ⟨*Every Party*⟩, all the Justices recommended. Two other Gents of his Acquaintance, men of Honour and figure. G.[3] concurred and urged, and dropped Hints if not Anecdotes, vs. the old one. Hints were dropped to him by others that I should employ Constables and so deprive him of his Profits. So that his Interest, his Vanity, his Honour, were all touched. It cost me much Pains, at least 2 Journeys to Boston, one to Mr. Niles', one to Germantown, one to Mr. [Bullards?], and Majr. Crosbeys. The Writing of a long Bond. The solicitation of Credentials, of sureties and of the office. More[4] solicitation procured it. And altho it was not much disguised or concealed, yet it was so silently conducted that I believe the [grand?] Adversary never once suspected it. All the Wiles and Malice of the old serpent would have been employed against it, if it had been known or suspected. But there was one Particular of mere Luck, to which we were much indebted—vizt. the Complaint of Cudworth against T. That unfriendly, unbrotherly, unneighbourly, as well as rash and unmannerly, Spurning of the Execution, and then sending it to Gould, where it was lost, gave the great Man an ill opinion of his sub.[5] and made him more willing and ready, at my solicitation, to constitute another, and even without consulting Thayer.

[1] To obtain the appointment of his brother Peter Boylston Adams as a deputy sheriff of Suffolk co. This was, as JA explained in his Autobiography, "in pursuance of my plan of reforming the practice of Sheriffs and Pettyfoggers" in drawing writs. A bill of costs from Peter for serving a long list of writs for JA, 1764–1766, remains in the Adams Papers, under the date of 26–27 Sept. 1766.

[2] A line across the page follows this paragraph in the MS, so that what follows may have been—and probably was—written one or more days later.

[3] Probably Stephen Greenleaf, sheriff of Suffolk co.

[4] Possibly "Mere," as rendered by CFA (JA, *Works*, 2:129).

[5] "subordinate"?

JUNE 20TH. 1761.

I have latterly arose much earlyer than Usual. Arose at five and at 6 O'clock, instead of 8 and 9. The Mornings are very long, and fine opportunities for Study. They are cool and pleasant. But I have not improved my Time, properly. I have dozed and sauntered away much of my Time. This morning is very fine. The clear sky, the bright sun, the clean Groves and Grass, after so fine a Rain are very pleasant. But the Books within this Chamber have a much better Title to my Attention than any of the rural scenes and objects without it. I have been latterly too much in the World, and too little in this Retreat. Abroad, my Appetites are solicited, my Passions inflamed, and my Understanding too much perverted, to judge wisely of Men or Things. But in this Retreat, where neither my Senses nor Appetites nor Passions are excited, am able to consider all Things more coolly, and sensibly. I was guilty of rash and profane Swearing, of rough ⟨and indecent⟩ Virulence vs. the Characters of Goffe, J. Russell, Lieutenant Governor, &c. Not but that there have been Faults in their Characters and Conduct, that every honest Man ought to resent.

SATURDAY JUNE 20TH. 1761.[1]

I have been interrupted from Reading this Institute ever since Feby. Amidst the Dissipations of Business, Pleasure, Conversation, Intrigue, Party &c. what mortal can give Attention to an old latin Institute of the Cannon Law? But it is certainly worth while to proceed and finish it, as I have already been 2/3 thro it.

[1] This second entry so dated is from D/JA/4, JA's desultory record of studies. The "Institute" here mentioned is Lancelotti's compilation of canon law; see entries of 27 Jan., above, and 17 Oct., below.

JULY 7TH. 1761.

Dined at Deacon Hills, with Sam Quincy and his Bride,[1] and with Mr. Cushing a Representative of Salisbury. Cushing seems a fair minded Countryman. Some free and friendly Conversation passed between Henry Hill and his father, about Advancement, and stock and setting up, and giving £1000 a Year. Henry said You ought to give me £1000 a Year or 10,000 right out, and then I maintain myself. You must give me Money or learn me to get it, or why did you make me? I'le go back again, &c.

Drank Tea, at Major Nobles, with Coll. Quincy, Deacon Whittemore, and the Man who is sued to this Court. I've forgot his Name. All in Consultation about defending their Lands in the Eastward.

¹ Samuel Quincy had married Hannah Hill of Boston, 16 June 1761 (Salisbury, *Family-Memorials*, 1:358).

AUGT. 1ST.

I am creating Enemies in every Quarter of the Town. The Clarks hate. Mother Hubbard, Thayer, Lamb, Tirrell, J. Brackett. This is multiplying and propagating Enemies, ⟨too⟩ fast. I shall have the Ill-Will of the whole Town.¹

Daniel White, Moses Adams.—This will not do.

Daniel Prat vs. Thos. Colson.—This Action was brot by Plaintiff vs. Colson as Administrator, on the Estate of Mr. Bolter, for Non-Performance of a Covenant of Indenture. Prat was a poor, fatherless Child and his Mother Unable to provide for him, bound him an Apprentice to Mr. Bolter. He was then under 10 Years of Age, and so was bound for Eleven Years, and some odd Months. In Consideration of this very long and unusual Term of Apprenticeship his Master covenanted to teach him to read, write and Cypher, and to teach him the Trade of a Weaver. But we ⟨contend⟩ complain that he never taught us either to read, write or Cypher, or to weave. Call the Proof.

The Law, Gentlemen, is extreamly tender and indulgent to such Actions as these. For such is the Benignity and Humanity of the English Constitution that all the weak, and helpless, and friendless Part of our Species are taken under its Peculiar Care and Protection. Women, Children, and Especially Widows and fatherless Children, have always, from the Compassion of the Law peculiar Priviledges and Indulgences allowed them. Therefore as a poor, fatherless, and friendless Child the Law would allow great Indulgence and Lenity to this Plantiff.

But he is to be favoured for Another Reason. Because the English Law greatly favours Education. In every English Country, some sort of Education, some Acquaintance with Letters, is necessary, that a Man may fill any station whatever. In the Countries of slavery, and Romish superstition, the Laity must not learn to read, least they should detect the gross Impostures of the Priesthood, and shake off the Yoke of Bondage. But in Protestant Countries and especially in England and its Colonies, Freedom of Enquiry is allowed to be not only the Priviledge but the Duty of every Individual. We know it to be our Duty, to read, examine and judge for ourselves, even of ourselves what is right. No Priest nor Pope has any Right to say what I shall believe, and I will not believe one Word they say, if I think it is not founded in Reason and in Revelation. Now how can I judge what My Bible justifies unless I can read my Bible.

The English Constitution is founded, tis bottomed And grounded on the Knowledge and good sense of the People. The very Ground of our Liberties, is the freedom of Elections. Every Man has in Politicks as well as Religion, a Right to think and speak and Act for himself. No man either King or Subject, Clergyman or Layman has any Right to dictate to me the Person I shall choose for my Legislator and Ruler. I must judge for myself, but how can I judge, how can any Man judge, unless his Mind has been opened and enlarged by Reading. A Man who can read, will find in his Bible, in the common sermon Books that common People have by them and even in the Almanack and News Papers, Rules and observations, that will enlarge his Range of Thought, and enable him the better to judge who has and who has not that Integrity of Heart, and that Compass of Knowledge and Understanding, which form the Statesman.

Mem[orandum]. To ask Seth Copeland, whether his Father White has a Copy of his Fathers Will? How came Eb. White possessed of that old Deed to his father, and how came Tho's White to have it? and whether he Tho's White has a Copy of that Deed. And Q[uery] of whom Capt. Thayer bought his share of the Landing? and of whom Holbrook bought his share of the Landing? And whether the Beech and Flatts, where Thayers and Holbrooks Wharffs now are, ever belonged to Tho's White the Testator.

[1] The several semidetached entries that follow may have been written any time from 2 Aug. to 9 Sept. 1761.

SEPTR. 10TH. 1761.

Spent Evening at Zabs with the Parson.

Wibirt. I have seen a Picture of Oliver Cromwell, with this Motto under it—

> Careat successibus opto
> Quisquis ab Eventu, facta notanda putat.[1]

I pray that he may want success, who thinks that Deeds are to be estimated from their Event, their success. Oliver was successful but not prudent nor honest, nor lawdable nor imitable.[2]

A certain Romish Priest had five young Nuns, committed to his Charge, i.e. he was appointed the Confessor to them. And after a while they all five proved with Child by him. He was summoned into the spiritual Court, to answer to the Charge of Fornication. The Judge told him he was charged with a criminal Correspondence with all five of the Nuns that had been entrusted to his Care. The Priest replies, Quinque mihi tradidit Dominus Talenta, Et Ecce alia quinque super lucratus sum.—The Judge was so well pleased with his Confession that he said Remittuntur tibi Peccata tua, Abi in Pace.

[1] From Ovid's *Heroids*, according to CFA (JA, *Works*, 2:132, note).
[2] It is impossible to tell from the MS whether or not the diarist intended to attribute to Parson Wibird the facetious story told in the paragraph that follows. See Matthew, 25:20.

OCTR. 17TH. 1761.

Read in Just[inian] and Lancelot.

OCTR. 17TH. 1761.[1]

I began Lancelotts Institute last Jany., and have read no farther than Lib[er] 3. Ti[tulus] 8. De Exceptionibus et Replicationibus.

[1] This entry, the second so dated, is from D/JA/4, JA's journal of studies.

OCTR. 18TH. 1761. SUNDAY.

Arose at 6. Read in Popes Satyrs. Nil Admirari &c. I last night read thro, both of Dr. Donnes Satyrs versifyed by Pope. Was most struck with these Lines

> Bear me some God! Oh! quickly bear me hence
> To wholsome solitude the Nurse of sense
> Where Contemplation prunes her ruffled Wings
> And the free soul looks down to pitty Kings.

Prayer! A post[ulant?]—Hands uplifted, and Eyes. A very proper Prayer for me to make when I'm in Boston. Solitude is a Personage, in a clean, wholsome Dress, the Nurse and Nourisher of sense. Contemplation a Personage, prunes, picks, smooths. Is she an Angell or a Bird—ruffled, rumpled, rugged, uneven, tumbled. Free soul, not enslaved, unshackled, no Bondage, no subjection, looks down, pitties George, Louis, Frederick, Phillip, Charles, &c.[1]

Among the numberless Imperfections of human Nature and society, there is none that deserves to be more lamented, because there is none that is the source of greater Evils, than the Tendency of great

Parts and Genius, to imprudent sallies and a Wrong Biass.[2] If We move back, thro the History of all ages and Nations, we shall find, that all the Tumults, Insurrections, and Revolutions, that have disturbed the Peace of society, and spilled oceans of Blood, have arisen from the giddy Rashness and Extravagance of the sublimest Minds. But in those Governments where the People have much Power, tho the best that can be found, the Danger from such spirits is the greatest of all. That unquenchable Thirst of superiority, and Power which, in such Governments, inkindles the Lust of Popularity, often precipitates Persons of [the] Character I describe, into the wildest Projects and Adventures, to set the World aware of their Parts and Persons, without attending to the Calamities that must ensue. Popular orators are generally opposite to the present Administration, blaming public Measures, and despizing or detesting Persons in Power, whether wise or foolish, wicked or upright, with all their Wit, and Knowledge, merely to make themselves the Idols of a slavish, timid People, who are always jealous and invidious of Power and therefore devoted to those that expose, ridicule or condemn it. Eloquence that may be employed wisely to persuade, is often employed wickedly to seduce, from the Eloquence of Greece and Rome down to the rude speeches of our American Town Meeting. I have more charity, than to believe, that these orators really intend an Injury to their Country; but so subtle are our Hearts in deceiving ourselves, we are so apt to think our own Parts so able and capable and necessary to the public, that we shall richly repair, by our Capacity in public station any Mischiefs we occasion in our Way to them. There is perhaps a sincere Patriotism in the Hearts of all such Persons; but it must be confessed, that the most refined Patriotism to which human Nature can be wrought, has in it an alloy of Ambition, of Pride and avarice that debases the Composition, and produces mischievous Effects.

As unhappy and blamable as such Persons are, the general Method in Use among Persons in Power of treating such spirits, is neither less unhappy, or blamable or hurtful. Such Minds, with a wise and delicate Management, may be made the ornaments and Blessings: but by an unskilfull and rough Usage, will be rendered desperate and therefore the Worst Blemishes and Plagues of their Country.

I therefore who am setting up for the Monitor of all future Legislators, a Character for which by my great Age, Experience, Sense and Learning I am well qualified, hereby advise the orator, to guard himself and his Country, against the Danger to which his Passions expose both, and the Man in Power, instead of thwarting, and insulting and over bearing a Person who perhaps is full as wise and good as he, to [soothe?] ³ and cool and soften by a mild obliging Behaviour, and a just Attention to the [former?].⁴

You have given me a fee.⁵ Now this Action may possibly bear 3 several Constructions.

1st. It might be considered as an Engagement in your suit vs. Cranch.

2d. It might be considered as an Engagement to give you, the Offer of my service in all Causes, before I should engage in favour of any other Person vs. you.

3. It may be considered, for aught I can say, merely as a sop for Cerberus, ⟨to hinder⟩ in short to silence me ⟨in this Case, to⟩ bearly ⁶ to prevent my engaging on the other side, and to secure me as an Under Worker to fetch and carry, prepare Evidence &c.

Now I frankly tell you, when I accepted a fee from you, I accepted it in the second sense And in that alone. And I will tell you my Reasons. I had often heard you say that you once gave Mr. Prat a retaining fee, and you explain[ed] yourself thus—a fee ⟨not to engage for⟩ to be on your side in all Causes if you desired it, and not to engage against you, without first letting you know it. And you said further that whenever any Cause happened, after you gave that fee, you again engaged him &c. Another Reason was some time since when you apprehended a Dispute with Deacon Palmer you ⟨told me you⟩ desired me if any Person should apply to me against you that I would not engage without letting you know it, and if upon such Information you did not offer me more than the other Party had, I should be at Liberty to engage for him. And you then subjoined, to secure You to this, I will give you a retaining fee if you will take it. By the Way I then made this objection. "For another Person I may be employed to conduct the Cause but you can never entrust a Cause in the Hands of your Son and me, and to employ me in Conjunction with another, in Neglect of your Son, would not do." You answered Yes, I should have the Conduct of the Causes for it was not proper a son [should?] argue a Cause for his father. Another Reason was you offered the fee to me as a retaining fee before you said one Word of any Particular Cause. Neither of Mr. Cranchs 3 suits, nor any Eastern Claims, nor Deacon Palmers Account nor any other Cause was mentioned to me, til after you had put the fee into my Hand, and with it you said if any Person shall apply to you against me, dont you engage till You let me [*remainder missing*]

Tuesday Night. *Col. Q.* If that House was builded in 1755 before my first Wifes Death &c. &c. I am the most lost to all sense of Truth that ever Man was.[7]

[1] There is little or no clue to the date of the three detached entries which follow and which conclude the entries in D/JA/7. One can only suppose they were written soon after the present entry, but because of variations in ink and intervals of blank space in the MS this is by no means certain.

[2] This entry is a draft of another essay probably intended for a newspaper and probably incomplete as it now stands. No printing has been found.

[3] MS: "sool."

[4] Reading uncertain; the final word may actually be crossed out and the sentence thus left incomplete.

[5] This draft letter to an unidentified legal client (probably Col. Josiah Quincy) is badly scrawled and at some points barely legible.

[6] Thus in MS.

[7] Hannah (Sturgis) Quincy, Col. Josiah Quincy's first wife, died in 1755, but the allusion to "that House" is obscure.

NOVR. IOTH. 1761.[1]

Another Year is come round, and I can recollect still less Reading, than I could last Novr. The Increase of my Business, within 12ve months, has been nothing. I drew fewer Writs last October Court than I drew the October Court before, tho I drew an uncommon Number at both.—Yet I have advanced a few Steps. Have procured my Brother, his office, abated Nathan Spears Writ, Battled it with Capt. Thayer at Majr. Crosbeys, recovered of Jo. Tirrell for Lambard, recovered of Lawrence for Tirrell, abated Kings Writ, conducted the Pet[ition] vs. Tav[erns]. All These Things have been done in one Year. Besides have bought some Books &c. but have read but little Law.

This morning I have been Reading Archbp. Sharps sermon, To the Upright there ariseth Light in the Darkness. His Character of the Upright man, &c. Same day read a Number of his sermons in his first Volume. He is a moving, affectionate Preacher—devotional, more than Tillotson, but not so moral.[2]

[1] This and the two following entries are from JA's journal of studies, D/JA/4, and conclude the entries in that booklet except for a single one made eleven years later (21 Nov. 1772, q.v.).

[2] JA owned a collection of the very popular *Works* of John Sharp, Archbishop of York, in 7 vols., London, 1754 (*Catalogue of JA's Library*).

NOVR. 14TH. 1761.

Brother Quincy and I were Sworn, before the Superiour Court.[1] It is now more than five Years since I began the study of the Law. And it is about three Years, since I was sworn at the Inferiour Court.

[1] "Upon a motion made by Jeremy Gridley Esqr. the Oath of an Attorney by the province Law prescribed was administred to Messrs. Samuel Quincy and John Adams in Order to their practising in this Court" (Superior Court of Judicature, Records, 1760–1762, p. 239). For the attorney's oath, adopted in 1701,

see *Province Laws*, 1:467. In his Autobiography JA merged his admission as
an attorney in the Superior Court with

his admission as a barrister the following
year.

NOVR. 20TH. 1761. MONDAY.

This day removed to my Chamber, and made a Fire. The Forenoon
was Spent in Conversation with Zab, in walking to Dr. Turners, and up
Pens Hill, and this afternoon in Conversation with Grindal Rawson
and Zab at Mrs. Marshes. Yet I have caught several snatches of Reading and Thinking, in Blackstone, Gilbert &c. But I, as usual, expect
great Things from this Chamber, and this Winter.[1]

[1] This entry fixes the date of JA's
fitting out and establishing himself in his
law office in the house now known as
the John Quincy Adams Birthplace,
which he had inherited from his father
(see entry of 24 Oct. 1762, note) and
which the Savils must by now have
vacated. The law office was in the south-
east room on the ground floor and JA
opened a new doorway into it from the
street. During the 19th century the
doorway was boarded over but it has
since been restored. See Waldo C.
Sprague, *The President John Adams and
President John Quincy Adams Birthplaces*, Quincy, 1959 (unpaged).

JUNE 5TH. 1762.[1]

Rode from Bass's to Secretary Olivers, in Company with Judge
Oliver.[2] The Judge soon opened upon Politicks. Says he, Major Stock-
bridge informs me, that Coll. Ruggles makes a very good Speaker.
He has behaved to universal approbation.

Soon afterwards, the Judge said, I never knew so easy an Election
in my Life. Some of the Bar interest themselves, very much in the
Matter. One Gentleman has interested himself most infamously, advanced that to be Law in the House which is not Law.—That the
Judges cant set in the House of Commons is certain because there is
an Act of Parliament against it. But the Judges may set and vote in
the House of Lords—i.e. they may if they are Peers. Ld. Mansfield—
think he dont set and vote.[3]—How can the Bar expect Protection from
the Court, if the Bar endeavours to bring the Court into Contempt.
He is forever abusing the Court. He said not long since in the Representatives Room, that take all the superiour Judges and every Inferiour
Judge in the Province, and put them all together and they would not
make one half of a Common Lawyer.

I said upon this "That was a distracted Speech. It is a pitty, that
Gentleman was not better guided. He has many fine Talents." The
Judge replyed quick, I have known him these 20 Years and I have
no opinion of his Head or his Heart. If Bedlamism is a Talent he has
it in Perfection.[4]

He will one Time say of the Lieutenant Governor, that he had rather have him than any Man he knows, in any one office, and the next Hour will represent him as the greatest Tyrant, and most despicable Creature living.

I have treated him with as much Friendship as ever I did a stranger in my Life, and he knows very well how he has treated me. I blush even to think of what he has said to me.

I have him in the Utmost Contempt. I have the Utmost Contempt of him. I had as live [lief] say it to him as not. I have the Utmost Contempt of him.

I have been twelve Years concerned in the Executive Courts, and I never knew so much ill Usage, given to the Court by all the Lawyers in the Province put it all together for all that Time, as I have known him give in one Term.

The origin of all his Bustle is very well known. I heard a Gentleman say he would give his oath, that Otis said to him if his father was not made a Judge, he would thro the Province into flames if it cost him his Life. For that one Speech, a Thousand other Persons would have been indicted.

[1] First entry in D/JA/8, a stitched gathering of leaves in a paper cover evidently added later and docketed by CFA: "Paper book. No. 8." At some unknown time this booklet strayed from the Adams Papers and was returned with an accompanying letter from Charles P. Greenough to CFA2, 2 July 1913, saying: "I found the enclosed among my papers and it occurred to me that you might be interested. I can't for the life of me remember where and when I got it." Three days later CFA2 sent on the estray with a note to Worthington C. Ford at the MHS, remarking that "The whole thing is very mysterious and very unpleasant." (Greenough was a Boston autograph collector. The letters here quoted are in the Adams Papers, Fourth Generation.)

The present booklet contains only a handful of scattered entries dating from June to Dec. 1762. Little documentation survives to fill the seven-month gap between the last preceding Diary entries and the beginning of D/JA/8, and very little either to fill the gaps in the latter. In the spring JA was concerned with the sale by the town of its South Commons (see *Braintree Town Records*, p. 383–384, 386). By fall he was actively court-ing Miss Nabby Smith of Weymouth (see his letter of 4 Oct. 1762, Adams Papers). He was also much occupied this year with improving the property he had inherited from his father in 1761 (see entry of 24 Oct., below).

[2] Peter Oliver, Harvard 1730, a judge of the Plymouth co. Court of Common Pleas since 1747 (later chief justice of the Superior Court of Judicature and an eminent loyalist), was a younger brother of Andrew Oliver, secretary of the Province (Sibley-Shipton, *Harvard Graduates*, 8:737–763).

[3] The dash in this sentence has been supplied to clarify it. Oliver is discussing the election of a speaker of the Massachusetts House of Representatives in the session that had begun on 26 May. Though James Otis Sr. was unanimously elected to succeed himself in this office, he declined to serve because "his living at such a Distance rendered his constant Attendance very uncertain." Thereupon Timothy Ruggles was nominated and elected (Mass., *House Jour.*, 1762–1763, p. 5). The account of this incident in Sibley-Shipton, *Harvard Graduates*, 9:207–208, confuses Otis Sr. with Otis Jr. But of course it was the younger

Otis who Oliver thought had "interested himself most infamously" in attempting to block Ruggles' election on the ground that judges ought not to sit in the House. (Ruggles was chief justice of the Worcester Court of Common Pleas.)

[4] Oliver's observations, though not in quotation marks, no doubt extend through the end of this entry.

JUNE 8TH. 1762.

Went to Taunton Court. To the Land of Leonards. Three Judges of the Common Pleas of that Name, each of whom has a Son, who was bred at a Colledge.

The Honl. George Leonard, the first Justice, seems to me arbitrary. He committed two old Gentlemen who were near 80 Years old, to the Custody of an officer, only for speaking loud, when they were both deaf and not conscious that they did speak loud. A Check, a Reproof, an Admonition, would have been enough.

He was unwilling that the sessions should adjourn for an Hour to take the Verdict of the Jury, in a Tryal upon a Presentment of a Riot, but would have had that Jury kept together all Night, till the Court should set again next Morning. No other Court in the Province, Superiour nor Inferiour, would have thought of keeping that Jury up.

He broke in most abruptly upon Bob Paine. He did not think it was right to run out against the Kings Witnesses. For his Part He did not love to hear it.—Three or four Times over—&c. Thus the hauty Tyrant treats the County.

I lodged the first Night at Corsmans [Crossmans], the second at Major Leonards of Rainham and the third at Captn. Cobbs with Paine. I dined the first day I was there wednesday at Captn. Cobbs with Coll. Otis and Paine, and the second at Coll. Whites. Drank Tea once at Coll. Whites with the three young Leonards, George, Zeph. and Daniel,[1] and I spent two Evenings at Cobbs with Coll. Otis, and Paine. And I rode from Taunton to Milton, with Coll. Otis. He is vastly easy and steady in his Temper. He is vastly good humoured and sociable and sensible. Learned he is not. But he is an easy, familiar Speaker. He gave me many Anecdotes both of his Law and Politicks.

[1] Daniel Leonard, Harvard 1760, attorney, loyalist, and author of the "Massachusettensis" papers, 1774–1775, to which JA replied over the name "Novanglus." On the Leonards and their circle (including a number of the persons mentioned here), see Ralph Davol, *Two Men of Taunton*, Taunton, 1912, *passim*.

AUG. 15TH. 1762.

Reading, Thinking, Writing—have I totally renounced all three? Tempora mutantur, et nos mutamur in illis. Yesterday I found in some of Crafts Books of Heraldry, a Coat of Arms given by Garter, King at Arms, about 130 Years ago, to one William Adams of the Middle Temple, Counsellor at Law. It consists of Three Martlets sable, on a Bend between two O's—bezants.

Jus et Libertas. Jus suum cuique tribuatur. Ope summâ, et alacri Studio, Leges accipite.

OCTOBER 22ND. 1762.

Spent last Monday in taking Pleasure, with Mr. Wibird. Met him in the Morning at Mr. Borlands, rode with him, to Squantum, to the very lowest Point of the Peninsula, next to Thompsons Island, to the high steep Rock, from where the Squaw threw herself, who gave the Name to the Place.[1] It is an hideous Craggy Precipice, nodding over the Ocean forty feet in hight. The Rocks seem to be a vast Collection of Pebbles, as big as hens Eggs, thrown into melted Cement, and cooled in. You may pull them to Pieces with your Fingers, as fast as you Please.

Various have been the Conjectures of the Learned, concerning this sort of Rocks. Upon this Part of the Peninsula, is a Number of Trees, which appear very much like the Lime Tree, of Europe, which Gentlemen are so fond of Planting in their Gardens for their beauty.

Returned to Mr. Borlands, dined, and after noon rode to Germantown, where we spent our Evening. Deacon Palmer shewed us his Lucern, growing in his Garden, of which he has cutt, as he tells us, four Crops this Year. The Deacon had his Lucern seeds of Mr. Greenleaf, of Abington, who had his of Judge Oliver. The Deacon watered his but twice this summer, and intends to expose it uncovered, to all the Weather of the Winter for a fair Tryal, whether it will endure our Winters or not. Each of his four Crops had attained a good Length. It has a rich fragrance for a Grass. He shewed us a Cut of it, in "Nature displayed," and another of St. Foin, and another of Trefoil. The Cut of the Lucern was exact enough. The Pod in which the seeds is is an odd Thing, a kind of Rams horn or [straw?].

We had a good deal of Conversation upon Husbandry. The Deacon has about 70 Bushells of Potatoes, this Year on about 1/4 of an Acre of Ground.

Trees of several sorts considered. The wild Cherry Tree. Bears a Fruit of some Value. The Wood is very good for the Cabinet-Maker, and is not bad to burn. It is a tree of much Beauty. Its leaves and Bark are handsome, and its shape.—The Locust, good Timber, fattening to soil, by its Leaves, Blossoms &c. Good Wood, quick growth, &c.—The

Larch Tree. There is but one in the Country, that in the Lieutenant Governors Yard at Milton. It looks somewhat like an Evergreen but is not. Sheds its Leaves.

I read in Thompsons Travels, in Turkey in Asia, mention of a Turpentine called by the Name of the Turpentine of Venice, which is not the Produce of Venice but of Dauphinè, and flows from the Larch Tree. It is thick and balsamic and used in several Arts, particularly that of Enameling.

[1] On the legend from which the neck of land still known as Squantum (forming the eastern shore of the mouth of the Neponset River) was supposed to have derived its name, see Pattee, *Old Braintree and Quincy*, p. 20, note.

OCTR. 23RD. 1762.

At my Swamp. Saw several Ginger Bushes. They Grow in Bunches like Willows and Alders, in low Grounds, between Upland and Meadows. They grow Eight feet high, and about an Inch thro at the Butt. They have Bark of a dark Colour, speckled over with little, white rough Spots, near the Ends of the Bows [Boughs] they branch out into a Multitude of little Sprigs. The Bush I saw had shed all its Leaves. All over the Branches and sprigs, are little fresh Buds at this season. It has a spicy Taste. The Spriggs and Buds and Bark have a spicy Taste.

Tirrell has cleared away all the Trees and Bushes, Willows, Alders, Arrow Wood, Dog Wood, Briars, Grape Vines, Elms, Ashes, Oaks, Birches, &c. that grew upon the Brook and burned them.

OCTR. 24TH. 1762.

Before [sun]rise. My Thoughts have taken a sudden Turn to Husbandry.[1] Have contracted with Jo. T[irrell?] to clear my swamp and to build me a long string of stone Wall, and with Isaac [Tirrell?] to build me 16 Rods more and with Jo Field to build me 6 Rods more. And my Thoughts are running continually from the orchard to the Pasture and from thence to the swamp, and thence to the House and Barn and Land adjoining. Sometimes I am at the orchard Ploughing up Acre after Acre and Planting, pruning Apple Trees, mending Fences, carting Dung. Sometimes in the Pasture, digging stones, clearing Bushes, Pruning Trees, building Wall to redeem Posts and Rails, and sometimes removing Button Trees down to my House. Sometimes I am at the old swamp, burning Bushes, digging stumps and Roots, cutting Ditches, across the Meadow, and against my Uncle, and am sometimes at the other End of the Town, buying Posts and Rails, to

Fence against my Uncle and against the Brook, and am sometimes Ploughing the Upland, with 6 Yoke of oxen, and planting Corn, Potatoes, &c. and digging up the Meadow and sowing onions, planting cabbages &c. &c.

Sometimes I am at the Homestead running Cross Fences, and planting Potatoes by the Acre, and Corn by the two Acres, and running a Ditch along the Line between me and Field, and a Fence along the Brook [against] my Brother and another Ditch in the Middle from Fields Line to the Meadow. Sometimes am Carting Gravel from the Neighboring Hills, and sometimes Dust from the streets upon the fresh Meadow. And sometimes plowing, sometimes digging those Meadows, to introduce Clover and other English Grasses.

[1] Deacon John Adams had died 25 May 1761. Under his Will, which was proved 10 July 1761 (copy in Adams Papers, Wills and Deeds), JA received a smaller bequest than his younger brothers because he had been given "a Libberal Education." He did, however, come into possession of substantial property: the cottage occupied by Dr. Savil and now known as the John Quincy Adams Birthplace, a barn, and 10 acres of adjoining land, together with some 30 acres of orchard, pasture, and woodland elsewhere in the town. His brother Peter Boylston inherited the Deacon's homestead (the John Adams Birthplace) and a larger farm, which in 1774 JA consolidated with his own (JA, notes on the copy of his father's Will in Adams Papers). As the present entry suggests, the young farmer's improvements to his property began promptly, and though there were long intervals when public office kept him away from his farm, they ended only with his death.

NOVEMBER 5TH. 1762.

The Cause of Jeffries Town Treasurer of Boston and Sewal and Edwards and several others being suits for the Penalties arising by the Law of the Province for building and covering those Building[s] not with slate nor Tile but with shingles.[1]

Mr. Gridley made a Motion that those Actions should be dismissed because the Judges were all Interested in the Event of them. Two of the Judges vizt. Wells and Foster Hutchinson, being Inhabitants of Boston, and the other two vizt. Eliakim Hutchinson and Watts, having real Estates in that Town, to the Poor of which those Penalties are appropriated. After a long Wrangle, as usual when Trowbridge is in a Case, the Court determined to continue the Action, that Application might be made to the Governor and Council for Special Judges. Wells and Foster declining to set, and Watts too.

The Case of a Witness was mentioned in the Argument. A Witness cannot depose, when he is interested. A Juryman may be challenged who is interested. But Persons belonging to Corporations, are allowed for the Necessity to testify, in Cases where those Corporations are interested. And Jurymen and Judges belonging to this Province sat in the Case of Gray and Paxton, tho interested, for the Necessity.

This Motion Mr. G. said could not be reduced to a Written Plea. He could not plead to the Jurisdiction of the Court. The Court of Common Pleas had undoubted Jurisdiction of the Cause but the Judges could not set because interested. Their Honours were not the Court of Common Pleas but the Justices of the Court of Common Pleas. The Court of Common Pleas was a Body Politic, an invisible system, a frame in the Mind, a fiction of the Law. The President and Fellows of H[arvard] Colledge are not H.C.

The Case in Strange was produced, in which Ld. Raymond went off the Bench, the Parish of Abbots Langley in which his Lordship lived being interested. An order of 2 Justices for the Removal of a Pauper, confined by the Sessions was carried to B.R.[2] by Certiorari.

Authorities from Hobarts and Cokes Rep[orts] were produced, to shew the Tenderness of the Law for this Maxim that a Man shall not be Judge in his own Cause, and that an Act of Parliament vs. natural Equity as that a Man should be judge in his own Cause would be void.

Mem. After the Court had given Judgment Mr. Gridley moved for a Minute of the Reasons of the Judgment. Wells said the Court was not accountable to the Bar for their Reasons. But Otis said the Courts at Home never refused their Reasons for any Judgment when the Bar requested them. Because if the Bar are left ignorant of the Reasons the Court go upon, they will not know how to advise and direct their Clients. And after some Debate, the Clerk was ordered to minute the Reason for the Continuance, which was that three of the Judges apprehended themselves interested and so not a Court competent to try the Cause.

G. contended that if the Court should continue the Causes, they could not refuse setting on the Tryal, because, an Imparlance was a Judicial Act, and so an Assumption of Jurisdiction. F[oster] H[utchinson] said that Dismissing the Actions would be a Judicial Act, as much as Continuing.

[1] From the names of the judges mentioned in the next paragraph it is clear that this case was tried in the Suffolk Inferior Court.

[2] Bancus Regis or King's Bench.

NOVR. 30TH. 1762.

Last Thursday Night, at Cranch's Wedding, Dr. Tufts, in the Room where the Gentlemen were, said We used to have on these Occasions, some good Matrimonial stories, to raise our spirits.[1] The story of B. Bicknal's Wife is a very clever one. She said, when she was married she was very anxious, she feared, she trembled, she could not go to Bed. But she recollected she had put her Hand to the Plow and could not look back, so she mustered up her Spirits, committed her soul to G[od] and her Body to B. Bicknal and into Bed she leaped—and in the Morning she was amazed, she could not think for her Life what it was that had scared her so.

P.[2] told a story of Elisha Marsh No. 2. when he was first married.

Q[uere]. The Humanity, The Utility, the Policy, the Piety of the sanguinary Laws against Robbery and Stealing.

[1] Richard Cranch married Mary Smith 25 Nov. 1762.
[2] This could be either Robert Treat Paine or, less likely, Joseph Palmer.

DECR. 28TH. 1762.

Mr. Cranch last fryday night discovered some Instances of his skill at a Bargain. He agreed to give Greenleaf £120 old Ten[or] for his Chaise. The Chaise is old, the Leather damnifyed thro careless Usage, the Wheels almost ruined, the spokes being loose &c., but G. asked that Price and he could not beat him down, he could not ask him to take less, because G. was poor, and it would look like Ungenerosity or Narrowness of Purse to desire it for less. This he was headstrong enough to do, against the Parsons repeated and enforced Advice. But a worse Instance of his Tameness and Credulity happened afterwards. G. offered him his Horse, told him the Horse stood him in £10 L.M.[1] and was an excellent Horse in the Harness tho unpleasant in a saddle. Cranch believed every Word he said, and was so secret about his Bargain, that he would not make it before me, who was then at his House but he must finish it, abroad, without Questioning the Horses Virtues or Abilities, or asking any Questions about the Price. He is to give £50 for the Horse. I would not give £10, for he is dull and lean, and weak, looks meanly and goes worse.—Thus the Man was fairly cheated in Jockey language out of £50, in one Hour. Besides his Buying the Horse was a Piece of ridiculous Foppery, at this Time. He had no Occasion for one. He cannot use one much this Winter, and it will cost him 3 Times so much as that Horse is worth to keep him till spring.

Miserably bubbled by his own Vanity and Credulity.

[1] New England "lawful money," which was worth slightly more than seven times "old tenor" money.

BOSTON. DECR. 30TH.

At Goldthwaits office, spent 1/4 of an Hour with Lt. Govr. Hutchinson. The first thing he said was a Question to Goldthwait, what was the Date of the Earlyest Records of the County Court? Goldthwait answered 1670. His Honor replyed there were County Courts for 40 Years before that—and said he wanted to settle something in his own Mind, concerning the origin and Constitution of the Courts. That Adultery was punished with death, by the first settlers, and many other offences were made capital, that are not now so. That Commissioners were sent over by K[ing] C[harles] in 1665, to enquire into the Constitution of the Colonies, tho their Authority was not owned. Goldthwait said, there were a great many odd Entries. One of a Prosecution of a Man for taking 6d. for an Horse, a Braintree man too, as unjust and unrighteous. His Honor told of a Record of a Woman condemned, for Adultery, because a Man had debauched her when she was drunk, and of another of a Boy imprisoned for a Capital Tryal for some of their trifling capital Crimes, stealing from his Master or something, which Boy was liberated by the Commissioners of 1665.

The story of Prats Death was told. His Honor said it would be a Loss to his family. He was in a fair Way to have raised it. But the New Yorkers will be glad of it.—This to be sure was Familiarity and Affability! But Goldthwait cringed down, and put on the timid, fawning face and Air and Tone.

BRAINTREE FEBY. 1ST. 1763. TUESDAY.[1]

Last Thursday afternoon, rode to Germantown, and there stayed at my friend Cs. till the last Night. Four Nights, and four days. Those 2 families well deserve the Character they hold of friendly, sensible, and Social.[2] The Men, Women and Children, are all sensible and obliging.

Mem. The notable Anecdote of Coll. Josa. Quincy. The Hydrostatical Experiment. And the other of Mrs. Lincoln, equally curious and instructive. The Pinching, and the Sprinkling, &c.

Mem. The other Anecdote of Mr. Erving. He has prophesyed so long, and with so much Confidence that Canada would be restored to the French that, because he begins to see his Predictions will not be fullfilled, he is now straining his Invention for Reasons, why we ought not to hold it. He says, the Restoration of that Province can alone prevent our becoming luxurious, effeminate, inattentive to any Danger and so an easy Prey to an Invader. He was so soundly bantered, the other day in the Council Chamber, that he snatched his Hat and Cloak and went off, in a Passion.

Mem. The other of a Piece sent to Fleet to be printed, upon the Unfitness of Mr. Mauduit to represent this Province, at the british Court, both in Point of Age and Knowledge. He is as that Writer says 70 Years old, an honest Man but avaricious, a Woolen Draper, a mere Cit, so ignorant of Court and public Business, that he knew not where the public offices were, and that he told Mr. Bollan, that he was Agent for New England. He says that all the other Agents laugh at this Province, for employing him. And that all Persons on that Side of the Water are surprized at us. That the Considerations on the present German War, were written by a Person unknown, who hired or persuaded Mr. Mauduitt to father it.[3]

Ob[servation]. The Character of Aunt Nell,[4] exemplified. Mrs. Eunice[5] told us the Catastrophe of two of her Teeth, she broke them out at Table in Company, and to avoid exposing her self, swallowed them.

I spent an Evening at Mrs. Palmers. Mrs. E[uni]c[e] was very sociable, she had the lead all the Evening. Gave us History's of her Journeys with her Brother, to Connecticutt, to Barnstable, Plymouth, Middleborough, Norton, &c. Descriptions of Seats and Roads, and Thicketts, Characters of Persons, of both sexes, and the hospitable offices of strangers, &c., and above all the Tittle, Tattle of the Town of Taunton, what Families Visit, and what not. The little female Miffs, and Bickerings. Dr. McInsters [McKinstrys], McWaters's, Fales, &c. &c.

The Temper and Habits of stale Virginity, are growing upon her. She is talkative. Q[uery], whether envious, sullen and passionate? She is no slanderer. She is tender of Characters and gives Merit its due Praise. The History of her Loves is curious, but not uncommon.

[...] or Di. was a constant feast.[6] Tender feeling, sensible, friendly. A friend. Not an imprudent, not an indelicate, not a disagreeable Word or Action. Prudent, modest, delicate, soft, sensible, obliging, active.

> Where all was full, possessing and possest
> no craving Void left Aching in the Breast.

Books, we read 5 Sermons in Dr. Shirlock [Sherlock], and several Chapters in the Inquiry into the origin of our Ideas of the Sublime and the beautiful.[7] The Chapter upon Sympathy, they all disapprove. The Author says we have a real Pleasure, in the Distresses and Misfortunes of others. Mem. To write a Letter to Sewal or Quincy, or Lowell[8] on the subject of that Chapter.

I employed however, too little of my Time in Reading and in Thinking. I might have spent much more. The Idea of M. de Vattell indeed, scowling and frowning, haunted me.

Q. Do we take Pleasure in the real Distresses of others? What is my Sensation, when I see Captn. Cunningham, laid up, with the Gout, and hear his plaintive Groans? What are the feelings of the Women, at Groanings? What is my feeling when I hear of an honest Mans loosing a ship at Sea? What when I hear [*sentence unfinished*]

[1] First entry in "Paper book No. 9" (our D/JA/9), a stitched gathering of leaves containing a few entries in Feb. 1763, a draft of a newspaper article that could not have been written before late June 1763, and some undated entries. The entries are not in chronological order in the MS.

This booklet contains the only Diary entries surviving for the year 1763. Fragmentary lists of JA's legal cases show that his practice was rapidly expanding, at least in the lower courts, and this year too he began to write with some frequency for the Boston newspapers. His surviving correspondence for 1763 is virtually all with Miss Abigail Smith of Weymouth.

[2] The Cranches and Palmers. Mrs. Palmer was a sister of Richard Cranch.

[3] In April 1762 the House voted to remove William Bollan, who had been Provincial agent in London since 1746 but was disliked by the Otises and others as a Churchman and a son-in-law of former Governor Shirley. He was replaced by Jasper Mauduit, a London woolen merchant and dissenter. Mauduit was dependent on his brother Israel, author of the tract mentioned in the text, for assistance, but their friends in Massachusetts failed to obtain a stipend for Israel as associate agent. The correspondence in *Jasper Mauduit ... 1762–1765* (MHS, *Colls.*, 74 [1918]) makes clear the sentiments and maneuvers of all parties in this petty but complex affair. See also 15 Aug. 1765, below.

[4] Unidentified.

[5] Mistress (Miss) Eunice Paine.

[6] One would like to believe that this refers to Abigail Smith, sister of the recently married Mary (Smith) Cranch. In the letters they exchanged at this time both Abigail and JA used the fanciful name Diana for her. But the preceding initial, which may be "H," cannot be explained.

[7] A *Philosophical Enquiry into the Origin of Our Ideas of the Sublime and Beautiful*, by Edmund Burke, was published anonymously in London, 1757.

[8] John Lowell, Harvard 1760, of Newburyport, trained or still training in the office of Oxenbridge Thacher for the bar; later a member of the Continental Congress and a federal judge.

FEB. 5TH. 1763.

Memorabilia of this Week.

The Bar agreed upon these 4 Rules.

1st. That the Clerk call the Plaintiff, and if any Body answer, except the Plaintiff or some sworn Attorney, his Power be demanded, and no general Power in such Case be admitted.

2dly. That no Attorneys Fee be taxed for the future where the Declaration was not drawn by the Plaintiff himself, or some sworn Attorney.

3dly. That no attendance be taxed, unless the Party attend personally, or by some sworn Attorney.

4. That no Attorney be allowed to Practice here unless sworn in this Court [1] or in the superiour Court.

Mr. Gridley read these Rules to the Court as unexceptionable Regulations, agreed upon by the Bar. Mr. Otis arose and said he had the Credit of the Motion, but he never had moved for any such Rules as these, for they were vs. the Province Law, vs. the Rights of Mankind, and he was amazed that so many wise Heads as that Bar was blessed with could think them practicable, and concluded that he was for one, entirely against them. And said that all schemes to suppress Petty fogger's must rest on the Honor of the Bar. Foster Hutchinson asked why then was the Court troubled with the Motion? Judge Watts said if the Bar was not agreed the Court could do nothing. And at last they determined to consider till April.

Thus with a whiff of Otis's pestilential Breath, was this whole system blown away.

But the Barr was in a great Rage!

Thatcher said to K[ent], A[uchmuty] and me, "whoever votes for him to be any Thing more than a Constable let him be Anathema maranatha. I pamphleteer for him again? No. Ile pamphleteer against him.

K[en]t damned him and said he had been abused by him personally, in such a manner as he never would forgive, unless he made him more satisfaction, than he imagined was in his Power.

Thatcher moved, that in the Cards to be sent to the Judges, the Expression should be "The Bar, exclusively of Mr. Otis, invites," and Auchmuty, Kent, Gridley and I, as well as Thatcher voted for it.

Auchmuty and Fitch were equally warm. They talked about renouncing all Commerce or Connection with him. Gridley talked about treating him dryly and decently.

Auchmuty said, the two Principles of all this were Popularity, and Avarice.

He made the Motion at first to get some of these Under strappers into his service. He could not bear that Q[uincy] and Auch. should have Underworkers and he none. And he objected to the Rules, to save his Popularity, with the Constables, Justices Story and Ruddock &c. and Pettyfoggers of the Town, and with the Pettyfoggers that he uses as Tools and Mirmidons in the House.

Mr. G. said he went off to avoid a Quarell, for he could not bear it. Such Tergiversation, such Trimming, such Behaviour.

K. and Auch. said they had born with his Insolence thinking him honest, tho hot and rash and passionate, but now he appeared to act against his Conscience.

Recipe to make a Patriot [2]

Take of the several Species of Malevolence, as Revenge, Malice, Envy, equal Quantities, of servility, fear, fury, Vanity, Prophaneness, and Ingratitude, equal Quantities, and infuse this Composition into the Brains of an ugly, surly, brutal Mortal and you have the Desideratum.

The Life of Furio.

In Croatia. His Descent. Education, at school, Colledge, at the Bar. Historians relate that he was grossly slandered, by a story of a Bastard on a Negro, his Wrath at Plymouth, at Boston he Heads the Trade, brings Actions, fails, is chosen Representative, quarrells with Governor, Lieutenant [Governor], Council, House, Custom house officers, Gentlemen of the Army, the Bar, retails prosody, writes upon Money, Prov[ince] sloop.

[1] The Suffolk co. Inferior Court of Common Pleas.
[2] It is not clear whether this and the following squib on Otis were composed or merely copied by JA. The second has the appearance of being notes for a satirical piece to be developed more fully.

FEBY. 10TH. 1763.

Belcher v. Hunt. This is an Action of Trover, for converting shingles to Hunts Use. The shingles were cutt upon Land which Jonathan White claims and has possessed for 20 Years.

There is a Question to be determined by the Court previously to the Tryal of his Action, vizt. whether a Title to Land can be given in Evidence, in the Tryal of these Actions of Trover.

Multa conceduntur per Obliquum quæ non conceduntur de directo. 6. Rep. 47. Debitum et Contractus sunt nullius Loci. 2. Inst. 231.

FEBY. 11TH. 1763.

Probate of Mr. Edwards's Will, Coram Governor and Council. John Edwards, one of the Heirs at Law of Samuel Edwards, appealed from the Decree of the Judge of Probate, 1st. because said Saml. at the Execution of said Writing and long after was not, nor for a long time before had been of a sound and disposing Mind and Memory, but was non Compos.

Quære. What is an Insanity, in Law? that disqualifies to make testament? and whether Saml. Edwards was so insane. Woods Inst. Page 336. Those who have not a sound, perfect and disposing Memory, for it is not sufficient that the Testator hath a Memory. 6. Rep. 23. Lunaticks in their Lucid Intervals may.

Dissertation on the word "perfect." A perfect Memory exists not —i.e. a Memory retentive of every Idea that ever was in the Mind. Nor is the Man who has the strongest Memory always the fittest to make a Will. For the observation is very common that Men of the strongest Memories have not always the soundest Judgments. The Memory of Xerxes or of Cæsar is not necessary to make a Will.

2nd. of James.

Our Case. I promise to pay A or order. I have paid A. and now I must pay the order too.[1]

[1] At this point in the MS appears the draft of JA's essay, signed "U.," which was printed in the *Boston Gazette*, 18 July 1763. The draft is printed below under that date, following the other entries in this booklet, all of which were undoubtedly written earlier than the essay even in its draft form.

BOSTON FEBY. 1763.

This day learned that the Caucas Clubb meets at certain Times in the Garret of Tom Daws, the Adjutant of the Boston Regiment.[1] He has a large House, and he has a moveable Partition in his Garrett, which he takes down and the whole Clubb meets in one Room. There they smoke tobacco till you cannot see from one End of the Garrett to the other. There they drink Phlip I suppose, and there they choose a Moderator, who puts Questions to the Vote regularly, and select Men, Assessors, Collectors, Wardens, Fire Wards, and Representatives are Regularly chosen before they are chosen in the Town. Uncle Fairfield,[2] Story, Ruddock, Adams,[3] Cooper, and a rudis indigestaque Moles of others are Members. They send Committees to wait on the Merchants Clubb and to propose, and join, in the Choice of Men and Measures. Captn. Cunningham[4] says they have often solicited him to go to these Caucas, they have assured him Benefit in his Business, &c.[5]

Propr[ietor]s of Wrentham v. [Metcalf.] [6]
2 Levinz. Scroaggs [Scroggs] C.J. It ought not to be a general Rule, that Members of Corporations shall or shall not be a Witness. But where the Int[erest] is inconsiderable they may.

Thatcher. It is a Rule that the Heir apparent shall not tho a Rem[ainde]r man shall be admitted because the last has no present Interest. A Guardian shall not be a Witness in Cause for his Ward because he is Party to the suit.

Auch[*muty*]. Proprs. Worcester v. Gates, the Inhabitants of Worcester were Admitted on Argument.

[1] Thomas Dawes, a bricklayer and militia officer, lived in Purchase Street, which ran eastwardly off Sumner close to the South End wharves (Thwing Cat.). This was therefore the South End "caucus"; see note 5, below.

[2] Presumably a relative of Samuel Adams, whose mother was born Mary Fyfield—a name spelled in a great variety of ways. JA frequently used "Uncle" or "Aunt" for an older person vaguely related to himself.

[3] This is the first mention in the Diary of Samuel Adams the politician, with whom JA was to be closely associated for a dozen or fifteen years to come despite sharp temperamental differences between the two men. JA and Sam Adams had the same great-grandfather, the 1st Joseph Adams of Braintree, son of Henry Adams the immigrant. Sam Adams' grandfather was John, a younger brother of JA's grandfather, the 2d Joseph of Braintree (Bartlett, *Henry Adams of Somersetshire*, p. 58).

[4] James Cunningham, glazier and militia officer; his wife was JA's Aunt Elizabeth (Boylston) Cunningham (*NEHGR*, 7 [1853]:147, 149; scattered Cunningham papers in MHi).

[5] The foregoing description, though only hearsay, is so vivid as to have become famous. According to William Gordon, writing before 1788, the Boston "caucuses" had been long established by 1763. "More than fifty years ago, Mr. Samuel Adams's father, and twenty others, one or two from the north end of the town, where all the ship business is carried on, used to meet, make a caucus, and lay their plan for introducing certain persons into places of trust and power. When they had settled it, they separated, and used each their particular influence within his own circle" by distributing ballots for the candidates agreed upon, &c. (*The History of the Rise, Progress, and Establishment of the Independence of the United States of America*, London, 1788, 1:365, note). Thus Sam Adams in some measure inherited his influence in these local political associations, the equivalent of ward clubs today, and at the time this Diary entry was written he was beginning to use that influence to fan the sparks of protest against royal authority into what became organized rebellion. The best account of the Boston caucuses, which were soon to emerge as the Sons of Liberty, is in Esther Forbes, *Paul Revere*, p. 119 ff.; see also John C. Miller, *Sam Adams, Pioneer in Propaganda*, Boston, 1936, *passim*. More detailed study of their membership and activities is still needed.

Elsewhere in the note cited above, William Gordon remarked that the terms *caucus* and *caucusing* were commonly used in Boston, "but my repeated applications to different gentlemen have not furnished me with a satisfactory account of [their] origin." There is still no satisfactory account though numerous explanations have been proposed. John Pickering, who compiled the first collection of Americanisms, suggested that since the meetings Gordon described were held where "*ship-business* [was] carried on," the word caucus "might be a corruption of *Caulkers*, the word meetings being understood," and he found that this was a common opinion in Boston and Salem (*A Vocabulary, or Collection of Words and Phrases . . . Peculiar to the United States of America*, Boston, 1816, p. 57). Whether correct or not, Pickering's explanation is certainly more plausible than that preferred by the latest authority, the *Dictionary of Americanisms*, namely that caucus derives from medieval Latin *caucus*, after Greek *kaukos*, a drinking vessel.

The early spellings of the word render this learned explanation extremely doubtful. Before Gordon's *History* no example spelled in the form that became standard in the 19th century has been found. Both the *Dictionary of Americanisms* and the earlier *Dictionary of American English* cite the form "West-Corcus in Boston" from the *Boston Evening Post*, suppl., 19 Aug. 1745, but the former authority rather surprisingly considers it probably "without significance." To the contrary, it would seem to be very significant, since a little later the caucus clubs were closely associated with districts of the town. The next recorded use is in a letter from Oxenbridge Thacher in Boston to Benjamin Prat in New York, without date but certainly written in 1762: "we daily see many of your predictions accomplished respecting the connections and discords of our politicians, corkusmen, plebeian tribunes, &ca., &ca." (MHS, *Procs.*, 1st ser., 20 [1882–1883]:48). In the present double use by JA both spellings are clearly "Caucas" in the MS, though "corrected" by CFA in printing the Diary. Two other early examples are worth citing. In the satirical song on James Otis entitled "Jemmibullero," published in the *Boston Evening Post*, 13 May 1765, this line appears: "And Jemmy's in the CAU-

CAS, and Jemmy's in the REPS." In a letter to James Warren, 22 Dec. 1773, JA wrote: "Yesterday, the Governor called a Council at Cambridge. Eight Members met at Brattles. This no doubt was concerted last Saturday, at Neponsit Hill [Governor Hutchinson's residence in Milton], where Brattle and Russell dined, by Way of Caucass I suppose" (MHi: Warren-Adams Coll.). In the only text of this letter by JA that has been published, the spelling is regularized to "caucus" (JA, *Works*, 9:334).

⁰ Defendant's name omitted in MS, but this case, an action of ejectment in Suffolk Superior Court, Feb. term, 1763, is reported more fully in Quincy, *Reports*, p. 36–37.

FEB.

This Action of Trover is an Innovation, one of the new and subtle Inventions in Derogation of the Common Law, that my Lord Coke has treated with so much righteous severity. It is in its Effects and Consequences subversive of all real Actions. It will destroy one of the strongest securities of our landed Property, the Rule that all real Titles[1] shall be tryed in the County where the Land lies. That it may be employed as an Instrument of endless Vexation to the poor People who live in distant Counties, who has the Honor of being the first Inventor I know not, but I hope your Honors will crush it as the illegitimate Production of a wanton Hour.[2]

It is true that, an incidental Question about a local Matter, may [be] decided, in the Tryal of a transitory Action—and it is equally true that, [a] Question may be tryed incidentally, by a Court that has no direct and original Jurisdiction of that Question. Multa conceduntur, per obliquum quæ non conceduntur de directo. But this is never suffered but in Cases of Necessity—where Justice cannot be done without it. And This Necessity seems to have been the sole Foundation of my Ld. Holts Opinion in the Case of Brown and Hedges. His Opinion was that an Incidental Question about the Title of Land should not bar the Plaintiff, because if it should, a Man might commit Wastes and Trespasses in Ireland, then take his flight to England and Escape Justice, for no Proscess from any Court in Ireland could run into England: Remedy must be sought in England or no where. But in these Cases there is no such Necessity. Actions may be brought in the County where the Lands lie, with the same Ease, and with much better Probability of fair and just Decision than out of them.

Dream of Mr. Pratt. He was seated on a Rock, in the Middle of the Sea, and reflecting on his Journey to N. York,[3] leaving his family &c., when the Clouds began to rise from all Quarters of the Horison, and soon thickened and blackened over his Head. The Thunders began to roar And the Lightnings to flash. At last, the Clouds opened and a glorious Luminary, in the shape of an Angel, made its Appearance and addressed Mr. Prat in these Lines

> Why mourns the Bard? Apollo bids thee rise,
> renounce the Dust, and Claim [thy] native skies.

Minutes of Dr. Marshes Testimony.

I was sent for. Mr. Edwards knew me, asked after my Health, and called me by my Name.

Afterward he gave me, by Word of Mouth the Minute of his Will. He said he intended to give his Wife, the Improvement of his whole Estate during Life. The Thought it seems came into his Mind of giving her the Improvement during her Widowhood, or while she remained his Widow and bore his Name, but that Thought he had Memory and Judgment enough to disapprove, and ordered it be given her for Life.

And after his Wifes Decease, he ordered his Estate to be divided equally between his own and his Wifes nearest Relatives.

And when he was asked, who he intended to make his Executors, he replyed you two, looking to his Brother Edwards and his Wifes Brother Smith who were then present.

The Degrees of Insanity, are infinite from the wildest symptoms of fury, when nothing but Chains can withold the Patient from doing Violence to himself or others, down to some fits of Passion, or some irrational Pangs of Affection. There is perhaps, in every human Mind, in some appearance or another, some Spice or Degree of Madness. The Hero that murders millions to sate his Revenge or Ambition, may surely by the soundest Understanding be denominated a Madman. Yet Alexander, or Charles of Sweeden had no doubt, a sufficient soundness of Mind to dispose of an Estate by Will. Nor can a perfect Memory be demanded. A perfect Memory cannot be believed to exist. Even Xerxes and Cæsar, who remembered every face and Name in their Armies, had not perfect Memories.

241

Swift v. Vose.

Hobarts Reports, 134. Weaver * and Ward. Skirmishing. No Justification only Excuse, unless Utterly without fault or Negligence.

1. Strange, 596. Underwood v. Hewson. Defendant was uncocking a Gun, and the Plaintiff was standing to see it, it went off and wounded him, and at the Tryal it was held might maintain Trespass. *Thatcher.—*

* Lords of Council's order to skirmish.

Tilt Turnament. Masters of Defence &c.

Mem. Case of Ideot, Lunatick &c. answerable in Trespass tho not criminal.

Affectation runs thro the whole Man. His Air, his Gate, his Tone, his Gestures, his Pronunciation. There is no Steadiness of Eye or Feature.

Fitch's Countenance is not Steady. He has a look of Jealousy, and of Diffidence. He has a look of Conceit, affectation, Suspicion, and Diffidence. His swell. His Puff. Gridley has a stedy and fixed face. His face is expressive. When he smiles, his whole face is lighted up. His Lips do not shew a smile when his Brows are frounding, and his Eye complaining. The Brow, the Eye, the Lips and the Voice all alike affected together.

Trowbridge. Oh says Mr. G. They object and say a ——. The officer he informs—why In that Case—redendo singula singulis.—Well —now—

To all young gent[lemen] between [10] and [20]—[4]

Many of the great sages, Phylosophers and statesmen, ancient and modern, have thought that the most effectual Exertion of their Talent Indulgence of the Benevolence for Mankind was by contriving and recommending to youth, Plans of Education and study, to train them early to right Habits of Thinking and of Acting, both for their own private Happiness as well as for the Tranquility, Wealth, Grandeur and Glory of their Country. I who have as much Benevolence, as any Sage, whatever, and Talents enough to advize my own young Countrymen, beg leave to advize them, (lest any one should suffer for want of such Advice tho I must own it is generally well understood that they by all Means, avoid every Appearance of Regard to any of those Properties, formerly respected under the Name of Wit, Humour, sense, Learning, Temperance, Justice, Industry,[5]

The Cyropedia of Xenophon, and the Treatises of Milton and

Lock upon Education, tho they might, (Longitude and Latitude considered) be well enough, are yet manifestly useless, at this Time and in this Place. There is it must be confessed, a natural faculty in the human mind (whether it sprang from the Protoplast or any other source I leave to Metaphysitians), that distinguishes between true and false, fair and foul, Virtue and Vice &c.–Now the great Aim of the abovementioned Writers on Education was to cultivate this faculty into the most delicate and exquisite Discernment: But believe me, This faculty is become in the Revolution of human Things not only useless, but destructive: believe me, the young man who is silly and obstinate enough to see and to say he sees, one spark of Parts or Virtues in Bluster and his followers e.g. shall with all the Benefactors to a man, be pronounced both a fool and a Knave: shall be opposed and abused on all occasions: e. contra if he sees, and says he sees, one fault, folly, Rashness, Indiscretion, Vice &c. in the same Persons or their Conduct, they and theirs will pronounce the same heavy sentence upon him. It is exactly so with the other side–if you have not a thourough Contempt for the Head and Detestation of the Heart of Bluster and all his followers, you are at once a seditious fellow, have no sense or Probity at all.[6]

So that the 1st Principle in Prov[incial] Education is to extinguish, stiffle, this most useless, troublesome, pernicious faculty, called the moral sense, [and] cultivate a total and absolute Indifference to Virtue and to Vice: In spight of natural Aversions press to your Bosom, with unbounded Confidence and Affection, the man who is of your side, after you have chosen any side, tho he may be prostitute and abandoned, destitute of every natural or moral Excellence.

Edwards's Will.
Godolphins orphans Legacy. Part 1. C. 8. Page 23.[7]

2. Such as are Mad Persons can make no Testament during the time of their Insanity of Mind, no not so much as ad Pios Usus. Nay the Testament made at such a Time shall not be good, tho afterward the Party recover his former Understanding; howbeit, if such Lunatick Persons have any Lucida Intervalla, or Intermissions then during the Time of such Freedom from the Lunacy they may make their Testaments betwixt the fitts. And here note, that every Person is presumed to be of perfect Mind and Memory, untill the Contrary be proved. So that he that objecteth Insanity of Mind, must prove the same, for which [*quotation breaks off thus in MS*]
C. 21.

Same Page 65. But regularly by the Laws and Customs of England, two Witnesses, without Exception, are requisite for the due Proof of a Testament and two are sufficient.

Swinbourne 77th. Page 78. Unless the Testator were besides himself but for a short Time and in some Peculiar Actions and not continually for a long space as for a Month or More, &c.

78. It is a hard and difficult Point to prove a Man not to have the Use or Understanding of Reason. And therefore, it is not sufficient for the Witnesses to depose that the Testator was mad or besides his Wits: unless they render a sufficient Reason to prove this their Deposition as that they did see him do such Things or heard him speak such Words as a Man having Reason would not have done or spoken.

78. lower down. If some Witnesses do depose that the Testator was of perfect Mind and Memory and others depose the Contrary, their Testimony is to be preferred which depose that he was of sound Memory, as well for that their Testimony tendeth to the favour And Validity of the Testament, as for that the same is more agreable to the Disposition of Nature, for every man is a Creature reasonable.

79. But if in the Testament there be Mixture of Wisdom and Folly it is to be presumed that the same was made during the Testators Frensy, insomuch that if there be but one Word sounding to Folly, it is presumed that the Testator was not of sound Mind.

Godolphin. Page 24. For it is a very tender and difficult Point to prove a Man not to have the Use of his Reason and Understanding; therefore it is not sufficient for the Witnesses to depose that the Person was mad, unless they render upon Knowledge a sufficient Reason therefor. Neither is one Witness sufficient to prove a Man mad, nor two in Case the one depose of the Testators Madness at one Time and the other of his Madness at another.

But in Contrary Depositions, those Witnesses are to be preferred, which depose that the Testator was of sound Memory: And if he Used to have Intervals of Reason and it be not certainly known, whether the Testament were made in or out of his fits of Lunacy; if no Argument of frenzy or folly can be collected by the Testament, it shall be presumed to be made during the Intermissions of the Lunacy, and so adjudged to be good.

One foolish Word may frustrate the Validity of the whole.

But if a Man who is of good and perfect Memory maketh his Will, and afterwards by the Visitation of God, he becomes of Unsound

Memory (as every Man is for the most Part, before his death) this Act of God shall not be a Revocation.

Dr. Groenvelt v. Dr. Burrell &c. Ld. Ray[mond] 252.

The Judge will not permit him to have a Copy of the Record if there was probable Cause of the Indictment.

There must be Evidence of express Rancour and Malice, for Innocence is not sufficient where it contains scandal or the Party has been imprisoned.

To be of sound and perfect Memory, is to have a reasonable Memory and Understanding to dispose of his Estate with Reason. 25.[8]

The Testators mind is the Testaments chief Essential.

Regularly, the Law will presume every man to be of sound Mind and Memory, and will cast the Onus Probandi on him who asserts the Contrary; which is but consonant to the Presumption of Nature itself.

[1] MS: "Tiller"—a curious inadvertence.

[2] The foregoing notes, like those in the following paragraph, evidently relate to the case of Gardiner *v.* Purrington, in Suffolk Superior Court, Feb. term, 1763; see Quincy, *Reports*, p. 59–62. The single other case that has been dated among the further detached legal notes below, that of Swift *v.* Vose, was settled in the same session of the same court (Superior Court of Judicature, Minute Book 79). These circumstances would seem to warrant dating this whole series of legal notes as Feb.–March 1763.

[3] Benjamin Prat was appointed chief justice of New York in March 1761; JA describes in his Autobiography how the members of the bar "waited on" Prat to Dedham when he left for his new post.

[4] Fragmentary draft of an essay intended for publication; no printing has been found. The figures in the salutation are illegible and have been guessed at; they are possibly "20" and "30." The first sentence, though much rewritten, is still defective.

[5] Sentence breaks off thus in the MS, and a short interval of space follows, but the ensuing paragraphs appear to belong to the same draft.

[6] The dash has been inserted in this sentence to clarify it.

[7] JA's own copies of the works cited here and below in connection with the Edwards will case are among his books in the Boston Public Library: John Godolphin, *The Orphan's Legacy: or, A Testamentary Abridgement . . .*, 4th edn., London, 1701; Henry Swinburne, *A Treatise of Testaments and Last Wills*, 5th edn., London, 1728.

[8] Here and in the following paragraphs JA is again quoting from Godolphin's *Orphan's Legacy.*

[DRAFT OF AN ESSAY ON AGRICULTURE IN THE *Boston Gazette*, 18 JULY 1763.] [1]

Among the Votaries of Science, and the numerous Competitors for Fame and Estimation, Utility seems to have been remarkably neglected. The Utmost subtlety of Wit, and all the labours of pertinacious Industry have been employed by Mathematicians to demonstrate little, unimportant Geometrical Niceties, or in searching for Demonstrations of other Propositions, which there is not the least Probability will ever be found. Philosophers have employed the Advantages of great Genius, Learning, Leisure, and Expense, in examining and displaying before the World, the formation of Shells, and Pebbles, and Insects, in which Mankind are no more interested, than they would be in a laborious Disquisition into or sage Conjectures about the Number of sands in the Moon or of Particles in the solar system. Many learned Pens are employed, much Time spent and much Mischeif and Malevolence occasioned, by Divines about Predestination, [the] Original of Evil, and other abstruse subjects, that having been to no good Purpose under learned Examination so many Centuries may by this Time be well enough concluded unfathomable by the human Line.

But all this while, Agriculture, the Nursing Mother of every Art, Science, Trade and Profession in civilized society, has been most ungratefully despized. It has been too much so in Europe, but infinitely more so in America, and perhaps not the least so in the Massachusetts Bay.

With Advantages of Soil, and Climate, that few Countries under Heaven can presume to boast, will any intelligent Person believe, we do not raise our own Bread? Capable as we are of making easily and at a very small Expence many very wholesome, palatable, and delicate Liquors, will it be believed that we send abroad every Year, at a very great Expence, for others that are unwholesome, disagreable and indelicate?

When it is in our Power, without any Difficulty, to raise many other Commodities, enough not only for our own Consumption, but for Exportation, will it be credited without surprize, that we send every Year, allmost the whole Globe over, to import such Commodities for our own Use?

Yet all these Facts, incredible as they would seem to some worthy People, are indisputably true. But it cannot long continue to be true. The sources of our Wealth are dried away. And unless we seek for Resources, from Improvements in our Agriculture and an Augmentation of our Commerce, we must forego the Pleasure of Delicacies and ornaments, if not the Comfort of real Necessaries, both in Diet and Apparell.

The Intention of this Paper then is to intreat my worthy Countrymen who have any Advantages of Leisure, Education, or Fortune to amuse themselves, at convenient opportunities, with the study, and the Practice too, of Husbandry. Nor let the narrow Circumstances of others who have Power to think and Act, discourage them from exerting their talents in the same Way, for

> haud facile emergunt, Quorum Virtutibus, obstat
> Res angusta Domi—

with all its Truth and Pathos, has done more Mischief in the World by soothing the Pride and Indolence of Genius, than it ever did good, by prompting the rich and Powerfull to seek the solitary Haunts of Merit to amplify its sphere.

In making Experiments, upon the Varieties of soils, and Manures, Grains and Grasses, Trees, and Bushes, and in your Enquiries into the Course and operation of Nature in the Production of these, you will find as much Employment for your Ingenuity, and as high a Gratification to a good Taste, as in any Business or Amusement you can chuse to pursue. The finest Productions of the Poet or the Painter, the statuary or the Architect, when they stand in Competition with the great and beautiful operations of Nature, in the Animal and Vegetable World, must be pronounced mean and despicable Baubles. The Mathematician, the Philosopher, the Chymist, and the Poet may here improve every Branch of their favorite sciences to the Advancement of their Health, the Increase of their Fortunes, and the Benefit of their Country.

But if I might descend without Presumption or offence to Particulars, I would recommend both the Theory and Practice of Husbandry, to Divines and Physicians, more than to any other orders.[2] For the former having more Leisure and better opportunities for study than any Men, will find this an agreable Relaxation from the arduous Labours of their Profession, an excellent Exercise for the Preservation of their Health, a means of supplying their families, with many Necessaries, at a trifling Expence that might otherwise cost them dear; and an excellent Example of Ingenuity, and Industry, removing many Temptations of Vice and Folly to the People under their Charge. Besides that their Acquaintance with the sciences subservient to Husbandry, will give them great Advantages, and in the Prosecution of such Enquiries, they will find their sentiments Exalted, their Ideas of divine Attributes displayed in the scenes of Nature, improved, and their Adoration of the great Creator and his Providence increased.

Physicians have many Advantages not only of the World in general, but of other liberal Professions. The Principles of those sciences which subserve more immediately their peculiar occupation are at the same Time the Foundation of all real [and] rational Improvements in Husbandry. Necessitated as they are to much Travel and frequent Conversations, with many sorts of People, they might, for their own Amusement and Diversion, remark the Appearances of Nature, and store their Minds with many useful observations, which they might communicate among their Patients, without the least loss of Time or Interruption to the Duties of their Profession.

These observations were occasioned by a late Piece in your Paper, signed H.P.[3]—Who was the Author of that Piece, what were his Intentions, in Writing, whether to do good or to do Evil, and why he chose that manner of conveying his Thoughts to the public, it concerns not me to enquire. His professed design is not only good but important. There is no subject, less understood, or less considered perhaps, by Men in general, in this Province, even of the liberal Professions, than the Theory of Agriculture. And the Writer, who should direct with success the Attention of inquisitive Minds, to that Branch of Learning, whether he intended to befriend the public or to blow it into flames, would certainly be the Occasion of much public Utility.

The particular subject which that Writer has chosen to recommend to the Consideration of the Province, promises, more fairly than any other, private Profit to the farmer and the Merchant, public Benefit to the Province, or perhaps Provinces in general, as well as to Great Britain, the Parent and the Protector of them all; whose society of Arts and &c. have discovered their kind concern for us, as well as their wise Care for their native Country, by offering Præmiums and Encouragements, for the Raising of this Commodity in New England as well as many other Ways. It is said that, "a Thousand Weight to an Acre is an ordinary Crop of Hemp." And it has been said too, by good authority, that "an Acre of Land well tilled will produce a Tun Weight" and that "a Tun of it, is worth sixty Pounds lawful Money." It is said also that "several hundred Thousand Pounds worth of foreign Hemp, are yearly expended in New England." And it is said too, that "Hemp may be raised on dreigned Lands," and that "if we can raise more than to supply our own Occasions we may send it Home."

It was not without good sense, then that Mr. Plough Jogger undertook to recommend this Plant to the Enquiries of the Curious, the Tryal of Husbandmen, the Encouragement of Statesmen and the Industry of the Laborious.

Give me Leave therefore to do myself the Honour, to claim the Merit with my Countrymen and their Posterity, of seconding without the least sneer or Banter, Mr. Ploughjogger, in his Attempt to introduce and recommend this subject so important to the Consideration and Industry of my fellow Countrymen, the Inhabitants of New England in General, and of this Province in Particular.

Hemp is a Plant of great Importance in the Arts and Manufactories, as it furnishes a great Variety of Threads, Cloths, and Cordage. It bears the nearest Resemblance and Analogy, to Flax, in its Nature, the Manner of its Cultivation, and the Purposes to which it serves. It must be annually sown afresh. It arises, in a little space of Time, into a tall, slim, shrub, with an hollow stem. It bears a small round seed, filled with a solid Pulp. Its Bark is a Tissue of Fibres, joined together with a soft substance, which easily rots it. There are two Kinds of Hemp, Male and Female. The Male only bears the seed, and from that seed arises both Male and Female.

The seed should be sown in the Month of May, in a warm, sandy, rich soil. They begin to gather it about [the first of *August*,] [4] the female being soonest Ripe. The Proofs of its Ripeness, are the alteration of the Colour of its leaves to Yellow, and its stalks to white. It must be pulled up by the Roots, and then bound in Bundles. The Male should stand 8 or 10 days in the Air, that the seed may ripen, which they afterwards get out, by cutting off the Heads and threshing or beating them. It must then be watered by laying it about a Week in a Pond, in order not to rot the Bark. I say a Pond, tho a Brook would be better if it did not give the Water an unwholesome Quality. After it is taken out and dryed the woody Part of the stem must be broken from the Bark which covers it, by crushing it in an Instrument called a Brake, beginning at the Roots. After it has been sufficiently broken, the small shivers must be swingled out, as we swingle Flax. When this is done it must be beat on a Block or in a Trough, with an Hammer or with Beetles, till it becomes soft and Pliable. When it has been well beaten, it must be heckled, or passed thro a toothed Instrument, like the Clothiers Comb, to seperate the shorter Tow, from that which is fit to be spun.

This is a very short Answer to Mr. Plough Joggers Inquiries, but if he or any other Person has a Curiosity to see a more particular Account of this Plant, (and give me leave to tell him and them there is not an Herb from the Cedar in Lebanon, to the Hyssop in the Wall, that can be studied to more Advantage) let them consult the Compleat Body of Husbandry, Chambers's Dictionary, the Præceptor and Nature delineated.

To conclude Let the World in general consider, that the Earth, and the seas and the Air, are to furnish all Animals, with food and Raiment; that mere animal strength, which is common to Beasts and Men, is not sufficient to avail us of any considerable Part of the bountiful Provision of Nature; that our Understandings, as well as our Arms and feet, must be employed in this service. And Let the few who have been distinguished by greater intellectual Abilities than Mankind in general, consider, that Nature intended them for Leaders of Industry. Let them be cautious of certain Airs of Wisdom and superiority by which some Gentlemen of real sense and Learning, and Public spirit, giving offence to the common People, have in some Measure defeated their own benevolent Intentions. Let them not be too sparing of their Application or Expence, lest failing of visible Profit and success they expose themselves to Ridicule and rational Husbandry itself to Disgrace among the common People. Human Nature is not so stupid or so abandoned, as many worthy men imagine, and even the common People, if their peculiar Customs and Modes of thinking are a little studied, [are not] so ungrateful, or untractible, but that their Labours may be conducted, by the Genius and Experience of a few, to very great and useful Purposes.   U.

¹ This draft appears in the middle of D/JA/9, between entries dated in Feb. 1763, but it could not have been written before late June since it was evoked by a piece signed "Humphrey Ploughjogger" in the *Boston Evening Post*, 20 June 1763. There is the strongest ground for believing that JA himself wrote this and the other Ploughjogger pieces that appeared in that paper this year, namely his own testimony, and that, accordingly, he was carrying on a dialogue with himself in the two leading Boston papers (though the draft itself shows that he first intended the present essay for the *Evening Post* rather than the *Boston Gazette*, where it eventually appeared). The question of his authorship of Ploughjogger's mildly facetious essays, all of them written in rustic dialect and phonetic spelling anticipating the school of Artemus Ward, cannot and need not be gone into here, but see JA to CA, 13 Feb. 1792 (MHi), and also a list of JA's writings compiled by his nephew William Smith Shaw, in the CFA Miscellany (Adams Papers, Microfilms, Reel No. 327).

The draft as it stands in the Diary is very rough and has a number of additions at the end, some of them keyed into the text by asterisks and some not. It could hardly have been rationalized at all if a printed text had not been found which shows the order of the material as JA finally wished it. The present text follows that final order, but only a few of the many differences in phrasing between the draft and the newspaper version have been noted.

² In the newspaper text JA added at this point: "without enquiring into the Truth of the Observation, that the Lawyers among us, are the most curious in Husbandry, which, if true, is unnatural and accidental."

³ The newspaper text reads, instead: "These Reflections have been occasion'd, by a late Piece in the *Evening-Post*, signed *Humphrey Ploughjogger*." The piece referred to appeared in the issue of 20 June and begins: "I arnt book larnt enuff, to rite so polytly, as the great gentlefolks, that rite in the News-Papers, about Pollyticks. I think it is pitty, they should know how to rite so well, saving they made better use ont. And that they might do, if they would rite about some-

thing else." Ploughjogger then suggests a fresh topic. "What I'me ater is, to get some great larnt gentleman, who has been to Old Ingland, and knows how they raise Hemp there, and can read books about it, and understand um, to print in your News, some direckshon, about it, that we may go to trying, for we cant afford to run venters, by working, may be, a month and then have nothing come of it for want of working right."

[4] Bracketed words supplied from the newspaper text for a blank in MS.

SODALITAS, A CLUBB OF FRIENDS.[1]

1765. JANY. 24TH. THURSDAY.[2]

Soon after I got to Boston, at Jany. Court Mr. Fitch came to me upon Change, and told me, that Mr. Gridley and he had something to communicate to me, that I should like, in Sacred Confidence however. I waited on Mr. Gridley, at his office, (after many Conjectures what the secret might be) and he told me, That He and Mr. Fitch had proposed a Law Clubb—a private Association, for the study of Law and oratory.—As to the Bar, he thought of them, as he did think of them— Otis, Thatcher, Auchmuty. He was considering, who was for the future to support the Honour and Dignity of the Bar. And he was determined to bring me into Practice, the first Practice, and Fitch too. He could easily do it, by recommending. And he was very desirous of forming a Junto, a small sodality, of himself and Fitch and me, and Dudley[3] if he pleased might come, in order to read in Concert the Feudal Law and Tullies orations. And for this Purpose he lent me, the Corpus Juris Civilis in 4 Partes distinctum, eruditissimis Dionysii Gothofredi J.C. clarissimi notis illustratum, at the End of which are the Feudorum Consuetudines Partim ex Editione vulgata partim ex Cujaciana vulgata, appositæ, as also the Epitome Feudorum Dionysio Gothofredo Authore.[4]

We accordingly agreed to meet the next Evening in one of Ballards back Chambers and determine upon Times, Places, and studies. We accordingly met the next Evening, Mr. Gridley, Fitch and I, and spent the whole Evening. Proposals were to read a Reign and the statutes of that Reign, to read Hurds Dialogues[5] and any new Pieces. But at last we determined to read The Feudal Law and Cicero only, least we should loose sight of our main Object, by attending to too many. Thursday Nights were agreed on, and to meet first at Mr. Gridleys office. There we accordingly met on the Thursday Night following, and suffered our Conversation to ramble upon Hurds Dialogues, the Pandects, their Discovery in Italy by Lotharius in 1127, in the Reign of Stephen, upon Lambard de priscis Anglorum Legibus, in Saxon and Latin, upon Ld. Kaims [Kames], Mr. Blackstone &c. But we agreed to meet the next Thursday night at Mr. Fitch's, and to read the Three first Titles of the feudal Law, and Tullies oration for Milo.

[1] This heading, written in a very large hand, is on the inside front cover of "Paper book No. 10" (D/JA/10), suggesting that JA planned to keep a separate record of the proceedings of this lawyers' study club. But after a few entries in Jan.-Feb. 1765 and some fragments of a first draft of his essay on canon and feudal law, written for the club, the record breaks off. Very likely the "sodality" itself did. A couple of extraneous entries made in Aug. 1765 follow in D/JA/10, but the last half of this booklet consists of nothing but blank leaves.

For the year 1764 there are no Diary entries at all. Lists of legal cases among his own papers indicate that JA continued to expand his practice; for example, a note from him to Samuel Quincy, 2 Jan. 1764 (MHi:Misc. Bound MSS), lists about forty cases JA wishes Quincy to enter for him in Boston. During the spring of 1764 he served on a town committee to report a plan for repairing the highways by a tax (*Braintree Town Records*, p. 395-398). Most of April and part of May he spent with other patients at his uncle James Cunningham's house in Boston undergoing the somewhat dangerous and extremely tedious process of inoculation against smallpox. His physician was Dr. Nathaniel Perkins, Harvard 1734, and JA's letters during this period probably embody as detailed an account as exists of the preparatory regimen and actual process of smallpox inoculation in the 1760's.

But the great event of 1764 was JA's marriage to Abigail Smith of Weymouth. As early as February they were trying to fix a date; see Hannah (Storer) Green to JA, 20 Feb. 1764 (Samuel Abbott

Green, *An Account of Percival and Ellen Green and Some of Their Descendants*, Groton, Mass., p. 56-57). They were married on 25 October.

[2] This entry appears to be retrospective and should probably have an earlier date. The meeting of the sodality that actually occurred on 24 Jan. is recorded in the following entry, the second so dated.

[3] Joseph Dudley, Harvard 1751; admitted attorney and barrister in the Superior Court, August term, 1762; died 1767 (Superior Court of Judicature, Minute Book 79; *Harvard Quinquennial Cat.*).

[4] It is not possible to tell which of the numerous editions of Denis Godefroy's *Corpus Juris Civilis*, first published in 1583, the club was using. As usual, JA's quotations, even when copying directly from a printed text, are careless.

[5] JA acquired his own copy of Richard Hurd's *Moral and Political Dialogues* (3d edn., London, 1765; 3 vols.) in 1769, and it remains among his books in the Boston Public Library. JA made a partial marginal digest of the book when he read it, but he wrote only one marginal comment. This appears at 3:40-41, where Hurd describes the awkward manners of the typical young man who has "been well whipped through one of our public schools." He is, says Hurd, "An absurd compound of abject sentiments, and bigoted notions, on the one hand; and of clownish, coarse, ungainly demeanour, on the other! In a word, both in mind and person the furthest in the world from any thing that is handsome, gentlemanlike, or of use and acceptance in good company!" Beside this JA wrote: "An exact description of a Dartmouth educated Schollar."

THURSDAY JANUARY 24TH. 1765.

I rode to Boston on Purpose to meet at Fitchs. Gridley came. We read the 3 first Titles of the feudal Law, and We read Gothofreds Notes and We looked into Strykius for the Explanation of many hard Words in those 3 Titles—The Valvasors, Capitanii, Guardia and Guastaldi.[1] This Strykius wrote an Examen Juris feudalis, by Way of

Question and Answer. His account of the original of the Consuetudines Feudorum is, that they were collected and written by Gerardus Niger, and Obertus, the Consulls of Milan.—We read also Part of Tully's Milo—and are to read the 4th. and 5th Title of The Feudal Law, and the rest of that oration next Thursday night.

The Law of Inheritances in England originates in the Feudal Law. Gilberts Tenures originate there. Robinsons[2] History of Scotland gives the clearest account of the Feudal system they say. Ld. Kaims has given us the Introduction of the Feudal Law in to Scotland.—Q. What say the Law Tracts and Dalrymple on this subject?

Gridley. Taylor observed to me when in England that no Books were more proper for Nisi prius oratory, than the Examiner, Craftsman and such Controversial Writings of the best Hands.

I expect the greatest Pleasure from this sodality, that I ever had in my Life—and a Pleasure too, that will not be painfull to my Reflection.

Milo was condemned and went into Banishment, at Marseilles. There He afterwards read the oration, which had been corrected and polished for his Perusal and sent to him by Cicero, for a Present and an Amusement. Reading it, he broke out "si sic ejecisses Marce Tulli barbatos Pisces non comedissem"—for he had been eating a sort of bearded Fishes, that he found at Marseilles.[3]

[1] Latin text has "valvasores," "capitanei," "guardiæ," and "gastaldiæ." Strykius is Samuel Stryk, 17th-century German jurisconsult.

[2] Silently corrected by CFA to "Robertson's." See entry of 21 Feb. and note 2 there.

[3] Various versions of this incident are recorded. According to JA's text, Milo said: "If you had thus delivered [your speech in my favor], Marcus Tullius, I would not have eaten bearded fishes [in Marseilles]."

THURSDAY. JANY. 31ST.

The snowy Weather prevented me from going to Dudleys. The Sodality however met and read the two Titles assigned, and assigned the three next vizt. the 6th. Episcopum, vel Abbatem vell Abbatissam, vel Dominum plebis feudum dare non posse. Tit. 7th. De Natura Feudi, and Tit. 8th. De successione Feudi.

THURSDAY. FEBRUARY 21ST. 1765.

At Boston, entertained the Sodality at Blodgets. We were never in better Spirits, or more Social. We began the 13th. Title of the feudal Law De Alienatione Feudi and read three Titles. Gridley proposed that we should mark all those Passages, which are adopted by the English Law, that when we come to read Ld. Coke we may recur back upon Occasion, to the originals of our Law.

The 14th. Title is De Feudo Marchiæ, vel Ducatus vel Comitatus. Here therefore we see the originals of English Dignities, Marquisates, Dukedoms, Countys &c. The 15th. Title is an Maritus succedat Uxori in Feudo.

I quoted to my Brothers, the Preface to the Historical Law Tracts, "The feudal Customs ought to be the Study of every Man, who proposes to reap Instruction from the History of the modern European Nations, because among these Nations, public Transactions not less than private Property, were some Centuries ago, regulated by the Feudal system.— Sovereigns formerly were many of them connected by the Relation of Superiour and Vassal. The King of England, for Example, by the feudal Tenure, held of the french King many fair Provinces."

I quoted also the sentiments of Rosseau, which are very inimical to the Feudal system.—"The Notion of Representatives, says he, is modern, descending to us, from the Feudal system, that most iniquitous and absurd Form of Government by which human Nature was so shamefully degraded." [1]

Fitch. The Feudal system was military. It was a martial system—a set of Regulations (as Robinsons [2] calls it) for the Incampment of a great Army—and it was a wise and good system, for a martial People in such Circumstances. For the feudal Connections and subordination, and services, were necessary for their Defence against the Inroads and Invasions of their Neighbours, &c.

Ego. I think that the Absurdity and Iniquity lies in this, that Nations at Peace and in Plenty who live by Commerce and Industry, have adopted such a system.

Gridley. There lies the Absurdity and Iniquity. And the observation you quote proves that Rosseau is shallow.

I might have quoted Ld. Kaims's British Antiquities, who says—"It is the Plan of the feudal Law to bestow the whole Land property upon the King and to subject to him the Bulk of the People, in Quality of Servants and Vassals; a Constitution so contradictory to all the Principles which govern Mankind can never be brought about, one should imagine, but by foreign Conquest, or native Usurpation." And in another Place he calls the feudal connection, the feudal Yoke.

These Epithets of absurd, iniquitous, unatural &c. are not very agreable to the Opinion of Strykius, who says in answer to the Question Unde Originem trahunt Feuda?—Certo modo et si formam feudorum genericam consideres, dici potest ex Jure Gentium. Hoc enim ratio naturalis, juncta necessitate publica, exigit, ut militibus potissimum Prædia, ab Hostibus occupata, pro bene meritis concederentur sub

Conditione tamen fidelitatis, quo eo securior esset Respublica, et ad Patriam defendendam magis allicerentur.

In Milo We read from the 27th. to the 34th section in Davidsons Translation. We begin the Peroration next. We had Guthries and Davidsons Translations. In Point of Accuracy And Spirit Davidson's is vastly Superiour.

Mr. Gridley produced a Book intituled in Herennium Commentarius, as an Introduction to Tully De Oratore—and read the Three sorts of orations, the Demonstrative, Deliberative and Judicial, and the several Parts of an oration, the Exordium &c.

Gridley. Our Plan must be, when we have finished the feudal Law, to read Coke Littleton, and after him a Reign and the Statutes of that Reign. It should also be a Part of our Plan, to improve ourselves in Writing, by reading carefully the best English Writers, and by Using ourselves to writing—for it should be a part of our Plan to publish Pieces, now and then. Let us form our Style upon the Ancients, and the best English Authors.

I hope and expect to see, at the Bar, in Consequence of this Sodality, a Purity, an Elegance, and a Spirit, surpassing any Thing that ever appeared in America.[3] Fich [Fitch] said that he would not say he had Abilities, but he would say he had Ambition enough to hope for the same Thing.

[1] A quotation from Jean Jacques Rousseau, *Du contrat social* (1762), a work of which JA eventually owned at least three copies, a pirated edition in French, Amsterdam, 1742 [i.e. 1762?], and two copies of the first English translation, *A Treatise on the Social Compact, or the Principles of Politic Law*, London, 1764; see *Catalogue of JA's Library*, p. 216. For an illuminating survey of JA's intellectual relations with Rousseau, see Haraszti, *JA and the Prophets of Prog*ress, ch. 5, "Rousseau and the Man of Nature."

[2] That is, William Robertson's *History of Scotland*, London, 1758–1759, a work with which JA was obviously not yet familiar.

[3] CFA arbitrarily placed quotation marks around this sentence and thereby attributed it to Gridley. The attribution is probably correct, but the sentence could be a reflection of JA's.

[FRAGMENTARY DRAFT OF A DISSERTATION ON CANON AND FEUDAL LAW, FEBRUARY 1765.]

This Sodality has given rise to the following Speculation of my own, which I commit to writing, as Hints for future Enquiries rather than as a satisfactory Theory.[1]

The Desire of ⟨Power⟩ ⟨Power⟩ Dominion, that encroaching, grasping, restless, and ungovernable Principle in human Nature, that Principle which has made so much Havock and Desolation, among the Works of God, in all the Variety of systems, that have been invented, for its Gratification, was never so successfull, as in the Invention and Establishment of the Cannon and the Feudal Law.—By the former the most refined, sublime, extensive, and astonishing Constitution of Policy, that was ever conceived by the Human Mind, was framed, by the Romish Clergy, for the Aggrandisement of their own order. This Constitution will be allowed to deserve all the Epithets I have given it, when it is considered, that they found Ways to make the World believe that God had entrusted them with Keys of Heaven whose Gates they might open and shut at Pleasure, with the Power of Dispensation over all the Rules and Types of Morality, the Power of licensing all sorts both of sins and Crimes, with the Power of Deposing Princes, and absolving all their subjects from their Allegiance, with the Power of Procuring or withholding the Rain of Heaven, and the Beams of the Sun, with the Power of Earthquakes, ⟨*Plagues,*⟩ Pestilence, Famine; nay with the Power of creating Blood Nay the Blood of God out of Wine, and Flesh the Flesh of God out of Bread. Thus was human Nature held for Ages, fast Bound in servitude, in a cruel, shameful, deplorable Bondage to him and his subordinate Tyrants who it was fortold in the Apocalypse, would exalt himself above all that is called God and that is worshiped.

By the latter another system was formed similar to the former in some Respects, and altho it was originally contrived perhaps for the necessary Defence of a barbarous ⟨*Nation*⟩ People against the Inroads and Invasions of her neighbouring Nations; yet it was soon adopted by almost all the Princes in Europe, and wrought into the Constitution of their Governments for the same Purposes of Tyranny, Cruelty and Lust. This Constitution was originally a Code of Laws for a vast Army, in a perpetual Encampment. The General was invested with the Property of all the Land within [*sentence unfinished*] [2]

It [3] was a Resolution formed by a sensible People almost in despair. They had become intelligent in general, and some of them learned but they had been galled, and fretted, and whipped and cropped, and hanged and burned. In short they had been so worried by Plagues and Tortures in every Shape, and they utterly despaired of Deliverance from these Miseries in their own Country, that they at last resolved to fly to the Wilderness, for Refuge from the temporal and spiritual Principalities and Powers, and Plagues and scourges of their Native Country.

After their Arrival here, they began their settlements and pursued their Plan both of Ecclesiastical and Civil Government in direct Opposition to the Cannon And the feudal systems.

5. THE BIRTHPLACES OF JOHN AND JOHN QUINCY ADAMS
IN 1822, BY ELIZA SUSAN QUINCY

6. MOUNT WOLLASTON, THE FORMER SEAT OF COLONEL JOHN QUINCY,
1822, BY ELIZA SUSAN QUINCY

7. QUINCY FROM PRESIDENTS HILL, 1822, BY ELIZA SUSAN QUINCY

8. EARLY VIEW OF LINCOLN COUNTY COURTHOUSE, POWNALBOROUGH, MAINE

Their first Concern was to preserve and propagate Knowledge. The leading Men among the first Settlers of America, were Men of sense and Learning. And the Clergymen, who came over first, were familiar with the Historians, Orators, Poets and Phylosophers of Greece and Rome, and many of them have left behind them Libraries which are still in Being consisting chiefly of Books, whose Character their great Grand sons can scarcely read.[4]

I always consider the settlement of America with Reverence and Wonder—as the Opening of a grand scene and Design in Providence, for the Illumination of the Ignorant and the Emancipation of the slavish Part of Mankind all over the Earth.

their great grand sons, tho educated at European Universities, can scarcely read. Archbishop King him self, (I think it was, for I say this upon Memory) observed of the Puritans in General, that they were much more intelligent, and better read than the Members of the Church whom he reproaches, and censures very warmly for that Reason.

Provision was early made by Law, that every Town should be accommodated with a grammar school—under a severe Penalty—so that even Negligence of Learning was made a Crime, a Stretch of Wisdom in Policy that was never equalled before nor since unless by the ancient Egyptians who made the Want of Generosity and Humanity a Capital Crime.

But besides the Obligation laid on every Town to provide the means of Learning, a Colledge nay a Number of Colledges were formed very early, and a very early Attention to them from the Legislature, exempted from Military Duties—exemptions from Taxes, and many other Encouragements have taken Place. And in fine We their Posterity, have seen the Fruits and Consequences of the Wisdom and Goodness of our Forefathers. All Ranks and orders of our People, are intelligent, are accomplished—a Native of America, especially of New England, who cannot read and wright is as rare a Phenomenon as a Comet.

Remainder of the Piece begun in our last.—

Thus accomplished were the first Settlers of these Colonies—and as has been said, Tyranny in every shape, was their Disdain and Abhorrence. No ⟨Kind of⟩ Fear of Punishment not even of Death itself, in exquisite Torture had been sufficient to conquer that steady, manly, pertinacious Spirit, with which they opposed the Tyrants of those Days in Church and state. And their greatest Concern seems to have been to establish a Government of the Church, more consistent with the scriptures, and a Government of the state more agreable to the Dignity of human Nature, than they had ever seen in Europe. They knew that beautiful were the feet &c. But They saw clearly, that of all the ⟨*ridiculous*⟩ Nonsense, Delusion, and Frenzy that had ever passed thro the Mind of Man, none had ever been more glaring and extravagant than the Notions of the Cannon Law, of the indellible Character, the perpetual succession, the virtuous and sanctified Effluvia from Episcopal Fingers, and all the rest of that dark Ribaldry which had thrown such a Glare of Mistery, Sanctity, Reverence and Right Reverence, Eminence and Holiness around the Idea of a Priest [*sentence unfinished*]

[1] The paragraphs that follow comprise JA's first thoughts for the important and eloquent essay to which he gave no name but which later became known as "A Dissertation on Canon and Feudal Law." (In his Autobiography JA observed that "It might as well have been called an Essay upon Forefathers Rock"— i.e. what is now known as Plymouth Rock.) The date here assigned to this very rough draft is conjectural, but since it immediately follows the Diary entry of 21 Feb. 1765, being separated from it only by a line across the page, we can say with some confidence that JA began putting down these detached thoughts late in February. He may, of course, have continued them in the following weeks or even months.

Much revised and expanded from the early draft, JA's essay was published in the *Boston Gazette*, without a signature of any kind, in four parts, 12 and 19 Aug., 30 Sept., and 21 Oct. 1765, whence it was reprinted in the *London Chronicle* in corresponding installments, 23 and 28 Nov., 3 and 26 Dec. 1765, under a title furnished by Thomas Hollis: "A DISSERTATION *on the* Feudal *and the* Canon Law." For its subsequent bibliographical history, see CFA's valuable

but not completely reliable introductory note to his reprint in JA's *Works*, 3:447–448. No attempt is made in the present text of the draft to show the variations between it and the published version, but readers who wish to see how JA used and revised his first thoughts will find nearly all of them embedded in the final version as reprinted in his *Works*, in the following order: p. 449–450, 451–452, 455–456, 452–453. It should be noted that the draft contains rudiments of only the first three parts of the essay as printed in the newspapers; the last installment, with its references to the Stamp Act (passed 22 March 1765), was doubtless composed later.

[2] An interval of space follows at this point in the MS, denoting a gap in the draft.

[3] That is, the Puritans' decision to leave England and settle in America. (In the next sentence JA wrote the word "Puritans" above the initial "They.")

[4] Last four words interlined. Evidently the next paragraph (which is the only substantial passage in the draft not in the text as printed in the *Boston Gazette*) was an afterthought, and the passage *after that* originally continued the present paragraph.

[ACCOUNTS ON THE EASTERN CIRCUIT, 7–12 JUNE 1765.] [1]

	£	s	d
June 7th. 1765. Paid at Goodwins for Dinners [2]	0:	10:	0
Paid at Lovejoys for Lodging Suppers &c	0:	8:	0

June 8th. Paid at Springers for Horse keeping 2s:8d, at Sewals for Lodging and Breakfast and Suppers 2s:6d and at Lovejoys for Lemmons Rum and sugar 1s:4d:	o:	6: 6
Paid at Springers for Reckoning 3s:2d: and for Shewing Horse 1s:2d	o:	4: 4
June 9th. paid at Bucknams and at Lorings	o:	3: 0
and at Tompsons	o:	o: 2
paid at Toms's for Horses 2s for Contribution 1s:2d	o:	3: 2
June 10th. at Millikins lodging Horse supper Breakfast	o:	3: 2
at Pattens	o:	o: 8
Highwaymen	o:	o: 8
at Jeffries's	o:	3: 8
June 11th. at Sewals 2s. at Leavitts 1s:4d at ferry 1s	o:	4: 4
at Hales 6d	o:	o: 6
June 12th. at Hunts in Rowley for Horse lodging and Breakfast	o:	2: 6
at Norwoods for Dinner &c 2s at two Houses before for oats 8d at Winnisimmit 10d at Boston for Tea and Horse 1s	o:	5: 6 [3]
	£2:	16: 2

[1] Loose sheet of accounts, docketed by JA: "Curious Minutes at Pownalborough," found among JA's legal papers (Adams Papers, Microfilms, Reel No. 185). The entries partially document JA's first trip to the District of Maine, where he argued a land case at Pownalborough on the Kennebec River, the seat of the newly established Lincoln co. (Pownalborough was later divided into several towns, including Dresden and Wiscasset, and disappeared as a place name.) The hardships of this trip into the Maine wilderness are graphically told in JA's Autobiography. The old wooden Lincoln Court House, built in 1761 within the parade grounds of Fort Shirley, still stands on the eastern bank of the Kennebec near Dresden Mills. An early view of it is reproduced as an illustration in this volume. See Fannie Scott Chase, *Wiscasset in Pownalborough*, Wiscasset, Me., 1941, p. 31, 71–75, 100–104; Federal Writers' Project, *Maine, A Guide "Down East,"* Boston, 1937, p. 350.

[2] This entry replaced a fuller one that is scored out on the facing page: "Pownalborough June 7th. 1765.–at Major Goodwins paid 10s. l[awful] M[oney] for 3 dinners & Tea once."

[3] Error for 4s. 6d.

AUGUST 15TH. 1765.[1]

I hope it will give no offence, to enquire into the Grounds and Reasons of the strange Conduct of Yesterday and last Night, at Boston.[2] Is there any Evidence, that Mr. Oliver ever wrote to the Ministry, or to any Body in England any unfavourable Representations, of the People of this Province? Has he ever placed the Character of the People, their

Manners, their Laws, their Principles in Religion or Government, their submission to order and Magistracy, in a false Light?

Is it known that he ever advised the Ministry to lay internal Taxes upon Us? That he ever solicited the office of Distributer of Stamps? or that he has ever done any Thing to injure the People, or to incur their Displeasure, besides barely accepting of that office? If there is no Proof at all of any such Injury done to the People by that Gentleman, has not the blind, undistinguishing Rage of the Rabble done him, irreparable Injustice? To be placed, only in Pageantry, in the most conspicuous Part of the Town, with such ignominous Devices around him, would be thought severity enough by any Man of common sensibility: But to be carried thro the Town, in such insolent Tryumph and burned on an Hill, to have his Garden torn in Pieces, his House broken open, his furniture destroyed and his whole family thrown into Confusion and Terror, is a very attrocious Violation of the Peace and of dangerous Tendency and Consequence.

But on the other Hand let us ask a few Questions. Has not his Honour the Lieutenant Governor discovered to the People in innumerable Instances, a very ambitious and avaricious Disposition? Has he not grasped four of the most important offices in the Province into his own Hands? Has not his Brother in Law Oliver another of the greatest Places in Government? Is not a Brother of the Secretary, a Judge of the Superiour Court? Has not that Brother a son in the House? Has not the secretary a son in the House, who is also a Judge in one of the Counties? Did not that son marry the Daughter of another of the Judges of the Superiour Court? Has not the Lieutenant Governor a Brother, a Judge of the Pleas in Boston? and a Namesake and near Relation who is another Judge? Has not the Lieutenant Governor a near Relation who is Register of his own Court of Probate, and Deputy Secretary? Has he not another near Relation who is Clerk of the House of Representatives? Is not this amazing ascendancy of one Family, Foundation sufficient on which to erect a Tyranny? Is it not enough to excite Jealousies among the People?

Quere further. Has not many a Member of both Houses, laboured to the Utmost of his Ability, to obtain a Resolution to send home some Petitions and Remonstrances to the King, Lords and Commons vs. the Impositions they saw were about to be laid upon Us. Has not the Lieutenant Governor all along been the very Gentleman who has prevented it, and wiped out every spirited, if not every sensible Expression out of those Petitions?

Quære further. When the Court was about to choose an Agent, did not the Governor, Lieutenant Governor, and Secretary, make Use of all their Influence to procure an Election for Mr. Jackson? [3] Was not Mr. Jackson [...] [4] a secretary to Mr. Greenville? Was not Mr. Greenville, the Author of the late Measures relative to the Colonies? Was not Mr. Jackson an Agent and a particular Friend of the Governor? Was not all this considering the natural Jealousy of Mankind, enough to excite suspicions among the Vulgar, that all these Gentlemen were in a Combination, to favour the Measures of the Ministry, at least to prevent any Thing from being done here to discourage the Minister from his rash, mad, and Dogmatical Proceedings?

Would it not be Prudence then in those Gentlemen at this alarming Conjuncture, and a Condescention that is due to the present Fears and Distresses of the People, (in some manner consistent with the Dignity of their stations and Characters,) to remove these Jealousies from the Minds of the People by giving an easy solution of these Difficulties?

[1] This is the first entry in the Diary since the rough draft of the essay on canon and feudal law, presumably begun in February. In March JA had been chosen one of the surveyors of highways in Braintree and also a member of a committee to lay out the North Commons in lots to be sold (*Braintree Town Records*, p. 399–402, 406–407). In April and May and again in July and August he attended sessions of Plymouth and Bristol Inferior Courts; in June he traveled the eastern circuit to Maine for the first time. On 14 July his first child, named for her mother and referred to in this work as AA2, was born.

[2] This entry is quite evidently a draft of another newspaper letter, but no printing has been found. On the morning of 14 Aug. a Boston mob hanged an effigy of Secretary Andrew Oliver, who according to reports had been appointed to distribute the stamps in Massachusetts when the Stamp Act went into effect on 1 November. In the afternoon the mob marched to the Province House and mockingly huzza'd Governor Bernard and the Council, proceeded to Oliver's new building at his dock on Kilby Street (where it was presumed the stamps would be distributed), destroyed it, built a bonfire on Fort Hill from the remnants of the building, and burned the effigy. Later that evening they pillaged Oliver's town residence and garden, and drove off Lt. Gov. Hutchinson and the sheriff with brickbats when they tried to interfere with the fun. See *Boston Gazette*, 19 Aug. 1765, suppl.; Rowe, *Letters and Diary*, p. 88–89; Edmund S. and Helen M. Morgan, *The Stamp Act Crisis*, Chapel Hill, 1953, p. 121–125.

[3] Richard Jackson (1721?–1787) was appointed provincial agent in London by the Massachusetts General Court, 24 Jan. 1765, to succeed Jasper Mauduit; see Hutchinson to Jackson, 25 Jan. 1765 (MHS, *Colls.*, 74 [1918]:179, note). According to James Otis and other anti-Hutchinsonians, Hutchinson had wanted Jackson appointed in 1762 "from views of interest hoping in him to have a private agent of his own invested with a publick character" (same, p. 78; see also p. 95, 115, 124, 127, note, 128; and entry of 1 Feb. 1763 and note, above).

[4] Corner of page torn off.

[AUGUST 1765.] [1]

Hannah Place vs. Atwood.

Introduced into the family at 13. Constant Understanding that she should be paid. A Pittance left to 'em by their Uncle. He [cutt?]. No particular Bargain for Wood or service.

Hannah Atwood. Had one of em constantly as a Maid. My Husband promised to pay her. The fore part of the Time Mary worked, the latter Hannah. Hannah worked but very little abroad the whole Time. She did some. They told me, both could not leave home at once. [....] [2] They bought their own Cloaths. From 47 to 56.

Richd. Mayberry. They worked at taylering for me. I paid em in sugar and Tea. I've seen them washing and laboring. And sowing seeds in Garden.

Daniel Barrows. About House work, fetching Water and Washing—no other Help.

Eliz. Halloway. Seen em Milking, Washing, Ironing, Baking. 3 of em lived there. Went out and took in Work.

Susannah Jones.

Wm. Halloway. Molly was weakly and made this her Home.

Eliz. Place. Father in Law employed one of my sisters constantly as a Maid and said he would pay her and all the rest of us were welcome to live there. Molly uneasy. He said his Word as good as the Bank. He found Room and Wood, and Provisions. Father borrowed the Wood of sister Hannah, to buy his Grave stones, pay her the Wood or the Money. Hired some Washing.

Abiel Whitmarsh. Something of an Account.

George Hallowell. Got me to milk.

George Ware. Conversation with Atwood about pay for Doctering. Chose to know what it is. Said he would agree with them and leave it to Men. Have known them to buy some Tea &c.

Paine. Troublesome family. No troublesome Company.—Family Witnesses.[3]

White. ⟨*Younger sister*⟩ Elder sister.
Witnesses.

Joseph Atwood. They worked out. The old Lady used to be the Maid, in the family. Never heard of any pay. Old Gentleman in kitchen. Weakly. Within 6 Year. My maid often sent for to help her up.

David Walker. They took several suits of Cloaths home. Never mistrusted their being Maids.

John Camp. Lived there 10 Year.[4]

[1] The following notes on the case of Hannah Place *v.* Ephraim Atwood Jr. can be dated from an entry in one of JA's lists of legal actions, in which this case is mentioned as coming up in Taunton (Bristol co.) Inferior Court,

Aug. 1765. JA probably served as the defendant's counsel.

² The omitted word was written between the lines and is illegible. It could be the name of another deponent or witness and at a guess is "Bayley."

³ Here a line is drawn across the page in the MS.

⁴ This note is on a page by itself and separated from the foregoing notes, but it probably relates to the case of Place *v.* Atwood.

BRAINTREE DECR. 18TH. 1765. WEDNESDAY.[1]

How great is my Loss, in neglecting to keep a regular Journal, through the last Spring, Summer, and Fall. In the Course of my Business, as a Surveyor of High-Ways, as one of the Committee, for dividing, planning, and selling the North-Commons, in the Course of my two great Journeys to Pounalborough and Marthas Vineyard, and in several smaller Journeys to Plymouth, Taunton and Boston, I had many fine Opportunities and Materials for Speculation.—The Year 1765 has been the most remarkable Year of my Life. That enormous Engine, fabricated by the british Parliament, for battering down all the Rights and Liberties of America, I mean the Stamp Act, has raised and spread, thro the whole Continent, a Spirit that will be recorded to our Honour, with all future Generations. In every Colony, from Georgia to New-Hampshire inclusively, the Stamp Distributors and Inspectors have been compelled, by the unconquerable Rage of the People, to renounce their offices. Such and so universal has been the Resentment of the People, that every Man who has dared to speak in favour of the Stamps, or to soften the detestation in which they are held, how great soever his Abilities and Virtues had been esteemed before, or whatever his fortune, Connections and Influence had been, has been seen to sink into universal Contempt and Ignominy.

The People, even to the lowest Ranks, have become more attentive to their Liberties, more inquisitive about them, and more determined to defend them, than they were ever before known or had occasion to be. Innumerable have been the Monuments of Wit, Humour, Sense, Learning, Spirit, Patriotism, and Heroism, erected in the several Colonies and Provinces, in the Course of this Year. Our Presses have groaned, our Pulpits have thundered, our Legislatures have resolved, our Towns have voted, The Crown Officers have every where trembled, and all their little Tools and Creatures, been afraid to Speak and ashamed to be seen.

This Spirit however has not yet been sufficient to banish, from Persons in Authority, that Timidity, which they have discovered from the Beginning. The executive Courts have not yet dared to adjudge the Stamp-Act void nor to proceed with Business as usual, tho it should seem that Necessity alone would be sufficient to justify Business, at present, tho the Act should be allowed to be obligatory. The Stamps are in the Castle. Mr. Oliver has no Commission. The Governor has no Authority to distribute, or even to unpack the Bales, the Act has never been proclaimed nor read in the Province; Yet the Probate office is shut, the Custom House is shut, the Courts of Justice are shut, and all Business seems at a Stand. Yesterday and the day before, the two last days of Service for January Term, only one Man asked me for a Writ, and he was soon determined to waive his Request. I have not drawn a Writ since 1st. Novr.

How long We are to remain in this languid Condition, this passive Obedience to the Stamp Act, is not certain. But such a Pause cannot be lasting. Debtors grow insolent. Creditors grow angry. And it is to be expected that the Public offices will very soon be forced open, unless such favourable Accounts should be received from England, as to draw away the Fears of the Great, or unless a greater Dread of the Multitude should drive away the Fear of Censure from G. Britain.

It is my Opinion that by this ⟨Timorous⟩ Inactivity we discover Cowardice, and too much Respect ⟨and Regard⟩ to the Act. This Rest appears to be by Implication at least an Acknowledgement of the Authority of Parliament to tax Us. And if this Authority is once acknowledged and established, the Ruin of America will become inevitable.

This long Interval of Indolence and Idleness will make a large Chasm in my affairs if it should not reduce me to Distress and incapacitate me to answer the Demands upon me. But I must endeavour in some degree to compensate the Disadvantage, by posting my Books, reducing my Accounts into better order, and by diminishing my Expences, but above all by improving the Leisure of this Winter, in a diligent Application to my Studies. I find that Idleness lies between Business and Study, i.e. The Transision from the Hurry of a multiplicity of Business, to the Tranquility that is necessary for intense Study, is not easy. There must be a Vacation, an Interval between them, for the Mind to recollect itself.

The Bar seem to me to behave like a Flock of shot Pidgeons. They seem to be stopped, the Net seems to be thrown over them, and they have scarcely Courage left to flounce and to flutter. So sudden an Interruption in my Career, is very unfortunate for me. I was but just getting into my Geers, just getting under Sail, and an Embargo is laid upon the Ship. Thirty Years of my Life are passed in Preparation for Business. I have had Poverty to struggle with—Envy and Jealousy and Malice of Enemies to encounter—no Friends, or but few to assist me, so that I have groped in dark Obscurity, till of late, and had but just become known, and gained a small degree of Reputation, when this execrable Project was set on foot for my Ruin as well as that of America in General, and of Great Britain.

¹ First entry in "Paper book No. 11" (our D/JA/11), which has on its cover, in JA's hand, the following couplet from Pope:
"Eye Nature's walks, Shoot folly as it flys And catch the Manners liveing as they rise."
JA's most important action in the interval since his last Diary entries in August was his composition of the "Braintree Instructions," denouncing the Stamp Act and denying Parliament's authority to tax the colonies without their consent. This paper is in the form of a letter from a special committee of the town to its representative in the General Court, Ebenezer Thayer, and is dated 24 Sept.

1765. A rough draft in JA's hand is in the Adams Papers. For the action of the town and the text of the Instructions as adopted, see *Braintree Town Records*, p. 404–406. In JA's *Works*, 3:464–468, the Instructions are reprinted from the *Boston Gazette*, 14 Oct., though the earliest printing was in Drapers' *Massachusetts Gazette and Boston News Letter*, 10 Oct. The open secret of JA's authorship of this spirited paper undoubtedly led to his being named in December one of the counsel for the Town of Boston to plead for the reopening of the courts; see the following entry.

DECR. 19TH. 1765.

A fair Morning after a severe Storm of 3 days and 4 Nights. A vast Quantity of rain fell.

About 12. O Clock came in Messrs. Crafts and Chase and gave me a particular Account of the Proceedings of the Sons of Liberty on Tuesday last, in prevailing on Mr. Oliver to renounce his Office of Distributor of Stamps, by a Declaration under his Hand, and under his Oath, taken before Justice Dana, in Hanover Square, under the very Tree of Liberty, nay under the very Limb where he had been hanged in Effigy, Aug. 14th. 1765. Their absolute Requisition of an Oath, and under that Tree, were Circumstances, extreamly humiliating and mortifying, as Punishment for his receiving a Deputation to be Distributor after his pretended Resignation, and for his faint and indirect Declaration in the News Papers last Monday.

About one O'Clock came in Mr. Clark, one of the Constables of the Town of Boston, with a Letter from Mr. Wm. Cooper their Town Clerk in these Words

Sir

I am directed by the Town to acquaint you, that they have this day voted unanimously, that Jeremiah Gridley, James Otis, and John Adams Esqrs. be applied to, as Council to appear before his Excellency the Governor in Council, in Support of their Memorial, praying that the Courts of Law in this Province may be opened. A Copy of said

Memorial will be handed you, on your coming to Town. I am sir, your most obedient hum. sert.,

Wm. Cooper Town Clerk

Boston Decr. 18th. 1765
John Adams Esqr.[1]

The Reasons which induced Boston to choose me, at a distance, and unknown as I am, The particular Persons concerned and measures concerted to bring this about, I am wholly at a loss to conjecture: as I am, what the future Effects and Consequences will be both with Regard to myself and the Public.

But when I recollect my own Reflections and Speculations Yesterday, a part of which were committed to Writing last Night, and may be seen under Decr. 18th, and compare them with the Proceedings of Boston Yesterday of which the foregoing Letter informed me, I cannot but Wonder, and call to Mind my Ld. Bacons Observation, about secret invisible Laws of Nature, a[nd] Communications and Influences between Places, that are not discoverable by Sense.

But I am now under all obligations of Interest and Ambition as well as Honour, Gratitude and Duty, to exert the Utmost of my Abilities, in this important Cause. How shall it be conducted? Shall we contend that the Stamp-Act is void? That the Parliament have no legal Authority to impose Internal Taxes upon Us?—Because We are not represented in it? And therefore that the Stamp Act ought to be waived by the Judges, as against natural Equity and the Constitution? Shall we use these, as Arguments for opening the Courts of Law? Or shall We ground ourselves on Necessity only.

[1] The original letter is in the Adams Papers. On 17 Dec., immediately following the forced resignation of Andrew Oliver, the custom house reopened for business without stamped paper, and next day a special town meeting was called to deal with the problem of reopening the courts without the use of stamps. Its proceedings, including the memorial mentioned here, are in Boston Record Commissioners, *16th Report*, p. 158–159.

FRYDAY. DECR. 20TH. 1765.

Went to Boston. Dined with Mr. Rowe,[1] in Company with Messrs. Gridley, Otis, Kent, and Dudley. After Dinner, went to the Town House, and Attended with the Committee of the Town of Boston and many other Gentlemen in the Representatives Room till about Dark, after Candle Light, when Mr. Adams, the Chairman of the Committee, received a Message from the Governor, by the Deputy Secretary, purporting that his Excellency and the Council were ready to hear the Memorial of the Town of Boston, and their Council in Support of it. But that no other Persons might attend.

We accordingly went in. His Excellency recommended it to Us, who were of Council for the Town, to divide the Points of Law and Topicks of Argument, among ourselves, that Repetition might as much as possible be avoided. Mr. Gridley answered, that, as he was to speak last, he would endeavour to avoid Repetition of what should be said by the two Gentlemen, who were to speak before him. Mr. Otis added that as he was to speak second, he would observe the same Rule.

Then it fell upon me, without one Moments Opportunity to consult any Authorities, to open an Argument, upon a Question that was never made before, and I wish I could hope it never would be made again, i.e. Whether the Courts of Law should be open, or not? My old Friend Thatchers Officina Justitiæ?

I grounded my Argument on the Invalidity of the Stamp Act, it not being in any sense our Act, having never consented to it. But least that foundation should not be sufficient, on the present Necessity to prevent a Failure of Justice, and the present Impossibility of carrying that Act into Execution.[2]

Mr. Otis reasoned with great Learning and Zeal, on the Judges Oaths, ⟨the⟩ &c.[3]

Mr. Gridley on the great ⟨Mischiefs⟩ Inconveniences that would ensue the Interuption of Justice.

The Governor said many of the Arguments used were very good ones to be used before the Judges of the Executive Courts. But he believed there had been no Instance in America of an Application to the Governor and Council, and said that if the Judges should receive any Directions from the King about a Point of Law, they would scorn to regard them, and would say that while they were in those Seats, they only were to determine Points of Law.

The Council adjourned to the Morning and I repaired to my Lodgings.

[1] John Rowe (1715–1787), the well-known Boston merchant, successful trimmer during the Revolution, and diarist; portions of his valuable diary from 1759 to 1779 have been published in *Letters and Diary of John Rowe*, ed. Anne Rowe Cunningham, Boston, 1903; the MS is in MHi. Rowe was a member of the committee appointed to present the Boston memorial to the Governor in Council.

[2] A page of notes and authorities presumably prepared for this argument, in JA's hand and headed "Right, Wrong and Remedy," is in the Adams Papers; though undated, it has been filed under the present date. CFA printed these notes in JA, *Works*, 2:159, note. As reported by Josiah Quincy, JA's argument on behalf of the Boston memorial does not follow the notes closely; see Quincy, *Reports*, p. 200–202.

[3] Otis "opened with Tears," according to Josiah Quincy. His argument and that of Gridley are in Quincy, *Reports*, p.

202–209, together with Governor Bernard's evasive proposal that the town's plea be taken to the judges, since the Governor and Council had no power to act on it.

SATURDAY DECR. 21ST. 1765.

Spent the Morning in sauntering about, and chatting with one and another—The Sherriff, Mr. Goldthw[ai]t, Brother Sewal &c.—upon the Times. Dined with Brother Kent; after Dinner received a Hint from the Committee that as I was of Council for the Town I not only had a Right, but it was expected I should attend the Meeting. I went accordingly. The Committee reported the Answer of the Board to their Petition. Which was, in Substance, that the Board had no Authority to direct the Courts of Law, in the manner prayed for. That the Memorial involved a Question of Law, vizt., whether the officers of the Government, in the present Circumstances of the Province, could be justified, in proceeding with Business without Stamps. That the Board were desirous that the Judges should decide that Question freely, without Apprehension of censure from the Board, and that the Board recomended it to the Judges of the Inferior Court for the County of Suffolk and to the other Judges of the other Courts in the Province to determine that Question as soon as may be, at or before their next respective Terms.

The Question was put whether that Paper should be recorded. Passed in the Affirmative.

The next Question was, Whether it was a satisfactory Answer to their Memorial. Unanimously in the Negative.[1]

Then several Motions were made, the first was, that the Meeting be adjourned to a future Day, and that the Towns Council be desired to consult together, and give the Town their Opinions, whether any other legal and Constitutional Steps can be taken by the Town, towards removing the obstructions to Justice. The second Motion was, that those of the Towns Council who were present should then give their opinion. The Third was that Application should be made to the Judges to determine the Question Speedily.

The second prevail'd and I was call'd upon to give my Opinion first. I agreed with Kent that an Application to the Judges might be out of Character both for the Town and the Judges, and that no Person could be in any danger of Penalties on the one Hand, or of having Proscesses adjudged void on the other. But many Persons might entertain Fears, and Jealousies and Doubts, which would everlastingly be a grievance. So that I had heard no Proposal yet made for the future

Conduct of the Town, which had not Difficulties and Objections attending it, so that I must conclude myself as yet in Doubt. And that I dared not give any opinion possitively, in a Matter of so much Importance without the most mature Deliberation.

Mr. Otis then gave his sentiments, and declared once for all, that he knew of no legal and Constitutional Course the Town could take but to direct their Representatives to request the Governor to call a Convention of the Members of both Houses, as he could not legally call an Assembly, and if his Excellency would not, to call one themselves, by requesting all the Members to meet. But concluded with observing, that as one of their Council was not present, and another was in Doubt, he thought it would be best to take further Time for Consideration. And the Town accordingly voted an Adjournment to next Thursday, 10 O'Clock.

A Consultation, therefore I must have with Messrs. Gridley and Otis, and We must all attend the Town-Meeting next Thursday. What Advice shall we give them?

The Question is "what legal and Constitutional Measures the Town can take to open the Courts of Law?"

The Town in their Memorial to his Excellency in Council, assert that "the Courts of Law within the Province, in which alone Justice can be distributed among the People, so far as respects civil Matters, are to all Intents and Purposes shut up. For which no just and legal Reason can be assigned."

The Record of the Board, sent down in Answer, admits that the Courts of Law are to all Intents and Purposes shut up, and says that before they can be opened a Point of Law must be decided vizt. whether the officers of the Government in the present Circumstances of the Province, can be justified in proceeding in their Offices without Stamps? which the Judges are to determine.

Are the Board then agreed with the Town that the Courts of Law are shut up? But I hope the Town will not agree with the Board that the Judges are the proper Persons to decide whether they shall be open or not. It is the first Time I believe, that such a Question was ever put, since Wm. the Conquerer, nay since the Days of King Lear. Should the twelve Judges of England, and all other officers of Justice Judicial and Ministerial, suddenly stop and shut up their offices, I believe the King, in Council, would hardly recommend any Points of Law to the Consideration of those Judges. The King it is true of his Prerogative could not remove the Judges, because in England a Judge is quite another Thing from what he is here. But I believe the Commons in Parliament would immediately impeach them all of high Treason.

My Advice to the Town will be, to take the Board at their Word, and to chuse a Committee immediately, in the first Place to wait on the Governor in Council, as the Supreme Court of Probate, and request of them a determination of the Point, whether the Officers of the Probate Courts in the Province, can be justifyed, in Proceeding with Business without Stamps, in the next Place to wait on the honorable the Judges of the Superiour Court to request their Determination of the same Question, and in the Third Place to wait on the Judges of the Inferior Court for the County of Suffolk with the same Request—in Pursuance of the Recommendation of the honorable Board— and unless a speedy Determination of the Question is obtained in all these Courts in this Way, to request of the Governor a Convention of the two Houses, and if that is refused to endeavour to call one, themselves.

What are the Consequences of the supposition that the Courts are shut up? The King is the Fountain of Justice by the Constitution—And it is a Maxim of the Law, that the King never dies.

Are not Protection and Allegiance reciprocal? And if We are out of the Kings Protection, are we not discharged from our Allegiance. Are not all the Ligaments of Government dissolved? Is it not ⟨a Declaration of⟩ an Abdication of the Throne? In short where will such an horrid Doctrine terminate? It would run us into Treason!

¹ The official record as printed breaks off here, stating that after this vote the meeting adjourned to the following Thursday (Boston Record Commissioners, *16th Report*, p. 160).

SUNDAY [22 DECEMBER].

At Home, with my family. Thinking.

1765. DECEMBER. 23D. MONDAY.

Went to Boston. After Dinner rambled after Messrs. Gridley and Otis but could find neither. Went into Mr. Dudleys, Mr. Dana's, Mr. Otis's office, and then to Mr. Adams's and went with him to the Monday night Clubb. There I found Otis, Cushing Wells, Pemberton, Gray, Austin, two Waldo's, Inches, Dr. Parker—And spent the Evening very agreably, indeed. Politicians all at this Clubb. We had many curious Anecdotes, about Governors, Councillors, Representatives, Demagogues, Merchants &c. The Behaviour of these Gentlemen is very familiar and friendly to each other, and very polite and complaisant to Strangers. Gray has a very tender Mind, is extreamly timid —he says when he meets a Man of the other Side he talks against him, when he meets a Man of our Side he opposes him, so that he fears, he shall be thought against every Body, and so every Body will be against him. But he hopes to prepare the Way for his Escape at next May from an Employment, that neither his Abilities, nor Circumstances nor turn of Mind, are fit for.

Cushing is steady and constant, and busy in the Interest of Liberty and the Opposition, is famed for Secrisy,[1] and his Talent at procuring Intelligence.[2]

Adams is zealous, ardent and keen in the Cause, is always for Softness, and Delicacy, and Prudence where they will do, but is stanch and stiff and strict and rigid and inflexible, in the Cause.

Otis is fiery and fev'rous. His Imagination flames, his Passions blaze. He is liable to great Inequalities of Temper—sometimes in Despondency, sometimes in a Rage. The Rashnesses and Imprudences, into which his Excess of Zeal have formerly transported him, have made him Enemies, whose malicious watch over him, occasion more Caution, and more Cunning and more inexplicable Passages in his Conduct than formerly. And perhaps Views at the Chair, or the Board, or possibly more expanded Views, beyond the Atlantic, may mingle now with his Patriotism.

The Il Penseroso, however, is discernible on the Faces of all four.

Adams I believe has the most thourough Understanding of Liberty, and her Resources, in the Temper and Character of the People, tho not in the Law and Constitution, as well as the most habitual, radical Love of it, of any of them—as well as the most correct, genteel and artful Pen. He is a Man of refined Policy, stedfast Integrity, exquisite Humanity, genteel Erudition, obliging, engaging Manners, real as well as professed Piety, and a universal good Character, unless it should be admitted that he is too attentive to the Public and not enough so, to himself and his family.

The Gentlemen were warm to have the Courts opened. Gridley had advised to wait for a Judicial Opinion of the Judges. I was for requesting of the Governor that the general Court might assemble at the Time to which they stood prorogued—and if the Town should think fit to request the Extrajudicial Opinion of the Judges. I was for petitioning the Governor and Council to determine the Question first as Supreme ordinary. Gridley will be absent, and so shall I. But I think the apparent Impatience of the Town must produce some spirited Measures, perhaps more spirited than prudent.

N.B. Lord Clarendon to William Pym.[3]

The Revolution which one Century has produced in your Principles is not quite so surprizing to me, as it seems to be to many others. You know very well that I always had a Jealousy that your Humanity was counterfeit, your Ardor for Liberty canker'd with simulation and your Integrity, problematical at least. Yet I confess, that so sudden a transition from Licentiousness to Despotism, so entire a transformation from a fiery Declaimer against arbitrary Power, to an abject Hireling of Corruption and Tyrany, gives me many painful Speculations on the frailty of human Nature, as well as a Clue to the Center of the great Labyrinth of your Politicks in 1641. It has confirmed in me, the Belief, of what was formerly suspected, vizt., that your Principles were very wicked and depraved, tho your Cunning was exquisite enough, to conceal your Crimes from the Public scrutiny. I am now brought to believe what was formerly only suspected, vizt. your subornation of Witnesses, your Perjuries, and your Briberies as well as your Cruelty.

Can any Thing less abominable, have prompted you, to commence an Enemy to human Liberty—an Enemy to human Nature—an Advocate for Courts, more frightful, infamous and detestable than the star Chamber and high Commission, for Taxations more grievous, arbitrary and unconstitutional, than ship Money; on which you and your Hampden, were known to ring eternal Changes, and indeed, of which you had so much Right to complain. If ever an Infant Country deserved to be cherished it is America, if ever a People merited Honor and Happiness, they are her Inhabitants. They have the high sentiments of Romans in the most prosperous and virtuous Times of that Commonwealth: Yet they have the tenderest feelings of Humanity and the noblest Benevolence of Christians. They have the most habitual, radical sense of Liberty, and the highest Reverence for Virtue. They are descended from a Race which, in a Confidence in Providence, set the seas and skies, Monsters and savages, Tyrants and Devils at Defyance, for the sake of their Liberty and Religion. Yet this is the People on whom you are contributing, for Hire, to rivit and confirm everlasting Oppression.

[1] A more or less conjectural reading for a word partly overwritten.

[2] Thomas Cushing (1725–1788), Harvard 1744, a Boston merchant and political moderate, became speaker of the Massachusetts House of Representatives in 1766 (as his father had been a generation earlier), served as a colleague of JA's in the first and second Continental Congresses, but was replaced by Elbridge Gerry in Dec. 1775 (see note 1 on entry of 24 Jan. 1776, below). He continued active in state politics, however, as a follower of John Hancock, and was elected first lieutenant governor under the Constitution of 1780.

There is a brief account of Cushing in *DAB*; the fullest biography, based on scattered but fairly extensive MS sources, is in Sibley-Shipton, *Harvard Graduates*, 11:377–395.

³ This is the first of a number of fragmentary drafts or first rough thoughts, scattered among the Diary entries from this point through 18 Jan. 1766, for JA's three letters signed "Clarendon" published in the *Boston Gazette* in January. Containing some of the author's most characteristic thinking on the British constitution and American rights, these papers were evoked by an article signed "William Pym" (a strange mistake for John Pym [1584–1643], the leader of the Long Parliament), first published in the *London Evening Post*, 20 Aug. 1765, and reprinted in the *Boston Evening Post*, 25 Nov. 1765. "Pym" loftily dismissed the colonial arguments against the validity of the Stamp Act with the simple assertion "that a resolution of the British parliament can at any time set aside all the charters that have ever been granted by our monarchs; and that consequently

nothing can be more idle than this pompous exclamation about their charter exemptions, whenever such a resolution has actually passed."

"Pym's" position was promptly attacked by "Hampden" (doubtless James Otis; see entry of 7 Jan. 1766 and note, below) in a series of six weekly articles that began in the *Boston Gazette* 9 Dec. 1765 and ended 27 Jan. 1766 with congratulatory remarks to "Clarendon," whose final letter also appeared in this issue.

In JA's *Works*, 3:469–483, CFA reprints the three "Clarendon" letters from the *Gazette*. The rough drafts in the Diary have not hitherto been printed. Greatly revised and somewhat expanded before publication, the drafts do not always present JA's ideas in the order in which he finally used them, and they contain some passages discarded before printing. The present earliest fragment embodies some material used in both the first and second "Clarendon" letters as printed (*Boston Gazette*, 13 Jan. 1766, suppl.; 20 Jan. 1766).

DECR. 24TH. 1765.

Returned from Boston. Spent the afternoon and Evening at Home.

DECR. 25TH. 1765. CHRISTMAS.

At Home. Thinking, reading, searching, concerning Taxation without Consent, concerning the great Pause and Rest in Business. By the Laws of England Justice flows, with an uninterupted Stream: In that Musick, the Law knows of neither Rests nor Pauses. Nothing but Violence, Invasion or Rebellion can obstruct the River or untune the Instrument.

Concerning a Compensation to the Sufferers by the late Riots in Boston.—Statute of Winchester. chap. 2. if the County will not answer the Bodies of the offenders, the People there shall be answerable for all the Robberies done, and also for the Damages.—Wingates Ab[ridgmen]t Tit[le] Robberies.

Nulli vendemus, nulli negabimus, aut deferemus Iustitiam. Every Writ supposes the King present in all his Courts of Justice.

Ld. Coke says, Against this ancient and fundamental Law, and in the face thereof, I find an Act of Parliament made, that As well Justices of Assize as Justices of Peace, without any finding or Presentment [by the verdict] of 12 Men, upon a bare Information for the K[ing] before them made, should have full Power and Authority, by their Discretions, to hear and determine all offences and Contempts, vs. the form, ordinance and Effect of any stat[ute] by Colour of which Act shaking this Fundamental Law, it is not credible what horrible Oppressions and Exactions were committed by Sir Richard Empson and Edmund Dudley. And upon this unjust and injurious Act a new Office was created, and they made Masters of the Kings Forfeitures. But at the Parliament 1 H. 8. this Act 11 H. 7. is recited, made void and repealed. The fearful End of these two Oppressors, should deter others from committing the like, and admonish Parliaments, that instead of this ordinary and precious Tryal Per Legem Terrae, they bring not in absolute and partial Tryals by Discretion.[1]

Went not to Christmas. Dined at Home. Drank Tea at Grandfather Quincys.[2] The old Gentleman, inquisitive about the Hearing before the Governor and Council, about the Governors and secretaries Looks and Behaviour, and about the final Determination of the Board. The old Lady as merry and chatty as ever, with her Stories out of the News Papers, of a Woman longing to throw beef Stakes in a Mans Face and giving him a Pipe of Madeira for humouring of her, and of the Doctor who could tell by a Persons Face all the Disorders he or she had suffered and would suffer.

Spent the Evening at Home, with my Partner and no other Company.

Mr. S. Adams told me he was glad I was nominated for several Reasons.—1st. Because he hoped that such an Instance of Respect from the Town of Boston, would make an Impression on my Mind, and secure my Friendship to the Town from Gratitude. 2dly. He was in Hopes such a Distinction from Boston, would be of Service to my Business and Interest. 3d. He hoped that Braintree, finding the Eyes of Boston were upon me, would fix their's on me too, next May. His Hopes, in the two first Particulars, may be well grounded, but I am sure not in the Third.

Clarendon to Pym.[3]

Pray recollect Mr. Pym, the cruel Exactions of Empson and Dudley, under an Act of Parliament, far less ⟨extravagant⟩ dangerous to Liberty than those which you defend. Recollect the old Sage Coke, and recollect Magna Charta which your Tribe used to think more sacred than scripture. Consider once more this hideous Taxation, more cruel and ruinous than Danegeld of old, which Speed says emptyed the Land of all the Coigne, the Kingdom of her Glory, the Commons of their Content, and the sovereign of his wonted Respects and Observance. Recollect, Mr. Pym, a scene in the Tragedy of K[ing] H[enry] 8th. I think you was once an Admirer of Shakespear. Vid. V. 5. 284. 285. 286.⁴ A scene which may be very properly recommended to modern Monarks, Queens, and Favourites. I will repeat it, Mr. Pym, for the Comfort of your Soul, for you always delighted in Ruin and Confusion—an hundred Years past you endeavoured to embroil as an Advocate for Liberty. Now it seems you are aiming at the same delightful object by enlisting under the bloody Banners of Tyranny.

You tell us that a Resolution of the B[ritish] Parliament can at any Time anull all the Charters of all our Monarcks. But would such an Act of Parliament do no wrong? Would it be obeyed? Would one Member of Parliament who voted for it, return to his Country alive? No You would have been the first Man in the Kingdom, when you was in the flesh, to have taken Arms against such a Law. You would have torn up the Foundations and demolished the whole Fabrick of the Government, and have suffered Democracy, Aristocracy, Monarchy, Anarchy, any thing or nothing to have arisen in its Place.

¹ A quotation, with inaccuracies and elisions, from Sir Edward Coke's commentary on Magna Charta in the *Second Institute*, cap. 29.

² Col. John Quincy of Mount Wollaston, AA's maternal grandfather. His wife was Elizabeth Norton of Hingham (Sibley-Shipton, *Harvard Graduates*, 5:445).

³ The following fragment contains part of the text of "Clarendon's" second letter to "Pym" as printed in the *Boston Gazette*, 20 Jan. 1766, together with some matter never printed.

⁴ This is a volume-and-page reference to JA's own set of Shakespeare's *Works* (Edinburgh, 1761), which remains, with some volumes missing, among his books in the Boston Public Library. The passage referred to in *Henry the Eighth* is in Act I, Scene ii (according to modern editions, but Scene iv according to JA's), in which Queen Katherine pleads successfully with the King for the removal of taxes burdensome to his subjects. See entry of 4 Jan. 1766, below.

DECR. 26TH. 1765 THURSDAY.

At Home by the Fireside viewing with Pleasure, the falling Snow and the Prospect of a large one.

Clarendon to Pym.¹

The gallant Struggle in America, is founded in Principles so indisputable, in the moral Law, in the revealed Law of God, in the true Constitution of great Britain, and in the most apparent Welfare of the Nation as well as the People in America, that I must confess it rejoices my very Soul. For you know, that altho I was always of the Royal Party, and for avoiding Violence and Confusion, and was oftentimes transported by my Loyalty and Zeal for the nations Peace, to some Excesses, Yet I never defended the real Infringments on the Constitution. I was as heartily for rectifying all those Abuses, and for procuring still further security of Freedom as any of you. For my Education had been in the Law the Grounds of which were so rivited in me that no Temptation could make me swerve from them: Besides you very well remember the surprizing Anecdote relative to my father and me. That Scene will remain with indelible Impressions on my soul throughout Duration. I see the good old Gentleman even at this Distance of Time. I see in his aged venerable Countenance that ardent parental affection to me, that Zeal for the Laws of his Country, that fervent Love of his Country, and that exalted Piety to God and good Will to all Mankind, which constituted his Character. I was upon one of the Circuits, which lead me down to my native Country, and I went to pay a Vizit to my Aged Father. He gave me an Invitation to take a Walk with him in the Field.—Says he, my Son, I am very old and this will probably be the last Time I shall ever see your Face. Your Welfare is near my Heart. The Reputation you have gained, for Learning, Probity, Skill and Eloquence in your Profession will in all Probability call you to manage the great Concerns of this nation in Parliament, and to Council your King in some of the greatest Offices of State. Give me Leave to warn you, against that Ambition which I have often observed in Men of your Profession, which will sacrifice all to their own Advancement. And I charge you, on my Blessing, never to forget this Nation, but to stand by the Law, the Constitution, and the real Welfare and Freedom of this Nation vs. all Temptations, &c.—The Words were scarcely pronounced before his Zeal and Conscience were too great for his strength and he fell dead before my Eyes. His Words sunk deep into my Heart, and no Temptation, no Byass or Prejudice could ever obliterate them. And you Mr. Pym are one Witness for me, that I never even excused the Nations real Grievances, while I sat in Parliament with you. And after the Restoration, when the Nation rushed into Madness with Loyalty, I was obliged to make a stand to Preserve even the Appearance of the Constitution: And in the Reign of my infamous and detestible tho royal son in Law James 2d. I chose to go into Banishment, rather than renounce the Liberties of the Nation.

You may easily believe therefore that the Conduct of the Americans, is quite agreable to me. My Resentment and Indignation is unutterable, when I see those worthy People chain'd and fettered by a few abandoned Villains in the Interest of France, Rome and Hell and even in the Reign of a wise, and good King.

Mr. Smith [2] and Dr. Tufts came in from Boston. Nothing remarkable.[3] Dr. Savil spent the Evening here. Chat about the Memorial and the Hearing.

A Dissertation Upon Seekers—of Elections, of Commissions from the Governour, of Commissions from the Crown.[4]

Of Elections when they give your [5] £100 l.M. towards building a new Meeting House, and an 100 Old Ten. towards repairing one, or 50 dollars, towards repairing High Ways, or Ten Dollars to the Treasury, towards the support of the poor of the Town—or when they are very liberal of their drams of Brandy, and lumps of Sugar, and of their Punch, &c. on May meeting days. These are commonly Persons, who have some further Views and Designs. These Largesses aim at something further than your Votes. These Persons aim at being Justices, Sheriffs, Judges, Colonells, and when they get to Court, they will be hired and sell their Votes, as you sold yours to them. But there is another Sort of seekers worse than the other two,—such as seek to be Governors, Lt. Governors, secretaries, Custom-House-Officers of all Sorts, Stamp officers of all sorts, in fine such as seek Appointments from the Crown. These Seekers are actuated by a more ravenous sort of Ambition and Avarice and they merit a more aggravated Condemnation. These ought to be avoided and dreaded as the Plague, as the destroying Angells. And the evil Spirits are as good Objects of your Trust as they. Let no such Man ever have the Vote of a Free holder or a Rep[resentative]. Let no such Man be trusted.

[1] This fragment contains portions of the second "Clarendon" letter as printed in the *Boston Gazette*, 20 Jan. 1766. The published text varies markedly from the draft.

[2] Probably Isaac Smith Sr. (1719–1787), AA's uncle, a Boston merchant and shipowner.

[3] This indicates that Smith and Tufts had not heard before leaving town of the proceedings of the Boston town meeting of this day, at which it was reported that the probate courts of the Province "would be opened" without stamped paper, that the Sheriff of Suffolk co. "had served and was ready to serve all Writts brought to him, and that the Court of Common Pleas for said County next in course to sit, would meet & proceed to Business." The meeting also voted that the Boston representatives in the General Court apply to Governor Bernard "humbly to desire that the General Assembly of this Province be not further prorogued." (Boston Record Commissioners, *16th Report*, p. 160–161.)

[4] This entry is obviously the beginning of another piece intended for a newspaper. No printing has been found.

[5] Thus in MS, but almost certainly an error for "you."

DECR. 27TH. 1765. FRYDAY.

In unforeseen Cases, i.e. when the State of things is found such as the Author of the Disposition has not foreseen, and could not have thought of, we should rather follow his Intention than his Words, and interpret the Act as he himself would have interpreted it, had he been present, or conformably to what he would have done if he had foreseen the Things that happened. This Rule is of great Use to Judges. Vattell. Page 230. B. 2. C. 17. §. 297. If a Case be presented, in which one cannot absolutely apply the well known Reason of a Law or a Promise, this Case ought to be excepted. B. 2. C. 17. §. 292. Every Interpretation that leads to an Absurdity, ought to be rejected. Page 222 B. 2. C. 17. §. 282. Every Impossibility, physical and moral is an Absurdity.

At Home all day. Mr. Shute call'd in the Evening, and gave us a Number of Anecdotes, about Governor Rogers and Secretary Potter, their Persecution in Boston, their flight to Rhode Island, their sufferings there; their Deliverance from Goal, and Voyage to Antigua, and Ireland without Money, their Reception in Ireland, and Voyage to England, their Distresses in England till they borrowed Money to get Rogers's Journal printed, and present it to his Majesty; which procured Each of them his Appointment at Michilimachana.[1]—Shute is a jolly, merry, droll, social Christian. He loves to laugh—tells a Story with a good Grace—delights in Banter. But yet reasons well, is inquisitive and judicious. Has an Eye that plays its Lightnings—sly, and waggish, and roguish. Is for sinking every Person who either favours the Stamps or Trims about them, into private Station—expects a great Mortality among the Councillors next May. In this I think he is right. If there is any Man, who, from wild Ideas of Power and Authority, from a Contempt of that Equality in Knowledge, Worth, and Power, which has prevailed in this Country, or from any other Cause, who can upon Principle, desire the Execution of the Stamp Act, those Principles are a total Forfeiture of the Confidence of the People.

If there is any one, who cannot see the Tendency of that Act to reduce the Body of the People to Ignorance, Poverty, Dependance, his Want of Eyesight is a Disqualification for public Employment. Let the Towns and the Representatives, therefore renounce every Stamp man and every Trimmer next May.

[1] Maj. Robert Rogers, the famous frontiersman, had recently gone to England seeking preferment and had been appointed commandant at Fort Michillimackinac, the farthest British outpost on the Lakes. He was not a "Governor," though he would like to have been one. There was a spectacular sequel to the episode that JA records here. In the summer of 1767 Rogers and his literary factotum, the former Brookline clergyman Nathaniel Potter (see first entry

of 18 Dec. 1760 and note), had a bitter quarrel. According to a deposition Potter made and signed at Quebec that fall, Rogers unfolded a plan for a separate Province of Michillimackinac, over which he would preside as governor. He warmly urged Potter to go to England to promote this scheme, and declared that if it was unsuccessful he would go over to the French, who he had reason to believe would give him "better encouragement" than he had had from the British. Potter virtuously declined the mission and raised questions about the pay Rogers had promised but never given him. Rogers then threatened Potter's life with "an Indian Spear" that was handy. There were more arguments and scuffles before Potter escaped from the remote post over which Rogers tyrannized. General Gage ordered the arrest of Rogers, who was brought in irons to Montreal, court-martialed, and eventually acquitted, but perhaps only because Potter, who had sailed for England with his budget of charges and woes, died in the English Channel before reaching port. (*DAB*, under Rogers; Gage, *Corr., passim*, especially 1:161–162; 2:55–56; *Documents Relative to the Colonial History of the State of New York*, Albany, 1856–1887, 7:988–992.)

DECR. 28TH. 1765. SATURDAY.

Went to Weymouth with my Wife. Dined at Father Smiths. Heard much of the Uneasiness among the People of Hingham, at a sermon preached by Mr. Gay, on the Day of Thanksgiving, from a Text in James, "Out of the same Mouth proceedeth Blessing and Cursing," in which he said that the ancient Weapons of the Church, were Prayers and Tears, not Clubbs, and inculcated Submission to Authority, in pretty strong Expressions. His People said that Mr. Gay would do very well for a Distributor, and they believed he had the Stamps in his House, and even threatned &c. This Uneasiness it seems was inflamed by a sermon preached there the sunday after by Mr. Smith, which they admired very much, and talk of printing as the best sermon, they ever heard him preach. This sermon of Mr. Smiths was from "render therefore to Cæsar, the Things that are Cæsars and unto God the Things that are Gods." The Tenor of it was to recommend Honour, Reward, and Obedience to good Rulers; and a Spirited Opposition to bad ones, interspersed with a good deal of animated Declamation upon Liberty and the Times.

It seems there is a Clubb, consisting of Coll. Lincoln, the two Captain Barkers, one of them an half Pay Officer, Coll. Thaxter [1] &c. who visit the Parson (Gay) every Sunday Evening, and this Clubb is wholly inclined to Passive Obedience—as the best Way to procure Redress. A very absurd Sentiment indeed! We have tryed Prayers and Tears, and humble Begging and timid tame submission as long as trying is good—and instead of Redress we have only increased our Burdens and aggravated our Condemnation.

Returned and spent the Evening at Home.

[1] John Thaxter Sr. (1721–1802), whose wife was Anna, daughter of Col. John Quincy, and who was thus AA's uncle by marriage (*History of the Town of Hingham* [Hingham,] 1893, 3:232). His son John Jr. became JA's law clerk, tutor to the Adams boys, JA's private secretary in Europe, 1779–1783, and a frequent correspondent of the Adamses; see 13 Nov. 1779 and note 2 there.

DECR. 29TH. 1765. SUNDAY.

Heard Parson Wibird. Hear O Heavens and give Ear O Earth, "I have nourished and brought up Children and they have rebelled against me."—I began to suspect a Tory Sermon on the Times from this Text. But the Preacher confined himself to Spirituals. But I expect, if the Tories should become the strongest, We shall hear many Sermons against the Ingratitude, Injustice, Disloyalty, Treason, Rebellion, Impiety, and ill Policy of refusing Obedience to the Stamp-Act. The Church Clergy to be sure will be very eloquent. The Church People are, many of them, Favourers of the stamp Act, at present. Major Miller, forsooth, is very fearful, that they will be *stomachful* at Home and angry and resentful. Mr. Vesey insists upon it that, We ought to pay our Proportion of the public Burdens. Mr. Cleverly is fully convinced that they i.e. the Parliament have a Right to tax Us. He thinks it is wrong to go on with Business. We had better stop, and wait till Spring, till we hear from home. He says We put the best face upon it, that Letters have been received in Boston, from the greatest Merchants in the Nation, blaming our Proceedings, and that the Merchants dont second us. Letters from old Mr. Lane, and from Mr. Dubert [De Berdt]. He says that Things go on here exactly as they did in the Reign of K[ing] C[harles] 1st. that blessed S[ain]t and Martyr.

Thus, that unaccountable Man goes about sowing his pernicious Seeds of Mischief, instilling wrong Principles in Church and State into the People, striving to divide and disunite them, and to excite fears to damp their Spirits and lower their Courage.

Etter is another of the poisonous Talkers, but not equally so. Cleverly and Vesey are Slaves in Principle. They are devout religious Slaves—and a religious Bigot is the worst of Men.

Cleverly converses of late at Mr. Lloyds with some of the Seekers of Appointments from the Crown—some of the Dozen in the Town of Boston, who ought as Hanncock says to be beheaded, or with some of those, who converse with the Governor, who ought as Tom Boylstone [1] says to be sent Home with all the other Governors on the Continent, with Chains about their Necks.

[1] Thomas Boylston (1721–1798), a cousin of JA's mother; Boston merchant and,

despite his warm feelings against the Stamp Act, eventually a loyalist (*NEHGR*, 7 [1853]:148; Sabine, *Loyalists*).

1765. DECR. 30TH. MONDAY.[1]

We are now concluding the Year 1765, tomorrow is the last day, of a Year in which America has shewn such Magnanimity and Spirit, as never before appeared, in any Country for such a Tract of Country. And Wednesday will open upon Us a new Year 1766, which I hope will procure Us, innumerable Testimonies from Europe in our favour and Applause, and which we all hope will produce the greatest and most extensive Joy ever felt in America, on the Repeal both of the stamp Act and sugar Act, at least of the former.

Q[uery]. Who is it, that has harrangued the Grand Juries in every County, and endeavoured to scatter Party Principles in Politicks?[2] Who has made it his constant Endeavour to discountenance the Odium in which Informers are held? Who has taken Occasion in fine spun, spick and span, spruce, nice, pretty, easy warbling Declamations to Grand Inquests to render the Characters of Informers, honourable and respectable? Who has frequently expressed his Apprehensions, that the form of Government in England was become too popular. Who is it, that has said in public Speeches, that the most compleat Monarchy in Europe was the Government of France? Who is it, that so often enlarges on the Excellency of the Government of Queen Elizabeth, and insists upon it so often, that the Constitution, about the Time of her Reign and under her Administration, was nearest the Point of Perfection? Who is it that has always given his opinion in Favour of Prerogative and Revenue, in every Case in which they have been brought into Question, without one Exception? Who is it that has endeavoured to biass simple Juries, by an Argument as warm and vehement, as those of the Bar, in a Case where the Province was contending vs. a Custom-House-Officer? And what were the other Means employed in that Cause vs. the Resolutions of the General Assembly? Who has monopolized almost all the Power, of the Government, to himself and his family, and who has been endeavouring to procure more, both on this side and the other side the Atlantic?

Read Shakespears Life of K. Henry 8th. Spent the Evening with the Company of Singers at Moses Adams's.

Clarendon to Pym.[3]

They are extreamly proud of their Country, and they have reason to be so. Millions, Tens and Hundreds of Millions of Freeborn Subjects, are familiar to their Imaginations, and they have a pious Horror, of consenting to any Thing, which may intail slavery on their Posterity. They think that the Liberties of Mankind and the Glory of human Nature is in their Keeping. They know that Liberty has been skulking about in Corners from the Creation, and has been hunted and persecuted, in all Countries, by cruel Power. But they flatter them selves that America was designed by Providence for the Theatre, on which Man was to make his true figure, on which science, Virtue, Liberty, Happiness and Glory were to exist in Peace.

Now have not they the same Reason to contend against Parliamentary Taxations, which you and your Hampden had against regal and ministerial Taxations.—What were your Reasons?

[1] First entry in "Paper book No. 12" (our D/JA/12), a gathering of leaves stitched into a cover cut from a copy of the *Boston Gazette*, 11 Feb. 1765.

[2] The references in this paragraph are to Thomas Hutchinson in his role as chief justice of the Superior Court, and especially to what JA and others considered Hutchinson's judicial favoritism in the appeals of the customs officer Charles Paxton in the related cases of Gray *v.* Paxton and Province *v.* Paxton, 1761–1762. See entry of 3 April 1761 and note 7 there; and Appendix II, by Samuel M. Quincy, in Quincy, *Reports*, p. 541–552.

[3] This remarkable fragment was not used in any of JA's published "Clarendon" letters.

1765. TUESDAY. DECR. 31ST.

Went to Mr. Jo. Bass's and there read Yesterdays Paper. Walked in the Afternoon into the Common and quite thro my Hemlock Swamp. [I] [1] find many fine Bunches of young Maples, and nothing else but Alders. Spent the Evening at Home with Neighbour Field.

The national Attention is fixed upon the Colonies. The Religion, Administration of Justice, Geography, Numbers, &c. of the Colonies are a fashionable Study. But what wretched Blunders do they make in attempting to regulate them. They know not the Character of Americans.

[1] MS: "A"—an obvious inadvertence.

ANNO DOMINI 1766
1766. JANUARY 1ST. WEDNESDAY.

Severe cold, and a Prospect of Snow.

We are now upon the Beginning of a Year of greater Expectation than any, that has passed before it. This Year brings Ruin or Salvation to the British Colonies. The Eyes of all America, are fixed on the B[ritish] Parliament. In short Britain and America are staring at each other.—And they will probably stare more and more for sometime.

At Home all day. Mr. Joshua Hayward Jur. dined with me. Town Politicks, the Subject. ⟨*Drank Tea*⟩ Dr. Tufts here in the Afternoon, American Politicks the Subject. Read, in the Evening a Letter from Mr. Du berdt our present Agent to Ld. Dartmouth, in which he considers three Questions.[1] 1st. Whether in Equity or Policy America ought to refund any Part of the Expence of driving away the French in the last War? 2d. Whether it is necessary for the Defence of the B[ritish] Plantations, to keep up an Army there? 3d. Whether, in Equity, the Parliament can tax Us? Each of which he discusses like a Man of Sense, Integrity and Humanity, well informed in the Nature of his Subject. In his Examination of the last Question he goes upon the Principle of the Ipswich Instructions,[2] vizt. that the first Settlers of America, were driven by Oppression from the Realm, and so dismembered from the Dominions, till at last they offered to make a Contract with the Nation, or the Crown, and to become subject to the Crown upon certain Conditions, which Contract, Subordination and Conditions were wrought into their Charters, which give them a Right to tax themselves. This is a Principle which has been advanced long ago. I remember in the Tryal of the Cause at Worcester between Governor Hopkins of Rhode Island and Mr. Ward[3] one of the Witnesses swore that he heard Governor Hopkins, some Years before, in a Banter with Coll. Amy, advancing that We were under no subjection to the British Parliament, that our Forefathers came from Leyden &c.—and indeed it appears from Hutchinsons History, and the Massachusetts Records, that the Colonies were considered formerly both here and at Home, as Allies rather than Subjects. The first Settlement certainly was not a national Act, i.e. not an Act of the People nor the Parliament. Nor was it a national Expence. Neither the People of England, nor their Representatives contributed any thing towards it. Nor was the Settlement made on a Territory belonging to the People nor the Crown of England.

Q[uery]. How far can the Concern the Council at Plymouth had, in the first Settlement, be considered as a national Act? How far can the Discoveries made by the Cabots, be considered as an Acquisition of Territory to the Nation or the Crown?—and Q. whether the Council at Plymouth or the Voyages of the Cabots, or of Sir Walter Rawleigh &c. were any Expence to the Nation?

In the Paper there are also, Remarks on the Proceedings of Parliament relating to the stamp Act taken from the London Magazine Septr. 1765.[4] This remarker says, as a great Number of new Offences, new Penalties, and new offices and officers, are by this Act created, We cannot wonder at its being extreamly disgustful to our Fellow Subjects in America. The patient and long suffering People of this Country would scarcely have born it at once—they were brought to it by Degrees—and they will be more inconvenient in America than they can be in England.

The Remarker says further, that the design of one Clause in the Stamp Act, seems to be, that there shall be no such Thing as a practising Lawyer in the Country, the Case of the Saxons. This design he says ludicrously, by compelling every man to manage and plead his own Cause, would prevent many delays and Perversions of Justice, and so be an Advantage to the People of America. But he seriously doubts whether the Tax will pay the Officers. People will trust to Honour, like Gamesters and Stockjobbers. He says he will not enter into the Question, whether the Americans are right or wrong in the Opinion they have been indulged in ever since their Establishment, that they could not be subjected to any Taxes, but such as should be imposed by their own respective Assemblies. He thinks a Land Tax the most just and convenient of any—an Extension of the British Land Tax to the American Dominions. But this would have occasioned a new Assessment of the improved Value of the Lands in England as well as here, which probably prevented the Scheme of a Land tax, for he hopes, no View of extending the corruptive Power of the Ministers of the Crown had any Effect.

It is said at N. York, that private Letters inform, the great Men are exceedingly irritated at the Tumults in America, and are determined to inforce the Act. This irritable Race, however, will have good Luck to inforce it. They will find it a more obstinate War, than the Conquest of Canada and Louisiana.

[1] Dennys De Berdt (1694?–1770) had been elected the Massachusetts House of Representatives' agent in London in Nov. 1765. The letter in question, from "an eminent Merchant in *London*, to a noble Lord in the present Ministry," was printed in the *Boston Evening Post*, 30 Dec. 1765, suppl., and in other Boston papers. It is without date, but the recipient's copy in the Dartmouth MSS is endorsed "Recd. Septr. 5. 1765" (Albert Matthews, "Letters of Dennys De Berdt, 1757–1770," Col. Soc. Mass., *Pubns.*, 13 [1912]:438).

[2] The relevant section of these remarkable instructions is quoted by CFA in JA, *Works*, 2:171, note.

[3] In 1759. See William Gammell, "Life of Samuel Ward," in Jared Sparks' *Library of American Biography*, 2d ser., Boston, 1844–1848, 9:260–263.

[4] In the *Boston Evening Post*, 30 Dec. 1765.

1766. JANY. 2D. THURSDAY.

A great Storm of Snow last night. Weather tempestuous all Day. Waddled thro the Snow, driving my Cattle to water at Dr. Savils. A fine Piece of glowing Exercise.—Brother spent the Evening here in chearful Chat.

At Phyladelphia, the Heart and Hand fire Company has expelled Mr. Hewes [Hughes] the Stamp Man for that Colony. The Freemen of Talbot County in Maryland have erected a Jibbet before the Door of the Court House 20 feet High, and have hanged on it, the Effigies of a Stamp Informer in Chains, in Terrorem, till the Stamp Act shall be repealed, and have resolved unanimously to hold in Utter Contempt and Abhorrence every Stamp Officer, and every Favourer of the Stamp Act, and to have no Communication with any such Person, not even to speak to him, unless to upbraid him with his Baseness.—So tryumphant is the Spirit of Liberty, every where.—Such an Union was never before known in America. In the Wars that have been with the french and Indians, a Union could never be effected.—I pitty my unhappy fellow Subjects in Quebeck and Hallifax, for the great Misfortune that has befallen them. Quebec consists chiefly of French Men who [are mixed][1] with a few English and awed by an Army—tho it seems the Discontent there is so great that the Gazette is drop'd. Hallifax consists of a sett of Fugitives and Vagabonds, who are also kept in fear by a Fleet and an Army. But can no Punishment be devised for Barbadoes and Port Royal in Jamaica? For their base Desertion of the Cause of Liberty? Their tame Surrender of the Rights of Britons? Their mean, timid Resignation to slavery? Meeching, sordid, stupid Creatures, below Contempt, below Pity. They deserve to be made Slaves to their own Negroes. But they live under the scortching Sun, which melts them, dissipates their Spirits and relaxes their Nerves. Yet their Negroes seem to have more of the Spirit of Liberty, than they. I think we sometimes read of Insurrections among their Negroes. I could wish that some of their Blacks had been appointed Distributors and Inspectors &c. over their Masters. This would have but a little aggravated the Indignity.

[1] CFA's conjecture for an inadvertent omission by the diarist.

1766. JANY. 3D. FRYDAY.

Fair Weather and Snow enough. Major Miller, Dr. Savil and Mr. Joseph Penniman spent the Evening, with me. Agriculture, Commerce, Fishery, Arts, Manufactures, Town, Provincial, American, and national Politicks the Subject.—Anecdote, in the Beginning of the Year, Deacon Penniman was for reducing the Salary of the School Master from 330 to 300£. The Master Penniman insisted on keeping half the time in the Middle Precinct, if he had but 300, to which the Select Men agreed. But when the Time came for Penniman to remove to the School in the Middle Precinct, Moses French, who had for many Winters kept the School there, and had been an active Advocate for Deacon Penniman, complained that he had depended on that School, and had not provided any other Business, and petitioned to keep it. So that the Deacon was obliged to move the select Men to agree afresh with Penniman and allow him his 330£ to keep at the North End. Thus it seems the Deacon did not see to the End of the Year when he began it.

1766. JANY. 4. SATURDAY.

Edes & Gill's Gazette brought in. I find that Somebody has published the very scene in Shakespears H[enry] 8, which I have put into Ld. Clarendons Letter to Pym.[1] This brings to my Mind again Ld. Bacons Doctrine of secret, invisible Connections and communications, and unknown undiscovered Laws of Nature. Hampden writes to Pym on the Failure of Justice in America, on the shutting up of the Courts of Justice, since October. He has given the Public Mr. Otis's Arguments before the Governor and Council, from Magna Charta, Ld. Coke, the Judges Oaths &c.—and promises to give more.

[1] See 25 Dec. 1765 and note, above. The scene from *Henry the Eighth* was printed in the *Boston Gazette*, 30 Dec. 1765, suppl., with an introductory note signed "A.B." As a result, JA did not use it in his "Clarendon" letters.

SUNDAY. JANY. 5TH. 1766.

Heard Mr. Wibird all Day. A Sacramental Sermon on "It is finished.—"

MONDAY [6 JANUARY].

At Home. Mr. Smith and Mr. Penniman dined here.

TUESDAY [7 JANUARY].

At Boston. Hampden has given us in Yesterdays Gazette, a long Letter to Pym upon shutting up the Courts, in which he proves from Holts and Pollexfens Arguments at the Revolution Conference, from Grotius De Jure Belli, B. 1. C. 3. §. 2. that shutting up the Courts is an Abdication of the Throne, a Discharge of the Subjects from their Allegiance, and a total Dissolution of Government and Reduction of all Men to a state of Nature. And he proves from Bracton that partial Tumults, &c. are not a Tempus Guerrium, (Bellorum) a Time of War.

Sam. Waterhouse has made a most malicious, ungenerous, Attack upon James Lovell Jur. the Usher of the Grammar school, and insinuated about feminine Gender and Conjunction Copulative—as Y.Z. and H. had attacked him, about Idleness and familiar Spirits, and Zanyship, and Expectancy of a Deputation &c.[1] This Way of reviling one another is very shocking to Humanity and very dangerous in its Consequences. To pry into a Mans private Life, and expose to the World, all the Vices, and Follies of Youth, to paint before the Public Eye, all the Blotts and Stains, in a Mans private Character, must excite the Commisseration of every Reader, to the Object, and his Indignation against the Author of such Abuse.

Spent half an Hour with Father Dana, another with Samuel Quincy, an Hour with Mr. Otis, &c. Otis is in high Spirits, is preparing for next Mondays Paper.[2] Says that Mr. Trail brings very comfortable News, that Conway told him the Stamp Act must be repealed, that there was some Difficulty about coming off with Honor and that America would boast that she had conquered Britain. But he hoped the Americans would Petition. He longed to receive some Petitions &c. John Wentworth writes his Uncle Saml., that the Marquis of Rockingham told him, he would give his Interest to repeal 100 stamp Acts, before he would run the Risque of such Confusions, as would be caused by Enforcing it. That he knew there were already 10,000 Workmen discharged from Business, in Consequence of the Advices from America.

Clarendon to Pym.[3]

Nothing gave me so much Regret, or such Remorse in my whole Life, as the Part I acted in conniving at some of King Charles's grievous and illegal Measures, and the Pains I took to support him, and his two oppressive Instruments Laud and Strafford. But my very zealous Attachment to the Church and the enthusiastical Spirit of Party, made me see many Objects in a Partial Light. I have condemned my self for these faults from that Time to this. And it grieves me to hear that the Barbadians have acted so vile a Part, in the Year 1765. That Island was settled, under the Protectorate of Cromwell, by zealous Partisans for Passive Obedience, and I suppose a Remnant of the servile Spirit of their Ancestors, and of those ruinous Doctrines have prevailed on them to submit. I said under the Protectorate for I must own I can scarcely prevail on my self to call it an Usurpation, or the struggle made by you and Hampden and others, a Rebellion. If I was to revise my History, I should alter many Things which the Rage of Party hurried me to record, and in Particular, the Tittle of that Work.

¹ These pieces appeared from time to time in both the *Boston Evening Post* and the *Boston Gazette*, Nov. 1765–Jan. 1766. They have decidedly lost their savor, if they ever had any. James Lovell (1737–1814), Harvard 1756, a teacher in the South Grammar School in Boston, achieved local celebrity by delivering the earliest of the anniversary orations on the "Boston Massacre," 1771. A zealous patriot, he was elected to the Continental Congress late in 1776, where he served for five years on (and for long periods *as*) the Committee for Foreign Affairs, distinguishing himself equally, according to Edmund C. Burnett, by his diligence and his love of intrigue and mystifica-

tion. In both his official capacity and as a family friend, Lovell corresponded voluminously with JA and AA, indiscriminately mixing international and personal affairs and views in his always lively letters. Burnett's short account of Lovell in *DAB* is masterly, but a more comprehensive biography, drawing on his widely dispersed papers, is badly needed.

² This can hardly mean anything else than that Otis was the author of the "Hampden" letters to "William Pym," and that Otis told JA so at this time.

³ Draft of a fragment of the second "Clarendon" letter as published in the *Boston Gazette*, 20 Jan. 1766.

WEDNESDAY JANY. 8TH. 1766.

At Home. Wrote &c.

THURSDAY JANY. 9TH. 1765 [*i.e.* 1766].

At Home.

> Tantone Novorum
> Proventu Scelerum quærunt uter imperet Urbi?
> Vix tanti fuerat Civilia Bella movere
> Ut Neuter.¹

Must such a Number of new Crimes be committed, to decide which of these two, Cæsar or Pompey, shall be master in Rome? One would hardly purchase at that Price, the good Fortune of having Neither of them for Master.

Clarendon to Pym.²

Grotius De Jure Belli et Pacis B. 2 C. 16. §. 22. N. 1. The Interpretation that restrains the Import of Words is taken either from an original Defect in the Will of the Speaker or from some Accident falling out inconsistent with his design. Note. 1. There are some Cases, which there is good Reason to believe, the Person who speaks either did or at least might foresee them; and yet that he never intended they should be included in the general Terms, tho he has not expressly

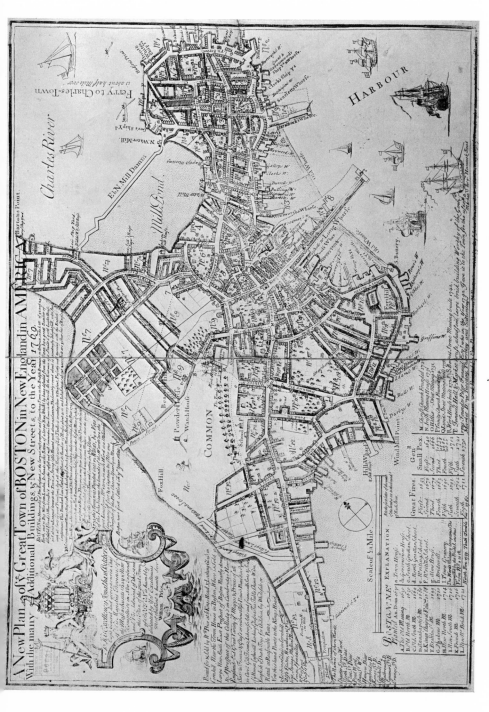

9. JOHN BONNER'S MAP OF BOSTON, 1769

Capt: Preston's Case.

2. H. H. P. C. 290. Tutius Semper est errare in acquietando, quam in puniendo ex Parte misericordiæ, quam ex Parte Justitiæ.

305. Tutius erratur ex Parte mitiori.

1. H. H. P. C. 509. The best Rule is in Dubiis, rather to incline to acquittal than Conviction.

300. quod dubitas, ne feceris, especially in Cases of Life.

2. H. H. P. C. 289. In some cases presumptive Evidences go far to prove a Person guilty, tho there be no express Proof of the fact to be committed by him, but then it must be very warily pressed, for it is better 5 guilty Persons should escape unpunished, ÿ one innocent Person should die.

Fortescue De Laudibus 59. indeed one would rather much rather, that twenty guilty Persons should escape the Punishment of Death, than that one innocent Person should be condemned & suffer capitally;

Law, no Passion can disturb. Tis void of Desire & fear, Lust & anger. Tis Mens Sine affectu, written Reason, retaining Some Measure of divine Perfection. It does not enjoin that which pleases a weak, frail Man, but without any Regard to Persons commands that which is good and punishes evil in all, whether rich or poor, high or low, Tis deaf, inexorable, inflexible.

10. NOTES BY JOHN ADAMS FOR THE DEFENSE OF
CAPTAIN THOMAS PRESTON, 1770

excepted them, because he supposed such an Exception clear in itself. There are other Cases which could not be foreseen but are such as if they could have come into the Mind of him who speaks, he would have excepted them. This is the Accident, inconsistent with his design.

§. 25. Tis also a very usual Inquiry, whether Acts are to be understood, with this tacit Condition *if things continue in the same Posture, they are now in*: and We frequently read in History, of Embassadors, who understanding that there was so great a Turn in Affairs, as would render the whole Matter and reason of their Embassy void, have returned home without opening their Commission at all. (implied Conditions, tacit Exceptions, tacit Restrictions.)

§. 26. Since it is impossible to foresee and specify every Accident, there is a Necessity for reserving the Liberty of exempting such Cases, as the Speaker would, were he present him self, exempt. One infallible Token that there ought to be such an Exemption is, when to adhere precisely to the Letter would be unlawful i.e. repugnant to the Laws of God and Nature. Another Token of Restriction shall be this, when to stick close to the Letter, is not absolutely, and of it self unlawful, but when upon Considering the Thing with Candor and Impartiality, it appears too grievous and burdensome. Seneca says, In the Law you say there is nothing excepted. But however, many Things which are not expressly excepted, are yet evidently implied to be so. The Letter indeed is narrow but the meaning extensive, and some Things are so very plain, as to want no Exception at all. And again, We engage to appear in Court on a certain day, and yet all those who do not appear, are not liable to the Penalty. There are some invincible Obstacles that excuse a Non Performance.

Thus all the Rules, that have been framed by Phylosophers, Civilians, and Common Lawyers, for the Interpretation of Promises, Covenants, nay Oaths, Treaties, Commissions, Instructions, Edicts and Acts of Parliament, are exactly coincident with the Maxim of Common sense, in the Conduct of private Life, that Cases of Necessity and Impossibility are always excepted. That there is a Necessity for proceeding with Business, has been proved by your old Friend Hampden, beyond all Contradiction. He has proved that Protection and Allegiance are reciprocal, that a Failure of Justice without actual Violence as in Cases of Invasion and Rebellion, is an Abdication of the Crown and Throne. So that if the Prevention of a total Dissolution of Government and an universal Reduction of all Men to a state of Nature, is a Case of Necessity, this Province is at present in that Case.

[1] "Lucan's Pharsalia, l. 2, v. 60" (CFA's note in JA, *Works*, 2:175).

² The following notes and extracts from Grotius were not used in any of JA's "Clarendon" letters as published.

THURSDAY. JANY. 9TH. 1766.

At Home all day. Mr. Smith, Dr. Tufts, Dr. Savil, Mr. Bass &c. here.

FRYDAY. JANY. 10TH. 1766.

Humphry Ploughjogger received a Letter from a Friend, thanking him for his good Advice and presenting him with a Crimson, Homespun Cap to wear with his Hide, as a Reward.¹—Mr. Etter came in before Dinner, about his Petition to the General Court for Assistance in his stocking Weaving Business.—Went in the afternoon with my Wife to her Grandfathers.—Mr. Cleverly here in the Evening. He says he is not so clear as he was that the Parliament has a Right to tax Us. He rather thinks it has not. Thus the Contagion of the Times has caught even that Bigot to passive Obedience and non Resistance. It has made him waver. It is almost the first Time I ever knew him converted or even brought to doubt and hesitate about any of his favourite Points, as the Authority of Parliament to tax us was one. Nay he used to assert possitively, that the King was as absolute in the Plantations as the great Turk in his dominions.

Mr. Quincy gave me, some Anecdotes about John Boylstone² and Jo. Green &c. Green refused to sign the Resolutions of Merchants at first, but was afterwards glad to send for the Paper. They were at first afraid of Salem, Newbury, Marblehead and Plymouth, but these Towns have agreed unanimously to the same Resolutions.

What will they say in England, when they see the Resolves of the American Legislatures, the Petitions from the united Colonies, the Resolutions of the Merchants in Boston, N. York, Phyladelphia &c.

¹ This letter has not been found. In his latest "Ploughjogger" letter to the *Boston Gazette*, 14 Oct. 1765, JA had declared that if the Stamp Act went into effect he would put away his English-made woolen coat and wear instead the hide of his own ox, like "the folks in England before Cæsar went there."

² John Boylston (1709–1795), son of the famous Dr. Zabdiel Boylston and thus a first cousin of JA's mother; he was a Boston merchant and became a loyalist (*NEHGR*, 7 [1853]:146; Sabine, *Loyalists*).

SATURDAY JANY. 11TH. 1766.

A Rain.

Clarendon to Pym.¹

In one particular, I must confess the Americans have not acted with their usual Acuteness of Understanding, and Firmness of Spirit. I mean in that very strange Piece of Conduct of their shutting the Courts of Justice. I call it their Conduct, tho it is apparently against the general Judgment of the People, and it ought to be charged on a few Individuals, who have Other Things in View besides Truth, Right, or Law. Indeed I could scarcely have believed, that the Fact was so, had not the Town of Boston asserted it, in their Memorial to his Excellency in Council, and had it not been admitted to be true, in the Answer of the honourable Board. Shutting the Courts of Law strictly speaking, which is to appear and be tryed by the Records, is a partial and temporary Dissolution of the Government, even in Cases of Invasion and Rebellion, and as I take it so far forth reduces the People to a state of Nature, and leaves every Man in every Case to do him self Justice, and to carve out his own Remedy with his Tongue, his fist or his Sword. Now, I should be very glad to know, whether it appears upon Record, that the Courts of Justice are shut. If it does, I apprehend that Record will justify me in judging in my own Cause, and becoming in all Cases where I am injured or have a Demand, my own Lawyer, Judge, Juror and sherriff. And the same Record will prove too that we are in a state of War foreign or domestic. But We are at Peace no doubt with all foreign Nations. Well then, the only Supposition that remains is that We are in a state of actual Rebellion, and that the Judges cannot sit in Judgment for fear of actual Violence. Will any Man pretend this is our Case? Has any Man within the Province appeared in Arms, unless it was out of Attachment to his Majestys Person and Government, as a Number of the Militia of the Town of Boston did? Has one overt act of Treason been committed within the Province? Was there ever such an Act committed within the Province from its first settlement? Nay, I may go further and ask, has there been a disrespectful Speech uttered of his Majesty or his Government, thro the whole memorable Year 1765, even at Midnight? over the Bowl or the Bottle?—I believe not one.—Oh, But there was a Riot which pull'd down an House.—So have there been an hundred Riots, an hundred skimmingtons Ridings, in which some of his Majestys subjects have received Damage, some by riding a Rail and some a Bull, some for one Misdemeanor and some for another. Nay there have been such Ridings in which some of his Majestys subjects have been slain, some in which the Kings officers, sherriffs have been killed in the Execution of his office. Pray was that an overt Act of high Treason in the whole Province, or in any one Person concerned in the Riot? Was that a Foundation for shutting the Courts? and recording the whole Province in a state of Rebellion? Will it be said that there is no Record of any shutting of Courts? no Record to prove any Invasion or Rebellion? How comes it then to have been admitted by the honorable Board that the Courts of Law, so far as respected civil Matters, were to all Intents and Purposes shutt up?

The Truth is here is a strange Ambiguity affected in this Matter. Courts will sit and suffer no Business to be done but adjourn, adjourn to next Spring. So that the Clerks are at a loss whether to make out Writs, the People are uncertain whether such Action will ever be sustained at all, and they know certainly that no Execution can be had till next Spring. So that they think it not worth while to be at the Expence of purchasing Writs. In this situation of Things we are as much deprived of the Kings Protection of our Persons and Properties, as unable to procure Justice, as if an actual Record was made of Invasion or Rebellion. So that the subject is as effectually deprived of the Benefit and Protection of the Law, as if the Laws were silent, drowned in the Din of War! We are therefore in Effect deprived of the Benefit of Magna Charta.

[1] This fragment does not appear in any of the "Clarendon" letters as published.

SUNDAY JANY. 12TH. 1766.

Heard Mr. Wibird all day, at Evening Mr. Etter, here.

MONDAY JANY. 13TH. 1766.

At Boston, the Inferiour Court of Common Pleas opened. Present Mr. Wells, Mr. Watts and Mr. Foster Hutchinson. More than 100 new Entries. The Actions all called over and many defaulted and some continued. So that The Court has rushed upon the thick Bosses of the Buckler and into the thickest of the Penalties and Forfeitures.[1] — Dined at Brother Dudleys, with Gridley, Swift,[2] Lowell and Mr. Fayerweather. Fayerweather is one of the genteel Folks. He said he was dressed in Black as Mourning for the Duke of Cumberland. He said he was wearing out his black Cloaths as fast as he could and was determined to get no more till the Stamp Act was repealed. He designed to wear out all his old Cloaths, and then go upon our own Manufactures, unless the stamp Act was repealed.

One Thompson came to me at Cunninghams in the Evening, and engaged me in a Cause of Lampson vs. Buttar, which is for entering a Vessell at Louisbourg and taking away 10 Bbls. Rum. Buttar was or pretended to be a naval Officer for the Port of Louisbourg, or Secretary to Governor Whitmore, and under Colour of that Authority, entered the Vessell and seized and brought off the Rum. Now Butter pretended to give Commissions to officers under him to attend the Wharfs and Keys of the Port and to examine all Goods imported and exported, and to stop the same, and report to him if illegal, or Contrary to the orders of the Governor, &c.[3]

Mr. Gridly was in a very trifling Humour to day after Dinner, telling tales about Overing &c. and Judges of Inferiour Courts formerly, and McCarty who built the Court by the Town House &c., and Stories about Coll. Choate of Ipswich, &c. The unsmotherable Pride of his own Heart, broke out in his account of his Disputes &c. with Choat. Choat was a Tyrant, Choat attempted Things too large for him. I have tumbled him over and over, and twisted and tossed and tumbled him, and Yet he could say to me sir I was here at 9 o Clock by Agreement and you was not come.—I answered him I was here, sir, at a Quarter after 9, and you was not here. Sir the Honour of attending me might at any Time dispense with a Quarter of an Hour.—This is not Pride. If Gridley had Pride, he would scorn such gross Vanity. A new England Church he said was one Object of Dispute between them.—The People in the Pale, the Deacons, and the Minister were the Picture of a N.E. Church. No Idea of it in the new Testament. Platform too was a bone of Contention.

Spent the Evening at Mr. Adams's, with him and Brother Swift, very socially.

[1] See Edmund S. and Helen M. Morgan, *The Stamp Act Crisis*, Chapel Hill, 1953, p. 140–143.

[2] Samuel Swift (1715–1775), Harvard 1735, one of the older generation of Boston lawyers (though not admitted to the Superior Court until Aug. term, 1761), and one of the radical leaders of Boston's North End (Superior Court of Judicature, Minute Book 79; Sibley-Shipton, *Harvard Graduates*, 9:580–583).

[3] This case is entered as Lamson *v.* Butter in JA's list of actions in the Suffolk Inferior Court, April term, 1766 (Adams Papers, Microfilms, Reel No. 182).

TUESDAY JANY. 14TH. 1766.

Dined at Mr. William Coopers with Messrs. Cushing, Story, and John Boylstone. Cushing, silent and sly as usual. Story I dont know what. Cooper and Boylstone principal Talkers. Boylstone, affecting a Phylosophical Indifference about Dress, Furniture, Entertainments &c., laughed at the affectation of nicely distinguishing Tastes, such as the several Degrees of Sweet till you come up to the first degree of bitter, laughed at the great Expences for Furniture, as Nick Boylstones Carpetts, Tables, Chairs, Glasses, Beds &c. which Cooper said were the richest in N. America.—The highest Taste and newest Fashion, would soon flatten and grow old.—A Curse or two upon the Climate, preferable however to Carolina. But every Part of Europe preferable to this.—Q[uery]. Is not this Nicety of Feeling, this Indisposition to be satisfyed with the Climate, of the same Nature with the Delicacy of Tastes, and the Curiosity about Furniture just before exploded.—Spent the Evening at Cunninghams.

WEDNESDAY. JANY. 15TH. 1766.

Dined at Mr. Isaac Smiths. No Company, no Conversation. Spent the Evening with the Sons of Liberty, at their own Apartment in Hanover Square, near the Tree of Liberty. It is a Compting Room in Chase & Speakmans Distillery. A very small Room it is.

John Avery Distiller or Merchant, of a liberal Education, John Smith the Brazier, Thomas Crafts the Painter, Edes the Printer, Stephen Cleverly the Brazier, Chase the Distiller, Joseph Field Master of a Vessell, Henry Bass, George Trott Jeweller, were present.

I was invited by Crafts and Trott, to go and spend an Evening with them and some others, Avery was mentioned to me as one. I went, and was very civilly and respectfully treated, by all Present. We had Punch, Wine, Pipes and Tobacco, Bisquit and Cheese—&c. I heard nothing but such Conversation as passes at all Clubbs among Gentlemen about the Times. No Plotts, no Machinations. They Chose a Committee to make Preparations for grand Rejoicings upon the Arrival of the News of a Repeal of the Stamp Act, and I heard afterwards they are to have such Illuminations, Bonfires, Piramids, Obelisks, such grand Exhibitions, and such Fireworks, as were never before seen in America.—I wish they mayn't be disappointed.

THURSDAY. JANY. 16TH. 1766.

Dined at Mr. Nick Boylstones, with the two Mr. Boylstones, two Mr. Smiths, Mr. Hallowel[1] and the Ladies. An elegant Dinner indeed! Went over the House to view the Furniture, which alone cost a thousand Pounds sterling. A Seat it is for a noble Man, a Prince. The Turkey Carpets, the painted Hangings, the Marble Tables, the rich Beds with crimson Damask Curtains and Counterpins, the beautiful Chimny Clock, the Spacious Garden, are the most magnificent of any Thing I have ever seen.

The Conversation of the two Boylstones and Hallowell is a Curiosity. Hotspurs all.—Tantivi.[2]—Nick. is a warm Friend of the Lieutenant

Governor, and inclining towards the Governor. Tom a firebrand against both. Tom is a perfect Viper—a Fiend—a Jew—a Devil—but is orthodox in Politicks however. Hallowell tells stories about Otis and drops Hints about Adams, &c., and about Mr. Dudley Atkins of Newbury. Otis told him, he says, that the Parliament had a Right to tax the Colonies and he was a d——d fool who deny'd it, and that this People never would be quiet till we had a Council from Home, till our Charter was taken away, and till we had regular Troops quartered upon Us.

⟨*He came up under the*⟩ He says he saw Adams under the Tree of Liberty, when the Effigies hung there and asked him who they were and what. He said he did not know, he could not tell. He wanted to enquire.

He says Mr. Dudley Atkins was too well acquainted with the Secret of some riots there, to be entirely depended on, in his Account, &c.

Nick Boylstone is full of Stories about Jemmy and Solomon Davis. Solomon says, Country man I dont see what Occasion there is for a Governor and Council and House. You and the Town would do well enough.

Spent the Evening at Bracketts with Gen. Winslow, Coll. Bradford, Mr. Otis, Father Danforth, Coll. Richmond, Mr. [Brinlys?], and Mr. [Caldwell?] and Captain Hayward. Mr. Otis gave Us some Account of Ruggles's Behaviour, at the Congress,[3] and Winslow told Us about catching Bass with Eeel Spears, at the North River. Otis says, that when they came to sign Ruggles moved that none of them should sign, but that the Petitions should be carried back to the assemblies, to see if they would adopt them. This would have defeated the whole Enterprize. This Ruggles has an inflexible Oddity about him, which has gained him a Character for Courage and Probity, but renders him a disagreable Companion in Business.

[1] Benjamin Hallowell (1725-1799), comptroller of the customs in Boston, had married Mary, a sister of Nicholas and Thomas Boylston and a first cousin of JA's mother. The Hallowells' son Ward (1747-1828), who in 1770 took the name Ward Nicholas Boylston upon the promise of a large inheritance from his uncle, was to be closely associated with two generations of the Adams family. (Robert Hallowell Gardiner, *Early Recollections*, Hallowell, Me., 1936, p. 4-11; Sabine, *Loyalists*, under Benjamin Hallowell and W. N. Boylston respectively; Francis E. Blake, *History of the Town of Princeton*, Princeton,

Mass., 1915, 1:278-280; 2:28.)

[2] That is, they ride at full gallop. CFA reads "Tantivy Nick," which was quite possibly what JA meant to write (the word being associated with high toryism; see *OED*), but the punctuation in the MS does not warrant such a reading.

[3] The Stamp Act Congress, held at New York in Oct. 1765, to which nine colonies sent delegates. Timothy Ruggles and the younger Otis were two of the three sent by Massachusetts, and Ruggles served as presiding officer. See Edmund S. and Helen M. Morgan, *The Stamp Act Crisis*, Chapel Hill, 1953, ch. 7.

FRYDAY [17 JANUARY].

Came home, and dined, and there stayed.

SATURDAY. JANY. 18TH. 1766.

At Home. The Dr. dined here.

Clarendon to Pym.[1]

There has been a great Inquiry, in some Parts of America, after a Diffinition of the british Constitution. Some have defined the Constitution to be the Practice of Parliament. Some have called it, Custom, some have call'd it the most perfect Combination of human Powers in society, that finite Wisdom has yet contrived and reduced to Practice, for the Preservation of Liberty, and the Production of Happiness. Some Have said that K[ing], Lords, and Commons make the Constitution. Some have said that the whole Body of the Laws are the Constitution.—I confess there is nothing in any one of these, that is satisfactory to my Mind. Yet I cannot say that I am at any Loss about my own or any Man's Meaning when he uses those Words "The british Constitution."

What do we mean by the human Constitution? The Constitution of the human Body? What by a strong and robust, or a weak and feeble Constitution? Do we not mean a certain Contexture of Nerves, fibres, Muscles, or certain Qualities of the Blood and Juices, as sizy or watery, flegmatic or fiery, acid or alkaline? These are the Ideas which enter into our Minds when we consider the human Constitution as productive of Health or Strength. And We always consider the Constitution in Relation to its End. And the Physician shall tell one Man, that certain Kinds of Exercise, or Dyet or Medicine are not adapted to or consistent with his Constitution, i.e. not compatible with that Mans Health, which he would say are the best adapted to Health in another. The Patients Habit, we will say, abounds with acid and acrimonious Juices, in too great a Quantity, will the Dr. order Vinegar, Lemmen Juice, Barberries and Cramberries, to work a Cure? These would be unconstitutional Remedies, calculated to increase the Evil, which arose for want of a Ballance between the acid and Alkaline Ingredients in his Composition. So if the Patients Nerves are braced overmuch, will the Physician order the Jesuits Bark? There is a certain Quantity of Exercise, Dyet, and Medicine, and they are of certain Sorts, which is best adapted to my Constitution, which will keep me in the best Health and Spirits, and will contribute the most to the Prolongation of my

Life. These determinate Quantities are not known to me perhaps or any other Person. And here is the proper Province of the Physician, to study my Constitution, and give me the best Advise he can, what and how much I may eat and drink, and sleep, how far I may ride or walk in a day, what Air and Weather I may improve for this Purpose and when I shall take Physick and of what sort it shall be, in order to preserve my Health and prolong my Life.

But there are moreover certain Parts of the human Constitution which may properly be called Stamina Vitæ, or essentials and Fundamentals—Parts without which Life itself cannot be preserved a Moment. I suppose that annihilate the Heart, the Lungs, the Brain, the Animal Spirits, the Blood, any one of these and Life will instantly depart. These may therefore be safely called fundament[al] Parts of the human Constitution. Yet the Limbs may be all amputated, the Eyes put out, and many other mutilations practiced on the Man, to impair his Strength, Activity and many other Attributes and yet the Fundamentals and Essentials to Life, may remain untouched and may last many Years.

Let me put the Case of a Machine, a Clock, a Watch, a Ship, or a Grist Mill.

A Clock also has a Constitution, i.e. a certain Combination of Weights, Springs, Wheels and Levers, calculated for certain Uses and Ends. This Use and End is the Mensuration of Time. Now the same Reasoning may be employed with equal Propriety, concerning a Clock as concerning the human Body. The Constitution of a Clock does not imply that the Weights and Wheels and other Movements should be so perfectly contrived and executed as never to go too fast or too slow, as never to gain nor loose a Second in a Year, or a Century. This is the Province of Quare and Graham and Tomlinson, to execute the Workmanship like Artists and come as near Perfection as the human Eye and finger will allow, i.e. as near an exact Mensuration of Time. But yet there are certain Parts in the Frame of a Watch without which it will not go att all—without which you can have no better Account from it of the Time of day than you can from the oar of Gold and silver and Brass and Iron out of which they are wrought. The Spring, some of the Wheels, the Dial Plate and the Hand—without any one of these you can have no Clock or Watch. These therefore are the Essentials and Fundamentals of a Watch.

Let Us now enquire if the same Reasoning is not applicable to Government. For Government is a Frame, a scheme, a system, a Combination of Powers, for a certain End vizt. the good of the whole Community. The public Good, the salus Populi is the professed End of all Government, the most despotic as well as the most free. I shall not enter into any Inquiry which Form of Government, whether Either of the Forms of the schools or any Mixture of them is the best calculated to this End the Salus Populi: This is the Inquiry of the Founders of Empires. I shall take for granted what I am sure no Briton will controvert, that Liberty is essential to human Happiness—to the public Good, the Salus Populi. And here lies the Difference between the british Constitution and other Constitutions of Government, vizt. that Liberty is its End—the preservation of Liberty is its End, its Use, its Designation, its Drift and scope, as much as Life and Health are the Ends of the Constitution of the human Body, as much as the Mensuration of Time is the End of the Constitution of a Watch, as much as Grinding Corn is the End of a Grist Mill, or the Transportation of Burdens the End of a Ship.

⟨*The British Constitution therefore is a Mixture*⟩[2]

The first grand Division of Power therefore in the British Constitution is into the Power of Legislation and that of Execution. The great Divisions of the Power of Legislation are into those of the King, the Lords, the Commons, and the People. I distinguish between the Commons and the People because there is a material Difference between the House of Commons and the People who depute them, and these last have as important a Power, in the Constitution as the former, the Power I mean of Election.

The Power of Execution also, consists of the King, Judges and Jurors.

So that two Branches of popular Power, are as essential and fundamental to the great End of the british Constitution, the Preservation of Liberty, and to preserve the Ballance and Mixture of the Government, and to prevent its running into an Oligarchy or Aristocracy, as the Lords and Commons are to prevent its becoming an absolute Monarchy.

The Branches of Power that I mean here are voting for Members of the House of Commons, and Tryals by Juries. This therefore is an Essential Wheel in the Watch, that the People should have a share in the making of Laws and in the Execution of them. In these two Wheels consist the security and Liberty of the People. They have no other Fortification against Power besides these, no other security against being ridden like Horses, and fleeced like Sheep, and worked like Cattle, and fed and Cloathed like Hoggs, and Hounds. Nay no other security against fines, Imprisonments, loss of Limbs, Whipping Posts, Gibbetts, Bastinadoes and Racks.

What a Fine Reflection is it to a Man, Pym, and Consolation—I can be subject to no Law that I do not make my self or constitute some of my Friends to make for me. My Father, Brother, Friend, Neighbour, a Man of my own Rank, nearly of my own Education, Fortune, Habits, Passions, Prejudices, one whose Life and Fortune and Liberty are to be affected like my own, by the Laws he shall consent to for himself and me!

What a Satisfaction is [it] to reflect, Mr. Pym, (I hope the infernal Regions have not made you forget all your humanity) that I can lye under the Imputation of no Guilt, be subject to no Punishment, lose none of my Property, or the ⟨Pleasures and⟩ Necessaries, Conveniences or Ornaments of Life which indulgent Providence has showered around me, but by the Judgment of my Peers, my equals, my Neighbours, Men who know me and to whom I am known, Men who have no End to serve by Punishing me, Men who wish to find me innocent if charged with a Crime and Men who are indifferent on which Side the Truth lies, if I dispute with my Neighbour.

[1] Rough draft of the greater part of JA's third "Clarendon" letter. The printed version, in the *Boston Gazette*, 27 Jan. 1766, varies widely from the draft; compare JA, *Works*, 3:477–483.

[2] Though broken off and scored out in the draft, this topic is developed in the letter as printed; see JA, *Works*, 3:480, first paragraph.

SUNDAY. JANY. 19TH. 1766.

Heard Mr. Robbins of Milton.

MONDAY. JANY 20TH. 1766.

Leonard gave me an Account of a Clubb that he belongs to, in Boston. It consists of John Lowell, Elisha Hutchinson, Frank Dana, Josiah Quincy,[1] and two other young Fellows, Strangers to me. Leonard had prepared a Collection of the Arguments, for and against the Right of Parliament to tax the Colonies, for said Clubb. His first Inquiry was whether the subject could be taxed without his Consent in Person or by his Representative? 2d. Whether We Americans are represented in Parliament or not?

Leonard says that Lowell is a Courtier, that he ripps about all who stand foremost in their opposition to the Stamp Act, at your Otis's and Adams's &c. and says that no Man can scribble about Politicks without bedaubing his fingers, and every one who does is a dirty fellow. He expresses great Resentment against that Line in Edes & Gill, "Retreat or you are ruined," and says they ought to be committed for that single stroke.—Thus it seems that the Air of Newbury, and the Vicinage of Farnham,[2] Chipman[3] &c. have obliterated all the Precepts, Admonitions, Instructions and Example of his Master Thatcher, and have made him in Thatchers Phrase a shoe licker and an A—se Kisser of Elisha Hutchinson. Lowel is however very warm, sudden, quick, and impetuous and all such People are unsteady. Too much Fire. Experientia docet.

Leonard gave me also a Relation of his going to Providence Court and Spending an Evening with the Political Clubb there. The Clubb consists of Governor Hopkins, Judge Jenks, Downer, Cole and others. They were impatient to have the Courts opened in this Province not choosing to proceed in Business alone. Were very inquisitive concerning all our Affairs. Had much to say of Hutchinson, Otis, &c. Admired the answer to the Governors Speech. Admired the Massachusetts Resolves. Hopkins said that nothing had been so much admired there through the whole Course of the Controversy, as the Answer to the Speech, tho the Massachusetts Resolves were the best digested and the best of any on the Continent. Enquired who was the Author of them.[4]

Enquired also who it was that burlesqued the Governors Speeches?[5] Who wrote Jemmybullero, &c.[6] Thought Hutchinsons History did not shine. Said his House was pulled down, to prevent his writing any more by destroying his Materials. Thought Otis was not an original Genius, nor a good Writer, but a Person who had done, and would continue to do much good service.

Were very inquisitive about McIntosh. Whether he was a Man of Abilities, or not? Whether he would probably rise, in Case this Contest should be carried into any Length.[7] Jo. Green, Waterhouse and Church were talk'd of as capable of Bullero and the Burlesques.

[1] Josiah Quincy Jr. (1744–1775), often called "the Patriot," to distinguish him from his father, "the Colonel," and his son, "the President" (of Harvard), since all three had the same name. Josiah Jr. was admitted to practice in the Inferior Court later this year (entry of 28 July, below), and in the Superior Court, Aug. term, 1768 (Superior Court of Judicature, Minute Book 86). He declined to become a barrister, objecting to "the Pomp and Magic of—the Long Robe" (Quincy, *Reports*, p. 317). This did not prevent his building up a lucrative practice, and he was frequently associated with JA at the bar in the following years, most notably in the trials growing out of what is called the Boston Massacre, 1770.

[2] Daniel Farnham (1719–1776), Harvard 1739, of Newburyport; read law with Edmund Trowbridge; admitted attorney in the Superior Court, 1745; barrister, 1762; though a loyalist in

sympathy, he was not driven into exile (Sibley-Shipton, *Harvard Graduates*, 10: 364–366; Superior Court of Judicature, Minute Book 79).

[3] John Chipman (1722–1768), Harvard 1738, of Marblehead; admitted to the Superior Court, 1751; barrister, 1762 (Sibley-Shipton, *Harvard Graduates*, 10:276–277; Superior Court of Judicature, Minute Book 79).

[4] Governor Francis Bernard's speech to the General Court on the Stamp Act, 25 Sept. 1765, the answer by the House, 25 Oct., and the Resolves of the House, 29 Oct., are most conveniently available in appendixes to Hutchinson, *Massachusetts Bay*, ed. Mayo, 3:334–344. Hutchinson in his text attributes both the answer and the Resolves to Sam Adams, who had just come into the House, succeeding Oxenbridge Thacher as a Boston representative (same, p. 96; see also Wells, *Samuel Adams*, 1:70–77).

[5] A long, dull parody in verse of Bernard's speeches appeared in the *Boston Gazette*, 25 Nov. 1765.

[6] "Jemmibullero: A Fragment of an Ode of Orpheus; Freely Translated from the original Tongue, and adapted to British Music. By Peter Minim, Esq;" was printed in the *Boston Evening Post*, 13 May 1765. It is a clever and thoroughly malicious satirical jingle on the younger Otis. CFA and others ascribe it to Samuel Waterhouse. A sample:
"As Jemmy is an envious dog, and
    Jemmy is ambitious,
And rage and slander, spite and
    dirt to Jemmy are delicious,
So Jemmy rail'd at *upper folks*
    while Jemmy's DAD was out,
But Jemmy's DAD has now *a place,*
    so Jemmy's turn'd about."

[7] Ebenezer Mackintosh (1737–1816), a South End shoemaker and leader of Pope's Day and Stamp Act riots. His life has been exhaustively studied in two articles by George P. Anderson, Col. Soc. Mass., *Pubns.*, 26 (1927):15–64, 348–361.

1766 MARCH 1ST. SATURDAY.[1]

Spent a Part of last Evening with Mr. Jo. Cleverly. He is a Tiptoe for Town Meeting. He has many Schemes and Improvements in his Head—vizt. for seperating the offices of Constable and Collector.—Collecting Taxes has laid the Foundation for the Ruin of many Families —John Vesey, Ben. Owen, Jed. Bass. He is for 5 select Men and will vote for the old ones Mr. Quincy,[2] and Major Miller. He hears they are for turning out all the old select Men and chusing a new sett: they [are] for having but 3 &c. The only Way is to oppose Schemes to Schemes, and so break in upon them.—Cleverly will become a great Town Meeting Man, and a great Speaker in Town Meeting. Q. What Effect will this have on the Town Affairs.

Brother tells me, that Wm. Vesey Jur. tells him, he has but one Objection against Jona. Bass, and that is, Bass is too forward.—When a Man is forward, We may conclude he has some selfish View, some self Ends.—Brother asked him if he and his Party would carry that Argument thro? It holds stronger vs. Captn. Thayer and Major Miller than it ever did against any Body in this Town excepting Coll. Gooch and Captn. Mills. But I desire the Proof of Bass's forwardness. Has he been more so than Major Miller?—Come Come Mr. Vesey, says Master Jo. Cleverly, dont you say too much. I ant of that mind.

Ego. Bass is an Active, capable Man, but no seeker by mean begging or buying of Votes.

[1] First entry in "Paper book No. 13" (our D/JA/13), a gathering of leaves stitched into a cover cut from a copy of the *Boston Gazette*, 29 Nov. 1762. For the period 21 Jan.–28 Feb. 1766 no Diary entries survive.

[2] Norton Quincy, Harvard 1736, son of Col. John Quincy of Mount Wollaston and thus an uncle of AA. In 1767 he inherited his father's large estate and devoted himself to farming in a gentlemanly manner, though he also had business interests.

SUNDAY [2 MARCH].

Heard Mr. Wibirt.

MONDAY. MARCH 3. 1766.

My Brother Peter, Mr. Etter and Mr. Field, having a Number of Votes prepared for Mr. Quincy and me, set themselves to scatter them in Town Meeting. The Town had been very silent and still, my Name had never been mentioned nor had our Friends ever talked of any new Select Men att all, excepting in the south Precinct. But as soon as they found their was an Attempt to be made, they fell in and assisted, and, altho there were 6 different Hatts, with Votes for as many different Persons, besides a considerable Number of Scattering Votes, I had the Major Vote of the Assembly, the first Time. Mr. Quincy had more than 160 Votes. I had but one Vote more than half. Some of the Church People, Mr. Jo. Cleverly, his Brother Ben. and Son &c. and Mr. Ben. Vesey of the Middle Precinct, Mr. James Faxon &c. I found were grieved and chagrined for the Loss of their dear Major Miller.[1]

Etter and my Brother took a skillful Method. They let a Number of young Fellows into the Design. John Ruggles, Peter Newcomb, &c. who were very well pleased with the Employment and put about a great many Votes. Many Persons, I hear acted slyly and deceitfully. This is always the Case.

I own it gave me much Pleasure to find I had so many Friends, and that my Conduct in Town, has been not disapproved. The Choice was quite unexpected to me. I thought the Project was so new and sudden that the People had not digested it, and would generally suppose, the Town would not like it, and so would not vote for it. But my Brothers answer was, that it had been talked of, last year, and some Years before, and that the Thought was familiar to the People in general, and was more agreable than any Thing of the Kind, that could be proposed to many. And for these Reasons his Hopes were strong.

But the Tryumph of the Party was very considerable, tho not compleat. For Thayer and Miller, and the late Lessees of the North Commons, and many of the Church People and many others, had determined to get out Deacon Penniman. But instead of that, their favourite was dropped, and I, more obnoxious to that Party than even Deacon Penniman, or any other Man, was chosen in his Room, and Deacon Penniman was saved with more than 130 Votes, a more reputable Election than even Thayer himself had.

Mr. Jo. Bass was extreamly sorry for the Loss of Major Miller, he would never come to another Meeting. Mr. Jo. Cleverly could not account for many Things done at Town Meetings. His Motion for Choosing Collectors was slighted—his Motion for lessening his fine was thrown out—and he made no Sort of figure as a Speaker. So that I believe Mr. Cleverly will make no Hand.

Elisha Niles says Sett a Knave to catch a Knave. A few days before a former March Meeting he told Thayer that he had a Mind to get in Deacon Penniman. Thayer asked him, who he would have with him? He answered Captain Allin. Thayer made him no Answer, but, when the Meeting came, was chosen himself.—Mr. Thomas Faxon of this End of the Town, told my Wife he never saw any Body chosen so neatly in his Life. Not a Word—not a Whisper before hand. Peter Newcomb gave him a Vote. He had one before for Miller, and had heard nothing of me. But He thought I should have one. So he dropped that for Miller. Jo. Nightingale asked my Wife, Mr. Adams will have too much Business, will he not. The Courts to attend—Select Man—and Representative at May, &c. Mr. John Baxter, the old Gentleman, told me, he was very well pleased with the Choice at the North End, &c. Old Mr. John Ruggles voted for me. But says that Thayer will [be elected] [2] at May. If I would set up, he would vote for me, and I should go, but Mr. Quincy will not. Lt. Holbrook I hear was much in my favour &c. Thus the Town is pretty generally disputing about me, I find. But this Choice will not disconcert Thayer at May, tho it will weaken him. But as I said before the Tryumph was not compleat. Cornet Bass had the most Votes the first Time, and would have come in the Second, but the North End People, his Friends, after putting in their Votes the first Time, withdrew for Refreshment, by which Accident he lost it, to their great Regrett.

Mark the Fruits of this Election, to me. Will the Church People be angry, and grow hot, and furious? Or will they be cooler and calmer for it? Will Thayers other Precinct friends resent it, and become more violent, or will they be less so?—In short, I cannot answer these Questions. Many of them will be disheartened I know. Some will be glad.

¹ At the town meeting this day four of the five selectmen then serving were reelected (Norton Quincy, James Penniman, Ebenezer Thayer, and Benjamin Porter), but Ebenezer Miller was replaced by JA. Since Miller was an Anglican and "inclined to the government," CFA rightly notes that this election marked "the first popular struggle of the Revolution in the town of Braintree" (JA, *Works*, 2:186, note).

² Inadvertent omission by the diarist. Thayer was reelected to the General Court, 19 May (*Braintree Town Records*, p. 411).

TUESDAY, WEDNESDAY, THURSDSAY, FRYDAY,
SATURDAY, SUNDAY [4–9 MARCH].

MONDAY. 10TH. 1766.

Last Week went to Boston, and to Weymouth, &c. I hear that Mr. Benjamin Cleverly has already bespoke Mr. John Ruggles Jur., against May Meeting. Promis'd him, as much as he can eat and drink of the best Sorts, if he will vote for Captn. Thayer. Told him he would not have acted as he did at March, if it had not been for Thos. Newcomb, and that he would vote for Thayer at May, if it was not for Thos. Newcomb. By this, the other Side are allarmed. The Craft they think is in danger. But I believe their Fears are groundless, tho I wish there was good Reason for them.

Drank Tea at Mr. Etters. He says all the Blame is laid to him, and that a certain Man takes it very ill of him.—By the Way, I heard to day that Major Miller and James Brackett Jur. were heard since March Meeting raving against Deacon Palmer, and said he was a Knave &c. Q. about this Quarrell?

I find the late Choice has brought upon me, a Multiplicity of new Cares. The Schools are one great Object of my Attention. It is a Thing of some difficulty to find out the best, most beneficial Method of expending the school Money. Captn. Adams says that each Parishes Proportion of the School Money, has not been settled, since my fathers day. Thos. Faxon says, it would be more profitable to the Children, to have a Number of Womens Schools about than to have a fixed Grammar School. Q. Whether he has not a Desire that his Wife should keep one? Jonathan Bass says the same. Q. his Wife is a School Mistress. So that two Points of Examination occur—the Proportion between the Parishes, i.e. the Sum which this Parish ought to have, and whether a standing Grammar school is preferable to a Number of school Mistresses Part of the Year and a Grammar School Part.

Another great Object, Are the Poor. Persons are soliciting for the

Priviledge of supplying the Poor, with Wood, Corn, Meat &c. The Care of supplying at Cash Price, and in Weight and Measure, is something. The Care of considering and deciding the Pretensions of the Claimants is something.

A Third, and the greatest is the Assessment. Here I am not so thorough. I must enquire a great While before I shall know the Polls, and Estates, real and personal, of all the Inhabitants of the Town or Parish.

The high Ways, the Districts to Surveyors, and laying out new Ways or altering old ones, are a 4th. Thing.

Perambulations of Lines, are another Thing.—Dorchester, Milton, Stoughton, Bridgwater, Abington, Weymouth. Orders, for Services of many Sorts, to &c.

It will increase my Connections, with the People.

TUESDAY 11TH.

Went to Boston. The C[hief] J[ustice] not there. A Piece of political Finess, to make the People believe he was under a Necessity of going a Journey this Week, but would be here by the next, was put about while Care was taken, to secure an Agreement to an Adjournment for 3 or 4 Weeks. So that Hutchinson is to trim, and shift, and luff up and bear away. And elude the Blame of the Ministry and the People.

Cushing Spoke out boldly and said he was ready to go on. He had no Difficulty about going on. Lynde said We are here. Oliver said here am I, in Duress, and if I must go on, I must. Thus Popular Compulsion, fear of Violence, of the Sons of Liberty, &c., was suggested to be the only Motive with him to go on.[1]

[1] Since no one (including the lawyers) wished to incur the possible penalties for proceeding without stamped paper, the judges like everyone else were playing the game of "Who will bell the cat?" Those named here were the younger John Cushing (1695–1778), of Scituate (Emory Washburn, *Sketches of the Judicial History of Massachusetts*, Boston, 1840, p. 298–299); the younger Benjamin Lynde (1700–1781), subsequently chief justice (Sibley-Shipton, *Harvard Graduates*, 6:250–257); and Peter Oliver, who has been mentioned earlier. Chief Justice Hutchinson's own account of the situation with respect to the Superior Court is in his *Massachusetts Bay*, ed. Mayo, 3:105–106. See also Quincy, *Reports*, p. 215–217; and the entries of 15 March, 15, 29 April, below.

WEDNESDAY. 12TH.

Returned to Braintree.

THURSDAY 13TH.

At home.

FRYDAY 14TH.

Yesterday and to day the severest Storm of Snow, we have had this Year.

SATURDAY 15TH. MARCH 1766.

The Snow is as deep and in as mountainous Banks, as it has been at any Time this Winter.—The unanimous Agreement of the Court and Bar, was, to try a few civil Causes, one at least, and then adjourn over.

SUNDAY 16TH. 1766.

Heard Mr. Wibirt all day.

MONDAY MARCH 17TH. 1766.

Rain. A Piece in Even[ing] Post March 10th. Remarks and Observations on Hutch[inson]'s History.[1] The Writer seems concerned least his Country men should incur the Censure of hissing from the stage all Merit of their own Growth.

But Q. Allowing Mr. Hutchinsons great Merit, what Disposition has his Country men discovered to hiss it from the Stage? Has not his Merit been sounded very high by his Country men?—for 20 Years? Have not his Countrymen loved, admired, revered, rewarded, nay almost adored him? Have not 99 in an 100 of them really thought him, the greatest and best Man in America? Has not the Perpetual Language of many Members of both Houses, and of a Majority of his Brother Councillors [been], that Mr. Hutchinson is a great Man, a pious, a wise, a learnd, a good Man, an eminent Saint, a Phylosopher &c., the greatest Man in the Province, the greatest on the Continent? ⟨Nay have not many proceeded almost to⟩ Nay has not the Affection and Admiration of his Countrymen, arisen so high, as often to style him, the greatest and best Man in the World? that they never saw nor heard, nor read of such a Man?—a Sort of Apotheosis like that of Alexander and that of Cæsar while they lived?

As to Rewards, have they not admitted him to the highest Honours, and Profits, in the Province? Have they not assisted him chearfully in raising himself and his family to allmost all the Honours and Profits—to the Exclusion of much better Men? Have they not rewarded him so far, as to form invincible Combinations to involve every Man of any

306

Learning and Ingenuity, in generall Detestation, Obloquy, and Ruin, who has been so unfortunate as to think him rather too craving?

There is also another Piece, in the same Paper, called Remarks on the Times, possibly by the same Hand—about Political Enthusiasm, disordered Pulses, Precipices, Vertigoes, falling on ragged Cliffs, Men of hot enthusiastical Turn of Mind, &c.[2]

Went to Town Meeting thro a fierce Wind, a soaking Rain, and miry Roads and Banks of Snow.[3]

[1] Signed "J." *The History of the Colony of Massachusets-Bay ...* [1628–1691], "By Mr. Hutchinson, Lieutenant-Governor of the Massachuse'ts Province," was printed by Thomas & John Fleet, Boston, 1764, the first of three volumes ultimately published.

[2] This piece is unsigned. CFA furnishes a sample from it in a footnote,

JA, *Works,* 2:190.

[3] This town meeting seems to have had no political overtones, being chiefly concerned with regulations to prevent obstructions to "the fish called Alewives" in the Monatiquot River and with the laying out of new roads (*Braintree Town Records,* p. 409–411).

TUESDAY. 18TH.

Went to Weymouth, found the Family mourning the Loss, and preparing for the Funeral of old Tom.—After my Return, rode to Mr. Halls,[1] and in my Return stopped at Mr. Jo. Basses, for the Papers. Major Miller soon afterwards came in, and he and I looked on each other, without Wrath or shame or Guilt, at least without any great Degree of Either, 'tho I must own I did not feel exactly as I used to in his Company, and I am sure by his Face and Eyes, that he did not in mine. We were very Social, &c.

[1] Probably John Hall (1698–1780), usually referred to in local records as "Lieutenant Hall," who in December of the present year married JA's widowed mother (Quincy, First Church, MS Records).

WEDNESDAY. MARCH 19TH. 1766.

At Home.

THURSDAY MARCH 20TH.

At Mrs. Baxters Funeral.

FRYDAY MARCH 21ST.

A fine Spring like Morning. The Birds of many Sorts, as sprightly and musical.

FRYDAY, MARCH 28TH. 1766.

I have omitted writing a Week. Dr. Tufts lodged here last Night with Yesterdays Paper. The Jany. Packet, arrived at N. York, has brought the K[ing]'s Speech, the Address of Lords and Commons, 14th. Jany., and many private Letters, which inform that Mr. Pitt was in the House of Commons and declared himself vs. Greenville [Grenville], and for a Repeal of the Stamp Act, upon Principle. Called it, the most impolitic, arbitrary, oppressive, and unconstitutional Act that ever was passed. Denyed that We were represented in the House of Commons. (Q. whether the House of Commons, or the Parliament). And asserted that the House granted Taxes in their Representative Capacity, not in their Legislative. And therefore, that the Parliament had not Right to tax the Colonies.

Q. What has been said in America which Mr. Pitt has not confirmed? Otis, Adams, Hopkins, &c. have said no more. Hampden, F.A., the Feudal System And Lord Clarendon, have gone no further than Pitt. No Epithets have been used in America worse than impolitic, arbitrary, oppressive, unconstitutional, unless it be cursed, damned, supercursed &c.

What shall we think of Mr. Pitt? What shall we call him? The Genius, and Guardian Angell of Britain and British America? Or what? Is it possible that Greenville, offensive to his K[ing], dissagreable to the People, should prevail vs. the whole new Ministry and Mr. Pitt?

FRYDAY APRIL 10TH. 1766.

At Plymouth. Court open and Business proceeding.[1]

[1] This was the Inferior Court of Common Pleas.

TUESDAY APRIL 15TH. 1766.

Went to Boston. The Superior Court adjourned again, for a fortnight. Hutchinson, Cushing and Oliver, present. What Insolence And Impudence, and Chickanery is this?

Fleet of Yesterday, gives us, a Piece from Lon[don] Gaz[ette] Jany. 8th. signed Vindex Patriæ. The sole Q[uestion] he says is, if the Americans are represented in Parliament?

Colonists by Charters shall have same Priviledges, as if born in England, i.e. that England shall be reputed their natale solum. Massachusetts by Fiction supposed to lye in England.—Q. whether this Thought was not suggested by the B[raintree] Instructions? "a fiction of Law insensible in Theory and injurious in Practice?"[1] All England is represented, then Massachusetts is.

[1] A not entirely accurate quotation from the Braintree Instructions written by JA; compare the text in his *Works*, 3:467.

SATURDAY APRIL 26TH. 1766.

The last Thurdsdays Paper is full.[1] The Resolves of the House of Commons, are the most interesting. The Bill which is to be brought in upon the first Resolve, and the Sixth has excited my Curiosity and Apprehensions the most.[2] The 1st. Resolve is that K., Lds. and Commons have an undoubted Right to make Laws for the Colonies in all Cases, whatever.—I am solicitous to know whether they will lay a Tax, in Consequence of that Resolution, or what Kind of a Law they will make.

The first Resolve is in these Words. "That the Kings Majesty, by and with the Advice and Consent of the Lords Spiritual and Temporal, and Commons of G. Britain in Parliament assembled, had, hath, and of right ought to have, full Power and Authority to make Laws and Statutes of sufficient Force and Validity to bind the Colonies and People of America, Subjects of the Crown of G. Britain, in all Cases whatever." Now upon this Resolution, a Bill is to be brought in. Q. What is the End and design of that Bill?

Another Resolution is, that all who have suffered Damages for their Desire to comply with any Act of Parliament, or to assist in the Execution of any, ought to be amply compensated.—But who are they, who have manifested a Desire to comply with the stamp Act, or to assist in the Execution of it? Winslow, Foster, Clap, Brown &c. were for Submission, in order to obtain a Repeal. Every Body has disowned any desire to comply or assist. Who will lay claim to the Character of dutiful and loyal Subjects, and to the Protection of the House of Commons in Consequence of the 5th Resolution?

Prophecies are the most airy, visionary Things in Nature. I remember the Time, when Pratt was universally call'd by the Hutchinsonians a bad Politician, and I never could hear any other Reason given, but this that his Prophecies about the K. of Prussia and General Amherst, did not turn out right. Now Hutchinson himself, Olivers, Trowbridges, Ruggles's, Winslows, have been prophesying, that Fleets and Armies would be sent to inforce the stamp Act. But they are as false Prophets as ever uttered oracles.

Foresight, Judgment, Sagacity, Penetration, &c. are but very feeble, infirm Things, in these great affairs of State and War. What Hutchinson [said][3] in the Probate office was as good a Way as any,—I never was more at a loss in my Life, about any Thing future! What the new Ministry will do, I know not. If Mr. Pitt was in I should be at no loss at all.—In this Way, an Air of deep important Wisdom is preserved, without danger of being proved mistaken by time.

¹ That is, the Drapers' *Massachusetts Gazette* (being the current title of the *Boston News Letter*) of Friday, 25 April, this issue having been published a day late. The resolves of the House of Commons quoted and summarized below were those of 24 Feb. 1766.

² The first resolve led to the Declaratory Act; the sixth excused from any penalty those who, "by Reason of the Tumults and Outrages in N. *America*," had been unable to procure stamped paper.

³ Word omitted by the diarist. The sentences that follow were presumably spoken by Hutchinson, and CFA supplied quotation marks around them.

SUNDAY APRIL 27TH. 1766.

Heard Mr. Smith.

In the Evening, I had a great deal of Conversation with Ezekiel Price, Yesterday[1] about Politicks, &c. I provoked him to speak freely by calling him an Hutchinsonian.—I swear says he I think the Lieutenant Governor an honest Man, and I think he has been most damnably abused and slandered and bely'd, &c. I know all his violent Opposers—I know them and what they are after, and their disciples in and about the Capital. There is no Man in the Province would fill any one of his offices, as he does. He is the best Judge of Probate, &c.— Flings about Otis and Adams, and about being one of their Disciples, &c.

[1] JA inserted this word above the line, possibly out of place (or perhaps he meant to cancel the words "In the Evening" at the beginning of the sentence). On Ezekiel Price (1727–1802), long active in town affairs in Boston and at this time crier of the Suffolk Court of General Sessions, there is a learned biographical note by John Noble in Col. Soc. Mass., *Pubns.*, 5 (1902):61–62.

MONDAY APRIL 28TH. 1766.

At Home.

TUESDAY APRIL 29TH. 1766.

At Boston. To this day the Superiour Court was adjourned: Hutchinson, Lynde and Cushing were present. Two of the Bar, agreed to continue an Action. Hutchinson leans over and orders Winthrop to minute an Agreement to continue. We will consider of it, says he. Another of the Bar, moved for a Continuance and no Opposition. Hutchinson orders the Clerk to enter it, a Motion for a Continuance, &c. Then the Court went to playing off a Farce, and to trying to get a Cause for the Jury. But none was then ready. Then Hutchinson proposed, what if we should adjourn to the first Tuesday in June. Then Otis and Swift moved that Complaints might be read and passed upon. Affirmed.[1] Hutchinson said, "I shall be very open in my Judgment. I am not for making up Judgment on any Complaints. I am upon Principle in it—it would not be regular, nor prudent at this critical Juncture." Cushing thought "that in some Cases of Necessity, it might be done"— with one of his most Jesuitical Looks. Lynde declared he would not belong to the General Court, in all Advents,[2] this Year. Hutchinson seemed in Tortures.—"He wanted to be out of Town, to be at Home. He was never so easy as when he was there. He did not love to spend his Time idly. If there was no Business to be done, he was for being where he could be imploy'd."

Thus the C.J. is now mustering up Fortitude enough to make public, to manifest his Desire to comply, with the Stamp-Act, and to assist in carrying it into Execution. In Order to lay claim to the Protection of the House of Commons, and to claim a Compensation for his Damages. Ay! he is now assuming the Character of a dutiful and loyal Subject.

I kept an obstinate Silence, the whole Time, I said not one Word for, or against the Adjournment. I saw the Court were determined before they came in, and they had no Right to expect that I would fall in with that Determination. And I had no Disposition to foment an opposition to it, because, an Opposition made with any Warmth might have ended in the Demolition of the Earthly House of his Honours Tabernacle.

But let me look back to the Sixth Page in this Book, i.e. to Tuesday. 11th. of March 1766, and read, What was said by Cushing, Lynde &c.—and can we be sufficiently amazed at the Chickanery, the Finess, the Prevarication, the Insincerity, the simulation, nay the Lyes and Falshoods of the Judges of the Superiour Court. These are harsh Words, but true. The Times are terrible, and made so at present by Hutch[inson] C.J. I cannot say, that Oliver fibbed, but Cushing did abominably on 11th. March.

Nathaniel Hatch says they are right—"for nothing hindered the Repeal of the Stamp Act, but what has been done here—the Riots, and Resolves, and doing Business &c."

Thus America will ring with Riots, Resolves, opening Courts, Instructions, Edes & Gills Gazette-Writers &c. All the Evil will be laid upon them—and the Congress too, and recalling Orders for Goods.

[1] CFA reads: "... passed upon or affirmed." In view of what follows, this makes better sense than the present reading, but there is no warrant for it in the MS.
[2] Thus in MS.

SUNDAY. MAY 4TH. 1766.

Returning from Meeting this Morning I saw for the first Time, a likely young Button Wood Tree, lately planted, on the Triangle made by the Three Roads, by the House of Mr. James Brackett.[1] The Tree is well set, well guarded, and has on it, an Inscription "The Tree of Liberty," and "cursed is he, who cutts this Tree."—Q. What will be the Consequences of this Thought? I never heard an Hint of it, till I saw it, but I hear that some Persons grumble and threaten to girdle it.

[1] James Brackett kept a "large and commodious" tavern on what is now the corner of Hancock and Elm Streets, Quincy (Pattee, *Old Braintree and Quincy*, p. 168-169).

SUNDAY. MAY 18TH. 1766.

Mem. to write some Speculations, upon the Union of Legislative and Executive Powers—and upon the Knot, the Junto, the Combination.

MONDAY MAY 26TH. 1766.

I have been very unfortunate, in running the Gauntlet, thro all the Rejoicings, for the Repeal of the Stamp-Act.[1]

Monday last at 2 O Clock, was our Town Meeting,[2] and the same Evening, were all the Rejoicings in Boston and in Plymouth. After Meeting I mounted for Plymouth, and reached Dr. Halls of Pembroke. The only Rejoicings, I heard or saw were at Hingham, where the Bells rung, Cannons were fired, Drums beaten, and Land Lady Cushing on the Plain, illuminated her House. The County of Plymouth has made a thorough Purgation, Winslow, Clap, Foster, Hayward, Keen, Oliver, Alden, are all omitted, and Warren, Seaver [Sever], Thomas, Turner, Vinal, Edson, Sprout are chosen. What a Change!

A duller Day, than last Monday, when the Province was in a Rapture for the Repeal of the Stamp Act, I do not remember to have passed. My Wife who had long depended on going to Boston, and my little Babe[3] were both very ill of an hooping Cough. My self, under Obligation to attend the Superiour Court at Plymouth, the next day, and therefore unable to go to Boston. And the Town of Braintree insensible to the Common Joy![4]

[1] News of the repeal of the Stamp Act, 19 March, was received in Boston on 19 May. The *Boston Gazette* of 26 May has extensive accounts of the celebrations.

[2] To elect a representative to the General Court. This proved to be Ebenezer Thayer, the incumbent. The *Braintree Town Records* give no indication of a contest between the partisans of Thayer and those of JA, but there probably was.

[3] AA2, now ten months old.

[4] Here follow six lines heavily inked out in the MS, apparently by JA and probably soon after they were written. In view of his habitual indiscretions in the Diary it is remarkable that JA felt impelled to obliterate this harmless expression of hurt pride. As imperfectly deciphered here, very doubtful words are enclosed in square brackets:

"I had [also] the mortification to see

that while allmost all the zealous opposers of the Stamp Act [were caressed]
by their Towns and chosen Representatives, Adams [*4 or 5 words*], Edson,
Doolittle and a multitude of others, I
was like to be neglected my self and that
all my friends in my own Town were
like to be neglected too."

WEDNESDAY. MAY 28TH.

General Election. At Boston. After Lecture, dined at Mr. Austins,
the Wine Cooper, with the Revd. Messrs. Prentice of Charlestown and
[Amos] Adams of Roxbury. Adams and Austin were the Disputants in
Politicks, Prentice a Moderator.

This Morning [Samuel] Adams was chosen Clerk, and Otis Speaker.
Govr. Bernard negatived him.[1] Cushing was chosen. In the Afternoon
they proceeded to choose Councillors, when Hutchinson, and the two
Olivers were dropp'd, and Trowbridge was dropped, and Mr. Pitts,
Coll. Gerrish, Coll. White, Bowers, Powel, and Mr. Saunders and
Dexter, were chosen.—What a Change! This Day seems to be the
litteral Accomplishment of a Prophecy of Mr. Otis, published two or
three Winters ago in the News Paper "The Day is hastening on, with
large Strides, when a dirty, very dirty, witless Rabble, I mean the
great Vulgar, shall go down with deserved Infamy to all Posterity."
Thus the Triumph of Otis and his Party are compleat. But what
changes are yet to come? Will not the other Party soon be uppermost?

[1] That is, James Otis Jr. as speaker. In the following entry it is James Otis Sr.
who is mentioned as negatived for membership in the Council. See Mass., *House
Jour.*, 1766–1767, p. 5, 8, 10, and entries of 11 Nov., 24 Dec., below.

THURSDAY, MAY 29TH.

The Governor negatived Otis, Sparhawk, Dexter, Saunders, Gerrish
and Bowers, and made the two Houses a most nitrous, sulphureous
Speech.[1]

What will be the Consequence?

This morning in Hatch's Office, Mr. Paxton came in. "This is the
lazyest Town upon the Globe—poor, proud and lazy is the Character
of this Town. They wont work. If the Neutrals[2] were gone, there
would be no body to throw the Water out of the long Boat in this
Town."

Trowbridge told Stories about the Virtue of some Neutrals—their
strict Justice, there Aversion to Prophaneness &c. Paxton said they
were never drunk, never disorderly, never before a Magistrate &c. &c.
&c. All this from Goffe and Paxton, was meant in favour of roman
Catholic Religion and civil slavery I doubt not.

Goffe said he had been reading the History of England, and he found that there had always arisen Men to defend Liberty, in the same manner, and from the same Principles, as they do here.

He said further that for himself, he felt so happily after his Death,[3] that he was pretty sure he had behaved well during his Lifetime. For himself, he was easy, but the poor Secretary is infirm; it will bear hard upon him. And for the Lieutenant Governor, now the Act is repeal'd, and considering how he has been used, instead of doing any Thing to make up his Loss, to leave him out of Council, and so to confirm in the Minds of the People a suspicion that he has been an Enemy to the Country, is very hard, for a Man who has behaved so well as he has.

[1] See Mass., *House Jour.*, 1766–1767, p. 11–13. A principal theme of Bernard's speech was that "the Inflammation of this Country has been a grand Object, with some Persons," and the implication was that those whom he had negatived were among those "Persons."

[2] The Acadian refugees.

[3] His political death, by his not being reelected to the Council.

JUNE 20TH. 1766.

Mem. to search the Books, with the Regard to the following Clause in the late Mr. Borlands Will, vizt. "Item, to my Son Francis Lindall Borland, who hath been long absent, and I fear is not now in Life, to him, if now living, I give all my Lands in Billerica, all my Lands in Sturbridge, my Messuage in Milk Street in Boston wherein Joseph Calef now lives, all the said Lands and Messuage to my said Son Francis Lindall and his Heirs forever. I give him allso the Sum of one Thousand Pounds l.M. of this Province, and my small Diamond Ring and my Gold Watch."

John Borland is afterwards made Residuary Legatee in these Words "Item, all the Rest and Residue of my Estate, real and personal, wheresoever the same may be, I give to my Son John his Heirs and Assigns for ever."

Q. Is this a lapsed Legacy? If a lapsed Legacy it must be parted and distributed among Francis Borlands Right Heirs.

But, I observe the Devise and Legacy is to him, if living. It has never yet been proved, probably never will be, that he was then dead, but admitting it certain he was not then living, would it follow that the Residuary Clause comprehended and extended to John what was before given conditionally to Francis.

[21] JULY 1766.[1]

Monday after Commencement. Last Saturday, I accidentally found a curious Volume, which Oaks Angier found in a Chest of Books belonging to an Uncle of his who died 45 Years ago. The Title Page and all the rest is gone till you come to the 18th. Page. It seems to be a Collection of Pamphlets, published in the memorable Year 1640, bound up together, in one Quarto Volume.

Lord Digbies Speech. 9. Novr. 1640, concerning Grievances and the Triennial Parliament.

Lord Digbies Speech Jany. 19. 1640 to the Bill for Triennial Parliaments.

Nathl. Fiennes his Speech 9th. Feby. 1640. concerning the Londoners Petition, and the Government of the Church by Archbishops, Bishops &c.

Francis Rous Esqrs. Speech before the Lords March 16th. 1640 upon presenting an Impeachment vs. Dr. Cossens, Dr. Maynwaring and Dr. Beale.

Nathl. Fiennes's 2d Speech touching the Subjects Liberty, against the late Cannons, and the new Oath.

Lord Digbies Speech, concerning Bishops and the City Petition Feby. 9th. 1640.

The Accusation and Impeachment of John Lord Finch Lord Keeper.

Lord Faulklands 2d Speech after reading the Articles vs. Lord Finch.

Four Speeches of Sir Edward Deering concerning Religion and the Government of Church.

Bagshaws Speech Feby. 9. 1640 concerning Episcopacy and the London Petition.

Three Speeches of Sir Benjamin Rudyer, concerning the Clergy, &c.

Message from Commons to Lords by Mr. Pym Novr. 11. 1640 requesting Strafford to be taken into Custody.

Articles of Impeachment vs. Thomas Earl of Strafford whereby he stands charg'd of High Treason.

Earl of Bristows Speech 7th. Decr. 1640.

Mr. Mainards Speech before both Houses. 24th. March in reply to Straffords Answer to his Articles at the Bar.

The London Petition, a Particular of Prelatical Grievances.

Articles vs. Secretary Windebanke.

Lord Finch's Speech, in the House of Commons, concerning Himself 21. Decr. 1640.

Harbottle Grimstones Speech 18th. Decr. 1640 moving for an Impeachment of the Archbishop. He calls him the great and common Enemy of all Goodness and good Men.

Message from the Queen to the Commons Feby. 5th. 1640.

Sir Thomas Roe's, concerning Trade 1640.

Lord Faulklands Speech concerning Episcopacy.

Pym's Speech after the Articles vs. Strafford were read.

Pym's Speech after the Articles vs. Sir George Ratcliffe were read.

[1] The day of the month can be supplied with certainty from the fact that commencement at Harvard in 1766 occurred on Wednesday, 16 July.

JULY 24TH. 1766.

Thanksgiving for the Repeal of the Stamp-Act. Mr. Smiths Text was "The Lord reigneth, let the Earth rejoice, and the Multitude of the Isles be glad thereof." Mr. Wibirts was Genesis 50th. 20th.—"But as for you, ye thought evil against me; but god meant it unto good, to bring to pass, as it is this Day, to save much People alive."—America is Joseph, the King Lords and Commons—Josephs Father and Brothers. Our Forefathers sold into Egypt, i.e. Persecuted into America, &c. Wibirt shone, they say.

MONDAY JULY 28TH. 1766.

At Boston. A Meeting of the Bar at the Coffee House, for the Admission of Three young Gentlemen, Mr. Oliver, Mr. Quincy and Mr. Blowers,[1] and another Meeting appointed next Fryday sennight, to consider of some Measures for Limitation, making a Pause, &c. They swarm and multiply. Sed, The Country grows amazingly, and the Time will not be long e're, many who are now upon the Stage will be in their Graves. Four Years must pass, before the 3 young Gentlemen, admitted this night, will assume the Gown. And four Years will make a great alteration in the Bar. It is not so long, since Pratt and Thatcher were in their Glory, at the Bar. Since Coll. Otis reigned in three southern Counties, &c. Mr. Gridley And Mr. Dana are between 60 and 70. Kent is near 60. Fitch, Otis, Auchmuty are about 40—Benj. Gridley[2] and Mr. Dudley are about 35—And Sewal, S. Quincy and I about 30. Within 4 Years possibly some of all these Ranks may depart. But the Bar has at last introduced a regular Progress, to the Gown, and seven Years must be the State of Probation.

Gridley, Otis and Auchmuty were the chief Speakers. Gridley however was not in Trim. I never saw him more out of Spirits. Otis told some Stories, Auch[muty] told more, and Scolded and rail'd about the lowness of the Fees. This is Auchmutys common Place Topick—In Jamaica, Barbadoes, South Carolina, and N. York, a Lawyer will make an Independent Fortune in Ten Years.

[1] Daniel Oliver, Josiah Quincy Jr., and Sampson Salter Blowers. Oliver (1743–1826), Harvard 1762, son of Secretary Oliver, was admitted to the Superior Court, Aug. term, 1768; barrister, Sept. term, 1772; loyalist (*NEHGR*, 19 [1865]:103; Superior Court of Judicature, Minute Book 79; Sabine, *Loyalists*). Blowers, Harvard 1763, admitted attorney and barrister in the Superior Court with Oliver, also became a loyalist; his later career, which was distinguished, is recorded in *DAB*.

[2] Benjamin Gridley, Harvard 1751, admitted attorney and barrister in the Superior Court, Aug. term, 1762 (Superior Court of Judicature, Minute Book 79). He too became a loyalist. JA records some amusing reminiscences by Benjamin of his famous uncle, Jeremy Gridley, in an entry dated Nov. 1769, below.

TUESDAY JULY 29TH. 1766.

At Boston—bought Gilberts Law of Evidence. Heard some Cases of Bastardy in the Sessions. William Douglass was charged by a Dutch Girl with being the father of a Bastard Child born of her Body. Auchmuty is employed, in sessions, and every where. The same heavy, dull, insipid Way of arguing every where—as many Repetitions as a presbyterian Parson in his Prayer—tedious as Applin. Volubility, voluble Repetition and repeated Volubility—fluent Reiterations, and reiterating Fluency. Such nauseous Eloquence always puts my Patience to the Torture. In what is this Man conspicuous? in Reasoning? in Imagination? in Painting? in the Pathetic? or what? In Confidence, in Dogmatism, &c. His Wit is flat, his Humour is affected, and dull.

To have this Man represented as the first at the Bar is a Libel upon it—a Reproach and disgrace to it.

WEDNESDAY [30 JULY].

At Boston. The Weather cloudy. Going to the Common Pleas to day. Let me take Minutes. Let me remark the Speakers, their Action, their Pronunciation, there Learning, their Reasoning, their Art and skill. Let me remark the Causes, the remarkable Circumstances, &c. and report [*sentence unfinished?*]

SUFFOLK SESSIONS JULY 1766.[1]

D[omin]us Rex vs. Francis Keen, for stealing Cask Molosses.

Dus. Rex vs. Mary Gardiner, for a common Scold, Quarreller and Disturber of the Peace.

Sewal. Hawkins—a common Scold is punishable by putting into the Ducking Stool. Prosecutions rare, 'tho the offence frequent. Other Crimes, not prosecuted here, as forestalling, Regrating &c.

W[escan?]. She gets drunk sometimes, and then curses and swears at her Husband, all Night, for several Nights together, and quarrells with her Neighbours.

Three Instances of Drunkeness prove a common Drunkard, 3 Acts of Barratry, prove a common Barrator, 3 Instances of Disceit, will prove a common Cheat. So 3 Instances of Brawling and Scolding to the common Disturbance of the Neighbourhood, proves a common Scold.

[1] This entry is inserted from "Paper book No. 14" (our D/JA/14), a stitched gathering of a few leaves, many of them blank, containing (except for these notes on cases in the Suffolk Court of General Sessions at the front of the booklet) entries dating exclusively in April and May 1767.

TUESDAY AUG. [5 *or* 12] 1766.

Satt out with my Wife for Salem—dined at Boston—drank Tea at Dr. Simons Tufts's at Medford[1]—lodg'd at Mr. Bishops.

[1] Simon Tufts (1727–1786), Harvard 1744, an older brother of AA's uncle by marriage, Dr. Cotton Tufts (Charles Brooks, *History of the Town of Medford*, Boston, 1855, p. 305–306).

WEDNESDAY AUG. [6 *or* 13] 1766.

Satt out from Mr. Bishops, oated, at Norwoods alias Martins, and reached Brother Cranches at 12 o Clock[1]—dined and drank Tea, and then rode down to the Neck Gate, and then back thro the common and down to Beverly Ferry, then back thro the common and round the back Part of the Town Home. Then Walked round the other Side of the Town to Coll. Browns, who not being at Home, we returned. The Town is situated on a Plain, a Level, a Flat—scarce an Eminence can be found, any where, to take a View. The Streets are broad, and strait and pretty clean. The Houses are the most elegant and grand, that I have seen in any of the maritime Towns.

[1] The Cranches had recently moved from the Germantown district of Braintree to Salem, where Richard Cranch established a watch and clockmaking business. Probably during either this first visit of the Adamses to the Cranches, or during a second visit in November of this year (see 3 Nov., below), JA and AA sat for their earliest known portraits, by Benjamin Blyth, a young and relatively little-known painter then working in Salem; see Henry Wilder Foote, "Benjamin Blyth of Salem: 18th Century Artist," MHS, *Procs.*, 71 (1953–1957): 69–71, 81–82. It is curious that JA says nothing in his Diary of these portraits, which now hang in the library of the Massachusetts Historical Society.

THURSDAY AUG. [7 *or* 14] 1766.

In the Morning rode a single Horse, in Company with Mrs. Cranch and Mrs. Adams in a Chaise, to Marblehead. The Road from Salem to Marblehead, 4 miles, is pleasant indeed. The Grass Plotts and Fields are delightfull. But Marblehead differs from Salem. The Streets are narrow, and rugged and dirty—but there are some very grand Buildings. Returned and din'd at Cranch's—after dinner walked to Witchcraft Hill—An Hill about 1/2 Mile from Cranches where the famous Persons formerly executed for Witches were buried. Somebody within a few Years has planted a Number of Locust Trees over the Graves, as a Memorial of that memorable Victory over the Prince of the Power of the Air. This Hill is in a large Common belonging to the Proprietors of Salem &c. From it you have a fair View of the Town, of the River, the North and South Fields—of Marble Head—of Judge Lynde's Pleasure House and of Salem Village &c.

MONDAY AUG. 18TH.

Went to Taunton. Lodged at McWhorters.

TUESDAY [19 AUGUST].

Dined at Captn. Cobbs with Coll. G. Leonard, Paine, Leonard, young Cobb &c.[1]

[1] John Rowe made a much fuller entry of the events of this day at Taunton court in his diary:

"19 August Tuesday Rose Very Early this morng. Reachd Taunton at Noon dind there with the Judges. Colo. Geo Leonard, Colo. Ephraim Leonard, Mr. Justice Williams and Mr. Justice Elisha Toby who was this [day] Swore into his Office also Mr. Justice Fales who is Clerk of this Court—had some Conversation with Colo. White and Mr. Adams on the Affairs of Ebenezer Stedson with B and Edwd. Davis and Gave Mr. Adams A Guinea as A fee. Spent the Evening at Mr. McQuarters with Mr. Adams, Mr. Leonard, Mr. Calef Mr. Amiel Mr. Wm. Speakman and young Mr. Cobb" (MS, MHi; this entry is partially printed under the erroneous date of 12 Aug. in Rowe, *Letters and Diary*, p. 106–107).

The case in which JA and Col. Samuel White of Taunton were serving as Rowe's counsel was that of "Benja. Davis and als. vs. Ebenezer Stetson. Coll. White appld. this. posted to Mr. Rowe" (JA's annotated list of actions in Taunton, Plymouth, and Barnstable courts, 1764–1767, Adams Papers, Microfilms, Reel No. 184).

WEDNESDAY [20 AUGUST].

Spent Evening at Lodgings with Charles Cushing, and Daniel Oliver of Middleborough,[1] Paine and Leonard—socially.

[1] Not the young lawyer of the same name mentioned under 28 July, above, but his first cousin, son of Judge (later Chief Justice) Peter Oliver. This Daniel Oliver died in 1768 at the age of 30 (*NEHGR*, 19 [1865]:104).

THURSDAY MORNING [21 AUGUST].

Fine Weather—feel well.

1766 NOVR. 3D. MONDAY.[1]

Sett off, with my Wife for Salem. Stopped 1/2 Hour att Boston, cross'd the Ferry, and at 3 O Clock arrived at Hill's the Tavern in Malden, the Sign of the rising Eagle, at the Brook, near Mr. Emmersons [Emerson's] Meeting House, 5 Miles from Norwoods, where vizt. at Hills we dined. Here we fell in Company with Kent and Sewal. We all oated at Martins, where we found the new Sherriff of Essex Coll. Saltonstal. We all rode into Town together. Arrived at my dear Brother Cranches, about 8 and drank Tea, and are all very happy. Sat and heard the Ladies talk about Ribbon, Catgut and Paris net, Riding hoods, Cloth, Silk and Lace.—Brother Cranch came Home, and a very happy Evening we had. Cranch is now in a good Situation for Business near the Court House and Mr. Bernards [Barnard's] Meeting house and on the Road to Marblehead—his House fronting the Wharffs, the Harbour, and Shipping, has a fine Prospect before it.

[1] Court records, together with notes among JA's own papers, show that in the interval since the last entry in his Diary he had attended Suffolk Superior Court in Boston when its long-delayed session began on 26 Aug., Worcester Superior Court in September, and Plymouth Inferior Court and Bristol Superior Court (Taunton) in October before starting for the November session of the Essex Superior Court at Salem. This may not be a complete list.

TUESDAY NOVR. 4TH.

A fine Morning. Attended Court all Day, heard the Charge to Grand Jury, and a Prayer by Mr. Barnard. Deacon Pickering was Foreman of one of the Juries. This Man, famous for his Writings in Newspapers concerning Church order and Government, they tell me is very rich.[1] His Appearance is perfectly plain, ⟨and coarse,⟩ like a Farmer. His smooth combed Locks flow behind him, like Deacon Cushing, tho not so grey. He has a quick Eye like ——. He has an hypocritical Demure on his Face like Deacon Foster. His mouth makes a Semicircle, when he puts on that devout Face. Deacon Penniman is somewhat like him tho Penniman has more of the grave Solemnity in his Behaviour than the other. The Picture of Govr. Endicott, &c. in the Council Chamber, is of this Sort. They are Puritanical Faces.

At this Court I also saw a young Gentleman lately sworn in the Inferiour Court, whose Name is Samuel Porter, he lived with Mr. Farnham, took his 2d. Degree last Year and lives at Ipswich.[2] Thus every County of the Province, Swarms with Pupils and students and young Practicers of Law.

[1] Timothy Pickering (1703–1778), deacon of the Third, or Tabernacle, Church in Salem, "famous" for his love of controversy and father of another Timothy, who became a prominent officer in the Revolution, secretary of state under Washington and JA, and more famous even than his father as a controversialist. See Harrison Ellery and Charles P. Bowditch, *The Pickering*

Genealogy . . . , Cambridge, 1897, 1: 81–85; James Duncan Phillips, *Salem in the Eighteenth Century*, Boston and N.Y., 1937, p. 266–268 and *passim*.

² Samuel Porter, Harvard 1763, of Salem; admitted attorney in the Superior Court, 1768; barrister, 1772; loyalist (Superior Court of Judicature, Minute Books 85, 97; Jones, *Loyalists of Mass.*, p. 237–238).

WEDNESDAY NOVR. 5TH.

Attended Court, heard the Tryal of an Action of Trespass brought by a Molatto Woman, for Damages, for restraining her of her Liberty.[1] This is call'd suing for Liberty; the first Action that ever I knew, of the Sort, tho I have heard there have been many. Heard another Action for Assault and Battery, of a Mariner by the Master of a Vessell; a little Fellow was produced as a Witness who is a Spaniard—speaks intelligible English—black Eyes, thin, sharp Features—has been among the English for 3 or 4 Years.

Here I saw Nathl. Peasley Sergeant of Methuen, 2 Years an Attorney of Superior Court, now commencing a Barister.[2] He took his Degree the Year I entered Colledge. He has the Character of Sense, Ingenuity &c. but not of fluency. He is a stout Man, not genteel nor sprightly. This is the Gentleman whom Thatcher recommended for a Justice and Admired for his Correctness and Conciseness, as another Father Reed.

Here I found the famous Joseph Eaton, at Law as usual. I knew him when I lived at Worcester where he had a Suit, I believe every Court while I lived there. He now lives at Lynn End, on the Borders between Essex and Middlesex. This is one of the stirring Instruments that Goffe has patronised and encouraged, for many Years. I remember to have heard Goffe celebrate him for self Government—for a cool steady command of his Passions, and for Firmness of Mind &c.

Eaton is now at Law with the Harts, whose Characters are as curious as his, and more so.

This Eaton Goffe set up, as Pynchon tells me, to be a Justice, but Thatcher got him indicted in the County of Essex for a Barrator, which defeated the scheme of Goffe, and he came near Conviction. Goffe grew warm and said that Eaton's Character was as good as any Mans at the Bar.

Spent the Evening at Mr. Pynchons, with Farnham, Sewal, Sergeant, Coll. Saltonstall &c., very agreably. Punch, Wine, bread and Cheese, Apples, Pipes and Tobacco. Popes and Bonfires this Evening at Salem, and a Swarm of tumultuous People attending them.[3]

¹ The case was that of Jenny Slew *v.* John Whipple Jr., in which Kent served as counsel for the appellant and Gridley for the appellee. The jury found for

the appellant (Superior Court of Judicature, Minute Book 85). Some fragmentary but interesting notes on the lawyers' arguments and the judges' queries and remarks remain among JA's legal papers (Microfilms, Reel No. 185).

[2] Nathaniel Peaslee Sargeant (1731–1791), a justice of the Massachusetts Superior (later Supreme) Court from 1776; chief justice, 1790–1791 (Emory Washburn, *Sketches of the Judicial History of Massachusetts*, Boston, 1840, p. 234–235).

[3] The 5th of November was Guy Fawkes Day, called Pope's Day in New England. See Forbes, *Paul Revere*, p. 93–97, 471–472.

NOVR. 6TH. THURSDAY.

A fine Morn. Oated at Martins where we saw 5 Boxes of Dollars containing as we were told about 18,000 of them, going in an Horse Cart from Salem Custom House to Boston, in Order to be shipp'd for England. A Guard of Armed Men, with swords, Hangers, Pistols and Musquets, attended it. We dined at Dr. Tufts's, in Medford.

There I first heard that the old Custom and Priviledge of Electing orators, Thesis Collectors, &c. by the Class, has been lately taken away, and that this Invasion of their Priviledges, contributed more than the Butter towards the late Spirit of Insurrection there.[1]

Drank Tea at Mrs. Kneelands. Got Home before 8 o Clock.

[1] The Harvard "Butter Rebellion" of 1766, a classic incident of its kind, has been graphically described by Samuel Eliot Morison in *Three Centuries of Harvard*, Cambridge, 1936, p. 117–118; see also Quincy, *History of Harvard Univ.*, 2:99–100. A ruling of 1765 required students to take all their commons at the College, but in the fall of the following year a revolt broke out over the imported Irish butter served by the steward after repeated and well-justified complaints that it was "bad and Unwholesome." The affair dragged on for weeks, proceeding through all the usual stages to an ultimate compromise. In the Adams Papers, though how it got there is unknown, is a copy of a MS memorial addressed by the undergraduates to the Overseers denying that they had entered "into Combination contrary to the Laws and Disrespectfull to the Government of the Colledge." This paper is unsigned and undated but has been filed at the end of the year 1766.

NOVR. 7TH.

Went up to my common Pasture, to give Directions about Trimming the Trees, i.e. lopping and Trimming the Walnuts and Oaks and felling the Pines and Savines and Hemlocks. An irregular, misshapen Pine will darken the whole scene in some Places. These I fell, without Mercy, to open the Prospect and let in the sun and air, that the other Wood may grow the faster and that Grass may get in for feed. I prune all the Trees I leave, Buttonwoods, Elmes, Maples, Oaks, Walnuts, Savines, Hemlocks and all. The Pines that grow in that Pasture are, i.e. the white Pines are, very knotty, crooked, unthrifty Things.—I am desirous of clearing out the Rocky Gutter, i.e. of clearing away the

Bushes and pruning all the Trees that we may see clearly the Course of the Water there and judge whether it is worth while to dig up the Rocks, and make a Ditch for the Water. And for another Reason too, vizt. to let in the sun and Air, because that rocky Gutter produces a great deal of Feed, which I would be glad to sweeten.

Afternoon, went to Major Crosbeys to see him execute a Codicil to his Will. The old Gentleman is very desirous that the Province should comply with the K[ing]'s Recommendation, to make up the Damages to the sufferers.[1]

[1] The sufferers at the hands of the anti-Stamp Act mobs. A legislative grant was at length made for this purpose, but to the annoyance of Bernard and Hutchinson it was linked with amnesty for the rioters (Hutchinson, *Massachusetts Bay*, ed. Mayo, 3:113–115).

1766. NOVR. 8TH. SATURDAY.

Fine Weather still.—Yesterday Clement Hayden came in to Major Crosbeys. He seem'd to hope, he said, that the Court would not vote to make up the Losses, but he heard to day that the King had requested it, and if that was true he knew not what to say. The K. had been so gracious, as to repeal the Stamp Act, and now to deny him such a Trifle would seem ungrateful and ungenerous. And it was our best Interest to be always in favour with him, and if we should refuse his request, it might be 10 times more damage to us, than to pay it. And He believed if this Town was to meet and to be fully informed, about it, they would not vote against it. In short Clem. talked like a reasonable Man. He said that, in all the Wars and all other Times, nothing ever happened that affected him like the Stamp Act. He said, if it had been insisted on, he knew it would not be born, and that he expected dismal scenes. The Repeal of it was great Joy, and he should be willing to do any Thing in Reason out of Duty to the K.

This Morning I asked John Clark some Questions, about it. He thinks if the King has requested it, it will be difficult to refuse it, but yet it will be hard upon us to pay it.

1766. NOVR. 9. SUNDAY.

Fine Weather Yet. Heard Mr. Penniman all Day. Spent Evening with Dr. Savil.

MONDAY [10 NOVEMBER].

Rain. Kill'd Cow. Read chiefly in the American Gazeteers, which are a very valuable Magazine of american Knowledge.

TUESDAY NOVR. 11TH.

Rain. Deacon Webb here at Tea, and put this strange Question to me, what do you think of the Lieutenant Governor, sir?

I told him, what I once thought of him, and that I now hoped I was mistaken in my Judgment. I told him I once thought, that his Death in a natural Way would have been a Smile of Providence upon the Public, and would have been the most joyful News to me that I could have heard.

The Deacon thought him a devout, pious Man, a Professer of Religion, a good Man, a Christian, &c., and a capable Man, and the best Judge of Probate that ever we had, this 40 year, and that he had been envyed. This Observation of his being envyed I have heard made by Nat Thayer before now.—He was capable, and greatly promoted and therefore envyed, at the same Time a craving Man.—[1]

I presume, it will not be deny'd, that this Province is at present, in a State of Peace, order and Tranquility: that the People are as quiet and submissive to Government, as any People under the sun—as little inclined to Tumults, Riots, Seditions, as they were ever known to be, since the first foundation of the Government.

The Repeal of the Stamp Act, has hushed into silence almost every popular Clamour, and composed every Wave of Popular Disorder into a smooth and peaceful Calm.

As the Indemnification, recommended by his Majesty, seems at present the reigning Topic of Conversation, a few Thoughts upon that Subject may not be improper.[2]

After the Repeal of the Stamp Act, every Newspaper and Pamphlet, every public And private Letter, which arrived in America from England seemed to breathe a Spirit of Benevolence, Tenderness and Generosity. The Utmost Delicacy was observed in all the State Papers, in the Choice of Expressions, that no unkind Impression might be left upon the Minds of the People in America. The Letters from the Ministry to the Governor, recommended the mildest, softest, most lenient and conciliating Measures, and even the Resolve of the House of Commons and the Recommendation from his Majesty, concerning an Indemnification to the Sufferers, was conceived in the most alluring Language. Oblivion of every disagreable Circumstance, which had happened, through the Warmth of the People in the late unhappy Times, was recommended—in the strongest Terms.

What Kind of Behaviour might have been expected from a Governor, in Consequence of such Advices from Home?

At such a Time, when the House of Representatives, newly chosen by the People, and an House which thought like the People, had proceeded with as much calm, composed Deliberation as was ever known, to the Choice [of] a Speaker, would it be expected that the Governor should Negative that Speaker? Especially as that Gentleman had been a long Time in great Esteem in the Province, had but just before been unanimously chosen upon the Congress at N. York and had executed that Trust, to the universal Acceptance of the Prov[ince]?

At such a Time, when the two Houses had proceeded, with equal Solemnity, to the Choice of Councillors, and had compleated the Election, could it be believed that a Governor should by his mighty Negative, slaughter six of the List at a blow, six of the most steady, capable, and Active Friends of the People in the whole Board?

After all this which was born without a Murmur, does it not exceed all Credibility, that this same Governor should meet the two Houses, and open the Session with a Speech—a Speech!—a Speech! I want Words to express my Sentiments of this Speech!

[1] Here a line is drawn across the page in the MS, suggesting that the following paragraphs were written after 11 November.

[2] Here another line is drawn across the page in the MS.

1766 DECR. 8TH. MONDAY.

Dined at Dr. Tufts's. Drank Tea at Dr. Halls Pembroke. Lodged at Captn. Littles Kingston.—I find a general Opposition in the County of Plymouth, to Compensation. Jacobs tells me, that Scituate voted vs. it with great Warmth. Judge Cushing Moderator did not think fit to say a Word, nor was there a Word said or an Hand up in favour of the Bill, tho they had voted for it in October. Keen of Pembroke was warm and stumped Sole [Soul *or* Soule] the Moderator to lay down the Money and prevent a Tax upon the Poor. Kingston was so fixed vs. it that they would not call a Meeting. The more considerate and sensible People however in all these Towns are in favour of it. Landlord and Landlady Little are full of Politicks. Mr. Little would get in General Winslow, and did get in Mr. Sever—and Mr. Sever is sensible of it. We had over the affair of Collector of Excise. Little dont like Judge Cushing nor Brig[adier] Ruggles, because they opposed his Collectorship, &c.

At Plymouth [1] the Province have been drawn in cleverly—to make themselves guilty of the Riots. Every Body out of the Prov[ince] will say so. The Province has been brought to pay what ought to have been paid by Boston, every farthing of it.

Paine. The Mistery of Iniquity opens more now in time of Peace than it did in Time of Confusion.

Sever said he believed Goffe would be glad to punish all the Transgressors in the late Times. Hally said he had tryed to persuade Goffe to enter a Nolle Pros. vs. the Rioters in Berkshire, but he would not and was very high &c. Paine said the Continent ought to have paid the Damage.

Nat Clap. These Town Meeting Laws are the most awful Things, and the Town of Boston ought to be stigmatized for setting the Example.

¹ Here supply the phrase "it is said" or its equivalent.

TUESDAY DECR. 23D. 1766.

I heard Yesterday, for the first Time, that young Jonathan Hayward, the Son of Lt. Joseph Hayward of the South Precinct, had got a Deputation from the Sherriff. Captn. Thayer was the Person, who went to the Sherriff and procur'd it for him. Silas Wild, Tho's Penniman, Stephen Penniman, Lt. Hayward and Zebulon Thayer were his Bondsmen—a goodly Class! a clever Groupe! a fine Company! a bright Cluster!

But what will be the Consequences of this Deputation?—and what were the Causes of it? My Brothers Disregard and neglect of the office and his Neglect to pay Greenleaf, were the Causes.

DECR. 24TH.¹

Who are to be understood by the better Sort of People?² There is in the Sight of God and indeed in the Consideration of a sincere Xtian or even of a good Philosopher, no Difference between one Man and another, but what real Merit creates. And I mean, by real Merit, that I may [be] as well understood as my Adversary, nothing more nor less than the Compound Ratio of Virtue and Knowledge. Now if the Gentleman means by the better sort of People, only such as are possessed of this real Merit, this Composition of Virtue and Ability, I am content to join Issue with him but who shall sit as judge between Us?—If a Whig shall be Judge, he will decide in favour of one set of Persons, if a Tory, he will give sentence for another; but if a Jacobite, he will be for a third.

But that I may be as little tedious as possible, I will take the Gentlemans own Difinition, and will understand those of every Rank of plain, good understanding, who by an uniform steady behaviour, testify their thorough sense of the Blessings of good Government, who without Affectation evince an habitual Regard for Peace, order, Justice and Civility, towards all Mankind. But I find myself again in the same Difficulty. And the Q. recurs, who shall be judge. Phylanthrop confidently denys that the better Sort according to this Deffinition, are either alarmed or offended at any Behaviour of the Governor. I as possitively affirm, that the better sort thro the Prov[ince] both in Boston and in the other seaport and Country Towns (I use Phylanthrops Language so will not answer for ⟨sense nor⟩ Accuracy of Writing or Grammar) are both alarmed and offended, at many Instances of the Governors Behaviour. I dont intend to submit this Question between Us to be decided by the Governor, nor by Philanthrop, nor any other of his Creatures, rich, nor poor, titled or untitled, powerful or impotent: Nor do I desire he should submit it to me, or any of my Particular Friends, Patrons or Connections.—No I appeal to the Public, to the Province, as Judges between Us, who are the better sort, in Phylanthrops sense of the Word. Let the whole Body of the Province then judge.—Well they have judged and by the happy Constitution of our Government, they must every Year determine who they esteem the better sort. The whole Body of the People, in every Yearly Election, depute a Number of Persons to represent them, and by their suffrages they declare such Persons to be the better sort of People among them, in their Estimation. This representative Body are in their Turn every Year, to chuse 28 out of the whole Province for Councillors, and by such Election, no doubt determine such to be of the very best sort, in their Understandings.

Thus far, It seems to me, I have proceeded on safe Ground, and may fairly conclude that the honourable his Majestys Council, and the honourable the House of Representatives, the Public, the Body of the People being Judges, are of the better sort of People in Phylanthrops own sense of the Words. I might go further here, and insist upon it, that the present Council, purifyed as it is, by the Governors Cathartic Negative, even his Excellency being Judge, consists entirely of the better sort of People. Otherwise, it is not to be supposed, at least by our scribler, that he would have approved of those Gentlemen. Let Us then enquire, whether his Majestys Council, and the honourable House have not exhibited abundant Proofs, that they are almost unanimously alarmed and offended at the Behaviour of the Governor.

The Council, in their Answer to the Governors Speech to both

327

Houses in May, have expressed as much Resentment against his Behaviour as can well be conveyed by Words, 'tho the Decorum and Dignity of the Board is preserved. They have flatly charged the Governor with bringing an unjust Accusation against the Province.

The honourable House in their Answers, which were adopted almost unanimously, tho they have been on their Guard, that no unwarrantable Expressions might escape them at that critical Conjuncture, have expressed as much just Indignation and disdain of his unworthy treatment of them, as was ever expressed by a british House of Commons, against a Tyrant on the Throne.

Answer to Governor['s] Speech last Session, in which the honourable House, 48 vs. 24 voted, with great Grief, and Concern and Alarm and Offence i[t]s Resentment, that the Governors Behaviour had been the sole Cause why Compensation was not made to the sufferers. This I should think was a Proof Instar omnium, that those 48 had taken alarm and offence.

Further, the House proceeded last session to the daring Enterprise of removing Mr. Jackson from the Agency, the Governors darling Friend and endearing Confederate, on whom the Governor had so set his Heart as to employ the most exceptionable ⟨Means⟩ Influence in order to get him chosen. This Removal was voted by 81 out of 87 in the House and unanimously in the Council, and the World believes, that Apprehensions of the Governors ill Intentions, and of the Danger to the Province from that Confederacy, influenced a Great Part of both House[s] to vote for the Dissolution of it.

To proceed a little further, the House are so allarmed and offended, at the Author of some late Misinformations and Misrepresentations to his Majesty, who appears beyond reasonable Doubt from Ld. Shelbournes Letter to be the Governor himself, that they have almost unanimously voted Letters to be sent to Ld. Shelbourne himself, and to their Agent, Mr. Debert, in order to remove those slanders and aspersions, in which their sense of the Ingratitude, Haughtiness and Cruelty of the Governor is expressed in very strong Terms.

But I will not confine my self to the two Houses of Assembly.

I ask whether those Gentlemen who have the Honour of his Majestys Commissions in his Revenue, are to be esteemed the better Sort of People, or not? If they are, I would ask again, have not the Customhouse Officers in General from the surveyor General downwards taken Offence at the Governor['s] Behaviour. I say [in][3] general—I would not be understood universally. I except a C—k-e[4] and a Paxton. These at least one of them, have always declared they would worship the sun while he was above the Horison, tho he should be covered all over with Clouds.

I ask further whether the Officers of his Majestys Navy, who have been occasionally on this station, will be allowed to be the better sort of People. If they should, is it not notorious that Govr. Bernards Conduct has been very disagreable and disgustful to them?

Where shall I go for better sort of People? The Judges of the superiour Court, move in so sublime an orbit—They tread in such exalted steps—That I dare not approach their Persons, so I cannot say what their sentiments of the Governors Conduct may be. They will not indulge themselves in speaking openly against any Person in Authority, so I believe they reserve their Opinion, till the Matter shall come judicially before them. Many [of] the Judges of the Inferiour Courts in many of the Counties, I can affirm, from Knowledge, because I have heard it from their own Mouths, have taken Alarm and offence, att all the Governors Negatives last May, at both his Speeches to the Assembly in May and June, at the Expression quoted in the Address of the Lords, and especially at his overbearing, threatning, wheedling Arts to get Mr. Jackson chosen Agent, and at his foolish Dismission of Military officers from Colonels down to little Ensigns— but most of all at his restless, impatient, uncontrou[la]ble, insatiable Machinations, by all Means, humane, inhumane, and diabolical, from his first Arrival in this Government to this moment, to enrich himself.

Thus I believe that it appears to all who consider the Matter, that almost all the People, whether better or worse, are of one Mind about the Governor and absolutely hate him and despize him—let Phylanthrop say what he will. And indeed I have very good Reasons to think that Phylanthrop lyed when he said that the better sort had taken no Offence, and absolutely endeavoured to impose a palpable falshood upon the Public.

[1] This entry is a draft of an essay, evidently never published, in reply to Jonathan Sewall, who had begun a series of articles over the name "Philanthrop" in the *Boston Evening Post*, 1 Dec. 1766 (and continuing more or less regularly through 2 March 1767), vindicating the conduct of Governor Bernard. "Philanthrop" depicted Bernard as an example of spotless virtue, and his articles drew out a swarm of writers on the other side of the question.

[2] See "Philanthrop" in the *Evening Post*, 22 Dec., p. 1, col. 1–2.

[3] MS: "I."

[4] James Cockle, a Salem customs officer; he had applied for the writ of assistance that led to the celebrated argument over such writs in 1761, and he was also concerned in dealings with Bernard that had been denounced by "Clarendon" (presumably JA) in a letter to the *Boston Gazette*, 19 May 1766. See Roger B. Berry, "John Adams: Two Further Contributions to the *Boston Gazette*, 1766–1768," NEQ, 31:90–95 (March 1958).

DECR. 31ST. 1766.[1]

"Whatever tends to create in the Minds of the People, a Contempt
of the Persons of those who hold the highest Offices in the State, tends
to a Belief that Subordination is not necessary, and is no essential
Part of Government."—Now I dont See the Truth of this. Should any
one say that the Steeple of Dr. Sewals Meeting was old, and decay'd
and rotten, and in danger of falling on the Heads of the People in the
Street, and say it in Print too, would this tend to induce in the Minds
of the People, that a Steeple was not necessary to a Meeting House,
and that the House might as well be turned topsy turvy, and the
steeple struck down into the Earth. Again suppose the sweep of my
Cyder Mill was cracked and shivered so that it had not strength to grind
an Apple or even to turn the Mill, if one of my Neighbours should come
in and tell me of this, would his telling me this tend to create in me a
Belief that a Sweep was no necessary Part of a Cyder Mill, and that the
Sweep might as well be placed where the Rolls are, or where the Hop-
per is, or the Trough, as where I commonly put it? Again, I take my
old Mare, which is not only old and lean, but is hipp'd and stifled and
spavined, has the Botts and has lost her Tail and both her Ears, and
put her into my Horse Cart and lead her thro the Town in the Sight
of all the People. I believe they would universally despize my old Mare,
and laugh at her too. But would all this their Contempt and Laughter
tend to induce in their Minds a Belief that an Horse was not necessary
to draw an Horse Cart, and that the Cart may as well be put before
the Horse, as the Horse before the Cart?

*Besides,[2] O—s has exerted himself so amazingly in the Cause of
America, to the loss of Estate, Health, ⟨*Trade and every Thing,*⟩ and
has had such Success, in saving her, that unless some Pains are taken
to ruin his Character ⟨*with the People*⟩ he will rise high into favour
and Power, and ever since the Affair of that Petition for a Grant to
supply the Insolvency I have hated him so, I have groaned for Revenge, and Revenge I will have, let him be as learned, spirited, sensible,
wise, generous, and disinterested as he will, I will maul him and
murder his Reputation. I will—I will. Oh the Disgrace of that Insolvency![3]

Revenge of that, made me write the Character of Bluster, Hector,
Wildfire, and Belzebub and 20 more. I have gone too far to retreat—
Nullar retror sum.[4] I will stab, sting, goad, maul, mangle and murder
his Rep[utation]—at least abroad, tho I cant do it at Home.

In fine such is the present Situation of Interests, that unless I exhibit some vigorous Exertion, unless I strike some bold daring Stroke, G—fe and I shall infallibly loose our Aim, and if we loose it now we loose it forever. Oh the chearing Rays, the benign Influences of that Office. It is worth 200 Lawful a year, besides the Reputation of it! My Children are multiplying about me, I love expensive living, and my meanes are very narrow. Good God what shall I do? Shall I starve and go to Goal? No, Self Preservation is the first Law of Nature, it can legitimate any Thing. I will not perish in this World, I will not starve and see my family suffer. I will say and write and do any Thing! I will vindicate the Governor, and will represent him roundly and dogmatically, as the best Governor, the mildest, most moderate, capable &c. that ever we had. Ay and I will pronounce boldly that I write only from Love of Order, Peace, Justice, Goodness and Truth—to support good Government, and much injured Innocence.

Much worse Things than this have been done from much less [worthy?] [5] Motives. Much greater falshoods, and [. . .] Wickedness have been used by Men in Affluence only to increase their Wealth and Power. Men who had not Hunger, and Children crying for bread to plead in their Excuse. Cæsar Borgia says whoever will arrive at Dominion, must necessarily remove all Obstacles out of the Way which obstruct his Greatness, and even forget the effeminate Tyes of Tenderness and Relation and with an undaunted Resolution run over the Thorns and Briars thrown in his Way, and with Intrepidity if need requires, even imbrue his Hands in his opposers Blood, and make a Dagger with Blindfolded Eyes, force a way to fortune.—Oh the Pangs, the pungent, excruciating Pangs of Ambition, Avarice, and Hunger.

There is a sense however in which my Professions are sincere.—I write from a Regard to the Peace of my family, and to silence the importunate Clamours of an empty craving stomack. I write to keep my Constitution in order for without something to eat, I am sure all will soon be in Confusion, with me. I write from a Regard to Justice, because that demands that my Creditors should be paid their Dues, And I write for injured Innocence, because my worthy Wife and my poor helpless Babe I am sure are innocent, and for them to suffer for want of Necessaries, I am sure, would be injurious.

This Soliloquy satisfy'd me! The whole Mystery was unriddled—all Phylanthrops facts, Anecdotes, Reasonings, Vapourings, all that he has said, done or wrote or can say, do or write is answered at once. There is no further occasion for scribling &c. nor for me to write any Thing more but the Name of

Misanthrop.

¹ This entry consists of partial drafts of two further replies to Jonathan Sewall's "Philanthrop" articles. The first sentence is quoted from Sewall's first article (*Boston Evening Post*, 1 Dec.), and the first paragraph was reworked and amplified by JA before publication over his old pen name "H. Ploughjogger" in the *Boston Gazette*, 5 Jan. 1767.

² The asterisk indicates that the paragraphs which follow must have been intended for insertion in another draft of a newspaper article which has not been found in either MS or printed form. Fragments of still other unpublished replies to "Philanthrop" remain among JA's papers (filed under the assigned date of Jan. 1767).

³ The allusions in this mock confession by "Philanthrop" are to Sewall's failure to obtain a grant by the Province to pay the debts of Chief Justice Stephen Sewall's estate. The Chief Justice was Jonathan's uncle, and JA always attributed the younger Sewall's feud with the Otises (who did not support the proposed grant), his political change of heart, his rewards in the form of crown offices, and his ultimate loyalism, to this incident. See JA, *Works*, 4:6–8.

⁴ Thus in MS. The intended meaning is "Not a step backward" or something similar.

⁵ Editorial conjecture for a word omitted in MS.

[1766?] ¹

Q[uery]. The Service done by Tommy Hutchinson, for the Province, for which he had a Grant of 40£. and his fathers application for Pay, for the same Service and saying, he never had any Pay for it.

The Bill drawn by Mr. Hutchinson, and carried in Council and sent down to the House, to enlarge the Power of the Judges of Probate, and empower them to appoint a few freeholders to set off Widows Dower—without any Action at Common Law, or Tryal by Jury.

Copies of the several Grants that have been made him, for drawing the state of the Prov[ince's] Claim to Sagadahock, Case of the Prov. and New York, Connecticutt [...]ing Lines &c. and the Prov. Claim on N. Hampshire—&c. Additional Grant as C[hief] J[ustice] &c.

Copy of his Petition last June was 12 months for a salary as Lieutenant Governor. It is in the Journal sent down together with a Message from the Governor 12 day of June A.D. 1765 Wednesday. Considered Fryday June 14. 1765 10 O clock.

¹ This and the following entry appear on a separate folded sheet laid in at the end of this Diary booklet (D/JA/13). The notes on the Hutchinsons, perhaps prepared for a newspaper communication, must almost certainly have been written before June 1766 because the references to events of "last June" can be verified as referring to events of June 1765. But it has seemed best to print the entry in the place where it is found in the Diary, after the last entries in 1766 and before the first in 1767.

SATURDAY MARCH 1767.

Went with Captn. Thayer to visit Robert Peacock and his poor distressed Family. We found them, in one Chamber, which serves them for Kitchen, Cellar, dining Room, Parlour, and Bedchamber. Two Beds, in one of which lay Peacock, where he told us he had lain for 7 Weeks, without going out of it farther than the Fire. He had a little Child in his Arms. Another Bed stood on one side of the Chamber where lay 3 other Children. The Mother only was up, by a fire, made of a few Chips, not larger than my Hand. The Chamber excessive cold and dirty.

These are the Conveniences and ornaments of a Life of Poverty. These the Comforts of the Poor. This is Want. This is Poverty! These the Comforts of the needy. The Bliss of the Necessitous.

We found upon Enquiry, that the Woman and her two oldest Children had been warned out of Boston. But the Man had not, and 3 Children had been born since.

Upon this Discovery we waited on Coll. Jackson, the first Select Man of Boston, and acquainted him with the facts and that we must be excused from any Expence for their Support.

When I was in that Chamber of Distress I felt the Meltings of Commiseration. This Office of Overseer of the Poor leads a Man into scenes of Distress, and is a continual Exercise of the benevolent Principles in his Mind. His Compassion is constantly excited, and his Benevolence encreased.[1]

[1] On 2 March JA had been reelected a selectman (*Braintree Town Records*, p. 414). Overseeing the poor was one of the duties of selectmen in Braintree until 1786; see same, p. 566, and CFA2, *Three Episodes*, 2:722 ff.

APRIL 4TH. 1767.[1]

Suits generally Spring from Passion. Jones vs. Bigelow, Cotton and Nye arose from Ambition. Jones and Bigelow were Competitors for Elections in the Town of Weston, Cotton and Nye were Rivals at Sandwich. Such Rivals have no Friendship for each other. From such Rivalries originate Contentions, Quarrells and Suits. Actions of Defamation are the usual Fruits of such Competitions. What affection can there be between two Rival Candidates for the Confidence of a Town. The famous Action of slander at Worcester between Hopkins and Ward, of Rhode Island, Sprouted from the same Stock. There the Aim was at the Confidence of the Colony.

Poor Nye of Sandwich, seems dejected. I should suspect by his Concern that Cotton gained Ground vs. him. He seems to be hipp'd. It fretts and worries and mortifies him. He cant sleep a Nights. His Health is infirm.

Cotton is insane, wild. His Proposal of giving his House and Farm at Sandwich to the Province, is a Proof of Insanity. He has Relations that are poor. Jno. Cotton is now poor enough. He has a Brother Josiah Cotton the Minister whom he procured to be removed to Woburn, and thereby to be ruin'd, who is very poor, maintained by Charity. Roland was Josiahs ruin; yet he did not choose to give his Estate to Josiah. Besides his Behaviour at Boston upon that occasion, was wild. His sitting down at the Council Table with his Hat on and Calling for his Deed and a Justice to acknowledge it, when the Council was sitting.

Cottons Method of getting Papers Signed by Members, in order to demolish poor Nye is new. The Certificate from Murray and Foster if genuine is a mean, scandalous Thing. It was mean in Murray and Foster to sign that Paper. For one Rep[resentative] to give a Constituent a Weapon to demolish another Rep., is ungentlemanlike.[2]

[1] First regular entry in "Paper book No. 14" (D/JA/14), though preceded by the detached notes on legal cases which have been inserted above under date of July 1766.

[2] The case of Roland Cotton *v.* Stephen Nye, the latter of whom had succeeded the former as representative from Sandwich in the General Court in 1761, was an action for defamation. The plaintiff was awarded damages in Barnstable Inferior Court in April. JA appealed for the defendant to the Superior Court at its Barnstable session in May but again lost; see the entries in May, below. Paine and Otis served as Cotton's counsel. Nye was obliged to pay £7 damages and £15 13s. 5d. costs. (JA, List of Cases in Bristol, Plymouth, and Barnstable Courts, 1764–1767, and notes on Cotton *v.* Nye, Adams Papers, Microfilms, Reels 184, 185; Superior Court of Judicature, Minute Book 82).

1767 APRIL 8TH. WEDNESDAY.

Mounted my Horse in a very Rainy Morning for Barnstable leaving my Dear Brother Cranch and his family at my House where they arrived last Night, and my Wife, all designing for Weymouth this Afternoon to Keep the fast with my father Smith and my Friend Tufts.—Arrived at Dr. Tufts's, where I found a fine Wild Goose on the Spit and Cramberries stewing in the Skillet for Dinner. Tufts as soon as he heard that Cranch was at Braintree determined to go over, and bring him and Wife and Child and my Wife and Child over to dine upon wild Goose and Cramberry Sause.

Proceeded without Baiting to Jacobs's where I dined. Lodged at Howlands. Rode next day, baited at Ellis's, dined at Newcombs and proceeded to Barnstable, lodged at Howes's and feel myself much better than I did when I came from Home. But I have had a very wet, cold, dirty, disagreable Journey of it.—Now I am on the stage and the scene is soon to open, what Part shall I act?—The People of the County I find are of opinion that Cotton will worry Nye. But Nye must come off, with flying Colours.

MAY [16], 1767. SATURDAY NIGHT.[1]

At Howlands in Plymouth. Returned this day from Barnstable. The Case of Cotton and Nye at Sandwich is remarkable. Cotton has been driving his Interest. This driving of an Interest, seldom succeeds. Jones of Weston, by driving his, drove it all away.—Where two Persons in a Town get into such a Quarrell, both must be very unhappy—Reproaching each other to their faces, relating facts concerning each other, to their Neighbours. These Relations are denied, repeated, misrepresented, additional and fictitious Circumstances put to them, Passions inflamed. Malice, Hatred, Envy, Pride fear, Rage, Despair, all take their Turns.

Father and son, Uncle and Nephew, Neighbour and Neighbour, Friend and Friend are all set together by the Ears. My Clients have been the Sufferers in both these Representative Causes. The Court was fixed in the Sandwich Case. Cotton is not only a Tory but a Relation of some of the Judges, Cushing particularly. Cushing married a Cotton, Sister of Jno. Cotton, the Register of Deeds at Plymouth. Cushing was very bitter, he was not for my arguing to the Jury the Question whether the Words were Actionable or not. He interrupted me—stopped me short, snapd me up.—"Keep to the Evidence—keep to the Point—dont ramble all over the World to ecclesiastical Councils—dont misrepresent the Evidence." This was his impartial Language. Oliver began his Speech to the Jury with—"A Disposition to slander and Defamation, is the most cursed Temper that ever the World was plagued with and I believe it is the Cause of the greatest Part of the Calamities that Mankind labour under." This was the fair, candid, impartial Judge. They adjudged solemnly, that I should not dispute to the Jury, whether the Words were actionable or not.

[1] To this and the next two entries (which conclude D/JA/14) the editors have assigned specific days of the month because they were obviously written on successive days almost immediately following JA's unsuccessful appeal in the case of Cotton *v.* Nye at Barnstable Superior Court. That appeal is known to have been heard on Thursday, 14 May; see note on entry of 4 April, above.

1767 MAY [17] SUNDAY.

At Plymouth, went to Mr. Robbins's Meeting in the Morning, and sat with Mr. Hovey. Dined with Coll. Warren.[1] Went to Mr. Bacons Meeting in the Afternoon and satt with Coll. Warren. Drank Tea at my Lodgings. Robbins preached upon doing the Will of God, and Bacon on Peace, and Goodwill. Judge Cushing was also at the Upper Meeting in the Morning and at the lower, in the Afternoon. Cushing has the sly, artfull, cunning—Artifice and Cunning is the reigning Characteristic in his face. The sly Sneer.—My Landlady Howland gives me a melancholly History of her Husbands Lawsuit, which lasted 20 Years, and brought him to Poverty. She says that Cushings father in Law Cotton, had an House on one Lott of Land that her Husband was Heir to in Tail, and her Husband was obliged to suffer a Common Recovery of that Lot and convey it to Cotton before Cushing would give Judgment. Saltonstall kept it 5 Years depending merely for his Opinion and Cushing many Years more. So that the Case of Roland Cotton last Week at Barnstable is not the only Case in which Cushing has at all Hazards supported the Interests of the Cotton Family. The father of Judge Cushings Wife, and Mr. Cotton the Register &c. was a Man of Figure in this County, Register of Deeds, Clerk of the Court and afterwards Judge—an odd, 'tho a sensible Man.

We shall see more of the cursed Cunning of this Cushing in the Case of Dumb Tom the Pauper. It was a Trick of his. The Secresy of the Removal was a Trick and Artifice of his. And he is now about to Certiorari him into Pembroke. He was first sent into Pembroke by secret Deviltry, and now is to be sent there again by open Deviltry. But Memento—Three Judges at Barnstable were for dismissing an Appeal to them from Marthas Vinyard because the Plaintiff had accepted of a bad Plea or no Plea. They said it was the Plaintiffs fault that he had accepted such a Plea. Now in the Case of Scituate, was it not the Select Mens fault that they had gone to Tryal without a written Answer?

A Question I shall make is, whether dumb Toms gaining a Settlement, at Tiverton or Bristol, has not annihilated his Settlement at Pembroke? No Pauper has two Settlements at once—a new settlement destroys an old one. He cant have a Settlement at Bristol and another at Pembroke at the same Time. Now is it not Scituates Duty to remove him to Bristol? But how can they?—But another Question is whether the secresy of the Removal, the Manifest Artifice and Trick, to charge Pembroke, shall not screen Pembroke? A Collusion it was. If a Woman pregnant of a Bastard Child is sent in the Night, private secretly into a Parish on Purpose that she may be delivered there, the Parish shall not be charged—for the Law will protect Parishes from such Frauds. Secresy never was more gross, nor fraud more manifest. Sent in the Night, 18 months old, by the Mother and a Negro, to a Squaws Wigwam, on purpose that it never might be suspected, but that it might be taken for an Indian. The Imposition was infinite upon the Poor Squaw.

Spent the Evening at Mr. Hoveys, with Deacon Foster and Dr. Thomas. The Deacon was very silent. The Dr. pretty sociable.

[1] James Warren, representative in the General Court from Plymouth and later prominent in Revolutionary politics. Warren's wife was the former Mercy Otis, a sister of the younger James Otis and an ambitious aspirant to fame as a poet and historian. Within a few years the Adamses and the Warrens formed a very intimate circle of friends and correspondents.

MONDAY MORNING [18 MAY].

A fine Sun and Air.

Cushing at Barnstable said to me—happy is he whom other Mens Errors, render wise.[1]—Otis by getting into the general Court, has lost his Business.—Felix quem faciunt aliena Pericula cautum—other Mens Dangers, Errors, Miscarriages, Mistakes, Misfortunes.

[1] From neither the punctuation nor the substance of this paragraph is it possible to tell where Judge Cushing's direct discourse ends, but most likely it ends here.

1768. JANUARY 30TH. SATURDAY NIGHT.[1]

To what Object, are my Views directed? What is the End and Purpose of my Studies, Journeys, Labours of all Kinds of Body and Mind, of Tongue and Pen? Am I grasping at Money, or Scheming for Power? Am I planning the Illustration of my Family or the Welfare of my Country? These are great Questions. In Truth, I am tossed about so much, from Post to Pillar, that I have not Leisure and Tranquillity enough, to consider distinctly my own Views, Objects and Feelings.— I am mostly intent at present, upon collecting a Library, and I find, that a great deal of Thought, and Care, as well as Money, are necessary to assemble an ample and well chosen Assortment of Books.—But when this is done, it is only a means, an Instrument. When ever I shall have compleated my Library, my End will not be answered. Fame, Fortune, Power say some, are the Ends intended by a Library. The Service of God, Country, Clients, Fellow Men, say others. Which of these lie nearest my Heart? Self Love but serves the virtuous Mind to wake as the small Pebble stirs the Peacefull Lake, The Center Moved, a Circle straight succeeds, another still and still another spreads. Friend, Parent, Neighbour, first it does embrace, our Country next and next all human Race.

I am certain however, that the Course I pursue will neither lead me to Fame, Fortune, Power Nor to the Service of my Friends, Clients or Country. What Plan of Reading or Reflection, or Business can be pursued by a Man, who is now at Pownalborough, then at Marthas Vineyard, next at Boston, then at Taunton, presently at Barnstable,

337

then at Concord, now at Salem, then at Cambridge, and afterwards at Worcester. Now at Sessions, then at Pleas, now in Admiralty, now at Superiour Court, then in the Gallery of the House. What a Dissipation must this be? Is it possible to pursue a regular Train of Thinking in this desultory Life?—By no Means.— It is a Life of *Here and every where*, to use the Expression, that is applyed to Othello, by Desdemona's Father. Here and there and every where, a rambling, roving, vagrant, vagabond Life. A wandering Life. At Meins Book store, at Bowes's Shop, at Danas House, at Fitches, Otis's office, and the Clerks office, in the Court Chamber, in the Gallery, at my own Fire, I am thinking on the same Plan.

[1] First entry in "Paper book No. 15" (our D/JA/15), a stitched gathering of leaves which, following the present entry, has a blank leaf and irregular entries from 10 Aug. 1769 to 22 Aug. 1770.

No Diary entries have been found for the period between late May 1767 and the end of Jan. 1768. The most important event in JA's domestic life during this interval was the birth at Braintree of a son and heir, 11 July 1767, who was, according to JA's Autobiography, "at the request of his Grandmother Smith christened by the Name of John Quincy on the day of the Death of his Great Grandfather, John Quincy of Mount Wollaston." After the excitements of the preceding winter, the remainder of the year 1767, at least until the arrival of the new customs commissioners in November, was compara-

tively quiet politically; at any rate, JA engaged in no further political activity or writing. But as a result of his growing prominence in both Braintree and Boston affairs his legal business expanded remarkably. By piecing together the evidence from his own papers and the Minute Books of the Superior Court, his itinerary during the second half of 1767 may be reconstructed as follows: in July at Plymouth Inferior Court; in August at Suffolk Superior Court; in September at Worcester Superior Court and Bristol Inferior Court; in October at Plymouth Inferior Court and Bristol and Middlesex (Cambridge) Superior Courts; in November at Middlesex (Charlestown) Inferior Court; in December at Barnstable and Plymouth Inferior Courts. Probably this is an incomplete list.

BOSTON AUGUST 10. 1769.[1]

John Tudor Esq. came to me, and for the third Time repeated his Request that I would take his Son William into my Office. I was not fond of the Proposal as I had but 10 days before taken Jona. Williams Austin, for 3 years. At last however I consented and Tudor is to come, tomorrow morning.[2]

What shall I do with 2 Clerks at a Time? And what will the Bar, and the World say? As to the last I am little solicitous, but my own Honour, Reputation and Conscience, are concerned in doing my best for their Education, and Advancement in the World. For their Advancement I can do little, for their Education, much, if I am not wanting to myself and them.

¹ A gap of a year and a half, indicated by only a single blank page in the MS, separates this entry from the preceding one. But the interval had been a busy one for JA and a critical one in the relations between the Province of Massachusetts Bay and the British government. Soon after the annual Braintree town meeting in March 1768 (at which JA declined to stand again for selectman and was thanked for this services during the past two years), JA and his family moved "into the White House as it was called in Brattle Square," formerly the residence of William Bollan (JA, *Works*, 2:210, note; Autobiography). On 28 Dec. his 2d daughter, Susanna, who lived only until 4 Feb. 1770, was born in this house and was baptized on New Year's Day by Dr. Samuel Cooper at the Brattle Street Church (HA2, *John Adams's Book, Being Notes on a Record of the Births, Marriages and Deaths of Three Generations of the Adams Family, 1734–1807*, Boston, 1934, p. 4–5). In the spring of 1769 he "removed to Cole Lane, to Mr. Fayerweathers House," which he occupied for about a year (second entry of 21 Nov. 1772, below).

Though JA rode the circuit with his usual regularity during these eighteen months (and in Sept. 1768 traveled for the first time as far as Springfield, there meeting Joseph Hawley, with whom he was to form an enduring friendship), his most important cases were related to the current political disputes. One of these was his defense of Michael Corbet and three other sailors in May–June 1769 for the killing of Lt. Panton of the British navy; see entry of 23 Dec. 1769 and note, below. Still more spectacular was his earlier defense, in the winter of 1768–1769, of John Hancock against charges of smuggling. This action *in personam* grew out of but was distinct from the action *in rem* concerning Hancock's sloop *Liberty*, condemned at the instance of the board of customs commissioners in the summer of 1768. "A painfull Drudgery I had of his cause," JA wrote in his

Autobiography. "There were few days through the whole Winter, when I was not summoned to attend the Court of Admiralty." JA's stubborn and successful defense in a trial lasting five months was one of his major accomplishments as a lawyer, but the necessary notes and references concerning it may be deferred to his discussion of it in his Autobiography.

In June 1768 and again in May 1769 JA was named on committees to prepare instructions for the Boston representatives to the General Court, and in both instances it was he who wrote the instructions. The first is mainly a protest against the seizure of the *Liberty* (*Works*, 3:501–504). The second is a recital of a series of grievances suffered by the town as the result of the presence of British troops since the preceding autumn, and also from the formidable and growing power of the admiralty courts (same, p. 505–510).

Life was not made up exclusively of drama and drudgery. An entry in John Rowe's Diary dated 4 Aug. 1769 begins: "fine Weather Din'd at John Champneys on A Pigy with the following Company —John Hancock, James Otis, John Adams," and thirteen others, including Robert Auchmuty, the admiralty judge (MS, MHi).

² Jonathan Williams Austin and William Tudor, both of the Harvard class of 1769, were JA's first law clerks, so far as we currently know. The ordinary term of service was three years, and both these young men were recommended by the bar for admission to practice as attorneys in July 1772 ("Suffolk Bar Book," MHS, *Procs.*, 1st ser., 19 [1881–1882]:150). Austin was admitted attorney in the Superior Court, Aug. term, 1778, but never became a barrister (Superior Court of Judicature, Minute Book 103). Tudor was admitted to practice in the Superior Court with Austin, served as first judge advocate of the Continental army, became a barrister, Feb. term, 1784, and was a lifelong friend and correspondent of JA.

AUG. 11TH. 1769. FRYDAY.

Mr. Tudor came, for the first Time and attended the Office, all

Day, and paid me £10 St.—In the Morning I went to take View of Mr. Copelys [Copley's] Pictures, and afterwards to hear News of the Letters arrived in Scott. The Mystery of Iniquity, seems to be unravelled.[1]

Spent the Evening at Mr. Wm. Coopers, the Dr. came in and was very social.[2] He came from a Meeting of the Overseers of the Colledge, at Cambridge, which was called to advise the Corporation to proceed to the Choice of a President.

[1] Capt. Scott of the *Boston Packet* arrived on 10 Aug. and brought "A new Freight of curious Letters of Sir *Francis Bernard* of *Nettleham*, Bart. the Commissioners, &c. . . . which will probably soon be publish'd" (*Boston Gazette*, 14 Aug. 1769). Bernard had just sailed for England. These letters and papers, furnishing a narrative of the recent "Troubles of this Town" from a government point of view and explaining only too clearly the role of the customs commissioners in bringing the regiments of British troops to Boston, were soon published under the title *Letters to the Ministry from Governor Bernard, General Gage, and Commodore Hood, and also Memorials to the Lords of the Treasury, from the Commissioners of the Customs*, Boston, 1769.

[2] William Cooper, perpetual town clerk of Boston and an active member of the Sons of Liberty, was the older brother of "the Dr.," i.e. Rev. Samuel Cooper, pastor of the Brattle Street Church (*NEHGR*, 44 [1890]:56–57).

1769. AUG. 12. SATURDAY.

Dined at Mr. Isaac Smiths and in the Evening went to Braintree.

AUG. 13. SUNDAY.

At Mr. Quincys.[1] Here is Solitude and Retirement. Still, calm, and serene, cool, tranquil, and peaceful. The Cell of the Hermit. Out at one Window, you see Mount Wollaston, the first Seat of our Ancestors, and beyond that Stony field Hill,[2] covered over with Corn and fruits.

At the other Window, an Orchard and beyond that the large Marsh called the broad Meadows. From the East Window of the opposite Chamber you see a fine Plain, covered with Corn and beyond that the whole Harbour and all the Islands. From the End Window of the East Chamber, you may see with a prospective Glass, every Ship, Sloop, Schooner, and Brigantine, that comes in, or goes out.

Heard Mr. Wibirt, Upon Resignation and Patience under Afflictions, in Imitation of the ancient Prophets and Apostles, a Sermon calculated for my Uncles family, whose Funeral was attended last Week. In the afternoon Elizabeth Adams the Widow of Micajah Adams lately deceased was baptized, and received into full Communion with the Church.[3] She never knew that she was not baptized in her Infancy till since her Husbands Decease, when her Aunt came from Lynn and informed her. Mr. Wibirt prayed, that the Loss of her Husband might be sanctified to her, this she bore with some firmness, but when he came to pray that the Loss might be made up to her little fatherless Children, the Tears could no longer be restrained. Then the Congregation sang an Hymn upon Submission under Afflictions to the Tune of the funeral Thought. The whole together was a moving Scene, and left scarcely a dry Eye in the House. After Meeting I went to Coll. Quincys to wait on Mr. Fisk of Salem 79 Year Old.

This Mr. Fisk and his Sister Madam Marsh, the former born in the very Month of the Revolution under Sir Edmund Andros, and the latter 10 Years before that, made a very venerable Appearance.

[1] Mount Wollaston Farm on the shore of Quincy Bay, the homestead of Norton Quincy, AA's uncle.

[2] The earliest name for what is now called Presidents Hill. JA later acquired this property and made it part of his homestead farm. In old age he occasion-ally dated letters from "Stony Field Hill."

[3] Ebenezer, brother of Deacon John Adams, died 6 Aug. 1769; his son Micajah had died 18 July (A. N. Adams, *Geneal. Hist. of Henry Adams of Braintree*, p. 395, 401).

MONDAY AUGUST 14.

Dined with 350 Sons of Liberty at Robinsons, the Sign of Liberty Tree in Dorchester. We had two Tables laid in the open Field by the Barn, with between 300 and 400 Plates, and an Arning of Sail Cloth overhead, and should have spent a most agreable Day had not the Rain made some Abatement in our Pleasures. Mr. Dickinson the Farmers Brother, and Mr. Reed the Secretary of New Jersey were there, both cool, reserved and guarded all day.[1] After Dinner was over and the Toasts drank we were diverted with Mr. Balch's Mimickry. He gave Us, the Lawyers Head, and the Hunting of a Bitch fox. We had also the Liberty Song—that by the Farmer, and that by Dr. Ch[urc]h, and the whole Company joined in the Chorus. This is cultivating the Sensations of Freedom. There was a large Collection of good Company. Otis and Adams are politick, in promoting these Festivals, for they tinge the Minds of the People, they impregnate them with the sentiments of Liberty. They render the People fond of their Leaders in the Cause, and averse and bitter against all opposers.

To the Honour of the Sons, I did not see one Person intoxicated, or near it.[2]

Between 4 and 5 O clock, the Carriages were all got ready and the Company rode off in Procession, Mr. Hancock first in his Charriot and another Charriot bringing up the Rear. I took my Leave of the Gentlemen and turned off for Taunton, oated at Doty's and arrived, long after Dark, at Noices.[3] There I put up. I should have been at Taunton if I had not turned back in the Morning from Roxbury—but I felt as if I ought not to loose this feast, as if it was my Duty to be there. I am not able to conjecture, of what Consequence it was whether I was there or not.

Jealousies arise from little Causes, and many might suspect, that I was not hearty in the Cause, if I had been absent whereas none of them are more sincere, and stedfast than I am.

¹ Philemon Dickinson, younger brother of "Farmer" John Dickinson; and Joseph Reed, who was then practicing law in Trenton, N.J.; see *DAB* under both names.

² This was sufficiently remarkable, considering that fourteen toasts were drunk at the Liberty Tree in Boston, followed by forty-five (in honor of John Wilkes' *North Briton*, No. 45) at the dinner—all enumerated in the account of the day's proceedings in the *Boston Gazette*, 21 Aug. 1769. A list of 355 Sons of Liberty present was compiled by William Palfrey, who was present, and is printed in MHS, *Procs.*, 1st ser., 11 (1869–1870):140.

³ Or Noyes', in Stoughton.

TUESDAY. AUG. 15.

Rode to Taunton, 16 miles before 9 O Clock, tho I stopped and breakfasted at Haywards in Easton 9 miles from Taunton. Spent all the Leisure moments I could snatch in Reading a Debate in Parliament, in 1744, upon a Motion to inquire into the Conduct of Admiral Mathews and Vice Admiral Lestock in the Mediterranean, when they had, and neglected so fine an Opportunity of destroying the combined Fleets of France and Spain off Toulon.

1769. SEPTR. 2. SATURDAY NIGHT.

Tho this Book has been in my Pocket, this fortnight, I have been too slothfull, to make Use of it.

Dined at Mr. Smiths. Heard that Messrs. Otis and Adams went Yesterday to Concert Hall, and there had each of them a Conference with each of the Commissioners, and that all the Commissioners met Mr. Otis, this Morning at 6 O Clock at the British Coffee House. The Cause, and End of these Conferences, are Subjects of much Speculation in Town.[1]

¹ If intended to prevent violence, the conferences failed, for on 5 Sept. Commissioner John Robinson, aided by others, assaulted James Otis at the British Coffee House, leading to a long lawsuit in which JA acted as one of Otis' counsel. See *Boston Gazette*, 11 Sept. 1769; Tudor, *James Otis*, p. 360–366, 503–506; entries of 25–27 July 1771, below. The most recent and authoritative discussion of the Robinson-Otis affair is in Mr. Shipton's biography of Otis, Sibley-Shipton, *Harvard Graduates*, 11:247–287.

SEPT. 3D. SUNDAY.

Heard Dr. Cooper in the forenoon, Mr. Champion of Connecticutt in the Afternoon and Mr. Pemberton in the Evening at the Charity Lecture. Spent the Remainder of the Evening and supped with Mr. Otis, in Company with Mr. Adams, Mr. Wm. Davis, and Mr. Jno. Gill. The Evening spent in preparing for the Next Days Newspaper— a curious Employment. Cooking up Paragraphs, Articles, Occurences, &c.—working the political Engine![1] Otis talks all. He grows the most talkative Man alive. No other Gentleman in Company can find a Space to put in a Word—as Dr. Swift expressed it, he leaves no Elbow Room. There is much Sense, Knowledge, Spirit and Humour in his Conversation. But he grows narrative, like an old Man. Abounds with Stories.

[1] One of the pieces thus cooked up led directly to the assault on Otis on the 5th, though that piece was signed by Otis himself, and there is nothing in the *Boston Gazette* of 4 Sept. that clearly reveals JA's hand.

MONDAY [4 SEPTEMBER].

Spent the Evening at Dr. Peckers, with the Clubb. Mr. Otis introduced a Stranger, a Gentleman from Georgia, recommended to him by the late Speaker of the House in that Province. Otis indulged himself in all his Airs. Attacked the Aldermen, Inches and Pemberton, for not calling a Town meeting to consider the Letters of the Governor, General, Commodore, Commissioners, Collector, Comptroller &c.— charged them with Timidity, Haughtiness, Arbitrary Dispositions, and Insolence of Office. But not the least Attention did he shew to his Friend the Georgian.—No Questions concerning his Province, their Measures against the Revenue Acts, their Growth, Manufactures, Husbandry, Commerce—No general Conversation, concerning the Continental Opposition—Nothing, but one continued Scene of bullying, bantering, reproaching and ridiculing the Select Men.—Airs and Vapours about his Moderatorship, and Membership, and Cushings Speakership.—There is no Politeness nor Delicacy, no Learning nor Ingenuity, no Taste or Sense in this Kind of Conversation.

WEDNESDAY. SEPTR. 6. 1769.

Mr. Cudworth told me on the Town house Steps, that Mr. Charles Paxton, the Commissioner, told him this day, that it was possible, he might be sent with some Proscess on board a Man of War, and he advised him, as a friend not to attempt to take any Man from on Board the Man of War; for you have no Right to, and if you attempt it, you'l never come away alive—and I want to see Otis the D[eputy] Sherriff [1] to give him the same Advice.—Cudworth told this to Otis in my Hearing, and Otis went directly to Mr. Paxtons as I since hear, and Mr. Paxton gave him the same Advice.[2]

[1] Joseph Otis and Benjamin Cudworth were both deputy sheriffs of Suffolk co.
[2] The passage is ambiguously punctuated, but it was clearly Paxton who warned Cudworth and wanted to warn Otis—and did so.

1769. OCTR. 19TH. THURSDAY.

Last night I spent the Evening, at the House of John Williams Esqr. the Revenue officer, in Company with Mr. Otis, Jona. Williams Esqr. and Mr. McDaniel a Scotch Gentleman, who has some Connection with the Commissioners, as Clerk, or something. Williams is as sly, secret and cunning a fellow, as need be. The Turn of his Eye, and Cast of his Countenance, is like Thayer of Braintree. In the Course of the Evening He said, that He knew that Lord Townsend borrowed Money of Paxton, when in America, to the amount of £500 st. at least that is not paid yet. He also said, in the Course of the Evening, that if he had drank a Glass of Wine, that came out of a seizure, he would take a Puke to throw it up. He had such a Contempt for the 3ds. of Seisures. He affects to speak slightly of the Commissioners and of their Conduct, tho guardedly, and to insinuate that his Connections, and Interest and Influence at Home with the Boards &c. are greater than theirs.

McDaniel is a composed, grave, steady Man to appearance, but his Eye has it's fire, still, if you view it attentively.—Otis bore his Part very well, conversible eno, but not extravagant, not rough, nor soure.

The morning at Bracketts upon the Case of the Whale.[1] The afternoon at the office posting Books.

[1] Joseph Doane *v.* Lot Gage, a protracted suit between two whalemen tried in the Court of Vice-Admiralty. Doane had sunk the first iron, but Gage had taken the whale. The question was whether Doane had been "fast" when Gage struck; if so, Doane was entitled to a one-eighth share of the value of the whale. JA represented Doane. Among his legal papers is a series of graphic depositions as well as notes for his own argument and those of the opposing counsel, Paine and Otis (Adams Papers, Microfilms, Reel No. 184).

1769. OCTR. 24TH.

Sunday last I rode to Braintree in the Morning, and heard Mr. Gay, of Hingham forenoon and afternoon, upon those Words in the Proverbs "The hoary Head is a Crown of Glory if it be found in the Way of Righteousness."—The good old Gentleman had been to the Funeral of his aged Brother at Dedham, and seemed to be very much affected. He said in his Prayer, that God in the Course of his Providence was admonishing him that he must very soon put off this Tabernacle, and prayed that the Dispensation might be sanctified to him—and he told the People in the Introduction to his Sermon, that this would probably be the last Exhortation they would ever hear from him their old Acquaintance.—I have not heard a more affecting, or more rational Entertainment on any Sabbath for many Years.

Dined with my Friend and Uncle Mr. Quincy, and returned after Meeting to Boston.

NOVEMBER 1769.

Saturday after attending Court in the Morning, I dined by particular Invitation at Mr. Winthrops the Clerk of the Superior Court with all the Bar, Messrs. Dana, Kent, Otis, Fitch, Reed, S. Quincy, B. Gridley, Cazneau,[1] Blowers.

Otis, B. Gridley, Kent, and S. Quincy, were the principal Talkers. Otis talked the most, B. Gridley next, Kent the next and S. Quincy, next. The rest of the Company said very little.

B. Gridley told us a Story of his Uncle Jeremiah the late Head of the Bar. "When I was a school Boy, at Master Lovells, Mr. Gridley my Uncle used to make me call at his Office, sometimes, to repeat my Lesson to him. I called there one Day for that Purpose.—Well, Ben! What have you to say, Ben? says he.—I am come to say my Lesson sir to you, says I.—Ay? Ben? what Book have you there? under your Arm?—Virgil sir.—Ay! Ben? Is that the Poet, Virgil?—Yes sir.—Well Ben, take it and read to me Ben. Read in the Beginning of the Æneids Ben.—Yes sir.—So I opened my Book and began.

Arma, Virumque Cāno, Trojæ, qui primus ab oris.

Arma, Virumque cāno! Ben! you Blockhead!—does John Lovell teach you to read so—read again.—So I began, again.

Arma Virumque cāno.—Cāno you Villain, canō—and gave me a tremendous Box on the Ear.—Arma Virumque canō, you Blockhead, is the true Reading.

Thinks I, what is this—I have Blockheading and boxing enough at Master Lovells, I wont have it repeated hear, and in a great Passion I threw the Virgil at his Head, hit him in the Face, and bruised his Lip, and ran away.

Ben! Ben! You Blockhead! You Villain, you Rascall, Ben!—

However away I went, and went home.

That evening, Uncle Jeremy came to our House, and sat down with my father.

Brother, I have something to say to you about that young Rogue of a son of yours, that Ben. He came to my Office, and I bid him read a Line in Virgil and he read it wrong and I box'd him, and he threw his Virgil in my face, and wounded me, he bruised me in my Lip—here is the Mark of it! You must lick him, you must thresh him Brother!

I was all this Time a listening, and heard my father justify me.— Ben did right says he—you had no Right to box him, you was not his Master and if he read wrong you should have taught him how to read right—not have boxed him.

Ay? Then I find you justify the Rogue.—Yes says father I think he did right.—Ay then you wont thresh him for it will you?—No I think he ought not to be threshed, I think you ought not to have box'd him.

What, justify the young Villain, in throwing his Book at me, and wounding me in this Manner?

About 2 or 3 Evenings Afterwards, Uncle Jeremy was at Clubb with Jo. Green, and John Lovell and others, and began, with great solemnity and sobriety—Jo.? What shall I do, two or three days ago, I was guilty of a bad Action and I dont know how to repair it. I boxed a little boy a Nephew of mine very unrighteously, and he is so little, so mere a Child that I cant ask his Pardon—and so in solemn Sadness told the whole Story to the Clubb." [2]

Whether there is any Truth in any Part of this Story or not I cant say. But if it is mere fiction, there are certainly strong Marks of Ingenuity, in the Invention. The Pride, Obstinacy, and Sauciness of Ben, are remembered in Ben, in the Circumstance of throwing the Virgil. The same Temper in his father is preserved in the Circumstance of his justifying it. The Suddenness, and Imperiousness of Jeremiah, in the Boxing, and his real Integrity, Candor, Benevolence, and good Nature in repenting of it at Clubb, and wishing to make Reparation.

B. Gridley, after this, gave us another Story of Coll. Byfield, and his marrying a Sailor which occasioned a great Laugh.

Upon the whole this same Ben. Gridley discovered a Capacity, a Genius—real Sentiment, Fancy, Wit, Humour, Judgment, and Observation. Yet he seems to be totally lost to the World. He has no Business of any Kind, lays abed till 10 'O Clock, drinks, laughs and frolicks, but, neither studies, nor practices, in his Profession.

Otis spent almost all the Afternoon in telling 2 stories, one of Gridleys offending the Suffolk Inferior Court, in the Dispute about introducing Demurrers, and of his making the Amende Honorable, making Concessions, &c. before that contemptible Tribunal—and another about a Conversation between Pratt, Kent and him. Kents asking the Question, what is the chief End of Man? and Pratts Answer to provide food &c. for other Animals, Cabbage Lice among the rest.

Before Dinner Kent proposed his Project of an Act of Parliament against Devils, like to that against Witches.

Otis catched at it, and proposed the Draught of a Bill.—Be it enacted &c.—that whereas many of the subjects of this Realm, have heretofore time out of Mind believed in certain imaginary Beings called Devils, therefore be it enacted, that no one shall mention the Devil, hereafter, &c., on Pain of high Treason, &c.

Thus are Mens Brains eternally at work according to the Proclamation of K[ing] James.

I dont think the World can furnish a more curious Collection of Characters than those that made up this Company—Otis, Kent, Dana, Gridley, Fitch, Winthrop, &c.

¹ Andrew Cazneau of Boston; admitted attorney in the Superior Court, 1765, and barrister, 1767; afterward a loyalist (Superior Court of Judicature, Minute Books 82, 85; Jones, *Loyalists of Mass.*, p. 78–79).

² The dialogue in young Gridley's anecdote was punctuated by JA more erratically than was usual even for him, and in the interest of clarity the punctuation has been slightly regularized by the editors.

1769. DECR. 23. SATURDAY NIGHT.

At my Office reading Sidney. I have been musing this evening upon a Report of the Case of the 4. Sailors, who were tryed last June, before the Special Court of Admiralty, for killing Lt. Panton. A Publication only of the Record, I mean the Articles, Plea to the Jurisdiction, Testimonies of Witnesses, &c. would be of great Utility. The Arguments which were used, are scarcely worth publishing. Those which might be used, would be well worth the Perusal of the Public. A great Variety of useful Learning might be brought into an History of that Case—and the great Curiosity of the World after the Case, would make it sell. I have half a Mind to undertake it.

The great Questions, concerning the Right of Juries in the Colonies, upon a Comparison of the 3 Statutes, and concerning the Right of impressing Seamen for his Majestys Service, whether with or without Warrants from the Lords of the Admiralty upon orders of the K[ing] in Council, are very important. Such a Pamphlet might suggest alterations in the Statutes, and might possibly procure us for the future the Benefit of Juries in such Cases. And the World ought to know, at least the American part of it, more than it does, of the true foundation of Impresses, if they have any.[1]

[1] This project was unfortunately not carried out, though the materials for it in JA's papers were (and still are) ample and important. Early in May 1769 Michael Corbet (whose name is variously spelled in the records) and three other sailors on the *Pitt Packet* of Marblehead resisted impressment when Lt. Henry Gibson Panton of the British frigate *Rose* boarded their vessel off Marblehead. From the forepeak they warned Panton that if he stepped toward them he was a dead man. Panton took a pinch of snuff and started for them with several armed companions. The next moment a harpoon severed Panton's jugular vein. A special court of admiralty was promptly held to try the case. Otis and JA, counsel for the sailors, moved first to obtain a jury trial but were thwarted by Hutchinson's influence with his fellow judges, among whom were Governors Bernard and Wentworth and Commodore Hood. The most telling point in JA's argument was his citation of the statute 6 Anne, ch. 37, sect. 9, which prohibited impressments in America. The verdict was that the sailors had killed Panton in self-defense. JA's brief is printed in an appendix to his *Works*, 2:526–534. His record of the testimony and of the argument of the crown lawyer, Samuel Fitch, are appended to a long article by BA on "The Convention of 1800 with France," MHS, *Procs.*, 44 (1910–1911):429–452. (The MSS are in the Adams Papers, Microfilms, Reel No. 184). Since the issues involved were so often of concern to JA in later life, he frequently discussed the case, and as usual with varying details. See especially his letters to JQA, 8 Jan. 1808 (printed by BA in the article cited above, p. 422–428); to Jedidiah Morse, 20 Jan. 1816 (*Works*, 10:204–210); and to William Tudor, 30 Dec. 1816 (same, 2:224, note). Hutchinson's account, with his explanation of the conduct of the trial, is in his *Massachusetts Bay*, ed. Mayo, 3:166–167. The chronology of the case is well set forth in the "Journal of the Times" as reprinted by Oliver M. Dickerson in *Boston under Military Rule*, 1768–1769, Boston, 1936, p. 94–95, 104, 110.

1770 JANUARY 16.

At my Office all Day.

Last Evening at Dr. Peckers with the Clubb.—Otis is in Confusion yet. He looses himself. He rambles and wanders like a Ship without an Helm. Attempted to tell a Story which took up almost all the Evening. The Story may at any Time be told in 3 minutes with all the Graces it is capable of, but he took an Hour. I fear he is not in his perfect Mind. The Nervous, Concise, and pithy were his Character, till lately. Now the verbose, roundabout and rambling, and long winded. He once said He hoped he should never see T.H. in Heaven. Dan. Waldo took offence at it, and made a serious Affair of it, said Otis very often bordered upon Prophaneness, if he was not strictly profane. Otis said, if he did see H. there he hoped it would be behind the Door.—In my fathers House are many Mansions, some more and some less honourable.

In one Word, Otis will spoil the Clubb. He talks so much and takes up so much of our Time, and fills it with Trash, Obsceneness, Profaneness, Nonsense and Distraction, that We have no [time] [1] left for rational Amusements or Enquiries.

He mentioned his Wife—said she was a good Wife, too good for him—but she was a tory, an high Tory. She gave him such Curtain Lectures, &c.[2]

In short, I never saw such an Object of Admiration, Reverence, Contempt and Compassion all at once as this. I fear, I tremble, I mourn for the Man, and for his Country. Many others mourne over him with Tears in their Eyes.

[1] Word omitted by the diarist.
[2] On Ruth (Cunningham) Otis, see Tudor, *James Otis*, p. 19–21.

[DRAFT OF A NEWSPAPER COMMUNICATION, JANUARY? 1770.][1]

"If I would but go to Hell for an eternal Moment or so, I might be knighted."

Governor Winthrop to the Inhabitants
of New England.

My dear Children—

You may well imagine, that no Lapse of Time, nor any Change whatever can render me totally inattentive or indifferent to your Interests. They are always near my Heart. I am as anxious as ever for your Welfare and as studious to avert the most distant Calamity that threatens or can befall you.

Your present Danger arises wholly from that general Cause of the Ruin of Mankind I mean Ambition. Your Agrarian Laws, and your frame of Government, are much better callculated than most others to oppose, to disarm, and restrain this fell Distroyer.

But, as no Government can possibly be contrived or conceived that shall wholly eradicate this Passion from human Nature, so yours is very far from being the best that can be conceived from [for?] preventing its ill Effects.

[1] Obviously incomplete as it stands, and no printing has been found. Other apparently related fragments will be found under Aug.? 1770 and 9 Feb. 1772, below.

1770. MONDAY FEBY. 26. OR THEREABOUTS.

Rode from Weymouth. Stoppd at my House, Veseys Blacksmith shop, my Brothers, my Mothers, and Robinsons.

These 5 Stops took up the day. When I came into Town, I saw a vast Collection of People, near Liberty Tree—enquired and found the funeral of the Child, lately kill'd by Richardson was to be attended. Went into Mr. Rowes, and warmed me, and then went out with him to the Funeral, a vast Number of Boys walked before the Coffin, a vast

Number of Women and Men after it, and a Number of Carriages. My Eyes never beheld such a funeral. The Procession extended further than can be well imagined.

This Shewes, there are many more Lives to spend if wanted in the Service of their Country.

It Shews, too that the Faction is not yet expiring—that the Ardor of the People is not to be quelled by the Slaughter of one Child and the Wounding of another.[1]

At Clubb this Evening, Mr. Scott and Mr. Cushing gave us a most alarming Account of O[tis]. He has been this afternoon raving Mad— raving vs. Father, Wife, Brother, Sister, Friend &c.[2]

[1] "Feb. 26. This afternoon the Boy that was killed by Richardson was buried. I am very sure two thousand people attended his Funerall" (Rowe, *Letters and Diary*, p. 197). The *Boston Gazette* of 5 March devoted half a column to these obsequies. The "Child" was Christopher Snider, eleven or twelve years old, who had been shot and killed by Ebenezer Richardson, an employee of the customs, on 22 Feb., when taunted in his house by a group of boys after a demonstration against a merchant known to have violated the nonimportation agreement. On April 20–21 Richardson and another customs man present at the shooting, George Wilmot, were indicted and tried for murder in Suffolk Superior Court. Wilmot was acquitted; Richardson was found guilty but was pardoned by the King. The affair was a dramatic prelude to the "Boston Massacre." See *Boston Gazette*, 26 Feb. 1770; Superior Court of Judicature, Minute Book 91; Hutchinson, *Massachusetts Bay*, ed. Mayo, 3:193–194, 206 and note; Oliver M. Dickerson, "The Commissioners of Customs and the 'Boston Massacre,'" *NEQ*, 27:310–312 (Sept. 1954). A copy of the defense counsel's argument, in an unidentified hand but docketed by JA, is in the Adams Papers, Microfilms, Reel No. 185. Robert Treat Paine acted for the crown (Paine, "Minutes of Law Cases, 1760–1774," MS, MHi).

[2] Inserted loose in the MS at this point is a receipted bill to JA from M. Cooke in the amount of £11 2s., for copying seventeen cases, here listed, for "March C[our]t 1770."

IPSWICH JUNE 19. 1770. TUESDAY MORNING.[1]

Rambled with Kent, round Landlord Treadwells Pastures, to see how our Horses fared. We found them in Grass, up to their Eyes. Excellent Pastures. This Hill on which stand the Meeting House and Court House, is a fine Elevation and We have here a fine Air, and the pleasant Prospect of the winding River, at the foot of the Hill.

[1] Preceding this entry is a gap of nearly four months in the Diary record, with no space left for it in the MS. Accordingly there is no strictly contemporary mention by JA of the episode known as the Boston Massacre, in the consequences of which he was to be so deeply involved, though in his Autobiography he gave an account of what he did and saw on the evening of 5 March and of the circumstances under which he agreed, next day, to defend Capt. Thomas Preston.

On 6 June JA was elected a delegate to the General Court from Boston in the room of James Bowdoin, who had been elected to the Council. He was at once caught up in the bitter and protracted dispute between the legislature and Lt. Gov. Hutchinson over the meeting-place of the General Court; see the *House Journal* for this year, *passim*. From June 1770 to April 1771, his single term as a member of the House, JA's name, as CFA remarked, "appears upon almost every important committee" (JA, *Works*, 1:109). An impressive tabulation of these committee assignments will be found in a long note in the same, 2:233–236.

JUNE 25. 1770. BOSTON.

Blowers. In the Reign of Richard the 2d. or Henry 6th. you may find Precedents for any Thing.

This Observation was echoed from some Tory, who applyed it to a late Quotation of the House of Representatives. It is true, Richard 2d. and H. 6. were weak and worthless Princes, and their Parliaments were bold and resolute, but weak Princes may arise hereafter, and then there will be need of daring and determined Parliaments. The Reigns of R. 2. and H. 6 were the Reigns of Evil Councillors and Favourites, and they exhibit notable Examples, of the public Mischiefs, arising from such Administrations, and of national and parliamentary Vengeance, on such wicked Minions.

JUNE 26.

Last of Service; very little Business this Court. The Bar and the Clerks universally complain of the Scarcity of Business. So little was perhaps never known, at July Term. The Cause must be the Non Importation agreement, and the Declension of Trade. So that the Lawyers loose as much by this Patriotic Measure as the Merchants, and Tradesmen.

Stephens the Connecticutt Hemp Man was at my Office, with Mr. Counsellor Powell and Mr. Kent. Stephens says that the whole Colony of Connecticutt has given more implicit Observance to a Letter from the Select Men of Boston than to their Bibles for some Years. And that in Consequence of it, the Country is vastly happier, than it was, for every Family has become a little manufactory House, and they raise and make within themselves, many Things, for which they used to run in debt to the Merchants and Traders. So that No Body is hurt but Boston, and the Maritime Towns.—I wish there was a Tax of 5s. st. on every Button, from England. It would be vastly for the good of this Country, &c. As to all the Bustle and Bombast about Tea, it has been begun by about 1/2 doz. Hollands Tea Smugglers, who could not find so much Profit in their Trade, since the Nine Pence was taken off in England.—Thus He. Some Sense and some Nonsense!

JUNE 27. WEDNESDAY MORN.

Very fine—likely to be hot—at my Office early. The only Way to compose myself and collect my Thoughts is to set down at my Table, place my Diary before me, and take my Pen into my Hand. This Apparatus takes off my Attention from other Objects. Pen, Ink and Paper and a sitting Posture, are great Helps to Attention and thinking.

Took an Airing in the Chaise with my Brother Sam. Adams, who returned and dined with me. He says he never looked forward in his Life, never planned, laid a scheme, or formed a design of laying up any Thing for himself or others after him. I told him, I could not say that of myself, if that had been true of me, you would never have seen my Face—and I think this was true. I was necessitated to ponder in my Youth, to consider of Ways and Means of raising a Subsistence, food and Rayment, and Books and Money to pay for my Education to the Bar. So that I must have sunk into total Contempt and Obscurity, if not perished for Want, if I had not planned for futurity. And it is no Damage to a young Man to learn the Art of living, early, if it is at the Expence of much musing and pondering and Anxiety.

JUNE 28. THURSDAY.

Mr. Goldthwait. Do you call tomorrow and dine with Us at flax Pond near Salem. Rowe, Davis, Brattle and half a dozen, as clever fellows as ever were born, are to dine there under the shady Trees, by the Pond, upon fish, and Bacon and Pees &c. and as to the Madeira, nothing can come up to it. Do you call. We'll give a genteell Dinner and fix you off on your Journey.[1]

Rumours of Ships and Troops, a Fleet and an Army, 10 Regiments and a No. of line of Battle Ships, were talked of to day.

If an Armament should come, what will be done by the People? Will they oppose them?

"If, by supporting the Rights of Mankind, and of invincible Truth, I shall contribute to save from the Agonies of Death one unfortunate Victim of Tyranny, or of Ignorance, equally fatal; his Blessing and Tears of Transport, will be a sufficient Consolation to me, for the Contempt of all Mankind." Essay on Crimes and Punishments. Page 42.[2]

I have received such Blessings and enjoyed such Tears of Transport—and there is no greater Pleasure, or Consolation! Journeying to Plymouth at a Tavern, I found a Man, who either knew me before, or by enquiring of some Person then present, discovered who I was. He went out and saddled my Horse and bridled him, and held the Stirrup while I mounted. Mr. Adams says he, as a Man of Liberty, I respect you. God bless you! I'le stand by you, while I live, and from hence to Cape Cod you wont find 10 Men amiss.—A few Years ago, a Person arrained for a Rape at Worcester, named me to the Court for his Council. I was appointed, and the Man was acquitted, but remanded in order to be tryed on another Indictment for an assault with Intention to ravish. When he had returned to Prison, he broke out of his own Accord—God bless Mr. Adams. God bless his Soul I am not to be hanged, and I dont care what else they do to me.—Here was his Blessing and his Transport which gave me more Pleasure, when I first heard the Relation and when I have recollected it since, than any fee would have done. This was a worthless fellow, but nihil humanum, alienum. His Joy, which I had in some Sense been instrumental in procuring, and his Blessings and good Wishes, occasioned very agreable Emotions in the Heart.[3]

This afternoon Mr. Wm. Frobisher gave me a Narration of his Services to the Province, in introducing the Manufacture of Pot ashes and Pearl ashes, and of his unsuccessfull Petitions to the General Court for a Compensation. He says he has suffered in his fortune, by his Labours and Expences, and has been instrumental of introducing and establishing the Manufacture And can obtain nothing. That £25,000 st. worth of Potashes have been exported from this Town, yearly for 5 Years past, and more than that Quantity for the last two Years as appears by the Custom House Books, and Mr. Sheaff the Collector was his Informer. That He has invented a Method of making Potashes, in much greater Quantity, and better Quality, than heretofore has been done, from the same materials, without any Augmentation of Expence. That he went to Hingham and worked with Mr. Lincoln a month, and has a Certificate from him, to the foregoing Purpose. That his new Method seperates from the Potash, a neutral Salt that is very pure and of valuable Use in medicine, &c. and that if his Method was adopted, no Russian Potash would sell at any Markett where American, was to be had.—Thus Projectors, ever restless.

[1] John Rowe describes this convivial gathering in his MS Diary (MHi) under date of 29 June. JA declined to attend.

[2] By Cesare, Marchese di Beccaria; first published, in Italian, in 1764. JA was probably using the English translation published in London, 1770. His own copy of Beccaria's *Dei delitti e delle pene* was bought in Paris in 1780 and is among his books in the Boston Public Library. He was to use this passage from Beccaria in opening his defense of Capt. Preston in October (Frederic Kidder, *History of the Boston Massacre* . . . , Albany, 1870, p. 232).

[3] This case was doubtless that of Rex *v.* Samuel Quinn, Worcester Superior Court, Sept. term, 1768. After being

adjudged not guilty of the rape of Agnis Brooks, Quinn pleaded guilty to a charge of assault with intent to ravish. "And the Court having considered his offense Order that the sd. Samuel Quinn be set upon the Gallows for the space of one hour that he be whipt thirty Stripes upon his bare Back viz ten stripes under the gallows and ten stripes in two other public places, that he suffer twelve months imprisonment, and that he pay costs of prosecution standing committed until the Sentence shall be performed" (Superior Court of Judicature, Minute Book 83).

JUNE 29. 1770. FRYDAY.

Began my Journey to Falmouth in Casco Bay. Baited my Horse at Martins in Lynn, where I saw T. Fletcher and his Wife, Mr. French &c. Dined at Goodhues in Salem, where I fell in Company with a Stranger, his Name I know not. He made a Genteell Appearance, was in a Chair himself with a Negro Servant. Seemed to have a general Knowledge of American Affairs, said he had been a Merchant in London, had been at Maryland, Phyladelphia, New York &c. One Year more he said would make Americans as quiet as Lambs. They could not do without Great Britain, they could not conquer their Luxury &c.

Oated my Horse and drank baume Tea at Treadwells in Ipswich, where I found Brother Porter and chatted with him 1/2 Hour, then rode to Rowley and lodged at Captn. Jewitts.—Jewitt had rather the House should sit all the Year round, than give up an Atom of Right or Priviledge.—The Governor cant frighten the People, with &c.—

JUNE 30TH. 1770. SATURDAY.

Arose not very early and drank a Pint of new Milk and set off. Oated my Horse at Newbury. Rode to Clarks at Greenland Meeting house, where I gave him Hay and Oats, and then set off for Newington. Turned in at a Gate by Colonel March's, and passed thro two Gates more before I came into the Road that carried me to my Uncles.[1] I found the old Gentleman in his 82d. Year, as hearty and alert as ever, his Son and daughter, well—their Children grown up, and every Thing strange to me. I find I had forgot the Place. It is 17 Years I presume since I was there. My Reception was friendly, cordial, and hospitable, as I could wish. Took a chearfull, agreable Dinner, and then Sat off for York, over Bloody Point Ferry, a Way I never went before, and arrived at Woodbridges 1/2 Hour after Sunset.

I have had a very unsentimental Journey, excepting this day at Dinner Time. Have been unfortunate eno, to ride alone all the Way, and have met with very few Characters or Adventures.

Soon after I alighted at Woodbridges in York, Mr. Winthrop, Mr.

Sewall and Mr. Farnum, returned from an Excursion they had made to Agamentacus, on a Party of Pleasure. It is the highest Mountain in this Part of the World, seen first by Sailors coming in from sea. It is in the Town of York, about 7 miles from the Court House. The Talk much, this Evening, of erecting [a] Beacon upon it.

I forgot Yesterday to mention, that I stopped and enquired the Name of a Pond, in Wenham, which I found was Wenham Pond, and also the Name of a remarkable little Hill at the mouth of the Pond, which resembles a high Loaf of our Country brown Bread, and found that it is called Peters's Hill to this day, from the famous Hugh Peters, who about the Year 1640 or before, preached from the Top of that Hillock, to the People who congregated round the Sides of it, without any Shelter for the Hearers, before any Buildings were erected, for public Worship.

By accidentally taking this new rout, I have avoided Portsmouth and my old Friend the Governor of it.[2] But I must make my Compliments to him, as I return. It is a Duty. He is my Friend And I am his. I should have seen enough of the Pomps and Vanities and Ceremonies of that little World, Portsmouth If I had gone there, but Formalities and Ceremonies are an abomination in my sight. I hate them, in Religion, Government, Science, Life.

[1] Joseph Adams, elder brother of Deacon John Adams; Harvard 1710. He was minister at Newington, N.H., for so many years that he became known as "the Bishop of Newington" (MHS, *Colls.*, 5th ser., 2 [1877]:212).

[2] JA's Harvard classmate John Wentworth.

JULY 1ST. 1770. SUNDAY.

Arose early at Paul Dudley Woodbridge's. A cloudy morning. Took a Walk to the Pasture, to see how my Horse fared. Saw my old Friend and Classmate David Sewall walking in his Garden. My little mare had provided for herself by leaping out of a bare Pasture into a neighbouring Lott of mowing Ground, and had filled herself, with Grass and Water. These are important Materials for History no doubt. My Biographer will scarcely introduce my little Mare, and her Adventures in quest of Feed and Water.

The Children of the House have got a young Crow, a Sight I never saw before. The Head and Bill are monstrous, the leggs and Clawes are long and sprawling. But the young Crow and the little mare are objects, that will not interest Posterity.

Landlord says David Sewall is not of the Liberty Side. The Moultons, Lymans, and Sewalls, and Sayward, are all of the Prerogative

Side.—They are afraid of their Commissions—and rather than hazard them, they would ruin the Country. We had a fair Tryal of them when we met to return Thanks to the 92 Antirescinders.[1] None of them voted for it, tho none of them, but Sayward and his Bookkeeper had Courage enough to hold up his Hand, when the Vote was put the Contrary Way.

This same Landlord I find is a high Son. He has upon his Sign Board, *Entertainment for the Sons of Liberty*, under the Portrait of Mr. Pitt.—Thus the Spirit of Liberty circulates thro every minute Artery of the Province.

Heard Mr. Lyman all day. They have 4 deacons and Three Elders in this Church. Bradbury[2] is an Elder, and Sayward is a Deacon. Lyman preached from "which Things the Angells desire to look into."

Drank Coffee at home, with Mr. Farnum, who came in to see me, and then went to D. Sewalls where I spent an Hour, with Farnum, Winthrop and Sewall and when I came away took a View of the Comet, which was then near the North Star—a large, bright Nucleus, in the Center of a nebulous Circle.

Came home, and took a Pipe after Supper with Landlord who is a staunch, zealous Son of Liberty. He speaks doubtfully of the new Councillor Gowing [Gowen] of Kittery. Says he always runs away till he sees how a Thing will go. Says he will lean to the other Side. Says, that He, (the Landlord) loves Peace, And should be very glad to have the Matter settled upon friendly Terms, without Bloodshed, but he would venture his own Life, and spend all he had in the World before he would give up.

He gives a sad Account of the Opposition and Persecution he has suffered from the Tories, for his Zeal and Firmness against their Schemes. Says they, i.e. the Moultons, Sewalls and Lymans, contrived every Way to thwart, vex, and distress him, and have got 1000 st[erling] from him at least, but he says that Providence has seemed to frown upon them, one running distracted and another &c., and has favoured him in Ways that he did not foresee.

[1] "Those members of the General Court who refused [30 June 1768] to rescind the resolution of the preceding House, directing a circular letter [11 Feb. 1768] to be sent to the several assemblies on the continent. This had given so great offence to the government at home, that it demanded some act of recantation. The vote stood ninety-two against, and seventeen for, rescinding" (note by CFA on this passage, JA, *Works*, 2:243). The text of the circular, which proposed that "constitutional measures" be taken by each of the colonies against the Townshend Revenue Act of 1767, is in Mass., *Speeches of the Governors, &c., 1765–1775*, p. 134–136. The names of the seventeen rescinders are recorded in Rowe, *Letters and Diary*, p. 167–168. One was Jonathan Sayward of York.

[2] John Bradbury, sometime member of the General Court and of the Council; not to be confused with his relative Theophilus, Harvard 1757, called "Brother Bradbury" by JA, a young lawyer of Falmouth (now Portland); see William B. Lapham, *Bradbury Memorial* ..., Portland, 1890, *passim*; and below, vol. 2:40, 41, 43, 62.

JULY 2. 1770.

Monday morning, in my Sulky before 5 o clock, Mr. Winthrop, Farnum and D. Sewall, with me on Horse back. Rode thro the Woods the Tide being too high to go over the Beach and to cross Cape Nittick [Neddick] River. Came to Littlefields in Wells 1/4 before 8 o clock. Stopped there and breakfasted. Afterwards Sewall and I stopped at the Door of our Classmate Hemenway, whom we found well, and very friendly, complaisant and hospitable, invited us to alight, to stop on our Return, and take a bed with him, and he enquired of me, where I lived in Boston. Said he would make it his Business to come and see me &c. Rode to Pattens of Arundel, and Mr. Winthrop and I turned our Horses into a little Close to roll and cool themselves and feed upon white honey suckle. Farnum and Sewal are gone forward to James Sullivans[1] to get Dinner ready.

Stopped at James Sullivans at Biddeford, and drank Punch, dined at Allens a Tavern at the Bridge. After Dinner Farnham, Winthrop, Sewall, Sullivan and I walked 1/4 of a mile down the River to see one [2] Poke, a Woman, at least 110 Years of age, some say 115. When we came to the House, nobody was at home but the old Woman and she lay in Bed asleep under the Window. We looked in at the Window, and saw an Object of Horror. Strong Muscles, withered and wrinkled to a Degree, that I never saw before.

After some Time her daughter came from a Neighbours House and we went in. The old Woman roused herself and looked round, very composedly upon Us, without saying a Word. The Daughter told her, "here is a Number of Gentlemen come to see you." Gentlemen, says the old antedeluvian, I am glad to see them. I want them to pray for me—my Prayers I fear are not answered. I used to think my Prayers were answered, but of late I think they are not I have been praying so long for deliverance. Oh living God, come in Mercy! Lord Jesus come in Mercy! Sweet Christ come in Mercy. I used to have comfort in God and set a good Example, but I fear—&c.

Her Mouth were full of large rugged Teeth, and her daughter says, since she was 100 Years old she had two new double Teeth come out. Her Hair is white as Snow, but there is a large Quantity of it on her Head. Her Arms are nothing but Bones covered over with a withered, wrinkled, Skin and Nerves. In short any Person will be convinced from the sight of her that she is as old as they say at least. She told us she was born in Ireland, within a Mile of Derry, came here in the Reign of K. William, she remembers the Reign of King Charles 2d., James 2d., Wm. and Mary. She remembers King James's Warrs, &c. But has got quite lost about her Age. Her daughter asked her how old she was. She said upwards of Three score, but she could not tell.

Got into my Chair after my Return from the old Woman, rode with Elder Bradbury thro Sir William Pepperells Woods, stopped and oated at Millikins, and rode into Falmouth, and putt up at Mr. Jonathan Webbs—Where I found my Classmate Charles Cushing, Mr. George Lyde, the Collector here, one Mr. Johnson and one Mr. Crocker.

[1] James Sullivan, afterward governor of Massachusetts, had just been admitted attorney in the Superior Court term at York in June; admitted barrister, 1772 (Superior Court of Judicature, Minute Books 92, 97).

[2] Space thus left in MS.

JULY 3. 1770. TUESDAY.

Rose in comfortable Health.

JULY 8. 1770 SUNDAY.

This Week has been taken up in the Hurry of the Court, and I have not been able to snatch a Moment to put down any Thing. The softly People where I lodge, Don Webb and his Wife, are the Opposites of every Thing great, spirited and enterprizing. His father was a dissenting Parson, and a Relation of mine, a zealous Puritan, and famous Preacher. This son however without the least Regard to his Education, his Connections, Relations, Reputation, or Examination into the controversy turns about and goes to Church, merely because an handfull of young foolish fellows here, took it into their Heads to go. Don never was, or aimed to be any Thing at Colledge but a silent Hearer of a few Rakes, and he continues to this day the same Man, rather the same softly living Thing that creepeth upon the face of the Earth. He attempted Trade but failed in that—now keeps School and takes Boarders, and his Wife longs to be genteel, to go to Dances, Assemblies, Dinners, suppers &c.—but cannot make it out for Want thereof. Such Imbicility of Genius, such Poverty of Spirit, such Impotence of Nerve, is often accompanied with a fribbling Affectation of Politeness, which is to me completely ridiculous—green Tea, if We could but get it—Madeira Wine, if I could but get it—Collectors[1] genteel Company, Dances, late suppers and Clubbs, &c. &c.

THURSDAY AFTERNOON [12 JULY].

3 O Clock, got into my Desobligeant to go home. 2 or 3 miles out of Town I overtook 2 Men on horseback. They rode sometimes before me, then would fall behind, and seemed a little unsteady. At last one of 'em came up. What is your Name? Why of what Consequence is it what my Name is? Why says he only as we are travelling the Road together, I wanted to know where you came from, and what your Name was. I told him my Name.—Where did you come from? Boston. Where have you been? To Falmouth. Upon a Frolick I suppose? No upon Business. What Business pray? Business at Court.

Thus far I humoured his Impertinence. Well now says he do you want to know my Name? Yes. My Name is Robert Jordan, I belong to Cape Elizabeth, and am now going round there. My forefathers came over here and settled a great many Years ago.—After a good deal more of this harmless Impertinence, he turned off, and left me.—I baited at Millikins and rode thro Saco Woods, and then rode from Saco Bridge, thro the Woods to Pattens after Night—many sharp, steep Hills, many Rocks, many deep Rutts, and not a Footstep of Man, except in the Road. It was vastly disagreable. Lodged at Pattens.

FRYDAY JULY 13. 1770.

Arose and walked with Patten to see the neighbouring Fields of English Grass and Grain and Indian Corn, consuming before the Worms. A long black Worm crawls up the Stalk of Rye or Grass and feeds upon the leaves. The Indian Corn looked stripped to a Skelleton, and that was black with the Worms. I found that they prevail very much in Arundell and Wells and so all along to Portsmouth and to Hampton.

Stopped two Hours at Mr. Hemenways, and then rode thro the Woods, in excessive Heat to York, dined at Woodbridges, who was much elated with his new Licence, and after Dinner was treating his friends, some of them. Spent an Hour at Mr. Sewalls with Elder Bradbury and then went to Portsmouth, crossed the Ferry after 9 O Clock and putt up at Tiltons the Sign of the Marquis of Rockingham—a very good House. I will call no more at Stavers's. I found very good Entertainment, and excellent Attendance—a very convenient House, a spacious Yard, good stables, and an excellent Garden, full of

Carrotts, Beets, Cabbages, Onions, Colliflowers, &c. This Tiltons is just behind the State House.

SATURDAY JULY 14. 1770.

Arose at 4. Got ready as soon as I could and rode out of Town a few Miles to Breakfast. Breakfasted at Lovatts in Hampton, 10 miles from Portsmouth and 12 from Newbury. Threatened with a very hot day. I hope I shall not be so overcome with Heat and Fatigue as I was Yesterday.

I fully intended to have made a long Visit to Governor Wentworth, upon this Occasion. But he was unluckily gone to Wolfborough, so that this Opportunity is lost.

1770. AUGUST. 9TH. THURSDAY.

Madam[1]

I received from Mr. Gill an Intimation, that a Letter from me would not be disagreable to you, and have been emboldened, by that Means, to run the Venture of giving you this Trouble. I have read with much Admiration, Mrs. Maccaulays History of England &c. It is formed upon the Plan, which I have ever wished to see adopted by Historians. It is calculated to strip off the Gilding and false Lustre from worthless Princes and Nobles, and to bestow the Reward of Virtue, Praise upon the generous and worthy only.[2]

No Charms of Eloquence, can atone for the Want of this exact Historical Morality. And I must be allowed to say, I have never seen an History in which it is more religiously regarded.

It was from this History, as well as from the concurrent Testimony, of all who have come to this Country from England, that I had formed the highest Opinion of the Author as one of the brightest ornaments not only of her Sex but of her Age and Country. I could not therefore, but esteem the Information given me by Mr. Gill, as one of the most agreable and fortunate Occurences of my Life.

Indeed it was rather a Mortification to me to find that a few fugitive Speculations in a News Paper, had excited your Curiosity to enquire after me. The Production, which some Person in England, I know not who, has been pleased to intitle a Dissertation on the cannon and the Feudal Law, was written, at Braintree about Eleven Miles from Boston in the Year 1765, written at Random weekly without any pre-conceived Plan, printed in the Newspapers, without Correction, and so little noticed or regarded here that the Author never thought it worth his while to give it Either a Title or a signature. And indeed the Editor in London, might with more Propriety have called it The What d ye call it, or as the Critical Reviewers did a flimsy lively Rhapsody than by the Title he has given it.[3]

But it seems it happened to hit the Taste of some one who has given [it] a longer Duration, than a few Weeks, by printing it in Conjunction with the Letters of the House of Representatives of this Province and by ascribing it to a very venerable, learned Name. I am sorry that Mr. Gridleys Name was affixed to it for many Reasons. The Mistakes, Inaccuracies and Want of Arrangement in it, are utterly unworthy of Mr. Gridlys great and deserved Character for Learning and the general Spirit and Sentiments of it, are by no Means reconcilable to his known Opinions and Principles in Politicks.

It was indeed written by your present Correspondent, who then had formed Designs, which he never has and never will attempt to execute. Oppressed and borne down as he is by the Infirmities of ill Health, and the Calls of a numerous growing Family, whose only Hopes are in his continual Application to the Drudgeries of his Profession, it is almost impossible for him to pursue any Enquiries or to enjoy any Pleasures of the literary Kind.

However, He has been informed that you have in Contemplation an History of the present Reign, or some other History in which the Affairs of America are to have a Share. If this is true it would give him infinite Pleasure—and whether it is or not, if he can by any Means in his Power, by Letters or otherways, contribute any Thing to your Assistance in any of your Enquiries, or to your Amusement he will always esteem himself very happy in attempting it.

Pray excuse the Trouble of this Letter, and believe me, with great Esteem and Admiration, your most obedient and very huml. servant.

[1] Catharine (Sawbridge) Macaulay (1731–1791), political pamphleteer and historian, whose multi-volume *History of England, from the Accession of James I to That of the Brunswick Line,* London, 1763–1783, was for a time a kind of Bible for political radicals in England and America. See Lucy M. Donnelly, "The Celebrated Mrs. Macaulay," *WMQ,* 3d ser., 6:173–207 (April 1949).

[2] The MS of the present draft is heavily corrected, but with the exception of a wholly canceled first paragraph the omissions and alterations do not seem important enough to record. The draft originally began as follows:

"With great Pleasure I received an Intimation from my Friend Mr. Gill that, you had enquired of Sophronia for the Author of a Speculation in a Newspaper which Some one has been pleased to call a Dissertation on the Cannon and feudal Law."

Who Sophronia was does not appear.

[3] The "Editor in London" was Thomas Hollis, who first reprinted JA's untitled newspaper essays of 1765 in the *London Chronicle* (see note on entry of Feb. 1765, above), and then issued them as the last part (p. 111–143) of a collection of papers he called *The True Sen-*

timents of America: ... *Together with
... a Dissertation on the Canon and the
Feudal Law*, London, 1768, remarking
in an introductory note to the latter that
"The Author of it, is said to have been,
JEREMY GRIDLEY, Esq; Attorney Gen-

eral of the Province of *Massachuset's
Bay*." Andrew Eliot informed Hollis of
his error, adding some interesting comments on the real author, in a letter
dated 27 Sept. 1768 (MHS, *Colls.*, 4th
ser., 4[1858]:426–427; see also p. 434).

1770. AUGUST 19. SUNDAY.

Last Fryday went to the Light House with the Committee of both Houses.[1]

Mr. Royal Tyler began to pick chat with me. Mr. Adams, have you ever read Dr. Souths sermon upon the Wisdom of this World? No. I'le lend it to you.—I should be much obliged.—Have you read the Fable of the Bees. Yes, and the Marquis of Hallifax's Character of a Trimmer and Hurds Dialogue upon Sincerity in the Commerce of Life—and Machiavell and Cæsar Borgia. Hard if these are not enough.

Tyler. The Author of the Fable of the Bees understood Human Nature and Mankind, better than any Man that ever lived. I can follow him as he goes along. Every Man in public Life ought to read that Book, to make him jealous and suspicious—&c.

Yesterday He sent the Book, and excellent Sermons they are. Concise and nervous and clear. Strong Ebullitions of the loyal Fanaticism of the Times he lived in, at and after the Restoration, but notwithstanding those Things there is a Degree of Sense and Spirit and Taste in them which will ever render them valuable.[2]

The sermon which Mr. Tyler recommended to my Perusal, is a sermon preached at Westminster Abbey Ap. 30. 1676. from 1. Cor. 3.19. For the Wisdom of this World, is Foolishness with God.—The Dr. undertakes to shew what are those Rules or Principles of Action, upon which the Policy, or Wisdom, in the Text proceeds, and he mentions 4. Rules or Principles. 1. A Man must maintain a constant continued Course of Dissimulation, in the whole Tenor of his Behaviour. 2. That Conscience and Religion ought to lay no Restraint upon Men at all, when it lies opposite to the Prosecution of their Interest—or in the Words of Machiavel, "that the Shew of Religion was helpfull to the Politician, but the Reality of it, hurtfull and pernicious." 3. That a Man ought to make himself, and not the Public, the chief if not the sole End of all his Actions. 4. That in shewing Kindness, or doing favours, no Respect at all is to be had to Friendship, Gratitude, or Sense of Honour; but that such favours are to be done only to the rich or potent, from whom a Man may receive a farther Advantage, or to his Enemies from whom he may otherwise fear a Mischief.

Mr. Winthrop, Mr. Adams and myself endeavoured to recollect the old Distich—Gutta cavat lapidem non vi, sed sepe cadendo. So far we got, but neither of these Gentlemen had ever heard the other Part, I, who had some Years ago been very familiar with it, could not recollect it—but it is

Sic, Homo fit doctus, non vi, sed sepe legendo.

Mr. Mason led us a Jaunt over sharp Rocks to the Point of the Island opposite to Nantasket, where in an hideous Cavern formed by a great Prominent Rock he shewed Us the Animal Plant or flower, a small, spungy muscular Substance, growing fast to the Rock, in figure and feeling resembling a young Girls Breast, shoot[ing] out at the Top of it, a flower, which shrinks in and disappears, upon touching the Substance.

[1] The expedition of this committee of inspection was to Little Brewster or Beacon Island, where Boston Light stood and still stands.

[2] Surviving among JA's books in the Boston Public Library is the first volume of Robert South's *Twelve Sermons Preached upon Several Occasions*, 5th edn., London, 1722.

1770 AUG. 20. MONDAY.

The first Maxim of worldly Wisdom, constant Dissimulation, may be good or evil as it is interpreted. If it means only a constant Concealment from others of such of our Sentiments, Actions, Desires, and Resolutions, as others have not a Right to know, it is not only lawful but commendable—because when these are once divulged, our Enemies may avail themselves of the Knowledge of them, to our Damage, Danger and Confusion. So that some Things which ought to be communicated to some of our Friends, that they may improve them to our Profit or Honour or Pleasure, should be concealed from our Enemies, and from indiscreet friends, least they should be turned to our Loss, Disgrace or Mortification. I am under no moral or other Obligation to publish to the World, how much my Expences or my Incomes amount to yearly. There are Times when and Persons to whom, I am not obliged to tell what are my Principles and Opinions in Politicks or Religion.

There are Persons whom in my Heart I despize; others I abhor. Yet I am not obliged to inform the one of my Contempt, nor the other of my Detestation. This Kind of Dissimulation, which is no more than Concealment, Secrecy, and Reserve, or in other Words, Prudence and Discretion, is a necessary Branch of Wisdom, and so far from being immoral and unlawfull, that [it] is a Duty and a Virtue.

Yet even this must be understood with certain Limitations, for there are Times, when the Cause of Religion, of Government, of Liberty, the Interest of the present Age and of Posterity, render it a necessary Duty for a Man to make known his Sentiments and Intentions boldly and publickly. So that it is difficult to establish any certain Rule, to determine what Things a Man may and what he may not lawfully conceal, and when. But it is no doubt clear, that there are many Things which may lawfully be concealed from many Persons at certain Times; and on the other Hand there are Things, which at certain Times it becomes mean and selfish, base, and wicked to conceal from some Persons.

1770. AUGUST 22. WEDNESDAY.

Rode to Cambridge in Company with Coll. Severn Ayers [Eyre] and Mr. Hewitt from Virginia, Mr. Bull and Mr. Trapier from South Carolina, Messrs. Cushing, Hancock, Adams, Thom. Brattle, Dr. Cooper and Wm. Cooper. Mr. Professor Winthrop shewed Us the Colledge, the Hall, Chappell, Phylosophy Room, Apparatus, Library and Musæum. We all dined at Stedmans, and had a very agreable Day. The Virginia Gentlemen are very full, and zealous in the Cause of American Liberty. Coll. Ayers is an intimate Friend of Mr. Patrick Henry, the first Mover of the Virginia Resolves in 1765, and is himself a Gentleman of great fortune, and of great Figure and Influence in the House of Burgesses. Both He and Mr. Hewit were bred at the Virginia Colledge, and appear to be Men of Genius and Learning. Ayers informed me that in the Reign of Charles 2d. an Act was sent over, from England, with an Instruction to the Governor, and he procured the Assembly to pass it granting a Duty of 2s. an Hogshead upon all Tobacco exported from the Colony, to his Majesty forever. This Duty amounts now to a Revenue of £5000 sterling a Year, which is given part to the Governor, part to the Judges &c. to the Amount of about £4000, and what becomes of the other 1000 is unknown. The Consequence of this is that the Governor calls an Assembly when he pleases, and that is only once in two Years.

These Gentlemen are all Valetudinarians and are taking the Northern Tour for their Health.

[DRAFT OF A NEWSPAPER COMMUNICATION, AUGUST? 1770.][1]

"If I would but go to Hell for an eternal Moment or so, I might be knighted." Shakespeare.

364

The Good of the governed is the End, and Rewards and Punishments are the Means of all Government. The Government of the Supream and alperfect Mind, over all his intellectual Creation, is by proportioning Rewards to Piety and Virtue, and Punishments to Disobedience and Vice. Virtue, by the Constitution of Nature carries in general its own Reward, and Vice its own Punishment, even in this World. But as many Exceptions to this Rule, take Place upon Earth, the Joys of Heaven are prepared, and the Horrors of Hell in a future State to render the moral Government of the Universe, perfect and compleat. Human Government is more or less perfect, as it approaches nearer or diverges farther from an Imitation of this perfect Plan of divine and moral Government. In Times of Simplicity and Innocence, Ability and Integrity will be the principal Recommendations to the public Service, and the sole Title to those Honours and Emoluments, which are in the Power of the Public to bestow. But when Elegance, Luxury and Effeminacy begin to be established, these Rewards will begin to be distributed to Vanity and folly. But when a Government becomes totally corrupted, the system of God Almighty in the Government of the World and the Rules of all good Government upon Earth will be reversed, and Virtue, Integrity and Ability will become the Objects of the Malice, Hatred and Revenge of the Men in Power, and folly, Vice, and Villany will be cherished and supported. In such Times you will see a Governor of a Province, for unwearied Industry in his Endeavours to ruin and destroy the People, whose Welfare he was under every moral obligation to study and promote, knighted and enobled. You will see a Philanthrop, for propagating as many Lies and Slanders against his Country as ever fell from the Pen of a sychophant, rewarded with the Places of Solicitor General, Attorney general, Advocate General, and Judge of Admiralty, with Six Thousands a Year. You will see 17 Rescinders, Wretches, without Sense or Sentiment, rewarded with Commissions to be Justices of Peace, Justices of the Common Pleas and presently Justices of the Kings Bench.

The Consequence of this will be that the Iron Rod of Power will be stretched out vs. the poor People in every [*sentence unfinished*]

¹ The date assigned is approximate. The draft was written at the end of D/JA/15, with a largely blank page preceding it. No printing of this fragmentary essay has been found. Other apparently related fragments will be found under Jan.? 1770, above, and 9 Feb. 1772, below.